CONTENTS

List of figures, tables and boxes   viii

Abbreviations   x

Notes on authors   xiii

Acknowledgements   xiv

Introduction   1
      Introducing social policy   1
      About this book   3
      A brief outline of the book   5

Part I: Approaching Irish social policy: from the past to the present   7

one   From the seventeenth century to the early twentieth century: the emergence of social policy in Ireland   9
      section one: Early social policy measures in Ireland   10
      section two: Irish social policy developments after 1800   13
      section three: Advances in Irish social policy in the late nineteenth and early twentieth century   23

two   From the 1920s to the 1970s: the development of social policy in Ireland   29
      section one: The 1920s to the late 1950s: the early decades of independence and the development of social policy   30
      section two: The late 1950s to the late 1970s: economic growth, social change and the gradual expansion of social policy provision   43

three   Irish social policy from the 1980s to the present: challenges, continuities and changes   53
      section one: Economic crisis and the social challenges of the 1980s   54
      section two: The 1990s and 2000s: new times and a new Ireland?   60
      section three: The return of economic crisis and austerity   68

Part II: Explaining social policy: politics, ideology and welfare states   77

four   Social policy and the welfare state: origins, developments and reform   79
      section one: The emergence of welfare: key developments of the nineteenth and early twentieth centuries   80
      section two: Emerging welfare states: the early and mid-twentieth century   87

section three: Welfare states and adaptation, retrenchment, and reform: from the late-twentieth century to the present ... 96

five   Political ideologies, welfare and social policy ... 111
        section one: Understanding perspectives on welfare ... 112
        section two: Political ideologies, welfare and social policy ... 117

six   Contemporary challenges for social policy and welfare states: Ireland in a wider context ... 141
        section one: Analysing contemporary challenges for the welfare state ... 142
        section two: Social policy and the EU: from subsidiarity, to fiscal surveillance, economic stability and social investment? ... 151
        section three: Challenges and contradictions impinging on the Irish welfare state ... 163

Part III: Analysing Irish social policy I: social services ... **173**

seven   Social protection policy ... 175
        section one: Social protection: definitions, values and systems ... 176
        section two: The development of social protection in Ireland ... 186
        section three: From the 1990s to the present: reform and contemporary issues in Irish social protection policy ... 192

eight   Health policy ... 205
        section one: Healthcare concepts, healthcare systems and recent trends ... 206
        section two: The development of the Irish healthcare system ... 215
        section three: The contemporary system: reform since the 1990s and continuing issues and challenges ... 223

nine   Education policy ... 239
        section one: Equality of opportunity and education policy ... 240
        section two: The development of education policy in Ireland ... 248
        section three: Education since the 1990s: an overview ... 255

ten   Housing policy ... 271
        section one: An overview of housing policy ... 272
        section two: The historical development of housing policy in Ireland ... 280
        section three: Irish housing policy since the mid-1990s: contemporary issues and developments ... 287

IRISH SOCIAL POLICY
A critical introduction

Fiona Dukelow and Mairéad Considine

First edition published in 2009 by Gill & Macmillan

First published in Great Britain in 2017 by

Policy Press
University of Bristol
1-9 Old Park Hill
Bristol
BS2 8BB
UK
t: +44 (0)117 954 5940
pp-info@bristol.ac.uk
www.policypress.co.uk

North America office:
Policy Press
c/o The University of Chicago Press
1427 East 60th Street
Chicago, IL 60637, USA
t: +1 773 702 7700
f: +1 773-702-9756
sales@press.uchicago.edu
www.press.uchicago.edu

© Policy Press 2017

British Library Cataloguing in Publication Data
A catalogue record for this book is available from the British Library

Library of Congress Cataloging-in-Publication Data
A catalog record for this book has been requested

ISBN 978-1-4473-2962-6 paperback
ISBN 978-1-4473-2961-9 hardcover
ISBN 978-1-4473-2963-3 ePub
ISBN 978-1-4473-2964-0 Mobi
ISBN 978-1-4473-2965-7 ePdf

The right of Fiona Dukelow and Mairéad Considine to be identified as authors of this work has been asserted by them in accordance with the Copyright, Designs and Patents Act 1988.

Cover design by Andrew Corbett
Front cover image: istock
Printed and bound in Great Britain by Clays Ltd, St Ives plc
Policy Press uses environmentally responsible print partners

For

Jim and Rebecca Dukelow

Nora and Tomás Ahern

Contents

Part IV: Analysing Irish social policy II: social groups, social policy and sustainability   **301**

eleven   Social policy and social groups: needs, rights and recognition   303
     section one: Social groups, recognition and citizenship   304
     section two: Children and Irish social policy   306
     section three: Older people and Irish social policy   314
     section four: People with disabilities and Irish social policy   320
     section five: Caring, carers and Irish social policy   327

twelve   Social policy and social groups: issues of diversity and discrimination   335
     section one: Immigration and Irish social policy   336
     section two: Travellers and Irish social policy   352
     section three: LGBT people and Irish social policy   362

thirteen   Social policy, the environment and sustainable development   371
     section one: Social policy and environmental concerns   372
     section two: Sustainable development and climate change   377
     section three: Social policy, transport and the environment   385

References   395

Index   455

List of figures, tables and boxes

Figures

2.1	Mother and child scheme explanatory booklet	40
3.1	1987 General Election poster	60
4.1	UK Ministry of National Insurance poster advertising the Family Allowance Act 1945	92
7.1	Expenditure on social protection as a percentage of GDP, Ireland, EU15 and EU28	196
7.2	Poverty rates in Ireland 2004-14 and Europe 2020 targets	202
8.1	A continuum of healthcare systems	209
8.2	Current health expenditure as a percentage of GDP in selected OECD countries	213
8.3	Current health expenditure, Ireland and OECD average, 1990-2015	225
8.4	Private, public and out-of-pocket share of current expenditure on health, 1990-2015	225
8.5	Life expectancy at birth by sex and social class, 2006/07	236
9.1	Expenditure per student, 2005-13	256
9.2	General government expenditure on education, 1995-2014	256
10.1	Local authority houses completed and local authority houses sold to tenants, 1980-94	285
10.2	Annual average property prices, 1995-2015	287
10.3	Social housing output and local authority houses sold, 1995-2015	290
12.1	Emigration, immigration and net migration, 1990-2016	339
12.2	Asylum-seeking trends, 1992-2015	339
13.1	Ireland's GHG emissions (total and transport), 1990-2015	387
13.2	Means of travel to work and total share of car drivers, 1991-2011	388
13.3	Ireland's ecological footprint	392

Tables

6.1	Major fiscal and economic policy responses to the Euro Crisis, 2010-16	161
7.1	Summary of the key characteristics of the main social protection systems	181
7.2	Summary of social protection measures introduced, 1908-89	190
9.1	Selected targets for participation in higher education	267
9.2	Estimated participation rate by socioeconomic background of new entrants to higher education in 2011	268
10.1	Housing tenure, 1946-91	283
10.2	Housing tenure, 2002-11	288
10.3	Homeless households, 1989-2013	298
13.1	CO_2 emissions, per capita, selected countries and country blocs, 2013	384

Boxes

4.1	Recent austerity and outcomes for the welfare state: illustrations from Europe	106
5.1	Right- and Left-wing approaches to social policy	114
6.1	Esping-Andersen's (1990) *Three Worlds of Welfare Capitalism*	147
6.2	Aspects of the worlds of welfare debate	148
6.3	Europe 2020 headline targets	155
7.1	Selected social protection policy developments	193
8.1	Where does the Irish healthcare system fit?	212
8.2	The two-tier health system	222
8.3	Main health policy documents and developments since the early 1990s	224
8.4	Categories of entitlement to public health services	229
8.5	The expansion and contraction of healthcare entitlements	231
8.6	Efforts to tackle waiting lists	233
9.1	Key differences between formal and substantive equality of opportunity	242
9.2	Key education policy and legislative developments	255
10.1	Key housing policy developments since 2000	289
11.1	Economic, social and cultural rights	305
11.2	Children: key policy and legislative developments	309
11.3	Older people: key policy and legislative developments	316
11.4	People with disabilities: key policy and legislative developments	324
11.5	Carers and caring: key policy and legislative developments	329
12.1	Key immigration policy and legislative developments	340
12.2	Roma in Ireland	342
12.3	Key policy and legislative developments with regard to Travellers	355
12.4	Key LGBT legislative and policy developments	365
13.1	Climate change: key global, EU and national commitments	381
13.2	Connections between climate change and climate justice	384
13.3	Dimensions of travel poverty	388

Abbreviations

ADC	Aid to Dependent Children
AFDC	Aid to Families with Dependent Children
AGS	Annual Growth Survey
ALMPs	active labour-market policies
CARE	Campaign for the Care of Deprived Children
CE	community employment
CICA	Commission to Inquire into Child Abuse
CNS	Community National Schools
CoP	Conference of Parties
COS	Charity Organisation Society
CPA	Combat Poverty Agency
CRA	Children's Rights Alliance
CRPD	Convention on the Rights of People with Disabilities
CSO	Central Statistics Office
DCYA	Department of Children and Youth Affairs
DECLG	Department of Environment, Community and Local Government
DEHLG	Department of Environment, Heritage, and Local Government
DEIS	Delivering Equality of Opportunity in Schools
DES	Department of Education and Skills
DESc	Department of Education and Science
DG ECFIN	Directorate General for Economics and Financial Affairs
DH	Department of Health
DHPCLG	Department of Housing, Planning, Community and Local Government
DJE	Department of Justice and Equality
DJELR	Department of Justice, Equality and Law Reform
DLG	Department of Local Government
DoE	Department of Environment
DoHC	Department of Health and Children
DoT	Department of Transport
DP	direct provision
DPER	Department of Public Expenditure and Reform
DSFA	Department of Social and Family Affairs
DSP	Department of Social Protection
EA	Euro Area
EC	European Commission
ECB	European Central Bank
ECCE	Early Childhood Care and Education
ECEC	Early Childhood Education and Care
ECSR	Economic, Cultural and Social Rights
EEA	European Economic Area

EEC	European Economic Community
EES	European Employment Strategy
EFSF	European Financial Stability Facility
EMU	Economic and Monetary Union
EPA	Environmental Protection Authority
EPSEN	Education for Persons with Special Educational Needs
ESF	European Social Fund
ESM	European Stability Mechanism
ESRI	Economic and Social Research Institute
ETB	Education Training Board
EU	European Union
EU15	Austria, Belgium, Denmark, Finland, France, Germany, Greece, Ireland, Italy, Luxembourg, Netherlands, Portugal, Spain, Sweden, United Kingdom
FERA	Federal Emergency Relief Administration
GAIE	Gross Average Industrial Earnings
GDP	gross domestic product
GHGs	greenhouse gases
GLEN	Gay and Lesbian Equality Network
GMS	General Medical Services Scheme
GNP	gross national product
GoI	Government of Ireland
GP	general practitioner
HAP	Housing Assistance Payment
HCP	Home Care Package
HEA	Higher Education Authority
HIA	Health Insurance Authority
HIQA	Health Information and Quality Authority
HRC	Habitual Residence Condition
HSE	Health Service Executive
IHREC	Irish Human Rights and Equality Commission
ILO	International Labour Organisation
IMF	International Monetary Fund
INOU	Irish National Organisation for the Unemployed
IPCC	Intergovernmental Panel on Climate Change
IQ	intelligence quotient
ISPCC	Irish Society for the Prevention of Cruelty to Children
IWLM	Irish Women's Liberation Movement
LCAP	Leaving Certificate Applied Programme
LCVP	Leaving Certificate Vocational Programme
LGBT	lesbian, gay, bisexual, transgender
MRCI	Migrant Rights Centre Ireland
NAI	National Archives of Ireland
NAMA	National Assets Management Agency

NAPS	National Anti-Poverty Strategy
NAS	National Advisory Service
NCCA	National Council for Curriculum and Assessment
NCCRI	National Consultative Committee on Racism and Interculturalism
NESC	National Economic and Social Council
NESF	National Economic and Social Forum
NGOs	non-governmental organisations
NHS	National Health Service
NSPCC	National Society for the Prevention of Cruelty to Children
NTPF	National Treatment Purchase Fund
NUI	National University of Ireland
OCO	Ombudsman for Children's Office
OECD	Organisation for Economic Co-operation and Development
OFP	One-Parent Family Payment
OMC	Open Method of Co-ordination
OMI	Office of the Minister for Integration
ORAC	Office of the Refugee Applications Commissioner
PISA	Programme for International Student Assessment
RAS	Rental Accommodation Scheme
REIT	real estate investment trusts
RIA	Reception and Integration Agency
RS	Rent Supplement
RTÉ	Raidió Teilifís Éireann
SARP	Special Assignee Relief Programme
SEN	Special Educational Needs
SGP	Stability and Growth Pact
SI	Social Investment
SILC	Statistics on Income and Living Conditions
SPCA	Society for the Prevention of Cruelty to Animals
SSI	Social Services Inspectorate
SUSI	Student Universal Support Ireland
TD	Teachta Dála (elected member of Dáil Eireann, Ireland's national parliament)
UK	United Kingdom
UNCRC	UN Convention on the Rights of the Child
UNFCCC	UN Framework Convention on Climate Change
UNHRC	United Nations Human Rights Council
US	United States
VEC	Vocational Education Committees
VHI	Voluntary Health Insurance
WCED	World Commission on Environment and Development
WHO	World Health Organisation

Notes on authors

Mairéad Considine was previously a lecturer in Social Policy at the School of Applied Social Studies, University College Cork, Ireland. Her research interests include social protection, pensions policy, social policy and welfare state change. Her publications include work on Irish pension reform, change to the Irish social protection system and analysis of Ireland's welfare state.

Fiona Dukelow is a lecturer in the School of Applied Social Studies, University College Cork, Ireland. Her research interests include critical welfare theory and various aspects of historical and contemporary Irish social policy and Irish welfare state change. Her previous publications include *Mobilising Classics: Reading Radical Writing in Ireland*, co-edited with Órla O'Donovan, *Defining Events: Power, Resistance and Identity in Twenty-First-Century Ireland*, co-edited with Rosie Meade, and *The Irish Welfare State in the Twenty-First Century: Challenges and Change*, co-edited with Mary P Murphy.

Acknowledgements

We would like to thank our colleagues and, in particular, our past and present students at the School of Applied Social Studies, University College Cork. Particular thanks go to Fred Powell and to Alastair Christie who, as Heads of School at various stages in the writing of this book, have been so supportive of this project. We are also really appreciative of the comments and feedback we received from colleagues in the wider Irish social policy community on the book's first edition.

Thanks to the staff at Policy Press for their help throughout the process of publication.

For permission to publish an image from the National Archives of Ireland we gratefully acknowledge the Director of the National Archives. We would also like to thank the Global Footprint Network for permission to use their Ireland Ecological Footprint graph and Derek Speirs for permission to reproduce a photograph.

Finally we would like to thank our families and friends for their encouragement and care. In particular Mairéad would like to thank John for his constant support, and Nora and Tomás too, who frequently asked how the book was going and inquired about word count and deadlines being met! Fiona would like to thank David for his never-ending inspiration, for this book and for everything else.

Introduction

Introducing social policy

Social policy is concerned with understanding the social and economic structures central to people's lives, life chances and quality of life. At its core, social policy is about the study of how human needs are met, how we respond to risks we face, and the ways in which well-being is interpreted and used to shape policy priorities and outcomes. Whether as individuals, families, communities or societies, people make decisions, or have decisions made for them, about needs such as education and training, healthcare, housing, working, caring and so on. As well as the many ways in which needs arise through the course of typical life experiences, we also face particular risks, such as not finding work or not having enough work, becoming ill, dealing with a failed or abusive relationship, becoming homeless and so on. Taken together, how we meet needs and deal with risks involves a concern with well-being, welfare or security.

While at an individual or personal level we try figure out what is the best thing to do to achieve well-being given the opportunities and constraints of our particular circumstances, social policy involves the study of this at a collective or social level; how do societies figure this out? This in turn involves addressing such questions as: What counts as a need or a risk? What social and economic challenges and changes arise over time? What values guide policy and provision? How are limited resources used? What impact does social policy have on different groups in society? How are resources shared or redistributed between different social groups? How is cultural diversity recognised? How are differences and inequalities dealt with? How are social relations, based on experiences of social class, gender, 'race', ethnicity, sexuality, disability and age, shaped as a result?

In responding to these issues, governments give direction to the level and extent of state intervention and guide policy priorities in any particular country. At the same time, various groups in society may mobilise around particular social needs and social issues, seeking social justice, rights and recognition. While words like welfare and well-being have a certain 'feel good' factor, the questions addressed in the study of social policy do not automatically produce positive answers. Social policy is a political and often contested activity, where different groups, who have different interests and needs, come into conflict. Different perspectives within social policy contribute to theoretical and political debates about how best to shape social policy provision and realise particular social outcomes. Linked to this, in practice, the design and implementation of social policies can often result in the opposite of welfare: such as economic insecurity and denial of, or differentiated, social rights. As a result, how needs are met and how risks are responded to can have very significant implications for the type of society we live in; whether, for example, it is broadly equal or unequal; and our position within that society.

If we look at some of the ways in which social policy relates to people's lives in Irish society many of these issues become more real. A good starting point is education. If you are reading this book as part of a course in social policy, then your participation in the education system will mean that you have had much personal and direct experience of the impact of social policy. Education is a major component of social policy provision and has a significant bearing on the early part of our lives and beyond. While day to day participation in the education system is quite a personal experience, it is shaped by the policy goals the state has for education. For example, only a basic form of education was treated as a need that the Irish state should pay for until the 1960s and there were substantial inequalities in Irish society between groups who could afford more than the free education provided until one reached 14 and those who could not. Religious thinking played a dominant role in the curriculum and in the overall aims of education. Education was also distinctly shaped by gender and ability norms: segregated schooling and very different expectations prevailed for different groups of children. Thus social class, gender and disability had a major bearing on the type of education different groups received and on social mobility. The placement of children needing care in industrial schools adds another layer of complexity and differentiation to how education was provided.

At the present time education is tied much more strongly to economic needs than to cultural ones, and policy, particularly at higher level, is strongly influenced by the need to provide a skilled and entrepreneurial labour force for our knowledge economy. Another frequently espoused goal is equality of opportunity. This broadly means that everyone is given a chance to succeed in the education system and should not face obstacles such as inability to pay for education. While there is still continuity with the past because the majority of schools are religiously owned, participation in the education system has increased enormously, particularly at third level. Only one in five school leavers went on to third level in 1980, compared to one in every two school leavers in 2011. The individual decisions we make about going to college and choosing courses to study are part of this wider policy context guided by economic needs and by the value placed upon equality of opportunity. These needs and values are, in turn, practically expressed through policy measures which moderate the cost of education and widen access. However equal participation has not been achieved. There are stark class and related spatial inequalities in who goes to college; while gender, as well as other social differences such as disability and ethnicity, also play a part in educational choices and constraints. Questions arise, such as how the needs and rights of different groups are recognised; how equality of opportunity is interpreted; how much money is spent and how it is distributed in the education system; how the system is driven and shaped by economic interests; and the extent to which education can address inequalities generated outside of the education system. How these issues are debated, researched, and addressed in policy make up some of the core elements of education as studied within the discipline of social policy. Education is taken here as one illustration of the importance of social policy in shaping the opportunities available to people. Examples could equally be given in areas such as housing, healthcare, social protection and social care – other key aspects of the social services.

The welfare state is a term often used to refer to the role, usually of the state, in these core areas of social policy. However, the idea of a welfare state is itself a contested one and definitions of it remain a source of disagreement. Narrower definitions tend to confine the concept of the welfare state to key social-service policy areas and while they do provide the main infrastructure of the welfare state, they cannot operate without reference to wider domains which define the nature, extent and quality of their provisions. In our view, social service provision cannot be separated from funding, allocation of resources, how resources are first generated and how they are then distributed to different welfare effects. In other words, the ways in which needs and risks are understood and met, in social protection, health, housing, education and social care policies need to be seen in terms of their wider connections. These connections include: finance and resources (tax collection and the provision of services); political ideas, government priorities and international influences (extent and type of state provision in different areas); the range of often competing interests (citizens, workers, industry, market providers) in any sphere of welfare; and the ways in which welfare policies interact and co-ordinate. A broader conceptualisation of the welfare state thus muddies the water significantly. It forces us to think about: Who decides what welfare we need and on what basis? Who pays? Who provides? Who benefits? To what ends? It requires critical consideration of issues such as power, in/ equality, redistribution, voice, participation, rights and how they influence and are influenced by the type of welfare state that exists.

About this book

This book is about social policy in the Irish context. It offers a way of understanding social policy in Ireland by looking at the past; introducing wider theoretical debates and issues; examining specific social-service areas and their development and current position in Ireland; and exploring the position and treatment of different social groups. In bringing the different elements of social policy together in this way we hope to provide, but also to go beyond, a descriptive account of issues and events, and encompass a critical examination of them.

The analysis of social policy presented here is shaped by attention to core social policy concepts which requires an openness to question and critique both the achievements and limits of social policy. In doing so we draw on critical traditions within social policy. We attempt to emphasise not only the importance of class inequalities but also wider critical frames related to, for example, gender, age and ethnicity, to consider different interpretations and views about the nature, development, scope and impact of Irish social policy and the Irish welfare state. This approach is taken to acknowledge the complexity of social policy processes and debates, and to offer an introduction to the discipline which both provokes and challenges discussion about Irish social policy, its limits and its potential. Our attempts to offer a relatively comprehensive and critical introduction also has drawbacks; attention to different issues and perspectives is at times uneven, more brief than we would have liked, and leaves many gaps.

The first edition of this book was completed at the end of 2008, just at the point when a major and enduring economic crisis was emerging in Ireland. At the time of completing the second edition by the end of 2016, practically all areas of Irish social policy have been significantly affected. Needs and risks associated with recession and economic precarity have escalated while social services have simultaneously had to cope with significant cutbacks and restructuring. Changes in the landscape of policy-making processes and policy drivers are also occurring, with shifts in the politics and ideas underpinning social policy, both nationally and internationally. Beyond the crisis-related changes of the past eight years, Irish society continues to undergo significant social and cultural change which is also impacting on social policy developments. In the second edition we have tried to capture the core elements of these changes and their significance. The period since the first edition has certainly been a period of 'policy hyperactivism' (Dunleavy and O'Leary, 1987) but what that means for the Irish welfare state and well-being is a complex question. Social policy seems to be made and contested in an increasingly cold climate. By this we mean that it is evolving in not only more financially straitened times but also under ideas which have further narrowed the conception of welfare to its compatibility with the economy and market interests, and, in the process, disarming welfare claims and critiques of social policy built on wider foundations of social justice. In the Irish context, this is not new and has indeed been a recurrent theme. Its most recent iteration following the crisis brings increased challenges. The diminished state of social policy seems ill-equipped to overcome or moderate the damage wrought by the hyper-globalised, hyper-competitive, hyper-divided world of twenty-first century capitalism. This endangering of social policy and the welfare state is not unique to Ireland, and we readily agree that there is a need to envisage 'a social policy future in which the state "reasserts collective (public) interests and enables collective (public) action"' (Newman and Clarke, 2014: 7-8 in Williams, 2016: 642).

A brief outline of the book

The book is divided into four parts. Part I traces the emergence and development of Irish social policy from its origins to the present, documenting in some historical detail its key phases, influences and changes over time. Part II turns to the wider discipline of social policy. The chapters in this part of the book highlight the political, ideological and other factors involved in the development of social policy and welfare states. They also discuss key disciplinary concepts and survey contemporary conditions and challenges in which social policy is made, including globalisation, financialisation and Europeanisation. In all instances the analysis is brought back to its relevance for understanding Irish social policy. Part III presents a detailed analysis of the four core social services areas: social protection, health, education and housing. Each chapter in Part III combines an introduction to the relevant policy area and its key concerns with a detailed analysis of the specific Irish context and contemporary situation. Part IV of the book contains an analysis of how social policy affects particular groups and shapes social relations in Irish society, including children, carers, people with disabilities, older people, migrants and LGBT (lesbian, gay, bisexual, transgender) people. The respective chapters also document how interest has grown in these areas in recent years, not least because such groups have drawn attention to enduring inequalities and the need for rights and recognition. For clarity of presentation, we look at each group separately; however, we recognise that aspects of identity such as age, ethnicity and disability are cross-cutting in how they shape people's lives and experiences of well-being, and we draw connections between them where possible in our analysis. The final chapter in Part IV extends the analysis to a relatively new and still under-examined element of social policy, namely sustainable development and the environment, which is a growing challenge that also needs understanding from a social policy perspective.

A note on data sources

Data is used at various points throughout the book to illustrate issues about welfare state expenditure and how Ireland compares with social policy in other countries. The full reference is not provided each time but note is made of the statistical provider; the main sources and their website addresses are listed below. These sources are regularly updated and should be consulted for updates on various measurements and indicators discussed in the book.

Eurostat (European Statistics provided by the European Commission): http://ec.europa.eu/eurostat/

OECD.Stat (Statistical data for OECD countries): http://stats.oecd.org/

CSO (Central Statistics Office, the official provider of Irish statistics): www.cso.ie/en/

Department of Public Expenditure and Reform Databank (statistics on Irish government expenditure provided by the Department of Public Expenditure and Reform): www.per.gov. ie/en/databank/

PART I
Approaching Irish social policy: from the past to the present

one

From the seventeenth century to the early twentieth century: the emergence of social policy in Ireland

This chapter sketches the key features of the emergence of social policy in Ireland. The chapter spans early state and charitable activity in the seventeenth and eighteenth centuries, through to the more extensive social policy measures and provisions during the nineteenth and early twentieth centuries before Ireland gained independence in 1921. The chapter documents the themes of care and social control which were intertwined in a mix of charitable and state provision during the seventeenth and eighteenth centuries. Provision dealt primarily with the 'problem of the poor'. During this period charitable efforts stand out, but these were primarily for categories of the 'deserving poor', principally children and the sick poor. State intervention was minimal and strongly linked to the control and punishment of the 'undeserving poor'. In the nineteenth century the establishment of the poor law continued the concern with poverty and social control, but within the context of a much larger institutional framework. The chapter also identifies the emergence of a more sustained debate about the nature of welfare by the end of the nineteenth century. This encompassed the idea that social policy and state intervention was a matter that went beyond the problems of the poor and resulted in recognition of the needs of some particular groups in the population, including children and older people.

Chapter outline
- The chapter first examines the roots of social policy by looking at the elements which existed prior to the nineteenth century.
- The second section looks at developments during the nineteenth century, which were dominated by the implementation of the poor law in Ireland from 1838.

• The final section explores the emergence of a modern strand to social policy development in the early twentieth century.

SECTION ONE
EARLY SOCIAL POLICY MEASURES IN IRELAND

[T]here are 34,425 strolling beggars in the kingdom; of which there are not 1 in 10 real objects (of compassion) ... so that we may suppose 30,000 of them able to work (Arthur Dobbs, Irish Surveyor General, 1729, in Powell, 1989: 72).

Early fragments of social policy emerged during the seventeenth and eighteenth centuries, before welfare provision became more easily recognised in the nineteenth century. The historical overview presented here refers directly to social policy developments and initiatives although this is not how such measures would have been identified at the time. Typically terms such as relief, correction and aid would have been used, reflecting the prevailing ethos of the time. Maintenance of social order superseded the meeting of needs, despite the existence of large-scale poverty in Ireland. The primary purpose of early provision was to group people who were considered undesirable together to impose order and control. Undesirability was associated with moving from place to place and being without work if one was physically capable of working or 'able-bodied'. Both of these qualities clashed with the emerging modern values of being settled in one place and at work. Therefore 'sturdy beggars' who contravened both of these values came

> **'Able-bodied' poor** referred to the poor who were assumed to be in a position to physically support themselves.

in for particular attention. This issue was not exclusive to Ireland; other European countries also perceived beggars as a threat to social stability and implemented measures to deal with this. In the Irish case the title of one of the earliest pieces of social policy related legislation includes an extensive list of individuals considered a problem. This was 'An Act for the Erecting of Houses of Correction and for Punishment of all Rogues, Vagabonds, Sturdy Beggars and other Lewd and Idle Persons', passed in 1635. The Act's title reflects the concern that idleness, and what were construed as illegitimate forms of movement, were to be dealt with using corrective treatment in an environment segregated from the rest of the population. Correction and punishment were implemented by setting people to labour and by administering 'moderate' whippings. This was intended as a form of deterrence for the rest of the poor as much as it acted as punishment for the idle poor (Powell, 1989). However, the legislation proved inoperable due to lack of financial provisions (Ó Cinnéide, 1969).

The 1635 Act was followed in 1703 by 'An Act for erecting a workhouse in the City of Dublin, for employing and maintaining the poor thereof'. The workhouse, also known as a house of industry, was built near James Street. Nicholls (1856: 37), in his history of the poor law in Ireland noted that this Act was the 'first in which a direct provision is made for the relief of poverty in Ireland'. However, while this Act marks an acknowledgement of poverty, the treatment of the poor continued to emphasise order and control. In 1735 an Act was passed to provide a similar workhouse in Cork, which was built on the Watercourse Road (O' Connor, 1995). Again the title of the Act reveals its purpose: 'An Act for erecting a workhouse in the city of Cork for employing and maintaining the poor, punishing vagabonds, and providing for and educating foundling children'. These workhouses operated jointly as 'foundling hospitals' for abandoned children. Abandonment, predominantly caused by family poverty, was not uncommon at the time. Funding was sourced from special local taxes, such as a tax on all imported coal in Cork and a house tax in Dublin. This legislation represented an early attempt to separate out different categories of need from the general mass of 'idle and lewd' persons. As Evason et al (1976) note, children were the first to benefit from recognition as a special category requiring more lenient attention. In the case of the 1703 Act for Dublin for example, Dublin Corporation was required to care for orphans and to 'apprentice out such children to any honest persons, being Protestants' (Evason et al, 1976: 4). In this case early social policy was also used as an instrument of proselytisation, specifically for promulgating Protestantism.

By the 1720s the Dublin workhouse became the Dublin Foundling Hospital, owing to the large numbers of children being abandoned. However, conditions within the Foundling Hospital were incredibly harsh, indicated by the number of children who died in the institution. Between 1790 and 1796 for example, of the 12,768 children who were admitted, 9,786 died (Raftery and O'Sullivan, 1999: 54). The hospital was later described by the Royal Commission on the Poor Laws of 1909 as 'the most gigantic baby-farming, nursing, boarding out and apprenticing institutions these countries have ever seen' (cited in Raftery and O'Sullivan, 1999: 54). In response to the awful conditions and the fact that children boarded out from there were brought up as Protestant, many Catholic orphanages were set up voluntarily by local parishes. These orphanages arranged for children to be boarded out to Catholic families, and thus 'rescued' them from the proselytising efforts of Protestants.

For adults, 'legitimate' or '**deserving**' beggars were recognised and distinguished from '**undeserving**' or 'sturdy' beggars, in an Act passed in 1772. This was 'An Act for badging such poor as shall be found

> **'Deserving'** and **'undeserving'** poor were terms used to distinguish between the poor who deserved support through charity or state provision and those who did not. The deserving poor included orphaned children, the sick and the disabled. In contrast, the undeserving poor, because they were able-bodied, did not deserve support.

unable to support themselves by labour, and otherwise providing for them, and for restraining such as shall be found able to support themselves by labour or industry from begging'. Beggars were separated into two groups: those whose activity was officially recognised and who were granted a badge to beg; and those who were 'able-bodied' and thus deemed fit to work. The latter were to be punished by being placed in stocks, with a three-hour stint for a first offence, and six hours for every re-offence (Nicholls, 1856). This Act also allowed for the erection of more workhouses, and by 1838 when the poor law was implemented, nine workhouses were in operation (Farley, 1964).

Outside of the workhouses, developments were also taking place in healthcare although such initiatives came mainly from charity or philanthropists, not the state. According to O'Brien (1999: 199),

> poor people in normal times fitted roughly into two categories: the sturdy beggars and the sick. ... The sick poor ... attracted sympathy rather than hostility. This reflected, partly, the popular recognition that sickness was not confined to the lower orders; partly also the realization that, whereas poverty was the result of improvidence and idleness, sickness was an act of God.

Therefore, as O'Brien (1999: 199) puts it, 'if you had the misfortune to be poor, you were better off being sick also'. This again reflects the distinction between the 'deserving' and 'undeserving' poor. The first voluntary hospital, founded by six surgeons, was opened on Cook Street in Dublin, with a mission to care for the 'maim'd and wound'd poor' (Kelly, 1999: 27). This became known as the Charitable Infirmary.[1] Another, the North Charitable Infirmary, opened in Cork in 1744.[2] Two other voluntary hospitals opened in Dublin, Dr Steeven's Hospital in 1733, initially funded by a legacy left by Dr Richard Steeven, and Mercer's Hospital, opened by Mary Mercer, in 1734. Following these general hospitals several more opened, often catering for more specific aspects of healthcare, such as fever hospitals and maternity hospitals, also known as 'lying in' hospitals. The **philanthropy** of the individuals involved in funding and running these hospitals were in part calculated to enhance their status in the community. And while the poor who availed of the hospitals did not have to pay, they were reminded of their status as objects of charity by

> **Philanthropy** is a form of charitable giving, often by wealthy individuals and corporate donors, reflecting personal interest in areas such as public health and medicine, poverty and education.

being expected to publicly acknowledge their indebtedness (Geary, 2004). All of these hospitals were supported by related charitable organisations. In Dublin for example, the proceeds of the first public performance of Handel's Messiah in 1742 went to Mercer's Hospital (Geary, 2004). However, charitable funding alone was insufficient. The high level of need among the sick meant that many of the hospitals went through several phases of expansion and eventually received public funding to supplement their charitable income.

These voluntary hospital initiatives did not extend outside of the main cities. A network of rural hospitals did not come about until the County Infirmaries Act 1765 provided for the creation of an infirmary in each county. These were funded by parliamentary grants, grand jury presentments and donations. However, these hospitals quickly became very run-down and, as Geary (2004: 53) notes, the Act 'was imperfect in many respects ... these institutions were too few, too small, and often inconveniently located. They were limited by the method of funding and staffing, and by the absence of proper supervision and control'. Dispensaries also began to emerge in the late eighteenth century, mainly in urban areas. These were designed to provide outpatient care, and included apothecaries, the precursor to pharmacies, which dispensed medicines to the poor. Again the dispensaries were a voluntary initiative, meeting the needs of the sick poor on money raised from voluntary subscriptions.

Education was also provided mostly outside of the state framework at this time. Again voluntary groups were the main actors, and the provision of education was divided along religious lines. Several Protestant societies, such as the Association for Discountenancing Vice and the Baptist Society for Promoting the Gospel in Ireland, ran primary and second-level schools. Their activities were assisted with some public funding, which was allocated as a means of spreading Protestantism and increasing the use of the English language (Coolahan, 1981). In contrast, the Penal Laws of the seventeenth century made life very difficult for Catholics and Catholic organisations were forbidden to establish schools. However, an unofficial system of hedge schools operated. Once the Penal Laws were repealed, the growth of Catholic-run schooling became significant, including education provided by the Christian Brothers and the Presentation Sisters. However, unlike the Protestant organisations, these groups did not initially receive state funding.

SECTION TWO
IRISH SOCIAL POLICY DEVELOPMENTS AFTER 1800

The nineteenth century began with the Act of Union 1800 and Ireland became part of the United Kingdom of Great Britain and Ireland. Ireland lost the political autonomy it had through a devolved parliament and any further developments depended on decisions taken in London. State intervention in matters of welfare grew throughout the century. However, as McPherson and Midgley (1987: 9 in Cousins, 2005a: 7) note, the nature of colonial administration meant that policy making was 'highly bureaucratic and extremely centralised – designed for control, maintenance of order and downward transmission of policies formulated elsewhere'.

In 1805 legislation was introduced to fund dispensaries in rural areas. If local voluntary funding could be raised then a similar amount would be provided by county grand juries through taxation. However, this initiative was uneven. Often, wealthier areas were more likely to raise the initial funding required, yet these areas would be less in need of dispensary services than poorer districts (Geary, 2004). Unequal access to healthcare, which is taken up again in Chapter Eight, has therefore a long history. In 1817 approval for the establishment of a network of public lunatic asylums made Ireland the first country in Europe to experience such a development (O'Brien, 1999). This was an improvement on the previous practice of consigning 'lunatics' to houses of industry and it mirrored a shift from punishment to the idea that mental illness could be medically treated. Twenty-two asylums were built between 1810 and 1869, and admission rates increased steadily over the nineteenth century (Malcolm, 1999).

The establishment of a national school system in 1831 was another development which put Ireland ahead of England. Education was increasingly recognised as an asset in developing industrial strength, but in Ireland's case, education was a powerful tool of cultural control in a colonised country. Several commissions were established to examine education in Ireland, and by 1831 the government decided to establish a Board of Commissioners for National Education whose members would be both Catholics and Protestants. This Board was given responsibility for funding and regulating schools. The arrangement was intended to develop multi-denominational schooling. However, the system gradually tilted towards denominational education, as none of the religious groupings were happy with a multi-denominational ethos (Coolahan, 1981).

While these initiatives were somewhat innovative, on the whole Ireland was not progressing economically or socially. Most of Ireland did not experience an industrial revolution; the economy remained largely agricultural, serving both its domestic needs as well as a growing market for food in the rest of the UK. An economic depression occurred in Ireland during the early to mid-1800s primarily due to events elsewhere in the UK, where a period of economic austerity reduced demand for Irish produce. Within Ireland, almost all land was owned by landlords who, as Daly (1981: 6) puts it 'represented the peak of the Irish social pyramid'. Below them were tenant farmers, many of whom got into difficulty paying rent at this time. Farm labourers, who gained work on a temporary basis, also fared badly. Landlord–tenant tensions rose as the effects of long leases became apparent: tenant farmers tended to further subdivide their land resulting in too many farmers on too-small holdings, unable to produce enough for survival or to pay their rents. Some landlords responded by reducing the length of new leases and consolidating farms by evicting small farmers and creating larger farms to rent. The scene was set for escalating levels of poverty and inequality. This was confirmed in the findings of the Poor Law Inquiry Commission appointed in 1835 to investigate poverty in Ireland; it concluded that the circumstances of three million out of the eight million people in Ireland would allow them to claim relief (Mokyr and Ó Gráda, 1988).

A Poor Law for Ireland

The Poor Law Inquiry Commission was the culmination of several investigations into the conditions of the poor in Ireland since the Act of Union; however, the various recommendations made were rarely acted on. This inaction changed with the growing feeling that there were too many Irish people availing of the poor law in England. Movement between the two countries was not uncommon, with a constant stream of migrant workers leaving Ireland for work in England, particularly after a regular steamboat crossing was set up in 1815. Some labourers, particularly those who also moved their families, became destitute. Even though they were not entitled to avail of poor relief until after five years of residence, it was, as McLoughlin (1990: 118) notes, 'the increasing visibility of these Irish poor on the English scene and their perceived threat to both wages and social order which provided the principal impetus for the 1838 Poor Law Act and the initiation of the workhouse system of relief'. This also indicates that debates about the implications of migration are not exclusive to the contemporary context (see Chapter Twelve). The poor law cast a long shadow over the development of Irish social policy, in terms of attitudes, administration, and rules and regulations attached to services, so it is important to examine it in greater detail. It must be acknowledged that this examination focuses on the general nature of the poor law in the broader context of the development of social policy in Ireland. In reality the poor law was 'fluid and diverse in character' (Crossman and Gray, 2011: 17) with variation in relation to, for example, local political and socioeconomic circumstances and individual workhouse practices, which are not possible to document here.

To understand the poor law in Ireland, we first need to look at its operation in Britain, where it was already well established. In 1601 an Act for the Relief of the Poor provided outdoor relief in Britain to 'able-bodied' adults. Outdoor relief meant that assistance, such as food or clothing, could be given in people's own homes, as opposed to requiring them to enter a workhouse. Two centuries later, however, the dominant ideas about welfare had changed and this approach was deemed too lenient and too expensive. The 1601 Act was amended in 1834 with a new Act, known as the 'new poor law' and entitled 'An Act for the Amendment and Better Administration of the Laws relating to the Poor in England and Wales'.

Two members of the Royal Commission appointed in 1832 to investigate the poor law in Britain, Edwin Chadwick and Nassau Senior, believed that the 1601 poor law had actually succeeded in encouraging **pauperism** by giving relief to the 'able-bodied' poor and had made living on relief more attractive than working. The prevailing view of poverty was that it was the fault of individuals and their particular character traits, such as idleness, rather than being caused by structural factors outside the

> **Pauperism** described a state of complete destitution symbolised by dependence on poor law provision.

control of individuals, such as lack of work. Thus it was felt that the existing poor law only encouraged 'the indolence and improvidence of the poor' (Jones, 1910: 361). In order to discourage this effect, Chadwick and Nassau Senior argued that relief to the 'able-bodied' poor should be given in workhouses only, where conditions would be less attractive than the standard of living one could achieve by earning a wage, however low. This was intended to deter those who were not truly destitute, and was otherwise known as the workhouse test.

The Royal Commission advocated the principle 'that the condition of paupers shall in no case be so eligible as the condition of persons of the lowest class subsisting on the fruits of their own industry' (cited in Ó Cinnéide, 1969: 286). This principle, known as the 'principle of less eligibility', dictated that relief for the able-bodied should only be available within workhouses. Entering the workhouse meant that one took on the status of a pauper, meaning one was not just poor but completely destitute. The overall character of the new poor law is summed up well by Jones (1910: 362):

> Destitution is the result of defective personal character; the firm and regular offer of the workhouse will convert the potential pauper into an independent labourer; in any case, the condition must be made worse than that of the free labourer; thrift, occupational improvement, manly independence, domestic peace, follow in the wake of strict administration. So runs the doctrine

The poor law was transferred to Ireland after the rejection of more progressive proposals made by the Royal Commission of Inquiry into the Condition of the Poorer Classes in Ireland. The Commission, headed by Dr Whately, the Protestant Archbishop of Dublin, took the view that a poor law would be inappropriate for Ireland; the conditions were so bad that the principle of 'less eligibility' would be inoperable. The Commission commented that, 'we see that the labouring class are eager for work; that work there is not for them, and that they are therefore, and not from any fault of their own, in permanent want' (cited in O'Connor, 1995: 54). The Commission recommended that Ireland's resources needed development to provide employment, and to supplement this, a scheme of assisted emigration was recommended to enable people to find work abroad.

The Commission's view clashed with the dominant ideas underpinning the new poor law in Britain and the Commission's recommendations were rejected. George Nicholls, already one of the Poor Law Commissioners in England and who fully endorsed the ideas behind the new poor law, was sent to investigate the feasibility of implementing it in Ireland. He produced a report after a six-week visit to Ireland, in which he emphatically recommended 'that, in Ireland, no relief should be given except in the workhouse. I do not propose to impart a right to relief, even to the destitute poor' (cited in Ó Cinnéide 1969: 288).

In keeping with the views of Chadwick and Nassau, Nicholls (1856: v) felt that the deterrent effect of the poor law would improve the character and conditions of the Irish people. He believed that it would, 'relieve the community from the demoralization as well as from the danger consequent on the prevalence of extensive and unmitigated destitution, and ... do this in such a way as shall have the least possible tendency to create the evil which it is sought to guard against'. Nicholls proposed that a poor law be introduced to Ireland by dividing the country into 130 poor law unions with a workhouse catering for 800 people in each union, run by a local board of guardians, paid for by poor law rates (a local property tax) and overseen by a Poor Law Commission located in London. This proposal was quickly adopted in the 'Act for the more effectual relief of the destitute poor in Ireland' 1838.

Implementation of the Irish poor law

There were two key components to what was considered effective relief in the application of the poor law. First, there was no automatic entitlement to relief, and second, life within the workhouses was to be highly regulated. The lack of a right to relief meant that entry was at the discretion of the board of guardians. As it quickly became apparent that the number of workhouses built was completely insufficient, women, children and the aged were prioritised over able-bodied but destitute men. However, if a man was granted relief in a workhouse, his family had to enter the workhouse as paupers with him. Once in the workhouse, classification systems were a central feature in the way workhouses were regulated. The interest in classifying people was part of a wider pattern in the emergence of social scientific knowledge at this time. Early social scientists, such as Bentham, aimed to create a body of knowledge about the social world, in a manner similar to how scientists were producing knowledge and classifying components of the physical world. The more knowledge produced about the social world, the more amenable it would be to reform and improvement. This thinking was applied with zeal in the workhouses; the more groups could be classified, the easier it would be to create order and to reform, and the whole enterprise was thought to operate on precise, scientific grounds as a result (Clarke, 2005).

The classification system in the workhouses laid down by the *Compendium of the Irish Poor Law; and general manual for Poor Law Guardians and their officers* published in 1887, was as follows:

1. Males above the age of 15 years
2. Boys above the age of 2 years, and under 15 years
3. Females above the age of 15 years
4. Girls above the age of 2 years, and under 15 years
5. Children under 2 years of age (cited in O Mahony, 2005: 6).

These groups were to have separate spaces in the workhouse, with further separation of the sick from the able-bodied. In some workhouses there were separate spaces for single mothers with more than one child and prostitutes, who were categorised as 'grossly immoral women' (Luddy, 2011: 111). All were given a workhouse uniform on entering, and different rations of 'monotonous and frugal' food (Crossman, 2006: 15). All adults, besides the sick, were expected to work and children were also assigned tasks when not being educated. However, this attempt at an ordered state of affairs failed as workhouses quickly descended into a dilapidated state. Lack of discipline within workhouses was often attributed to poor implementation of the classification system, and when separate categories were allowed to mix, it was felt that it paved the way for 'moral contagion' (Englander, 1998). Attempts at more stringent implementation of workhouse regulations paled into insignificance as the onset of the famine in 1845 resulted in a crisis for the workhouse system.

The poor law during the Great Famine and beyond

> The Workhouse is filled beyond what prudence would suggest as safe to the health of the inmate, or that of the city. At most, it can shelter but a few hundreds more – while every lane in the city has *hundreds* of starving poor – while every parish in the city swarms with THOUSANDS of destitute men, women and children (*The Cork Examiner*, 14 May 1847).

During the Great Famine (1845-47), levels of destitution escalated due to the failure of the potato crop, which was the main food source for the majority of the population. People who were previously reluctant to enter the workhouse now had to resort to it as the sole source of relief. Overcrowding was the inevitable result. One million people died during the famine, yet state intervention was based on a workhouse system which was designed to cater for approximately 110,000 people. By 1851 there were 217,000 inmates in the workhouses (O'Connor, 1995).

The government's response to this scale of failure was minimal and significant changes were not implemented until voluntary initiatives paved the way. Voluntary organisations, such as the Society of Friends, known as Quakers, raised money to set up soup kitchens. In 1847 there was public outcry in Britain after artists' depictions of the famine were printed in the British media. This led to government-funded soup kitchens to give relief to those who could not gain admittance to the overcrowded workhouses (O'Connor, 1995). Subsequently, a significant piece of legislation was introduced: the Irish Poor Relief Extension Act 1847. The Act introduced a right to relief and allowed boards of guardians to provide outdoor relief. Outdoor relief was given in the form of food only, by 'relieving officers'. As a deterrence only certain groups of people were entitled to this relief, including the sick, the aged, and the widowed, provided they had two or more dependent, legitimate children. Outdoor relief for the able-bodied was only allowed when the workhouse was full or overcome by fever, for fear that giving outdoor relief would encourage idleness among those capable of working

(Crossman and Gray, 2011). The Poor Law Commissioners' decision to begin displaying the names of those receiving indoor and outdoor relief acted as another deterrent. While the list was to inform the ratepayers who were funding the service, it also acted as a measure of fraud detection by encouraging 'all trustworthy persons in the union' to give information 'on circumstances of persons receiving relief' (First Report of the Irish Poor Law Commissioners 1848, cited in Burke, 1987: 135). This practice continued until the 1920s. The provision of relief became a little more generous by 1880 with the Relief of Distress Act, which extended outdoor relief to all categories of need. The origins of one component of the contemporary social protection system, the Supplementary Welfare Allowance, can be traced back to the introduction of outdoor relief.

An assisted emigration scheme also emerged out of the crisis of the workhouse system during the famine. Boards of guardians became empowered to assist paupers to emigrate to other British colonies experiencing a labour shortage, such as Canada and Australia. Boards of guardians were particularly keen to arrange for the emigration of their female inmates because, as the famine receded, the population within the workhouses tended towards a greater proportion of women, as more work became available for men. There was a fear that women and children would become a long-term burden and were described as 'permanent deadweight' (Moran, 2004: 123). In addition, it was felt that if the surplus poor emigrated, improvement would follow for the rest of the population. As Duffy (2004: 80) points out, 'the idea of overpopulation as an "encumbrance on society", restricting improvements in moral and social order and civilisation, was fashionable in colonial discourse'. Emigration under the poor law system began in 1849 and continued until 1906, during which time approximately 45,000 people were assisted to emigrate (Moran, 2004). This figure is part of a much larger number of people who emigrated in the decades after the famine. Many were assisted by voluntary organisations or by landlords. Landlords found emigration schemes attractive, calculating that it would cost them less to assist people to emigrate than to continue funding them via the workhouse, given the rising poor law rates they had to pay during the famine.

Rising levels of sickness and disease were an inevitable consequence of the famine, and legislation was introduced in 1846 to require poor law unions to build fever hospitals on workhouse grounds. This expanded the role of the poor law system in providing healthcare, as previously workhouses only had a sick ward. Pauper graveyards also became part of the system after 1847. The role of the poor law system in administering health services expanded greatly in 1851, as the boards of guardians took over the running of dispensaries, thus extending the 'outdoor' nature of relief available under the poor law. This was legislated for under the Medical Charities (Ireland) Act 1851. Under this legislation, existing dispensaries were reorganised across the poor law unions. Each poor law union was divided into a number of dispensary districts and services were to be funded by the poor rate. Boards of guardians had to look after dispensary buildings, supply medicines and pay the dispensary doctor attached to each district. Dispensary doctors were charged with the care of people who couldn't afford to pay for their own healthcare and who had obtained a ticket from the management committee appointed by the board of guardians to run the service. The tickets issued were known as black and red tickets; black indicating that the bearer was entitled to receive care and medicine at the dispensary, and red indicating that the recipient's condition required home visits by the doctor (Cassell, 1997). The decision as to who was entitled to a ticket was left to the discretion of the management committee, who judged each individual case. The legislation used the words 'poor persons' as opposed to paupers when referring to who could access free healthcare from a dispensary; however, no guidelines to aid decision making were included in the legislation. As a result, while the right to healthcare was not introduced, the legislation expanded the numbers of people who could potentially be granted medical relief. Following this, the role of the poor law in providing hospital care was also expanded through the Poor Law (Ireland) Amendment Act 1861. This provided for the conversion of workhouse infirmaries into general hospitals, where poor persons with non-contagious diseases could be admitted.

Within the workhouse hospitals nuns became an important part of the nursing staff and by 1903 nuns were responsible for the nursing duties in 84 workhouse hospitals (Luddy, 1999). Nuns performing nursing work were attractive to boards of guardians because they generally worked for low pay and 'would bring with them into the workhouse all those virtues with which "good" women were credited. They would also, more importantly, create a docile and passive inmate and a more moral female patient' (Luddy, 1999: 107). The influence of the nuns was welcomed at this time because, by the 1850s, as Luddy documents, female poverty and the rising number of women presenting at the workhouses was conflated with sexual immorality. The presence of nuns was therefore perceived to help prevent the risk of moral contamination these women posed.

However, it is also important to note ways in which people responded to and used the workhouses, and the ways in which workhouse practices embodied complexity and were not uniformly and unremittingly harsh. Crossman (2013), for example, cautions against an interpretation of workhouse users as passive victims of an oppressive system. People rioted against poor quality food; complained about ill-treatment; and used the system in strategic ways by, for example, entering on a Saturday and leaving on a Monday to avoid the work regime, or entering to avail of assisted emigration. By the late nineteenth century the composition of workhouse users also changed: besides greater numbers of women, those entering more likely to be older and/or sick. The workhouse regime also changed, becoming less punitive and more focused on quality of care (Crossman, 2006). In 1862 a system of boarding out children from the workhouses began. This reflected concerns with the high level of child mortality in the workhouse and the conviction that living in a family environment was preferable for child welfare (Skehill, 2011). Boarding out remained a relatively marginal practice but forms the roots of contemporary foster care. The balance between indoor and outdoor relief also changed; by the 1890s average daily numbers in receipt of indoor relief stood at 40,000 in contrast to 59,000 for outdoor relief (Crossman and Gray, 2011).

The growth of the Catholic Church as a provider of social services from the mid-nineteenth century

The entry of nuns to staff the workhouse hospitals was part of a growing trend of Catholic involvement in welfare provision. As already discussed, charitable activity was long established; however, the mid-nineteenth century marked the development of a stronger and more organised Catholic Church. It was particularly keen to take over existing activities, such as small local orphanages, and to develop bigger institutions in the fields of health, education and childcare, with women and children foremost in their work. Their activity also focused on countering the conversion efforts of Protestant charities. However, both groups had similar attitudes to the poor they set out to help. As Preston (1998: 106) notes, 'many charities noted in their statement of intent that they helped only those who "deserved aid"'. Thus the distinction between the 'deserving' and 'undeserving' poor was not exclusive to state-provided welfare or solely imposed by a colonial administration. Deservingness was evident in the names of some of the charities, for example, the Dublin-based 'House of Protection for Distressed Young Women of Unblemished Character' and the 'House of Refuge for Industrious and Distressed Females of Good Character'. For women who had 'fallen' and whose character was considered redeemable, there was the female penitentiary or 'Magdalen' system, which aimed to house and reform women. Named after the biblical figure Mary Magdalen as a model of repentance, Magdalen homes initially targeted prostitutes, and subsequently unmarried mothers (Smith, 2007). The first Magdalen home was established in Dublin in 1767, but as congregations of religious women grew, a network of Magdalen asylums formed, including, most notably, homes run by the Good Shepherd Sisters (Finnegan, 2001). A strict disciplinary regime was followed in the Magdalen homes, based on penitence and obedience, with laundry work, carried out in silence, being the women's daily activity. Far from being unknown to the wider community, these homes advertised for laundry as a way of funding their operations:

The Magdalen Asylum Laundry. [Waterford]

The Community of the Good Shepherd beg to inform the public that in the new Magdalen Asylum Laundry, under their care, washing is done most carefully and satisfactorily as can be testified by the gentry of both County and City. The Community earnestly solicit the County and City Clubs, and also private families to send their washing, as the work in the Laundry at present is not sufficient to keep the penitents employed, and is besides, inadequate for the maintenance of the daily increasing numbers who make application for admission. The

Magdalen Asylum Laundry van will call to any place in and around the City for washing, and will deliver it in due time when done (*Waterford Chronicle*, 14 December 1895 cited in Finnegan, 2001: 47).

Besides the Magdalen homes, disciplinary control also featured heavily in the industrial and reformatory schools which began to open from the late 1850s. Unlike the Magdalen homes, these were funded by the state but still managed by religious groups. Moreover, the practice of boarding children out from workhouses remained marginal, engulfed by the growth of a system of institutional childcare via industrial and reformatory schools (Skehill, 2011). The first schools opened in Dublin; the first reformatory in Drumcondra in 1858, and the first industrial school in Sandymount in 1869. The industrial schools operated on the principle of taking children 'in their early childhood, training them to industry and good conduct' (Hill 1856 in Raftery and O'Sullivan, 1999: 63). The children placed in industrial schools included those whose parents were poor and considered unfit or unable to look after their children, as well as orphans, and children of unmarried mothers. Many of these children would have previously ended up in the workhouses; now they were brought up in industrial schools, an environment considered more appropriate for children. But there were other considerations as well. Echoing some of the logic behind the poor law, the industrial school system was considered, 'by far the cheapest and best in every point of view, since it saves the expense of prosecuting and imprisoning the children; and what is more important, by preventing them from becoming criminals, protects the community from the losses and evils they would inflict upon it' (Hill 1856 in Raftery and O'Sullivan, 1999: 63).

Reformatories catered for children sentenced by the courts, after committing an offence, usually something minor. Running these schools was an attractive proposition for the Catholic Church, because it gave them an opportunity to 'save the souls' of these children, and the institutional model of care represented 'an efficient means of maintaining the maximum control over the recipients of this care' (Raftery and O'Sullivan, 1999: 57). Thus both types of school expanded rapidly, despite the fact that early inspectors of the schools were critical both of the expansion of the system and the substandard levels of care they found in many of the schools. Overall the institutionalisation of children became an increasingly significant trend. Luddy (2014) calculates from the 1901 census that 4.5% of the population of children aged under 14 were in some institution or other. We return to the issue of institutionalised welfare post-independence in Chapters Two and Three, and examine how abuse in these institutions eventually became the subject of historical investigation and redress.

SECTION THREE
ADVANCES IN IRISH SOCIAL POLICY IN THE LATE NINETEENTH AND EARLY TWENTIETH CENTURY

> That one-half of the world knows not how the other half lives is a truth, not always acknowledged by us, but one that is strikingly emphasised when one descends into the lives and homes of those who are destined to live perpetually on the border line of subsistence, and work out a hand-to-mouth existence from day to day (MacSweeney, *A study of poverty in Cork City*, 1915: 93).

Some important developments in the late nineteenth century marked the roots of modern social policy. These were underpinned by a change, or at least a partial shift, in attitudes about poverty and poor people, and in thinking about welfare. The view of poverty as a personal failing was challenged by links established between poverty and problems beyond individual control, such as unemployment. The idea that welfare was something for the poor only, which rich people paid for but didn't avail of, and the impulse to control recipients of relief faded somewhat. Welfare began to be perceived as a matter of rights, where an individual's needs were met as a member of society or as a citizen, not as a matter of charity calibrated by notions of deservingness. However, this was not a rapid transformation; changes were often the outcome of conflict between those who maintained the view that the poor law was the most effective solution for social problems, and those who felt that people should be compensated for the problems encountered in an industrial society, such as unemployment and old age.

In Britain, emerging research about the extent of poverty, the growing strength of the labour movement and the establishment of the Fabian Society all contributed to the push towards newer social policy developments (these themes are dealt with in more detail in Chapter Four). These developments, which were implemented in Ireland as well, were not so radical as to completely overthrow the poor law system. Instead, developments occurred by recognising particular categories of people, not as paupers, but as people entitled to welfare as a right. The first legislation contributing to a structure of provision outside the poor law was the Workmen's Compensation Act 1897. This Act was significant because it was based on the recognition that a person's inability to work could be due to accidents at work, for example, which merited compensation, rather than leading to destitution and the workhouse.

The introduction of old age pensions, which had long been campaigned for as a matter of right completely detached from any notion of pauperism, was a particularly notable advance. The Old Age Pension Act 1908 meant that people over 70 could qualify for a pension and the rate at which they received the payment depended on their means. However, there were some conditions attached to entitlement. One of the reasons the pension was introduced was because of the high numbers of aged poor residing in workhouses. It was felt that the pension would help this group leave behind the workhouse and the 'disreputable inmates' with whom they were forced to live. Consequently, to ensure that the pension went to the 'deserving aged' only, several disqualifications applied. These included being in receipt of outdoor relief, being convicted under the 1898 Inebriates Act, and being detained in a lunatic asylum. Those who '"habitually failed to work" according to their ability, opportunity and need for their maintenance' (Farley, 1964: 18) were also disqualified. At the same time, the introduction of the pension was quite a radical departure from previous welfare provision. Older people in Ireland fared particularly well, as the rates set were referenced against wages and living standards in Britain which were higher than in Ireland. For many men it meant that they returned to live with their extended families, with the pension contributing to the household income, while it enhanced the status and independence of many older women (Guinnane, 1993). There was, however, the feeling that the initial number of claimants in Ireland did not accurately reflect the actual number of people who were over 70. This was complicated by the fact that a system of birth registrations was not fully functioning until 1864. As a result, some people got their pension early, with divine intervention getting the better of the pension administrators: 'Grateful thanks to the Sacred Heart of Jesus for obtaining my Old Age Pension five years before it was due' (Thanksgiving notice published in a provincial newspaper cited in Ó Gráda, 2002: 134).

Growing interest in child welfare is also evident by the late nineteenth century, reflected in philanthropic concern about child neglect, and in greater state intervention into familial child cruelty (Luddy, 2014). A Children's Act, commonly known as the *Children's Charter* was introduced in 1908. It was the first comprehensive piece of legislation to deal with children and was considered progressive in its time. The Act sought, in the words of its instigator Herbert Samuel, to rescue children from the 'bad home' (cited in Dawson 1910: 388). It provided for regulation and inspection of the guardians of children and protected children against assault, ill-treatment and danger to life or health by any person caring for them. For the greater part of the twentieth century child welfare services were founded on this Act and its later amendments (Raftery and O'Sullivan, 1999).

Alongside legislation in these areas, progress was notable in housing and rural development, demonstrated by several pieces of legislation which dealt with circumstances specific to Ireland. These circumstances had to do with increasing unrest, particularly in relation to land matters under colonial rule. One strand of this was the establishment of the Congested Districts Board in 1891. It was charged with the task of developing the poorer western regions of the country and dealing with congestion, or overcrowding. It attempted to consolidate unviable smallholdings by buying up and then redistributing land, and it also aimed to create sustainable livelihoods by developing agricultural and fishery resources. This was, as Fahey and McLaughlin (1999: 120) note, 'a unique experiment in state-led development at the time'. It went against the grain of minimal intervention and minimal redistribution, which had been the prevailing state ethos. The Board was also active in building new houses and improving the existing housing stock and in this respect it was part of a larger housing initiative which again was unique to Ireland. A series of Labourers' Acts (1883-1906) were designed to build houses for rent by landless agricultural labourers and a total of 41,000 houses were built by 1921. This initiative was, according to Aalen (1992: 140 in Fahey and McLaughlin, 1999: 120), 'the first public housing programme in the British Isles and probably in Europe'. The rural example led to pressure for similar funding of urban housing and in 1908 a Housing Act was passed to provide for urban housing development. Consequently the provision of Irish urban housing was well ahead of British provision in the early decades of the twentieth century (Fahey, 2002).

One final significant development prior to Ireland gaining independence in 1921 was the introduction of the National Insurance Act 1911. This again gave workers something to rely on as a right outside of the poor law, and established the beginnings of social insurance. The Act was based on contributory insurance with contributions coming from three sources: the employee, the employer and the state. The proposed Act was composed of two parts. The first part provided health insurance giving entitlements to medical benefits including a free general practitioner service and free prescription medicine, set apart from the dispensary service. The second part provided national insurance, giving benefits in the event of sickness or unemployment. Thus structural causes of unemployment were gaining some recognition and the language of the 'able-bodied poor' began to fade. Despite the security offered to workers by the Act, it was opposed by many groups in Ireland including the Catholic Church, the medical profession and the Irish Party on grounds such as cost and whether a predominantly agricultural country needed such a measure (Powell, 1992). On foot of this opposition, a compromise was reached which meant that while the National Insurance Act was applied to Ireland, medical benefit was excluded and an opportunity to develop an insurance-based health system was lost. Another long-lasting implication of this Act was that it laid the foundations of a **male bread winner model** of social protection. The Act operated on the assumption that the man as head of the household was the most important or sole wage earner. Women, whether married or single, were considered less important earners and were treated

> The **male bread winner model** describes the extent to which welfare states and social protection systems in particular, have been 'gendered' with certain assumptions around the roles of women and men in society.

differently in terms of contributions and benefits (Yeates, 1997). These differences, though modified over time, left a significant legacy in terms of inequalities between men and women in the social protection system.

Many women's groups were active in Ireland at this time, and women became more involved in public life beyond charity work. As Luddy (2002: 72) notes, 'by the beginning of the twentieth century women had created a diverse group of formal organisations that allowed them political expression. In addition to reform societies, which had originally been connected with women's philanthropic work, unionist, nationalist, suffrage, cultural and labour organisations had also been created'. The first suffrage society in Ireland had been established by Isabella Tod in 1871; in 1908 the Irish Women's Franchise League was formed and 'the vote' was finally granted to women over 30 in 1918. Local government reform in the late nineteenth century also widened women's participation, by affording them elected positions as poor law guardians and members of urban and district councils.

In overall terms, the range of activity and organizations of women fighting for equality and the improvement of social conditions (including the Irish Women's Workers Union and United Irishwomen), as well as the contribution of women such as Cumann na mBan – the 'League of Women' – to the nationalist agenda, seemed promising in terms of the potential for social reform once Ireland gained independence. Within the nationalist movement the promise of equality mentioned in the 1916 Proclamation, and the principles included in the Democratic Programme adopted by Sinn Féin at the first session of the Revolutionary National Assembly or Dáil Éireann in January 1919 provided grounds for optimism. For example, the Democratic Programme (Dáil Éireann, 1919) promised the abolition of the poor law and placed a strong emphasis on redistribution and equality.

Finally, and specifically with regard to gender equality, the activism of women's groups in Ireland during the early twentieth century provided further grounds for optimism about the capacity for change. The hard-fought success of the suffrage movement in securing the right to vote for women in the Representation of People Act 1918 served as a concrete example of what was possible. Despite the age restriction contained in the Act (only women over 30 were entitled to vote initially), a small group of Irish feminists continued to highlight the wider impediments to equality:

> We want equal pay for equal work, equal marriage laws, the abolition of legal disabilities, the right of women to enter the hitherto banned learned professions, women jurors and justices, in short, the complete abolition of various taboos and barriers – social, economic and political – that still impede women's progress and consequently that of the race (Editorial from the *Irish Citizen*, 1919 cited in Cullen Owens, 1984: 132).

However, these aspirations were all but ignored in Ireland in the years that followed. The equality demands of women in early-twentieth-century Ireland were given some short-lived credence but ultimately did not result in change. This change was to take the better part of the century to achieve and forms part of a more complex story about the development of social policy which is continued in the next two chapters.

Chapter summary

- This chapter provided an account of the emergence and developments of welfare measures in Ireland since the seventeenth to the early twentieth century. The earliest measures were balanced between aid and punishment, and aimed exclusively at the poor. However, the poor were categorised into 'deserving' and 'undeserving' groups, with aid for the former and punishment for the latter.
- State provision grew during the nineteenth century with the introduction of the poor law to Ireland. The network of workhouses established under the poor law represented a larger-scale effort to deal with poverty; however, the thinking behind the system remained essentially the same as heretofore.
- By the late nineteenth and early twentieth centuries, other factors became significant in the development of welfare. One was the growth of the Catholic Church as a charitable provider of welfare, but the impulse to categorise and control was something it shared with existing state provision. Another strand, which we would recognise today as the roots of modern social policy, is the shift away from workhouse provision towards cash payments in the form of pensions and national insurance.
- However, the development of social policy is not a simple story of linear progress, where each new phase succeeds in eradicating the influences of a less developed past. The history of social policy, from the past to the present, can be marked as much by repetition and regression as progression, as different strands and influences have varying weight over time, depending on the wider political, economic and cultural context.

Discussion points

- Think about your local area in terms of early social interventions. Trace the origins of institutions such as county hospitals, schools and voluntary associations, and locate their development in the wider history of social policy.
- Examine the differences between Whately's and Nicholl's proposals for a poor law for Ireland in terms of solutions to poverty.
- Consider the distinction between the deserving and undeserving poor: a relic of the past or still influential?

Further reading list

Crossman, V (2006) *The Poor Law in Ireland 1838-1948*, Dundalk: Economic and Social History Society of Ireland

Crossman, V (2013) *Poverty and the Poor Law in Ireland, 1850-1914*, Liverpool: Liverpool UP

Powell, FW (1992) *The Politics of Irish Social Policy 1600-1990*, New York: Edwin Mellen Press

Raftery, M and O'Sullivan, E (1999) *Suffer the little children: The inside story of Ireland's industrial schools*, Dublin: New Island

Notes

1. The Charitable Infirmary later became Jervis Street Hospital. The hospital was closed in 1987 and the site was subsequently developed as the Jervis Street shopping centre.
2. The North Charitable Infirmary remained open until 1988 and since became a hotel.

two

From the 1920s to the 1970s: the development of social policy in Ireland

This chapter examines the context in which social policy developed in Ireland from 1921, when the country gained independence, to the 1970s by which time modernisation had taken hold. Though there are continuities throughout this period, the chapter is very much a matter of two halves, documenting two quite different eras in which social policy evolved; the first spanning 1921 to the late 1950s and the second covering the late 1950s to the late 1970s. From the perspective of social policy developments, the first period is marked by little progress. The early decades of independence had the hallmarks of a state finding its feet, trying to carve out an identity and attempting to impose order, with few resources and little inclination to progress social policy. Not only were the economic conditions conservative, so too was the social and cultural environment in which the new state operated. This environment was dominated by the Catholic Church and ruralist values. This overall context shaped the types of social policy developments which did take place in areas such as housing and social welfare, while a turn to more coercive institutionalised responses can be discerned in other areas, such as the needs of children and unmarried mothers. The second period marks a gradual transformation of the conditions that previously inhibited social policy developments. Economic growth and a broad set of social and cultural changes provided the impetus for social policy change. Gradual reform led to the expansion of the main social services together with some recognition of issues such as poverty and discrimination, and of the needs of groups who had been neglected by the main actors and interests that had shaped social policy until the 1950s. While some progress was made it also is important not to overstress the degree and intensity of societal and social policy change during the 1960s and 1970s.

Chapter outline

- Section one examines social policy developments and the context in which they emerged during the period from the early 1920s to the end of the 1950s. The section highlights the roles of conservatism and Catholicism in social policy making and discusses key social policy developments over these decades.
- Section two reviews the main ways Ireland changed economically and socially from the late 1950s onwards. The impact of these changes on social policy is examined by looking at how the main social services expanded and how new thinking and issues came to the fore, making for a period that represented both continuity and change with the past.

SECTION ONE

THE 1920s TO THE LATE 1950s: THE EARLY DECADES OF INDEPENDENCE AND THE DEVELOPMENT OF SOCIAL POLICY

1920s: economic conservatism and social policy as social control

Contrary to the promising signs for the development of social policy as discussed at the end of Chapter One, economic and religious influences gained the upper hand over concerns with equality and social rights once Ireland achieved independence. Thus the early decades of independence were marked by a conservative and cautious approach to welfare expenditure. In addition, there was a strong Catholic influence on policy making and a value system based on rural, **patriarchal** living dominated. There was little appetite for redistributive policies, leaving class distinctions, gender inequalities and unequal childhoods undisturbed and obscured by a vision of a harmonious and morally pure agrarian society.

Patriarchy refers to both the structures and relations of male power involved in the subordination of women in the private and the public domain.

In the first decade of independence (1922–32) Cumann na nGaedheal (a new party composed of those within Sinn Féin who accepted the 1921 Treaty with Britain that granted Ireland independence as a free state, renamed Fine Gael in 1930) held power. It governed the country through what O'Connor Lysaght (1991: 49) describes as 'refurbished' versions of institutions that existed under colonial rule. A key element of this refurbishment was a highly centralised approach to policy making, which has remained more or less intact since then. At the centre of this was the Department of Finance, which kept a strong check on government expenditure. Another theme inherited from the previous century was a suspicion of welfare and its effect on character, with government minsters fearful that expansion of state welfare would make people overly dependent. For example, in 1924 the Minister for Local Government, PJ

Burke, argued that: 'one of the most serious defects of the Irish character is this tendency to dependence of one kind or another... The number of people who lead a parasitic existence ...[is] increasing relative to the number of people who are striving to make an honest living' (cited in Ó Gráda 1997: 91). The Old Age Pension was one of the first social policy measures to bear the brunt of these attitudes, and early on there was, as Ó Gráda (2002: 148) puts it, 'signs of nerves' about how much pensions were costing. In 1924 pension payments were reduced, and income taxes were lowered from 25% to 15% between 1924 and 1926.

These changes were also influenced by the state of the economy and the power of key economic actors. The Irish economy was impoverished after independence, and hampered by the effects of colonisation and a subsequent civil war, which meant that there was little industrial infrastructure and few resources for economic investment. Furthermore, agricultural interests and actors lay at the heart of class politics and represented a more influential force than the labour movement and the working classes. As Garvin (2005: 34-5) notes, 'there was a new, and large, middle class of over 200,000 farmers with between fifteen and 100 acres, which dominated society and politics because of its massive collective presence in the form of demographic weight, cultural identity and electoral political clout.'

Securing the prosperity of the farming classes was therefore an important goal for the government. Cumann na nGaedheal's economic strategy was to use agriculture as the motor for growth of the economy. Its aim was to reduce the costs of production by lowering taxation and limiting government expenditure. Other areas of social policy also suffered under this regime. The substance of the poor law remained, with some changes made to its administration. Under the Local Government (Temporary Provisions) Act 1923 many workhouses were closed, the remainder became county homes and outdoor relief was renamed 'home assistance'. Home assistance was the only payment available other than pensions and national insurance payments; any person in need and not entitled to these had to apply for home assistance to their county Board of Health and Public Assistance, which under the 1923 Act replaced Boards of Guardians. A poor person was defined under the scheme as a 'person who is unable to provide by his own industry or other lawful means the necessaries of life' (cited in Ó Cinnéide, 1970: 3). This regime remained largely in place until the 1970s. Each application was assessed by an assistance officer. The means-testing involved a household or family means test, which meant that the income of other people in a household was taken into account in making a decision and assistance was ultimately at the discretion of the Board of Health and Public Assistance. For the most part, poverty was recognised only in a very narrow way, and a family would have to display destitution in order for the applicant to receive assistance. Distinctions between the deserving and undeserving poor continued to be made, with assistance officers often making judgements on the basis of character and behaviour (Maguire, 2009). The system continued to be highly stigmatising and it was women who frequently bore the brunt of this. More women than men, including widows, deserted wives and unmarried mothers, applied for home assistance for themselves and their children. Besides this financial help, county homes cast a wide net covering a diverse range of groups, needs and 'problems' in one institution. As described by the Report of an Inter-departmental Committee on County Homes (1951 in Luddy, 2011: 115), they 'became repositories for all types and conditions of poor persons, the majority of whom were aged and infirm; but who also included considerable numbers of mental defectives, unmarried mothers, children both legitimate and illegitimate, persons suffering from long-term illnesses and some able-bodied destitute.'

County homes were part of a wider network which O'Sullivan and O'Donnell (2012: 2) identify with the practice of 'coercive confinement'. This idea relates to how such institutions, whose purpose was apparently welfare oriented, were inherently punitive in how they were run and how individuals experienced them. Coercive confinement therefore also marks how so much of social policy in the early decades of independence manifested as the institutionalised social control of vulnerable groups, while underlying social conditions such as poverty and lack of educational and employment opportunities, particularly for women, were not recognised. The institutions involved included not only county homes, but Magdalen homes, Mother and Baby homes, reformatory and industrial schools, prisons and psychiatric hospitals in the case of patients being involuntarily admitted. All of these institutions, with the exception of Mother and Baby homes, existed prior to independence. However, post-independence there seemed to be a shift in how they were used, moving further away from their philanthropic origins to increasingly becoming places of incarceration. Moreover, while none were exclusively Irish nor Catholic, relatively unique aspects of their use in Ireland included the rate of confinement which, O'Sullivan and O'Donnell (2012) suggest, was 1% of the population. Smith (2007) uses the concept of the 'architecture of containment' to describe a similar set of institutions and their legislative and policy context. For him the longevity of containment, with institutions lasting well into the mid-twentieth century while other countries were closing such institutions down, is another unique aspect of this type of social policy in Ireland.

The question of what shaped this dimension of Ireland's social policy history is a complex and contested one. Recent accounts emphasise different factors. These principally focus either on the role of the Catholic Church, in particular its role in providing social services and in dictating matters of sexual and social morality; or on the role of the state, characterised by its lack of resources, reluctance to intervene and deference to the Church. O'Sullivan and O'Donnell (2012: 267) add a third element, that is, the role of the family who strategically used institutions to 'divest themselves of a problematic [family] member'. In explaining this, they suggest that 'rural fundamentalism' and 'raw economics' (O'Sullivan and O'Donnell, 2012: 272, 273) drove such use of institutions, particularly in rural areas, where land ownership and the preservation of family farms mattered enormously. The likelihood is that all factors, religious, state and familial, constitute partial explanations and were mutually reinforcing.

At the same time it must be acknowledged that the everyday experiences and encounters of people with the social policy regime of the time, particularly people who were marginalised, remain a largely hidden element of Ireland's social policy history. Echoing recent research on how people used the poor law, as mentioned in Chapter One, emerging research on the post-independence context has looked at how working-class women were active agents who used various strategies to resist, or at least not passively accept, the ways in which their lives were regulated (Brophy and Delay, 2015). Earner-Byrne (2015) has, for example, looked at how women whose families were in severe poverty used the church and state ideal of motherhood to make their case in seeking financial assistance from the Catholic Church. Maguire (2009: 49) documents the fact that not all unmarried mothers were coercively confined, noting that ISPCC archives demonstrate 'the almost heroic efforts some women made, sometimes with the help of family and friends and sometimes entirely on their own, to keep their children'. Such findings do not belie the fact that the social policy in the decades after independence was predominantly conservative and controlling. Yet they also suggest that an awareness of diversity and complexity is needed in interpreting how people experienced and negotiated the landscape of social provision. Bearing this in mind we turn to look in more detail at the key ways in which the state and the Catholic Church together shaped and delivered social policy post-independence, and in particular the impact this had on women and children.

The Catholic Church, the state and social policy

> The Church speaks to the state as fully an equal, not as a subordinate part, or in any way dependent on, or drawing its powers from, the State (Coyne, 1951: 132).

Once the country gained independence, the Catholic Church sought to consolidate its position in Irish society. The Church saw itself as equal to the state and having a higher authority than any other group in society when it came to commenting on or criticising state activity. And while the Church was in the business of securing people's eternal salvation, in practice this meant that the Church felt it had as much authority on social questions as moral questions, because it did not see the two as mutually exclusive spheres. This was made clear in *Quadragesimo Anno*, a Papal Encyclical written by Pope Pius XI in 1931:

> It is Our right and Our duty to deal authoritatively with social and economic problems. ... the deposit of truth entrusted to Us by God, and Our weighty office of declaring, interpreting and urging, in season and out of season, the entire moral law, demand that both the social order and economic life be brought within our supreme jurisdiction (cited in Coyne, 1951: 136).

Much of the Church's focus on authority and morality was expressed through attempts to control women and families, seen as the foundation of social order in the newly independent state. For women, the Church prescribed the role of motherhood, which included strict regulation of sexuality. This thinking resulted in policies that discriminated against women. Women's rights were denied in many areas and instead of pursuing the vision of equality contained in the 1916 Proclamation, discrimination and inequality was legitimised by the state. For the state as for the Church, the regulation of sexuality and sexual desire by tying it to marriage in which women were subordinate partners, was central to social order and social control. This need to maintain order was heightened in the early decades of independence as the new state tried to define its national identity in the aftermath of colonisation and curb any risk of instability or ungovernability (Valiulis, 2011). In this scheme of things unmarried mothers in particular were judged to bring '"shame" to the nation and their families' (Luddy, 2011: 112). Reflecting O'Sullivan and O'Donnell's (2012) observations about the role of the family in coercive confinement, concern about illegitimacy also suited the economic interests of the land-owning class, as the emphasis on land ownership dominated all other spheres of life, including decisions about marriage. Children born outside of wedlock upset this order (Inglis, 2005).

Regarding the regulation of sexuality, three influential reports were written between 1927 and 1931. In 1927, the *Report of the Committee on Evil Literature* and the *Report of the Commission on the Relief of the Sick and Destitute Poor Including the Insane Poor* were both published. These were followed in 1931 by the *Report of the Committee on the Criminal Law Amendment Acts (1880-5) and Juvenile Prostitution*, referred to as the Carrigan report. However this report remained unpublished due to what was regarded as the sensitive nature of its content. The concerns of these reports provide the background to the Censorship of Publications Act 1929, which prohibited literature advertising contraceptives, and the Criminal Law Amendment Act 1935, which went further by prohibiting the importation and sale of contraceptives. The 1935 legislation was also aided by the 1930 Papal Encyclical, *Casti Connubii*, which condemned contraception, abortion and sterilisation regardless of the circumstances.

Concern with unmarried mothers preoccupied the members of the *Commission on the Relief of the Sick and Destitute Poor Including the Insane Poor*. Economics and morality were intertwined in this concern: there was a feeling that the number of unmarried mothers residing in county homes was a strain on resources, and there was also uneasiness about unmarried mothers mixing with the 'deserving' poor and sick (McAvoy, 1999). The Commission suggested that unmarried mothers be divided into two categories, those capable of being reformed, or 'first offenders', and 'less hopeful cases' who had 'fallen' more than once and had more than one 'illegitimate' child. The Commission recommended that the first group could be reformed by character and training. Mother and Baby homes, set up during the 1920s and 1930s and run by religious orders, but aided by the state, were considered suitable institutions for the first group. Such homes included Bessborough House in Cork city run by the Sisters of the Sacred Heart of Jesus and Mary, and St Patrick's Home, run by the Sisters of Charity in Dublin. However, the regime within such institutions appeared as punitive as that within Magdalen homes, which were recommended as places of detention for the less hopeful cases, who, it was considered, posed the threat of contagion.

Children born outside of marriage, particularly those in Mother and Baby homes, were also part of unregulated, informal and, in some cases, forced adoption system. Catholic charities arranged for the overseas adoption of these children, predominantly to American Catholic families; a practice which continued until the 1970s (Maguire, 2002). Adoption was not officially recognised until the Adoption Act 1952. Legislated for much later than other European countries, strong resistance was mounted by the Church which felt that adoption, along with fostering, posed a risk to the religious welfare of the children involved.

As for other children in need, the use of industrial and reformatory schools continued, accentuating the trend of an institutionalised response to child welfare identified pre-independence. In practice, the number of children in industrial schools far outweighed those in reformatories. Moreover, as Ferriter (2004: 325) notes 'by 1924 there were more children in industrial schools in the Irish Free State than there were in all of the industrial schools in England, Scotland, Wales and Northern Ireland combined. Abolished in England in 1933, the system was tenaciously clung to in Ireland'. Conditions within the Catholic managed schools were incredibly tough and children were at risk of starvation, abuse and neglect. These conditions were highlighted by school inspections, yet nothing was done by either Church or state to improve or abolish the system, despite critical comments from inspection reports emerging as early as the 1940s (Holohan, 2011). The state, in particular, was reluctant to take responsibility for the care of those Gilligan (2014: 157) terms 'public children', that is those who required support and care beyond the private domain of the family and who were more likely also to come from 'humble and impoverished background[s]'. Unemployment, poverty, malnutrition, and unsanitary and over-crowded housing were in many cases the reasons underlying child neglect and deprivation, and why children were removed from their families and placed in industrial schools. These social conditions were in turn symptomatic of a lack of state supports for working-class families (Maguire, 2009) and children of the aforementioned 'less hopeful' category of unmarried mother were also likely to end up in industrial schools.

1930s: the influence of early Fianna Fáil governments

> If there are to be hair shirts at all, it will be hair shirts all round. Ultimately I hope the day will come when the hair shirt will give way to the silk shirt all round (de Valera, 1932 in Moynihan, 1980: 205).

By the early 1930s Fianna Fáil was in government, having taken power from Fine Gael in 1932. Fianna Fáil was a new party founded by Éamon de Valera in

1926, comprising people within Sinn Féin who opposed the 1921 treaty. Fianna Fáil took a more active stance on social problems and its electoral strategy of a cross-class alliance was designed to overpower Fine Gael and its more well-off supporters. While coercive confinement continued, Fianna Fáil did succeed in implementing some positive social policy measures, particularly in relation to housing, and to a lesser extent in relation to social welfare. The Church still remained dominant, with its armour strengthened by the publication of *Quadragesimo Anno*. The Encyclical stated that 'it is an injustice, ... a grave evil and a disturbance of right order, for a larger and higher association to arrogate to itself functions which can be performed efficiently by smaller and lower societies' (1931, paras 79–80 cited in Powell 1992, 232). This is known as the principle of **subsidiarity** and the implication for the state is that it should not take on the responsibility for providing social services where needs could be met by smaller entities, such as individuals themselves, their families or through voluntary organisations. In the Irish context this became a mechanism which shaped the relationship between the state and families; the state only intervened in ways which were consistent with the Church's perspective.

> **Subsidiarity** is a principle which originates in, but is not exclusive to, Catholic social teaching, which considers that matters of policy and provision should be handled by the smallest, most local or least centralised unit possible.

The state of the economy and the economic policy Fianna Fáil chose to pursue was another factor shaping social policy. A worldwide economic depression during the 1930s impacted on Ireland by closing off opportunities to emigrate and creating a dramatic rise in unemployment. The number of unemployed people rose from 29,331 in December 1931 to 102,619 in December 1932 (Powell, 1992). Fianna Fáil's approach to the economy was to pursue a policy of protectionism. This policy was instrumental in shaping Irish society according the party's vision of a self-sufficient, non-materialistic country, able to shake off any external influences, be they cultural or economic. Economic protectionism was implemented by imposing high import taxes on foreign goods and by discouraging foreign investment in the Irish economy. Instead, Irish industries were encouraged to produce Irish goods for Irish consumption; a strategy underpinned by the value of frugality.

While the state of the economy meant that little wealth was generated, Fianna Fáil partly carved out its identity by distinguishing itself from the harsher approach Cumann na nGaedheal took to social policy. It used pensions in particular to mark itself out as different, and once in government it eased the means test applied to state pensions. And while Cumann na nGaedheal's greatest activity in social policy was in housing, as it built approximately 14,000 homes for smallholders in congested districts and for urban artisans, Fianna Fáil became even more active in housing. This allowed Fianna Fáil to gain extra electoral support, especially from people who might otherwise have voted for the Labour Party. At the same time, its housing policy efforts, especially in relation to rural housing, reflected an important symbolic vision on de Valera's part. As Walsh (1999: 50) explains,

> for de Valera, the labourer epitomised the cultural and economic values of a rural idyll. But the idyll was tarnished by poverty, poor health and housing conditions. The resulting high levels of emigration caused uneasiness in government circles. It was felt that a cottage and small plot at a low rent would provide the labourer with a mainstay at all times and root him in the land. It was not envisioned that this would lead to a luxurious life-style.

Thus the Housing Act 1932 allowed for compulsory acquisition of land and increased the finance available to local authorities for cottage building. Between 1931 and 1942, 82,000 dwellings were constructed (Curry, 2011). In 1936 a Labourer's Act provided for the sale of cottages to labourers; however, the Act defined a labourer very widely to encourage home ownership among rural dwellers. This marked the beginnings of the strong preoccupation with home ownership in Irish housing policy. This continued throughout the twentieth century as more and more groups of people were considered eligible to buy the homes they were renting from a local authority. Home ownership was elevated for the sense of security and protection it offered otherwise poor people and was supported by all political parties.

Another factor motivating Fianna Fáil's social policy initiatives was the growth of more radical left-wing groups in the 1930s responding to the economic crisis and the growth of unemployment. For de Valera

> If men are hungry they will not be too particular about the ultimate principles of the organisation they would join, if that organisation promises to give them bread ... what we have got to do is to remove the breeding ground of attachment to false principle. That breeding ground is there in the present economic situation (de Valera cited in Daly, 2011: 31).

This reasoning not only stimulated investment in housing but was also a factor in the introduction of public relief works for those on the unemployment register and the introduction of the Unemployment Assistance Act 1933. Unemployment assistance was designed to provide means-tested relief for the unemployed without entitlement to national insurance or whose entitlement had expired. However, when it was introduced the severity of means-testing meant that far fewer people actually received payment than those who initially applied. Only 60,000 people had qualified out of 200,000 applicants by May 1934 (Powell, 1992). Strong protest from the unemployed poor resulted in some changes to the severity of the means-testing.

Another method of dealing with the unemployment problem was to further restrict women's right to work. In 1932 Fianna Fáil introduced a marriage bar requiring women to retire from teaching and the civil service upon marriage. Women's right to work was further curtailed in the Conditions of Employment Act 1936 which gave power to the Minister for Industry to restrict the number of women in industry. This was debated in terms of fitness for work and women were not considered fit for many forms of employment. This view was bolstered by the assumption that the man in a family would be the breadwinner and that the growth of female employment would threaten male employment. These issues went unopposed by the trade union movement with the exception of the Irish Women Workers' Union and some female senators, such as Kathleen Clarke (Hutton, 1991). The dominant thinking however meant that, as Conroy-Jackson (1993: 77) put it: 'unemployment was merely a theoretical concept for women'.

This thinking on the position of women was cemented in the new Irish Constitution, introduced by de Valera in 1937. Ireland already had a Free State constitution; however, this was felt to be too heavily laden with 'the "repugnant symbols" of imperialism' (Keogh, 1987: 6). In de Valera's constitution colonial influences were replaced by religious influences as well as nationalist and republican strands of thinking. Catholic social principles were strongly evident, especially in sections relating to the family (Article 41), education (Article 42) and religion (Article 44). Yet, these articles, as Murray (2016: 502) argues, contained 'a minimal set of socio-economic rights, primarily those of property, education and child welfare provision'. Other areas of social policy were more weakly expressed as directive principles, meaning that they were not legally binding.

A draft of the constitution was published in May 1937. Many women's organisations, such as the Joint Committee of Women's Societies and Social Workers, and the Irish Women's Workers Union, were opposed to several of the articles for undermining women's rights and for posing differentiated citizenship for men and women (Beaumont, 1997). In particular they were opposed to Article 41.2 on the family, which is based on very different roles, rights and responsibilities for men and women. However despite opposition, in its final form the Article reads as follows:

> 41.2.1 In particular, the State recognises that by her life within the home, woman gives to the state a support without which the common good cannot be achieved.

> 41.2.2 The State shall therefore, endeavour to ensure that all mothers shall not be obliged by economic necessity to engage in labour to the neglect of their duties in the home (Constitution of Ireland, 1937).

The idea of an all-encompassing sexual difference between men and women appeared again in Article 45, where a reference was made to the state's intention to protect women and children from unsuitable 'avocations' because of their 'inadequate strength'. The women's groups opposition succeeded in having the phrase 'inadequate strength' dropped (O'Callaghan, 2002). However the final version of Article 45.4.2 still assumes a sexual division of labour: 'the state shall endeavour to ensure that the strength and health of workers, men and women, and the tender age of children shall not be abused and that citizens shall not be forced by economic necessity to enter avocations unsuited to their sex, age or strength' (Constitution of Ireland, 1937).

1940s: developments in relation to children and to health

In the 1940s one of the most significant developments in social policy was the introduction of a Children's Allowance in 1944. The Irish Women's Citizen's and Local Government Association had been promoting the idea of a children's allowance since the 1920s, suggesting that it would contribute to child welfare, and at the same time give wives 'a sense of contributing to her share of the family exchequer' (United Irishwomen, 1926 in Beaumont, 1997: 176). However, the eventual implementation of the Act did not quite meet their aspirations, as the payment was made to the father as the head of the household, a stipulation that remained until 1974. Yet, as a social policy measure, Ó Gráda (2002) suggests that it was the most radical development since the introduction of the Old Age Pension in 1908. Part of its significance lay in the fact that it was introduced as a universal rather than as a means–tested payment. That is, it was made available to all families with children, regardless of their income. Additionally the expenditure involved represented a major commitment; it initially added 25% to the government's social welfare expenditure, all the more significant for occurring during the Second World War (Cousins, 1999). The financial implications of the Act did not go unopposed, as the Department of Finance voiced its conservative opinion. It argued that: 'The principle has not been generally accepted that the State has responsibility for the relief of poverty in all its degrees. The State's responsibility lay only in relation to the relief of destitution: i.e. extreme cases where employment and the minimum necessities of existence are lacking' (cited in Cousins, 1999: 42).

This reflected attitudes towards poverty that had prevailed since the nineteenth century; however, as Cousins (1999: 50) suggests, the 1930s and 1940s became a time when 'the domains of life for which the state was perceived as having some responsibility were expanding'. The 'domain of life' that was relevant here was family poverty, and Lemass, the Minister for Industry and Commerce who introduced the Children's Allowance, couched it in terms of alleviating the poverty experienced by large families. Therefore, the payment was initially only made to families with three or more children. Interestingly, the introduction of the Children's Allowance was approved by the Catholic Church, which was of the opinion that it did not contravene the principle of subsidiarity. In its view the payment would supplement the family wage, not supplant it. However, three years later, another universal scheme, this time in the area of healthcare, did not meet with the same approval by the Church. This gave rise to a key episode in social policy development in the twentieth century: the mother and child controversy.

The proposed mother and child scheme revealed the extent not only of Church control and influence on social policy, but also the power of the medical profession in shaping heath policy. Health services had not progressed very far since independence. The health status of the population did not compare favourably with other European countries and hospitals 'were old, rundown, ill equipped to the extent that they were more of a danger or hazard to health than they were capable of restoring patients to health' according to Noël Browne (1986: 140), the Minister for Health during the inter-party government of 1948-51. The basis of the mother and child scheme already existed in Fianna Fáil's plans for health reform during the late 1940s. These plans were prompted by growing concern with the health status of the population. Ill health particularly affected the poorest sections of the population whose living conditions were very meagre and lacked adequate sanitation. These conditions affected children in particular and the mortality rate for infants was very high. In 1945 the Department of Local Government and Public Health prepared proposals for the development of the health services, which over time were intended to cover the whole of the population.

The mother and child element of the scheme was designed to provide a comprehensive package of healthcare free to mothers and children up to 16 years, exclusive of both compulsion and means-testing. The scheme was to be delivered through the dispensary system, to be improved with extra staffing and better accommodation. Services provided in the dispensary would be augmented by home visits during the child's early years and school visits once a child reached school age (McCarthy, 2004). It was felt that this would be an effective way of tackling the health problems that came to the fore in the 1940s. It would also represent a very definite move forward in terms of developing Ireland's welfare state and expanding social rights. However, the idea of a welfare state was not welcomed by everyone. The Department of Finance again rowed in with its conservative views, with McElligott, the Secretary of the Department of Finance, feeling that comprehensively provided state healthcare would have a detrimental effect on character:

Figure 2.1: Mother and child scheme explanatory booklet

WHAT THE NEW SERVICE MEANS TO EVERY FAMILY

Source: NAI, TSCH/3/S14997A

There was at one time in the country the belief – perhaps it still persists – that to take a 'red ticket' involved a certain loss of caste and that the doctor should be paid if the money could be found at all. That very proper pride will surely be steadily diminished if the farmers' sons and daughters can get this medical benefit without any transfer of cash. That spirit of independence was very valuable, and I am not actuated by financial considerations when I say it is a pity that it should be helped to disappear (McElligott, 1944 in McKee, 1986: 166).

Nevertheless a Health Act reflecting the Department of Local Government and Public Health's proposals was passed in 1947. Fianna Fáil lost power in a general election in 1948 that saw a coalition government forming, consisting of Fine Gael, the Labour Party and Clann na Poblachta, of which Browne was a member. Browne became the new Minister for Health and had the task of implementing part 3 of the 1947 Act, which comprised the mother and child scheme. For the Church however, this signalled the advent of overly interventionist state provision and it opposed the notion of universal entitlement to healthcare for mothers and children. The banner of subsidiarity was brought to bear in their opposition:

The right to provide for the health of children belongs to parents not the State. The State has a right to intervene only in a subsidiary capacity ... It may help indigent or neglectful parents; it may not deprive 90% of parents of their rights because of 10% necessitous or negligent parents (Staunton, 1950 in Powell, 1992: 257).

The Church also opposed the scheme on the grounds that there was no guarantee that the healthcare delivered would be in accordance with Catholic social principles. It feared that the care provided would include advice on birth control, and that Catholic women might be cared for by Protestant doctors. Therefore the scheme was deemed, by the Archbishop of Dublin, Dr Charles McQuaid, to be 'entirely contrary to Catholic social teaching, the rights of the family, the rights of the church in education, and the rights of the medical profession and of voluntary institutions' (cited in Whyte, 1971: 143). It seemed that McQuaid was defending everybody's rights but those who needed the service.

The mention of the medical profession here points to the fact that it was also strongly opposed to the scheme. The medical profession's preference as outlined in a plan previously submitted to the Department of Local Government and Public Health was for 'free medical relief for the poor, a contributory service for wage earners, and the preservation of the upper income field as a battleground for the more enterprising practitioners' (cited in McKee, 1986: 163). Essentially the medical profession felt the scheme threatened its right to practice and profit from private medicine, therefore it opposed the idea of a mother and child scheme without means-testing.

Browne did not agree with the reasoning of either the Church or the medical profession. In a series of exchanges Browne had with the Church and with other members of the inter-party government, he was adamant that means-testing was not the way to proceed and the differences became irresolvable. The outcome was that Browne was forced to resign and the new Fianna Fáil government, elected in 1951 introduced a new Health Act in 1953. It contained a scheme similar to that of the mother and child scheme but with vital differences. A means test was imposed and services were to be made available only until a child reached six weeks rather than 16 years of age. After Browne resigned he published correspondence between himself and the Church in the *Irish Times* newspaper. This made public for the first time the strength of Church–state relations. However, it also shielded the medical profession's power to obstruct change. The 1953 Act was still unpalatable to the medical profession and a compromise was reached by the promise of the development of a voluntary insurance scheme, which would assist people in paying for private care. An opportunity to develop a comprehensive health service free at the point of use therefore failed and the legacy of this lost opportunity remains to the present time.

1950s: economic failure, unemployment and emigration

Over the 1950s the economy became the main focus of attention and by the end of the decade the policy of economic protectionism finally came to an end. The failure of protectionism became more apparent in the aftermath of the Second World War when other European countries experienced post-war economic growth and improved standards of living. While Ireland did experience some of the benefits of post-war economic growth, by the 1950s this had petered out. Balance of payments crises in the 1950s highlighted the unsustainability of protectionism as goods imported far exceeded goods exported. Demand for imports was dampened by higher taxes and public spending cutbacks. The result of this austerity was a stagnant economy. By 1957, unemployment peaked at 78,000. Agricultural employment was in decline and government cutbacks also affected particular trades, especially building. An equally worrying trend was the rising emigration levels, which were a direct consequence of unemployment and without which unemployment would have been much higher. Emigration levels also peaked in 1957, with 78,000 people leaving the country that year. This was part of a larger net loss of 408,800 people between the 1951 and 1961 (O'Hanlon, 2004).

Emigrating rather than struggling with unemployment therefore seemed to be the more common choice. Living standards were undeniably higher in Britain, which was where most people went. In addition, life as an emigrant was also preferable to many, particularly women, who had more options and rights abroad (Yeates, 2004). For married women for example, in Britain 40% of Irish-born married women participated in the labour force, compared to only 7% in Ireland (O'Hanlon, 2004). Many of these women worked in professions such as nursing, reflecting the fact that emigrating gave these women the opportunity to develop their careers, an option that the marriage bar denied them in Ireland. The growth of the welfare state in Britain also highlighted the underdeveloped and stigmatising versions of welfare offered in Ireland. Donál MacAmhlaigh in an account of his life as an Irish emigrant labourer in England in the 1950s wrote of the way that the British welfare state highlighted the class inequality and degradation that existed in parts of Ireland:

> it has many qualities that are closer to Christian values than much at home in Ireland ... at home, such as I saw it, if you can get a ticket to go to the doctor, you have to wait in an old ruin of a house. Look around you and all you see is poverty, despair and dirt, both on people themselves and on their clothes. The people go in to the doctor as they used to go into the aristocrats or the landlords long ago – shaking with humility. In England he'll give you to understand that you are a person and not a beggar (cited in Ferriter, 2004: 478).

While the general response to emigration seemed to be one of ambivalence nevertheless a decision was made to set up a Commission on Emigration and Other Population Problems during the coalition government of 1948-51. It reported in 1954, during the period of a second coalition government, between 1954 and 1957 (this time a coalition of Fine Gael, the Labour Party and Clann na Talmhan). The Commission was, as Connolly (2004: 87) notes, the first, 'conscious effort made by an Irish administration to study population trends with particular emphasis on emigration'. Most of the Commission's recommendations centred on economic development which would result in rising living standards. However, it seemed pessimistic about the likelihood of economic development occurring because of a lack of resources. The Commission also acknowledged the need to improve welfare through diet, clothing and housing. It focused particularly on the need for rural development, through measures such as rural electrification, and the improvement of postal, telephone, transport and health services. In itself, the work of the Commission did little to halt emigration. However, by the late 1950s increasing attention was given to the state of the economy and the need to find new solutions for the lack of the economic progress. This became a pivotal point at which economic policy and, to a lesser extent social policy, altered course.

SECTION TWO

THE LATE 1950s TO THE LATE 1970s: ECONOMIC GROWTH, SOCIAL CHANGE AND THE GRADUAL EXPANSION OF SOCIAL POLICY PROVISION

In November 1958 the government published a *Programme for Economic Expansion* which was to provide the impetus for a new path of industrial development. This was preceded by an influential paper, *Economic Development*, written by TK Whitaker in May 1958 (Department of Finance, 1958). At this point Fianna Fáil was again back in power and its outlook began to change as Seán Lemass took over leadership of the party from de Valera in 1959. Prior to that he had been the Minister for Industry and Commerce and had long been campaigning for a change of direction in economic policy. By 1958, in the *Programme for Economic Expansion*, the government admitted the need to 'redefine the objectives of economic policy' (GoI [Government of Ireland], 1958: 7) in order to tackle emigration and unemployment. It also wanted to prevent Irish standards of living falling further behind the rest of Europe, which was now forging ahead with the creation of the EU (then the European Economic Community [EEC]) in 1958. The *Programme* envisaged radical changes in industrial policy: 'we must be prepared to welcome foreign participation, financial and technical, in new industrial activities aimed at exports' (GoI, 1958: 36). A strong role for the state was envisaged through the financing of various schemes designed to encourage industrial development, the promotion of exports through the agency Coras Tráchtála Teo., and the attraction of foreign investment through the Industrial Development Authority. Alongside these measures aimed at stimulating private enterprise, the state also expanded the semi-state sector, and development of its own activities in steel, shipping, public transport, electricity, turf, civic aviation, telephones, mining and tourism.

The late 1950s and early 1960s therefore marked the beginning of the period that saw Ireland become a much more open economy, with a significant focus on trade, exports and foreign direct investment as the recipe for economic growth and increased standard of living. As will be explored in Chapter Three, the model has mutated over time and has not, for a variety of reasons, proved particularly stable. Over the 1960s and 1970s significant economic expansion was achieved and the structure of the economy shifted from agriculture to industry and services. The economy grew at an annual average of 4.4% of GDP between 1960 and 1973, and 4.9% of GDP between 1973 and 1979 (OECD, 1999). Initially emphasis was placed on productive spending, or spending that would directly benefit the economy, which meant that social policy had to take a back seat. Resources were eventually channelled to develop some social services; however, the view that social policy is subordinate to economic policy remained strong. Yet economic thinking was the not the only driver of social policy developments during the 1960s and 1970s. These decades were also witness to a period of acute social and cultural change.

Social change and social policy

Over the 1960s conservative values and attitudes were gradually changing and Ireland slowly became a more open, secular and urbanised society. A number of factors contributed to this. The media became influential as an agent of change. By the 1960s news media had grown substantially, and with it the growth of social reporting, represented, for example, by articles written by journalist Michael Viney on the relatively hidden subjects such as unmarried mothers, alcoholism and childhood deprivation. The introduction of television (Telifís Éireann) in

1961 also had a significant impact. As Lee (1979: 173, 172) observes, television became a 'major conduit of imported mass cultural influences' which coincided with 'a questioning mentality and a receptivity to change'. The media also enabled various groups and movements to generate public concern for their various causes. In the case of children and industrial schools, for example, Daly (2016: 171) notes 'a range of interest groups began to scrutinise conditions in the industrial schools, asking awkward questions and publicising their concerns'. Notable among these groups were the Joint Committee of Women's Societies and Women Social Workers, and the group Tuairim, whose 1966 report, *Some of our children: A report on the residential care of the deprived child in Ireland*, gained significant media attention (Finn, 2012).

The Catholic Church was one of the established actors in social policy that began being open to question as, 'before the mid-1960s it was unheard of for an Irish bishop to submit himself to interview' (Whyte, 1971: 79). The Church itself also developed a more critical view of the state's activity in social policy and 'government departments were increasingly likely to be criticised for not doing enough, rather than for doing too much' (Whyte, 1971: 76). This partly reflected the influence of the second Vatican Council, held in Rome between 1962 and 1965, which reviewed the position of the Church in a modernising world, and oriented its message more towards the need for social justice. The decline in vocations was also influential, leading to a gradual decline in the number of religious working in key areas of the social services such as hospitals and schools.

Ireland's rural way of life was also changing. By the 1971 census more people lived in urban rather than rural areas for the first time (Ferriter, 2012). Another first was the fact that Ireland actually encountered a period of inward migration, with immigration of 109,000 recorded for 1971-79 (Blackwell, 1982). Lifestyles and expectations were rapidly changing. As the economy was expanding standards of living were on the increase. While some political and religious leaders worried about the effects of modernisation, dissatisfaction with how wealth was distributed, inequities in income and taxation and the uneven impact of economic growth were also coming to the fore. Some of this made an impact on how the main political parties positioned themselves. As early as 1963 Lemass (1963), leader of Fianna Fáil declared that 'I believe that the time has come when national policy should take a shift to the left', by which he meant economic progress should be translated into improved social conditions and social services. Fine Gael (1965) issued a document called *Towards a Just Society* in 1965, suggesting it was also becoming more attuned to social justice issues (Meehan, 2013), while in 1967 the Labour Party promised that the 'seventies will be socialist' (Puirséil, 2007).

The 1970s more generally was a decade of radicalism and protest for some organised groups including community and women's groups and the trade union movement. These groups made their voices heard in different ways and ultimately left their mark in core social policy areas including gender equality, access to public services, responses to poverty and in generally challenging the status quo.

The renewal of the Irish women's movement acted as a significant force for change, and highlighted how social policy developments still left a lot to be desired in terms of women's welfare. One consequence of this was the establishment of the Commission on the Status of Women in 1970. This was the result of campaigning by a long-established women's group, the Irish Housewives Association, which joined with other groups to form an Ad Hoc Committee of Women's Organisations for the purpose of lobbying the government to set up the Commission. The bulk of the Commission's work focused on equal pay and equal work conditions for women, as well as equality in areas such as social welfare, focusing particularly on the social welfare needs of marginalised women such as deserted wives, widows and unmarried mothers (Commission on the Status of Women, 1972). Another strand of the women's movement was represented by the emergence of more radical groups, including the Irish Women's Liberation Movement (IWLM) formed in 1970 and Irish Women United formed in 1975. Preferring direct action they challenged the confining roles mapped out for women in Irish society. In this regard for example, the IWLM picketed the GPO (General Post Office) in protest of the fact that Children's Allowances were still automatically paid to the father. In another event, IWLM members took the train to Belfast and returned to Dublin with contraceptives, thus contravening the ban on importation and sale of contraceptives under the Criminal Law Amendment Act 1935 and challenging customs officials to arrest them. Lack of access to contraception also motivated the establishment of the Irish Family Planning Association in 1969 (initially called the Irish Fertility Company) which also challenged the 1935 Act by opening clinics in Dublin providing guidance on and access to contraception (Daly, 2016).

The emergence of women's groups along with other community-based organisations marked a shift in emphasis from 'charity' towards an ethos of participation and empowerment, which were important values in the growth of community activism (Donoghue, 1999). Such activism was also more likely to oppose the state, pointing out the ways in which state action actually 'played an important role in underpinning patterns of disadvantage' (Curtin and Varley, 1995: 380), rather than alleviating it. This was particularly the case for emerging tenants' groups and housing action groups, such as the Dublin Housing Action Committee, who were critical of the economic development as it was unfolding, because of its effects on poorer communities in both urban and rural areas (Irish Times, 1968). Advocacy groups also formed such as CARE (Campaign for the Care of Deprived Children), reflecting a growing childcare movement who argued that substantial improvements needed to be made in how deprived children were looked after by the state, as a matter of social justice, not charity. This movement was also influenced by the growth of new understandings of childhood and children's needs, including developmental needs focusing on emotional and psychological development as well as physical welfare (O'Sullivan, 1979).

Greater attention to poverty also evolved via the so-called 'rediscovery of poverty'. This saw the emergence of evidence, first in the US and UK and later in Ireland, that 'poverty hadn't gone away'. In their landmark UK study, Abel-Smith and Townsend (1965) were instrumental in reconceptualising poverty and its measurement. Their approach was based on a relative understanding of poverty, which considered the circumstances of individuals relative to the rest of the society in which they lived. In Ireland, the first research incorporating this perspective was presented at the Kilkenny Conference on Poverty, organised by the Catholic Church's newly formed Council for Social Welfare, in 1971. Despite improvements in the economy, Ó Cinnéide (1972) found that at least 24% of the population fell below the poverty line. This research confirmed the existence of significant social problems which others had also highlighted. It also exposed the inadequacies of Irish welfare provision and its limited capacity to deal with poverty. This pioneering work marked the beginning of more sustained attention to and research on the causes and incidence of poverty in Ireland.

The wider issue of wealth distribution also gained attention in the early 1970s. The degree of wealth inequality in Ireland was highlighted in a study by economist Patrick Lyons (1972). His research, based on Estate Duty returns (a tax paid on the value of a person's estate at the time of their death) estimated that 5% of people in the Republic owned 72% of the estate capital, whereas 47% of estate capital was owned by the top 5% in the North. The media attention the research generated facilitated the introduction of a short-lived wealth tax by the Fine Gael/Labour government in 1975 (Sandford and Morrissey, 1985).

Some social policy developments were also aided by membership of the EEC, which Ireland joined in 1973. Though more commonly associated with the economic benefits it brought, membership brought social benefits as well. Joining the EEC forced Ireland to pay much more attention to equality policies, specifically in relation to equality of opportunity for women in the workforce. The establishment of an EEC anti-poverty programme in Ireland, as Donoghue (1998a: 20) notes, 'provided another building block in community activism as this emphasised the structural causes of poverty and promoted a process of community empowerment'. Ireland also benefited from economic and social investment under the EEC's distributive policies which made structural funding available to its poorer member states.

State capacity in terms of social policy making also expanded with the establishment of the National Economic and Social Council (NESC) in 1973. This body, whose members were drawn from a range of interests, was noteworthy both as an emerging structure of national social partnership and in terms of enhancing 'the flow of information and intelligence available to such decision-makers as choose to take cognisance of them' (Lee, 1989: 365). Work produced by the NESC in its early years examined previously neglected debates in Irish social policy including universal and selective provision of services, issues of distribution and the objectives of social policy. While the NESC makes policy recommendations to government, these do not have to be accepted or implemented. Nevertheless, the emergence of an advisory body with such a focus represented a major boost for development of social policy debate in Ireland at that time.

Developments in social policy

Greater policy engagement and rising social expenditure can be seen from the early 1960s onwards. Following a decade of stagnation from 1952 to 1962 when the annual real growth rate in social expenditure rose by 1.5%, the period 1963-75 was one of major expansion when social expenditure rose in annual real terms by 8.8%. Expenditure increases slowed after the first oil price shock in 1973 and later grew again leading to an annual expenditure growth rate of 4.8% overall for the second half of the 1970s (Maguire, 1986).

One of the first areas of social policy to benefit from the change in economic policy was education. The 1960s saw a shift away from an elite model of education to a mass model, with a growing role for the state, which had previously been minimal, as provision was left to the various churches. Education was justified as productive spending, reflecting the popularity of the idea of education as human capital in the 1960s; in other words, investment in people by educating and training them is an important source of economic growth. A report entitled *Investment in Education* followed in 1965, which was jointly published by the Irish government and the OECD (OECD, 1965). Unsurprisingly, it found that significant class and regional inequalities existed in education participation rates and, given the rate of economic growth, the education system would not be fulfilling the needs of the economy by the 1970s. It suggested therefore that expanding the education system and increasing participation would be both economically prudent and contribute to equality of opportunity.

A major step forward was the introduction of free post-primary level education in 1967-68, so that people would no longer have to come from a wealthy background or gain a scholarship to remain in school until their Leaving Certificate. As for third level, which was even more elitist, a Local Authority (Higher Education Grant) Act was passed in 1968 to enable students from less well-off backgrounds to participate in third-level education. This was followed by a major expansion of the third-level sector with the establishment of Regional Technical Colleges, now known as Institutes of Technology.

Population growth and the growth in urbanisation led to significant increases in house building. A mass model of housing development was followed in the local authority housing sector as a policy of maximum units for minimum cost was pursued, epitomised by the construction of large housing estates such as Ballymun in Dublin. The construction of large owner-occupied estates took off, particularly in the 1970s. The share of people owning their own homes increased greatly while the price of houses also rose significantly, resulting in a housing boom by the late 1970s.

In terms of healthcare, a White Paper entitled *The Health Services and Their Further Development* (GoI, 1966) focused on streamlining the health system. The White Paper proposed that specialised healthcare could be most effectively organised from national and regional centres. The subsequent Health Act 1970 provided for the creation of eight regional health boards. Another milestone was the replacement of the dispensary system of healthcare with the General Medical Services Scheme in 1972. This finally ended the ticket system. These were replaced by medical cards which allowed a choice of doctor and chemist to those who were eligible.

The social welfare system also expanded in the 1960s and 1970s, as new needs and new groups of people were recognised. This was true of the 1970s in particular, reflecting the fact that increases in expenditure in the 'non-productive' area of social welfare came later than 'productive' spending in areas such as education and housing. Much of the expansion in the system, reflecting the influence of the Commission on the Status of Women, concerned the needs of women who had hitherto been excluded from the social welfare system. The introduction of Unmarried Mothers Allowance in 1973 for example, marked the first significant recognition of single mothers in Ireland, and Kennedy (2001: 219) remarks that its introduction was like 'stepping on to a new planet'. Home Assistance was replaced by the Supplementary Welfare Allowance scheme in 1977. Though still a means-tested payment of last resort, it was now based on statutory standards as opposed to individual local authority decisions. Besides changes to social welfare, women's dependent status was also modified by EEC membership. A process of gradual reform followed with the introduction of the Anti-Discrimination Pay Act 1974 and the Employment Equality Act 1977, and the establishment of the Employment Equality Agency in 1977 to oversee the operation of this legislation. The Civil Service (Employment of Married Women) Act 1973 removed the marriage bar in the civil service.

Outside of the main social services, various reports and commissions signalled the emergence of some attention towards minority groups, and to the area of services traditionally known as the personal social services, catering for specific needs beyond the remit of mainstream income, housing, health and education services. These included a report on Travellers in 1963 entitled *Report of the Commission on Itinerancy* (Commission on Itinerancy, 1963). This report at least recognised the Travelling population in Ireland, which at that time were referred to as itinerants, but paradoxically the main thrust of the report was the absorption the Travelling population into the settled community, thus negating their specific identity. People with intellectual disabilities, then referred to as the mentally handicapped, came to attention in the Report of the Commission of Inquiry on Mental Handicap (Commission of Inquiry on Mental Handicap, 1965), while older people were the concern of *The Care of the Aged* (Inter-Departmental Committee, 1968). A substantial proportion of both groups were cared for in county homes and both reports recommended greater community supports and community care, and more specialised services in areas such as education for young people with intellectual disabilities.

A long-overdue report on children in industrial and reformatory schools was published in 1970. This was the *Reformatory and Industrial Schools Systems Report* (GoI, 1970), known as the Kennedy Report, after the chairperson of the reporting body, District Justice Eileen Kennedy. Described as a 'pivotal moment in the history of residential child care in Ireland' (E O'Sullivan, 2014: 126) the report signalled the end of the era of industrial and reform schools. This report came only a few years after an Inter-Departmental Committee on the Prevention of Crime and Treatment of Offenders investigated industrial and reformatory schools in the early 1960s as part of its remit (Keating, 2015). It found appalling conditions and treatment of children. These findings were, however, downplayed in the final report which, Keating (2015) argues, reflected Church and state interests of the time. Though it would take decades before relevant legislation, administration and services were transformed, the Kennedy Report instigated this process along with the shift to family and community services, foster care, smaller residential centres and special schools underpinned by an expanded professional social work and childcare service. Reflecting changes in social values and support of single mothers, the use of Mother and Baby homes and Magdalen homes also faded out by the late 1970s, though the final Magdalen home, on Sean McDermott Street in Dublin, did not close until 1996.

A common theme of the reports on children and other groups was, as O'Sullivan (1979: 214) notes, 'a disenchantment with institutionalisation as a form of intervention' and a preference for community- and family-based care. The voluntary nature of much of the provision for these groups was also recognised, as in many cases voluntary organisations delivered the only services available in the absence of state provision. Despite expanding state provision during the 1960s, these reports encouraged the further development of voluntary provision, but with more formalised state funding and support. Thus a trend developed of more state-sponsored but not state-delivered services (Donoghue, 1998b). The Catholic Church also continued to run many of these voluntary services.

In terms of wider social norms, public debate generated by the women's movement about the availability of contraceptives and the decision of the Supreme Court in the McGee case (ruling in 1973 that there was a right to marital privacy under the Constitution) did not result in legislative change until 1979. The Health (Family Planning) Act 1979 introduced by the Fianna Fáil government allowed for contraceptives to be available but only under prescription and to bona fide married couples for family planning purposes. This was the legislative compromise put forward, given the wider opposition to the availability of contraceptives by many, including campaigning by The Council for Social Concern and The League of Decency. It was in this context that the contraception legislation enacted in 1979 was assessed as: 'a genuine attempt to accommodate to the old values *and* the new, an impossible task, breeding a piece of legislation ignored in practice and condemned on all sides' (Kerrigan, 1983: 8).

The tension between tradition and modernisation embodied in the contraception legislation raises the wider question of how deep the social policy changes of the 1960s and 1970s were. The expansion of social service provision and the recognition of the needs of groups that were previously hidden or treated in discriminatory or unjust ways ultimately had mixed effects. Though expenditure on social policy grew, new social services were characterised by a heavy reliance on means-testing, most notably in social welfare and health. In addition the recognition of particular groups, such as women in the social security system, did not necessarily mean an end to discriminatory treatment. As Conroy-Jackson (1993: 91) notes, the inclusion of women in social welfare was 'as a separate but unequal category within the system as wives and mothers'. Essentially many of the payments introduced were for women as wives and mothers without husbands. In the case of Travellers, in some ways the 1963 report read more as a legitimation of continued discrimination and lack of recognition than any fundamental change in attitude towards this group. Furthermore the limits of state investment were particularly apparent in the case of groups such as people with disabilities and older people; voluntary groups were still expected to be at the forefront of provision. Successive governments' commitments to addressing poverty were also questioned. According to Brown's (1981: 149) assessment of the time, 'the problem of poverty remains marginal to economic and social planning'. Ultimately while social policy was changing the nature of that change was ambiguous: the legacy of past caution, conservatism and inequalities remained. Many of the social problems highlighted, as well as proposals for reform, would continue to resonate in the succeeding decades. This more broadly points to the limits of change and modernisation in the 1960s and 1970s, which is highlighted in accounts of these decades by Daly (2016) and Ferriter (2012). Girvin (2010) goes further, suggesting that Ireland remained a predominantly conservative country until the 1990s, characterising the period 1959-89 as a period of 'change without modernisation'.

Underlying all of this was the health of the economy and by the late 1970s, a range of frailties were appearing. These included the reliance on multinational companies for job creation while indigenous companies were failing in their ability to compete in a more open economy. Internationally the oil price crises in 1973 and 1979 led to a massive increase in the cost of oil, resulting a worldwide recession. Inflation and greater wage demands became a significant difficulty in Ireland over the course of the 1970s. In addition, government borrowing emerged as an issue after the long-standing policy of balancing current expenditure with current revenue was abandoned in 1972 (Kennedy et al, 1988). By the end of the decade cracks were beginning to appear in the Irish economy; workers protested over their dissatisfaction with the equity of the tax system, demands for wage increases were considered increasingly unsustainable, and the national debt was mounting. Trouble was being stored up for the 1980s, which became an austere era for social policy and is taken up in Chapter Three.

Chapter summary

- This chapter profiled the main developments in the Irish economy and society from the 1920s to the 1970s and broadly considered their impact on social policy developments.
- For the most part it can be said that developments in social policy left a lot to be desired. Powerful interests and conservative attitudes combined with lack of economic development conspired to inhibit the emergence of new welfare programmes and ultimately the welfare state in Ireland.
- This lack of development impacted on the most vulnerable and minority groups, including poor people, children and women in particular.
- Signs of growth and innovation were evident by the 1960s and the needs of some previously excluded and/or hidden groups gained some recognition. Drivers and movements for change gathered momentum, particularly by the 1970s, and the language of social justice began to enter social policy discourse. Yet significant inequalities and social injustices have persisted until the present time.

Discussion points

- Choose one or more of the various actors in Irish society over the 1920s to the 1970s – such as the Catholic Church, prominent politicians, farmers and business interests, trade unions, women's groups – and assess the their influence on social policy developments.
- If a policy of economic protectionism was not pursued from the 1930s to the 1950s do you think Irish social policy would have developed differently?
- Discuss the changing experiences of women in relation to social policy over the 1920s-1970s.
- 'The more things change the more they stay the same': consider in relation to social policy in the 1970s and now.

Further reading list

Browne, N (1986) *Against the tide*, Dublin: Gill & Macmillan

Ferriter, D (2004) *The transformation of Ireland 1900-2000*, London: Profile Books

Litton, F (ed) (1982) *Unequal achievement: The Irish experience 1957-1982*, Dublin: IPA

O'Sullivan, E and O'Donnell, I (2012) *Coercive confinement in post-independence Ireland: Patients, prisoners and penitents*, Manchester: Manchester UP

three

Irish social policy from the 1980s to the present: challenges, continuities and changes

This chapter sets the context for understanding the development of social policy in Ireland since the 1980s and the scene for the more detailed treatment of particular areas of social policy in Parts II and III of the book. The decades since the 1980s have been marked by a series of social and economic changes which have posed both opportunities and challenges for social policy. In turn, social policy can be characterised by patterns of continuity and change in how it has developed over this period. Economic transformation and instability sets the widest frame for the chapter as a sequence of economic bust, boom and bust has dominated Ireland's recent path of social policy development. Socially and culturally Ireland has also seen much change. A conservative turn in the 1980s was gradually overturned by trends towards an increasingly modernised, secularised and diverse society, though this has not happened without contest. This transformation has since seen the revisiting of Ireland's social policy history, and the examination of past social policy failures, particularly in regard to institutional abuse and lack of social rights. This is a history which continues to resonate as the legacy of the most recent economic crisis and austerity endures in social terms, and certain issues of state neglect demonstrate that lessons from history are not only about overcoming past problems.

Chapter outline
- The first section reviews the particularly fraught decade of the 1980s, which was characterised by economic recession and social conflict, and it considers the consequences of these issues for social policy.
- The second section sketches the intense period of economic and social change occurring between the early 1990s and mid-2000s and looks at how this brought aspects of social policy into sharper focus.

• The third section reviews the 2008 economic crisis and its aftermath for social policy. The wider landscape of social change is also reviewed, including the continued struggle for rights and recognition, and the revisiting of the 'wrongs' of historical social policy provision.

SECTION ONE

ECONOMIC CRISIS AND THE SOCIAL CHALLENGES OF THE 1980s

> Will the last TD to leave the Dáil please switch off the light at the end of the tunnel (Browne, 1982 in Magill, January 1982: 21).

The 1980s is not a decade that is fondly remembered – massive emigration, high unemployment, high interest rates, high inflation, cutbacks in social services and inadequate social welfare payments made life a tough grind for many. The country experienced poor economic performance for much of the 1980s, the origins of which are frequently attributed to political decisions taken in the decade before. Fianna Fáil won the 1977 general election with a large majority and their manifesto is frequently referred to as an ambitious and expensive programme for government, which it transpired the country could ill afford. Taxes were cut and borrowing bolstered government spending during the late 1970s at a time when it could have done without, and this was compounded by the second oil price shock in 1979. The national debt rose from 53.6% of GDP in 1970 to 123.1% of GDP (gross domestic product) by 1987 (DG ECFIN, 2003). In addition, the steady decline in the numbers at work in agriculture, along with serious job losses in the manufacturing sector throughout the 1970s and 1980s outstripped the gains made in creating new employment. Larger-scale factory closures which had a very serious impact included Ferenka in Limerick in 1978, and the Ford and Dunlop manufacturing plants in Cork in the 1980s. Shortcomings in social service and welfare provisions also became more apparent. It was clear that many social groups continued to live on the margins due to poverty and a lack of opportunities, and the fact that the services on which many were reliant belonged to an earlier era. The social and economic difficulties were compounded by a lack of political stability, particularly during the early 1980s. There were three governments between mid-1981 and the end of 1982 when a Fine Gael/Labour coalition secured office until 1987.

Demographic pressures, poverty, unemployment and emigration

The demographic profile of the country presented a considerable challenge in terms of the massive need for employment and social services. The fact that fertility rates in Ireland remained high until 1980, long after the post-war baby boom had subsided elsewhere, meant that there was a large cohort of young people and families requiring social services. This is understood as a high dependency ratio, that is, the number of 'dependants' in proportion to those 'economically active'. As Fahey and Fitz Gerald (1997: 98) note, 'The mid-1980s witnessed peak levels of *economic* dependency ... a very small workforce was supporting a very large child population, a very large number of unemployed and a reasonably large elderly population. The number of women involved in home duties was also very large.' This demographic profile imposed a heavy financial burden on the state, an impact felt more acutely in the context of persistently high unemployment. Unemployment increased from just under 10% in 1981 to a peak of almost 17% by 1987 and the phenomenon of long-term unemployment became a particularly difficult problem.

Poverty studies indicated the extent to which the social services and welfare system fell short (Kennedy, 1981). Unemployed people and their children, women, single parent families, older people, people in institutional care and the Travelling Community, were all identified at particular risk of poverty (Fitzgerald, 1981). Furthermore, poverty was not only the preserve of 'at risk' groups; there was evidence of a 'working poor' phenomenon with at least one person working in almost half of the poorest 30% of households (Trench and Brennan, 1980). Research by the ESRI (Economic and Social Research Institute) indicated that three out of five households where the head was unemployed fell below the poverty line (Callan et al, 1989). A study of the scale and impact of the poverty experienced by women in Ireland found that 274,000 adult women (slightly over 30%) lived in poverty (Daly, 1989). In addition, female participation in the labour force remained low throughout the decade with a 30% female participation rate in 1985 (CSO, 2006). Women who did work outside the home continued to earn less than men. In 1987, the average gross weekly wage of women in industry was 40% below that of men. The continued absence of opportunities or infrastructure (for example in childcare) along with the persistence of traditional attitudes about the role of women in society, denied many women the chance of labour force participation on the same basis as men.

The lack of work resulted in renewed emigration on a scale comparable with 1950s Ireland. Young people in particular left; 70.6% of those who emigrated between 1981 and 1986 were aged 15-24 (NESC, 1991). The proportion of university graduates emigrating during this period highlighted the scale of the problem; in 1988, for instance 26.1% of graduates left the country (Ó Gráda, 1997). O'Toole (1988) argued that the scale of graduate emigration meant that the main beneficiaries of educating graduates to this level were foreign governments and multinationals. The government response appears to have been yet again one of ambivalence, exemplified by Minister Lenihan's famous remark that 'after all, we can't all life on a small island' in an interview published in *Newsweek* in October, 1987 (Lenihan in Whelan, 1987).

Social policy development during the 1980s: emerging recognition but few resources and little reform

In the midst of so many social problems the Fine Gael/Labour government commissioned the first ever review of the Irish social welfare system in 1983. The *Report of the Commission on Social Welfare* (Commission on Social Welfare, 1986) made many recommendations for the reform of the system, not least of which related to improving the adequacy of social welfare payments and the establishment of a minimum adequate income. The report however, came at the height of the economic crisis, which essentially prevented implementation of its recommendations on cost grounds (Curry, 2011). Nevertheless, the report was widely publicised and its relevance was indisputable in the context of the significant demands on the social welfare system at that time.

Despite the scarce resources of the 1980s, policy documents were drawn up in a number of previously neglected areas. An examination of the mental-health services *The Psychiatric Services: Planning for the Future* (Study Group on the Development of Psychiatric Services, 1984) provided the policy framework for deinstitutionalisation and the development of community-based services where possible, although issues did arise with its implementation. With regard to the needs of older people, a Working Party on Services for the Elderly (1988) completed a report entitled *The Years Ahead – A Policy for the Elderly* which reviewed relevant health and welfare services; however, many of its recommendations remained unimplemented until recent years. *Towards a Full Life: A Green Paper on Services for Disabled People* (Department of Health and Social Welfare, 1984) marked the beginning of greater recognition of the needs of people with disabilities, although it was into the 1990s and 2000s before much of the necessary legislation was enacted. The position of the Travelling Community was considered in *The Report of the Travelling People Review Body* (Travelling People Review Body, 1983). The report made a significant leap from the earlier Commission on Itinerancy Report (1963) in recognising the distinct identity of Travellers; however, no particular resources were made available to affect this recognition (Crowley, 1999). Youth policy reports (O'Sullivan Committee, 1980; National Youth Policy Committee, 1984) reviewed the position of youth work in Ireland and made recommendations about the future development of the area but these were not implemented (Jenkinson, 1996). In response to the problem of emigration, NESC (1991) published a report entitled the *Economic and Social Implications of Emigration*. It made recommendations both to halt the flow of emigration and to assist those who emigrated to Britain in particular. Ultimately, however, the issue of emigration was resolved by an upturn in the economy rather than any specific government efforts in the area.

In short, the 1980s saw the emergence of greater attention to the needs of many different and previously neglected sectors of Irish society but this was not necessarily translated into policy implementation. It seemed that such groups would need to demand political attention and policy change and many subsequently did during the 1990s and beyond as discussed later in the chapter.

The stalled 'liberal agenda' and Irish solutions to Irish problems

In addition to economic troubles and the challenges these posed for social policy, the 1980s was also marked by a resurgence of Catholic social teaching and conflict in areas such as sexuality, contraception, divorce, the family and the role of the state in people's lives. As Inglis (2002: 7) puts it, 'While there is no evidence of a causal connection, the economic recession coincided with the emergence of a new strident Catholic morality.' The advances made by the women's movement and the increased attention given to issues of equality in the 1970s therefore did not indicate a seamless process of change in social values and attitudes in Irish society during the 1980s. This decade was to be a bleak one for many Irish women in particular; in Smyth's assessment (1993: 265), 'women were subjected to unprecedented social, psychic, and moral battering.'

The extent of state regulation of matters of private morality was exemplified in the case of a female teacher who lost her job when, in February 1984, the Employment Appeals Tribunal upheld the right of an order of nuns to sack her because she had become pregnant by the married man with whom she lived. This dismissal was later upheld in the High Court in July 1984 (Inglis, 2002). In January of the same year, a 15-year-old schoolgirl gave birth at the foot of a grotto in County Longford, where both she and her baby died. In 1984, too, the case of the Kerry Babies came to prominence when the Garda investigation into the death of two newborn babies collapsed and was followed by a Public Tribunal of Inquiry into the case. The Tribunal lasted 84 days, during which time there was much public vilification of the woman at centre of the case, despite the fact that the case being made was rejected by one of the expert witnesses for the prosecution (Inglis, 2002).

Small moves forward were evident in debate carried over from the 1970s about 'illegitimate children', and the absence of rights for children born outside of marriage was the subject of a Law Reform Commission Report in 1983. It recommended 'that the legislation remove the concept of illegitimacy from the law and equalise the rights of children born outside marriage with those of children born within marriage' (in Kennedy, 2001: 234). The matter was given greater impetus after a Supreme Court ruling in 1984 upheld the discrimination of children born outside of marriage. It ruled that the Succession Act 1965 gave no succession rights to 'illegitimate' children and that the Act was in accordance with Article 41 on the family in the Constitution (Kennedy, 2001). The subsequent Status of Children Act 1987 offered greater recognition to the guardianship, maintenance and inheritance rights to the children of unmarried parents.

Some progress was also made in widening access to contraception with the passing of the Health (Family Planning) (Amendment) Act 1985. The Act allowed for the sale of condoms to those over 18, but in a restricted set of locations, including chemists and family planning clinics. Efforts to introduce divorce in the 1980s were not as successful. In a 1986 referendum the right to divorce was rejected by 63.5%, notwithstanding the fact that polls conducted as early as 1977 had indicated that public opinion would favour the legalisation of divorce (Magill, 1977). The power of the Catholic Church, which may have been perceived to be waning, was considerable in the divorce referendum and highlighted the sustained influence of Catholic social teaching on social policy.

When it comes to struggles over abortion, which erupted in the early 1980s and have resonated ever since, the influence of the Catholic Church was even more evident. Illegal under the Offences Against the Persons Act 1861, abortion became an issue in the context of proposed legislative change in the UK and probably more importantly as a result of the issue of abortion referral, which was not a crime in Ireland. Movement to tighten Ireland's regime gained ground with the establishment of the Irish Society for the Protection of the Unborn Child in 1980. Other groups subsequently entered the fray (including The Irish Catholic Doctors' Guild and The Responsible Society), culminating in the emergence of the Pro-Life Amendment Campaign in April 1981 (Brennan, 1982). Following nearly two years of divisive debate, an abortion referendum was carried by a two-to-one majority which, by virtue of the wording, made abortion unconstitutional in Ireland in 1983.

The Eighth Amendment to the Constitution, Article 40.3.3, reads as follows: 'The State acknowledges the right to life of the unborn and, with due regard to the equal right to life of the mother, guarantees in its laws to respect, and, as far as practicable, by its laws to defend and vindicate that right.' Referred to as a 'legal timebomb' by then attorney general Peter Sutherland (cited in Lord, 2015: 91), a series of issues and crises have made abortion a problematic issue ever since, which we address later in the chapter.

Responding to the economic crisis: cutbacks and consensus

Returning to the state of the economy and government finances, government debt reached crisis point. As the debt level rose so, too, did the cost of servicing it, with four out of every five pounds collected in income tax needed to cover the interest on the national debt alone (Mac Sharry, 2000). Fianna Fáil was returned to office in 1987 as a minority government. Although they ran the election campaign slogan *Health Cuts Hurt the Old the Sick and the Handicapped: There is a Better Way*, their budgetary actions quickly placed them in retrenchment mode. This was indicated by the establishment of the Expenditure Review Group, popularly known as An Bórd Snip. This was a small group of three civil servants working with the advice of economist Colm McCarthy who were given the task of reviewing where expenditure cuts could be made (Cromien, 2011). Cutbacks, described as 'the most dramatic ... in public expenditure which any Government had ever undertaken' (Cromien, 2011) included the closure of hospitals and hospital beds, the lack of maintenance of basic social infrastructure such as school buildings, the selling off of local authority houses, an early retirement scheme, a freeze on recruitment and the postponement of special pay awards in the public service. Examples of state agency cuts included budgetary and staff allocations that were 50% less than what the Combat Poverty Agency, an agency established only two years earlier in 1986, required (CPA, 1987). The National Adult Literacy Agency also had its budget cut by one third (Trench et al, 1987). While social welfare payments were not directly cut, particular groups were effected, such as young people on training schemes, who had their allowances reduced by one third (CPA, 1987).

The mood was grim but several factors appear to have worked to offer a greater sense of shared purpose around the need for economic and fiscal reform. This included the **bipartisan** strategy of Fine Gael, known as the 'Tallaght Strategy' by which the party agreed to offer its support to Fianna Fáil's minority administration. The emergence of a **social partnership** approach to policy making also contributed. This involved deliberation between the government, employer bodies and trade unions, with trade union participation motivated by the more hostile treatment meted out to unions in the UK under Thatcherism (Mjøset, 1992). The outcome was a *Programme for National Recovery*, agreed in 1987 (GoI, 1987), which set out a path to reduce borrowing and stabilise the national debt, while unions agreed to pay restraint in return for income tax concessions. This was the start of a policy-making process that was to endure until Ireland hit another severe crisis in the late 2000s.

> A **bipartisan** approach in politics occurs when two political parties, who may typically oppose each other, agree to compromise, or cooperate and jointly support a particular policy or piece of legislation.

> **Social partners** are representatives of particular groups (including trade unions, employers/business, farmers and the community/voluntary sector) that may be consulted and/or engage in a process with government to secure agreement on specific aspects of policy.

The economic situation showed signs of improvement from 1988 onwards. The economic growth rate improved, the debt to GDP ratio started to fall as did interest rates. It took somewhat longer for the improved economic circumstances to filter down to the population at large. Emigration, persistent unemployment and, in particular, youth unemployment, continued for the remainder of the 1980s and the early 1990s, but over the course of the 1990s there was much change to come.

Figure 3.1: 1987 General Election poster

Copyright: Derek Speirs

SECTION TWO

THE 1990s AND 2000s: NEW TIMES AND A NEW IRELAND?

> Ireland's transformation is so dazzling ... one of the most remarkable
> economic transformations of recent times: from basket case to 'emerald
> tiger' in ten years (*The Economist*, 17 May 1997 in Sweeney, 1999: 8).

The period from the early 1990s to the late 2000s is marked by an enormous leap in economic growth and prosperity, some of which later turned out to be illusory as the subsequent economic crash indicated. Known as the 'Celtic Tiger', the label was first applied to the Irish economy by Kevin Gardiner of the investment bank Morgan Stanley in August 1994 (O'Hearn, 1997). From 1994 the economy began to grow significantly, the annual GDP growth rate averaged 9.4% between 1994 and 2000 and 5.4% between 2001 and 2006. This was notably higher than EU15 growth rates over both these periods: 2.8% and 2% (Eurostat). Ireland also became much wealthier. Measured as GDP per capita, Ireland converged with the EU15 by the late 1990s and subsequently surpassed the EU15 on this measure.

Employment grew by an annual average of 4.3% between 1994 and 2006 and the total number at work grew from 1.23 million to 2.05 million. More women entered the workforce and the total number of women in work grew by 90% in comparison to 53% for men. The unemployment rate dropped to 4.5% by 2006

(Eurostat). Such economic data was unprecedented for Ireland and so too was its experience of migration. Over the course of the 1990s and 2000s emigration was not only halted, large-scale immigration became a new reality for Ireland reflecting an unprecedented labour shortage. By 1996, as Ruhs and Quinn (2009) note, 'Ireland reached its migration "turning point" making it the last EU Member State to become a country of net immigration'. Subsequently the pace of change accelerated and by 2002 'the estimated share of non-nationals in Ireland's population had surpassed those of the UK and France, countries with much longer immigration histories' (Ruhs, 2005: 10). The longer term legacy, as Fanning (2016) observes, is that Ireland has become a multi-ethnic society.

This was a remarkable about-turn in economic fortunes, and all in a relatively short period of time. Assessments of the factors that contributed to the success of the Irish economy during the 1990s vary in emphasis. First, there was an improvement in external economic conditions and an intensification of global economic activity which provided a suitable climate to continue the policy of supporting foreign direct investment and attracting multinational corporations to locate in Ireland. Second, the internal dynamics of the Irish economy were also more favourable. Social partnership was considered to have brought about greater stability in industrial relations, and the conditions for economic competitiveness and growth had been enhanced through various grants, incentives and tax reform, including a corporate tax rate of 12.5%, one of the lowest in Europe. Third, there was an easing of the demographic pressures on social services and the availability of a young well-educated, English-speaking workforce was an important 'selling point' to potential foreign investors. Finally, the impact of EU membership (the single market, EMU [Economic and Monetary Union] and the benefit derived from structural and cohesion funds) is also among the factors widely regarded as important to creating the conditions for unparalleled economic growth. In short, Ireland developed over the course of the 1990s to become a much more flexible, open and globalised economy.

Though not part of mainstream analysis and debate at the time, this growth pattern, particularly as it evolved over the 2000s, reflected underlying frailties of the Irish economy, which were exacerbated by its exposure to external risks. In particular Ireland opened itself up to global financial services investment in the late 1980s with the establishment of the International Financial Services Centre. As well as its efforts to attract foreign investment with low corporation tax, its 'light touch' approach to financial regulation also became part of this package. With the full implementation of EMU, finance from the European core countries flowed into Ireland. Irish domestic banks, also lightly regulated, became increasingly dependent on this source of funding which was lent under an increasingly lax lending regime. Mortgage lending to private customers grew by almost 400% and property related business lending rose by almost 800% (O'Hearn, 2011). Credit tripled relative to GNP (gross national product), as bank lending grew from 60% of GNP in 1997 to over 200% of GNP by 2008 whereas normal levels of bank lending internationally stood at 80 to 100% of GNP (Kelly, 2009). In the 'real' economy, this resulted in a switch in focus in economic activity and growth from production of goods and services for export to construction. This created a property boom and a bubble economy, which was not seriously recognised as such until after it crashed. We return to the unfolding of the crash and its implications for social policy later. For now we continue to document the context in which social policy was developed in the 1990s and 2000s by looking at the way Ireland transformed socially as well as economically.

Social change in the 1990s

In contrast to the conservative currents of the 1980s, Irish society began to change markedly from the 1990s onwards. As well as becoming more socially diverse because of immigration, other developments also suggested that Ireland was gradually becoming a more open, modern society. Such developments did not occur overnight but were the product of sustained campaigning for change, and they have not always been clear-cut in terms of positive outcomes. Notable milestones included the decriminalisation of homosexuality with the passing of the Criminal Law (Sexual Offences) Act 1993. Also in 1993, access to contraceptives was further liberalised. In the context of heightened fears about HIV transmission and campaigning by groups such as the Irish Family Planning Association, sale of condoms was completely liberalised under the Health (Family Planning) Amendment Act 1993, meaning that age restrictions were lifted and condoms could be sold anywhere, including from vending machines. After a referendum in 1995 passed by an extremely narrow margin: 50.28% in favour and 49.72% against, the right to divorce was introduced with the Family Law (Divorce) Act 1996. Ultimately however, the divorce legislation generated what Fahey (2012) refers to as a 'small bang' in terms of changing family patterns in Ireland, with an increase in marital breakdown and alternative family forms preceding the introduction of divorce.

While policy change in areas such as homosexuality, divorce and contraception might be taken to signify a growing shift in social values, this did not extend to the issue of abortion. An indicator of continued tension between liberalism and conservativism, abortion remained a troubling issue. The impact of the Eighth Amendment quickly became apparent when Irish courts ruled in 1986 that information on the procurement of an abortion abroad could not be made available in Ireland, because, as argued by the Society for the Protection of the Unborn Child, it 'amounted to a breach of the constitutional right to life of the unborn' (Bacik, 2015: 108). In 1992, this was challenged in the European Court of Human Rights in a case brought by Open Door Counselling and the Dublin Well Woman Centre. The Court found that a ban on information on abortion was contrary to Article 10 of the European Convention on Human Rights. In February of that year, the law was applied to prevent a 14-year-old girl who became pregnant as a result of rape from travelling abroad for an abortion, demonstrating the conflict between the right to life of the mother and the unborn in the Eighth Amendment.

The X case, as it became known, caused public outcry and the government was forced to respond. The Supreme Court ruled that an abortion was permissible if the girl was suicidal and there was therefore 'a real and substantial risk to the life, as distinct from the health, of the mother'. In November 1992 the government proposed three further amendments to Article 40.3.3. These included the ruling out of suicide as a threat to the life of a pregnant women (that is, overruling the Supreme Court decision in the X case), the right to information and the right to travel. The first amendment was not carried, but the right to information and travel were passed (Bacik, 2015).

What followed was a further series of crisis cases including the C Case in 1997, the D Case in 2007 and the ABC Case in 2010, all demonstrating how problematic the Eighth Amendment was, as well as pointing to the need for legislation in response to the X case. Some attempts to address the issue were made by a *Green Paper on Abortion* (Department of the Taoiseach, 1999) and The All-Party Oireachtas Committee on the Constitution (2000) which set out different options for constitutional and legislative change. Pressure by the anti-abortion movement resulted in another referendum in 2002 on amending the Constitution, in which the reversal of the decision on the X case was again proposed, but it was not carried (see Quilty et al, 2015 for a timeline of abortion issues). Further substantial change did not occur until 2013 which we review towards the end of this chapter.

Turning to another area of social change, the issue of child abuse in variety of contexts, familial, institutional and clerical, gained increasing attention. Early in the 1990s the Kilkenny Incest Case and the West of Ireland Farmer Case, as they were known, highlighted in a very stark way the extreme abuse that could happen within the confines of the family. These cases exposed the inadequacies in the Irish child protection system but they also raised public consciousness about the existence of child abuse and contributed to the full implementation of the Child Care Act 1991 by 1996. The 1991 Act replaced the Children Act 1908 and substantially strengthened the responsibility and resourcing of Health Boards to care for abused and neglected children. There was a significant increase in notified cases of child abuse throughout the 1990s (Ferguson and O'Reilly, 2001), probably reflecting growing awareness of the issue. However, Ireland's typically slow response to social issues and to enacting change is also particularly well illustrated in the case of child protection. The origins of the Child Care Act can be traced to a Task Force on Child Care set up in 1980 on foot of the Kennedy Report, published in 1970 (and discussed in Chapter Two). The Task Force reported in 1981 and the legislation it recommended did not materialise until the 1991 Act (E O'Sullivan, 2014).

A process of uncovering historical institutional child abuse began in the 1990s, although the degree to which this was a process of exposing a hidden past is open to question. As O'Sullivan and O'Donnell (2012: 278) assert, institutions were 'widely known', 'extensively utilised' and 'not part of a hidden Ireland that was only exposed in the 1990s and beyond'. The 1990s did, however, mark the start of a process of recognising and dealing with this past. In 1996, RTÉ broadcast *Dear Daughter* which dealt with the abuses in the Goldenbridge Orphanage (Kennedy, 2001). Three years later, a three-part documentary series *States of Fear* gave a harrowing account of the abuses suffered in Industrial Schools (see Raftery and O'Sullivan, 1999). Survivor testimony and survivor campaign groups, such as One in Four, also contributed to what Powell et al (2013: 12) describe as a process of transforming 'Irish public consciousness regarding the significance of child abuse in Irish society'.

Accounts of clerical sexual abuse also came to light, the pain of which, for many victims, was compounded by the non-management/mismanagement of the issue by senior religious figures in many dioceses. The failure of the Catholic Church to respond effectively to allegations of child sexual abuse among some of its practising priests damaged its reputation in the public mind both in Ireland and elsewhere, leading to an acceleration of its decline as a moral authority in Irish society.

Following growing debate and public concern, in 1999 then Taoiseach Bertie Ahern issued an apology on behalf of the state to victims of child abuse in industrial and reformatory schools. A Commission to Inquire into Child Abuse (CICA) was established to investigate the abuse and make recommendations to address the effects of abuse on the victims as well as prevent future institutional abuse (Brennan, 2007). The work of CICA culminated in the publication of the five-volume Ryan Report (named after the chair of the Commission Mr Justice Sean Ryan) in 2009. In addition to CICA a number of government inquiries into allegations of clerical sex abuse and how these were handled by both the Church and state institutions were also instigated. These resulted in the Ferns Report (Ferns Inquiry, 2005) relating to abuse in the Catholic diocese of Ferns Co. Wexford, the Murphy Report (Commission of Investigation, 2009) concerning the Dublin Catholic Archdiocese and the Cloyne Report (Commission of Investigation, 2010) investigating clerical abuse in the Catholic Diocese of Cloyne. We return to the aftermath and outcomes of these reports towards the end of the chapter.

A new climate for the development of social policy? The widening agenda, actors and scope of social policy

What effect did economic and social transformation have on social policy? For the first time in its history, Ireland generated employment sufficient to meet demand, and it had resources available on an unprecedented scale to develop and invest in the social services and in key areas of infrastructure. In many ways economic prosperity allowed a process of 'catch up' as the cutbacks of the 1980s had taken their toll on social services that had endured decades of underinvestment and were in serious need of modernisation. Taken in absolute terms, there was unprecedented investment in social and public services. Overall government expenditure grew from €21.6bn in 1995 to €70.7bn in 2007, while government revenue grew from €20.5bn to €71.3bn over the same period (Eurostat). Several social services saw much greater levels of investment and many important policy developments. In health substantial, albeit uneven, investment took place in hospital and primary care services. Initiatives to address educational disadvantage and to widen access and participation, including the introduction of free third-level education in 1995, were notable in the education system. Early Childhood Care and Education services, a particularly neglected area of policy and provision saw significant developments and expansion. The social welfare system underwent considerable reform in terms of meeting the targets set by the Commission on Social Welfare (1986) and in modernising its operations through the provision of more accessible information on citizens' rights and entitlements.

Specifically with regard to poverty and **social exclusion**, the development of the National Anti-Poverty Strategy (NAPS; GoI, 1997) provides a useful illustration of social policy innovation and the beginnings of a more extensive policy response to poverty. The NAPS provided

> **Social exclusion** is a concept used to refer to the consequences of poverty and inequality, where people are 'left out' and unable to participate fully in society.

the official definition of poverty adopted in Ireland, it set specific policy targets for poverty reduction and Ireland was the first EU member state to adopt these targets. The structural developments attached to its implementation (for example a designated Cabinet Sub-Committee, the establishment of a NAPS unit in the Department of Social and Family Affairs and later the setting-up of the Office for Social Inclusion), and the targets developed in this regard are noteworthy policy initiatives which focused attention on poverty and inequality but that, as we have seen, were a long time in the making. The NAPS achieved its target of reducing consistent poverty well in advance of its deadline. However, relative poverty and inequality as measured by the Gini coefficient remained relatively high for the majority of the celtic tiger years.

Besides the positive effects of the growth in resources on social policy developments, the more explicit campaigning and lobbying activities of many organisations also helped to put the rights of particular groups on the political agenda. Some of these groups had their origins in the 1980s, including the Irish National Organisation for the Unemployed (INOU) the first national organisation to represent unemployed people (Allen, 1998). The INOU together with other non-governmental organisations (NGOs) such as the Community Workers Co-operative and the National Women's Council of Ireland, also founded in the 1980s, became more significant in terms of the broader politics of policy making. The disability rights movement became a more visible and influential force, including activist groups such as the Centre for Independent Living established in 1992 and organisations focusing on advocacy, such as Inclusion Ireland (originally established as Namhi in 1961) and the National Disability Authority set up in 2000. Children's rights campaigners also became more prominent, with a number of children's rights NGOs coming together to form the Children's Rights Alliance in 1995.

Social partnership was a vehicle by which certain civil society groups became more involved, and potentially more influential in setting the social policy agenda and realising social policy change. The community and voluntary sector were invited to participate in the national social partnership talks in 1997 and continued to do so through successive agreements until social partnership collapsed in 2009. However, the extent to which such participation was effective and the actual weight given to the sector in negotiations, in a process characterised by Larragy (2014) as 'asymmetric engagement', posed a dilemma for many groups. Many within the sector remained critical and sometimes cynical about their involvement and the extent to which they really had a say in the final agreements.

Other policy, legislative and institutional developments reflected growing attention to issues of recognition and redistribution, and to the growing diversity of Irish society. If social policy developments in the area of poverty and inequality are considered central to the notion of redistribution, then the emergence of more sustained attention to issues of discrimination and exclusion highlight the relevance of the concept of recognition for social policy. The recognition of various marginalised groups in Irish society was an issue that gained prominence and helped to move services beyond what was still largely a charity model in many sectors. Significant policy documents were published including the National Children's Strategy (2000), the National Disability Strategy (DJELR, 2004) and the National Action Plan Against Racism 2005-2008 (DJLER, 2005b). The Office of the Minister for Children in 2005, which preceded the Department of Children and Youth Affairs established in 2011, instigated a more integrated and strengthened approach to policy issues pertaining to children and young people. Another notable development was the establishment in 1998 of the National Consultative Committee on Racism and Interculturalism (NCCRI). It was tasked with developing an inclusive approach to combat racism and to promote an intercultural society by providing advice and training to government and NGOs, monitoring racist incidents, providing information and raising public awareness.

The establishment of the Equality Authority in 1999 represented another step in improving the recognition and protection of individuals and social groups. The passing of significant equality legislation including the Equality Acts 1998 and 2004 and the Equal Status Acts 2000 and 2004 marked a milestone in the development of the '**equality agenda**' in Ireland. This legislation prohibits discrimination (in the provision of goods and services, employment, training, advertising, collective agreements and other opportunities to which the public generally has access) on nine grounds: gender, marital status, sexual orientation, family status, disability, age, race, religion and membership of the Travelling Community.

> The **equality agenda** refers to the pursuit of recognition and equality for all individuals and groups in society.

The limits to expansionary social policy

These developments, however, should not be interpreted as an unequivocal expansion of the welfare state or the extension of social rights. Despite the increased availability of resources during Ireland's years of prosperity, Ireland remained one of the low social spenders in comparative terms. Measured as a percentage of GDP, Ireland's overall government expenditure stood at 40.8% in contrast to 51.7% in the EU15. By 2007 general government expenditure fell to 33.9% of GDP compared to 45.2% in the EU15 (Eurostat). Given this performance during a period of substantial growth in resources, many civil society actors argued that Ireland's social development lagged behind economic development and that a Nordic model of welfare, built on a much stronger platform of social rights and universal services was both desirable and achievable (Kirby and Murphy, 2008). On the other hand, the notion of the limits of what a small state in a global economy could do and the need to remain competitive and attractive to foreign direct investment seemed to increasingly dominate government discourse (Dukelow, 2005), which dovetailed with the long-held view that social policy is subordinate to economic policy.

More broadly, it seems that social rights remained a **contested concept**; while there undoubtedly were improvements in the services to which individuals are entitled, there were also limits to the quality of, or access to, certain entitlements relative to what might be available in the private sector. This contradiction is illustrated in parallel

> A **contested concept** is one which is subject to differing interpretations around which there is no universal agreement of meaning.

developments demonstrating the emergence of a more distinctive benefit to be drawn from the private as opposed to the public spheres. Access to healthcare, housing, the rise of the private school phenomenon in education and the growth of private sector care services for older people provide notable examples. These trends point to the fact that market choices in key areas were consolidated during this era, but only for those who could afford to pay. Moreover, private provision of services was encouraged through increased cash benefits for childcare and substantial tax reliefs for pension, health and housing costs. The expansion of social services during the boom years, therefore, might be characterised as somewhat reformist but the outcomes were not always inclusive or redistributive.

The extent to which the 'equality agenda' was fully progressed is also open to question. In the case of the Equality Authority, for example, despite being one of the most positive social policy initiatives in this period, Baker et al (2015) note the Equality Authority's efforts to progress equality quickly met the limits of what governments were prepared to act on. They point out that: 'its repeated recommendations for including socio-economic disadvantage and other new grounds of discrimination, for removing exemptions from public functions, and for introducing positive duties to promote equality ... were ignored by government.

The Equality Acts were improved, but mostly as a result of EU directives' (Baker et al, 2015: 184).

In short, developments during the 1990s and 2000s appeared to reflect a growing level of political acceptance of the necessity to listen to and acknowledge the needs of particular social groups and their representatives. Yet there were also political limits to action that would mean more fundamental transformation of existing social relations and power structures in Irish society.

Some of these concerns were addressed in what was probably the most extensive assessment of the Irish welfare state during this period, namely *The Developmental Welfare State* (DWS) published by the NESC (2005). This offered a comprehensive appraisal of the welfare state and an attempt to redirect its focus in tandem with Ireland's economic transformation. Inspired by the growing idea of a social investment perspective at European level, it argued that the goals of the Irish welfare state needed to be 'recast' and become 'developmental'. It acknowledged that social expenditure remained below international norms, but also argued that recent increases did not produce expected improvements in welfare outcomes. In particular it articulated the problem of a 'deepening dualism' within Irish social policy, involving 'a growing majority who are able to supplement very basic levels of public service provision with additional protection they purchase for themselves', while 'a significant minority [...] rely nearly entirely on public provision, and in doing so are further removed from the mainstream of Irish society and less likely to experience mobility into it' (NESC, 2005: 163). However, the DWS received both a mixed and remarkably low-key response. The lack of debate may be symptomatic of a wider ambivalence or reluctance to be explicit about 'the direction' of the Irish welfare state and which allowed significant investment without fundamentally tackling social inequalities during the boom years. Moreover, the potential for more progressive developments in social policy took a significant turn for the worse shortly after. Ireland became consumed by a new economic crisis which began to unfold in late 2008 and which has shaped the landscape of social policy developments since.

SECTION THREE
THE RETURN OF ECONOMIC CRISIS AND AUSTERITY

> Ireland jumped with both feet into the brave new world of unsupervised markets. .... Then the bubble burst (Paul Krugman, The lessons of Ireland, *The Guardian*, 21 April 2009).

Gradually building since the mid-2000s, by autumn 2008 a full blown 'credit crunch' severely hampered the US economy. It quickly reverberated across the global economy as massively inflated property and related financial assets bubbles burst, and financial institutions collapsed or came near to the brink of collapse (see Gamble, 2009). As a very small open economy with a significant financial services sector Ireland was particularly exposed to global economic trends. However, as mentioned earlier, Ireland's domestic economic dynamics meant that much of its economic troubles were of its own making, given the way the economy developed over the 2000s. As a result of instabilities and risks built up over this period, Ireland became one of the most severely damaged economies in Europe and the first in the Eurozone to enter a recession in September 2008. Real GDP fell by approximately 9% between 2007 and 2010, with a second smaller recessionary dip in 2012.

As the economy shrunk Ireland's debt and deficit levels rapidly grew, peaking at levels higher than the 1980s crisis. The **government deficit** peaked at 32% in 2010, a particularly high figure due to the amount of capital channelled into financial institutions in that year, and the general government debt peaked at 120% in 2012 (Eurostat). One of the main ways in which the 2008 crisis differed from crises in the 1970s and 1980s was its **financialised** nature. Financial flows and financial interests had come to dominate the global economy and this was mirrored in the way the Irish economy had also grown and become so unstable (Ó Riain, 2014). As a result, Ireland's banking crisis and the way the government responded to it had a significant impact on the state finances, and limited options in other areas of economic and social policy as the crisis continued. Ireland's controversial attempts to rescue its collapsing banking sector, including a blanket bank guarantee and the setting-up of a 'bad bank', the National Assets Management Agency (NAMA) led to the most costly banking crisis among advanced economies since the 1930s (Laeven and Valencia, 2012) and contributed approximately one third of the increase in debt (Irish Fiscal Advisory Council, 2014).

> A **government deficit** arises when a government spends more than it receives in revenue (mostly tax receipts) in a single year. Each year's deficit adds to the government debt, which is the total outstanding amount owed by government. It can also be referred to as national debt or sovereign debt.

> **Financialisation** refers to the variety of ways in which finance has changed the structure of economies since the 1970s. This includes change to how wealth is created (making money from financial investments rather than the production of goods and services); to how it is distributed (with a growing gap between the top 1% and the rest), and to the exercise and influence of corporate power and its relationship with the state.

Despite introducing **austerity** as early as July 2008, by autumn 2010 Ireland's crisis had become a sovereign debt crisis, when interest rates on Irish government borrowing became prohibitively high. Ireland followed Greece to become the

> **Austerity** is a term used to describe typically severe policy measures, including expenditure cutbacks and tax increases, with the intent of reducing government budget deficits.

second country in the Eurozone to require a loan conditional on more austerity, and structural and financial sector reforms, along with direct supervision from the EC/IMF/ECB, known as the Troika, during the disbursement period of the loan from late 2010 to late 2013. This again marked a new departure for Ireland and a level of external surveillance and intrusion on policy making not previously encountered.

There were, however, some similarities with previous crises, particularly in terms of how the crisis was understood and responded to in the way that the welfare state is implicated. Despite Ireland's economic weaknesses and the fact that its public expenditure remained below the European average, the idea that excessive social expenditure played a key role in causing the crisis echoed debates in the 1970s and 1980s. In particular, ideas around overly-generous welfare payments and the idea of welfare as a disincentive to work were similarly articulated in past crises (Dukelow, 2011, and forthcoming). The setting-up of a Special Group on Public Service Numbers and Expenditure Programmes in 2008 to advise the government on cutbacks mirrored the approach taken in 1987 as previously discussed, and popularly became known as 'An Bórd Snip Nua'. There were also certain parallels in how cutbacks were imposed on particular groups and particular state agencies, though the degree and duration of austerity ran much deeper this time.

The socioeconomic effects of the crisis quickly followed. There was a return to high levels of unemployment, rising from 4.5% in 2006 to a high of 14.7% in 2011 and 2012, with youth unemployment and long-term unemployment becoming particularly acute. Underemployment also became a problem with a substantial increase in involuntary part-time work, rising from 13.6% of total part-time work in 2008 to a peak of 43.1% in 2013 (Eurostat). Consistent poverty and, in particular, the rate of deprivation rose significantly, with the former rising from 4.2% in 2008 to a peak of 9.1% in 2013 and the latter from 13.7% in 2008 to a peak of 30.5% in 2013. The financialised nature of the economy also meant that consumer debt and in particular housing debt, became a significant problem, with a marked rise in mortgage arrears (Stamp, 2016). Emigration also returned, tripling between 2008 and 2012 and peaking at 89,000 people in 2013, thus surpassing previous highs. As with the 1980s wave of emigration, young people and third-level graduates were disproportionately represented, though unlike the 1980s, this wave was also characterised by immigrants deciding to leave and people leaving because of dissatisfaction with their jobs and future prospects (Glynn et al, 2015). A rise in mental-health problems, and in suicide and self-harm (Corcoran et al, 2015) also indicated the severity of the social impact of the crisis. For people in poverty, or on low incomes, and living with the everyday reality of cumulative cuts to social services, austerity caused enormous hardship and fear for the future (Community Platform, 2014).

The impact of austerity on social policy

The impact of austerity further exacerbated the social dimensions of the crisis. In total, between 2008 and 2014 austerity of approximately 18% of GDP was undertaken with the balance set between approximately one third tax increases and two thirds spending cuts. The overall effect of austerity had a significant impact on the lowest 10% income group, who bore the second highest drop in disposable income after the top 10% income group (Callan et al, 2015). While social protection expenditure noticeably increased due to rising demand, this masked significant cutbacks at programme level, particularly concerning payments to young people and lone parents. Substantial cuts were also made in health and environment group (especially social housing) expenditure. Arts, Heritage and Gaeltacht (Irish-language speaking regions), responsible for funding some community sector initiatives also suffered major cuts; its budget fell by 63% between 2008 and 2013 (authors' calculations based on DPER data). As Harvey (2012, 2014) found, the community and voluntary sector has been significantly 'downsized' as a result. This in turn has resulted in cutbacks in community development and services to disadvantaged communities, including women's youth and Traveller organisations; and drug and family support services. The restructuring of community development and the introduction of competitive tendering as opposed to grants for projects has meant that the sector's role as an independent and critical voice has been significantly curtailed. Consequently, the sector is being remodelled by the state to fulfil a remit of service delivery only (Forde et al, 2016). This is something Harvey (2016) suggests was a deliberate state strategy of suppressing dissent, a factor which has been central to a historical unease the state has had with civil society activism.

This dovetails with another strand of austerity that Baker et al (2015) describe as 'cutting back on equality'. Many of the institutional developments which progressed equality, rights and recognition over the previous period were rolled back. As Baker et al (2015: 187) document, 'groups representing or supporting Travellers, people with disabilities, women, children, carers and those living in poverty, among others, were all adversely affected'. Some state agencies were shut down including the NCCRI in 2009, while the Equality Authority had its budget cut by 43% in 2009. It was later amalgamated with the Irish Human Rights Commission to become the Irish Human Rights and Equality Commission (IHREC) in 2014. The Combat Poverty Agency ceased to be a separate agency, and was absorbed into what eventually became the Social Inclusion Division of the Department of Social Protection. One of the very few examples of the establishment of a new agency in recent times is the creation of Tusla, the Child and Family Agency, in 2014, representing a dedicated, independent body taking over responsibility for child welfare from the Health Service Executive. This event reflects the fact that although the economic crisis and its aftermath looms large, it is not the only recent factor shaping social policy. Ireland has continued to undergo significant social and cultural change, regarding issues such as children's rights, the family and equality, and we close the chapter by taking up this theme again from where we left off earlier in the chapter.

Recent social change and its impact on social policy

Assessed as 'the most important event in the history of Irish childcare' (Powell et al, 2013: 12–13), the publication of the Ryan Report in 2009 sparked considerable soul-searching about how Ireland treated vulnerable children. Described as a 'map of an Irish hell' (Irish Times, 2009: 19) the report was anchored in survivor testimony of 1,090 women and men who gave evidence to CICA. It unrelentingly documented the horrific, endemic child abuse – physical, sexual, emotional and neglect – in industrial and reformatory schools and related settings. The failures the report pointed to in relation to regulation by the Department of Education were equally disturbing.

Although there were many problems with how CICA was run, and how prosecutions of perpetrators and remedies to victims were subsequently dealt with (UNHRC, 2014), the content of the report and the media attention it garnered helped to push forward a number of reforms. These reforms, much like the earlier phase of reforms in the 1990s, were the product of lengthy campaigning, contestation and previous report recommendations, beginning with the *Report of the Kilkenny Incest Investigation* 1993 (O'Mahony, 2016). The 1937 Constitution placed great emphasis on parental rights and on the (marital) family, reflective of Catholic social teaching. This limited state intervention in child protection and welfare cases to detrimental effect. A constitutional referendum on the rights of the child was held in 2012, designed to elevate the rights of the child in the Constitution. The referendum was carried with 58% of the vote in an extremely low voter turn-out of 33.5% (McGing, 2014). After the outcome of the referendum was the subject of a failed legal challenge, a specific article on children (Article 42A) was inserted into the Constitution in 2015, though the practical implications of the new article have yet to be seen. The establishment of Tusla also potentially marks a stronger commitment to child welfare, but whether it will be adequately resourced remains to be seen. Another outcome of the Ryan Report is the way that it furthered demands for justice in other cases of Ireland's history of 'coercive confinement'. This led to an Inter-Departmental Committee to establish the facts of state involvement with the Magdalen laundries (Inter-Departmental Committee, 2013) and a Commission of Investigation into Mother and Baby Homes (Garrett, 2015).

The Ryan Report also sparked a debate about explanatory factors as to why so many children were institutionalised and why so many were the victims of abuse. Contributors to this debate have pointed to the role of actors such as the Catholic Religious Congregations, the state, the NSPCC/ISPCC, civil society, and the role of factors such as social class and family circumstances, and the construction of child abuse (Ferguson, 2007; Garrett, 2013; Powell et al, 2013; O'Sullivan, 2015). While undoubtedly the Catholic Church features at the centre of the problem, it has possibly been 'hyper-responsibilized' (Garrett, 2013: 61) in subsequent debates, meaning that other factors, and how they interact have not been given adequate critical consideration. Central to this is the way that the state steered social policy developments. As noted by Holohan (2011: 31),

> A historical legacy of voluntary provision, deference to agents of the Catholic Church, negative attitudes towards the working class family, a failure to address the issue of sexual crime appropriately, and the low priority afforded to children in the care of the State, are all factors that affected the responses of agents of the State to allegations and incidents of child abuse, and to failings in the system of residential institutions.

This debate and analysis of factors is important, not only because it is a matter of redressing past failures, but also because of how it provides a lens with which to evaluate contemporary social policy and social change. As McGregor (2014) suggests in the case of setting up Tusla, there is an impulse to purge past failures and to frame the contemporary social policy landscape as completely new and separate. Equally there is a risk of overemphasising the 2012 referendum on children's rights, and the more recent legalisation of same-sex marriage following the marriage equality referendum in 2015, as indictors of a decisive shift in the Irish state's commitment to social justice and to social rights. However dualisms, contradictions and deficiencies remain all too contemporary. As already discussed, the recent wave of austerity demonstrates the uneven application of cutbacks, thus aggravating existing inequalities and the vulnerabilities of particular social groups (Community Platform, 2014). Cutbacks to state agencies also point to ways in which the state can simultaneously cut back and 'roll out' measures of equality and recognition. Moreover, there are ongoing deficiencies in how the state cares for and protects vulnerable children in general; and particular groups of children, such as asylum-seeking and homeless children, together with their families. Despite the establishment of the Health Information and Quality Authority (HIQA) in 2007, responsible among other things for setting standards and monitoring the quality of health and related care services, institutional care continues to raise concerns around its adequacy, appropriateness and the degree to which it is regulated in the case of people with disabilities and older people (IHREC, 2015).

There is also persistent concern about women's reproductive rights. This concern came to a head again in 2012 when Savita Halappanavar, a woman 17 weeks pregnant and miscarrying, died from sepsis at Galway University Hospital. The public alarm and anger over this tragedy, together with pressure for a response to the European Court of Human Rights in the ABC case in 2010, which found that Ireland violated human rights by not providing lawful abortion when a woman's life is at risk, resulted in the passing of the Protection of Life During Pregnancy Act 2013. The Act also finally responded to the Supreme Court ruling in the X case. The highly restrictive legislation does not, however, allow for lawful abortion in cases such as rape, fatal foetal abnormalities or serious health risks. The UNHRC (2014), in its periodic review of the state in 2014, quickly criticised the Act for the way that, among other things, it criminalised abortion in the aforementioned circumstances and discriminated against women who were unable to travel abroad for an abortion.

In summary, therefore, Ireland has experienced great upheaval in the last decade. The latest round of what appears to be cyclical instability in Ireland's economy has posed great challenges for social policy having to do 'more with less'. At the same time decisions on where austerity was imposed reveals continuing vulnerabilities of particular social groups in terms of redistribution and recognition. This pattern of vulnerability and limits to rights is reinforced when we look at the wider landscape of social change. Despite many positive developments and the efforts to deal with past social policy failures, social discrimination and social marginality remain pressing social policy issues in early twenty-first century Ireland.

Chapter summary

- This chapter outlined the social, political and economic backdrop to the development of social policy in Ireland since 1980, from which we can discern waves of challenge, continuity and change.
- The 1980s were marked by a series of tribulations – economic, political, social and moral – providing a hostile climate for the development of social policy.
- The 1990s to the late 2000s was a period of significant economic growth and rapid social change in Irish society. While welfare provision improved in certain areas, there was also limited commitment to rights-based social services. Continuities and contradictions were also evident in the persistence of poverty and relatively high levels of inequality.
- The dramatic collapse of the Irish economy in the late 2000s revealed many weakness of the Irish economic model. The social impact of the crisis as well as the constraints posed by austerity resulted in a period of severe challenges for social policy. Currents of social change and social activism, in some cases building from as far back as the 1980s and 1990s, are also significant in this period, resulting in reconceptualised and augmented rights in some areas, but not without continuing areas of conflict and state neglect.
- Throughout the different phases of the period reviewed in this chapter, therefore, while the economy, and the way politics and economics interact are clearly major factors shaping opportunities and challenges in social policy, social policy developments are also driven by social politics. Both sets of factors shape the context for change and limits to change in social policy over time.

Discussion points

- Discuss the extent of continuity and change in evolution of social policy from the 1980s to the present.
- Select any decade discussed in this chapter and analyse the major influences on social policy during that time.

• Discuss the recent periods of austerity and 'recovery' – to what extent are the 'pain' and 'gain' of these respective periods evenly experienced?

Further reading list

Kirby, P and Murphy, MP (2011) *Towards a second republic? Irish politics after the celtic tiger*, London: Pluto

Meade, R and Dukelow, F (eds) *Defining events: Power, resistance and identity in twenty-first-century Ireland*, Manchester: Manchester UP

Murphy, MP and Dukelow, F (eds) (2016) *The Irish welfare state in the twenty-first century: Challenges and change*, Basingstoke: Palgrave Macmillan

Nolan, B, O'Connell, PJ and Whelan, CT (eds) (2000) *Bust to boom? The Irish experience of growth and inequality*, Dublin: IPA

Ó Riain, S (2014) *The rise and fall of Ireland's celtic tiger: Liberalism, boom and bust*, Cambridge: Cambridge UP

PART II
Explaining social policy: politics, ideology and welfare states

four

Social policy and the welfare state: origins, developments and reform

The aim of this chapter is to provide a wider exploration of the origins and development of welfare and social services from the latter part of the nineteenth century onwards. It maps the broader context of the emergence of welfare issues and the development of welfare states, offering a point of contrast between the experience in Ireland and elsewhere. There is a particular focus on Britain, where the historical development of social policy was 'shared' in terms of early inherited legislation and because of its subsequently differing welfare trajectory during the so-called 'golden age' of the welfare state, if not thereafter. Such an examination provides another dimension to the study of social policy because, in contrast to the relatively delayed development of the discipline in Ireland, in other countries, social policy – or social administration as it was previously called – became the subject of academic scrutiny and social policy issues came more to the fore of political debate throughout the twentieth century. The chapter identifies a range of influences on the development of welfare states including the emergence of new ideas, political movements and changing social attitudes along with economic expansion which shaped the context for social change and welfare reform over the twentieth century. There are, however, severe limitations to such a 'potted history' of welfare and what we provide is a sketch of certain major social policy developments and debates which should be followed up with supplementary reading. The chapter introduces various concepts that inform different perspectives on the role of social policy and in the final section it outlines some of the foremost influences on welfare state change in recent decades.

Chapter outline

- The first section traces the growing attention given to welfare-related issues since the latter part of the nineteenth century. The emergence of competing ideas about the organisation of society, the development of economies, and questions about meeting basic needs and acknowledging risks are considered.
- The foundations of the welfare state which were laid in the early part of the twentieth century are explored along with the wider political, economic and social influences including the emergence of a more collectivist perspective, underpinned by Keynesianism, during the mid-twentieth century. The subsequent contestation of some of the core assumptions on which the welfare state was established are then outlined.
- The final section examines the impact of shifting welfare discourses influenced by the New Right and the rise of neo-liberalism since the 1980s. We document the range of pressures and challenges welfare states have come under, and how they continue to adapt.

SECTION ONE

THE EMERGENCE OF WELFARE: KEY DEVELOPMENTS OF THE NINETEENTH AND EARLY TWENTIETH CENTURIES

Individualism and the ethos of the poor law

The examination of the Irish poor law in Chapter One highlighted its severity and its categorisation of poor people as 'deserving', 'undeserving', 'able-bodied' and 'impotent poor'. The implementation of the poor law, particularly as seen in its emphasis on personal responsibility, individual failure and associated negligence held an underlying philosophy of individual and familial responsibility in which collective responses to poverty were minimal. The overriding concern was to protect the ethos of **individualism** and to promote individual responsibility including, where necessary, to contain and control those in abject poverty, rather than to acknowledge the structural causes which contributed to the situation. The pervading philosophy of the time was similar elsewhere. For example, in Germany a system of poor relief was also in operation where legislation placed responsibility for the poor with local rather than national government. Rosenhaft's (1994: 26) account of this period in Germany notes how

Individualism is a belief which confers a central role on individuals in maintaining their own well-being.

> State law fixed the obligations of the municipalities, but it implied neither an obligation on its own part nor a right to support on the part of the poor; indeed, those who were dependent on poor relief

were deprived of most civil rights, including the franchise. Nineteenth-century poor law represented the minimum intervention necessary to protect public order against the threat posed by unrelieved hardship.

Katz (1996: 3) describes public welfare provided through poorhouses in the US:

> Poorhouses, which shut the old and sick away from their friends and relatives, were supposed to deter the working class from asking for poor relief. They were, in fact, the ultimate defense against the erosion of the work ethic in early industrial America. Miserable, poorly managed, underfunded institutions, trapped by their own contradictions, poorhouses failed to meet any of the goals so confidently predicted by their sponsors.

Notwithstanding the obvious hardships endured, the legacy of poor relief remains important because it was the first system of state intervention to deal with poverty and deliver a most basic form of provision, albeit one of last resort. Ultimately, the poor law system marked the opening phase in what was to become a more complex and less grudging acceptance of the role of the state in the provision of welfare.

The emphasis on individual responsibility had been a hallmark value of the early nineteenth century; based on a laissez-faire philosophy, it stressed the importance of self-responsibility at the core of Victorian values, in which class boundaries were also rigid. The class system was part of 'the natural order of things' and as such people were not expected to move beyond the class into which they were born. The wider implications of this way of thinking were evident in relation to children, who 'should be seen but not heard' and also in the dependent roles ascribed to women. These values extended to the use of the incarceration of particular people in institutions who were deemed to require such intervention, as outlined in Chapter Two with reference to the Irish case. Ultimately though, the traditional and extended family continued to be the primary source of welfare. Outside providers, where available, were only called upon if absolutely necessary. The aim of Victorian governments was 'to provide a framework of rules and guidelines designed to enable society very largely to run itself' (Harris, 1990: 67 in Lewis, 1999: 14).

A number of forces did coalesce, however, to bring about some shift in the level of state intervention in support for people and in meeting their needs. Taken together, these influences marked the emergence of a changed climate in terms of attitudes to human need, risk, different life stages and vulnerabilities. This is not to say that a change in opinion about the provision of welfare was universal or the result of unanimous support. However, the arrival of competing ideas about how best to support individuals and their families, and the identification of needs specific to certain groups, such as workers, children and older people, paved the way for significant change in the provision of welfare and social services during the twentieth century.

Social change, activism and philanthropy

The mid-nineteenth century was a period of immense social and economic change. Industrialisation and urbanisation in countries like Britain, Germany and America prompted massive transformation, from rural to urban living, the growing specialisation of skills, and the emergence of the factory as a major site of production and employment. The 'social consequences of industrialisation' according to Fraser (1984: 5), 'provided the fieldwork with which social policy had to deal, and they were broadly of three sorts, affecting the individual, his work and his environment.' In terms of the individual, people found themselves having to relate to each other, and to authority, in a more sophisticated but sometimes less secure way. As Fraser (1984: 5) explains, 'In place of the security of a cohesive *vertical* social structure in which every individual had a formal or informal connection with those above and below, there was the uncertainty of a mass society in which a *horizontal* class structure gradually emerged.'

In terms of work, the nature and types of activity changed enormously and the demand for particular skills grew, while others became obsolete. Monitoring and regulation of new places of employment came to be critical to the protection of workers and these interventions emerged as a formative aspect of social policy affecting the lives of individuals. Known as *arbeiterschutz* in Germany, the regulation of working conditions was important in 'the developing system of industrial wage labour' (Rosenhaft, 1994: 26). Tampke (1981), for example, describes early social legislation introduced in Prussia to cover employees in the coal-mining industry. From 1776 (and enforced until 1865), work in the mines was restricted to eight hours, with a guaranteed minimum income and medical treatment for accident or illness and payments during such periods. No women and children were permitted to work in mining. Wider restrictions on the employment of children were introduced in 1839 and the Office of Factory Inspector was set up to supervise these regulations. In the UK, the Children's Employment Commission in Mines and Factories 1842 highlighted the inadequate regulation and sometimes shocking working conditions which prevailed during the industrial revolution. Legislation began to regulate conditions of employment through a series of Factory Acts, culminating in the abolition of child labour from factories in 1901.

Industrialisation bore witness to the earliest work-related benefits (now known as occupational benefits); these benefits accrue to the employee from the employer as part of their conditions of employment. Various large-scale, wealthy employers provided accommodation through the development of 'model villages' attached to their factories. Examples of such housing developments include those undertaken by WH Lever, Wedgwood, Rowntree and Cadbury in the UK. Some of the first pensions were delivered as work-based occupational benefits in the 1870s by railroad companies such as Grand Trunk Railway and American Express in the

US and Canada. Critically though, these welfare initiatives were at the discretion of employers and only available to some employees.

At its most basic, industrialisation and urbanisation highlighted in even more stark terms the risks presented by poverty and poor housing conditions, overcrowding and inadequate sanitation. Taken together, these problems emerged as **social risks** that had the potential to damage the existing social structure of society and gradually these were acknowledged as issues that were not going to go away without significant investment and intervention by a larger body. Public health measures were among the first which gave recognition to large-scale needs. Inadequate systems of sewerage and drainage, access to water, cleaning the streets and overcrowding were the main areas for which local authorities were gradually given greater powers and responsibility. Significant public health legislation was passed in both Britain and the US by the late 1870s.

> **Social risks** refer to both probabilities and dangers that are beyond the control of an individual; they are shared in the sense that there are certain risks to which all of us are exposed in various ways.

Some of the most notable developments of this period occurred outside of the domain of the state, in civil society. The emergence of what we now call the voluntary sector goes back to this time when a lead role was played by voluntary groups in highlighting and responding to welfare needs. One element of this was the practice of forming support systems within social groups and communities, known as **mutual aid**, which grew during the nineteenth century. Examples of mutual aid organisations include cooperatives, housing associations, credit unions and friendly societies. Friendly societies worked on the basis of people in particular trades or guilds each contributing to a fund, in return for which an amount could be received in the event of a death in the family, illness and so on. They operated as a preventative or proactive welfare strategy; however, friendly societies had their drawbacks – they were mainly closed associations available only to those who had work and income sufficient to contribute. Eventually their costs began to mount and some became bankrupt. Yet mutual aid gave rise to the principle of shared or socialised risk which subsequently formed the basis of many social security systems around the world.

> **Mutual aid** refers to non-state reciprocal help or support; it can be financial or social in orientation.

In terms of the voluntary sector more generally, charitable groups grew and were at the forefront of seeking to address issues of poverty and human need. Specifically, the significance of philanthropy developed over the course of the nineteenth century. Upper-middle-class women in particular engaged in charitable work, especially in urban areas. The growth and widening scope of the sector is evident from about 1870 onwards when a number of high-profile organisations were established including the Dr Barnardo's Home, the Society of Saint Vincent de Paul, the Salvation Army, the Peabody Foundation and the Charity Organisation Society (COS).

Motivations for engagement in charitable work varied and for some the threat of the spread of disease or crime prompted intervention by the middle class. Regardless of the motivation, the growth in charitable activity during this period was remarkable, particularly among women, with an estimated 500,000 female volunteers in the UK in 1893 (Thane, 1996). The charitable sector was also significant in terms of its resources. By the end of the nineteenth century £8 million per annum was transferred to charities in London, more than the total national poor law expenditure at that time (Thane, 1996). Women's groups in particular advocated a range of social measures such as the provision of school meals, medical inspections, improvement in the quality of food and better maternity services. In terms of women's volunteerism as Thane (1996: 18) points out: 'Though unpaid, many of them were highly committed professionals. They created new approaches to social policy, some of which (e.g. district nurses, health visitors) were later adopted by the statutory sector.'

One such example was the COS founded in Britain in 1869. It sought to cooperate with the poor law provisions and to better coordinate the activities of charitable agencies, and branches were established in Germany, France and in America (Trattner, 1999; Ziliak, 2004). The stated aims of the COS included: 'to promote, as far as possible, the general welfare of the poor by means of social and sanitary reforms, and by the inculcation of habits of providence and self-dependence' (COS in Mooney, 1998: 69). This was done through the development of casework involving direct work with individuals and their families, an approach which subsequently became influential in social work.

However, the ethos of personal responsibility and self-help underpinning the work of the COS distinguished between 'deserving' and 'undeserving' cases. This philosophy was not without its critics, mainly because, as Jones (2000: 36) asserts

> Their approach, both with their clients and with more compassionate relief organizations, was so abrasive that it earned much of the opprobrium which has since been directed against philanthropy in general. Their diagnosis of the problems of large-scale Victorian philanthropy was sound enough; but their proposed cure gave the whole movement a bad name.

Overall, the growth of voluntary welfare provision in the latter part of the nineteenth century is significant in that it offered practical assistance, agitated for reform, while often motivated by an underlying religious philosophy and frequently shaped by varying belief systems. Some of these beliefs tended to re-enforce the tenet of personal responsibility which was discretionary in its allocation of welfare. In addition, and notwithstanding its pioneering role in many countries, philanthropy was, by its nature 'unevenly spread and frequently could only offer palliatives rather than fundamental solutions to the problems it encountered' (Stevenson, 1984: 24). More broadly, the limits of philanthropy must be set in the wider context of the confines of state support, as Thane (1996: 19) notes 'in 1870, and still in 1900, support from agencies of either central or local government was the least sought and usually the last resort. The family was almost certainly the first resort'. In short, the emerging social policy was arrived at by means of a complicated, reluctant and reactionary response to events and issues, and not based on any long-term strategy about meeting need.

Knowledge, democracy and ideology

Increased political activism and the emergence of political rights over the latter part of the nineteenth century and particularly 'one person, one vote' meant that individuals could finally express, through the ballot box at least, a preference for a certain point of view. As Flora (1981: 353) puts it, 'the development towards mass democracy inevitably brought new tasks for governments, but it equally strengthened the legitimacy of their demands for resources.' Enfranchisement occurred alongside the emergence of the trade union movement and the legal right of individuals to associate in groups, marking a new phase in highlighting class and social divisions. Trade union legislation passed during the 1870s in Britain gave recognition to unions before the law and made peaceful protest legal. The concurrent emergence of Marxist thinking offered a radical analysis of the unequal relationship between the working class and the owners of production, highlighting the insecurity of workers' lives and the nature of class divisions endemic to the capitalist system (see Chapter Five). The growth of the labour movement brought working conditions and the everyday experiences of working people into sharper focus. Events such as the international trade union conference held in 1890 sought a reduction in the number of working hours per day, restrictions on dangerous occupations, a ban on women working in mines and on night work, and the provision of four weeks' maternity leave (ILO, 1921 in Rowbotham, 1994). Though these resolutions were not binding they highlighted the need for regulation of the workplace and contributed to more sustained debate about the role of the state in protecting workers' rights.

Debate was shaped by considerations outside of the factories too, in particular living conditions. Early surveys provided the first scientific appreciation of the scale and depth of poverty which persisted in poor law times. In Britain, the first attempt to quantify the problem of poverty came in the late 1880s, in the research conducted by Charles Booth in London and Seebohm Rowntree in York. These landmark studies marked the emergence of social inquiry into the nature and prevalence of poverty. Despite taking different measurement approaches, when the findings were compared Rowntree concluded that 'we are faced with the startling probability that from 25 per cent to 30 per cent of the town population of the United Kingdom are living in poverty' (in Thane, 1996: 8). Both recorded the statistical incidence of poverty using particular indicators and wider impressions of poverty. What Booth did for the first time was to lay claim to the identification of poor people and poverty in Britain and in so doing supplanted 'stereotypes and prejudice with factual answers' (Jones, 2000: 50).

Rowntree subsequently developed his approach to analysing poverty by conducting over 11,000 working-class household surveys to establish family budgets and expenditure. His distinction between primary poverty (where earnings were insufficient for physical survival) and secondary poverty (where resources were sufficient for physical survival but not much else) presented a turning point because he challenged the conventional wisdom that absence of poverty equated with mere physical efficiency. In addition, he highlighted the possibility of a cycle of poverty at distinct times in the life of a labourer including childhood, the early years of one's family and child rearing, and old age (Fraser, 1984). Ultimately Rowntree presented the first indication of the need for a more sophisticated discussion about the nature, measurement and responses to poverty, a debate which continues ever since.

The emergence of the Fabian Society in the 1880s was another important development in advancing social policy issues. The Society was founded by a group of upper-middle-class intellectuals, based in London, including HG Wells, GB Shaw, and Sidney and Beatrice Webb. **Fabianism** became significant for the new ideological agenda it put forward for a collectivist philosophy, which sought to promote a gradual move towards socialism. The Fabians were essentially socialist in thought but differed substantially from Marxism in their belief that society could be reformed incrementally. Their arguments were based on the idea of social reform and promoting the values of collectivism. The Fabians advocated state intervention in the organisation of society, seeing it as a largely positive and benevolent force. They were to become pivotal to the development of the discipline of Social Policy, with their emphasis on awareness-raising through empirical research, in order to make, in Shaw's words: 'the public conscious of the evil condition of society under the present system' (cited in Lee and Raban, 1988: 15). The Fabian Society was also influential in the establishment of the British Labour Party in 1900.

> **Fabianism** describes the perspective of the Fabian Society which challenged conventional wisdom by arguing for a more extensive/interventionist role for the state in matters of welfare.

By the end of the nineteenth century some important social policy developments were apparent; there was direct state intervention in areas of education and public health and a growing momentum in relation to the need for protections for workers. Democratisation, political activism and social change became key drivers of an agenda that demanded a different approach to meeting human needs. The debates that surrounded securing political rights, establishing rights for workers and managing social change paved the way for more sustained attention to questions about the organisation of society and the role of the state. Essentially, the foundations of state welfare were being laid.

SECTION TWO
EMERGING WELFARE STATES: THE EARLY AND
MID-TWENTIETH CENTURY

The emergence of more concrete state intervention gained pace in the first decade of the twentieth century and thus began a century in which matters of welfare came to occupy a prominent position in political debate. A distinct literature later emerged offering a number of theories that aid in our overall understanding of the development of state welfare. The earliest of these theories (for example Wilensky, 1975) emphasises the significance of structural features including the stage of capitalism, economic development and industrialisation. Others (for example Korpi, 1983) stress the importance of political forces such as the relative influence of political traditions and political parties in the expansion of social policy. Esping-Andersen's (1990) analysis of welfare state development highlights the significance of historical legacy and the influence of political structures along with the potential for working-class mobilisation. The debate on exact cause and effect is complex precisely because countries' political cultures and policy processes differ although the stage of economic development, or the 'logic of industrialisation', remains important to our overall understanding (Cousins, 2005b).

The establishment of the first system of compulsory social insurance in Germany in the 1880s marked a watershed in the development of social security benefits. German workers now had a right to protection (by means of a minimal benefit) in the event of illness, accident, disability or old age. Although widely considered groundbreaking, Bismarck's introduction of social insurance was motivated primarily by concerns about the strength of the Social Democratic Party and socialist trade unions rather than a wider progressive vision about the capacity of social security. In the event, Bismarck's original plan was to have low, non-earning-related contributions and benefits, but what emerged was contribution led (both employers and employees contributed) with separate schemes for 'blue collar' and 'white collar' workers and civil servants (Clasen, 1994). The development of these policy initiatives in Germany did have a wider impact, particularly in Scandinavia. State contributions to accident, sickness and old-age insurance were introduced in Sweden, for example, between 1891 and 1913 (Berend, 2005).

Landmark welfare measures were subsequently initiated in many countries, although the basis of their introduction was quite different. A non-contributory old age pension was set up in Denmark in 1891 and in New Zealand in 1898. Similarly, in the UK and Ireland, the Old Age Pension Act 1908 provided state pensions on a non-contributory basis. Payments were low but their provision on a basis separate from the poor law, and not reliant on previous work-based contributions, was significant.

The emergence of welfare provisions in the core areas of pensions, unemployment, illness and disability represented the beginning of an acknowledgement of distinct phases of the life course with particular needs, risks and vulnerabilities. The social security initially offered was largely designed to protect individuals as workers, but the introduction of protective legislation for children and the provision of old age pensions indicated a growing acknowledgement of 'lifecycle risk'. The harsh living conditions and the sometimes awful treatment of children, for instance, began to enter public consciousness by the latter part of the nineteenth century. The establishment of Societies for the Prevention of Cruelty to Children in the US, the UK and Ireland contributed to raising awareness about the welfare of children in general. In the UK the *Children's Charter* 1889 provided the first legal basis for state intervention in child–parent relations. Legislation pertaining to the protection of children was developed with the introduction of the National Society for the Prevention of Cruelty to Children (NSPCC) inspectors in the Prevention of Cruelty Act 1904. These inspectors had the right to remove children from their homes on the grounds of abuse or neglect, on the approval of a Justice of the Peace (NSPCC, nd), although protection of many these children thereafter was woefully neglected by the state. Overall, the early twentieth century saw the first challenge to conventional views about the position of children in society marking the beginning of a long struggle for the recognition of children as individuals in their own right, subject to certain risks, and entitled to protection.

Other important developments indicated the dawn of a more extensive role for the state in key areas of social policy. In the UK, for example, the introduction of labour exchanges and the National Insurance Act 1911 paved the way for benefits during periods of sickness and unemployment, although unemployment benefit covered far fewer workers and for a shorter timeframe than elsewhere (McCashin, 2004). The rise in the level of state provision was matched with a wider span of taxation measures. The 'People's Budget' introduced by Lloyd George in 1909 for example, contained new land taxes including a levy on land sales and a tax on the capital value of undeveloped land (Lund, 2002).

From welfare efforts to welfare states: key developments and debates

Sweden continues to be popularly recognised as the 'model' welfare state, although that characterisation has been open to greater debate in recent times. In historical terms Sweden was indeed at the forefront of welfare state development, and while influenced by the earlier Bismarckian initiatives, the Swedish application is assessed as more inclusive than was actually the case in Germany. Collective ideals had been actively promoted in political discourse since the late 1920s. Known as the People's Home Speech, the soon to become Prime Minister Hansson of Sweden made a famous parliamentary speech in 1928 (cited in Olsen, 1992: 98 in Salonen, 2001: 146):

> The basis of the home is community and the feeling of togetherness. The good home knows no privileged or disadvantaged individuals, no favourites and step-children. There, one does not look down upon another; there, nobody tries to gain an advantage at the cost of another, the strong one does not hold down and plunder the weak. In the good home equality, consideration, helpfulness prevail. Applied to the great people's and citizens' home, this would mean the breaking down of all social and economic barriers, which now divide citizens into privileged and disadvantaged, into rulers and dependants, into rich and poor, propertied and miserable, plunderers and plundered.

The sustained success of the Social Democratic Party, which held power from 1932 to 1976, was undoubtedly a decisive factor in the subsequent welfare state that developed in Sweden.

The US followed a different welfare state trajectory as local and voluntary sources remained the primary sources of assistance outside of the family. This was the case until the economic depression and unemployment crisis of the 1930s, even though many groups had long argued the merits of state or federal provision. The election of Franklin D. Roosevelt in 1933 offered a political leader apparently more open to ameliorating the difficulties associated with large-scale unemployment. The Federal Emergency Relief Administration (FERA) was established and provided, for the first time, federal assistance to unemployed persons and while it brought welcome support to the many unemployed, the scheme itself was short-lived and emphasis fast shifted to work-based schemes for the 'able-bodied' unemployed. The abolition of FERA in 1936 indicated the reluctance of the federal state to provide assistance for people affected by unemployment (Piven and Cloward, 1993). These people had no option but to rely on local agencies which, once again, were under pressure to provide relief. It is against this backdrop that the Social Security Act 1935 is assessed as a milestone in US social policy. It introduced a national social insurance pension, a federal system of unemployment insurance (administered by individual states) and a system of Aid to Dependent Children (ADC). These were significant developments in securing welfare provisions but it is important to note that, for example, in the case of unemployment insurance payments, these were set at local level, coverage was for a limited period and many workers were actually not covered by the scheme (Trattner, 1999). The ADC was also administered locally on the basis of stringent means-testing and strict eligibility criteria, indicating the conditional nature of the new schemes and the limits of state welfare expansionism in America at this time. Characterisations of a 'work and relief state' (Amenta, 1998 in Clarke, 2001: 115) and a 'semi-welfare state' (Katz, 1986 in Clarke, 2001: 118) capture the defining features of this period in American social policy history and stand in contrast to the more comprehensive approach to welfare provision which subsequently emerged in Europe.

Economic and welfare interventions: the impact of Keynes and Beveridge

The more comprehensive approach to welfare adopted in some European countries was largely shaped by a new approach to economic management which became highly influential for much of the twentieth century. The work of the economist JM Keynes was central to the argument for a greater role for the state in economic matters and in the development of employment policy from the late 1930s onwards. The fact that he offered the first theoretical rationale for state intervention in the economy was to prove vital in the welfare state expansion that subsequently occurred. Specifically, Keynes suggested that the state could intervene to regulate the worst aspects of economic cycles in order to engage in 'demand management' (and thus economic growth) and to maintain employment, where appropriate. **Keynesian economics**, as it became known, was instrumental to the development of the welfare state, particularly with its attention to the role of government and the importance of employment policy to the wider welfare agenda. Critically, the impact of Keynesianism marked a break with the predominance of classical economics. As Mullard and Spicker (1998: 29) point out, 'Keynesians sought to offer a revolution in thinking about government and economy and therefore aimed to break with the classical paradigm that a *laissez-faire* economy was the only solution for the well-being of a society.' In offering an economic rationale for greater state intervention, Keynesian economics became the mechanism by which more extensive state supports were both possible and justifiable, and its impact was immense.

> **Keynesian economics**, so named after economist JM Keynes, advocated state intervention in the economy (as appropriate to the economic conditions which prevailed), challenging the long-standing classical economic laissez-faire position.

Published at the height of the Second World War in 1942, *Social Insurance and Allied Services*, the *Beveridge Report* as it became known, is probably the most well-known social policy report of the twentieth century. The author, William Beveridge, was set the task of sorting out the muddled system of social insurance which had evolved over the years. His report offered a plan for the future of social policy in Britain. Beveridge (1942: 6) provided a vision of welfare which was much more all-encompassing than social insurance alone:

> organisation of social insurance should be treated as one part only of a comprehensive policy of social progress. Social insurance fully developed may provide income security: it is an attack upon Want. But Want is one only of five giants on the road of reconstruction and in some ways the easiest to attack. The others are Disease, Ignorance, Squalor and Idleness.

Healthcare, education, housing and work were the antidotes to these social problems and the reconstruction which followed the Second World War allowed for major policy developments in these respective areas. The fulsome acknowledgement of the range of issues which arise in meeting human needs marked a watershed in defining the role of the social services in providing welfare. In so doing, the idea of a baseline or 'national minimum' under which no one should fall, became a new but seemingly feasible policy objective, which appealed to people's sense of social solidarity particularly in the aftermath of the war. In addition, the centrality of employment, as a policy objective and as the economic linchpin on which welfare provision was possible, was crucial. Availability of work was accepted as a central element of social and economic policy for the future. Critically, though, while a responsive and expanded role for the state was being carved out in the formative years of the British welfare state, this was not to happen at the expense of economic progress. While advocating a greater role for the state in the abolition of want and in meeting basic needs, Beveridge (1942: 6) noted that an appropriate balance had to be struck,

> social security must be achieved by co-operation between the State and the individual. The State should offer security for service and contribution. The State in organising security should not stifle incentive, opportunity, responsibility; in establishing a national minimum, it should leave room and encouragement for voluntary action by each individual to provide more than that minimum for himself and his family.

The collectivist philosophy at the core of a national minimum was circumscribed by a keenness to see individual responsibility maintained in any new welfare balance. 'Reluctant collectivists' (George and Wilding, 1985) was the term subsequently used to describe advocates of this approach to welfare provision.

Turning this plan into a reality in Britain became the job of the Labour Party, returned after a landmark election victory in 1945, which secured the first majority in their history. In general terms, the Labour Party was considered a solid supporter of the Beveridge Report and efforts were made to implement the proposals in the years that followed. While these were not realised in full (Glennerster, 1995), some core policy areas saw milestone developments. Labour inherited the Education Act 1944 which had abolished fees for secondary education along with legislation for the provision of Family Allowances. In 1945, the provision of family allowances, delivered in the form of a cash benefit for the second and subsequent children of all families on a non-means-tested and on a non-contributory basis, represented the introduction of the first quintessential universal benefit in Britain. Wider elements of public policy incorporated state control of some economic activities to protect core utilities in the national economic and public interest. Several major industries were nationalised by the 1940s including civil aviation, coal, transport, electricity and gas.

Figure 4.1: UK Ministry of National Insurance poster advertising the Family Allowance Act 1945

Source: The National Archives, UK

Much was done to consolidate the organisation of the health and social security systems in Britain between 1945 and 1951. While the Mother and Child Scheme controversy exposed the various opponents of a collectivist vision for healthcare in Ireland, in the UK Aneurin Bevan succeeded in passing the National Health Service Act 1946, despite the objections of many medical professionals. Private consultant practice was allowed to continue but the Act provided a national health service (NHS), largely paid for through general taxation. Services provided by the NHS included free treatment by the citizen's doctor of choice, free prescriptions and no charge for hospital care (Glennerster, 1995).

The extent to which the suffering experienced during the Second World War and the reconstruction required for national recovery in Britain precipitated support for the welfare state project is debated but it was undoubtedly a crucial part of the context within which the Beveridge Report was received. A headline from the *Daily Mirror* on 5 July 1948 (in Fraser, 1984: xxi) gives a snapshot of the significance attached to the emerging health and welfare rights: 'The great day has arrived. You wanted the State to assume greater responsibility for individual citizens. You wanted social security. From today you have it'. The Beveridge Report made the headlines in Ireland too and its popularity prompted a debate about the nature of Irish social policy (Ó Cinnéide, 2000) as discussed in Chapter Seven. The Beveridge Plan received considerable scrutiny in Germany, even if the ideas around social insurance were 'by no means a novelty in German eyes' (Hockerts, 1981: 324). A report produced on social security in Canada in 1943 which 'was not as comprehensive as its British counterpart [...] nevertheless firmly placed Canada in the Keynes-Beveridge tradition' (Lightman and Riches, 2001: 51) and universal family allowances and old age pensions were introduced there in 1945 and 1952 respectively.

Overall this period was marked by a significant shift in thinking around welfare. The focus moved from 'individuals with problems' and 'troubles' which needed to be 'fixed' to an acknowledgement of the possibilities associated with a more **collectivist approach** underpinned by **universal provision** of some basic level of welfare and social services. The period after the Second World War was therefore a formative one in which the basis for comprehensive social services had been established. The so-called 'golden age' of the welfare state lasted from the late 1940s until the mid-1970s; social services were set up and access improved and widened, particularly in the areas of health, education and social security. Looking at welfare states across Europe, Cousins (2005b) outlines how benefits expanded from 1950 to 1970 and notes the significantly wider reach of state welfare during this period. Social policy had moved from concentrating on how best to deal with the poor, to looking at how access to social services might be the preserve or entitlement of all citizens.

Understanding the emergent welfare state as the expansion of citizenship, TH Marshall's seminal essay 'Citizenship and Social Class' written in 1949 (Marshall, 1964) offered a historical evolutionary analysis of the development of **citizenship** rights in Britain. He saw citizenship as evolving from the emergence of civil rights (the right to freedom of expression, freedom of religion and justice before the law) during the eighteenth century, to the establishment of political rights (the right to vote and the right to stand for public office) over the course of the nineteenth century and the development of social rights (the right to a modicum of economic welfare and security) in the twentieth century. He defined citizenship as a 'status bestowed on those who are full members of a community' (Marshall, 1964: 84) the social element of which included a 'whole range from a right to share a modicum of economic welfare and security to the right to share to the full in the social heritage and to live the life of a civilised being according to the standards prevailing in the society' (Marshall, 1964: 84). He suggested that the institutions most closely connected with this idea of social citizenship are the education system and the social services and emphasised the common experiences social rights would produce, regardless of one's class position, and suggested that social citizenship would modify patterns of social inequality. In short, civil and political rights were viewed as necessary components for the development of capitalism and the emergence of social rights offered a solution to some of the inequalities inherent in capitalist society. The expansionary phase of welfare provision in Britain at that time was clearly relevant to such an analysis,

> A **collectivist approach** sees groups, communities and societies as the basic unit of social structure. Need and risk are to be met on a 'shared' rather than individualised basis, thereby apportioning greater responsibility to society (often through the medium of the state) in meeting them.

> **Universal provision** refers to the delivery of a social service or social protection as a matter of right, satisfying a certain core criterion without the use of a means test or other measure of differentiation.

> **Marshallian citizenship** refers to TH Marshall's three-prong identification of citizenship rights as having civil, political and social elements. His conception of social citizenship was constructed around the role of the state in abating class inequalities in the context of the nation state.

although subsequent assessments of Marshall's theory of citizenship challenged its core assumptions and questioned its broader application. The idea of more expansive welfare access to deliver social rights based on a particular notion of citizenship emerged as a problematic one. Regarding women, for example, it quickly became clear that they were treated as 'second-class' citizens in aspects of welfare provision, while some groups, notably immigrants, were denied access to services on the basis of not being citizens.

Contesting social norms and welfare assumptions

It was evident, even at the time of the publication of the Beveridge Report, that the proposals were framed with reference to re-enforcing certain 'social norms', particularly with regard to the role of women as housewives and mothers. In 1943, Abbott and Bompass (in J Pratt, 2006) highlighted the unequal treatment of married women where Beveridge had proposed the removal of women's social insurance rights on marriage, that contributions would be voluntary rather than compulsory and that benefits would be payable at a lower rate to that of men. The predominance of these assumptions paved the way for welfare provision based on what is now known as the male breadwinner model, with married women assigned a dependent status within the family and not recognised as individuals in their own right. While countries such as Sweden and Denmark made greater advances after the late 1960s with the introduction of day care, parental leave and amended tax policies contributing to higher female labour-market participation, a strong male breadwinner model persisted in Britain, Ireland and Germany (Lewis and Åström, 1997). The dependent status imposed on women, constructed around particular familial and domestic ideals, severely restricted the lives of women and much of the invisible work done by women in the home continued to be ignored. Feminist agitation to address the discriminatory structure of the UK welfare state as well as others gained ground by the 1970s and a number of issues were tackled such as inequalities in pay and in the formal labour market. While these reforms were welcome and long overdue, they primarily addressed the inherent **institutional discrimination** which existed and could no longer be ignored.

Williams (1989) argues that the model of solidarity espoused by Beveridge allowed for institutional inequalities not only in the treatment of women but that the social rights of other groups were also not vindicated. The residency requirements attached to many welfare provisions excluded many 'non-citizens' living in Britain from accessing the social services, even though it was within these services that many migrant people worked. As Williams (1989: 162) puts it, 'when Beveridge announced his attack on the five giants – Want, Squalor, Idleness, Ignorance and Disease – he hid the giants Racism and Sexism, and the fights against them, behind statues to the Nation and

> **Institutional discrimination**
> refers to direct or indirect bias in policies and/or services against particular groups of people, given less favourable rights and/or access than the rest of the population.

the White Family.' Similar issues came to the fore in the US, and ultimately the Civil Rights movement of the 1960s became central to the demands for welfare reform. Apart from the obvious unrest caused by racial discrimination and conflict, the limitations of the existing welfare provisions also garnered greater scrutiny. The federal local mix of welfare provision and in particular the conditions attached to the ADC highlighted the 'moral' conditions that were attached to benefit receipt. According to Gordon (1994: 298 in Clarke, 2001: 118),

> ADC was unique among all welfare programs in its subjection of applicants to a morals test. The most frequent measurement of a 'suitable home' was sexual behaviours. The presence of a man in the house, or the birth of an illegitimate child, made the home unsuitable. These provisions also permitted racist policies. For example, black–white relationships were particularly likely to make a child's home declared unsuitable. The search for these 'moral' infractions produced intense supervision and invasions of privacy.

Besides these shortcomings, other political, economic and social issues also presented the impetus for a wider welfare debate with criticism emanating from Left and Right, including from supporters of the welfare state who felt it had fallen short of its stated objectives and could do better. In the 1960s, the 'rediscovery' of poverty highlighted problems with the capacity of the welfare state to address issues of poverty and inequality. A study conducted by Abel-Smith and Townsend (1965) entitled *The Poor and the Poorest* demonstrated the extent of poverty particularly among large low-income families in Britain. A number of direct action groups campaigned on this issue including the Child Poverty Action Group and the Low Pay Unit (Jones, 2000). The 1970s also saw the emergence of community development projects which facilitated important work with people, mainly in disadvantaged areas. Jones (2000), for example, identifies the emergent Welfare Rights and Law Centres movements in Britain as significant in providing welfare information and advice. At a more general level, the growth in community development became a more critical voice about the shortcomings of the welfare state. It is clear that the ethos and culture of the welfare state was under pressure to be more responsive than the original traditional structures would allow.

A more radical critique of the welfare state, based on a revival of Marxist thinking, or neo-Marxism (O'Connor, 1973; Ginsburg, 1979; Gough, 1979), delivered a challenging assessment of the role of the welfare state in promoting and protecting capitalism. In general terms, this literature highlighted the 'contradictions of the welfare state' (Offe, 1982, 1984) in providing the necessary conditions for the maintenance of capitalism (see Chapter Five).

In economic terms, the oil crises of the 1970s, rapid inflation and increasing unemployment meant that Keynesian economics was no longer considered the panacea in addressing the worst excesses of the economic cycle. Workers were unhappy, too, with high inflation eroding the real value of their wages and in some cases threatening their jobs. With the economic justification for state intervention and welfare provision under attack, the political and ideological grounds for state intervention became increasingly difficult to defend. As the UK Labour Minister, Anthony Crosland put it in 1975, the 'party is over' (in Hill, 2003: 36). Many academics confirmed the onset of the 'crisis of the welfare state' although this, in retrospect, turned out to be largely intellectual (Alber, 1988) and ideological rather than a 'practical crisis' of its ability to perform existing day-to-day functions.

Criticisms of the welfare state project were grounded in differing perspectives and shaped by conflicting ideological values but the cumulative effect remained significant; there was an appetite for change, demonstrated in the collapse in support for the Labour Party in Britain in the late 1970s and by the 18 years of Conservative government which followed from 1979 to 1997. The wider resurgence in right-wing thinking was evident elsewhere too with the election of Ronald Reagan in the US in 1980 and in Canada the Conservative Party won a considerable majority in 1984 (Mishra, 1990). While the political and economic climate changed and became more hostile to the welfare state it is important to note that welfare states in Europe continued to grow and spending continued to rise.

SECTION THREE

WELFARE STATES AND ADAPTATION, RETRENCHMENT AND REFORM: FROM THE LATE TWENTIETH CENTURY TO THE PRESENT

So far this chapter has mapped the broad story of the development of the welfare state with particular emphasis on the key ideas and influences on its evolution. Debates about the optimum functions of welfare states have always been a source of ideological and political contestation and as Gamble notes (2016: 56), 'for much of the twentieth century, the moral argument was generally won by those arguing for extending state provision and reducing the risks and uncertainties individuals faced in their lives'. The demise of Keynesianism was aided by the strengthening political and policy preferences of neo-liberalism which came to prominence since the 1980s. By the 2000s, welfare state reform had become a prominent feature of social policy discourse across Europe. Issues of cost containment, sustainability and the need to modernise the welfare state dominated. Inevitably, reforms have not conformed along a singular track, given the distinct institutional features and the mediating forces that come to bear, especially on the domestic politics of welfare reform. Despite all of the structural reforms initiated, overall social expenditure continued to grow between 1980 and 2005. In some countries, this is due, in part at least, to increased social investment spending. A productive turn is also evident in welfare state reforms since the late 1990s, exemplified by the development of employment and activation policy. Wider ideas around the role of social investment gained some ground during the 2000s. The different and uneven impact of austerity since the late 2000s marks the latest instalment in the story of the welfare state, with evidence mounting of a shift to a supply-side welfare state. In short, advanced European welfare states moved from a golden era (1940s-1970s), to a period of crisis with resilience (1980s), to one of modification, cost containment and labour market oriented reforms (1990s-2000s), to a new phase of crisis and austerity with more market-conforming reforms (2010s). The final section of this chapter attempts to broadly map out the circumstances, politics, concepts and policies that have shaped this period of welfare state change.

Rolling back the welfare state

Reducing the role of the state in all aspects of economic and social life was the major purpose of the **New Right**. This largely anti-collectivist thinking was exemplified by the Thatcher government elected in Britain in 1979. Following the theoretical guidance of Friedrich von Hayek, Margaret Thatcher valued, 'a society in which the vast majority of

> The **New Right** is an all-encompassing title for the right-wing political values that gained prominence during the 1980s. Various strands of thinking have been influential including neo-liberalism and neo-conservatism.

men and women are encouraged and helped to accept responsibility for themselves and their families, and to live their lives with a maximum of independence and self-reliance' (Thatcher, 1977 in George and Wilding, 1985: 22).

The New Right philosophy sought to reduce the role of the state in the lives of individuals and radically reform the welfare state, which it was argued had created over-reliance, and was inefficient and wasteful. The infrastructure of the welfare state was pared back and in Britain over 200 advisory bodies were abolished and official statistical services were curtailed (Jones, 2000). The state was also considered to have overstepped its position in the ownership of key utilities, such as British Gas and British Telecom, and **privatisation** became a core policy objective. The application of market principles to areas of the public services took many forms. Thatcher's ambition to encourage stakeholder capitalism among ordinary people was epitomised in the Right to Buy scheme which encouraged the sale of local authority

> **Privatisation** refers to the process through which previously state-owned companies (often utilities, such as electricity, transport) are sold by the state to private enterprise.

houses to tenants. The overall approach sought to re-enforce classical liberal values of individualism and the merits of the free market, the principles of which were also to be adopted in the public services.

New Public Management refers to the development of a business and commercial ethos and management style in the public service.

Marketisation describes various processes by which public/social services are made to operate on a basis more like that of the private market. **Quasi-markets** are established within the public sector to encourage market-type efficiency gains. **Contracting out** refers to the process by which certain services within the public sphere are put out to tender to private enterprise or voluntary sector organisations.

The emergence of **New Public Management** during the 1980s sought to apply private sector practices in the management, budgets and finance of the public service. In turn, outcomes were measured closely in terms of performance and efficiency. Application of new public management principles included the creation of internal markets within the social services in Britain, most notably in health, local government and education, and certain functions (for example cleaning and catering) within the services were put out to tender. The introduction of **marketisation** via **quasi-markets** or some level of market competition within the social services meant that while the state continued to fund/purchase elements of a service, it may not be the actual provider. The **contracting out** of various parts of services subsequently became more widespread and increasingly common elsewhere. This led to both voluntary and private providers entering formal service agreements with the state around the delivery of particular social services.

For the New Right, extolling the virtues of the free market meant tackling the vested interests outside the state as well. Taking on the trades unions, which the Conservative Party viewed as too powerful, was central to restoring the values of capitalism. A combination of legislation and infamous standoffs (most notably with the miners) led to confrontation between state and workers on a scale not seen for many years. The lack of work weakened the union position, as unemployment was a very real prospect. Films such as *Brassed Off* (1996) and *Billy Elliot* (2000) offer a vivid insight into the social tensions and divisions which emerged in Britain at the time. Unemployment rose sharply in the early 1980s but in the New Right assessment it was the market and not the state which would solve the unemployment problem. Unemployment also rose in the US but it wasn't just the scale of the unemployment that was problematic; cutbacks and tighter benefit eligibility criteria meant that only 25% of those unemployed received benefits by 1984, compared with 75% in 1975 (Mishra, 1990). Similarly in the UK, social security was made increasingly conditional. Examples include the application of penalties to unemployed people who refused training or left jobs; the replacement of two universal welfare benefits (the maternity grant and the death grant) with means–tested schemes and the reform of the national pension system to encourage people away from it and into private schemes (Hill, 2003).

The hostile ideological climate in Britain, which was also in evidence in the US, undermined the solidaristic basis of welfare provision and portrayed many welfare recipients as 'deviants'. A wider academic discourse re-enforced a confrontational approach to welfare debate with Murray (1984) and others referring to an 'underclass' of society. However ill-defined (see Lister, 1996 for analysis of the debate), the term was frequently taken to refer to individual or familial behaviour argued to contribute to poverty and welfare dependency. The 'underclass' debate was trenchantly argued, along with other 'dependency politics' (Mead, 1992) theories, which put forward the view that the welfare state sapped people's initiative and encouraged dependency on the state. This view was cogently rebutted (Dean and Taylor-Gooby, 1992), by reference to the absence of work in the first instance and the severity of the social exclusion experienced by many of the most disadvantaged social groups.

A 'tough love' approach manifested itself in the welfare to work or **workfare** agenda of the 1990s, evidenced in social policy developments in the US. In 1994 the ADC (then Aid to Families with Dependent Children (AFDC)) was replaced with a programme called Temporary Assistance to Needy Families which imposed work requirements and time limits on lone mothers

> **Workfare** refers to welfare arrangements in which a specific requirement to work (often without additional payment) is a condition of eligibility.

receiving assistance. The Personal Responsibility Act 1996 similarly sought that families be independent through work. In practice, this meant a maximum of two years' benefit before the state could begin withdrawing support. Furthermore, the Act aimed to promote marriage and two-parent families; in fact, states could refuse additional benefit for any child born whose mother was already in receipt of welfare (Clarke and Piven, 2001). The Act, and in particular the abolition of the AFDC, 'eliminated any national entitlement to welfare' and 'reflected a resurgence of a number of fundamental themes of colonial poor law, its more unworkable, or at least unfair and punitive provisions' (Trattner, 1999: 397).

Notwithstanding the impact of New Right thinking on welfare benefits and the increased conditions attached to them, it is important to note that the welfare state did, broadly speaking, 'survive' plans to dismantle it. This is true even in countries like the UK and the US, where the impact of New Right politics was greatest. Recognition of the resilience of welfare states brought to the fore new scholarship about the politics of welfare roll back or retrenchment (Pierson, 1994, 1996). Pierson drew attention to the different dynamics at play where welfare retrenchment is concerned. Pre-existing welfare arrangements contribute to a social policy legacy or feedback with commitments and interest groups that are not easily overturned. Institutional structures are also key; they 'establish the rules of the game for political struggles – influencing group identities, policy preferences, and coalitional choices, and enhancing the bargaining power of some groups while devaluing that of others. Institutions also affect government capacities – their administrative and financial resources for fashioning policy interventions' (Pierson, 1996: 152). History, institutions and politics therefore matter a great deal to how, and to what extent, welfare retrenchment is pursued. At the same time, these welfare states did not emerge unscathed. The nature and extent of the role of the state as a provider and funder of welfare services was revised in certain important respects; the application of market principles in contracting out core social services, adherence to ideals of new public management, privatisation of key utilities, increasing individualisation of risks, the cumulative effect of which was to rebalance the welfare mix. The aforementioned developments aligned with the broader thrust of neo-liberalism influential in Anglo-American welfare states in particular.

Welfare states: adaptation and structural reforms

Partly in response to the rise of neo-liberalism, the 1990s saw a marked shift in political thinking on the Left, most notably by the Labour Party in Britain (re-named New Labour), and also in Germany, the Netherlands and in the US during Bill Clinton's administration. The emergence of a so-called Third Way offered a perspective that was not bound by old ideological values of Left and Right and as advocates of the Third Way argued, it acknowledged the changed nature of society, especially in terms of globalisation, and the need to change with it. Applying the Third Way perspective to economic and social policy meant taking more nuanced positions on social rights, withdrawing from the 'old' unconditional notion of social rights in favour of 'no rights without responsibilities'. In terms of the role of the private sector, New Labour was more pro-market than their 'Old Labour' predecessors; they sought to stress the benefits of the market and in that sense made a clear break with their previous more socialist leanings. The Third Way approach to welfare showed some continuity with the reforms of the 1980s while at the same time developing priorities for promoting equality of opportunity through investment in children and in education, marking the beginnings of a policy agenda also influenced by selected ideas pertaining to a **social investment state** (Giddens, 1998). The emerging idea of social investment sought to invest in human capital, namely people, with a view to maximising their economic and productive capacity. The development of the social investment concept and its various policy interpretations are considered in Chapter Six.

> **Social investment state** describes ideas related to reorienting welfare to make it more focused on building human capital capacity via a more active and enabling welfare state. A 'prepair' as opposed to a 'repair' approach, it seeks to invest in social supports (childcare, education, activation) to maximise opportunities for (labour market) participation.

While the rhetoric of the Left had clearly changed, some of its core policy objectives, at least, had not. Reducing child and family poverty was a major policy objective of Britain's New Labour governments (1997-2010). The objective to reduce poverty was tackled using not only conventional cash transfers, as attention shifted to the role of services in tackling poverty. Underpinned by the notion that investing in services would address social disadvantage and level the playing field for all,

equality of opportunity emerged as a central plank of Third Way policy. Greater access to education, early childhood care and low-income family supports was to provide the basis for better opportunities for all. Less attention was paid to income inequality and redistribution although the gap between rich and poor continued to widen. New Labour concentrated their efforts on the bottom half of the income distribution and not the top (Lupton et al, 2013), which they did not seem to view as a concern any longer. As the Prime Minister, Tony Blair (cited in Lupton et al, 2013: 16), acknowledged: 'It's not a burning ambition of mine to make sure that David Beckham earns less money'. Growing **income inequality** has been a feature of most advanced economies since the 1970s particularly in the US, UK and Canada, where the share of income going to the top 1% of earners has doubled and their share of overall wealth also increased (Piketty, 2014). The significance of increased inequality and its consequences has been long argued by Tony Atkinson (see Atkinson, 2015 for a recent contribution). Other academics (Wilkinson and Pickett, 2009; Dorling, 2010; Stiglitz, 2012) also added to our understanding of inequality and assisted in bringing the issue to greater public prominence in recent years.

> **Equality of opportunity** broadly refers to the notion that everyone is given an equal chance to succeed regardless of factors such as class, gender, disability, race or any other aspect of identity.

> **Income inequality** refers to the gap in income differences which result in unequal and uneven distributions of income across different groups or the population as a whole.

During the 1990s and 2000s however, increased inequality was overshadowed by the dominant political narrative around the assumed potential of opportunities for all, to be achieved in increasingly liberalised market economies to which welfare states would have to adapt. Relatedly, the '"competitiveness imperative" … drives a determination to activate policies to sustain higher levels of productive employment and lower state spending on dependent groups, so that benefits are targeted and the private sector expands' (Taylor-Gooby, 2001: x). These ideas played a decisive role in European welfare state change since the 1990s. The role of greater European economic integration also played a part. EU member states joining the Economic and Monetary Union (EMU) had to adhere to the Maastricht criteria which included limits on government deficits and debt, and rules on inflation, interest rates and exchange rate stability which restrained national governments' room for fiscal manoeuvre on spending (see Chapter Six).

Simultaneously, the maturation of welfare states across Europe meant that the notion of 'welfare states under pressure' (Taylor-Gooby, 2001) sustained and intensified. The ideological assault on the welfare state was nowhere as strong as that of Britain but welfare reforms were also initiated across Europe since the 1990s which were initially framed more by the logic of protecting the welfare state. Pension reforms initiated in Germany and France in the 1990s, for example, were then presented as necessary to maintain their strong social insurance,

Bismarckian-based, systems in the face of growing economic, demographic and fiscal pressures. However, as Palier and Martin (2008) identify, reforms and subsequent path-breaking developments in the 2000s created new programmes following new rules, including greater use of means-tested provisions, a more significant role for the private sector in pensions and health, and some weakening of social insurance instruments. These reforms highlight how cost containment and other pressures came to bear upon what were often considered the most inert European welfare states. Taking a longer view, two decades of industrial relations, labour market and welfare state change in France and Germany, are assessed to have brought about significant change resulting in 'the institutionalization of new forms of **dualism** ... now explicitly underwritten by state policy' (Palier and Thelen, 2010: 119).

> **Dualism** refers to the ways in which the administration of welfare and the objectives of welfare states can result in new and changing divisions between insiders (with access to welfare/social protection) and outsiders (those excluded from protection).

Another important aspect of social exclusion that comes to the fore in welfare states relates more broadly to conceptions of citizenship as tied to nationality and the nation state. Where citizenship denoted formal membership of a country together with a shared national culture or identity, immigration disrupted this understanding. As Joppke (1999: 629) points out,

> The movement of people across states revealed that citizenship is not only a set of rights, but also a mechanism of closure that sharply demarcates the boundaries of states. ... As a mechanism of closure, citizenship (commonly ascribed at birth) is like a filing mechanism, distributing people to just one of the world's many states. ... for those who manage to enter the territory of another state, access to this state's citizenship is generally denied, and available only if demanding (residence and personal) characteristics are fulfilled, which are differently conceived in different states.

Therefore when immigrants became a significant part of the population, rules relating to citizenship came to the fore, as well as how welfare states developed policies which reflect and respect the needs of more multi-ethnic societies. For instance, where immigrants and new ethnic groups have become citizens, further issues arise in relation to recognition and respect, and the degree to which citizenship accommodates cultural diversity. This can also involve discussion of cultural rights, based on particular group characteristics, such as language and particular religious requirements, in addition to individual rights that accompany citizenship (Koopmans, 2013).

Over time, multiculturalism became a distinct aspect of public policy in some countries, most notably in Canada and Australia, and in the UK during the

New Labour years. Its 'philosophical orientation recognizes *de facto* pluralism in a society, and celebrates that diversity', thus multiculturalism 'requires governments and institutions to encourage pluralism through public policy, though the precise way this is done can vary across places and time' (Bloemraad, 2011). Policies vary greatly, however, and both the concept and aspects of multicultural policy adopted in different nation states remain contested, as discussed in Chapter Twelve in the case of Ireland.

Returning to conceptualisations of welfare state reform more generally, by the early 2000s there was a growing recognition of a range of **new social risks** (Jaeger and Kvist, 2003; Taylor-Gooby, 2004; Bonoli, 2007) that distinguished between 'old' established social risks dealt with by the traditional welfare state and those risks which, historically ignored, also require attention. Welfare states still offer greatest protection to those with a full-time, long-standing employment record but changes in the nature of work and in conditions of employment in post-industrial society has led to the 'de-standardisation of employment' (Bonoli, 2007: 500) which moves from the full-time, job-for-life model and exposes the risks exemplified by the position

> **New social risks** refer to a variety of needs and risks including labour market marginalisation and unemployment often due to post-industrialisation, the reconciliation of work and family life, different family forms and caring.

of part-time, casual workers as well the unemployed. The increased participation of women in the labour market is also included within the framework of new social risks although it 'is obviously not a source of social risk per se. … Rather, a new risk stems from the inability to combine motherhood and child rearing with paid employment' (Bonoli, 2007: 499). Caring responsibilities and changes in family forms are also incorporated in new social risks because welfare states are often ill-equipped to recognise and accommodate them. Proponents of a 'new welfare state' (Esping-Andersen et al, 2002) argued that attention to new social risks provided justification for a recasting of welfare states. In short, things had moved on, the traditional protective and transfer functions of the welfare state were, on their own, insufficient to meet the needs, risks and diversity of contemporary society. More enabling and active social policies were required to address marginalisation from the labour market and difficulties reconciling work, care and family life. In terms of the latter, some limited, but very uneven, progress has been made. At one end are the North European countries with a long history of investment in families and children, and supports for high rates of female labour-market participation. Family policies have expanded over the last two decades but significant divergence remains (Ferragina and Seeleib-Kaiser, 2015) in the scale of investment and priority accorded to this area. Policy developments in activation have been much more decisive over the same timeframe and the shift towards **activation**-based policies has been widespread. While Ireland was a comparatively late converter (see Chapter Seven), countries such as Sweden and Finland have a long history of active labour-market policies

> **Activation** seeks to maximise labour market participation via a range of interventions from access to education/training, and supported employment to stricter welfare eligibility including welfare sanctions for non-compliance in activation programmes.

(ALMPs). Sweden, in particular, 'always embodied the idea that everyone has both a right and a duty to work and that only paid work will uphold the welfare state' (Timonen, 2003: 156). While considerable policy divergence remains in the operating frameworks of ALMPs, in overall terms, 'activation is driven by the goal of increasing overall labor market participation and particularly the employability of those at the margins of the labor market' (Obinger and Starke, 2014: 16). In seeking to realise this goal, ALMPs are linked to social assistance, education, training and family policies, across different welfare states.

The activation turn is part of wider, albeit very uneven, trend towards greater social investment type policies during the 2000s, regardless of welfare state type (Hemerijck, 2013). In basic terms, the period since the 1990s up until the emergence of the financial crisis at least, were marked by continuous bouts of welfare reform, shaped by the key imperatives of economic sustainability and cost containment, giving rise to the notion of 'permanent austerity' (Pierson, 2001) and a transition to the 'silver age of the welfare state' (Taylor-Gooby, 2002). Although pressures intensified, and welfare states adapted (to varying degrees), they were not in decline per se. The emphasis of welfare reform shifted since the 2000s with a particular focus on the productive role of social policy as espoused through ideas of enabling and active social policies and the wider 'social investment turn' (Hemerijck, 2013: 35) prior to the financial crisis. These concepts gained greater policy traction contributing to the emergence of what Obinger and Starke (2014: 19) term a 'supply-side welfare state' reflecting,

> the concern about individual (dis)incentives in terms of labor market participation, investment and other supply-side factors that underlies much current social policy-making. The term is broad enough to include activation, employability and social investment and to reflect the growing importance of incentives based on internal markets and market-compatible social provision.

As a concept, the supply-side welfare state captures the range and extent of welfare state change over recent decades, marking a distinct point of contrast with the Keynesian demand-sided policies of the earlier post-war welfare state (Obinger and Starke, 2014). In short, welfare states continue to exist but they have changed, in potentially transformative ways. Developments highlighted in our discussion indicate that their objectives broadened and policy instruments have been expanded in ways that are multidirectional. The overall trend towards increasing 'enabling' supports for labour-market participation has occurred alongside greater inequality, a growing preference for more market-conforming reforms of the welfare state, which includes new modes of dualisation and a degree of transfer of risk back to the individual.

Competing perspectives on the roles and responsibilities of the state in relation to welfare and human well-being have shifted over time, as this chapter has sought to demonstrate. This observation applies not only to questions about who provides and who pays for welfare but also who is entitled to welfare and on what basis. One aspect of the contemporary politics of welfare debate has focused on the welfare rights of immigrants and the basis of their inclusion in society. There has been something of a backlash against multiculturalism over the 2000s; the term has been dropped from use in policy in Britain and Germany and references to diversity policy are increasingly applied instead (Vertovec and Wessendorf, 2010). Predicated on the idea that different cultures cannot assimilate or integrate, that we cannot live with difference, multiculturalism has become a political target for what are complex issues relating to how differences in culture and religion for instance can respectfully coexist. However when actual policies are examined, Banting and Kymlicka (2012: 3) note that, with the exception of the Netherlands, 'most countries that adopted multicultural approaches in the later part of the twentieth century have maintained their programs ... and a significant number of countries have added new ones'. The political discounting of multiculturalism comes at a time when political leadership on issues of diversity is urgently needed across Europe. Specifically in terms of the ramifications for the welfare state, does it mean a decline in solidarity upon which welfare states have been built? Banting and Kymlicka (2012: 19) argue that this is not necessarily the case, pointing to evidence from their index which tracks the strength of multicultural policies and programmes: 'efforts to strengthen civic integration are being layered over older programs recognizing and supporting diversity, generating a multicultural version of civic integration'. The problem is that the political debate appears headed in the direction of a return to assimilationist forms of identity whereby all groups identify with same national culture. This also lends credence to ideas around **welfare chauvinism** whereby 'targeting migrants is part of a broader neoliberal restructuring of the welfare state and of welfare retrenchment' (Keskinen et al, 2016: 322) thus adding another strand to the broader politics of welfare retrenchment and neo-liberalism that remains in ascendance at present.

> **Welfare chauvinism** refers to the idea that welfare spending should prioritise the needs of the indigenous population, even at the expense of the welfare provisions available to other people, usually migrants.

The impact of the global financial crisis and its aftermath on welfare states

The most recent phase of welfare state change has been defined by policies of fiscal consolidation and austerity generated in the aftermath of the global financial crisis of 2008. Subsequent policy responses reflect and confirm 'the strange non-death of neoliberalism' (Crouch, 2011), despite the fact that the crisis origins lie within the core architecture of neo-liberalism. Initial crisis management policy responses were broadly Keynesian in orientation. However a significant U-turn quickly followed in which 'the financial crisis was redefined as a crisis of fiscal profligacy, requiring tough and prolonged public austerity' (Hemerijck and Vandenbroucke, 2012: 201). Austerity policies and structural reforms have been the order of the day for countries most severely affected by the financial, and subsequently sovereign debt and Euro crises (see Chapter Six). The impact of the crises has been immense and uneven (see Box 4.1).

Box 4.1: Recent austerity and outcomes for the welfare state: illustrations from Europe

Fiscal consolidation was most severe in Greece (23% of GDP), followed by Latvia (16%), Ireland (14%), Romania (13%), Cyprus (13%), Spain (11%) and Lithuania (10%). In Estonia, Portugal, Slovakia, Bulgaria, Slovenia, Czech Republic, Poland, Italy, the UK and the Netherlands, fiscal consolidation amounted to 5%-10% of GDP. Sweden was the only EU member state to utilise fiscal stimulus (approximately 2.5% of GDP between 2007 and 2013) (Darvas et al, 2014).

Drawing on Vaughan-Whitehead's (2014) analysis of the decline of the European social model in the aftermath of the crisis, the following provides a brief illustration of the impacts.

- **Work and the minimum wage:** a minimum wage rate-freeze or restrictions were imposed in France, Czech Republic, Portugal, Spain and the UK (younger workers) and in Greece it was cut by 22%; increased flexibilisation of work contracts and a growth in agency contracts evident; in the UK and Ireland the emergence of zero-hour contracts; upturn in contract conversion from full to part time work in Greece, Italy, France, Cyprus and Ireland.
- **Social protection** has been retrenched and reformed: stricter eligibility requirements for unemployment assistance was common; the duration of benefit entitlement was reduced in Portugal, Ireland and Estonia; the value of unemployment benefits cut in several countries including Greece (22%), Portugal (after six months 20%) and Romania (15%). Spending on family and child tax and social protection supports was curtailed in many countries. Shifts towards targeting and means-tested provision also occurred, especially in Greece.
- **Wider welfare state spending cuts** in other areas were also severe, most notably in healthcare and education. Education spending was cut by 33% in Greece (2008-13), 23% in Latvia (2008-10) and 18.4% in Portugal.
- **Public sector:** subjected to 'unprecedented shock' (Vaughan-Whitehead, 2014: 28). A recruitment embargo was introduced in Ireland in 2009. In Greece, in 2010, this was accompanied by a replacement rate of one for every ten exits in 2010 and one for every five exits from 2012-16. There were no such cuts in the Nordic countries and job cuts were limited in Germany, the Netherlands and Croatia. The scale of public sector wage cuts varied significantly: there were none in Germany and Sweden, cuts averaged 5%-10% in Croatia,

Estonia and the UK. In Greece these wages were cut by 15%-30% in 2010 and a further 17% on average in 2012.

Taking Britain as just one example of the impact of austerity on the welfare state in recent times, the unprecedented welfare and public expenditure cuts, the emphasis on expanding the role of private and not-for-profit providers and greater 'responsibilisation of individuals and families' (Bochel and Powell, 2016: 19) have brought welfare issues into sharp focus once again. With the significant exception of the NHS it would seem that the defining features of the Beveridge welfare state have, at this point, all but disappeared. The shift from the Beveridgean welfare state began in the 1980s and it looks as if Britain has since made an almost fulsome shift to a market-oriented and much less rights-based welfare system. Ken Loach's film (2016) *I, Daniel Blake* brings these issues to life with particular effect. Grimshaw and Rubery (2015: 216) assert that recent austerity policies further eroded Britain's social model (including welfare and employment) to the extent that 'both reinforced long-term trends and introduced a distinctive shift toward an ideal-type neoliberal model.' They note the implications of the 'shrinking public realm', highlighting the increasing privatisation of public services, the commodification of citizens' rights and the downgrading of remaining public services. The extent to which these observations resonate in other welfare states across Europe is an altogether bigger question, also requiring consideration far beyond what is possible here.

In terms of European welfare states more generally, tighter fiscal and budgetary surveillance mechanisms became the overriding policy solution, especially for EU member states in most difficulty (see Chapter Six), delivering an austerity centred response, making way for what Streeck (2015: 1) terms the 'European consolidation state' involving 'a deep rebuilding of the political institutions of postwar democratic capitalism and its international order, in particular in Europe where consolidation coincides with an unprecedented increase in the scale of political rule under European Monetary Union ... and the transformation of the latter into an asymmetric fiscal stabilization regime'.

In the aftermath of the Great Recession, assessments are still being made about the full ramifications for welfare states. It is a period of continuing uncertainty and the overhang from the crisis is far from resolved. Welfare retrenchment and ongoing cost containment dominate institutional and political welfare discourse, especially in European countries most deeply affected by the crisis. However, recent evidence also points to welfare retrenchment occurring alongside, albeit very uneven, developments in some social investment policies (van Kersbergen et al, 2014). Nearly a decade of austerity on, it is clear that some European welfare states (mainly peripheral and newer member states) now face their toughest resilience challenge yet.

If the welfare story of the last hundred years tells us anything, it is that welfare states emerged in unplanned and often ad hoc ways, that positive change often came about as a result of social movements and social change, that politics matters and that welfare states are more adaptable to reform than many thought possible. On the other hand, the broad political picture, such as it currently stands, is dominated by a right-wing agenda which, for now at least, remains seemingly hostile to advancing more progressive welfare measures. The failure of the Left to successfully challenge austerity and protect the interests of those it proports to represent, presents a significant obstacle and these themes are taken up again in the subsequent chapters.

Chapter summary

- This chapter traced the emergence of the welfare state by outlining the main factors that have influenced its development over the late nineteenth and twentieth centuries.
- Formative influences in the latter part of the nineteenth century included political activism, philanthropy and the establishment of democratic rights. The poor law remained the first element of welfare provision in many countries until the significant need and demand for intervention brought about state involvement in public health and education was followed by social security measures.
- The next phase of welfare state development occurred after the Second World War when a more collectivist approach saw the establishment of core social services on a more comprehensive basis. This expansionary phase lasted through to the 1970s, when the 'welfare state project' came under increasing scrutiny for its assumptions around citizenship, work and the role of women. Persisting poverty and the rising costs associated with the welfare state led to mounting criticism of its objectives and results.
- The 1980s saw the New Right promote welfare retrenchment in many countries and a wider discourse of welfare state reform followed over subsequent debates.
- Since the 1990s advanced welfare states have variously sought to confront considerable challenges brought about by major economic and social changes which have altered both the context and need for welfare states to adapt. Recession and austerity dominated the narrative of the welfare reform agenda in many counties over recent years with lasting implications for social policy.

Discussion points

- Choose an area of welfare provision in a particular country (for example pensions, unemployment) and examine availability and entitlement conditions in 1920, 1990 and today.
- Discuss the proposition that Beveridge's approach to welfare was formative but flawed.
- Have we reached the limits of the welfare state? What should be included in a blueprint for welfare states in the twenty-first century?

Further reading list

Gamble, A (2016) *Can the welfare state survive?* Cambridge: Polity

Hemerijck, A (2013) *Changing welfare states*, Oxford: Oxford UP

Jones, K (2000) *The making of social policy in Britain: From the poor law to New Labour* (3rd edn), London: The Athlone Press

Williams, F (1989) *Social policy: A critical introduction: issues of race, gender and class,* Cambridge: Polity

Williams, F (2016) 'Critical thinking in social policy: The challenges of past, present and future', *Social Policy & Administration,* 50:6, 628-47

five

Political ideologies, welfare and social policy

Social policy has historically been shaped by many factors, not least different and competing political ideas, perspectives on welfare and the functions of the state, which influence the scope of social policy and the types of welfare states in existence. Ideologies of welfare are an important area of study because they impact on the breadth of policy debate and shape political positions on core aspects of social policy, which in turn affects individuals' well-being and quality of life. Ideologies of welfare may be understood as a set of ideas and associated principles or values which, when taken together, offer a rationale for a particular approach to welfare and social policy issues. Ideologies of welfare have evolved prior to, and in tandem with, welfare state development and as such are themselves subject to some modification, particularly over time and in light of changing circumstances. However, that is not to imply that ideologies of welfare are 'highly moveable' because at their core should be some 'first principles' which continue to influence their thinking, even in the context of social change. This chapter outlines some of the major ideological perspectives influential in political debate on many matters of importance to social policy. The key principles underpinning the different perspectives are explained and the implications of each political ideology is explored with reference to issues such as welfare, the economy and the role of the state, the significance and interpretation of equality, and the overall functions and scope of social policy.

Chapter outline

- The first section maps the relevance of welfare ideologies to the study of social policy. Attention is given to the parameters of Left and Right that often accompany discussions of ideological positions, and to the concepts of freedom and equality which are of significant explanatory value in understanding the various perspectives on welfare and social policy. The wider political economy in which these perspectives are debated is also briefly considered.
- The core features of key ideologies including liberalism, conservatism, Christian democracy, socialism, social democracy, feminism and greenism are outlined in section two. While this is

not an exhaustive examination of relevant 'isms', a number of the key perspectives that aid in our understanding of the interplay between politics, ideology and social policy are outlined.

SECTION ONE
UNDERSTANDING PERSPECTIVES ON WELFARE

Take a topic such as education and its provision. Should students at risk of leaving school early be paid to attend? Should students be free to wear clothing and jewellery that has religious significance? Should free school meals be provided to all pupils? Should religious instruction be part of the school day? Should third-level students pay fees? There are no wrong or right answers to these questions. They are rather a matter of debate involving different values and perspectives about the role of the state, the position of religion, the importance of individual freedom and choice, the extent to which **equality** should be pursued, and views about individual behaviour and how it can or should be influenced. In debating these issues most of us will have some opinions and reasons for our viewpoint, and it is likely that our responses will be influenced by our life experiences, including educational experiences and opportunities, social class, religious beliefs and familial values. While we may not recognise our views in terms of a fully fledged ideology or coherent set of values, at the same time, as Heywood (2012: 3) suggests, 'whether consciously or subconsciously, everyone subscribes to a set of political beliefs and values that guide their behaviour and influence their conduct. Political ideas and ideologies thus set goals that inspire political activism.'

> **Equality** refers to the principle of addressing unequal circumstances which prevail in society. The extent to which equality is perceived and pursued differs widely, with divergent interpretations of the concept (for example, equality of opportunity versus equality of condition).

Social policy is strongly influenced by political beliefs that belong to different ideological traditions. A core element of the discussion of the influence of ideology on social policy is the significance of the extent to which various ideologies differ. Social policies are not devised and implemented in a political vacuum; they are subject to conflicting and often contested aims and values. Another important aspect of ideology in relation to social policy is the relationship between principles and practice. An ideology, in outlining its 'first principles' or ideals is normative in its prescriptions about how certain issues *should* be dealt with. Their normative component highlights the 'vision' or 'ideal' being put forward. The reality of course is often different. Real life, politics and current social and economic issues frequently force a more pragmatic approach, and 'realpolitik' usually results in a dilution of core values in the transition from theory to practice. This does not make ideologies redundant; it acknowledges the political (and other) realities within which they are applied. Outside of the domestic political domain are a range of wider public policy making influences. These include the role of international and global policy actors (for example, the EU, IMF, World Bank) and key interests (capital/corporate, labour). While recent decades have seen an intensification of global actors and corporate interests (discussed in Chapter Six), politics and political ideologies still matter and remain the key site of social policy contestation and debate.

Left and Right

At a basic level, competing ideologies are often identified in terms of Left and Right of the political spectrum. This Left/Right analogy of political ideologies provides a popular shorthand characterisation of the political domain. However, its application needs to be mindful of the context in which it is used and in light of perspectives such as feminism and greenism that don't fit neatly within its confines and are often marginalised from discussions as a result. According to Heywood (2003: 17-18):

> The weakness of the linear spectrum is that it tries to reduce politics to a single dimension, and suggests that political views can be classified according to merely one criterion, be it one's attitude to change, view of equality or economic philosophy. Political ideologies are in fact highly complex collections of beliefs, values and doctrines, which any kind of spectrum is forced to oversimplify.

Nevertheless, the Left/Right characterisation of political ideas and political parties remains in widespread use providing a useful opening prism within which to identify the key defining concepts associated with the different ideologies of welfare. The Left/Right labels originate from the seating arrangements taken in the French Parliament after the 1798 revolution. In general terms, the 'Left-wing' approach to social policy is associated with state intervention, collective provision, universalism, and a concern with addressing inequalities and delivering social rights. The Right is typically regarded in social policy terms for its emphasis on the free market, individualism and limited welfare provisions.

Simply put, it can be argued that what distinguishes Left and Right is the starting point adopted. For the Right, the individual is the primary focus; for the Left, society, and the way it is organised and structured, is central to fully understand, include, and respond to, all individuals. Differences in ideology can usefully be identified with reference to two core concepts: freedom and equality (George and Wilding, 1985) and the position taken in respect of them.

Box 5.1: Right- and Left-wing approaches to social policy

Right	Left
Individualism	Collectivism
'Negative' freedom	'Positive' freedom
Pro-market	Pro-state
Advocates private and/or charitable provision of welfare/social services	Advocates statutory provision of welfare/social services
Selectivism	Universalism
Rights defined primarily in the context of the civil and political domain (for example, equal treatment before the law)	Rights considered in a more extensive way, including civil, political, economic and social rights
Equality understood in a formal sense: fair and same treatment for all	Equality understood in structural or relational terms: emphasis on the need to address inequalities through state intervention, redistribution, positive discrimination etc.
Equality of opportunity: minimalist approach	Equality of opportunity: maximalist approach and for some, a commitment to equality of condition
Meritocratic	Egalitarian

Freedom and equality

Freedom and equality are among the most pivotal concepts in shaping our 'world view'. Both concepts are the subject of extensive philosophical and political debate to which justice cannot be done here. Turning briefly to freedom, the work of Amartya Sen has been influential in bringing new conceptions of freedom into the field of social policy debate. He draws distinctions between commodities, capabilities and functioning and makes the case for 'an integrated analysis of economic, social and political activities, involving a variety of institutions and many interactive agencies' (Sen, 1999: xii). Sen's capabilities approach connects freedom with resources and ultimately the ability to achieve. Focusing on a wide range of institutions from the state to the market, to political parties, media and the wider public sphere, he casts an extensive net to assess 'their contribution to enhancing and guaranteeing the substantive freedoms of individuals, seen as active agents of change, rather than as passive recipients of dispensed benefits' (Sen, 1999: xiii). Sen's work is part of an ongoing philosophical debate about differing interpretations of freedom and social justice.

The multiple layers of ideas attaching to contemporary debates on interpretations of freedom stand in contrast to the more rigid 'positive' and 'negative' interpretations of freedom historically associated with the traditional Left and Right of the political spectrum. Isaiah Berlin (1909–97) distinguished between positive and negative freedom. Positive freedom refers to the notion of being 'free to do' something whereas negative freedom refers to 'freedom from' interference or constraint. The Right stresses the need for individual freedom, in the 'negative' sense, to be free from interference including from the state. The Right, broadly speaking, argues that social issues such as poverty are best addressed through 'natural' free-market forces and accepts that a certain level of inequality is inevitable. In contrast, the Left sees equality as an objective to be pursued by society; it acknowledges a range of forces which present as obstacles to equality and seeks to address these barriers. Individual liberty is also valued by those on the Left, but their approach to freedom, characterised as 'positive', suggests that in order for individuals to really be 'free', they must have opportunity, they must be facilitated to exercise their freedom. Individuals who do not have the means or the opportunity do not have their right to freedom vindicated. Fitzpatrick (2001: 54) explains the dilemma as follows:

> In a formal sense it is true that the beggar is free to dine at the Ritz, just as the banker is free to sleep under a bridge, but this conception of liberty deprives the principle of any meaningful content. For the Left, being prevented from doing something implies more than physical constraints, it also implies financial constraints (so the beggar *is* less free than the banker).

This illustration also raises issues of equality and inequality – in this case between the beggar and the banker – and the extent to which their equal worth is interpreted in different conceptions of equality. Discussions of equality are complicated by the fact that interpretations vary and the intended meaning is often not clear. In basic terms, the principle of equality is taken to refer to the idea of fair or equal treatment for all; all human beings are of equal worth and entitled to the same rights and protections. Understood as foundational equality, this version of equality provides a crucial starting point and is widely endorsed, including by those on the Right of the political spectrum. However, foundational equality does not take account of difference and the disadvantage people may experience. In social policy terms, questions therefore arise about how equality is pursued, not only in ways that ensure the same rights and protections for all but also how policy may or should serve to remove disadvantage and reduce inequalities, which 'sameness of treatment' does not necessarily address. Distinctions between equality of opportunity and equality of outcome are frequently drawn upon to offer greater clarity in this regard. Equality of opportunity refers to addressing existing obstacles or disadvantage to the extent that a 'level playing field' or 'equal starting point' is achieved. Equality of outcome (or social equality), on the other hand, includes a much wider set of structural factors (including the overall distribution of resources), which present as barriers to equality. These distinctions are taken up again in Chapter Nine in relation to education, where debates on equality are particularly relevant.

Contemporary context of ideological debate

The idea of a dichotomous Left and Right politics was challenged by a number of developments during the 1990s. First, the collapse of communism across Eastern Europe resulted in a new era in international politics no longer defined in terms of communism versus capitalism. Fukuyama (1992) wrote of 'the end of history' in which liberal democratic capitalism would inevitably prevail. At an ideological level, there were calls for movement beyond the old ideological boundaries of Right and Left. Giddens (1994: 12), for example, argued for 'a reconstituted radical politics, one which draws on philosophic conservatism but preserves some of the core values hitherto associated with socialist thought'. The Third Way project which subsequently emerged gave practical effect to these ideas, refashioning the values of the centre Left using concepts more closely aligned with Right-wing thinking (see below). Third, the Rightward shift of many centre Left political parties during this period, which was also marked by intensifying economic integration, was significant in facilitating the constellation of more favourable political conditions in which deeper market liberalisation could become embedded. The revival of laissez-faire economics and the predominance of market neo-liberalism has since become the major challenge of our times. Its particular relevance for social policy lies in the fact that, as Gamble (2016: 56) asserts, 'it challenges the reason for welfare states to continue to exist'.

The financial crisis of 2008, essentially a crisis of capitalism, exposed major flaws in the 'neo-liberal order' (Gamble, 2014a), with massive consequences for ordinary people. It seemed as if a critical moment had been reached from which the neo-liberal model could never feasibly recover. Instead, it remains intact, 'preparing for another spin of the wheel as though nothing had happened' (Gamble, 2014a: 4). The resilience that masks its instability is likely to be temporary, however. The crisis has been widely assessed as structural one, requiring radical reform (Crouch, 2011; Gamble, 2014a; Streeck, 2014). The discontent engendered by the crisis and the policy responses to it, especially regarding bailing out the banks while imposing austerity, brought about greater public awareness of the contradictions at the core of the neo-liberal order. The emergence of various social movements over the last decade (Anti-Austerity and Occupy, for example) indicates a shift in politics away from older 'establishment' parties as new alliances emerge to challenge the status quo. As Reich (2015) notes,

> the interminable debate over the merits of the 'free market' versus an activist government has diverted attention from how the market, both in Britain and in the United States, has come to be organised differently from the way it was half a century ago, why its current organisation is failing to deliver the widely shared prosperity it delivered then and what the basic rules of the market should be. This means that the fracture in politics will move from left to right to the anti-establishment versus establishment.

The established political mainstream on both the Right and the Left have not adequately analysed the big changes in the nature of capitalism in recent decades and this presents a significant challenge for their futures. This deficit provides the conditions in which anti-establishment sentiment may well thrive as traditionally ideologically opposing cohorts find themselves on the same side of key debates but for completely different reasons. To what extent this will redefine the politics of the twenty-first century is an altogether bigger question, probably to be shaped to a large degree by the will, capacity and power of nation states to address democratic deficits, reform and rebalance their policy actions in favour of their peoples. New chasms have opened up in Europe, too, as the ongoing impact of the Euro crisis are felt with economic stagnation and austerity, while the fiscal conditionalities emanating from the European institutions re-enforce the notion of core and peripheral member states. The migrant crisis lacks a coherent or solidaristic policy response across the EU, while Brexit has brought forth further instability about the future of the Union.

SECTION TWO
POLITICAL IDEOLOGIES, WELFARE AND SOCIAL POLICY

This section outlines the main features of the most influential ideologies of welfare. The discussion of each ideology is brief and the aim is to provide a useful starting point for examining ideologies of welfare and their impact on social policy.

Liberalism

Classical liberalism draws on the work of the 'founding father' of economics, Adam Smith (1723-90), best known for arguing the benefits of free-market capitalism in generating wealth. This, he believed, would be achieved by leaving market forces to produce the best outcome in terms of competition, prices and wealth generation, without interference by the state. The application of a laissez-faire (leave alone to do) philosophy to the workings of the economy is believed to provide greater benefit to all; for Smith, an 'invisible hand' guides and promotes general prosperity, even when this is not the primary objective. Left to its natural devices, the economic rule of supply and demand ensures competitors in markets, which is good for consumers, promotes economic growth and from which overall prosperity results.

It is important to note that modern liberalism has a distinct meaning in ideological terms that is different from the connotations drawn from both the classical and neo-liberal positions. This distinction rests primarily on the less hostile approach adopted by modern liberals to the functions of the state. The everyday use of the term 'liberal' for instance is considered to be 'progressive' or 'broadminded' in terms of social issues in particular. This may present as a point of confusion in ideological terms with classical and neo-liberalism more clearly associated with the Right of the political spectrum. Focus here is centred on the core values of the classical liberal position which in social policy terms is noted for its emphasis on individualism, the free market and a limited role for the state.

According to the liberal perspective, individualism is a core value. It is the role of individuals, rather than any other entity, which should be emphasised in organising society and in analysing social issues. The individual is therefore the basic source of action, freedom and responsibility. The personal freedom associated with individualism is celebrated, although it is defined in the negative sense of being 'free from' interference and state coercion. Individualism promotes self-responsibility and liberals argue that individuals know what is best for them, and how this should be achieved. In pure terms, the only condition attached is that individuals do not harm others in the pursuit of their own interests. To protect against that possibility, classical liberals accept the need for a legal/justice system to ensure the right to due process before the law if another individual's right to freedom is breached. In terms of equality, it is acceptable as far as it provides 'equality of general rules, that is that laws apply to all citizens equally – equality of civil and political rights – and equality of opportunity' (George and Wilding, 1985: 24). Anti-collectivists do not find equality of opportunity necessarily objectionable because, in their view, 'it does not presuppose any particular social arrangements as desirable' (George and Wilding, 1985: 24). Ultimately, because liberalism sees individuals as autonomous and independent, it subscribes that individuals fare best in a free-market context and are opposed to social rights and state intervention as far as practicable.

Libertarianism

Libertarianism is the term used to describe a perspective which values individual liberty over all other principles. Right-wing libertarianism is our focus here; it defines freedom in negative terms and refutes the need for state intervention (outside of the requirement for a legal and justice system). Pure libertarians reject state intervention in the economy, in society and in the private affairs of individuals. In short, libertarians are 'on the Right' in terms of the economy, but in following through on their principles may be 'on the Left' in matters of personal liberty and the non-regulation of individual behaviour, in so far as it doesn't harm another. For instance, a pure libertarian is likely to argue that drug-taking is a matter of personal choice and individuals are free to make such choices, even if detrimental to them, if not to others.

The pursuit of distributional equality is dismissed by Right-wing libertarians given that redistribution would require people to pay tax, which is considered an imposition on individuals' freedom. Robert Nozick (1938-2002), one of the best-known libertarian thinkers, argued that 'taxation of earnings from labor is on a par with forced labor' (Nozick, 1974: 169). Libertarians therefore reject the concept of redistribution and the associated welfare state, seeing such interventions as anathema to individual liberty that compromises the benefits of free-market forces, in which individuals as consumers can maximise choices in relation to their own welfare. Taken overall, libertarians relegate the role of the state as far as practicable, in defence of individual freedom. It adopts a radically anti-state position regarding matters of social policy. Libertarianism is promoted by think tanks such as the Cato Institute and Heritage Foundation in the US while in Britain the Adam Smith Institute similarly advocates free market and libertarian ideas.

The application of libertarian principles to the economy resonates with the classical liberal position although it is worth noting that some eminent thinkers of the classical liberal perspective acknowledged a role for the state in certain matters of social policy. Friedrich von Hayek (1899-1992), for example, considered that people may have to be compelled to protect against need arising from 'those common hazards of life' (Hayek, 1960 in George and Wilding, 1985: 36), namely unemployment, illness and old age. This departure from the principles outlined earlier is circumscribed by concern that the goalposts will quickly shift from basic minimum needs to something more demanding in terms of taking individuals' resources, damaging the values of freedom and individualism, and undermining free-market capitalism in the process. In addition, the pursuit of social justice is rejected as inherently flawed. In Hayek's view, the notion of social justice presents a threat 'to most other values of a free civilisation' (Hayek, 1976 in Lund, 2006: 114) and the welfare state is considered a major risk in this regard.

The critique of the welfare state stems from the perceived threat to libertarian starting principles of individual freedom, individualism and the merits of the free market. Hayek (2006 [1960]: 226) argues that the idea of the welfare state was not adequately defined: 'What goes under that name is a conglomerate of so many diverse and even contradictory elements that, while some of them may make a free society more attractive, others are incompatible with it or may at least constitute potential threats to its existence'. Aside from compromising individual freedom, the welfare state is thought to be paternalistic in deciding what is best for individuals. State provision of a range of services is also argued to produce distortions in welfare markets, through monopolistic provision, leading to inefficiency, bureaucracy, over-regulation of individuals, business, and the economy in general, and poor value for taxpayers' money (see Chapter Four for illustrations of these arguments).

Public choice theory

The emergence of public choice theory, most notably in the US since the 1960s, provides an additional strand to the critique of the welfare state. Taking a 'politics without romance' (Buchanan, 2003: 13) approach, they apply an economic analysis to politics and argue that the absence of limits to the role of government is flawed and that 'bureaucratic oversupply' cannot be curbed. Public choice theory offers the view that both politicians and public servants are motivated primarily by the need to maintain their position, and the promises offered are not necessarily in the best interests of the country but can in some cases amount to a collage of different policies designed to secure re-election. In this view, politicians are considered to act in their own best interest, unrestrained by economic considerations of cost or the long-term consequences of their actions. This assessment of politics and those elected to public office uses economic theory to account for political and policy decisions and does not incorporate wider societal phenomena into their analysis. The solutions offered by public choice theory are similarly derived and include privatisation and the imposition of strict spending limits on governments.

Neo-liberalism

Frequently assessed as the dominant, or hegemonic, ideology since the mid-1980s the term neo-liberalism is employed widely but often too loosely, rendering its core meaning ill-defined, because it is seemingly all pervasive and everyone is expected to know what it is! In brief, the origins of neo-liberalism go back to the ideas of Hayek, Friedman and others from the so-called Chicago School of Economics, which sought to challenge the Keynesian economics that held sway until 1970s. The evolution of neo-liberalism from a relatively marginal intellectual perspective in the 1940s to its emergence as a mainstream political influence in the 1980s has been characterised as 'an intellectual professional project' (Mudge, 2008: 708), in which 'a well-trodden system of economic thought and a faith in the promise of "the market"' (2008: 724) was driven by professional and intellectual elites during that time. Harvey (2005) emphasises the role of the corporate capitalist class in the creation of neo-liberalism as a political project since the 1960s. When the economic crisis of the 1970s took hold, neo-liberals were well placed to provide an alternative to the interventionist, state-managed Keynesianism that had shaped the policy landscape of the mid-twentieth century.

In summary, neo-liberalism draws on a combination of classic liberal economics and libertarian values to promote the benefits of the market in both economic and social order. Neo-liberalism asserts the merits of the (global) free market, in what Heywood (2012: 49) describes as 'a form of market fundamentalism'. Challenging the growth of welfare states and the role of the state therein, neo-liberalism resists extensive state intervention in matters of human welfare. Instead, neo-liberals draw 'a clear and fundamental distinction between the legal and political rights at the core of classical liberalism and the putative claims of a right to welfare' (A Pratt, 2006a: 21). This allows for a division between civil and political rights on the one hand and social and economic rights on the other. Realigning the discourse of rights in favour of moral values associated with classical liberalism in which 'all human beings are to be treated as equal, but the most important fact which makes them equal is their capacity for liberty' (Gamble, 2016: 47) sets the conceptual framework for an alternative vision. Influenced by market libertarian ideals in which 'the direction of policy should always be to reduce state spending and taxation so as to enlarge the sphere of individual liberty' (Gamble,

2016: 49), neo–liberals seek to dismantle the welfare state. Market providers would inevitably step in and individuals as consumers would be free to purchase whatever they require.

Additionally, according to Monbiot (2016), 'Neoliberalism sees competition as the defining characteristic of human relations. It redefines citizens as consumers, whose democratic choices are best exercised by buying and selling, a process that rewards merit and punishes inefficiency. It maintains that "the market" delivers benefits that could never be achieved by planning.' Aligned with this, belief in the superiority of the market provides a logic for greater privatisation, deregulation, minimal taxation and reduced welfare entitlements, in favour of market-based provision (see Chapter Four for policy examples). However, for all of the above, the central paradox of contemporary neo–liberalism is that it favours a strong state – so long as it works in the interests of the market. Economic liberalism, as Gamble (2014b: 29-30) explains,

> elevates the market above all other institutions and wants a politics–free world in which decisions are taken according to market logic rather than political logic. To achieve this, however, requires a very active state, and a political movement and ideology to underpin it. The separation of the state and the market which economic liberalism seeks is an illusion, and is revealed as such whenever there is a major crisis and the state is called upon to intervene and guarantee the market order.

Neo–liberal ideas have long been espoused by think tanks supported by interests seeking to promote their particular perspective (A Pratt, 2006a; Mudge, 2008). Manifestations of neo–liberalism are evident in the political rhetoric and policies of the Right, particularly in political systems where the liberal perspective has always held sway, most notably in the US and Britain, although this is not say that it has been insignificant elsewhere. Its impact on alternative perspectives on welfare may yet be its greatest legacy, acting as a 'pull factor', drawing competing perspectives in their direction. However, for all its considerable influence over recent times, it is ironic that, as Mudge (2014: 87) notes,

> Self-identified neo–liberals are hard to come by; there is no political party or national regime that touts the 'neo–liberal' moniker; it does not denote a definite professional position in economics or anywhere else. And yet many take the view that neo–liberalism's continued reign is among the most perplexing puzzles of our time. How does one engage with, or hope to critique, a shadow?

Conservatism

Conservatism is a position associated with an affinity for tradition and order and a resistance to change; 'a philosophy of limits and restraint' (Fitzpatrick, 2001:

125). Conservative ideas first emerged in the context of significant economic and social change in the late eighteenth and early nineteenth centuries, challenging the concurrent growth of liberalism, socialism and nationalism. The core principles of conservatism include tradition, pragmatism, human imperfection, organic society, hierarchy, authority and property ownership (Heywood, 2002). Edmund Burke's (1729-97) 'change in order to conserve' philosophy has been an important element in refining the thinking itself (Heywood, 2002). In terms of tradition, conservatives regard established institutions, customs and practice as important in recognising established wisdom, appreciating it and providing a sense of identity. They believe in pragmatism to deal with reality and 'to do what works'. Humans are regarded as fallible (and sometimes flawed), and in need of security and protection. This belief, along with their acceptance of hierarchy and authority, particularly taken with their emphasis on individual duties, provides the justification for a tough approach to crime and justice and a commitment to 'strong' government in dealing with such matters. In practical terms, conservatism seeks to preserve stability and manage forces of social change, particularly those thought to present a threat to social order. The family, for instance, is viewed as an essential element of society and, although averse to state intervention in other instances, conservatives argue that the state has a central role in maintaining core social structures, rather than risk the uncertainty that could accompany more dramatic social change.

Harold Macmillan's (1938) *The Middle Way*, influenced the shift towards more 'planned capitalism' and a greater acceptance of social reform by Conservatives in Britain by the 1950s. They steered a more moderate 'middle way' between the economic and the social although this was not embraced by all and wasn't sustained in the long-term (Ritschel, 1995). By the 1970s the emergent critique of the role of the state in the economy and of the welfare state culminated in overtly New Right policies during the Thatcher era. The economic policies of Conservative governments of the 1980s drew heavily on the classical liberal position (Pinker, 2008). This neo-liberal turn was not 'typically' conservative; social policies adopted during the 1990s such as measures designed to promote the 'work ethic' and end 'welfare dependency' along with the 'back to basics' approach were more reflective of traditional conservative thought.

Prominent contemporary conservative politicians in Britain such as David Cameron, Theresa May and Boris Johnson identify their values in terms of one-nation conservatism, the origins of which lie with the philosophy of Benjamin Disraeli. Author, and prime minister in the 1860s, Disraeli made the case for state support for the working class on the grounds of mutual obligations between the classes and also because failure to protect social stability could lead to instability and revolution. A pragmatic approach, the rhetoric of contemporary one-nation conservatism seeks to appeal to an alienated working class.

Neo-conservatism

Neo-conservatism draws on the economic liberal perspective of the free market and shares with it a negative view of the capacity of the state in matters of human welfare generally. However, in seeking to restore traditional conservative values, particularly those associated with 'the family, religion and the nation' (Heywood, 2002: 50) they advocate robust state intervention to uphold traditional values, particularly in the context of the nation state. Conservative nationalist parties, such as the UK Independence Party and the National Front in France, hold a strong anti-immigrant perspective and are to the fore in arguing against multiculturalism. Anti-establishment and anti-EU sentiment is also a key feature of their perspectives. Using populism and resentment politics (Liang, 2007) conservative nationalist parties frequently argue that the political elite is out of touch with ordinary people. This populism claims to encourage '"plain speaking" and they believe they represent the common man from the street whom the traditional leadership elite has forsaken' (Liang, 2007: 5). Populist radical Right parties exist in diverse forms across Europe and it is important not to lose sight of their varying values and objectives in assessing their impacts (Adler, 2016). At the extreme of the spectrum are far-Right parties (such as Golden Dawn in Greece) which are racist, xenophobic and neo-Nazi sympathisers.

Returning to neo-conservatism in the general sense, it takes the view that the state, as an authority, has an important role in maintaining 'social order and public morality' (Heywood, 2012: 91) with policy centred on promoting traditional family values and adopting a robust approach to crime and antisocial behaviour. It is also associated with promoting privatisation of social security and advocating that religious and other voluntary agencies provide welfare. The term neo-conservatism has taken on a particular usage and is commonly applied to specific political 'neocon' viewpoints espoused in the US, where elements of conservatism were pushed to new and controversial limits especially during the early 2000s, when the merits of unilateral decisions and interventionist foreign policies were advocated in the common good.

Christian democracy

The Christian democratic tradition, while sharing aspects of the conservative approach to social order and stability, is more accepting of a role for the state, albeit defined by religious principles, particularly Catholic ones, drawing on concepts such as subsidiarity. This refers to the ideal of support being availed of at the lowest level possible, that is, the family as first resort followed by local rather than national sources. The concept of the 'social market economy' is also employed and demonstrates the balance sought by Christian democracy in social and economic terms. Heywood (2012: 84) explains the social market economy as 'structured by market principles but which operates in the context of a society in which cohesion is maintained through a comprehensive welfare system and effective public services'. It emphasises the significance of community and the family and the role of significant institutions in society, such as the Church, trade unions and business representatives and, in so doing, accord them a particular 'status' in a corporatist approach to policy making. This approach facilitates a type of cross-class appeal, accommodating different groups, allowing for the emergence of pragmatic 'catch-all' political parties, especially as they evolved in post-war Europe. In addition, as Kalyvas and van Kersbergen (2010: 189) observe, 'by stressing the cross-class nature of the movement, Christian democratic parties managed to attract voters by appealing to "catholicity" in its literal sense'.

In terms of social policy, European Christian democrats historically demonstrated a strong attachment to the male breadwinner model of social security in keeping with their traditional values. Social protection is considered an important aspect of welfare provision in which continuity of employment is rewarded. This gives rise to particular social divisions in the quality and duration of welfare entitlements available, resulting in insider/outsider divisions between those with continuous employment record and those without (discussed in Chapter Seven).

Family policy reforms initiated by the Grand Coalition in the late 2000s of which the Christian Democrats in Germany were part, suggests a shift to more employment-centred family policy through earnings-related parental leave and more extensive childcare provision. These policy departures imply some modernisation of Christian Democratic family policy in Germany although as Fleckenstein (2011) notes, policy change was contested internally and remains somewhat incomplete. Family policy is but one example of the policy challenges facing Christian Democrats in recent decades but overall it is important to note that its fate has not been shown to be tied to secularisation. Utilising the idea of a modern version of 'unsecular politics', Kalyvas and van Kersbergen (2010: 204) remind us not to 'underestimate how religious parties themselves are active producers' of unsecular politics, which captures 'the often uneasy attempt to strip off the explicitly and exclusively religious ideological baggage, while at the same time constructing a new religiously inspired package of beliefs, values, and norms'. This pragmatism coupled with its historical cross-class appeal will be important in its future evolution and is perhaps relevant also to the wider politics of the EU, where the European People's Party, founded by Christian Democrats, remains a major political force in the European Parliament.

Socialism

There is a range of thinking to be considered under the umbrella term of socialism. Marxism, socialism, communism and Fabianism are the major perspectives representing different 'shades' of the Left. Social democracy was similarly borne out of the emergence of socialism, although its post-Second World War trajectory put clearer distance between it and contemporary socialism and it is therefore dealt with separately, below. In the broadest sense, socialism developed in response to challenges associated the emergence of capitalism over the course of the nineteenth century, although some eminent socialist thinkers (such as Comte de Saint-Simon (1760-1825) and Robert Owen (1771-1858)) predate this period. The impact of industrialisation and urbanisation raised fundamental questions about who benefited from these changes. The growth of the trade union movement and emerging recognition of need, poverty and social class brought about a new political era, where class divisions and associated inequalities could no longer be ignored (as outlined in Chapter Four).

The starting point of socialist thinking is collectivist and humanitarian in orientation. In other words, it is argued that people do not live in isolation from one another and therefore society needs to be viewed in terms of the structural forces and dynamics that make up its being, and how these impact on individuals in society. Human well-being is of central importance. In taking this approach socialism is clear that the way society is organised, and the way control and ownership of resources are distributed, is critical. The various strands of socialist thought are linked by a shared identification of class as 'the key parameter of social inequality' (Ginsburg, 2003: 94) and a concern with the pursuit of social equality, although the means of its achievement differ substantially. Equality of outcome (rather than equality of opportunity) is a core objective of socialism, with emphasis placed on the right of all human beings to share in the available resources of a society.

Socialism is also concerned with liberty although the socialist conception of freedom is fundamentally different from that held by liberals. Writing in 1949, Richard H Tawney (1880-1962) (in George and Wilding, 1985: 74) provides an illustration of their position: 'The increase in the freedom of ordinary men and women during the last two generations has taken place, not in spite of the action of governments, but because of it…. The mother of liberty has, in fact, been law.' Government 'facilitation' of freedom is not necessarily a position on freedom that all socialists would accept; Marxists in particular are likely to reject the possibility of enhanced individual liberty in the context of capitalism at all. The varieties of socialism that emerged present a challenge in the overall conceptualisation of this perspective of welfare. For instance, it is often thought that socialism and Marxism are 'more or less' the same thing; this is not the case. As Baradat (2000: 185) puts it: 'All Marxists are socialists, but not all socialists are Marxists.' Crucially, a distinction exists between socialists who seek an evolutionary approach to socialism and those who advocate revolutionary means to secure socialism. The gradualist (or reformist) approach of the Fabian Socialists contrasts with the revolutionary (or transformative) approach of Marxism.

Fabian socialism

Fabian socialists are collectivist in orientation; their ideas are based upon the values of freedom, equality and fellowship, along with democratic participation and humanitarianism (George and Wilding, 1985). Influenced by intellectuals within the Fabian Society (see Chapter Four), they seek improvements in society through democratic means to address the inequalities precipitating from capitalism. In *The Future of Socialism* (Crosland, 1956: 215 in George and Wilding, 1985: 71) Anthony Crosland (1918-77) asserted that: 'If social mobility is low ... and people cannot easily move up from the lower or middle reaches to the top, then the ruling elite becomes hereditary and self-perpetuating; and whatever one may concede to inherited or family advantages, this must involve a waste of talent'. Inequality is seen as an outcome of capitalism which threatens social cohesion, is wasteful in economic terms and 'diminishes people's basic humanity' (George and Wilding, 1985: 72). In contrast to Marxism, Fabian Socialists seek a gradual or 'evolutionist' strategy in changing the organisation of society in order that a collectivist and redistributive socialist agenda can be pursued through parliamentary politics and democratic means. They believe strongly in the need for, and capacity of, government and reject the anti-collectivist position adopted by classical liberals, as indicated by Tawney (1953: 87 in Deakin and Wright, 1995: 140):

> It is constantly assumed by privileged classes that, when the state refrains from intervening in any department of economic or social affairs, what remains as a result of its inaction is liberty. In reality, as far as the mass of mankind are concerned, what commonly remains is, not liberty, but tyranny.

They also consider issues of class conflict and its impact in their writings although not to the same extent as within the Marxist tradition.

One of the most influential social policy thinkers of the twentieth century, Richard Titmuss (1907-73) advocated universalist and comprehensive social services, regarding this as central to promoting social solidarity, in which access could be assured to all. This would provide the bedrock of a better society by promoting social cohesion in a manner not possible where distinctions are made between individuals, as happens when services are provided on a selectivist basis. In addition, Titmuss offered an analysis of welfare divisions which challenged conventional wisdom around the provision of welfare. He argued that it was more accurate to analyse the various systems of welfare that existed – not just social welfare but also occupational welfare and fiscal welfare. In this respect, he encouraged a fuller analysis of all means of welfare, not just welfare as provided through social services. Titmuss laid the foundations for the development of more robust conceptual tools of welfare analysis that take a more systematic approach to the various methods of redistribution and their respective impacts (see Chapter Seven).

Fabian socialism was highly influential in the architecture of the original welfare state in Britain. It sought to provide a comprehensive and accessible range of services for its citizens (see Chapter Four). This position was based on the capacity of the state to deliver social citizenship rights but this became a matter of debate as the capacity of the 'traditional top-down approach ... where the state decided what was good for people and then delivered it, resulted in a failure to meet the real needs and preferences of individuals and families' (A Pratt, 2006b: 43). However, how much of this was the fault of Fabians is questionable, as they argued the importance of local government and municipal ownership too (Fitzpatrick, 2006). The Fabian Society is Britain's oldest think tank; it was influential in the development of the Labour Party to which it remains affiliated as a Socialist Society. Fitzpatrick (2006: 444) notes that 'the Society is now more receptive to neo-liberal ideas and is no longer quite the leftist think tank of old', reflective perhaps of the wider shift in social democratic politics of recent decades.

Marxist socialism

Marxism shares a commitment to social equality and individual freedom with evolutionary socialism; 'from each according to his abilities, to each according to his needs' was to be the distributive principle of communism and its core values are derived primarily from its fundamental critique of capitalism. Based on the writings of Karl Marx (1818-83), he provided 'a relentless critique of the inhumanity of the capitalist system as it existed during his lifetime' (George and Wilding, 1985: 96). Marxism highlights the injustices of the class system inherent to capitalism and the unequal and exploitative relations at the core of its existence. The nature of the relationship between the owners of production (the capitalists or bourgeoisie) and workers (the proletariat) highlights the divisions and inequalities that exist within capitalism, the alienation that results and the class conflict that is inevitable. This critique is founded on a 'materialist conception of history' where according to Marx (in George and Wilding, 1985: 99): 'The mode of production in material life determines the general character of the social, political and spiritual processes of life. It is not the consciousness of men that determines their existence but, on the contrary, their social existence determines their consciousness'.

The inevitable class conflict would give rise to revolution, making way for a classless society organised on the basis of common ownership, where the state would 'wither away' (Dean, 2008: 88). However, this did not happen in any of the countries (such as the former USSR, Cuba, North Korea) where communism took hold. This fact gives rise to much scepticism about the application of Marxist theory in practice. Nevertheless, Marxist theory offers a cogent critique of capitalism and its shortcomings; how it assesses the welfare state and the structures that emerged to deal with the worst excesses of capitalism is the issue to which we now turn.

Neo-Marxism

Neo-Marxism refers to the revival of Marxist theory in the 1970s which offers a critique of contemporary capitalism and examines the position of the welfare state in that context. The term 'welfare state' is generally rejected in favour of 'welfare capitalism' as a more accurate reflection of reality. The development of welfare provisions is largely seen as the outcome of class conflict but not necessarily a victory for the working class. From a neo-Marxist perspective, welfare measures support and uphold capitalism, providing, and maintaining, the conditions in which capitalism continues to prosper. According to this view, the welfare state 'is a device to stabilise rather than a step in the transformation of capitalist society' (Offe, 1982: 12). Offe argues this on three main grounds: (1) the welfare state is ineffective and inefficient, (2) it is repressive and (3) it offers a false perspective on the organisation of society where 'the structural arrangements of the welfare state tend to make people ignore or forget that the needs and contingencies which the welfare state responds to are themselves constituted, directly or indirectly, in the sphere of work and production' (Offe, 1982: 13).

The welfare state is considered ineffective because it largely failed to address the disparities in income distribution between labour and capital and because it compensates for capitalism rather than dealing with the causes of need and insecurity (that is, capitalism) in the first place. The social control or 'repressiveness of the welfare state' (Offe, 1982: 13) is highlighted in terms of the requirements imposed for the receipt of benefits, many of which seek to re-enforce particular views such as the 'deserving' client. Lavalette (2006: 55) points to the control exercised 'within the daily functioning of welfare services and institutions' where, for example, aspects of education, juvenile justice and family support services involve regulation of families, children and young people. Finally, the 'politico-ideological control function' (Offe, 1982: 13) refers to the impact of the welfare state in diffusing rather than challenging the causes and effects of capitalism. In other words, the welfare state produces a false sense of social harmony which glosses over the fundamental inequalities that persist within the capitalist system.

Gough's (1979) *Political Economy of the Welfare State* focuses on the relationship between capitalism and the welfare state, highlighting the contradictory pressures of the welfare state for capitalism which requires steady economic growth to sustain it, but from which it also benefits. In the longer term, he concludes that 'either accumulation and economic growth or political and social rights must be sacrificed' (Gough, 1979: 152). The subsequent emergence of neo-liberal capitalism and the most recent crisis sets the context for Gough's (2012) analysis. He notes the erosion of influence of the countervailing forces of labour and trades unions as against powerful corporate and financial interests. He expects varieties of capitalism to continue and contends that current pessimism about Anglo-capitalism notwithstanding, 'only nation states can supply or support these countervailing functions' which implies 'extensive and reformed international institutions' will be needed to reverse 'the shift from "organised" to "unorganised" capitalism' (Gough, 2012: 590), and generate more robust state responses and social policies to meet need and provide social investment. Gough's (1979) earlier conclusion that the relationship between capitalism and the welfare state would result in welfare cuts, privatisation and the rise of low pay proved prescient (Hill, 2012) and his recent predictions for the future are worth quoting:

> In the end ... democratic states in reacting to the ongoing crisis will slowly act to curb elite greed and reverse their grab of an inordinate share of the social surplus in order to preserve the capitalist system. ... But a reforming state will undertake this task under most unpropitious fiscal circumstances. It will need simultaneously to address social investment, social transfers, future pension costs, public debt, infrastructure investment, new green investment and 'eco-system maintenance'. In other words, it will entail substantial collective intervention in national resource allocation. My own view is that this restructuring will be aided by the threats of faltering growth, climate change and energy insecurity. The result would be some form of 'eco-welfare state' (Gough, 2012: 590).

While an eco-welfare state may work within the framework of capitalism, it is not, in his view, compatible with the unorganised version of neo-liberal capitalism. Ultimately, eco-social policies will be faced with the limits of growth conundrum, economic growth on which all welfare states have relied will catch up with us as climate change 'presents the definitive challenge' (Gough, 2012: 591) to all welfare states. Only then, Gough concludes is it that 'the relationship between capitalism and the welfare state including the eco-welfare state will likely become incompatible' (2012: 591). This is a discussion that is also of relevance to environmentalism which we review later in this chapter and to the broader issue of social policy and the environment as discussed in Chapter Thirteen.

Social democracy

The social democratic perspective evolved, and some would argue changed significantly, over the course of the twentieth century. Its origins date back to the emergence of workers' movements during the latter part of the nineteenth century and the subsequent establishment of social democratic, labour or workers' political parties across Europe. This coincided with a period during which democracy was still in its infancy and full voting rights had not been secured for all citizens. Its belief in the importance of democracy is one of its defining features, as illustrated by Berger (2002: 17) who quotes the 1869 Eisenach programme of the German Social Democratic Workers Party: 'political freedom is the most indispensable precondition for the economic emancipation of the working classes. Hence the social question is indivisible from the political question. The solution to the former is conditional on the solution of the latter, and possible only in the democratic state'. Initially influenced by both Marxist thinking and the Fabian Socialist positions, the orientation of social democracy was largely guided by the evolutionary approach advocated by the latter.

The core features of 'old' social democracy included a socialist vision, a positive interpretation of freedom in the context of democracy, and a concern about inequality and the need to tackle it, mainly through state interventions to promote redistribution. The objective was to humanise capitalism, to address the inequalities that arise while at the same time acknowledging that resources have to be generated before they can be redistributed. Social democracy was historically noted for its enthusiasm for the welfare state project, including nationalisation and public ownership. While socialist in aspiration, the social democratic perspective married this with an acceptance of economic imperatives as the necessary mechanism for generating wealth and through which redistribution could address class divisions and inequalities.

The high point of social democracy is commonly acknowledged to coincide with 'the golden era of the welfare state', from the end of the Second World War until the mid-1970s. Sweden emerged as the archetype for post-war social democracy and the Keynesian rationale for economic and social planning offered a policy mechanism through which the welfare state project could be pursued. However, Keynesian economic principles were increasingly challenged during the 1970s and 'by 1990 ... the left-wing exuberance of the 1970s had almost completed disappeared' (Callaghan, 2003: 129). Thus began a period of reflection by many social democrats on their core values resulting in the 'Third Way' perspective which came to prominence during the 1990s and early 2000s although it was not to endure and had all but faded from the political lexicon of European social democratic parties by the mid-2000s.

The Third Way marked an important turn in social democracy. It is most associated with the emergence of New Labour in Britain, but it was also prominent during Bill Clinton's presidency in the US and in the Schröder period in Germany. Governments in Sweden, Belgium and the Netherlands also adopted Third Way policies during the 1990s. In Britain, Anthony Giddens (1998, 2000) provided an academic rationale for modernising social democratic thinking, challenging the outmoded views of the Left, highlighting the impact of globalisation and advocating a new approach for new times.

Particularly noted for a language of compromise and what Powell (2008: 93) describes as 'a rhetoric of reconciliation' illustrated by phrases such as '"economic dynamism as well as social justice"', the Third Way drew on the values of the Right and the Left, rendering its core ideological make-up difficult to discern. In relation to equality, for example, the Third Way accepted equality as critical to social inclusion. Specifically, equality of opportunity was the core objective. This marked a distinction from 'old Left' values that saw equality more in terms of equality of outcome. Equality of outcome was rejected, because 'predetermined results imposed ... by a central authority and decided irrespective of work, effort or contribution to the community, is not a socialist dream but other people's nightmare of socialism' (Brown, 1999: 42 in Page, 2005: 286).

The Third Way espoused equality of opportunity and equality of respect, 'whatever their background, capability, creed or race' (Blair, 1998: 3). Families and communities were to be supported to realise the potential of all. The welfare state was central to providing such supports, although some of its traditional features were considered inefficient and the old objectives at odds with the new realities that now pertained. The Third Way welfare state was to be active and responsive, promote self-responsibility and self-realisation, be prudent yet caring and target resources to those most in need of them. Communities were to be supported to be strong and antisocial behaviour was not to be tolerated. These ideas were captured in various soundbites such as 'work is the best form of welfare', the welfare state should provide a 'hand up not a hand out', and that it is time to be 'tough on crime, tough on the causes of crime'. Influenced by **communitarianism**, the Third Way stressed the rights and the duties of individuals to themselves and to the wider community. In addition to the 'rights with responsibilities' approach to welfare came an enthusiastic endorsement of the market and market-based principles, from which the public sector should learn. The most enduring policy examples of the impact of the Third Way emanate from Britain where the Labour Party enjoyed unprecedented electoral

> **Communitarianism** situates individuals in the context of the wider community. Variously interpreted, this concept implies a rejection of pure individualism while also promoting the duties of individuals within communities.

success, holding government from 1997 to 2010. Their shift in social democratic thinking brought about a changed policy focus to match the new Left ideals (see Chapter Four). The policy changes informed by this updated left–of–centre thinking were variously appraised, by some as a betrayal of traditional social democratic values and by others as a legitimate and practical modernisation of its core objectives.

Taking the social democratic philosophy as a whole, Keating and McCrone (2013: 2) consider it is a 'multidimensional' concept and that 'there has never been a single social democratic model' with variations evident over time and in different countries. What is clear at this juncture is that social democratic parties are in difficulty across Europe (Keating and McCrone, 2013), as structural occupational and class changes mean there is no longer a coherent unionised or unified working class, a cohort social democrats traditionally represented and from whom they garnered support. Now much less ideologically distinct from its political opponents than in the past, social democracy appears to be reeling still from its capitulation to the assumed necessities of global capitalism in the twenty-first century. The financial crisis exposed the fault lines of particular aspects of contemporary neo–liberal capitalism; under–regulated, under–taxed and over-supported by states and associated institutional policy actors. Any intuitive sense that social democrats would become the harbingers of greater electoral support in the aftermath of the financial crisis did not materialise. Instead the 'existential crisis of social democracy finds its ultimate expression in the continuing crisis of capitalism. If the historic goal of social democracy is to humanise capitalism, then the way in which public finances have been used to bail out the banks at the expense of the people who are capitalism's victims, proves the paucity of the social democrat position' (Lawson, 2014).

Crouch (2013) asserts that social democrats will have to provide a critique of corporate behaviour and pursue the regulation of the corporation much more rigorously, which will also require a shift in its predominant nation–state focus. This is likely to require a coordinated effort by social democrats across Europe to find a more robust way of managing capitalism in the interests of people.

In ideological terms, the Third Way turn left a significant legacy from which it seems social democracy has yet to recover. By becoming more similar to the Right, social democrats allowed the 'bourgeois *imaginaire*' (Bauman, 2013) to win out. Based on assumptions of the merits of unrelenting economic growth, consumption and meritocracy for society, the bourgeois ideology is flawed and unsustainable, but, as yet, they have 'no alternative vision, no "utopia"' (Bauman, 2013: 4). The crisis of democratic institutions presents a real dilemma for social democrats. In Bauman's view 'the divorce between power and politics' (2013: 5) leaves politicians without the means to deliver. Lawson's (2013: 1) analysis brings together 'the twin and interlinked crises of Europe and social democracy' which he considers 'structural and existential' requiring radical steps for action, including

> meaningful economic reforms that change the balance of power between people and capital, creating jobs (in environmentally sustainable areas in particular), economic security and much greater equality across Europe. This should be allied to deep-rooted democratic changes to European political institutions to ensure legitimacy and accountability for the new project (Lawson, 2013: 1).

How these challenges will be taken up by social democratic parties across Europe remains to be seen.

Feminism

Feminism is often thought of as a twentieth-century social movement particularly associated with the women's liberation movement of the 1960s and 1970s; it has in fact a much longer history, with women highlighting aspects of women's inequality throughout the nineteenth century. The suffrage movement, the involvement of women in trade unions, voluntary, community and advocacy work (although not so called at the time) marked the arrival of 'first wave' feminism, and the beginnings of a long and continuing debate about the nature of women's rights. The second wave refers to the period of the late 1960s and 1970s, during which time women again mobilised to challenge continuing discrimination and raise fundamental questions about existing assumptions regarding the role and position of women. In contemporary terms, there is no singular feminist perspective, rather a variety of feminisms have developed over time. In this context, the different types of feminist ideology are briefly outlined here, some of which connect their overall perspective to the ideologies already discussed. bell hooks (2015: 1) provides a concise definition of feminism to begin with: 'Simply put, feminism is a movement to end sexism, sexist exploitation, and oppression.' She goes on to say that 'it is a definition which implies that all sexist thinking and action is the problem, whether those who perpetuate it are female or male, child or adult. It is also broad enough to include an understanding of systemic institutionalized sexism'. The possibilities for and of feminism are drawn together by hooks in a way that dispels many of the myths that frequently surround feminism.

Feminism may be seen as a political ideology in its own right, or as one that aligns itself with other perspectives to promote a particular type of feminism. Drawing on liberal values as outlined earlier, liberal feminism seeks equal rights and equal treatment for women and men. In their pursuit of 'formal' equality, emphasis is placed on the rights of women to be protected and promoted, primarily with reference to the public sphere (Williams, 1989). Liberal feminists are reformist and broadly view the state as a positive avenue for change, via policy and legislative tools. Little attention is given to the private domain, such as women's family lives.

Socialist feminism, in contrast, offers an assessment of the position of women in society that highlights the unequal relations in capitalist society. While critical of the relative neglect of the oppression of women in classical Marxist thinking, socialist feminism often draws on the Marxist perspective to highlight structural dimensions of inequality that are relevant. The effects of capitalism are therefore considered in terms of its impact on women's lives in the formal sphere of the paid labour market and within the household. In Young's (1981: 58 in McLaughlin, 2003: 51) assessment, for example, 'the marginalization of women and thereby our functioning as a secondary labour force is an essential and fundamental characteristic of capitalism'. The concept of patriarchy is also applied in this context and has been variously defined by feminists. Interpretations of patriarchy (introduced to feminist thought in Kate Millet's (1970) *Sexual Politics*) have evolved over time but at its core it refers to both the structures and relations of male power involved in the subordination of women in society. For socialist feminists what is of concern is the interplay between capitalism and patriarchy, conveyed by the concept of capitalist patriarchy, and its impact on the lives of women. This marks an important distinction from liberal feminism because, it is an effort, as Williams (1989: 64) explains, 'on the one hand to acknowledge the significance of institutionalized power relationships between men and women which produce gender inequalities, and, on the other, an acknowledgement that capitalism gives rise to *differential* experiences of oppression by women of different classes.' This emphasis on the structured relations between men and women in society and on the needs and position of all women, and how they may differ are issues not acknowledged by liberal feminism.

Radical feminism emerged during second-wave feminism, when the wider political climate was also shaped by several demands for social change. In political terms, the radical feminist message was built around two main concepts; that of patriarchy and the notion that 'the personal is political'. In drawing attention to what was traditionally understood as the 'private' sphere, radical feminists highlighted what they saw as other (and previously hidden) areas of oppression, particularly with regard to sexuality and the family, both of which are regarded by radical feminists as 'instruments of patriarchal domination' (Bryson, 2003: 163). In practical terms, many radical feminist activists played a vital role in establishing important services such as well-woman and health clinics, refuges for women in abusive relationships and in advocating the individual rights of women to define their own sexuality (Williams, 1989).

One of the criticisms most frequently levelled at feminism in general is that its agenda is predominantly shaped by white middle-class heterosexual women, to the neglect of others. Black feminists were among the first to highlight some of the shortcomings associated with feminism, particularly its failure to acknowledge the diversity of women who are part of the wider feminist struggle, and the 'classist' and racist nature of the mainstream movement. bell hooks (1982: 145) in *Ain't I a Woman?* for example, argued that 'not all women are equally oppressed because some women are able to use their class, race, and educational privilege to effectively resist sexist oppression'. The questioning of the notion of a unified category of women with common experiences upon which solidarity can be premised, and the recognition of difference(s) among women, subsequently became important issues for feminist thinking and activism. Essentially more fluid understandings of women and men and their diverse range of identities, experiences and values came to the fore.

For example, feminist scholarship on intersectionality, a concept that denotes the experiences of black women who are oppressed in sexist and racist terms, seeks to understand the multiple intersecting differences that comprise the experiences of different groups of people and shape the power differentials between them. Intersectionality thus draws attention to multiple systems of power, 'race, gender, class, sexuality, ability, age, country of origin, citizenship status' (Hill Collins and Chepp, 2013: 60), that both make up and to some extent change women's experiences over time, as they, for example, migrate, become a mother, become older, come out and so on. This is reflected in the diverse range of feminisms, hybrid feminisms and feminist campaigning which proliferates beyond the typology of liberal, radical and socialist feminism, including for example, postcolonial feminism, anti-racist feminism, critical feminist disability studies and trans-feminism (Dhamoon, 2013).

Another key intervention has been Judith Butler's (1990) work, *Gender Trouble: Feminism and the Subversion of Identity*. Butler deconstructed the difference between sex as a biological category and gender as a socially constructed category, and the binaries of male and female, masculine and feminine; distinctions central to second-wave feminism. As a result, Butler raised challenging questions about 'what is a woman?' This goes further than making the point that different women have different experiences, to ask whether it is possible to assume that woman as a unified subject, arising from the 'bodily and social experiences of being a woman', exists at all (Dhamoon, 2013: 98). It is impossible to convey here both the complexity of Butler's contribution and of how its implications for feminist politics has been subsequently interpreted and misinterpreted. At its core, however, is the notion that gender is performative, or is something we 'do'; it does not exist beyond repeated performances of the cultural norms of what is taken as masculine and feminine, implying that categories such as man and woman are not fixed, and that there are several genders, understood as expressions of one's gender identity (MacKay, 2015). For all this multiplicity and diversity however, as MacKay (2015: 55) puts it, 'for some activists today ... the label of just "feminist" alone is quite enough. It is often seen as a label that is radical enough yet broad enough to contain a myriad of views and standpoints'.

The feminist movement might also be said to have evolved from third wave to fourth wave, though these categories are not as solidly defined or as commonly used as first- and second-wave feminism. If the current era of feminist thinking can be taken as fourth-wave feminism, it comes after and critically appraises 1980s and 1990s third-wave feminism, which focused on the cultural politics of identity, individual empowerment, and freedom of choice (Tong, 2007). Contemporary feminist movement, which has seen a resurgence in the last decade, aims to acknowledge both intersectionality and structural inequality. It thus returns to the importance of critically analysing capitalism and patriarchy in their twenty-first century forms.

Although Nancy Fraser does not use the labels of third and fourth wave, her reflections on what has been achieved by feminism and where it now stands are instructive. For her, feminism from the 1970s onwards seemed to slide into 'a "dangerous liaison" with neoliberalism' (Eisenstein, 2005 in Fraser, 2009: 109). Central to Fraser's (2009, 2016) argument is that emancipation through paid work and the hope of gender equality in economic terms, both of which were central to second-wave feminism, have had ambiguous outcomes. In particular the valorisation of paid work and the dual-earner family, which have been given a 'feminist aura' by contemporary neo-liberal capitalism, have instead been associated with growing labour market insecurity and declining living standards (Fraser, 2016: 114). This is made even more demanding for women when combined with care or more broadly social reproduction, that is, the nurturing of relationships and of community upon which societies depend but which neo-liberalism neither recognises nor values, unless in commodified form. Fraser thus speaks of a reinvigorated socialist feminism for the twenty-first century that rebalances the cultural politics of recent feminism with a critique of contemporary capitalism. This would involve 'a massive reorganization of the relation between production and reproduction: for social arrangements that could enable people of every class, gender, sexuality and colour to combine social-reproductive activities with safe, interesting and well-remunerated work' (Fraser, 2016: 16).

While Fraser's account is one of many perspectives on twenty-first century feminism (see also for example Power, 2009; MacKay, 2015), it is one which resonates with long-standing feminist debates in social policy. Feminism began to impact on social policy during the 1970s and 1980s. Arguably more than any other perspective on welfare, feminism has challenged the 'traditionalism' of the original welfare state project and sought a fuller engagement with the pursuit of equality and respect for difference in social policy. Feminist perspectives offer a forceful critique of the exclusionary nature of citizenship (for example, Young, 1989; Lister, 2003; Siim, 2000) which have continued to highlight the limitations attached to the gendered assumptions underpinning the welfare state, particularly regarding the family, work and care. Feminist social policy has therefore, among other things, interrogated the meaning of gender equality with respect to work and welfare (Lewis, 1992, 1997); highlighted the importance of the family for a full understanding of how welfare is 'produced', going beyond a focus on states and markets and questioning the public/private divide (Lister, 2010); and contested and reworked key concepts such as interdependence, care and citizenship, by proposing a **feminist ethic of care** (Lister, 2003). Within these debates there are a range of views, and as Lister (2010) suggests, feminist critique of social policy draws eclectically on wider strands of feminist ideology.

> **The feminist 'ethic of care'** highlights the need to conceptualise and take account of care issues, both with regard to the cared for person and the carer, to promote and realise a more inclusive type of citizenship.

Reflecting wider contemporary debates, there is also a questioning within feminist social policy scholarship of the 'selective mainstreaming of feminism', in social policy and social policy discourse (Williams, 2015: 504). This has led to considerable scepticism and a continued interrogation of how gender equality is constructed in contemporary social policy, especially in terms of work and care, around which gender inequalities are particularly resilient (Jenson, 2015). Challenging these inequalities and the way that feminism has been incorporated into mainstream social policy, contemporary feminist social policy scholarship and activism traverses the cultural and economic domain and, as Hobson et al. (2015) see it, connects with anti-racist, anti-poverty, anti-austerity and environmentalist campaigns. In this regard, issues such as 'gender-based violence, militarism, everyday and racialized misogyny, lack of equal pay … migration especially domestic work, and trafficking; … challenging the illusions of post-feminist and post-racial equalities' (Hobson et al., 2015: 504) provide an indication of the range of issues twenty-first century feminist social policy addresses.

Greenism

The 1970s saw a growth of concern for the environment, to which the terms greenism and environmentalism, which are often used interchangeably, refer. Concern for the environment manifested as both a social movement and as a related set of ideas. These ideas addressed questions about the relationship between society and the environment; the root causes of environmental problems, such as pollution, the loss of biodiversity and species habitat; and what needed to be done about them. Dryzek (2005: 225) suggests that 'in the last three decades or so green radicalism has come from nowhere to develop a comprehensive critique of the environmental, social, political and economic shortcomings of industrial society. As such, it represents perhaps the most significant ideological development of the late twentieth century'. In addition green thinking has influenced mainstream politics, as evidenced by the growth of environmental policy as an area of government, and the appropriation of green ideas by existing political ideologies. To make sense of the diversity of green thinking, different strands are typically divided into two overarching approaches. These are variously described as 'dark' versus 'light' green, deep versus shallow green, radical versus reformist, technocentric versus ecocentric, and environmentalist versus ecologist approaches.

Here we use the radical versus reformist divide to explore in more detail the key differences between core green thinking and the adoption of green thinking by existing political ideologies. The adoption of green ideas by existing Left- and Right-wing ideologies including social democracy and liberalism is generally reflective of a reformist approach. This approach does recognise environmental problems; however, it believes that either capitalist markets will always produce solutions to overcome problems such as dwindling resources, and continued growth will be ensured; or that by careful economic and environmental management, problems can be overcome to the extent that it is possible to have both economic growth and environmental protection. In either case faith is placed in the usefulness of conventional scientific, technological and economic knowledge and expertise. It follows that this view stresses management over participation, and individuals and local communities do not have a significant role to play in dealing with environmental problems. Debates about values are also of minimal importance. This view is therefore **anthropocentric**. Generally the reformist approach does not envisage radical alteration of society and its institutions, however those on the Left advocate gradual change (Pepper, 1996). Much contemporary environmental and sustainable development policy can be located within this approach.

> **Anthropocentrism** refers to valuing the non-human world, such as plants and animals, for instrumental reasons, that is, for how it can benefit humans.

Radical greenism on the other hand sees itself as a distinct ideology, exemplified by a slogan of the German green party, 'neither right nor left but in front'. As Heywood (2012) suggests, this ideology is distinct from both the politics of material distribution, which the central concern of the classical ideologies falling along the Left/Right-wing spectrum; and from the newer ideologies based on the politics of identity, such as feminism. In contrast, radical greenism is a 'politics of sensibilities' (Heywood, 2012: 253) whose chief concern is to alter the relationship between humans and nature. From green political parties to direct action groups to alternative communities, there is within deep green thinking a considerable diversity among positions including eco-socialism, ecofeminism, deep ecology, social ecology and environmental justice movements. Some of these positions have opposing ideas, some emphasise the primacy of values and principles while others are more practically oriented and it would not be possible to discuss the range of ideas in detail here. We look briefly at some of the main ideas illustrative of the overall approach (see Dryzek and Schlosberg (2005) and Carter (2007) for more on the range of green ideas and debates).

The idea of limits is central to radical green thinking; the human world is understood as part of a global ecosystem and is therefore subject to ecological laws. These laws ultimately constrain human action, particularly in terms of economic and population growth and levels of consumption (Pepper, 1996). In other words, the natural world simply cannot sustain unlimited growth. Radical green thinking (except for eco-socialism), therefore, rejects both capitalism and socialism because both are underpinned by industrialism premised on the notion of continued economic growth (George and Wilding, 1994). Acceptance of the limits to growth implies that there must be a reduction in economic growth and consumption, and population. Some radical greens therefore advocate the notion of a steady state economy as proposed by Herman Daly. Daly critiqued the 'growthmania' of conventional economics which views economic growth as the solution to every problem, be it social, economic or environmental. A steady state economy in contrast is 'an economy with constant stocks of artefacts and people' where the throughput of people and goods is 'limited in scale so as to be within the regenerative and assimilative capacities of the ecosystem' (Daly, 1995: 331). Related ideas are being mobilised by the contemporary de-growth movement (Martínez-Alier et al, 2010).

Even if unlimited growth were possible, radical greens question the desirability of limitless consumption, arguing that the 'iron cage of consumerism' makes for anxious, individualistic, competitive, acquisitive and ultimately unequal societies (Jackson, 2009: 9). It is thus believed that ending the perpetual search for economic growth and material prosperity is an intrinsic good because it leads to richer and more fulfilling lives. In addition, radical greens argue that the pursuit of economic growth aimed at continuously rising living standards averts the need for radical redistributive policies within and between countries, in particular between developed and developing countries, which is needed in the context of limits to growth.

Radical greens also advocate decentralisation and small-scale participatory democracy. This would have environmental benefits because the creation of small-scale self-sufficient communities would cease the environmental destruction caused by large-scale globalised industrial production. It is also argued that this would have social benefits because 'a decentralized, participatory and egalitarian society is one that recognizes each person's value as an important and respected member of the community' (Garner, 1996: 38). This would encourage conservation, reduce waste and pollution, and be more participatory. The main trade and exchange would be within ecoregions, and this would entail less movement of people and goods. There are many problems with the practical application of eco- or bioregionalism, and in the more immediate term radical greens emphasise community values such as participation, empowerment and self-reliance, sharing of resources, and local solutions to local problems and local needs. Promotion of the third sector and the social economy are seen as ways of realising these values and principles in practice. This is part of the wider aim to transform society along the lines of communalism where 'economic relations are intimately connected with social relations and feelings of belonging, sharing, caring and surviving' (O'Riordan, 1981: 89-90). Influenced by the work of André Gorz in particular, the reduction of working time and the introduction of basic income policies are seen as means of achieving this transformation.

In contrast to the reformist trust in science and technology, radical greens are critical or at least ambivalent about the resort to complex large-scale technology used in areas such as industry, agriculture and medicine (George and Wilding, 1994). It encourages overconsumption of resources and potentially creates further problems. The production of biofuel as a solution to climate change, for example, leads to the problem of rising food costs which particularly effect those on low incomes. Informed by writers such as Ivan Illich, radical greens advocate alternative technologies 'partly because they are considered environmentally benign, but also because they are potentially "democratic". That is, unlike high technology, they can be owned, understood, maintained and used by individuals and groups with little economic or political power' (Pepper 1996: 38). Finally, this approach is **ecocentric** as opposed to anthropocentric: there is deep respect for nature in its own right, not just in terms of how it can benefit humans. In this view, nature contains its own purpose which should be respected as a matter of ethical principle, termed bioethics (O'Riordan, 1981). Respect is central here because, as

> **Ecocentrism** takes the fact that humankind is part of the global ecosystem seriously; human action is therefore subject to ecological laws and limits, and the non-human parts of the ecosystem are given equal respect as humans and are intrinsically valued.

most radical green thinkers acknowledge, the implementation of ideas such as species equality would be untenable. In practice, typical policies include banning or phasing out blood sports, animal experiments and intensive livestock farming (George and Wilding, 1994). This approach to the non-human world also informs the radical green view of relationships between people, which should similarly be informed by principles of respect, equality and social justice.

As for an overall assessment of green thinking on policy making and the welfare state; green parties have had some influence and electoral success, particularly in Northern and Western Europe. In practice, green parties tend to combine radical positions on the environment together with Left-wing positions on other social and economic issues, though the experience of government means they invariably have to compromise on and downplay their radical environmental positions (Carter, 2013). The wider context here is the typically pessimistic assessment of the receptivity to radical green ideas by the electorates of developed nations accustomed to growth and consumerism. The global corporate interests driving twenty-first century capitalism are clearly another major block to the progress of green thinking of either radical or reformist hue; an issue we take up again in Chapter Thirteen when we look more closely at social policy and environmental issues.

Chapter summary
- This chapter examined the role of political ideologies in social policy debate. It provided a brief conceptual map of political perspectives in terms of their core values. These values shape positions on welfare and matters of social policy and illustrate the political nature of social policy decisions and outcomes.
- The liberal perspective emphasises individual freedom as a core value to be protected. Classical liberalism applies this principle to the economy through its laissez-faire philosophy. It rejects the welfare state, highlighting what it sees as an inefficient and monopolistic creation which damages individual freedom. The neo-liberal variant has dominated in recent decades and contributed to a substantial rebalancing of power in favour of corporate and capital interests.
- The socialist perspective sees class divisions and inequality as the inevitable outcome of capitalism and it advocates a collective approach to society and its organisation. Different socialist perspectives exist; some Marxist and others of a less radical and more gradualist character.
- The feminist perspective challenges certain assumptions about the role and rights of women in society. Feminism has sought to address not only overt discrimination but also to highlight the gender-blind and hence exclusionary construction of key aspects of social policy, including citizenship, social rights and the welfare state.
- The green perspective stresses the limits to growth and the need to consider the finite nature of resources. Policies need to acknowledge and address issues of environmental sustainability. In this context, there are different 'shades of green', some reformist and others radical.

Discussion points
- Critically examine the main features of an ideological perspective with reference to its impact on social policy.
- Analyse the work of a key political thinker/activist and assess their contribution to social policy discourse.
- Does politics still matter?

Further reading list
Fitzpatrick, T (2011) *Welfare theory: An introduction* (2nd edn), Basingstoke: Palgrave Macmillan

Heywood, A (2017) *Political ideologies: An introduction* (6th edn), London: Palgrave Macmillan

Taylor, G (2007) *Ideology and welfare: Historical and theoretical perspectives*, Basingstoke: Palgrave Macmillan

six

Contemporary challenges for social policy and welfare states: Ireland in a wider context

The study of social policy and welfare states is shaped by various theoretical debates and different perspectives on how best to understand welfare systems, the influences on their development and reform, and the challenges they face. The chapter builds on the broad narrative of the welfare state offered in Chapter Four, and the role of political ideas and values mapped out in Chapter Five, to provide an outline of various perspectives, concepts and debates which consider both external factors and the internal influences on the changing scope and trajectory of social policy. In a sense this chapter introduces key 'bigger picture' welfare state issues and debates, and identifies drivers of welfare state reform that assist in deepening our analysis of contemporary social policy in Ireland and elsewhere.

Chapter outline
- Section one sets out some disparate but cumulatively influential areas of welfare state research. It maps out a number of the major challenges confronting welfare states and briefly overviews the productive turn in social policy and the social investment agenda which has since emerged.
- Section two charts the uneven development of EU social policy. It outlines the impact of the Euro crisis and the policy responses to it and considers the unsettled outlook for the social policy agenda of the EU.
- Section three draws on the themes of the earlier sections to develop a critical assessment of the contemporary politics of Irish social policy and its impacts on Ireland's welfare state.

SECTION ONE

ANALYSING CONTEMPORARY CHALLENGES FOR THE WELFARE STATE

Post-industrialisation, globalisation and financialisation

Apart from the potential impact of the logic of globalisation on politics and public policy (discussed below), **post-industrialisation** and economic globalisation have been significant factors shaping economies in the wake of the economic crisis of the 1970s and 1980s. Advanced economies have gradually become post-industrialised as they experience a decline in manufacturing-based employment and a growth in services, information technology, and financial services-based occupations. For example, in 1975 over one third of workers in OECD countries worked in manufacturing, compared with just a fifth by the 2010s (Hall, 2015). Shifting occupational structures have resulted in debate about polarisation of employment structures in recent decades. On the one hand, in line with educational expansion, there is evidence of occupational upgrading with growth in professional- and managerial-type jobs, and a decline in production and clerical work (Oesch, 2013). Growth in both high- and low-ranking jobs has occurred alongside a decline in mid-ranking job employment share, reflecting the so-called 'hollowing-out' of the labour market, which in turn contributes to a more unequal distribution of market incomes and the risk of less social mobility (Hall, 2015). The increased prevalence of low pay is found not just in liberal market economies like the US and the UK but also in countries such as Germany. In addition, the rise in long-term unemployment, increased wage inequalities, the flexibilisation of employment contracts and the growth of atypical employment, indicates the extent of labour market change (Emmenegger et al, 2012). However, labour market changes are mediated by states and the policies in place. Characterising developments in recent decades as 'the age of dualization', Emmenegger et al (2012: 10) focus on the process and politics of change, whereby 'policies increasingly differentiate rights, entitlements, and services provided to different categories of recipients'. This leads to different varieties of dualisation with new and different insider/outsider divides in and between different welfare state regimes. Welfare states thus play a key role in managing the impacts of post-industrialisation.

> **Post-industrialisation** describes the shift from manufacturing to service- and knowledge-based economic activity.

Often considered 'a series of processes of integration that emerge from the exchange of ideas, goods and culture' (Artaraz and Hill, 2016: 17), globalisation captures various processes of change relating to: (1) the extension of social, economic and political activities beyond national borders, (2) the increasing scale of these activities, (3) the impacts stemming from these activities especially where national borders do not protect against events elsewhere and (4) the emergence of technical and other means which enable the changes outlined to occur (Held et al, 1999 in Artaraz and Hill, 2016). These processes of change are relevant to social policy in many respects, from the role of global policy actors and institutions to the impact on people and their well-being. The nation state, as the original bedrock of the welfare state, is also exposed to and involved in these processes of change associated with globalisation. Different perspectives have emerged on globalisation as it relates to welfare states and social policy development. These range from the view that globalisation causes welfare states to cut their spending resulting in a 'race to the bottom' (known as the efficiency hypothesis); to the view that welfare states use social expenditure to compensate for its effects (known as the compensatory hypothesis); to the view that the make-up of different welfare states and how they respond to globalisation means that globalisation has divergent impacts (Swank, 2010).

While the impact of globalisation on welfare states remains contested, economic globalisation has undoubtedly intensified this shift towards post-industrialism. **Economic globalisation** refers to the process whereby production, business and finance has become increasingly more mobile and internationalised. Hemerijck (2013) identifies five interrelated factors that have contributed to accelerated economic internationalisation since the 1980s; trade competition, the globalisation of finance, an austerity bias in macroeconomic policy, tax competition and the 'political logic' of globalisation, which is often brought to bear on domestic policies. This logic reflects the ability of powerful, often corporate, interests, to exert pressure on nation states to conform with its policy preferences, especially where the threat of capital mobility and relocation is considered to weaken the positions of trades unions and workers. Maintaining and improving international competitiveness is considered a key element of economic policy and the affordability of public services and a welfare state is increasingly framed by the imperative of competitiveness. The result can be that countries experience greater competition in attracting foreign investment and in honing the policy instruments used to maximise their competitive advantage. Recent political debates about corporate taxation regimes and their impacts illustrates the fallout at the level of the nation state. The US president Barack Obama brought attention to this issue during his presidency, highlighting how tax loopholes in other countries facilitate large US multinational corporations to avoid paying tax on their profits in the US.

> **Economic globalisation** describes the process whereby economies operate on a more open basis and are influenced by increasingly 'global' financial imperatives around trade, investment and competitiveness.

The globalisation of finance is best understood with reference to financialisation, which refers to the various ways in which finance has emerged at the centre of a structural change to capitalist economic development, particularly since the early

1980s when the conditions for greater financialisation intensified in liberal market economies. Deregulation brought about a decisive shift from long-established banking activities of deposits and loans to a more speculative approach to finance (Seguino, 2011). Powerful interests lobbied policy makers, resulting in a form of 'regulatory capture: public agencies charged with regulating in the public interest instead acted in favor of the financial sector (or turned a blind eye to the practices) they were charged with regulating' (Seguino, 2011: 2). Although less is known about the impact of financialisation outside of Anglo–American economies (Van der Zwan, 2014), and the scholarship around financialisation is still taking shape, there are elements of truth at its core. The global financial crisis put the spotlight on the dysfunctionality of contemporary capitalism (Streeck, 2014; Gamble, 2014). Specifically in relation to arguments made in financialisation studies, Van der Zwan (2014a: 120) notes that these 'have been vindicated by the subprime mortgage crisis of 2008' as it:

> exposed the shaky fundaments on which our economies are based: frantic trade in inscrutable financial products like derivatives and asset-backed security; a Wall Street bonus culture that incentivised risk-taking and speculation; predatory lending practices that convicted low- and middle-income individuals to a lifetime of debt; and lax oversight by government and private monitoring agencies, rife with conflicts of interest.

The documentary *Inside Job* (2010) and the film *The Big Short* (2015) provide some insights into this previously largely unexposed world.

Van der Zwan (2014) distinguishes three strands in the financialisation literature: a new regime of accumulation, the growth of the shareholder value orientation and the financialisation of everyday life. In the first approach, Krippner (2005: 174) describes 'a pattern of accumulation in which profits accrue primarily through financial channels rather than through trade and commodity production'. The substantial shift from productive activities to financial sector profit-making highlights the nature of the change in recent decades. The growth of shareholder value orientation refers to changes in corporate practices which intensified the need to maximise shareholder value, with concentration on short-term profits over stability, employment or the longer-term growth of the firm. Corporate governance and decision making became increasingly based on 'downsize and distribute' rather than 'retain and reinvest' (Lazonick and O'Sullivan 2000 in Stockhammer, 2010: 4). Clark (2015: 48) notes that by the 2000s 'the shareholder focus had diffused broadly across the whole economy, and companies had come to be seen as vehicles for maximising financial returns regardless of geographic location or the implications for domestic employment'. The implications are ones to which we have become accustomed: company profits are used to pay out higher dividends to shareholders, short-term financial gain is prized over the long-term development of non-financial companies and workers loose out to shareholders with job and wage cuts. These trends in turn impact on the share of income going to labour, which declined relative to capital.

In short, financialisation ultimately became a key enabler of the profit-led growth which began in the 1970s, as distinct from the wage-led growth of earlier years. The rising inequality it precipitated is aggravated by pressure to reduce government spending and the policy focus on inflation and interest rates with less attention to price stability and employment (Seguino, 2011). In this context, depressed wages meant that finance played a growing role in the form of debt accumulation among individuals and households (for example mortgages, loans to fund education and healthcare costs) but, on the flipside, finance also influenced household asset accumulation (life insurance, pensions, housing). In both ways, workers income became financialised, and a source of profit extraction for banks and other financial institutions (Lapavitsas, 2011), reflecting both the need for access to credit and the financialisation of everyday life.

Post-industrialisation, economic globalisation and financialisation capture something of the degree to which capitalism has changed in recent decades with precipitous consequences for the pressure for welfare state change. Ostensibly seen as exogenous or external challenges, as they have become embedded in contemporary capitalism the parameters of national macroeconomic policy have also been altered. This is not to say that, for example, globalisation causes welfare state change per se, rather the international political economy context in which welfare states exist are affected by its changed and multifaceted nature. In reality, the context in which states now operate and steer their economies has changed and 'national welfare states are no longer closed systems. More than ever, domestic social policy is conditioned by the parameters set by other countries' (Hemerijck, 2013: 52). European economic integration as it has evolved, has also become a major player in setting these parameters, as we discuss in Section Two.

Domestic challenges: the example of demography

What are often considered more endogenous, or domestic, drivers of welfare state pressure must also be examined: demographic, family and societal changes such as increased life expectancy, ageing populations, higher female labour market participation rates and differing family forms; and migration and cultural change, reflecting the range of new social risks (see Chapter Four) which challenge the efficacy of the traditional architecture of welfare states. To take just one, shifting demographic patterns, most notably declining fertility rates and increased life expectancy in advanced industrial countries have resulted in considerable focus on the capacity of welfare states to continue to fund the redistribution of resources between the generations (Gamble, 2016). Greater longevity, one of the key successes of the twentieth-century welfare state, is a problem for twenty-first century welfare states because of the reduced pool of workers available to fund the growing number of pensioners. Global (World Bank, OECD) and European (European Commission) policy actors feature prominently in diagnosing the problems and recommending policy reforms. The extent of the demographic change forecast for some European welfare states by the middle of this century has precipitated much concern about the long-term sustainability of some pension systems. Using a combination of policy measures including higher contribution requirements, tighter eligibility criteria for state pensions, increasing the retirement age and encouraging private pension provision, welfare states are engaging in pension system reform almost everywhere. Marketisation and privatisation have become a particularly notable aspect of pension reform in Europe (Ebbinghaus, 2015). In the case of pensions, at least, the social protection frameworks for old social risks are being reformed, even if the pace and scale of the reforms remain diverse and are more medium to long term in impact. The power of old social risks may make reform more difficult but it continues to happen. Pensions remain a massive policy headache, frequently assessed as a major drain on resources especially where future dependence on the state is considered unsustainable. However, increased marketisation and privatisation of pensions is a risky policy solution (as the massive losses sustained by private pension funds during the global financial crisis demonstrates). Robust state action and regulation is required which, as Crouch (2014: 18) warns, may present its own dangers as

> growing stress is placed on state regulation as a solution, to make private providers meet social expectation. The result is arguably less a privatization of pensions than a reconstruction of private provision to serve public purposes. However, the more the state directs private provider operations, the more likely it will be held responsible for future failures. Further, the pressure on fund managers for secure returns (passed on to traders as targets and benchmarks against which performance is assessed) feeds financial market instability, speeds up market trading ('the fidgeting fingers of the hidden hand'), fostering speculation, instability and possibly the next financial crash.

Domestic politics and institutions still matter, however, and can act as important mediating influences on how welfare states adapt. Existing and established approaches to national welfare matters also to how welfare state problem pressures are addressed. The role of national politics, key actors, veto players and alliances, administrative structures, pervading welfare ethos, in addition to the degree of economic development and the role(s) of the state are among the relevant factors which mediate the types of welfare settlements in place at national level. While accepting that no two welfare states are the same, given the unique features bound up in all of the above, testing the ideas associated with distinguishing between welfare regimes (see Boxes 6.1 and 6.2 for a brief overview), and how and why they change, has been a major focus of welfare state research over recent decades.

Welfare regimes: a brief overview

Box 6.1: Esping-Andersen's (1990) *Three Worlds of Welfare Capitalism*

Esping-Andersen's (1990) contribution remains the benchmark study of typologies of welfare (Box 6.1). Esping-Andersen (1990: 37) defined decommodification as 'the degree to which individuals, or families, can uphold a socially acceptable standard of living independently of market participation.' The other major element of his analysis is consideration of 'the welfare state as a system of stratification' by which is meant that the welfare state itself 'is not just a mechanism that intervenes in, and possibly corrects, the structure of inequality; it is, in its own right, a system of stratification. It is an active force in the ordering of social relations' (Esping-Andersen, 1990: 23). Taking three core elements of social security; pensions, sickness and unemployment arrangements, a decommodification index was generated to empirically analyse the extent to which welfare states decommodify, thus 'capturing the degree of market-independence for an average worker' (Esping-Andersen, 1990: 50).

- **Liberal welfare states** (the US, Canada and Australia) demonstrated a limited development of welfare rights, a strong emphasis on protection of the 'work-ethic', means-tested assistance and modest social insurance benefits with strict entitlement criteria leaving ample space for private/market-based welfare.
- **Conservative/corporatist cluster** (Germany, Austria, Italy and France) demonstrated the Christian democratic influence with a tendency towards subsidiarity but at the same time an acceptance of social rights, framed, first, in terms of social insurance, thereby limiting the redistributive capacity of the welfare state overall. Commitment to social insurance in a way that re-enforces the position of the traditional family.
- **Social democratic regime** (Sweden, Norway and Denmark) provides the highest level of social protection and had the greatest decommodifying capacity. Characterised by a high degree of universalism and a commitment to equality. Social insurance is solidaristic and universal 'yet benefits are graduated according to accustomed earnings' (Esping-Andersen, 1990: 28).

The identification of these welfare regimes provides a framework for understanding welfare states although as Esping-Andersen (1990: 28-9) himself notes:

> welfare states cluster, but we must recognize that there is no single pure case. The Scandinavian countries may be predominantly social democratic, but they are not free of crucial liberal elements. Neither are the liberal regimes pure types. The American social-security system is redistributive, compulsory and far from actuarial. At least in its early formulation, the New Deal was as social democratic as was contemporary Scandinavian social democracy. And European conservative regimes have incorporated both liberal and social democratic impulses. Over the decades, they have become less corporativist and less authoritarian.

Box 6.2: Aspects of the worlds of welfare debate

Considered to have 'become a classic' (Emmenegger et al, 2015: 3), Esping-Andersen's (1990) work has had a decisive impact on welfare state research whilst also generating much debate:

More than three worlds of welfare: Leibfried (1992) identifies the Scandinavian countries, the 'Bismarck' countries (Germany and Austria), Anglo-Saxon countries (US, UK, Australia and New Zealand) and the 'Latin-Rim' countries of Spain, Portugal, Greece, Southern Italy. The fourth type is distinguished by its residualism and the lack of an explicit right to welfare, influenced by traditional values and characterised as a 'rudimentary welfare state'. Ferrera (1996) similarly identifies a distinct 'Southern model' where relatively generous provisions exist in some areas (for example, pensions) while basic provisions for those without contributory-based entitlements are not necessarily assured. Kwon (1997) argued that although some similarities exist, Japan and Korea do not fit into the conservative welfare regime type and the case is made for a distinct East Asian welfare regime type. The challenges associated with welfare state 'typologising' are also evident when individual country cases are examined. Ireland proved difficult to classify, appearing across clusters. Arts and Gelissen (2002: 151) highlighted the 'hybrid cases' of the Netherlands and Switzerland. While Esping-Andersen's work remains a benchmark, subsequent research thus points to ways in which the worlds of welfare need to account for more and hybrid types of welfare states.

Women: Feminists note the extent to which the position of women was overlooked. The lack of attention to the value of unpaid work frequently carried out by women meant that 'concepts such as "decommodification" or "dependency" have a gendered meaning that is rarely acknowledged' and 'while Esping-Andersen (1990) writes of de-commodification as a necessary prerequisite for workers' political mobilization, the worker he has in mind is male and his mobilization may depend as much on unpaid female household labour as state policies' (Lewis, 1997: 161). Lewis drew on the male breadwinner model to demonstrate the differing extents to which women have had particular roles (and relationships with the labour market) assigned to them.

Care and family: Daly and Lewis (2000) highlighted the need to extend the analysis to include the concept of care, in a way that considers cash benefits, services and incorporates the different domains of care work; public, private, voluntary and informal. They also argued that inclusion of social care: 'can also enhance the quality and depth of welfare state analysis in general ... helping to overcome both the fragmentation in existing scholarship between the cash and service dimensions of welfare states and the relative neglect of the latter' (Daly and Lewis, 2000: 296). Jensen (2008: 152) argued for distinction between welfare arrangements that relate to decommodification and those that relate to defamilisation because 'even though both concepts actually refer to transfers as well as services ... it might be helpful to view decommodification as predominantly linked to transfers, and defamilization as predominantly linked to welfare services'.

Recent contributions also focus on methods and the distinction between welfare regimes as **typologies** (classifications based on specified empirical data) and **ideal-types** (theoretically based and which assess how/the degree to which a case corresponds or 'fits') (See Van Kersbergen, 2013, Van Kersbergen and Vis, 2015; Rice, 2013).

Responding to contemporary challenges: social investment as a new direction for welfare states?

There are several strands to the genesis of the social investment perspective, including the external and internal pressures on welfare states to adapt their social policies to the effects of globalisation and post-industrialisation together with the need to respond social needs and risks of typical late twentieth and early twenty-first century lifecourses and biographies. Additionally social investment as an emerging paradigm of model of social policy was crafted as a response to the dominance of neo-liberalism. Social Investment (SI) ideas emerged in the 1990s (Giddens, 1998; Esping-Andersen, 1999) and started to permeate European social policy discourse during the 2000s. The EU commissioned the *Why We Need A New Welfare State* (Esping-Andersen et al, 2002: 25) study which noted that 'the single greatest challenge we face today is how to rethink social policy so that, once again, labor markets and families are welfare optimizers and a good guarantee that tomorrow's adult workers will be as productive and resourceful as possible'. Essentially, it argued that 'the staying power of male-breadwinner employment-based social insurance increasingly fostered suboptimal life chances for large parts of the population' (Hemerijck, 2015: 245). Both the European Employment Strategy and the Lisbon Strategy drew on aspects of the SI agenda, most notably linking policies to tackle unemployment within an activation framework (Leoni, 2015).

The SI perspective underlines the productive capacity of social policy by seeking to promote policies which invest in human capital – people – with a view to maximising their potential. Social spending should therefore prioritise 'activating people ... to maintain responsibility for their well-being via market incomes, rather than towards passive benefits' (Morel et al, 2012: 9-10). Emphasis centres around policies that 'prepare' people for the risks attaching to contemporary society, via education, training, upskilling, early childhood supports, childcare and family supports, thereby promoting social inclusion and minimising the 'repair' functions considered a less desirable by-product of the traditional welfare state. Jenson (2012) considers SI a new paradigm with ideas, means and goals that are distinct from both Keynesianism and neo-liberalism. In short, SI advocates a shift from passive to active social policies in which greater prominence is given to equality of opportunity, meeting lifecycle needs and on the 'carrying capacity' (Hemerijck, 2015) of the welfare state for future productive generations via an enabling and activating welfare state. SI views social policy as an essential precondition for economic growth and stresses its productive potential, providing an economic rationale for state investment in people, moulded to meet the changed needs of the twenty-first century.

A burgeoning literature is emerging on the SI perspective and there are many questions that remain to be considered. On the one hand, SI ideas have taken root in important domains such as labour market activation and in respect of family policy in some countries in Europe. SI-directed policies were already well established in the Nordic countries, with a long-standing preference towards comprehensive childcare provisions, progressive family supports, significant investment in education and life-long learning alongside decent minimum income supports. Some recent SI-type policies have been identified in countries such as Austria, France, Germany, Slovenia and the Netherlands, while another group which includes the UK and Ireland lacks an integrated SI approach although new targeted policy initiatives have been introduced. A third cluster of countries displays least evidence of an SI orientation including Greece, Italy and many of the post-communist member states of the EU (Hemerijck, 2015). While many of the challenges outlined are common to all, it is likely that just as welfare states do not conform to a uniform type, adoption of SI ideas is also likely to give rise to distinct variants of SI into the future.

It may be that the infiltration of SI ideas into the European policy mainstream now amounts to the establishment of a social investment paradigm 'in a rather quiet but nonetheless robust manner over the past two decades across Europe' (Hemerijck, 2015: 244). However, critical issues remain in relation to the SI perspective which have potentially far-reaching implications for future welfare reforms and the wider attributed role of social policy. Concerns with the SI perspective highlight significant welfare dilemmas including: (1) insufficient attention to poverty, class inequality, the position of vulnerable groups and redistribution in the present (see Cantillon, 2011), (2) an instrumentalist approach to female employment which undermines any notion of a gender inclusive citizenship (see Saraceno, 2015) and (3) emphasis on the investment components of social expenditure, runs the risk of weakening welfare efforts thought not to produce a return in economic terms (see Nolan, 2013). Relatedly, the emphasis on productive social policies may help to provide economic justification for new welfare measures, especially for politicians, but it does not do enough to validate important existing protective welfare provisions that do not fall under the remit of social investment.

It is likely that the emergence of the SI perspective will be considered a positive and viable policy alternative by many, especially given the predominance of neo-liberal imperatives in shaping the welfare reform agenda over recent decades. However, Pierson's (2001) assertion that welfare states would continue to face significant pressures and would likely operate in a 'context of permanent austerity' has proved prescient and remains relevant. This is demonstrated in national and European welfare debates, especially where the impact of deepening economic integration presents considerable challenges in managing national economic and social policies particularly given the fiscal restraints imposed by governments as a policy response to the Great Recession. The use of austerity policies as a solution to the problems brought about by the financial crisis has not been uniform across welfare states, as discussed in Chapter Four. However, the impact of economic integration, particularly for member states of the EMU, and the fiscal and budgetary requirements therein, have a notable impact on the adaptive capacity and autonomy of welfare states. It is to the theme of social policy and the EU to which we now turn.

SECTION TWO

SOCIAL POLICY AND THE EU: FROM SUBSIDIARITY, TO FISCAL SURVEILLANCE, ECONOMIC STABILITY AND SOCIAL INVESTMENT?

Founded in the 1950s with six member states, the European Economic Community (EEC) sought to expand trade links and to build on the objectives of the European Coal and Steel Community. The Treaty of Rome, signed in 1957, provided the legal framework for the EEC and the establishment of its various institutions. Articles 117–28 of the Treaty covered specified social policy matters; these promoted member state cooperation in areas of employment, training, working conditions, social security, collective bargaining and the principle of equal pay (Hantrais, 2008). However, apart from the equal pay principle, these were not legally binding and overall 'social policy was considered as an adjunct to economic policy' (European Parliament, 2004).

The Social Action Programme was set up in 1974 in response to a call for action from some heads of state. The programme was 'designed to achieve the three goals of full and better employment; an improvement in living and working conditions; and greater involvement of management and labour' (Kleinman, 2002: 85). A number of European poverty programmes were established from 1975 (1975-80, 1985-89, 1989-94), which, while limited in terms of their overall impact, raised the profile of issues of poverty and social exclusion at EU level. At national level, the evolution of these programmes contributed to the development of different approaches to tackling poverty and social exclusion, such as support for community development and area-based initiatives (Frazer, 2007). Separately, a series of directives (legally binding on all member states and enforceable in law) on equal treatment (arising out of Article 119 of the Treaty of Rome) delivered during the 1970s and 1980s were crucial to the development of the principle of gender equality. Therefore, the defining features of emergent EU social policy can be identified in terms of: a concern with social cohesion in tandem with economic development; equal access to protection, rights and equity within the

> **EU subsidiarity** seeks to ensure that interventions come primarily from the 'national' domain. This protects the primacy of member states' rights to shape and manage their own policy affairs, unless agreement to the contrary is reached.

workplace and investment and support for local and regional disadvantaged areas.

In overall terms, **subsidiarity** is considered a core guiding principle in the operation of the EU, which was formally set out as such in the Maastricht Treaty (1992). Adherence to this principle largely maintains the status of national social policy. Subsidiarity is also considered necessary, in Delors' (cited in Rayle, 2015) words, 'to preserve our roots in the shape of our nations and regions.' In short, the EU can only act 'when its aims can be better achieved at European rather than at national level, and the burden of proof is on the European institutions to show that action is necessary at that level, and also to show that binding instruments are necessary rather than support measures and framework directives' (Kleinman, 2002: 90).

The (uneven) development of EU social policy

During the late 1980s, the Commission president Jacques Delors was keen to develop a more social Europe alongside the development of the single European market as initiated through the Single European Act 1986. On the social policy front, the Council of Ministers adopted a resolution to combat social exclusion; member states were to review their policies and the Commission was to monitor developments via the Observatory on National Policies to Combat Social Exclusion (Ó Cinnéide, 2010). Developments such as the Community Charter of Basic Social Rights for Workers in 1989 was to go some way towards 'a more balanced integration process' (Copeland, 2015: 97). Noted for its recognition of workers' rights and the rights of men and women on an equal basis, the Charter also marked the first recognition of the rights of older people and people with disabilities at this level (Harvey, 2003). However, references to citizens, as opposed to workers, evident in earlier drafts, did not appear in the final version (Hantrais, 2000). Although the Charter was not binding (and was vetoed by the UK government), the Commission was tasked with devising an action plan for implementation of aspects within the EU's remit. Progress was mixed (and the UK negotiated several exceptions) but over the longer term it resulted in a number of important social policy directives on working time, the safety of pregnant workers and young workers (Anderson, 2015). Another illustration of the tensions between member states around EU competency in matters of social policy arose when proposals for a fourth European Poverty Programme were opposed by the UK and Germany. When the Commission proposed in early 1995 that it would grant-aid some of the Programme the issue was referred to the European Court of Justice who ruled that the Commission was in breach of Article 4(1) in committing to the expenditure and thus was to be cancelled (Ó Cinnéide, 2010).

In contrast to the still-evolving scope of EU competency in matters of social policy, the development of closer economic and monetary integration moved apace throughout the 1990s. The Treaty on European Union (Maastricht Treaty), set the framework for EMU and included formal convergence criteria for member states in the lead up to full EMU which included: inflation rates of not more than 2%-3%, managing deficit reductions, improving competitiveness and requiring government deficits be limited to 3% of GDP and government debt be kept under 60% of GDP. The Stability and Growth Pact (SGP) introduced in 1997 sought to strengthen oversight of these requirements. However, these were not always adhered to and became a source of controversy during the 2000s, when France and Germany were in breach of the SGP and the EC's recommendation to take sanctions against them was rejected by EU finance ministers.

Considered something of a high point in terms of developing a social agenda for the EU, the Amsterdam Treaty 1997 provided some strengthening of the social objectives with the inclusion of established areas such as employment, vocational training, education, young people and equal pay along with developing equality objectives particularly gender 'mainstreaming', equal opportunities and equal treatment and combating discrimination. It also provided official recognition of the European objective to combat social exclusion and the possibility of initiating programmes in this regard. At the same time, slow economic growth rates, ageing populations and rising unemployment meant that the impact of post-industrialisation and economic globalisation became particularly evident in a number of member states and employment trends and prospects became a central focus. The European Employment Strategy (EES) was launched following the inclusion of employment as a 'common concern' in the Amsterdam Treaty and the Luxembourg Jobs Summit held in 1997. The objectives of the EES included a commitment to a high level of employment in the EU and the establishment of various structures including an Employment Committee and a 'country surveillance procedure' to monitor and offer guidance and recommendations on the basis of the National Action Plans on Employment submitted by the member states. The EES objectives were initially formulated with attention to four pillars: employability, entrepreneurship, adaptability and equal opportunities. The first of these reflected the growing focus on activation policies. The second pillar focused on supporting the efforts of new and small businesses to maximise their potential for growth and development. Adaptability refers to the objective of 'modernising work organisation' to develop and upgrade the skills of workers and to promote efficiency. The availability of childcare, career breaks, part-time work and parental leave was identified to support the increasing employment rates of women and equal opportunities. The European Social Fund (ESF) was the major funding source for initiatives in these areas.

The Lisbon Strategy marks another chapter in the uneven history of social policy in the EU. The ambitious objective arising from the Lisbon European Council in 2000 was that, by 2020, the EU would be 'the most competitive and dynamic knowledge-based economy in the world capable of sustainable economic growth with more and better jobs and greater social cohesion'. Economic, employment and social policy were formally brought together in what became known as the 'Lisbon triangle' (and to which the environmental pillar was added in 2001). Targets were set to increase the employment rate within the EU to 70%, a 60% target for women and a 50% target for older workers (55–64 years) was also added in 2001. In terms of poverty and social inclusion, the Lisbon Strategy agreed 'on the need to take steps to make a decisive impact on the eradication of poverty' (Council of the European Union, 2002: 4). Four Common Objectives were put forward: (1) to facilitate participation in employment and access by all to resources, rights, goods and services, (2) to prevent the risks of exclusion, (3) to help the most vulnerable and (4) to mobilise all relevant bodies.

By 2005 however, given poor economic growth and a critical review of its implementation, the Lisbon Strategy was relaunched, with a revised focus. Greater emphasis was placed on the need to strengthen the bases for economic growth; new guidelines produced on economic and employment policy excluded attention to social exclusion, which was to be dealt with separately. In terms of social policy, Daly (2008) highlighted the shift away from social exclusion, the conceptual preference for 'active social inclusion' and the lack of attention to preventive measures. Dieckhoff and Gallie (2007: 499) noted that 'the reformed Lisbon processes led to few policy initiatives that could be expected to make a significant reduction in the vulnerability of the socially disadvantaged.' The relaunch of Lisbon was also critically assessed for its focusing 'on competitiveness at the expense of social and environmental issues' (Magnusson, 2010: 18). Overall, while the EES and the ideas behind the original Lisbon Strategy were broadly considered a belated yet ambitious attempt to develop the architecture for the social dimension of the EU, final assessments were much less positive. Sluggish economic growth rates coupled with the unfolding impact of the financial crisis meant that when the Swedish prime minister, Fredrik Reinfeldt, described the Lisbon Strategy as a 'failure' in 2009, it was an assessment he could proffer 'without fear of contradiction' (Teasdale, 2012), given that its targets were not in sight of being reached and the financial crisis was setting objectives back further.

Despite pessimism about the overall direction and achievements of the Lisbon Strategy, it did bring certain innovations in EU modes of governance relevant to social policy, most notably the Social **Open Method of Coordination** (OMC). First officially unveiled in the context of Lisbon and since revised, the Social OMC provided a forum for social policy dialogue in which policy dissemination and learning could take place. National Action Plans/Reports submitted by member states were evaluated by the Commission and the Council and a Joint Report issued providing a synthesis of the position across the member states on a range of issues, highlighting priorities in key areas and noting examples of good

> The **open method of coordination** refers to the process whereby member states monitor policy developments, targets and outcomes through cooperation and in 'non-directive' terms.

practice. In this context, peer review and mutual policy learning was seen on the one hand as a particularly innovative element of the OMC. Yet others remain critical of this 'soft' approach to policy making, which is not legally binding and does not have any sanctions attached, unlike areas of economic policy.

Following some initial lack of clarity regarding the role of the Social OMC in Europe 2020, the process is now overseen by the Social Protection Committee (an EU advisory policy committee for Employment and Social Affairs Ministers in the Employment and Social Affairs Council) and is understood as 'a voluntary process for political cooperation based on agreeing common objectives and measuring progress towards these goals using common indicators. The process also involves close co-operation with stakeholders, including Social Partners and civil society'.[1] Member states prepare National Social Reports covering policy developments in the areas of social inclusion, health and long-term care and pensions.

Europe 2020 was launched in 2010 against the backdrop of the global financial crisis and recession. Its strategic objective is to make the EU a 'smart, sustainable and inclusive economy, delivering high levels of employment, productivity and social cohesion' and it 'sets out a vision of Europe's social market economy for the 21st century' (EC, 2010: 3). Considered as mutually reinforcing priorities, the Strategy sets out five headline targets (Box 6.3) and member states set national targets, the progression of which is monitored via the European Semester (discussed in the next section). Seven flagship initiatives are included in Europe 2020 reflecting the emphasis on growth and jobs in the smart, sustainable and inclusive economy.

Box 6.3: Europe 2020 headline targets

Employment:
• 75% of 20- to 64-year-old men and women to be employed

Research and development:
• 3% of GDP to be invested in this sector

Climate change and energy sustainability:
• Reduce greenhouse gas emissions by 20% compared to 1990 levels
• Increase the share of renewables in final energy consumption to 20%
• Increase energy efficiency by 20%

Education:
• Reduce the rates of early school leaving to below 10%
• At least 40% of 30- to 34-year-olds to have completed tertiary or equivalent education

Fighting poverty and social exclusion:

• Reduce poverty by lifting at least 20 million people out of the risk of poverty and social exclusion

Widely regarded as laudable, many welcomed the specificity attaching to the Europe 2020 objectives, the explicit target in respect of poverty and social exclusion and so on. However, the wider crisis context seems not to have been absorbed in the framing of overarching economic and social objectives for the 2010s. Europe 2020 reads as a continuation of the Lisbon Strategy and lessons of its weaknesses appear not to have been learned. Its strategic objective is noted to be 'extremely close to the famous slogan of the Lisbon Strategy, except that, interestingly, the reference to job quality has been dropped, replaced by productivity' (Peña-Casas, 2013: 132). Furthermore, de la Porte and Heins (2015: 24) argue that as 'the instrument designed to coordinate employment and social policy and further develop the European Social Model', Europe 2020 'is comparatively weak compared with the sharpened objectives, surveillance and enforcement mechanisms in EMU'. In this regard, Copeland and Daly (2014: 358) identify 'a hierarchy of priorities in which some objectives are deemed more important than others'. They point to the low priority accorded to monitoring the poverty targets, evidenced in the absence of any reference to them in the Annual Growth Surveys (AGS) (except in the Annex) for 2011 and 2012. Since 2013 there are some tentative signs that social policy priorities are gaining visibility in AGSs and that key policy actors such as the Employment and Social Protection Committees sought to strengthen their analytical tools, such as the introduction of scoreboard of key economic and social indicators, and new social reporting initiatives. Overall, the evolution of EU social policy reflects what Hemerijck (2013: 292) terms 'the "double bind" of social Europe, an institutional predicament or catch-22 that immediately follows from the twofold commitment to domestic social protection and European market integration'. Overcoming this conundrum presents a monumental challenge to the EU especially in a crisis context, which has generated much uncertainty accompanied by an unprecedented lack of confidence in the EU.

European leaders have indicated that more needs to be done to improve the application of subsidiarity in practice. In this regard, the European Commission President Jean-Claude Juncker, 2014, notes that 'What we are doing, however, is not sufficient. Our speeches last longer than our efforts to make real headway in reducing red tape, and to ensure that the European Commission – and the European Union – concerns itself with the really major European issues instead of interfering from all angles in every detail of people's lives'. Even if the principle of subsidiarity is revamped to shore up presently ailing support for the EU among its citizens, there is a wider tension of most relevance to the 19 Euro Area (EA) member states which may be most difficult to resolve. Greater European economic integration brought with it a 'constitutional asymmetry' (Scharpf, 2002: 645), in which,

National welfare states are legally and economically constrained by European rules of economic integration, liberalisation and competition law, whereas efforts to adopt European social policies are politically impeded by the diversity of national welfare states, differing not only in levels of economic development and hence in their ability to pay for social transfers and services but, even more significantly, in their normative aspirations and institutional structures.

The Euro crisis subsequently laid bare the consequences of this asymmetry.

The Euro crisis: policy responses and implications for social policy

Several years on, the Euro crisis which (formally) began in 2008, remains on the horizon, with continuing economic and social implications for EU citizens. Job losses, indebtedness, lack of work, benefit cuts, housing difficulties, problems accessing affordable education, health and social care are but some of the social consequences, even if this reality is not adequately captured in the overarching narrative of the crisis. At the macroeconomic level, the crisis precipitated prolonged recession followed by modest economic growth and while unemployment has declined, youth unemployment remains a particularly intractable problem, particularly in Southern Europe. In this section, we briefly outline the emergence of and policy responses to the Euro crisis before noting some persistent problems and prospects for the future.

The global financial crisis that first emerged in the US in 2007 marked the first warning sign that deregulation of banking and lending activities, the easy availability of credit and greater financialisation in increasingly liberalised market economies could trigger a full-blown crisis and recession. Deeper economic integration and more integrated money markets post-EMU meant that, in Europe too, banks and financial institutions were free to extend their lending and borrowing capacities. This unprecedented level of access to borrowing via money markets was largely unproblematised and was more often seen as a positive by-product of financialisation. In European terms, economic balances within the Euro area masked significant imbalances within it where, for example, smaller banks could readily access funds from larger financial institutions in Europe. A strong flow of funds from the banks of core Euro countries (Germany, France, Austria, Belgium and the Netherlands) to banks of so-called peripheral ones (Greece, Ireland, Italy, Spain and Portugal) meant that the 'interlinkage between core-nation banks and periphery-nation borrowers created one of the fragilities that made the Crisis politically difficult to manage' (Baldwin et al, 2015: 7). This exposed design flaws in EMU which did not adequately monitor cross-border activities of the banks. More generally, as Nicaise and Schepers (2013: 198) note, 'for an economic and monetary union to function well, it must have some means of dealing with divergent developments among its Member States. ... This necessity had been ignored when designing the monetary union'. Divergence, national growth strategies and different models of capitalism were also a factor underpinning the extent to which some countries were at risk (Hall, 2014; Verdun, 2013), as exemplified by the Irish case (Dukelow and Considine, 2014a).

By mid-2008, a number of banks had to be bailed out by their governments, significantly increasing their national debt. Confidence in global financial markets began to dissipate, 'the European financial system appeared increasingly fragile, panic broke out in the stock market, market valuations of financial institutions evaporated and interbank lending practically ceased' (Copeland, 2015: 100). The early EU policy response (2008-09) was actually countercyclical; the ECB provided liquidity for EA banks and the European Economic Recovery Plan allowed for deficits to go above 3% to stimulate investment, protect **automatic stabilisers** and support employment schemes, representing a 'short-lived Keynesian moment to stabilize the economy to buffer the downturn' (Hemerijck, 2016: 30). This approach was not to last.

> **Automatic stabilisers** refer to existing tax and welfare programmes/transfers and budget initiatives which can lessen the impact of economic fluctuations.

When Greece announced the true size of its government deficit in 2009, already jittery markets began to consider if other nations were also at risk. The result was a '"sudden stop" in cross-border lending' (Baldwin et al, 2015: 2) that laid bare the scale to which overextended banks could no longer borrow on the international money markets and the ECB had to become their lender of last resort. A private debt and banking crisis became a sovereign debt crisis when some governments (notably Ireland) took on the debts of their banks. Despite common misconceptions, the Euro crisis was not caused by out of control public debt levels, they became unmanageable where substantial private bank losses were taken on by the state. In fact, the debt-to-GDP ratio of Euro countries declined from 72% in 1999 to 66% in 2007 and both Ireland and Spain 'were paragons of fiscal rectitude' with ratios well below the 60% Maastricht limit in 2007 (Baldwin et al, 2015: 5).

De Grauwe (2013: 15) explains the wider consequences of misdiagnosing the causes of the crisis:

> the diagnosis that was made by the Eurozone leaders, i.e. the German government, the ECB and the European Commission, is that government profligacy was to blame. The effect of this misdiagnosis was that budgetary austerity was imposed as the cure to solve the crisis. … the Southern Eurozone countries that were forced to swallow most of the wrong medicine pushed their economies in deep economic depressions. The latter, instead of improving the fiscal situations of the governments of these countries made these worse. It also led to an increasing social and political rejection of the austerity strategy and weakened the social acceptability of the Eurozone itself.

When Euro Area countries found themselves in difficulty pre-existing structural EMU weakness was again exposed; these governments effectively had no lender of last resort, nor was the option of devaluation available to them (Baldwin et al, 2015). Faced with the risk of contagion and the prospect of insolvent states within the Euro Area, EU leaders, the EU, and especially the institutions charged with responsibility for EMU, were plunged into a crisis for which a set of policy responses had to be developed (Table 6.1). After some deliberation and much criticism for its lack of decisive action, a major but largely one directional procyclical policy response began to emerge. The European Financial Stability Facility (EFSF) was established in 2010, providing a temporary mechanism through which member states requiring support could enter a Programme of Financial Assistance which was 'offered within the framework of a macroeconomic adjustment programme' (Verdun, 2015: 226). Finance was made available via the European Commission, the ECB and the IMF (the Troika) based on Memoranda of Understanding drawn up with the individual member states containing detailed policy objectives and timelines for their implementation, closely monitored by the country representatives of the Troika. The loan facility to Greece in May 2010 supplied the template for the EFSF (Verdun, 2015). Ireland subsequently entered a Programme of Financial Assistance in November 2010, followed by Portugal in 2011 and Cyprus in 2012. The EFSF was replaced by a permanent European Stability Mechanism (ESM) in 2012. Efforts by the ECB to stem the crisis were also stepped up through a bond purchasing programme with Mario Draghi announcing that the ECB was ready to do 'whatever it takes to preserve the euro' (in Copelovitch et al, 2016: 816). In addition to reforms in the banking sector, a wider set of macroeconomic and budgetary EU oversight measures (the Six-Pack, the Two-Pack, the Fiscal Compact and the European Semester) were introduced between 2010 and 2013 to strengthen the requirements of the SGP and put in place more robust fiscal rules and tighter budgetary surveillance of EA member states (see Table 6.1 for details).

The **European Semester** refers to the cycle of macroeconomic surveillance undertaken by the Commission, the role of the European Council, member states and the European Parliament. The European Semester has a significant impact on both the macroeconomic objectives and timeframe of the budget making processes of member states. Implementation of Country Specific Recommendations has however been variable (see Gros and Alcidi, 2015). First introduced in 2010, the European Semester was revised in 2016 on foot of the Five Presidents' Report (Juncker et al, 2015).

The Five Presidents' Report (Juncker et al, 2015) essentially sets out their vision for the future of EMU and its staged completion over the coming decade.

> **European semester** is part of the governance framework of the EU which incorporates an annual programme of macroeconomic policy coordination and surveillance. The European Commission examines fiscal and structural reform programmes, issues recommendations and monitors implementation in all member states.

Stage 1 (2015-17) seeks to make best use of existing structures to enhance 'competitiveness and structural convergence, completing the Financial Union, achieving and maintaining responsible fiscal policies at national and euro area level, and enhancing democratic accountability' (Juncker et al, 2015: 5). Stage 2 (2017 onwards) suggests further more substantive action to be agreed, particularly around the convergence process, to complete the institutional structures of EMU. Stage 3, that is complete EMU, is to be achieved by 2025 at the latest. Taking this longer-term view, the Report provides important insights for what EA member states should expect in return for their participation in EMU over the coming years. Reissl and Stockhammer (2016) assert that the Report 'represents the most comprehensive single statement by the European institutions thus far about the direction EMU should be heading' although their assessment does not provide much grounds for optimism regarding the future of a more social Europe.

Taking a wider view of EU policy developments over the last decade, it is difficult to discern any certainty about the prospects for a social Europe, or even an EU with a robust social policy focus. Much concern arises from the ultimate priority presently accorded to fiscal and budgetary discipline above all other policy objectives. This priority has been (re)operationalised via the major policy instruments developed since 2010 (Table 6.1). Copeland (2015: 94) asserts that the single market and EMU have been privileged since their introduction resulting in an 'asymmetrical system of governance' in which social and employment standards were worn down over time. In responding to the Euro crisis, monetary integration via budgetary and fiscal discipline has become 'the EU's first-order priority' (Copeland, 2015: 102), the single European market is second, employment policy third and social policy comes as a fourth priority in this hierarchy. The result is that 'the social dimension has shifted from a historic "add-on" to economic integration, to that of "dependence upon" economic objectives' (Copeland, 2015: 102). Essentially, recent EU governance reforms have resulted in 'a shift of political power from the Member States to the EU' with political consequences inevitable from this 'massive transfer of power' (Natali, 2013: 253). The strengthened role of the Commission in budgetary and fiscal surveillance is a particular focus in this power shift. In this regard, Crespy and Menz (2015: 761-2) take the view that 'the Commission has actively contributed to shaping and enforcing austerity policies' and has also ultimately contributed 'to the further subordination of social policy objectives to the reduction of the public deficit, thus rendering their achievement de facto nearly impossible'. Accepting this as a possibility puts the political consequences of the crisis and recent reforms into sharper focus. Hemerijck (2016: 46) draws attention to two particular political problems pressures:

> First, there is the overarching challenge to keep the single currency afloat. Economic divergences and social imbalances can still undermine the sustainability of EMU. The second conundrum concerns the populist temptation of national welfare chauvinist closure. An honest

Table 6.1: Major fiscal and economic policy responses to the Euro Crisis, 2010-16

Facility	Mandate	Characteristics of this institution (scope) and Contents of agreement
Greek Loan FacilityMay 2010	Provide loans to EA member state in need (in first instance: Greece).	Memorandum of understanding signed by EA member states. Commission coordinates and disburses the bilateral loans (provided by member states). IMF also contributes.
European Financial Stability Facility June 2010	Safeguard financial stability in the EU by providing financial assistance to EA countries.	A special purpose vehicle that serves as a temporary rescue mechanism. Provides financial assistance to EA member states within the framework of a macroeconomic adjustment programme. No new financing programmes after July 2013 but continued the ongoing programmes for Greece, Portugal and Ireland.
European Stability Mechanism October 2012	Safeguard financial stability in the EU by providing financial assistance to EA countries.	Permanent rescue mechanism. Issues debt instruments to finance loans and other financial instruments to EA member states. Intergovernmental organisation under public law. From November 2014, with the single supervisory mechanism in place, it may recapitalise banks directly.
Six-Pack December 2011	Strengthens the SGP (stricter application of fiscal rules and greater macroeconomic surveillance).	Five regulations and a directive (EU Secondary Law). Defines deviation from the Medium Term Objectives; focuses more on the debt than the earlier SGP did. Financial sanctions more gradual. Reverse qualified majority vote is introduced. This vote is needed for the Council to reverse a Commission recommendation or proposal otherwise it is adopted.
European Semester September 2010	Coordinate economic policy; ensure member states meet objectives.	European Commission adopts Annual Growth Survey; European Council provides policy orientations; member states submit their economic plans; Commission makes detailed analysis of member states' economic programmes and offers recommendations for the next 12-18 months (discussed by Council; endorsed by the European Council); formal adoption of country-specific recommendation by Council.
Two-Pack May 2013	Improve budgetary surveillance procedure (early warning system for budgets of EA member states).	Two regulations; the first one is addressed to all EA member states; the second facilitates enhanced surveillance for EA member states facing budgetary difficulties. They introduce a common budgetary timeline.
Fiscal Compact or 'Fiscal stability treaty' January 2013	Signatory states agree to alter national laws so as to ensure they limit their budgetary deficits.	Stricter version of the SGP. Commitment by Member States to amend national laws to ensure budgetary deficits remain below 0.5% of GDP or less than 1.0% of GDP if their debt/GDP ratio is significantly below 60%.

Source: adapted from Verdun (2015)

recognition of the economic, social and political limits of austerity reform, on the one hand, and the full recognition of the positive track record of social investment innovation, on the other hand, are sine qua non for constructing an overlapping political consensus in the political centre of a currency union based on an employment-friendly macroeconomic 'holding environment' that allows EMU and active European welfare states to prosper in tandem.

Continued divergence in the economic, fiscal and social profiles of member states is inevitable in the absence of policy reform which specifically addresses this reality. Such a reform move would be politically contentious, especially in the context of rising national welfare chauvinism and diminished confidence in the EU but neither problem can be addressed without significant political action and leadership. The economic crisis resulted in a political crisis and ultimately, as Hall (2014: 1259) asserts, a 'legitimacy crisis', evident in the rise in Euroscepticism, decline in support for its open borders where 'it has become harder for ordinary people, as well as observers, to discern just what the European Union stands for' (Hall, 2014: 1239). He suggests that those advocating 'more Europe' need to explain what this would actually mean. As Hall (2014: 1239) concludes, 'the motto of the EU is not "uniformity" but, rather, "unity in diversity" – and the future of European integration will depend on Europe's capacity to give substance to that slogan'.

Finally, recent evaluations of the social dimension of the European Semester (Zeitlin and Vanhercke, 2015; Vanhercke et al, 2015) find 'a partial but progressive "socialization" of the Semester, in terms both of its substantive policy content and of its governance procedures' (Vanhercke et al, 2015: 21) since 2011. Aspects of the AGS 2016 (EC, 2015: 9) may be considered somewhat encouraging although framed in terms of labour market participation; it contains reference to social investment in healthcare, childcare, housing support and rehabilitation services, in order 'to strengthen people's current and future capacities to engage in the labour market and adapt'. In terms of social protection, the AGS (EC, 2015: 12) states that 'more effective social protection systems are needed to confront poverty and social exclusion, while preserving sustainable public finances and incentives to work'. Activation is clearly the primary objective, but decent jobs need to exist too. Better implementation and monitoring of the Europe 2020 goals are also highlighted as an objective of the Commission to be achieved via the European Semester. Overall though, even sanguine assessments of the future of social Europe remain, at best, guarded, circumspect and only cautiously hopeful of a breakthrough. Given the policy priorities and hierarchy attaching to recent EU governance reforms and the political and legitimacy problems that pervade, it seems that the idea that 'Europe's ambition should be to earn a "social triple A"' (Juncker et al, 2015: 8) remains a distinct prospect for now.

SECTION THREE
CHALLENGES AND CONTRADICTIONS IMPINGING ON THE IRISH WELFARE STATE

Utilising some of the relevant drivers and pressures on welfare states identified earlier in the chapter, in this section we focus on key economic, political and institutional intersections that have impacted upon the Irish social policy landscape to further our understanding of the competing challenges that Ireland's welfare state future is faced with.

'Ireland: still riding the globalisation wave'[2]?

Ireland has ranked highly in economic globalisation indicators since the 1990s and the development of pro-globalisation policies have over time become deeply embedded in Ireland's growth strategy. The comparatively early policy strategy of making and maintaining Ireland as a key site for foreign direct investment placed it 'well ahead of the field' (Ruane and Görg, 1997: 20). Even so, pursuit of this policy objective, which began in the late 1950s, did not protect against economic cycles of boom and bust that have characterised the Irish economy over recent decades, the social and economic consequences of which are discussed in Chapters Two and Three. The intensification of competitiveness pressures during the 1990s outlined earlier also applied in the Irish case and the role of the state has been crucial in mediating the changing dynamics of contemporary capitalism.

Internally, the national policy-making framework of social partnership that emerged in response to the economic crisis of the 1980s subsequently developed alongside Ireland's rapid economic growth, but largely operated within the policy parameters of the dominant and increasingly neo-liberal economic paradigm, until it collapsed in 2009. Never an equal partnership, government was central to its operation and continuity. The Irish version of social partnership was notably different from more robust models of corporatism operating elsewhere in Europe, not least because, 'the "Celtic Tiger" boom coupled with a quasi-corporatist partnership regime obscured the extent of Ireland's integration with global neo-liberal structures' (McDonough and Dundon, 2010: 544).

Much has changed in Ireland and elsewhere since Esping-Andersen's (1990) study of welfare regimes, in which Ireland failed to rank in a way that was consistent with the worlds of welfare identified. Displaying both liberal and corporatist features, Cochrane (1993: 15) described the Irish welfare state as 'an uneasy mix of corporatism and liberalism'. Ginsburg (2001) considered that Ireland displayed some characteristics associated with the Southern European model in terms of its economic development, Catholic influence and the role of the voluntary sector in social service provision while also demonstrating a liberal orientation similar to Britain with comparable use of means-testing and poverty levels. In respect of economic globalisation, Ginsburg (2001: 183) noted how in the cases of both Ireland and Britain 'they certainly have many liberal features that have been enhanced by their state-sponsored exposure to economic globalisation since the 1980s'. Earlier in this chapter we noted various perspectives on globalisation and the welfare state. One such view highlights the role of national policy in globalising processes in which, as Yeates (2007: 631) asserts, 'states have not been idle, passive, powerless actors in these processes. Indeed, different states have enthusiastically followed pro-globalization policies'. In the Irish case, the state has been an active player in the development of pro-globalisation policies to underpin this component of Ireland's growth strategy. Ireland, never a fully industrialised economy in the first place, made strategic moves to develop its readiness for the shift from industry to services and in particular it embraced the liberalisation of international markets associated with the 1990s wave of financialisation. Light touch regulation and a favourable tax regime provided ideal conditions for such services to locate in Ireland (Considine and Dukelow, 2014). A recent globalisation study makes specific mention of 'the importance of Ireland's capital, Dublin, as a financial centre means that the country is in a top ranking position in terms of international capital flows' (Böhmer et al, 2016: 11).

Considered the 'poorest of the rich' in Europe in the 1980s (The Economist, 1988), a 'Celtic tiger' in the 1990s (Gardiner, 1994 in O'Hearn, 1997), Ireland featured as 'Erin go broke' (Krugman, 2009) in the New York Times in 2009 and was labelled 'the comeback kid of Europe's crisis-hit economies' (Gurria in Barber, 2016) by the head of the OECD in 2016. These headlines provide a snapshot of the serious boom–bust cycles that have characterised the Irish economy in recent decades. As a small, open and globalised economy, it is noteworthy that not much attention is given to the vulnerability and risks inherent to the Irish growth model (Kirby, 2010). Globalisation and the processes therein have been, and remain, relatively uncontested in the political and public domains in Ireland. Antoniades (2007: 314) notes how 'the main "objects" of economic globalisation (e.g. deregulation, privatisation, tax cuts) were ever-present in Irish politics. Yet, these objects did not define a new zone of contestation, but rather a set of taken-for-granted policies and practices'. This remains the case in terms of post-crisis policy. The largely benign interpretation of economic globalisation has additionally been framed in terms of opportunity that must be taken; Ireland needs to be prepared to take advantage of via attractive corporation tax rates and honed policy instruments which maximise Ireland's competitive advantage for foreign direct investment. Much less consideration is given to the related exposure to global market volatility and risk. There continues to be little critical scrutiny of the state's approach to globalisation, not to mention financialisation and, the scale and depth of the recent Irish crisis notwithstanding, the dominant policy paradigm has been maintained and perhaps even renewed, with relative political ease. This is significant from a social policy perspective because, as Hemerijck (2016: 10) puts it, 'every macroeconomic policy regime harbours a theory of the state'. Kirby and Murphy (2011b) assess two competing perspectives of relevance to the Irish case, that of the competition state and the developmental state. They find that both logics have informed the approach of the state at different stages and in different policy areas but that overall 'the overriding logic is that of the competition state' (Kirby and Murphy, 2011b: 33). The stronger competition state logic privileges economic competitiveness over redistribution, social cohesion and welfare priorities.

The competition state logic is problematic for the Irish welfare state in many respects; insufficient attention is given to the potential impacts of exposure to global market risks for the state or for the individual. Competitiveness pressures can bear down on taxation and wage policy priorities which in turn impinge on social spending and redistributive policy priorities. The latter issues are less central where competition state logic dominates and fail to feature in the same way as fiscal pressures and competitiveness considerations do. Income inequalities, low wages and insecure work are thus largely accepted as part of the post-industrialised and globalised norm of Irish society. Public and social services can also be subject to competitive and market logics: such as a market-led approach to childcare (Hayes, 2016) and the impact of new managerialism in higher education (Grummell and Lynch, 2016). Dualisation of welfare has become increasingly embedded in the fabric of the Irish welfare state over time as illustrated in the areas of healthcare (Burke, 2016a) and pensions (Hughes and Maher, 2016).

Instability in government revenue remains a risk in open liberal market economies like Ireland although the need for a wider and more sustainable tax base was one of the first lessons emanating from the recent crisis. Exposure to global market volatility and trends implies that the welfare state needs to have the capacity to respond to downturns or shocks that affect the labour market, employment, activation policy and so on, as the most recent crisis also demonstrated. Robust welfare systems provide important automatic stabilisers in crisis circumstances (Hemerijck, 2013), providing another significant insight as to why more rather than less comprehensive welfare arrangements matter. These crisis lessons have not, so far, altered the trajectory of the Irish model.

Ireland and the EU: still the outlier?

Ireland's membership of the EU has been a critical aspect of its development over recent decades. Laffan and Tonra (2010: 430) note that for Ireland, 'membership of the European Union since 1973 provided this small open polity with a framework within which it could mediate the forces of growing interdependence and, more recently, globalisation'. Ireland's accession to the EEC was crucial to its subsequent economic development. Early economic benefits came mainly in the form of the Common Agricultural Policy, which was followed later by the trading advantages accruing from the single market, as well as being a major beneficiary of EU regional and structural funds for over 30 years. In political terms, Ireland has been largely positive about the value of its EU membership. Benefits were often framed in terms of enhancing the national identity of a small state on the periphery and establishing Ireland's place in Europe (Dukelow and Considine, 2014a).

The overall impact of EU membership on Irish social policy is difficult to quantify. Tied to the wider ups and downs of the social dimension of the EU, discussed earlier, it has had both diffuse and concrete effects over time. Early examples of the EU impact on Irish social policy include the EU anti-poverty programmes, while limited in number and reach, helped to widen the scope of Irish poverty policy interventions. The first equality directives brought important domestic legislative change regarding the rights of women in the workplace. Over time, EU directives have also been important in a wide range of areas including anti-discrimination and workplace health and safety. Also in the Irish case, the social OMC is sometimes credited with bringing about greater policy learning opportunities and instruments and some, albeit limited, stakeholder involvement to the process. Overall though significant weaknesses remain, not least 'insufficient integration between micro social policy and macro-economic policy' (Murphy, 2014: 16).

EU regional and structural funds supported public investment initiatives, especially during the 1990s, by which time Ireland had caught up with average living standards across the EU and was preparing for entry to EMU. Ireland's entry was regarded generally as positive and a logical next step which would provide the basis for sound public finances and be good for the Irish economy. Apart from one episode in 2001, the fiscal requirements and adherence to the SGP presented no major problems for Ireland. However, Ireland's economic cycle was out of step with the more modest growth rates in the major EA countries. It was also the only liberal market economy in the Euro Area, 'the outlier inside' (Hay et al, 2008). When Ireland's export boom of the late 1990s is distinguished from the credit and property boom of the 2000s, the problem of low interest rates, set by the ECB, exacerbated the credit-driven property bubble then in full swing. When and since the crisis hit in 2008, Ireland's crisis experience and the policy responses to it have exposed various fault lines in: the Irish growth model; EMU; the lack of robust internal or external assessment of the full array of risks associated with Ireland's pro-financialisation, pro-globalisation strategy; Ireland and the EU's lack of readiness for crisis especially among the EA member states, and the precise hierarchy of national/European responsibility in relation to fiscal and monetary policy in crisis circumstances.

Ireland's entry into its Programme of Financial Assistance with the Troika is outlined in Chapter Three. On the face of it, by 2016 Ireland appeared to have out-recovered the rest of Europe, despite making sovereign the debts of Irish banks and holding the distinction of creating the costliest bank rescue programme in the world. Ireland's continuing 'outlier' status in European economic terms is reflected more recently in the publication of unreal growth figures (GDP growth of 26.3% in 2015), driven by the activities of some multinationals, and which generated much curiosity and some ridicule. Ireland's post-crisis economic growth may have occurred 'thanks to Ireland's huge pool of foreign investment and success in the third great globalisation wave' (Haugh, 2016b) but nothing has changed its degree of exposure to global market risks and volatility. So the challenges remain and are likely to intensify in the context of high-profile controversies and recent political and policy developments relating to: global firms and how much and where their taxes should be paid; a new wave of protectionist-oriented political rhetoric in both Britain and the US; the election of Donald Trump in the US; the still-unfolding consequences of Brexit; any future tax harmonisation proposals within the EU; and the enhanced fiscal surveillance architecture attached to EMU.

The EMU reform initiatives detailed earlier in this chapter provides the overarching macroeconomic and fiscal policy framework in which Ireland conducts its budgetary processes and objectives. In its present form, there is little room for manoeuvre and from a social policy perspective, 'social targets are at once integrated into, but residual to economic and fiscal targets' (Murphy, 2014: 16). If this position holds, the outlook for the Irish welfare state is that the status quo, that is the subordination of social policy objectives over economic priorities, more or less remains intact. Other possibilities exist, depending on the policy priorities adopted by the EU in the coming years. In this regard, Murphy (2014: 17-18) notes that

> While still emerging, further extensive EU coordination of taxation and fiscal policy has potentially positive and negative implications for Irish social policy. If a low tax Ireland is forced to converge toward the average EU tax model, this may have positive repercussions for funding Irish social policy. On the other hand, an EU banking policy with no retrospective sovereign debt relief does not augur well for Irish social policy. Good social policy requires banking and fiscal union capable of automatically transferring funds to member states suffering from asymmetric economic shocks or high unemployment.

For now, however, the positive scenario outlined by Murphy remains very much an open question.

Ireland: politics, ideological ambiguity and the welfare state

Chapter Five presented the major political and ideological perspectives brought to bear on welfare policies and welfare state debates over many decades across Europe and beyond. Students of Social Policy living in Ireland may well struggle to see the relevance of that chapter to a book on Irish Social Policy, given that so many of the concepts and political ideologies, remain distant and unfamiliar in the Irish political context. We seek to explain that conundrum here. Essentially, the liberal leaning and globalising tendencies of the Irish model is underpinned by a pragmatic and apparently non-ideological approach by the established political mainstream. There is, as Lynch (2010: 11) puts it, 'a denial of ideology at the heart of party politics. Ireland's main political parties are populist; they conceal their own ideological roots'. Irish politics is not non-ideological, far from it, but there is a long-standing reluctance to articulate and connect with the language and values associated with political ideologies.

This ideological ambiguity is often accounted for in part at least by the political heritage of the two largest parties, Fianna Fáil and Fine Gael, whose origins lie in their opposing positions on the Anglo Irish Treaty 1921 that formed the basis for the establishment of the Irish Free State. The national question provided the main political dividing line in Ireland's fledgling state. Furthermore, the overarching Catholic, conservative liberalism that came to dominate the early decades of the Irish state downplayed the relevance of class politics and associated social divisions. The Irish Labour Party found it difficult to grow its support base and was outflanked by Fianna Fáil in particular, who managed to appeal to many working-class people, considered the natural constituency of Labour. By the mid-twentieth century and in contrast to much of the rest of Europe, social democracy had failed to gain a political foothold in Ireland. Irish political culture was insular in its orientation, populist and strongly clientelistic in its connection with people. While Irish politics became much more outward-looking by the 1960s, the pragmatic 'non-ideological' orientation of Irish political discourse largely continued even after the dominance of Catholic liberalism was increasingly challenged in the 1970s and 1980s (discussed in Chapter Two). Smaller political parties, and some independent politicians have been, and remain, much better at naming their politics. Fianna Fáil, in contrast, often refers to 'the national interest' to appeal to a support base that would not focus on social and class divisions, but rather 'come together' to avoid such challenges, with 'give and take' all round. Framed in this way, Fianna Fáil 'deliberately set its face against any attempts to translate social conflict into politics' (Mair and Weeks, 2005: 147). In government in 1932-48, 1951-54, 1957-73, 1977-81, February to November 1982, 1987-94 and 1997-2011, this position served Fianna Fáil well and the cross-class support it enjoyed sustained its electoral success throughout the twentieth century.

The hegemonic role of this 'catch-all' party in Irish politics came to an abrupt halt with the collapse in their support in 2011. The dramatic almost-obliteration of Fianna Fáil in the 2011 general election created some anticipation about the prospect of radical transformation of the Irish political landscape, though this did not transpire. The vote was for change in the governing parties and Fine Gael and Labour held office with a comfortable majority from 2011 to 2016. But this change in governing parties did not generate a shift in policy direction. Fine Gael and Labour largely conformed with the conditions set down by the Troika and were assessed to have taken 'strong ownership of the goals of the EU-IMF program' (DG ECFIN, 2011: 3). The overarching policy responses to the crisis were marked by a high degree of continuity, regardless of whether Fianna Fáil or Fine Gael was in government. The Labour Party, for its part, promised much more than it delivered during its time in government and it, in turn, was roundly rejected in the 2016 election. A Fine Gael-led minority government was formed with the support of nine independent TDs with a Confidence and

Supply agreement with Fianna Fáil in 2016. In short, Fine Gael and Fianna Fáil together had the numbers but not the appetite to form a government. Their deep and long-established political rivalry belies their now very proximate ideological positions, especially on economic policy.

The dominance of the centre-Right, though rarely labelled as such, adopts a largely non-ideological, common-sense neo-liberal approach with spill-over effects for the welfare state. While there has long been class dynamics at play within and between the establishment parties of the centre-Right, these have not translated into class-based politics. The electoral advances of Sinn Féin over the last two decades along with the more recent growth in Left-leaning alliances such as People Before Profit suggest that a more overtly class-based politics might be beginning to emerge in Ireland. Independents have also gained a higher proportion of the vote over the last decade. These developments reflect, in part at least, the anti-establishment sentiment that is also present, although overall the centre ground of Irish politics appears reasonably solid. However, as Reidy (2016: 6) notes, 'voter loyalties to the large centrist parties of the twentieth century are weakening and there is growing political fragmentation'. The actual scale and impact of this fragmentation on the political landscape in Ireland will be one to watch.

The reason why all of this matters so much is captured by Lynch (2010: 1) in her identification of 'invisible barriers that control public consciousness and do not allow us to think differently'. These barriers are associated with the lack of ideological forthrightness in Irish political culture. Lynch (2010: 1-2) draws attention to 'the implications of ideological closure, and the implicit censorship of new political ideas and concepts in Ireland' arguing 'that this closure has brought us to a place where neo-liberal capitalism and deep patriarchal values are entrenched in Irish public policy without any major political articulation as to their negative implications for so many people's well-being'. This shortcoming is not new but has had considerable implications for the development of Irish social policy, as outlined in Part I of this book.

In brief, the story of the delayed and uneven development of the Irish welfare state is connected to the wider political ambiguity around the objectives associated with it. Piecemeal and breakthrough developments in particular areas over the decades provide important illustrations of the state taking responsibility for the well-being of its people, such as: the provision of housing in the early decades of the Irish state, making post-primary education available to all children in the late 1960s, the expansion of social welfare entitlements in the 1970s and the development of anti-poverty measures in the 1990s. Each of these policy advances could be matched with significant examples of state inaction down the decades. Ireland inherited some founding welfare state measures pre-independence but the architecture of the Irish welfare state was moulded by Catholic social teaching and the, largely Catholic, charitable provision of social services. The unravelling of that legacy remains a work in progress. There was no Irish Beveridge moment and no 'golden age' from which a more comprehensive welfare state could take root. Neither was there any notable rights-based social policy culture of which to speak. Greater investment in welfare services during the latter part of the twentieth century brought substantial improvements in the availability of services in some areas of the welfare state but Ireland has largely been behind the curve and trying to catch up with the needs and risks it might be expected to address.

A mass of contradictions emerge in relation to our sociopolitical engagement with the welfare state and its role and objectives in Irish society: politically we are still supposed to be able to 'do more with less' somehow, while public discourse is filled with stories of overstretched and inadequate public and social services and frustrated citizens, who often want better social services but cannot afford to pay more taxes. Various forms of welfare dualism have become increasingly embedded in the Irish welfare state in recent decades, which, in addition to the inequities that arise, obscures and often undermines the social solidarity on which welfare states depend. Put plainly, people who pay for some services (e.g. health insurance) often contend that they benefit little from publicly provided social services, even though they usually do or have at some point (e.g. school, college, pension, public hospital, child benefit, tax relief on health insurance/pensions/mortgages etc.). In overall terms, social policy in Ireland has some distance to go in raising awareness of how all these themes connect to the quality and type of welfare state that exists and what policy alternatives are possible. Prominent, too, in public discourse is the notion of the burdening cost associated with social welfare and the social services generally, while fiscal and corporate welfare arrangements remain relatively under-examined. Public sector pay, numbers and pensions are the subject of important scrutiny but frequently in isolation from related issues regarding wages, taxation, access to pensions and income inequalities across the labour market, not to mention wider expectations and policy objectives for the public and social services. The paucity of political ambition regarding social policy objectives adds to the challenges that already abound regarding the adaptive capacity of the Irish welfare state at this juncture. The mounting pressures and challenges facing the core social services of the Irish welfare state are examined in more detail in the next Part of this book.

Chapter summary

- The intensification of welfare state pressures emanating from economic globalisation, financialisation and the increasingly liberalised tendencies of global markets present considerable challenges to post-industrial states; their role and policy responses to these pressures remains critical to welfare state futures. The concurrent recognition of a wider range of social risks along with significant demographic, economic and sociocultural change has led to new lines of welfare thinking since the 1990s.
- The argument for moving to a social investment state has gained some policy traction in recent years but questions remain about this, as yet very uneven, directional shift. The wider move to austerity as a policy response to the fallout from the recent financial crisis has

eroded the protective capacity of welfare states, especially in the worst affected countries (notably Greece) and repairing now diminished welfare states remains a critical challenge.

- The role of the EU in contributing to the scale of austerity in some of its member states remains highly contested. Section two outlined the consequences emanating from the responses to the Euro crisis and the severe problems that persist.

- Section three positioned the Irish welfare state and its particular challenges in the wider analytical context of this part of the book. It identified how aspects of the Irish growth model are brought to bear on welfare state thinking and it highlighted a political and ideological ambiguity that belies the liberal tendencies inherent in the prevailing economic paradigm, with inevitable consequences for Ireland's welfare state future. In their current form, EU fiscal and macroeconomic policy reforms seem likely to provide another constraining influence on developing the capacity and scope of the Irish welfare state.

Discussion points

- How can the state mediate the impact of globalisation?
- Assess the benefits and drawbacks of economic globalisation for Ireland.
- Critically assess the trajectory of EU economic and social policy priorities.
- How do you think Ireland would have fared outside of the EU?
- Examine the stated values of Irish political parties and assess them against their core policy objectives (and where appropriate what they actually delivered in government). How/do they align on the left/right ideological spectrum?

Further reading list

Greve, B (2015) *Welfare and the welfare state: Present and future*, Abingdon: Routledge

Kirby, P and Murphy, MP (2011) *Towards a second republic? Irish politics after the celtic tiger*, London: Pluto

Morel, N, Palier, B and Palme J (eds) (2012) *Towards a social investment welfare state? Ideas, policies and challenges*, Bristol: Policy Press

Vanhercke B, Natali D and Bouget D (eds) (2016) *Social policy in the European Union: State of play 2016*, Brussels: ETUI and OSE [annual publication – see etui.org for updates]

Notes

1. http://ec.europa.eu/social/main.jsp?catId=750.
2. Haugh, 2016a.

PART III
Analysing Irish social policy I: social services

seven

Social protection policy

Social protection is one of the most central aspects of social policy provision. Virtually everyone is connected in some way to the social protection system, whether as a recipient of a particular payment during various stages of the lifecourse, as a contributor via taxation or social insurance, or both. It is a central expression of how we live in society and how far duties and rights extend. Social protection is underpinned by competing ideological traditions and values which have different views of the system and what it is for. These range from the idea that social protection is about reducing inequality in society; to the idea that it is about providing a safety net to those who have no other source of income; to the idea that access to social protection should come with certain conditions such as the duty to work.

Sparked by economic crises of the 1970s, social protection has been at the centre of debate since then about welfare states under pressure. This is a debate which continues in the form of discussions about welfare reform; it has been influenced by a number of factors including the changing nature of economies, the changing nature of social risks, and the impact of subsequent economic crises. Social protection represents both an expression of particular values and a substantial commitment in terms of resources; and both the values informing the system and its costs have come under scrutiny, with social protection undergoing substantial reforms as a result. The 2008 economic crisis and the subsequent 'era of austerity' intensified pressures to reform and questions about the role of social protection, its affordability and its adaptability to changing economic and social circumstances continue to be pressing issues.

Chapter outline

- The chapter begins with a broad examination of social protection policy, defining it and looking at the factors that underpin its emergence and development, with particular reference to the concepts of social justice and redistribution. This section also looks at the main types of social protection payments, and the systems of social protection associated with different types of payments. Some of the main elements of the reform of social protection systems since the 1990s, shaped by austerity and activation, are also discussed.
- In section two we trace the development of the Irish social protection system from pre-independence to the 1980s, looking at how it evolved in terms of influences and programme design, and how various social needs were recognised.
- In section three we look at the contemporary system, presenting a broad overview of how the system evolved since the 1990s, with particular attention to the notion of permanent austerity. The section then looks in more detail at the theme of activation. The final part of section three briefly considers the wider context of poverty and anti-poverty policy, which is often overlooked in recent discussions about social protection reform.

SECTION ONE
SOCIAL PROTECTION: DEFINITIONS, VALUES AND SYSTEMS

Defining social protection

Social protection is a term used interchangeably with terms such as social security, social welfare and income maintenance. In the past these latter terms would have been more frequently used; however, in recent years the term 'social protection' is more commonly used, although differences remain depending on national context. In Ireland the government department responsible for dealing with social welfare changed its name to the Department of Social Protection (DSP) in 2010, reflecting use of this term at EU level. Despite the variations in the term, the key word 'social' indicates that the system implicates all of society or that it is a shared system that broadly involves everyone, whether as a contributor or recipient or both (Millar, 2009). The second element of the term, whether it be security, protection or welfare, all point to a similar meaning: that the system is about ensuring security, protection or well-being, in a financial sense, in the face of particular needs or contingencies. These arise out of circumstances which impinge on individuals' and families' abilities to generate their own income; such as unemployment, ill health, disability, old age, and insufficient income due to low-paid work. Income provided through social protection means that individuals are not left to rely on the market, families or charity if particular circumstances materialise. The needs and risks recognised by social protection systems have changed and grown over time, and as a result, the scope of social protection systems widened greatly since their inception in the late nineteenth century. Correspondingly, government expenditure, and contributions in the form of tax and social insurance, have grown substantially. In the early 1950s most European countries spent less than 10% of GDP on social protection (Ferrera, 2008); by 2014 the EU average was 19.5% and it accounts for the largest share of government expenditure (Eurostat).

Social protection, redistribution and social justice

Social protection systems are also an expression of particular values or normative concerns. As Millar (2009: 6) points out 'social protection provisions involve various forms of redistribution that are an expression of our values as a society and our commitments to social and economic justice'. Money collected through taxation and social insurance contributions gets distributed in the form of unemployment payments, pensions, maternity benefits and so on.

While factors such as the political context and levels of national wealth determine the amounts of money involved and who gets what, the foundation of these decisions rests on notions of justice, specifically distributive or social justice. Distributive or social justice are terms that can be used interchangeably, but they basically refer to 'how a society or group should allocate its scarce resources or product among individuals with competing needs or claims' (Roemer, 1996: 1 in Lund, 2006: 107). Justice in this sense involves rights and duties, it means giving people what is due to them, and not giving them what is not due to them. It goes beyond charity to mean 'what is morally required that we, perhaps collectively through our political and social institutions, do to and for one another. Not just to what it would be morally good to do, but what we have a duty to do' (Swift, 2014: 13). The notion of distributive justice began 'creeping into use from about 1850 on' (Swift, 2014: 11) and by the early twentieth century, 'theorising about social justice became a major concern' (Miller, 1999: 4 in Lund, 2006: 108). This coincided with changes in thinking about people's position in society, so that it was no longer seen as something rigidly fixed, but something which could be affected by government intervention. With this change in thinking, ideas such as social justice became meaningful. However, it was not the idea of social justice alone that gave rise to social protection systems. Debates about social justice coincided with the growth of industrialisation and national wealth, and the growth of democracy and rights as discussed in Chapter Four. By 1948, access to social protection was considered a fundamental human right, as proclaimed in the 1948 Universal Declaration of Human Rights (Articles 22 and 25) (Dixon, 1999).

Types of social protection

Broadly speaking, there are three different ways in which social protection programmes are designed. These are insurance-based programmes, assistance-based programmes and universal programmes. Most welfare states have a mix of programmes; however, one type usually tends to be more dominant, depending on historical, economic, political and social factors, such as levels of economic development, the relative power of different actors (such as trade unions and employers), and attitudes towards welfare. The type of social protection system a country has is therefore a good indicator or expression of its overall welfare state regime.

Social insurance

Social insurance-based programmes are also known as contributory programmes. These involve specific contributions, usually made by workers, employers and the state. These contributions form a state social insurance fund which is used to cover risks such as unemployment, sickness and retirement. Payments made into the fund are usually income-related. That is, the higher one's salary, the greater the contribution made, and payments made from the fund may be either pay-related, so that those earning more receive more; or they may be made at a flat rate, whereby every recipient receives the same regardless of their prior income. Unemployment and sickness payments made from the fund are usually limited by time. This kind of social protection involves a limited sense of redistribution, where only those workers deemed eligible to contribute benefit. The type of redistribution which occurs is known as **horizontal redistribution**. Social insurance thus works as a form of a 'piggy bank' (Barr, 2001). Social insurance is also built upon the values of collective responsibility and solidarity. Responsibility is collective in the sense that contributions are drawn from three strands: workers, employers and the state. Solidarity is also based on these three strands alongside the notion of a shared response to social risks.

> **Horizontal redistribution** occurs across similar income groups, such as during different lifecycle stages, when resources are distributed from working people to retired workers through pensions.

Since the inception of social insurance-based programmes there has been a gradual widening of participation; from a handful of occupations to virtually all occupations, as well as the inclusion of part-time workers and the self-employed. The widening process has also meant increasing inclusion for women. Married women, for example, were typically excluded in earlier programmes, while the inclusion of part-time workers has had the greatest impact on women, as they make up the majority of part-time workers. However, growing labour market insecurity counteracts these trends, resulting in a new socioeconomic group called the 'precariat' by Guy Standing (2014). In terms of social insurance, labour market insecurity has meant that particular groups, including young people and migrants, don't fully benefit. This is because these groups are at higher risk of insecure and low-paid employment and consequently don't build up a sufficient contribution record to access social insurance. In addition, social insurance does not offer protection for those who may never enter the labour market, as the opportunity to make contributions does not arise. Social insurance-based payments are therefore often referred to as earned rights, based on attachment to the labour market. The system is sometimes also assessed as causing a dualisation between insiders (those with good social insurance coverage and benefits) and outsiders (those with weaker attachment to the labour market and weaker social rights as a result).

As noted in Chapter Four, over the course of the 1880s Germany became the first country to introduce social protection. Following Germany's example, other European countries also introduced social insurance programmes. These programmes emerged in a relatively short time span from the 1890s to the first decade of the twentieth century. Countries where insurance-based programmes are dominant belong to the conservative/corporatist welfare regime, of which Germany is still one of the main members. Other countries in which this model is influential include France, Austria and the Netherlands.

Social assistance

The second design template for social protection involves social assistance-based payments. These are also known as non-contributory payments. Here eligibility is decided on the basis of need, which is usually organised through categories. As with social insurance, the needs recognised under social assistance have grown over time, from those associated with old age and widowhood, to those associated with caring, disability and so on. Under social assistance, need is measured through means–testing. Thus having means, including income and assets, below a certain threshold qualifies one for payment. This method is intended to ensure that resources go to those most in need, as well as 'stopping benefits going to others' (Spicker, 2011: 15), and this is referred to as a **selective** approach to social protection. Payments are funded through general taxation, and here the principle of **vertical redistribution** applies. Assistance payments tend not to be as generous as insurance-based payments and they have more of a direct lineage with the poor law, marked by their selective focus on need and means-testing. As Marshall (1965 in Dixon 1999: 43) notes '"need" per se does not generate a "right" to social security; it merely justifies "public charity"'. However, these types of payments have a stronger redistributive effect than insurance-based payments, exhibiting what Barr (2001) calls a 'Robin Hood' function. Yet this targeted approach may also have

> **Selectivism** is an approach which targets payments to groups, usually based on need and measured by means-testing.

> **Vertical redistribution** refers to redistribution up and down the income scale, usually but not always, from higher-income groups to lower-income groups.

> **Stigma** is a feeling of shame associated with having to apply for means-tested or otherwise selective benefits, the determination of which can involve intrusiveness and potentially mark the recipient as different, or needier than the general population.

a **stigmatising** effect, unlike payments based on the principle of rights.

Countries which rely more heavily on social assistance belong to the liberal welfare regime. Individualism is a core value and payments are based on the minimum necessary to alleviate poverty. In Europe, the UK has become the closest proponent of this model of welfare in recent times.

Universal payments and universalism

The word 'universal' has a number of related meanings in the context of social protection and welfare states. Universality refers narrowly to the method of redistribution embedded in universal payments or the universal model of welfare, while universalism, taken more broadly, may apply to the principles and ideals behind such welfare states, such as equality and integration (Anttonen and Sipilä, 2012). Nordic welfare states, based on social democracy, are generally most associated with universalism, though the British welfare state as informed by Beveridgean principles after the Second World War (see Chapter Four) reminds us that the Nordic model is not the only example. There are two distinguishing factors of universality: membership and allocation (Kildal and Kuhnle, 2005). On the first, this means that practically everyone in a population is covered on the basis of membership as a resident or as a citizen. Benefits are available on the basis of individual social rights and belonging to a certain population category, which is usually, but not solely, associated with a particular stage or condition during the lifecourse, such as families with children, older people or sick people. In terms of allocation, as Kildal and Kuhnle (2005: 14) note, 'no comprehensive universal welfare state manages without discretionary allocations', though this applies more to social services than to social protection. Universalism does not necessarily imply that the same is given to all, which is known as flat-rate universalism; universal social protection benefits can also include an earnings-related component. However, though not all commentators agree that this strictly reflects the meaning of universalism (Anttonen and Sipilä, 2012). Allocation of universal payments can also be based on what Titmuss (1968) referred to as positive selective discrimination, whereby those with greater need benefit more.

The universal model of welfare places a heavier emphasis on equality and redistribution than the two previous models. Both horizontal and vertical redistribution take place, and payments aim to prevent poverty rather than alleviate it. Though practices vary from country to country, this model is generally financed with a combination of general taxation and social protection contributions. A high value is also placed on labour market participation to help generate the resources to fund such a system.

The universal model has generated much debate about whether it really contributes to equality, or whether it means that people who can afford their own welfare receive payments they don't need, and as a result the model is expensive and inefficient. An influential study countering the latter idea suggested that the Nordic model embodies a paradox of redistribution (Korpi and Palme, 1998). Korpi and Palme found that the poor do better in welfare states where the middle classes also benefit. This means that a greater proportion of the population have a stake in ensuring benefits and services remain generous and high quality; residual or assistance-based systems that cater for the poor only will not be as well-funded or regarded. As welfare states come under increasing financial and political pressure, questions are raised about whether universalism is in decline and whether the Nordic model is as distinct as it used to be. This is evident in trends in Nordic countries, such as growing inequality, and reforms leading to differential treatment of different groups of pensioners and unemployed people, thus diminishing the universality of social protection (Kvist et al, 2012).

Table 7.1: Summary of the key characteristics of the main social protection systems

	Qualifying criteria	Source of funding
Social insurance	Available to those who have made the necessary insurance contributions	Social insurance fund
Social assistance	Available to those in need based on means testing	General taxation
Universal	Available as a right to all those who belong to the relevant category	Predominantly general taxation

Fiscal welfare and occupational welfare

Besides these forms of social protection, there are other, less visible, variants of welfare; namely, fiscal welfare and occupational welfare. These were first highlighted by Richard Titmuss, who developed the idea of the social division of welfare to include social welfare, encompassing the three types of social protection already discussed, and fiscal welfare and occupational welfare (Titmuss, 1987 [1956]).

Fiscal welfare refers to 'allowances and reliefs from income tax' such that 'the tax saving that accrues to the individual is, in effect, a transfer payment' (Titmuss, 1987 [1956]: 48). Examples include tax allowances on gross income in recognition of particular activities such as childcare, and tax relief on income spent on private pension contributions and private health insurance. Income transferred in this way has the potential to be regressive, as access to tax benefits may disproportionately benefit those who earn higher incomes, particularly where the allowances are provided at the marginal rate of income tax. Fiscal welfare is often referred to as hidden welfare because it is typically not calculated as part of public welfare expenditure (Greve, 2015), or acknowledged in public discourse, especially in terms of how welfare states benefit middle- and high-income earners, and thus result in 'upside-down redistribution' (Sinfield, 2013: 23). In recent years, tax credits, which are reductions in tax liability, have become a popular policy preference in liberal welfare states such as the US, Australia and the UK to support the working poor and 'make work pay'. As Clegg (2015: 493) notes, politically, tax credits are more acceptable than traditional social protection benefits because they are 'meant to reconcile redistribution and poverty reduction with goals more valued on the political right, such as limiting burdens on employers, improving incentives for participation in paid work and combating "dependency"'. Yet they also raise the question of whether they are simply subsidising low-paid work and are as much of a benefit to the employer as the employee.

Occupational welfare or the 'social policy of the firm' as Martin Rein (1982) calls it, refers to benefits, in cash or in kind, provided by employers. This may include provisions such as occupational pensions, redundancy payments and sickness benefits, and may also extend to items such as health insurance and education and training supports. Some of these payments are **statutory** and the state plays a role in their regulation. In other

> **Statutory** refers to provisions required by law, **non-statutory** are provisions made voluntarily.

cases, payments and benefits are **non-statutory** and are entirely private forms of welfare designed to attract and reward the workforce. As noted by Titmuss (1987 [1956]: 51) occupational welfare duplicates and overlaps with social and fiscal welfare and may 'function as concealed multipliers of occupational success'. In this sense, occupational welfare can redistribute resources regressively as greater benefits accrue to those who are better off. Occupational welfare is very unevenly spread across companies, and not only do higher earners tend to benefit more, it is also gendered, with men tending to benefit more (Farnsworth, 2004). However, occupational welfare is increasingly encouraged by governments because, as Farnsworth (2004: 437) notes, 'contemporary political and economic pressures have reduced the room for governments to borrow and raise additional revenue from higher personal and corporate taxes'.

Social protection challenges and recent reforms

> **Replacement ratio** is the ratio of income received through welfare payments compared to the income received in work. Social protection systems often aim to set welfare payments at a particular replacement rate.

The 1950s to the 1970s was known as the golden age of welfare, when welfare states grew significantly and social protection systems expanded (see Chapter Four). They widened their scope, and **replacement ratios** rose so that the amount of income social protection replaced from earnings grew (Glyn, 2006). However, the 1980s was a decade of crisis that provoked much debate about social protection. A combination of declining growth and rising unemployment meant that social protection systems found their main sources of revenue, that is, tax and social insurance contributions, decline at the same time as the demands on them were higher than ever. This contributed to the notion of a fiscal crisis confronting welfare states. At the same time welfare states and social protection systems were being attacked ideologically. Neo-liberal thinking was on the ascendant and it had very different views of justice and responsibility, prioritising the individual over the social. Social rights were criticised for placing too much emphasis on rights and not enough on responsibility. Instead of providing security, payments were considered to make people **dependent**, reluctant to work and producing over time a 'culture of dependency' transmitted from one generation to the next.

> **Welfare dependency** is a (contested) term which emerged from the New Right critique of social protection. It suggests that welfare recipients are not only financially dependent on welfare but psychologically dependent, losing their sense of self-reliance and motivation to work.

International trends in social protection since the 1990s did not quite fulfil the predictions made about the demise of welfare states and social protection. Social protection systems were not obliterated by neo-liberalism, yet neo-liberal ideas and economics remained common sense and influenced politics across the political spectrum (Mudge, 2008). As a result, the neo-liberal expression of collective interests in individualistic terms, such as the 'tax payer', and the supplanting of commitments to social justice and redistribution with jobs and growth, frame the policy environment in which social protection policy evolves in many countries. The term unemployment has been replaced with terms such as 'jobseeking', 'worklessness' and 'economic inactivity'. These terms change the meaning of unemployment from a social problem for which we have collective responsibility to one of individual responsibility and personal failure (Raffass, 2016).

Besides operating under these dominant ideas, welfare states and their social protection systems were also felt to have entered a 'silver age of permanent austerity' (Ferrera, 2008: 83) as they faced challenges of financial sustainability and external and internal constraints forcing them to adapt and restructure. Externally generated constraints include the implications of economic globalisation and European integration as discussed in Chapter Six, and which have eroded national autonomy over social spending and revenue raising. The 'Great Recession' has added to the pressure, as welfare states are dealing with escalated levels of public debt, which grew from an average of 57% of GDP in the EU28 in 2007 to 85% in 2015 (Eurostat). Dealing with the debt is compounded by the disciplinary power of international financial markets, and poor economic and employment growth.

Internal or domestic sociodemographic trends also impact on social protection, contributing to the silver age of permanent austerity. A key concern is population ageing: the proportion of the world population aged 60 and over is expected to rise from 11% in 2000 to 22% by 2050. However, this rise is not evenly spread. In most developed countries which also have the most mature welfare states, the current share, 20%, is expected to rise to 30% by 2050 (Bloom and McKinnon, 2010). This trend, together with the fact that global life expectancy is also rising – from 68 in 2010 to 75 in 2045 – a phenomenon known as 'double ageing' (Kvist et al, 2012), raises enormous challenges for the long-term affordability and sustainability of pension systems.

Another significant sociodemographic trend is changing family and household structures. Family norms based on stable unions of heterosexual couples with a male breadwinner have given way to a myriad of other family forms which parallel other changes such as individualisation, increased female labour-force participation and changing work practices. However, these changes have also raised issues such as the need for greater recognition of caring; and an examination of ways in which social protection systems, historically based on the norm of full-time and stable work, can facilitate flexibility in relation to work/life balance. Similarly patterns of family formation have changed, manifested in trends such as the increasing prevalence of sole-parent families, a family form more likely associated with unemployment and thus higher risk of poverty (OECD, 2011).

The rise of sole-parent families overlaps with what has been called 'new social risk groups' (Taylor-Gooby, 2004) who don't fare well in social protection systems originally designed in the context of industrialised societies. Earnings inequalities, flexible work patterns, and labour market insecurities in globalised, post-industrialised and financialised societies, as well as more fluid family formations, have generated new needs and vulnerabilities to which social protection systems need to respond. Such vulnerabilities include underemployment and in-work poverty, which disproportionately affect young people, families with children, lone parents, low-skilled people and migrant ethnic minorities; groups which have been bundled together in the aforementioned concept of the precariat (Standing, 2014).

These trends have led to the restructuring of social protection systems in a number of ways, two of which are particularly significant, namely cost containment and connecting welfare to work. With regard to cost containment, payments related to old age, unemployment, sickness, disability and lone parenthood have been subjected to measures such as tightening eligibility criteria or conditions attached to payments. Increased **conditionality**, which is evident across the OECD (Kangas and Kvist, 2013), aims among other things to dampen demand. The impulse of cost containment has intensified in recent years as austerity spread in response to the Great Recession (Farnsworth and Irving, 2015).

Some of the conditions attached to payments, such as undertaking training while receiving an unemployment payment, are part of the broader efforts to connect welfare with work. The focus of

Conditionality refers to the eligibility rules attached to accessing benefits. The trend of increasing conditionality includes measures such as extending contribution periods and stipulating particular actions such as engaging with activation provisions, including job-searching services, employment or training programmes.

social protection therefore shifts from income maintenance to employment promotion, and this has become a major feature of the direction in which social protection systems are moving. This is variously referred to as activation, insertion or workfare and such policies are increasingly targeted at people of '**working age**'. This means that the policy focus has extended to people for whom it was previously legitimate

> **Working age** is a term increasingly used in connection with social protection systems, to encompass all people, not just the unemployed, in relation to measures that seek to progress people from welfare to work.

not to participate in the labour market, such as people with disabilities and lone parents. Clasen and Clegg (2011: 8) describe this as a process of 'risk re-categorisation' which has the effect of blurring the boundaries between social protection traditionally associated with the unemployed and other social protection programmes, and between social insurance and social assistance. This change is mirrored in changes to how social protection is administered and delivered, with a growth in a 'one-stop shop' approach, so that social protection is no longer a separate service, but integrated with labour market policy and labour market services (Minas, 2014). There are various types of activation, as indicated by Bonoli's (2011) typology of incentive reinforcement, employment assistance, occupation and human capital investment. Approaches to activation are also distinguished by whether they offer 'carrots' or 'sticks'; in other words, whether they support or coerce people into work. The latter approach is traditionally associated with liberal welfare regimes (Barbier, 2004). However, there seems to be a general trend in Europe, even among the Nordic welfare states usually associated with a more supportive activation regime, towards a coercive approach with an emphasis on 'work first' over human capital investment such as upskilling (Kvist et al, 2012).

This restructuring of social protection towards a greater focus on work connects with the broader trend of emerging social investment states (discussed in Chapter Six). When looked at from the point of view of social protection, policy motivated by social investment shifts from 'passive' income maintenance to 'active' measures such as training and work placement, or from the redistribution of income to access to job opportunities. Social expenditure is thus less focused on 'old' spending, which compensates or protects people in the context of risks such as unemployment, focusing instead on 'new' spending, enabling people to develop the capacity to deal with evolving risks and opportunities in post-industrial labour markets. This shift also encompasses related policy areas such as family policy, which appears to be expanding in many welfare states (Ferragina and Seeleib-Kaiser, 2015). From a social investment perspective, family policy is designed to enhance services and benefits related to childcare and family leave to facilitate flexible working lives. However, as noted in Chapter Six, social investment remains an unsettled and problematic policy shift. From a social protection point of view, it is questionable whether social investment can address poverty more effectively than traditional social protection policies, or help people secure better quality employment (Taylor-Gooby et al, 2015). In addition, the individualised focus of social investment, as Taylor-Gooby et al (2015: 100) note, 'downplays the enhanced structural power of capital in a more globalised world' which has led to more deregulated labour markets and more precarious employment.

SECTION TWO
THE DEVELOPMENT OF SOCIAL PROTECTION IN IRELAND

Pre-independence to the early 1940s

As indicated in Chapter One, Ireland's early welfare infrastructure was dominated by the poor law, with subsequent developments involving provision for unemployment and old age originating in Britain. Thus, prior to gaining independence Ireland had a basic structure of Workmen's Compensation (1897), Old Age Pensions (1908) and National Insurance covering sickness and unemployment (1911) in place. This reflected a mix of social assistance (Old Age Pensions) and social insurance (Workmen's Compensation and National Insurance). Various extensions to these programmes occurred up to 1921, including the introduction of a Blind Pension for people over 50, and the inclusion of dependants' allowances for wives and children in national insurance payments. Despite these changes, the overall thrust of the social protection system remained one of poverty alleviation through minimal payment levels. In the Irish context this minimalism was reinforced by the resistance of various Irish actors, including the Catholic Church and the Irish Party, to the introduction of national insurance in Ireland. An amended version of national insurance was implemented in Ireland which included sickness benefit, but not medical benefit. This had important consequences for the further development of the Irish social protection system. It set Ireland apart from the way in which social protection developed in many other European countries, where access to healthcare was included in social insurance. Another important point to note in terms of gender and the future development of the system, is that with the exception of the Old Age Pension which treated men and women equally, there was greater coverage of men than women in the fledgling social protection system. This is because the system included more male-dominated occupations, and excluded domestic service, which was typically female employment. The introduction of dependant's allowances for wives and children, but not for husbands, also set the system on the path of a male breadwinner model.

After independence, some of the key factors associated with the development of social protection, such as industrialisation, wealth and a commitment to social justice, were in scarce supply. While the Irish social protection system shared similar developments with the rest of Europe; such as dismantling poor law structures; dealing with rising unemployment; developing children's allowances and more comprehensive insurance systems; the key influences on social protection in Ireland ensured that they tended to be less comprehensive and at the low end of the scale in terms of expenditure.

In addition to the colonial legacy, indigenous factors reinforced the largely liberal nature of developments post-independence. These factors included a lack of resources, as poor economic development inhibited the development of extensive social protection programmes. Fahey (2002) and Carey (2005) argue that agrarianism, that is, the influence of agricultural interests, is a significant factor in the path of development taken by the Irish welfare state and the social protection system in particular. The predominance of small family farms providing relatively secure subsistence-based lifestyles bolstered arguments that Ireland could not afford, nor did it need, extensive social insurance-based programmes designed to meet the needs of industrial workers. Social assistance programmes funded from general taxation were felt to be more appropriate.

This preference for a liberal-oriented welfare state also sat comfortably with the Catholic Church. The Church promoted charity over state payments in response to need, and as noted in the previous section, social assistance is closer in character to charity than social insurance. Overall however, as Fahey and McLaughlin (1999: 125) note, the Church held 'a suspicion of state schemes of income distribution and other social services' and this stance mirrored liberalism's preference for a minimal state.

One final factor militating against expansive developments in social welfare was the prevailing attitude among a number of key government ministers and civil servants in the early decades of independence. This was particularly the case with JJ McElligott, the Secretary of the Department of Finance between 1927 and 1953, described by Ó Gráda (1997: 227) as the 'Dr No' of Irish economic policy. Influenced by fiscal liberalism, he made every effort to keep state expenditure to a minimum and to foster a character of self-reliance. Thus poverty alleviation at minimal levels was a recurring theme.

Turning to actual developments during the first decades of independence, reform began with the partial dismantling of the poor law in the 1920s. Developments, as discussed in Chapter Two, included the replacement of Outdoor Relief with Home Assistance in 1923, the introduction of Unemployment Assistance in 1933, the introduction of Widows and Orphans Pensions in 1935, and the introduction of the Children's Allowance in 1944. The introduction of the Children's Allowance is particularly significant because it was the first universal payment introduced in Ireland, made available to everyone who had children, funded from general taxation and not tied to insurance- or assistance-based principles, as was the case with children's allowances in many other European countries (Kaim-Caudle, 1967).

Late 1940s and the 1950s

The late 1940s and early 1950s were an important time in the development of social protection. Many European countries were entering a period of expansion and improvement of their social protection schemes, in the aftermath of the Second World War. Ireland also participated in this general trend. The publication of the Beveridge report 'created a stir in Ireland' (Ó Cinnéide 2000: 21) and questions were raised as to whether Ireland could also develop its social protection system along the lines proposed by Beveridge for Britain. This was not countenanced by the government at the time, who criticised Beveridge-style proposals for being too costly and unsuitable to Irish conditions. Outside of government circles Dr John Dignan, the Bishop of Clonfert, produced a pamphlet in 1945, known as the Dignan plan. Dignan proposed a system of comprehensive insurance, influenced not only by the Beveridge plan but also by developments in other continental European welfare states. If considered, this would have represented a major departure from the existing system, and it also represented thinking which deviated from the Catholic Church's position on social protection. Again the plan was rejected by the government who were not happy with the lack of costing in the proposals and in a rare case of role reversal, the government also criticised the cleric's proposals for not leaving enough room for charity (Kaim-Caudle, 1967).

The starting point for actual reform was administrative reorganisation with the creation of a separate Department of Social Welfare in 1947. This department took over social welfare programmes previously scattered between different departments. One of the first actions of the department was to produce a white paper outlining proposals to combine existing social insurance-based payments and to develop them into a more comprehensive social insurance system (Department of Social Welfare, 1949). The White Paper was published under William Norton, the Minister for Social Welfare and leader of the Labour party in the inter-party government of the time. Norton's proposals included the creation of one social insurance scheme, incorporating the existing schemes, which would be open to all employees except self-employed persons. The proposal contained many traits of the Beveridge report, such as a flat-rate system and the assumption of a male breadwinner. The flat-rate system was preferred because it would leave room for the habits of saving and thrift, it would be less costly to administer, and it would reduce the moral dangers associated with malingering (Kaim-Caudle, 1967). The new Fianna Fáil government implemented a restricted version of the proposals in the Social Welfare Act 1952, an approach described by Bew and Patterson (1982: 63 in Cousins, 2003: 173) as 'mild social reform with financial orthodoxy'. The legislation introduced a system less comprehensive than Norton envisaged by imposing an income ceiling and excluding particular categories of workers altogether. Some of the benefits Norton proposed, including a contributory pension and a death grant, were not included. However, it did include a maternity allowance, payable for 12 weeks, and improvements to sickness and disability benefit.

Overall, despite the advances made in relation to social insurance, the system was still heavily based on social assistance. The system also continued to discriminate on the basis of gender, particularly in the case of married women. Unless married women were employed, and most were not, they did not qualify for benefits. However, married women who were employed and subsequently claimed a benefit were paid at a lower rate than unemployed married men (Cousins, 2005b).

Subsequent to these reforms, the introduction of Disabled Persons Maintenance Allowance in 1954, administered by the Department of Health was another notable development. It represented a widening of the system by recognising the financial needs associated with having a disability. This was a means-tested payment and it took disabled persons who did not qualify for Unemployment Benefit or Assistance out of the Home Assistance net.

1960s and 1970s

Following the economic and social changes of the 1960s and 1970s, the social welfare system also changed and grew, but not in a systematic way. Several new schemes, in addition to modifications to existing ones, were introduced. Some involved the implementation of earlier proposals, others were in response to newly recognised needs and gaps in the system which gained greater visibility as a result of the changing social environment, profiled in Chapter Two.

The 1960s saw the implementation of some of the measures proposed in the previous decade related to social insurance. These included the introduction of a contributory Old Age Pension in 1961. Workmen's Compensation was replaced by an Occupational Injuries scheme in 1967; this provided a social insurance-based payment to workers for work-related injuries and illnesses. On the social assistance front, Smallholders Assistance was introduced in 1966. This was a means-tested payment made to small farmers who had been excluded from the Social Welfare Act 1952.

The 1960s are also significant for the first recognition of informal caring in the social protection system. This came about with the introduction in 1968 of a Prescribed Relative Allowance. This was paid as an increase in pension payments to pensioners who required full-time care in their homes, to be provided by a 'prescribed female relative', such as a daughter, who lived with the pensioner. However, the scheme remained very restrictive in terms of the female relatives who qualified, and the payment was made to the old age pensioner not to the carer. In addition the carer was not allowed to participate in paid employment. The payment also reflected the assumption that caring was a female role.

The 1970s brought much more activity, as the benefits under social insurance expanded, and a range of new assistance-based payments were introduced. Social insurance benefits were extended in the early 1970s by the introduction of Invalidity Pensions (which were made payable to individuals with a long-term illness and who had been claiming disability benefit), and payments to deserted wives. Pay-related benefits were introduced for unemployment and disability payments in 1974. Between 1973 and 1977 the qualifying age for the old age pension was reduced from 70 to 66. New assistance-based payments were introduced which were targeted at women in particular. These included a Deserted Wife's Allowance (1970), Unmarried Mothers Allowance (1973), Prisoner's Wife's Allowance (1974) and Single Women Aged 58 to 68 Allowance (1974). These payments represented a response to the lack of provision for women in the absence of a male breadwinner. Heretofore, the only payment available to these women was Home Assistance. This was also replaced by Supplementary Welfare Allowance in 1977, which made a minimum payment a legal right.

While the changes during the 1960s and 1970s increased the scope of the social protection system, they were still problematic. Cook (1986: 78) argues that 'a

Table 7.2: Summary of social protection measures introduced, 1908-89

Year	Social insurance	Social assistance	Universal
1908		Old Age Pension	
1911	Unemployment Benefit Sickness Benefit		
1920		Blind Pension	
1923		Home Assistance Replaced Outdoor Relief	
1933		Unemployment Assistance	
1935	Widow's and Orphan's Pension	Widow's and Orphan's Pension	
1944			Children's Allowance
1954		Disabled Person's Maintenance Allowance	
1961	Old Age Pension		
1966		Smallholder's Assistance	
1967	Occupational Injuries		
1968		Prescribed Relative Allowance	
1970	Retirement Pension Invalidity Pension	Deserted Wife's Allowance	
1973	Deserted Wife's Benefit	Unmarried Mother's Allowance	
1974	Pay-Related Benefit	Single Woman's Allowance Prisoner's Wife's Allowance	
1977		Supplementary Welfare Allowance	
1980	Christmas Bonus	Christmas Bonus	
1981	Maternity Benefit		
1984		Family Income Supplement	
1989		Lone Parent's Allowance	

Source: adapted from Curry, 2011

highly categorical system of social insurance became even more highly categorised' and that the system 'became extremely complex. The identification of the appropriate benefit and separate claims procedures often made the establishment of welfare rights difficult, particularly when certain schemes were stigmatising to claimants, and the visibility and cause of claimant status were reinforced by the categorical nature of the system'. This problem applied to women in particular, who were predominantly left to rely on the highly categorical social assistance-based payments.

On the other hand, by the end the 1970s, the social insurance element of the system was also gradually widening and becoming more comprehensive. In 1974 insurance was extended to all full-time employees as the income ceiling was abolished; pay-related benefit was also introduced and was fully phased in by 1979. At this stage, as Cousins (2000: 33) notes, 'in many ways, the Irish system was moving away from the classic Beveridgean flat rate approach towards a more continental pay-related model'.

1980s: social protection in the context of economic crisis

The shift towards a continental system did not continue into the 1980s. For much of this decade Ireland was transfixed by a severe economic crisis, as discussed in Chapter Three. Consequently, the social protection system had to cope with mass unemployment and rising numbers of people claiming Unemployment Assistance, as people's entitlement to Unemployment Benefit ran out. Unlike the UK, where Thatcherism dominated the 1980s and both the social protection system and its beneficiaries came under attack, Right-wing thinking and critique remained more muted in the Irish context. Some attempts were made to curb rising costs and rising levels of dependency on the social protection system. For example, pay-related benefits were reduced in 1984, only five years after they were fully implemented. A 'genuinely seeking work' requirement was applied to claimants of Unemployment Benefit, which added a new element of conditionality to the payment. Previously this requirement only applied to claimants of Unemployment Assistance (Cousins, 2005b). Attempts were also made to maintain people with families in low-paid employment, with the introduction of Family Income Supplement in 1984. Various schemes were introduced to provide work, such as a Social Employment Scheme (1985); to encourage job seeking, through Jobsearch (1987); and to encourage further education, through an Educational Opportunities Scheme (1986). These measures mark the origins of activation in Ireland.

One positive aspect of social protection in the 1980s related to improvements for women, which went against the tide of cutbacks and crisis. These changes stemmed from EU legislation. An EU directive on equal treatment in social protection in 1979 meant that many of the inequalities married women experienced in the social protection system surrounding rates, duration of benefit and assumptions about dependency were removed, but at a slow pace (Cook and McCashin, 1997). Also, maternity leave was introduced in 1981 which provided

14 weeks' leave from work. This was implemented alongside Maternity Benefit intended to replace women's income from work while on maternity leave.

The 1980s are also significant for the fact that the first (and to the date the only) comprehensive review of the social protection system was undertaken. A Commission on Social Welfare was appointed in 1983 and its report (Commission on Social Welfare, 1986) made recommendations consistent with a gradual development of the existing system. The Commission recommended the broadening of the insurance base together with the enhancement of means-tested schemes, to respond to those in greatest poverty, and to address the hierarchy between those treated most generously in the social protection system (old age pensioners and widows) and those treated the most parsimoniously (the unemployed and those claiming supplementary welfare allowance). However, it envisaged that if the social insurance element of the system was to expand then eventually the role of social assistance would diminish. It also outlined some guiding principles for the future development of the system. This was the first time any principles were articulated in connection with social protection policy and these were adequacy, redistribution, comprehensiveness, consistency and simplicity. One of the key recommendations related to adequacy, and the Commission recommended that a minimally adequate social welfare payment should amount to approximately half of net average industrial earnings.

As Curry (1986), the Chairman of the Commission noted, government reaction to the report focused on cost implications. This led to the decision to postpone the implementation of any recommendations, as economic circumstances did not permit the expenditure entailed. The first social partnership agreement in 1987 included a commitment not to cut social welfare payments, and gradually over the course of agreements in the 1990s some of the main recommendations were implemented. Some of these changes are discussed further in section three.

SECTION THREE
FROM THE 1990s TO THE PRESENT: REFORM AND CONTEMPORARY ISSUES IN IRISH SOCIAL PROTECTION POLICY

The delayed onset of permanent austerity?

In the Irish context the effects of economic globalisation and post-industrialisation proved very successful in economic terms, transforming the crisis of the 1980s into a period of unprecedented growth between the mid-1990s and mid-2000s. Despite a series of tax cuts in the late 1990s and early 2000s, more resources became available for social expenditure as the economy grew, with revenue collected from construction-based taxes growing enormously. Instead of permanent austerity, the Irish social protection system seemed increasingly inclusive and expansive, contrary to attempts at cost containment that prevailed elsewhere. Replacement rates improved and put Ireland in a comparatively higher position internationally; in particular Ireland's historical relationship with the UK was reversed in this regard (NESC, 2011). However since the Commission on Social Welfare Report (1986), there has been no overarching policy vision for social protection. A pattern of piecemeal and ad hoc change continues and when pressures mount, such as during the economic crisis, the changes made often amount to muddling through. In Box 7.1 we outline the most significant policy developments since the 1990s. More reports have been published, particularly in recent years, but have not been particularly influential; our selection is limited to those most clearly associated with changes to the system.

Box 7.1: Selected social protection policy developments

1996	Report of the Expert Working Group on the Integration of Tax and Social Welfare Systems
1997	Sharing in Progress: National Anti-Poverty Strategy
2001	Report of the Social Welfare Benchmarking and Indexation Group
2002	Building an Inclusive Society: Review of the National Anti-Poverty Strategy under the Programme for Fairness and Prosperity
2006	Government Discussion Paper, Proposals for Supporting Lone Parents
2007	National Action Plan for Social Inclusion 2007-2016
2009	OECD Report Activation policies in Ireland
2010	National Pensions Framework
2012	Launch of Intreo
2012/2013/2015	Pathways to Work
2016	Pathways to Work 2016-2020

A number of changes and improvements were made to payments for adults in a way that downplayed the fact that they were of 'working age'. While unemployment was still high, a pre-retirement allowance was introduced in 1990 for those over 55 in receipt of unemployment assistance, and this allowance did not require recipients to sign on the Live Register, that is, seek work. A Carer's Allowance was also introduced in 1990 and Carer's Benefit in 2000. Various efforts were made to streamline payments, signified by the introduction of Disability Allowance (1996), One-Parent Family Payment (OFP) (1997) and Farm Assist (1999). These replaced and consolidated existing payments in these areas and in some cases relaxed conditions such as earnings disregards (earnings of a certain amount per week not taken into account in the means-test) to afford recipients greater incentive to combine work and welfare. With unemployment falling over the late 1990s and early 2000s, and the numbers in receipt of unemployment payments in decline, the numbers in other payment categories increased, including OFP and Disability Allowance. A similar trend occurred in social protection payments in other countries and efforts were made to activate these groups (Immervoll and Scarpetta, 2012). However, in Ireland the main focus remained on income transfers, combined with an approach to activation that focused mainly on positive incentives.

This strategy was reinforced by a growing anti-poverty focus, beginning with the publication of the National Anti-Poverty Strategy (NAPS) in 1997 (discussed in the final section of this chapter). As a result, policy attention shifted to payment increases across all payment types (see also Box 7.1). By 2002, under a revised NAPS, *Building an Inclusive Society*, which took into account Ireland's continued prosperity and the recommendations of the Social Welfare Benchmarking and Indexation Group (2001), targets were adopted in relation to the value of welfare payments. These set a target rate of €150 per week in 2002 terms for the lowest rates of social welfare by 2007, equivalent to 30% of Gross Average Industrial Earnings (GAIE) at the time. This was achieved by the 2007 Budget due to a series of payment increases, particularly between 2005 and 2007. State pension payments reached 34% of GAIE, reaching the pension policy target set in 1998.

While significant improvements were made to the social protection system under benign economic conditions, this period was also punctuated by periods of cost containment. In particular, when economic growth faltered, in the early 2000s, a set of cuts known as the 'savage sixteen' were implemented in 2004 (Murphy, 2012). While the system was not in permanent austerity mode, commentators questioned the degree of ambition in improving the social protection system when the resources, were available to do so (Murphy, 2012). Despite what seemed like an upgrade in Ireland's wealth and resources, the social protection system, as McCashin and O'Shea (2007) note, maintained its focus on poverty alleviation with only limited emphasis on redistribution. The overall structure of the system remained unchanged and means-testing remained a key feature, with Ireland typically ranking highest on this indicator in the EU. In 2008, 25.2% of all payments were means-tested, compared to an 11.1% average for the EU27 (Eurostat). Similarly EU assessments of the Irish system observed that while economic growth masked 'very significant investment in welfare benefits ... the underlying high proportion at risk of poverty also reflects the structure of the Irish welfare system (based on flat-rate benefits) and points to a continued level of inequality in Irish society which must be a matter for concern' (DG EMPL, 2007: 220). Another problem being stored up was that social expenditure was based on increasingly precarious sources, which was exposed by the economic crisis.

The effect of the economic crisis and its continuing legacy has markedly changed the environment in which social protection policy is now made, with constraints and challenges more closely approximating Pierson's (2001) notion of permanent austerity. The immediate problems for the social protection system included the sharp rise in unemployment and long-term unemployment. Consequently, the amount spent on social protection rose rapidly in the most acute years of the crisis (Figure 7.1). The collapsing property market meant that a significant portion of revenue successive governments relied on also collapsed. The structure and role of the social protection system also came under greater scrutiny. Attention rapidly turned to seeing the social protection system as 'overly generous and poorly policed' (NESC, 2011: 2) and a contributor to the fiscal crisis, though this perception was strongly contested. Ideas such as the system being 'no longer fit for purpose' and the need to transform it from a 'passive' to an 'active' system began to circulate more frequently in policy discourse (Dukelow and Considine, 2014b). External actors such as the OECD, and the IMF and the European Commission as part of the Troika, also became more influential in the push for reform. In these conditions a relatively intense period of cutbacks and reforms unfolded between 2009 and 2014. As the crisis abated the pace of reform also slowed; however, the outcome is that the system has been tightened in terms of conditions and entitlements, and it is also more focused on activation.

In terms of cutbacks, a number of social protection programmes saw nominal rates cut in 2010 and 2011, the cumulate average cut being approximately 10% (when cuts to the Christmas Bonus are included). State pensions were the only payments to avoid cuts to weekly rates. Cuts in payments to particular groups were greater, including younger people. By 2014, the rate of Jobseekers Allowance and Supplementary Welfare Allowance for those aged 18-24 was cut by 51% to €100 and, for those aged 25, the rate was cut 30% by to €144. Entitlement to OFP was also significantly curtailed. Until 2012 OFP was applicable until the claimant's youngest child was 18, or 22 if in full-time education. Since 2015 entitlement ends once a claimant's youngest child reaches age seven. Plans to transfer lone parents to Jobseekers Assistance and thus subject them to activation processes that come with being classified as being available for work were altered following campaigning by lone-parent groups. Consequently Jobseekers Transitional payment has been introduced for lone parents. This payment exempts lone parents from the condition of being available for work until their youngest child reaches age 14. Child Benefit rates were also cut, though this was also the first payment to be increased once budgetary conditions improved somewhat in 2015. The Early Childcare Supplement, introduced in 2006, was replaced in 2010 with the less costly entitlement to a free preschool year of care and education on a part-time basis. This was extended to a second year, or to all children once they reach the age of three, in 2016. Reforms such as this, along with the introduction of two weeks' paternity leave in 2016, signify some reform in the direction of social investment (Daly, 2015), though they must also be balanced against the fact that Ireland has the most costly childcare in the OECD for most family situations.

Reforms which potentially have a longer-term structural effect on the system were also implemented. These include increased conditionality, further weakening the social insurance element of the system. The principal changes to conditions include a doubling of the contributions required to qualify for Jobseekers Benefit and Illness Benefit (paid to workers who become ill and are unable to work). These changes were coupled with reductions in the duration of the payment. Illness Benefit changed from being indefinite in duration to a one- to two-year payment depending on number of contributions paid, while Jobseeker's Benefit was reduced from 15/12 months to 9/6 months also depending on the number of contributions paid. Future state pension entitlements are curtailed by the intention, announced in 2011, to increase the qualifying age for the state pension to 68 by 2028, by which time it will be the highest qualifying age in Europe alongside the Czech Republic (OECD, 2015a). The number of social insurance contributions required for qualification for the contributory state pension doubled in 2012 and there are proposals in the National Pensions Framework (GoI, 2010) to move to a 'total contributions approach' by 2020. This would, according to the Framework, 'see a reduction in the levels at which pensions are paid' (GoI, 2010: 22). Budget 2015 marked the end of the current period of retrenchment, when as mentioned, Child Benefit rates were raised and other minor improvements were made. A wider set of rate increases to weekly payments were introduced in Budget 2017. Budget 2015 also introduced a new in-work payment, Back to Work Family Dividend, to which long-term unemployed social protection recipients are eligible during the first two years of their return to work. When set in the context of the extensive changes to Ireland's activation regime as discussed in the following section, it is suggestive of a more productive turn in Irish social protection; however, it is also a more punitive one in many respects.

Before we turn to activation, we close this section by looking briefly at Ireland's social expenditure over time and in a comparative context. Figure 7.1 compares social protection expenditure in Ireland as a percentage of GDP with the EU15 from 1995 and the EU28 from 2008. Before the economic crisis social expenditure across the EU remained relatively stable, despite various attempts at reform and cost containment across different welfare states. Irish expenditure typically remained

Figure 7.1: Expenditure on social protection as a percentage of GDP, Ireland, EU15 and EU28

Data source: Eurostat

below the EU average, reflecting its characterisation as a comparatively low social spender. However, evaluating welfare on the basis of expenditure as a percentage of GDP needs some qualification. Over the 2000s substantial economic growth outpaced, and thus masked, what was also significant growth in social expenditure. During the height of the crisis GDP dropped sharply while social expenditure grew rapidly, reflecting rising need, even though individual programmes were cut back. As the crisis has eased, Irish expenditure as a percentage of GDP is declining and returning to 'normal' rates, and the gap between it and the European average is again widening.

Activation: from 'passive' to 'active' welfare?

Until recently, activation focused heavily on training and direct job creation, which was a legacy of Irish activation policy's roots in the context of mass long-term unemployment in the 1980s. Then, as Bonoli (2011) notes, activation across Europe had a strong social cohesion focus. While no overall policy or strategy developed, activation did garner greater attention when the growing economy had little effect on unemployment, particularly long-term unemployment. Concern was also rising about poverty and unemployment traps in the way the social protection and taxation systems interacted. A cluster of allowances was introduced over the 1990s: Back to Education Allowance (1990), Back to Work Allowance (1993) and Back to Enterprise Allowance (1999). All three allowed recipients to retain a portion of their social welfare payments for a period after taking up employment. Direct job creation also became important as indicated by growing numbers on Community Employment (CE), which replaced the Social Employment Scheme in 1994. The primary function of CEs is to provide direct employment with a training element in the social/non-market economy to the long-term unemployed in order to enhance participants' employability and to provide local services. Recipients could retain a portion of their social welfare payment and receive a CE wage. The programme quickly grew to 40,000 participants.

The nature of Ireland's heavily means-tested social protection system makes it particularly prone to **unemployment traps**. These, which together with **poverty traps** became the focus an Expert Working Group on the Integration of Tax and Social Welfare Systems (1996). The setting up of the Group reflected growing concern with obstacles to becoming and remaining employed. Following the Group's report, measures were implemented to curtail the effects

Unemployment traps occur when the interaction between the social protection system and the taxation system create a situation where there is no financial incentive for a person to move from welfare to work. **Poverty traps** occur in work, at a particular income threshold when the effects of income tax combined with the withdrawal of in-work benefits leaves the worker less well-off compared to when they were earning a lower gross wage.

of unemployment and poverty traps. These involved tax reform, including a reduction in income tax rates and the introduction of a minimum wage; and a more tapered withdrawal of benefits associated with Back to Work Allowance and related schemes; a more generous application of Family Income Supplement; and an increase in earnings disregards. Altogether these measures aimed to positively incentivise people to move from welfare to work and remain in work, or in other words, to make work pay.

Positive steps to making work pay were balanced with the introduction of some compulsion, or at least 'quasi-compulsion' (Grubb et al, 2009: 55), to activation. Since introducing a requirement that 18-19-year-olds who were unemployed for more than six months register with FÁS (the state's training agency, replaced in 2013 by Solas) in 1996, the National Employment Action Plan introduced in 1998 gradually widened this activation process. By 2007, all those unemployed for three months or more aged 18-64 were required to register and attend an activation interview with FÁS.

Prior to the economic crisis, efforts to shift from a 'passive' to an 'active' system and to gradually recategorise all adult social protection recipients as 'working age' first and foremost, were evident. The *Government Discussion Paper: Proposals for Supporting Lone Parents* (DSFA, 2006) for example, proposed the introduction of compulsory engagement with employment services once the parent's youngest child reaches a certain age, for example age five or seven, and the withdrawal of OFP at another older age threshold. In addition, plans were in train to develop more targeted employment supports for people with disabilities (DSFA, 2008). *NAPinclusion 2007-2016*, the ten-year successor programme to NAPS (1997) also signalled a stronger connection between anti-poverty policy and activation.

These tentative steps towards stronger activation were overtaken by the economic crisis and the mounting problems of unemployment. In a similar manner to how social protection payments were criticised for being overly generous, Ireland's activation system also came in for critical scrutiny. In particular, an invited OECD review was likened to finding 'the emperor who had no clothes' (Martin, 2015: 9) as Ireland's system was criticised for its lack of compulsion and poor implementation. Similarly ESRI research noted 'the lax nature of the activation process' (McGuinness et al, 2013: 1), while the Troika also pushed for a modernised and more intensive activation process.

Paralleling cuts to social protection, payment rates and other conditions such as scheme duration were cut back in all activation schemes and entry conditions were tightened, while sanctions for non-participation have also increased. In terms of Bonoli's (2011) typology of activation, occupation or direct job elements of the Irish system have been curbed and incentive reinforcement has been strengthened, particularly negative reinforcement. In this way, Ireland's system aligns more closely with more coercive, 'work first' reforms occurring elsewhere. The policy guiding transformation of the system is *Pathways to Work*, whose initial development was required under the Troika reforms. Four iterations of the policy document have been published to date, taking account of changing economic conditions, all of which emphasise greater engagement with the unemployed, greater targeting of activation programmes, incentivisation or 'making work pay' and institutional reform. The most recent, *Pathways to Work 2016-2020*, contains plans for 'activation in a time of recovery and growth' (GoI, 2016a: 4), which proposes to extend activation to groups in the social protection system not classified as seeking work or 'non-active', such as people with disabilities and carers.

Looking at changes to the occupational dimensions of activation, the crisis has seen an effort to curtail the main occupational scheme, CE. It was criticised in particular for its lack of employment progression to the open job market. There has been only a modest rise in CE participants in recent years (21,142 participants in 2008 to 22,813 in 2015) and the payments participants receive were also curtailed. Such changes have, however, been criticised for how they overlook the potential of CE, which tends reach those harder to activate/further away from the labour market (Collins, 2013).

As well as CE reform, two new less-generous direct occupational programmes were established: Tús in 2011 and Gateway in 2013. Both offer non-market work placements, the former in local community and voluntary services and the latter in local authorities. Recruitment to these schemes illustrates the growing compulsive nature of Ireland's activation regime. In the case of Tús as described by the DSP (2012: 20):

> Participants are randomly selected from the Live Register and sanctions apply to those who do not avail of offer of placements. While the scheme aims to contribute to the work readiness of the long-term unemployed, it also contributes to the management of the Live Register in highlighting those who are unemployed but may not be actively seeking work.

Gateway operates in a similar manner, though eligible participants can also voluntarily apply.

In addition to direct work schemes, JobBridge, operating between 2011 and 2016, reflects the policy aspiration to reorient Ireland's activation system to a greater focus on labour market reintegration. JobBridge host-organisations, principally private companies but also public sector bodies and voluntary and community organisations, provided six- or nine-month placements advertised as internships. JobBridge generated considerable controversy for the variable quality of work experience it provided, lack of support for interns, and the inadequacy of the top-up to the intern's social protection payment in meeting costs associated with participation (Doorley, 2015). Its potential for deadweight, job displacement and driving down wages were also raised (Murphy, 2015). Partly in response to these controversies, in late 2016 the scheme was closed to new entrants. This does not necessarily halt this model of activation; a new scheme, targeting the longer-term unemployed is due to replace it.

Other activation schemes have also been transformed. The Back to Work Allowance was closed to new participants in 2009 while the move from unemployment to self-employment was encouraged by the introduction of the Short Term Enterprise Allowance in 2009. The role of the DSP in activation has been more broadly transformed in major institutional reforms in train since 2011. Employment services have been transferred from FÁS to the DSP and integrated with benefit provision in a new service provision model called Intreo. This reflects the international turn to one-stop shops integrating social protection and activation. In turn, FÁS was disbanded and its training services became the remit of a new further education and training agency, Solas, established in 2013.

Under Intreo, instead of the previously used time-based intervention system, on becoming unemployed, individuals are assessed and assigned a Probability of Exit (Pex) score based on how long they are likely to remain unemployed. This score is used to determine the appropriate level of service intervention. Reflecting a lack of resources in the public sector, for the long-term unemployed activation services are provided by a new private service called JobPath, introduced in 2015. Contracted service providers are paid on a payment-by-results basis for placement in the labour market. A tailored activation process for disadvantaged young people called First Steps has also developed. Part of Ireland's EU youth guarantee, it provides internships which are effectively mandatory for participants who are selected by the DSP.

The introduction of new sanctions, and their greater use, also reflects a stronger disciplinary dimension, or 'negative reinforcement' in how unemployed people are activated. The Social Welfare Miscellaneous Provisions Act 2010 introduced penalty rates to payments to the unemployed for failure to participate in approved training and other programmes. The Social Welfare Act 2013 widened the circumstances that would attract a penalty rate of payment, to include refusal or failure to attend activation meetings. If refusal or failure to attend continued under the penalty rate, the Act provides for a disqualification from the payment for up to nine weeks. Since their introduction, the number of penalty rates applied to those in receipt of jobseeker payments has steadily increased from 359 in 2011 to 6,743 in 2015 (Dáil Debates, 2016).

Ireland's greater focus on activation and the introduction of new schemes and services is taken as a potentially stronger turn towards social investment (Daly, 2015). However, echoing criticisms of social investment outlined earlier, the nature of changes have also been questioned for the type of labour market participation they lead to and whether they become a route to more precarious, low-paid work in Ireland post-crisis (Collins and Murphy, 2016). In this regard, the push towards activation, which Murphy (2016: 447) suggests is underpinned by a philosophy that 'any job is better than none', undermines the so-called 'passive' protective functions of social protection with respect to poverty.

Social protection and poverty

The Irish social protection system performs well in reducing poverty when pre-transfer income is compared with post-transfer income. By this metric, 'at risk of poverty' levels in Ireland pre-transfer are among the highest in Europe, but fall to about average after social protection transfers for working-age people, to below average for children and to one of the lowest for older people (Watson and Maître, 2013). This reinforces the important role social protection payments play in society, though it must also be remembered that the majority of working-age social protection payments fall below the 'at risk of poverty' threshold of 60% of median income (€228 per week in 2015). Additionally a mixed picture emerges when we look at anti-poverty policy and how Ireland has performed across different measurements of poverty, particularly in recent years.

Anti-poverty policy originally gained considerable momentum with the adoption of NAPS in 1997 when, for the first time, Irish policy targets were set to reduce poverty. The strategy also preceded EU efforts initiated in 2000 to develop national action planning on poverty and social inclusion as part of its open method of coordination (see Chapter Six). NAPS provided a definition of relative poverty used in successive policy documents:

> People are in poverty if their income and resources (material, cultural and social) are so inadequate as to preclude them from having a standard of living which is regarded as acceptable by Irish society generally. As a result of inadequate income and resources, people may be excluded and marginalised from participating in activities where are considered the norm for other people in society (GoI, 1997: 3).

NAPS targets were informed by a measurement of poverty known as consistent poverty; a measure which 'identifies the proportion of people, from those with an income below a certain threshold, (less than 60% of the median income), who are deprived of one or more goods or services considered essential for a basic standard of living' (GoI, 2007: 24). Currently the deprivation component of consistent poverty comprises 11 indicators, in use from 2007, including items such as two pairs of strong shoes, keeping the home adequately warm, and buying presents for friends or family at least once a year (Maître et al, 2006).

While Ireland's official measure is consistent poverty, in the EU context 'relative income poverty' has been the key measure of poverty, where the percentage of people in a population below 60% of median income is expressed as the 'at risk of poverty rate'. There is, as Walsh (2007) notes, a tension between measuring poverty in consistent and relative terms. Successive Irish governments have been keen to downplay the relative income poverty measure, arguing it is not a useful measure when standards of living are rising, which they did in Ireland over the 1990s until the late 2000s. In the event, relative income poverty, which was substantially higher in Ireland than the European average over the 1990s, fell significantly by the mid-

2000s. On the other hand, anti–poverty advocates have found the consistent poverty measure wanting, particularly in terms of how deprivation indicators are decided.

The original poverty reduction target in NAPS was to reduce the level of consistent poverty from 9%-15% (depending on the median income threshold used) to 5%-10% by 2007. Consistent poverty rates fell quite quickly from 1997 to 2001, and the revised NAPS strategy in 2002 aimed to reduce consistent poverty to below 2% and potentially eliminate it altogether. While this aim was not met, consistent poverty continued to fall until 2008 when it reached 4.2% (see Figure 7.2). The *National Action Plan for Social Inclusion 2007-2016* (GoI, 2007) followed, to guide policy until 2016. The Plan made a commitment to reduce consistent poverty to between 2% and 4% by 2012, and to eliminate it by 2016. However, the economic crisis led to a significant rise in consistent poverty, along with a dramatic rise in the enforced deprivation rate which measures material deprivation alone (Figure 7.2). Children in particular are more vulnerable to consistent poverty and material deprivation and across household types lone-parent families generally have the highest consistent poverty, relative poverty and enforced deprivation rates (CSO EU-SILC).

Figure 7.2: Poverty rates in Ireland 2004-14 and Europe 2020 targets

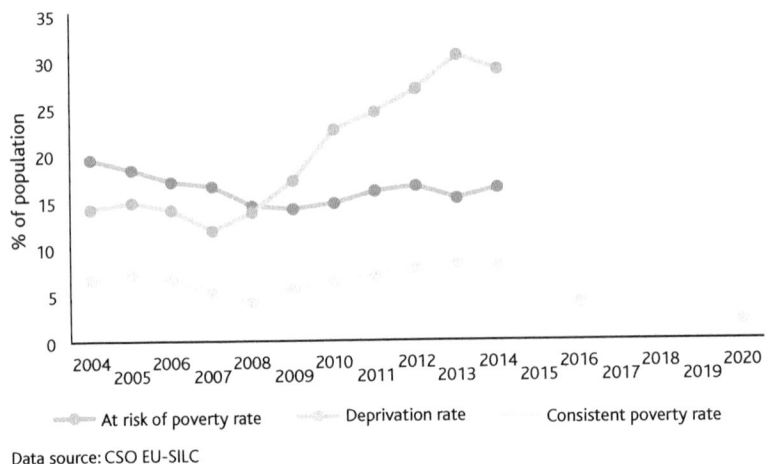

Data source: CSO EU-SILC

In the meantime Europe's strategy for growth Europe 2020 (see Chapter Six) included a specific target on poverty; the first time such a quantitative social target was included in EU policy (Copeland and Daly, 2012). Member states were also permitted to use their own equivalent measures which led to the Irish government using consistent poverty. As its contribution to this target, Ireland revised its NAPinclusion target to reduce consistent poverty to 4% in 2016 and to 2% or less by 2020, based on a 2010 baseline rate of 6.2%. However, Ireland's targets under this plan prove elusive as consistent poverty rates remained high.

None of this of course tells us anything about the everyday lived reality of poverty and the impact of policy on people's lives. Statistical measures and 'counting the poor' are important to inform and evaluate policy. However, the reality of poverty, the struggles of 'existing, not living' and the relational/symbolic dimensions of poverty associated with 'lack of voice, respect and self-esteem, isolation and humiliation' (Lister, 2004: 13), also need to be understood and responded to in the policy decisions that impact on the lives of poor people. As Lister argues (2015) the lack of recognition of these dimensions of poverty constitutes a form of symbolic injustice. Understanding poverty in this way means that we should consider questions of social welfare rates, cuts and coercive activation not only for their individual financial impact and for their effect on poverty trends and targets, but for what they tell us about recognition of people's worth and their impact on people's ability to live decent and meaningful lives.

Chapter summary
- The first section examined the relationship between social justice, redistribution and social protection, and reviewed the range of approaches to the formation and development of social protection systems, including social insurance, social assistance and universal-type systems. Challenges faced by all social protection systems, including economic and sociodemographic trends, impacting on the values and cost of all systems in various ways, were also examined. Within this context, the trends of cost containment and of reorienting systems towards the needs and activation of people of 'working age' was noted in particular.
- The second section reviewed the development of the Irish social protection system and explained the reasons why it has relied strongly on social assistance with limited potential for redistribution. The gradual growth of the system to include recognition of a wider range of needs, but within a highly categorical framework since the 1960s was also discussed. This section ended with a review of the 1980s; a decade which posed serious challenges for the social protection system and under which it managed to stay intact without major erosion.
- Section three considered reforms within the system since the 1990s: a period heavily impacted by the fluctuating fortunes of the economy. The social protection system benefited from economic growth in the earlier period but has been retrenched and restructured to varying degrees during the recent period of austerity. The longer-term legacy may be a strengthened activation system integrated with social protection, but the direction in which it is being restructured raises questions about the nature of social protection in the early twenty-first century. To what extent can we still talk about social justice, redistribution and protection?

Discussion points
- What are the main differences between social insurance, social assistance and universalism?
- What is poverty?
- Is social investment is the best response to twenty-first century social risks?
- Is any job better than none?

Further reading list
Cousins, M (2003) *The birth of social welfare in Ireland, 1922-52*, Dublin: Four Courts Press

McCashin, A (2004) *Social security in Ireland*, Dublin: Gill & Macmillan

Murphy, M (2012) 'Interests, institutions and ideas: Explaining Irish social security policy', *Politics & Policy*, 40:3, 347-65

eight

Health policy

The notion of crisis is a familiar one in the context of Irish health policy. Health is one of the most contested and debated areas of social policy and gains an enormous amount of media attention. Waves of stories about waiting lists, public patients versus private patients, chaotic accident and emergency services, misdiagnoses, patient deaths, unhygienic hospitals, elder abuse in nursing homes, and problems with health budgets abound. These issues raise wider questions about the extent to which equity or equal access for all is pursued, the way the Irish health system is organised and managed, and the extent to which scarce resources are put to the most efficient use. These questions are not exclusive to the Irish system but are shared across all healthcare systems at a time when health policy is undergoing what appears to be constant reform. This chapter aims to look therefore at the broad context of healthcare and current healthcare issues before examining the development of the Irish system and the current key issues and challenges it faces.

Chapter outline
- Section one introduces the core concepts and issues associated with healthcare, including the diversity of systems in which states create and deliver healthcare, and it also briefly reviews some contemporary reform issues.
- In section two we look at the historical development of the Irish system, tracing its roots and subsequent development over the twentieth century and locating it within the broader context for understanding healthcare outlined in section one.
- Section three examines the contemporary Irish healthcare system, focusing on policy reform since the 1990s and the issue of equity of access to healthcare in particular.

SECTION ONE
HEALTHCARE CONCEPTS, HEALTHCARE SYSTEMS AND RECENT TRENDS

Healthcare concepts

Health inequality, inequity and equity

Health is a fundamental resource for human life and human flourishing. Ill health can have a ripple effect, leading to problems in other areas of our lives, such as the ability to obtain and remain in employment, and to participate in society. Conversely, good health can be an important resource in overcoming social disadvantage (Braveman and Gruskin, 2003). Differences in health status are therefore an important issue for health policy.

The term 'health inequality' is used to refer broadly to differences in health status. However, it has a range of meanings. Graham (2007) identifies three interpretations of health inequalities. These are differences in health status between (1) individuals, (2) population groups and (3) groups occupying unequal positions in society, such as people in poverty or ethnic minorities. The first meaning focuses on individualised patterns of health and simply sees them as differences among people 'ungrouped'. The second approach acknowledges a social pattern to health, in other words, different groups in the population, such as older people, women or social classes vary according to health status. The third meaning explicitly links health differences with people's unequal position in society. These differences matter in terms of policy formation and practical consequences. They can influence commitments to measuring health inequalities and the allocation of resources to address these inequalities (Braveman, 2006).

The use of the term 'health inequality' associated with Graham's third interpretation suggests an acknowledgement of injustice. In contrast, terms such as variations or disparities, reflecting the first and second of Graham's interpretations, describe a situation without necessarily implying there is anything to be done about such inequalities. When health differences are considered unjust these are referred to as **health inequities**. If health inequalities are acknowledged as unfair then health policy becomes concerned with the challenge of trying to ensure equity. This involves a movement beyond the commitment to equity as an ethical principle, to trying to achieve equity in a practical and measurable way. The World Health Organization (WHO) suggests that 'health equity has two important strands: improving average health of countries and abolishing avoidable inequalities in health between countries. In both cases ... the aim should be to

> **Health inequity** exists where differences in health are present across different income and social groups, and are considered to be avoidable and unfair.

bring the health of those worse off up to the level of the best' (WHO, 2008: 29). The policy implications of this generally extend beyond the remit of health policy to include areas that affect the social determinants of health such as income redistribution, housing and education. As the WHO (2008: 26) states:

> Certainly, maldistribution of health care – not delivering care to those who most need it – is one of the social determinants of health. But the high burden of illness responsible for appalling premature loss of life arises in large part because of the conditions in which people are born, grow, live, work and age. ... Poor and unequal conditions are, in their turn, the consequence of deeper structural conditions that together fashion the way societies are organised – poor social policies and programmes, unfair economic arrangements, and bad politics.

The impact of wider societal inequalities on health has been notably demonstrated by Wilkinson and Pickett's (2009) work on income inequality, showing that more equal societies perform better on a range of health outcomes related to physical and mental health, such as life expectancy and depression; and to wider public health issues, such as obesity. This relationship matters not only in material terms (more money equates with access to better healthcare and so on) but also in social terms because of 'status syndrome' (Marmot, 2015). The stress or social pain of being compared and held in poor esteem matters in terms of health. These issues are all the more important because of the trend of growing inequality both between and within societies, leading to widening gaps in health status between rich and poor. This is a trend affecting almost all countries, the main difference being the rate or speed at which the gap is widening, with the UK and the US 'leading' the way (Hunter, 2016). In the realm of health policy, at a broad level, equity involves consideration of 'need rather than underlying social advantage ... in decisions about resource allocation that affect health' (WHO, 1998: 2). In other words, need for healthcare, rather than ability to pay, should be the chief determinant of the allocation of healthcare resources.

Public health systems in general articulate some notion of fairness around how healthcare is provided; however, in practice this may be vague or ambiguous. Generally speaking, European health systems have evolved towards a system of universal access: the public health system is made available to everyone on an equal basis. This means offering universal coverage to the core elements of the healthcare system, including **primary, secondary and tertiary care**, without having to pay at the point of use. This, for the most part, was achieved by almost all European states by the 1980s (Freeman, 2000). This embodies the principle of equal access to available care for equal need.

> **Primary care** covers the first points of contact within a health system in the community. It encompasses access to curative and preventive care by healthcare professionals such as general practitioners, public health nurses and dentists. **Secondary care** includes more specialised care following primary care referral, including outpatient and emergency hospital department services and specialised non-hospital services such as psychiatry and occupational therapy. **Tertiary care** refers to inpatient hospital care.

Efficiency

Health systems also have to work under economic principles, most importantly the principle of efficiency. Healthcare has the potential to absorb what seems like limitless amounts of money. As health services have to be paid for and resources are not unlimited, it is important that the most efficient use of resources available is made. The allocation of resources therefore involves a trade-off between fairness and efficiency. Efficiency is also linked to the challenge of cost containment, something all healthcare systems increasingly grapple with.

Simply defined, economic efficiency is about 'making the best use of limited resources given people's tastes' (Barr, 2004: 66). LeGrand et al (1992: 41) define an efficient level of healthcare 'as one that maximizes the difference between benefits and costs'. In economic theory this is about finding the point where the distance between the benefits and costs of producing a particular good is the greatest. For example, an efficient number of hospitals within a city would mean the benefits produced by the hospitals outweigh the costs of building and running the hospitals to the greatest degree. Opening another hospital would cost more than the benefits to be gained from having another hospital in the region. However, like equity, efficiency is contested concept. One of the main reasons is because efficiency can be difficult to measure, particularly when it comes to measuring benefits. As Duff (1997: 62) points out 'it is extremely difficult to define what maximum benefit or output means in health care. ... it could be the number of days it takes to heal after taking a prescription, or how well one feels, or some other indicator'. There is also ongoing debate about whether markets or governments are best placed to deliver efficient healthcare. Recent decades have seen a turn towards market-based reforms in the delivery of healthcare services, driven by new public management thinking and the assumption that market-like principles in the public system will drive efficiency. This is something we return to later.

Healthcare systems

Three main types of healthcare system have been identified: national health systems, social health insurance systems and private health insurance systems. One of the first typologies was produced by the OECD, which constructed a continuum from the principle of social equity to patient sovereignty (Figure 8.1) and located each model along this continuum.

Figure 8.1: A continuum of healthcare systems

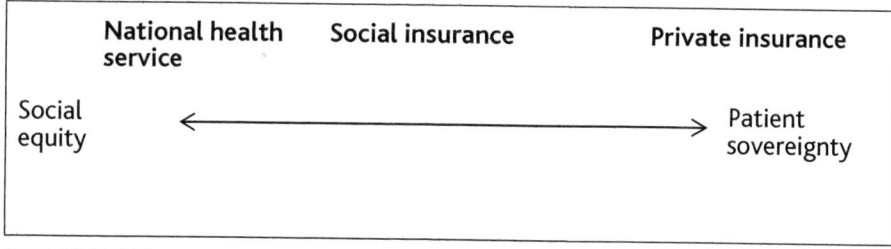

Source: OECD, 1987

The OECD classification focused on funding as the main element influencing the organisation of healthcare systems, which in turn impacts on the balance between equity and individual choice. This classification was developed in the context of concerns about the cost of health and how to pay for it, and how to make the most efficient use of money spent on healthcare, which has increasingly preoccupied debate since the 1970s.

Since the OECD study others have identified further significant factors that shape an individual country's health system (see Wendt et al, 2009, for an overview). This research broadened the focus of health system typologies beyond health economics to looking at how health systems are also inherently political. One of the most systematic and comprehensive typologies is offered by Moran (1999, 2000). Moran's work draws attention to the politics of healthcare, in particular the distributive struggles about who gets what kind healthcare and who pays for it, and the role of healthcare within an economy. In this regard Moran suggests that the healthcare state has three 'faces'. The first concerns welfare and setting out access to health services. The second relates to the economic activity of regulating the industrial aspects of health, primarily the production of pharmaceuticals and medical equipment. The third involves the regulation of health interests. This includes not only industrial interests, but also very significant professional interests, especially doctors, whose actions, particularly relating to their power in deciding the consumption of healthcare, are a key component in understanding healthcare provision and policy making.

Moran offers a typology involving four basic types: secure and insecure command and control type systems, corporatist systems and supply systems. The first two roughly correspond with the national health model, the third with social insurance and the fourth with private insurance. Though more nuanced, Moran's work also demonstrates the basic utility of the national health system, social health insurance system and private health system typology. Wendt's (2014) work also shows that when comparative dimensions are widened to include, for example, indicators of eligibility for services and the degree to which systems change over time, this trifold classification remains largely relevant.

National health systems

In national health systems healthcare is publicly provided on a universal basis and funded through general taxation. All citizens are therefore entitled to basic healthcare, including hospital and general practitioner (GP) services and medicines, which they do not pay for at the point of use. Healthcare infrastructure such as hospitals and primary care services are publicly owned and/or controlled. This type of healthcare system was first established in New Zealand in 1938; however, it is most directly identified with the British system, founded in the 1940s as part of the Beveridge reforms. This model was also adopted in Scandinavian countries. As it is strongly motivated by equity, need rather than the ability to pay is the main factor influencing healthcare in this system.

Moran (1999, 2000) refers to this as a command and control system because the state is heavily implicated in the control and allocation of resources. This allows for the pursuit of an equitable distribution of healthcare between people of different social classes and between different regions, and for the pursuit of efficiency through administrative means such as rationing. Hunter (2016) suggests that this system is actually the most efficient type of health system. This, however, also depends on the strength of the state to control expenditure and other system actors, such as medical professionals and pharmaceutical companies.

Moran's account differentiates between secure and insecure command and control systems. The latter include national health-type systems developed later, specifically in Italy (1978), Portugal (1979) Greece (1983) and Spain (1986). These systems have been described as 'formally ambitious but under-resourced' (Freeman, 2000: 6) meaning that they have not been able to reach the level of equal resource distribution that the earlier systems achieved. Moreover, as Moran (2000) notes, these later systems have had to survive in a harsher economic climate, compared to the 'golden age' in which the earlier national systems grew. However, the older established systems are also struggling, especially in the context of recent austerity, with fewer resources and rising costs. Therefore both the secure and insecure systems share similar problems.

Social health insurance

This model is also referred to as corporatist-type health systems and it is common in continental Europe. Under this system healthcare is paid for by insurance based on employer and employee contributions. The state subsidises individuals who cannot afford to pay. There are different versions of this model, depending on how the insurance funds are regulated. Some countries operate under a single public-fund system, many European countries have competing public and private insurance funds, and, in a limited number of cases, all funds are private, though the way the private insurers are regulated means that it is still considered a social insurance model (Wendt, 2014). These insurance funds usually contract services from both public and private hospitals and from independent doctors. Individuals may also take out supplementary private insurance to cover care not provided under social insurance.

The social character of the insurance system means that it has similarities with the tax-based national health model and differences that set it apart from private insurance. In contrast to private health insurance, social insurance is usually compulsory and the system is essentially collectivist; risk is pooled without taking account of differences in health status between contributors. Also, as Freeman (2000) points out regarding funding, there is little to distinguish national health and social insurance-based systems: both are essentially funded through taxes. However, in terms of expenditure, social insurance systems tend to cost more, because of greater administrative costs and the tendencies within the model towards over-treating and over-pricing (Street, 2015). This appears to be borne out in health expenditure trends among countries included in Figure 8.2.

Private health insurance

Private health insurance companies enter the health insurance market in order to make a profit, and they operate predominantly in countries with weak public healthcare provision. Private insurance differs from social insurance because it is predominantly funded by the individual, is voluntary and the cost of insurance is usually risk-related. This means that differences in the health status of individuals are reflected in different premiums. People with a history of particular illnesses may have to pay higher premiums, and payments may also be loaded if an individual engages in what is considered risky behaviour, such as smoking. Private health insurance therefore does not have the solidaristic quality of social insurance systems.

The US most closely approximates the private health insurance model, which is also referred to as the supply healthcare state (Moran, 2000). Advocates argue that it promotes individual choice or patient sovereignty, because individuals choose what insurance to take out, what doctors to see and what hospitals to go to. Consequently health providers have to compete for customers, which helps to ensure efficiency, and the supply-led nature of the system drives innovation in medical technology (Moran, 1999). This argument, however, ignores the fact that the system is built on making profits. The US, therefore, has been beset by the costliness of the model and the lack of access for people who could not afford to pay and who did not qualify for the two public schemes, Medicare for older people and Medicaid for low-income people (see also Figure 8.2). After struggling with enormous ideological and corporate resistance the Patient Protection and Affordable Care Act 2010, known as Obamacare, aimed to somewhat transform the system by ensuring affordable access to health insurance and by restricting the risk-related premium setting of its private health insurance operators (Béland et al., 2016). At the time of writing, whether these reforms hold is deeply uncertain, given Donald Trump's election as president and his intention to dismantle Obamacare.

Box 8.1: Where does the Irish healthcare system fit?

No country fits exactly within healthcare model and every country can to some extent be considered a mixed system. This is particularly true in the Irish case, which contains elements of both a national health and a private system. In terms of publicly provided services, hospital care is available to everyone and funded primarily from general taxation, along with a capped hospital charge, while GP care is only available free to those who qualify (see Box 8.4). This sets Ireland apart from other European healthcare systems; it is the only one not to provide GP care free at the point of use (Thomson et al, 2014). Private care is a significant feature of the Irish system, the main benefits being access to private hospitals and timelier care. This is known as a duplicate system: the services provided by private insurers are also available in the public service. The only other OECD country to have a similarly high rate of duplication is Australia (OECD, 2015b). Another relatively unique feature of the Irish system is the entangled relationship between the public system and private insurance: besides private hospitals, a substantial amount of private care is delivered within the public system. This has produced many inequities and inefficiencies, discussed in sections two and three.

Trends and issues across healthcare systems

Cost containment has become one of the biggest challenges in healthcare systems in recent decades, in the context of rising expenditure. Figure 8.2 shows that the total expenditure (both public and private) on health as a percentage of GDP has risen significantly since the 1970s. The rate of growth has been relatively consistent over time. The US stands out as exceptional, having a particularly high level of health expenditure, over half of which is private and is explained by its particular healthcare system.

Cost containment is related to a number of other challenges health systems are facing. These include demographic changes, changes in the nature of illness and disease, rising expectations and medical progress. The demographic profile of Western nations has changed considerably with a decline in birth rates coupled with an increase in life expectancy, meaning that populations are ageing and older people tend to need greater healthcare. While the origins of many systems were tied to concerns about workers' health, in contemporary healthcare systems the health problems of those outside the labour market require as much, if not more, attention. This includes not just older people but also the chronically (long-term) sick as the incidence of chronic sickness has risen in recent decades. This is partly a reflection of medical progress which has allowed people with chronic illnesses to live longer, yet this also means that greater demands are made of health services. Another related challenge is the rise of so-called diseases of affluence and lifestyle, such as obesity, alcohol misuse and mental ill health, but which in many cases are driven by the characteristics of contemporary capitalism,

Figure 8.2: Current health expenditure as a percentage of GDP in selected OECD countries

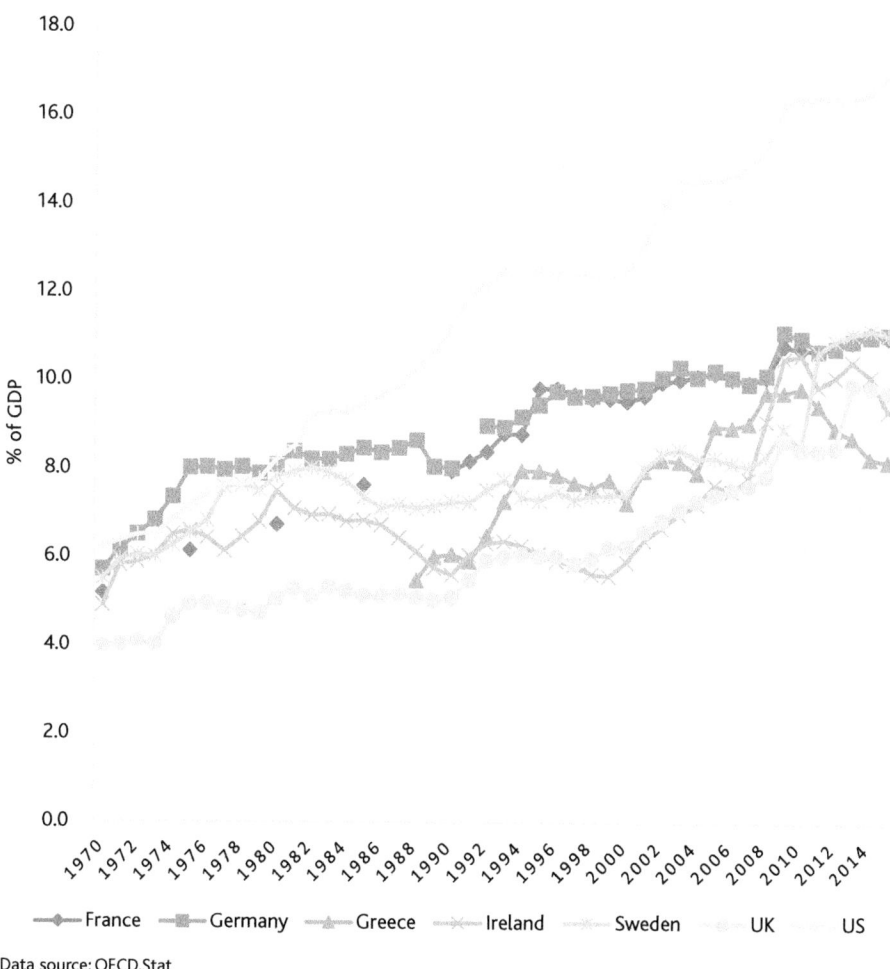

Data source: OECD.Stat

not least of which is inequality, meaning that many of these health problems are patterned by social class.

The rise in chronic illness is related to two other phenomena: medical progress and rising patient expectations. People have become more informed about the illnesses they are experiencing and the quality of care they expect from health providers (Lenaghan, 1997). The rise of health activism, particularly through patient interest groups, means that some groups of patients at least may no longer accurately be depicted as a 'repressed structural interest' within the system (Alford, 1975: 15). Advances in medicine and medical technology also put increasing pressure on healthcare systems. Advances tend to be related to high-cost technologies and procedures involving highly skilled labour. Initially these may be accessed by patients with private insurance, which in turn puts pressure on public systems to make the procedures and medicines available on the grounds of equity.

If these are the issues influencing rising costs, on the other side healthcare states have been trying to contain costs. Like social protection, health expenditure also constitutes a large proportion of public expenditure, and cost containment in this case has been particularly tied to new public management. Debate about the need for reform as well as actual reforms that have taken place is thus 'informed by a market-based ideology in which private sector practice is claimed to be superior and as providing a model for the transformation of allegedly underperforming, low-quality public services, and weak public sector management' (Hunter, 2016: 11). This dovetails with rising expectations which are translated into the need to offer patients, framed as consumers, more choice in how care is provided and more information about the quality and performance of healthcare providers. This has seen the principle of market competition and other elements of private sector management thinking applied to the organisation, funding and delivery of healthcare. The application of market principles, combined with the objective of containing costs can result in attempts to shift the costs of healthcare from the state to the individual. This is a regressive or inequitable step: ability to pay rather than need begins to creep into the allocation of healthcare and this affects hardest those with the least ability to pay. This also erodes universal access.

However, such reform is an unsettled process and change swings back and forth between greater and lesser levels of competition and marketisation. Reform seems to be a permanent feature of health policy and, as Toth (2010: 87) observes, 'most of the problems afflicting healthcare systems in the early 1990s remain largely unsolved even today'. Alford's (1972) earlier characterisation of health policy as 'dynamics without change' continues to be an apt description of health service reform.

The type of changes occurring in national health services, such as in the UK and in Sweden, include the use of quasi- or internal markets. The state still controls the overall amount of the health budget, but the budget is allocated according to principles of supply and demand. Different areas of the health services are split into buyers, such as doctors, and sellers, such as hospitals, who compete for their custom. Money thus 'follows the patient'. In national healthcare systems rationing has also become more significant. Rationing has always been part of the way these systems operated; however, it has become more problematic compared to the 1950s, when many of these systems were established and rationing was more easily accepted. The use of waiting lists is one of the most well-known methods of rationing. These may be used in conjunction with performance management techniques, such as target setting and penalties for not reaching them, in order to reduce waiting times and waiting lists. Use of private care services in a bid to reduce waiting lists is also a way in which private healthcare grows while public health service activity is curtailed. One of the ways social health insurance systems have responded to the problem of rising costs is by introducing competition through choice of insurer, which, it is assumed, will drive down costs.

Developments common to both national health and social health insurance systems include restriction in the use of, or insurance coverage for, certain drugs and services. This can prompt a rise in the take-up of private health insurance in countries with national health-type systems and supplementary insurance in social insurance systems. Another common feature is the increasing use of 'out-of-pocket' payments, implying that the sick take on a greater burden for how care is paid for. Examples include increasing co-payments for items such as drugs, and the extension of user charges for services such as inpatient treatment and dental services (Blank and Burau, 2014). Because of such trends the solidaristic nature of public health systems can begin to erode and the boundaries blur between public and private healthcare (Moran, 2000). The equitable base on public healthcare is also threatened as such moves impede access to services and are regressive in their impact, disproportionately affecting poorer health users (Blank and Burau, 2014). These trends have translated into a relative retreat of public health spending. Public expenditure has risen more slowly than private expenditure: its share of overall expenditure has fallen from an OECD average of 80% in 1980 to 75% in 2005 (Rothgang et al, 2010 in Wendt, 2013).

Such trends have become acute in the last decade, particularly in European countries heavily affected by the 2008 economic crisis and undergoing prolonged austerity. While cost containment typically achieves only a slow-down in the rate of expenditure increase, trends across Europe in the early 2010s produced the rarer outcome of reductions in health expenditure in real terms (OECD, 2015b). Cost containment has been particularly ramped up in Spain, Greece, Italy, Portugal and Ireland, some of which was imposed under EU/IMF loan conditions. Measures include capping health budgets; increasing out-of-pocket payments; reducing the amount paid for pharmaceuticals resulting in medicine shortage in some cases; reducing the number of public hospital beds and the opening hours of services; and cutting budgets for preventive care, such as vaccines. These restrictions were compounded by the negative effects of the economic crisis on health. The crisis was found to have a worsening effect on mental health in particular, demonstrated by the increasing incidence of anxiety, depression and suicide (Karanikolos et al, 2016).

SECTION TWO
THE DEVELOPMENT OF THE IRISH HEALTHCARE SYSTEM

Pre-independence

Early state involvement in healthcare across Europe was primarily tied to the threat the spread of disease posed to the population at large. Early hospitals, like workhouses, served as institutions to contain the sick and prevent contagion. Public health measures originating from the mid-1800s onwards were similarly concerned with controlling outbreaks of disease and epidemics. These developments sprung as much from voluntary charitable efforts as they did from the state. Charitable efforts were often religiously motivated and there is a long history of religious bodies caring for the sick across Europe prior to state intervention.

In Ireland and elsewhere, hospitals were not associated with cure but were places of last resort. Admission to hospital was a sign of inability to pay for care in the home and a sign of the divide between the rich and the poor. The rich accessed the services of private physicians in their own homes, allowing them to minimise the risk of contagion. The rich/poor divide also applied to maternity care (Barrington, 1987). In the case of mental illness those with enough money tended to send their 'insane' to private institutions abroad while the 'insane poor' had to enter existing houses of industry (Finnane, 1981).

The earliest Irish hospitals and dispensaries (clinics which distributed medicines and provided the services of a dispensary doctor), built in the early to mid-1700s, were the product of charitable efforts. The hospitals were classed as 'charitable infirmaries' and later known as voluntary hospitals. By the mid-1800s more vigorous and sustained state effort in healthcare for the sick poor came about under the poor law, which provided an administrative framework for an expanding range of healthcare services. Poor law institutions took over the running of dispensaries in 1851 and services were provided to all those deemed unable to afford medical help, not just the destitute as before. Workhouse infirmaries gradually accommodated more people, especially those not treatable in the existing network of infirmaries, and their role gradually transformed into one of a general hospital (Earner-Byrne, 2007).

The public health movement of the mid-nineteenth century was primarily concerned with attempting to control the spread of infectious diseases such as typhus and cholera, which were a major problem, especially in urban areas. Other public health measures included the Births and Deaths Registration (Ireland) Act 1864, the Public Health Act 1878 and the Compulsory Vaccination (Ireland) Act 1885. These Acts represented the growth of state intervention in health in the name of prevention, regulation and control. However, implementation of this legislation was challenging. There was an air of apathy and helplessness among the public health authorities, who were hampered by the reluctance to impose higher taxes necessary to fund services, and by the scale of poverty and squalor (Barrington, 1987). As was the case previously with the development of infirmaries, voluntary efforts often took the lead in public health measures in areas such as tuberculosis, and maternity and child welfare (Earner-Byrne, 2007).

The 1880s is commonly identified as the beginnings of a marked increase in state involvement in healthcare (Freeman, 2000). In the Irish case, increased state involvement was dependent on developments in Britain. A collective insurance-based response to the health needs of workers was not introduced in the UK until 1911, when health insurance was introduced as part of the National Insurance Act. As discussed in Chapter One, this entitled workers under a certain income limit to medical benefit which took them out of the dispensary service and gave them free use of GP services and medicines. In Ireland the health insurance part of the Act was not passed, as the strength of those who opposed it outweighed those in favour. The Irish Party was concerned about the costs of the scheme and it was considered an unfair form of taxation. The medical profession were divided on the basis of who was to gain and lose income under the proposals. The strongest opposition came from the Catholic Church who, paying scant regard to the needs of the working class, saw nothing in health insurance for agricultural and business interests (Barrington, 1987; Powell, 1992). Social insurance as a funding mechanism for GP services therefore did not take root in Ireland. The dispensary service remained, with eligibility determined by income and need. For everyone else, GP services would continue to be accessed privately. This episode represented a significant juncture in the history of Irish health policy. The introduction of health insurance in various forms across Europe set countries on a path of gradually extending access to medical services. By contrast Ireland lacked this foundation on which to build health services and improve access.

1920s and 1930s

In common with the other social services, few changes occurred in healthcare once Ireland gained independence. Administrative changes came on foot of the Ministers and Secretaries Act 1924 which led to the creation of a Department of Local Government and Public Health. Administrative reform did not lead to new services; old ones were recycled. Workhouses were converted into public hospitals either in the form of county homes (to cater mainly for older people), county hospitals (one per county to act as the main hospital), and district or local hospitals. The Commission on the Relief of the Sick and Destitute Poor 1929 was severely critical of the services provided under this framework, finding the network of public hospitals underfunded and inadequate (Robins, 1960). Two of the biggest health problems of the early twentieth century – infant mortality and tuberculosis – were neglected. Mother and infant services were left mainly to voluntary initiatives. Tuberculosis services shared a similar fate, with shortage of accommodation a particular problem. Consequently, while other countries experienced an improvement in the death rates because fewer people were dying from tuberculosis, the rate of decline in Ireland was minimal.

By the 1930s the focus turned to attempting to rationalise the network of hospitals. This was prompted by the financial crisis experienced by the voluntary hospital sector, giving rise to the hospital sweepstakes. The Public Charitable Hospitals Act 1930 legalised sweepstakes on horse races for the purposes of raising funds for hospitals. (The hospital sweepstakes operated until 1986 when it was replaced by the National Lottery, under which health services continue to receive funding.) The sweepstakes were very successful during their first decade, and marked 'the first step towards much greater involvement by public authorities in the affairs of hospitals' (Barrington, 1987: 111-12). The increasing cost of and demand for hospital care and specialist treatment also posed a challenge, as this had the potential to widen the gulf between the rich and poor in terms of accessing healthcare.

The Fianna Fáil government established a Hospitals Commission in 1933 to survey existing services and plan a coherent approach to future hospital provision. It recommended 12 main hospital centres and the amalgamation of some of the voluntary hospitals so as to improve their facilities and coordinate their services. The rationale for these developments included an attempt to have some equality of treatment between fee-paying patients and non-fee-paying patients, make efficient use of services, and avoid a situation where private patients would be treated in voluntary hospitals and the poor in public hospitals. Public hospitals on the whole were less popular and held the stigma of their workhouse origins (Robbins and Lapsley, 2008). The Commission recommended that voluntary hospitals be required to maintain a certain proportion of non-fee-paying patients and the practice of a public/private mix in Irish hospitals began. Consultants in the voluntary hospitals and to a lesser extent in the local authority hospitals were allowed to use private beds and hospital services for private patients, treating non-fee-paying patients in return (NESF, 2002). By now the sweepstakes were administered through a Hospital Trust Fund and the money was used to finance the construction of new public hospitals as well as support the voluntary ones (Barrington, 1987). In the case of voluntary hospitals, public funding generally increased over time, yet these hospitals were not nationalised as in Britain (Finn and Hardiman, 2012). The easy availability of funding also obscured questions of rationalisation and efficiency, storing up problems for later decades. However, despite this intense period of capital investment, the overall health status of the population left a lot to be desired. Life expectancy lagged behind the UK, infant mortality was still high and tuberculosis remained a significant problem. This situation was in part a reflection on the fact that services required to address these issues continued to be under-resourced.

1940s and 1950s

The 1940s marked the emergence of a new phase in state involvement in healthcare across Europe, with growing universalisation of access to healthcare. These developments did not occur without controversy, and more radical reforms arose in countries which had stronger Left-wing parties twinned with less than coherent opposition from existing interests such as the medical profession and insurance funds (Freeman, 2000). In Ireland, debates about healthcare were influenced to a degree by the developing welfare state in Britain and the establishment of the National Health Service (NHS) in 1948. While Aneurin Bevan, the minister for health, succeeded in overcoming opposition to the NHS, attempts to widen access to health services in Ireland entailed much more of a struggle with structural interests. These included the medical profession, the Catholic Church and the Catholic-owned voluntary hospitals. All feared further state encroachment into existing practices, which would mean a loss of autonomy, damage to the prevailing Catholic ethos, and in the case of the medical practitioners, potential loss of income from private practice. These oppositional forces came to a head in the Mother and Child controversy over the late 1940s and early 1950s. The controversy is discussed in Chapter Two, here the focus is on the implications the outcome had for the overall development of the healthcare system, and how events in Ireland can be understood in the wider context of universalising access during this period.

The eventual outcome of the controversy was the Health Act 1953 which offered a much more limited Mother and Child service, as part of wider health reforms. These reforms included the extension of free hospital services and the institution of three categories of eligibility for health services. Category one, those with the lowest incomes, were provided with free access to all services. Category two, the middle 50% of income earners, were provided with free hospital care, but not GP care. Category three users, roughly the top 15% of income earners, had to pay for almost all services, except those for tuberculosis. While it has since been modified, this arrangement set in the 1950s remains the cornerstone of access and entitlement in the Irish healthcare system, with different categories of entitlement based on income.

The whole episode therefore significantly curtailed efforts to develop a universal health service free at the point of use, which would have seen the majority of the medical profession working for the public service and paid a salary. Under the 1953 legislation the public/private mix in public hospitals became more entrenched because the legislation provided for payments to consultants treating public patients in voluntary hospitals and this subsequently become the norm (NESF, 2002). In addition, Voluntary Health Insurance (VHI) was introduced in 1956 in response to the continuing opposition by the Irish Medial Association to the 1953 reforms because of the loss of private patients. A state-sponsored VHI Board was set up offering insurance cover on a non-profit basis for the hospital costs incurred by category three health users and the hospital costs incurred by category two users who opted for private care. Although it was initially intended to cater for the small number of people not entitled to public care, this turned out not to be the case and the take-up of private insurance grew substantially. However, the period also held out some positive developments. For example, while Noël Browne was minister for health he used the Hospital Trust Fund to embark on a major programme of upgrading and building hospitals, making a greater range of diagnostic tools and surgical procedures available in county hospitals. This expansionary programme was continued by successive governments in the 1950s to meet the growing demands for healthcare as a result of increased entitlements to public healthcare following the 1953 Act. Building on the efforts of earlier doctors, such as Dorothy Price working with children who acquired the disease, Browne also recognised the significance of vaccination against tuberculosis. The implementation of a nationwide vaccination programme in the early 1950s meant that by the end of the decade, tuberculosis ceased to be a major problem (Ó hÓgartaigh, 1999).

1960s and 1970s

During this period the focus of the health system turned towards administrative reform and continuing attempts to rationalise services, which were expanding greatly. There were more hospitals and services to run, and they were in demand by the larger proportion of the population who were entitled to services free, as together category one and two health users amounted to approximately 85% of the population. While health improved in terms of tuberculosis, life expectancy and infant mortality, new health problems were replacing them, especially heart disease, cancer, diseases related to ageing, drug and alcohol dependency, and deaths due to accidents. Costs rose significantly, as the proportion of GDP devoted to health expenditure increased from 3.7% in 1960 to 5.1% in 1970 (OECD, 2008). In 1966 the Fianna Fáil government published a White Paper entitled *The Health Services and their Further Development* (GoI, 1966). This White Paper is significant for being the road map for many of the developments which have since occurred. However, at the outset it declared that the state did not have 'a duty to provide unconditionally for all medical services free of cost for everyone' (Barrington, 1987: 261) which basically confirmed existing eligibility arrangements.

The White Paper recommended that category one individuals be granted a choice of doctor and a choice of pharmacist instead of receiving drugs directly from the dispensary doctor, and doctors would be obliged to treat category one patients in the same facilities as private patients. These changes signalled the end of the dispensary system, which was replaced by a General Medical Services Scheme (GMS) in 1972. While the end of the dispensary system and the division between public and private GP patients was most welcome, the creation of the GMS was problematic, principally because, after doctor opposition, doctors were paid a fee per service rather than a typically less costly annual lump sum per patient.

The White Paper also assessed trends and problems in hospital services. It ascertained that county hospitals were no longer suitable as the main hospital for a region: these needed to be based in larger regions and tied to regional rather than county-based administration. The task of formulating a plan to implement this was given to a Consultative Council on the General Hospital Services in 1967. The Council's report, known as the Fitzgerald Report, proposed a systematic but controversial plan by recommending fewer and larger hospitals. The report was not well received at local level, with each area defending its own hospital against what was perceived as downgrading to a community health centre, and regional hospitals were considered too far away from many rural areas (Barrington, 1987). In any event, hospital services did not undergo a major rationalisation until the 1980s.

The Health Act 1970 brought many of the changes outlined in the 1966 White Paper to fruition. Eight regional Health Boards replaced county-based administration. Health Boards became the main operational centres for administering and delivering services. To appease local interests, local authority representatives comprised the majority of Board members. Eligibility for hospital services was extended in 1979 when then minister for health Charles Haughey implemented a plan for free hospital care for all three user categories. However, category three users were still liable to pay consultant charges. On the whole the 1970s delivered another phase of expansion which entailed significant increases in expenditure. While all health funding was now under the control of central government this did not actually put a brake on expenditure (see Figure 8.1), which can be partly explained by population growth.

The 1980s

The economic climate of 1980s and the consequent turn to cost containment marked a turning point, entrenching the inequities of the health system. Inequitable access, referred to as the two-tier health system, unfolded during the 1980s in the context of two significant trends: public health cutbacks and private health expansion. One of the most visible ways in which health services were cut back was through hospital closures: the first serious rationalisation of hospital services occurred in contrast with earlier decades when rationalisation plans were not followed through. Part of the rationale of cutting hospital services was to promote alternatives. These included community care as envisaged in *Planning for the Future* (Study Group on the Development of Psychiatric Services, 1984) and primary care and **health promotion** as opposed to 'repair' as envisaged in *Health the Wider Dimensions* (DoH, 1986). However, in the climate of fiscal restraint at the time these ideals were not adequately realised. Despite strong local resistance, many district and long-running voluntary hospitals closed. Consequently the number of hospital beds fell by 20% between 1987 and 1993 (OECD.Stat). Other examples of cost containment included the controversial introduction of user charges in 1987; hospital users without a medical card became liable for a charge for overnight hospital stays and outpatient visits. The GMS was also reformed in 1988 to a fee-per-capita system.

> **Health promotion** focuses on health improvement and optimal health, and the individual and social, economic and environmental conditions for its fulfilment.

On the other hand, the provision of private health services grew and the public/ private mix in the system became more entrenched. These trends stemmed in part from the implementation of a common consultants contract in 1981. This contract put consultants in Health Board and voluntary hospitals on the same footing. It provided for a salaried consultant service in all public hospitals and allowed consultants to practice privately either in the public hospital in which they carried out their salaried work or in a private hospital. Crucially, however, this contract did not provide for monitoring consultant time devoted to public patients, and the extent to which consultants could engage in private practice was unspecified. This paved the way for the expansion of private medicine and 'turned heavily state subsidised, private medicine into a growth industry' (Wren, 2003: 57). Regarding private hospitals, the Mater Private and the Blackrock Clinic both opened in Dublin in 1986. The Mater Private was established by the Sisters of Mercy to replace an existing private hospital the order ran. It was subsequently sold to a management group in 2000. The Blackrock clinic was established by Jimmy Sheehan, an orthopaedic consultant, who promoted the notion of health as a commodity:

> The state cannot provide for everyone. ... I think health is a bit like housing. People are entitled to different levels of housing. If they want to put their effort into providing for better housing, they have to work very hard for it and people have forgotten about that in relation to their own health (Sheehan, 2002 in Wren, 2003: 69).

The growth in private hospital care paralleled the growth in private health insurance; the number insured grew from 26.1% of the population in 1979 to 34.4% by 1990. The volume of private activity in public hospitals also grew. In the context of health cutbacks, the extra revenue hospitals could raise by providing private bed accommodation incentivised the transformation of public into private wards, and the proportion of private beds in public hospitals grew from approximately 10% in 1972 to 20% in 1987 (Wren, 2003). The public/private mix has evolved over many decades; however, the sense that it was problematic did not become widespread until the 1980s (NESF, 2002) when the implications of the two-tier system became more visible due to the cutbacks.

Box 8.2: The two-tier health system

The two-tier system refers to two tiers of access and care in the public hospital system. Two-tier access became apparent as public patients experienced growing waiting times for care, while private patients avoided these waiting times and received faster private access to the same hospitals. Two-tiered care emerged, where private patients benefit from a consultant-provided service, whereas care for public patients is consultant-led. This arrangement reflects the fact that consultants are paid a fee per patient in the private system, while their remuneration for the treatment of public patients is salary based. For public patients, besides long waiting times, frontline services are more likely to be provided by trainee non-consultant hospital doctors.

This position is exacerbated by the way in which the public/private mix works in the Irish system, translating to a situation where 'public patients help pay for their own subordination' (Tussing and Wren, 2006: 139). The private component of the public health system does not pay its own way but is publicly subsided. Although modified in recent years, public subsidisation occurs in three principal ways. First, public hospitals do not charge the full costs of providing private care. Second, and in turn, insurance subscription rates do not reflect the full cost of private care and third, these costs are lowered further by the provision of tax relief on insurance premiums. In brief, public money subsidises private health care, which is inefficient use of scarce public resources and inequitable, given the faster access and potentially superior care afforded to private users of hospital care. In terms of health equity, while broadly equity of access is defined in terms of equal access for equal need, in this situation income rather than medical need determines access to hospital care.

One of the first efforts to address the two-tier health service came with the establishment of a Commission on Health Funding in 1987 to examine how an equitable, comprehensive and cost-effective service could be funded. To achieve equity of access, the Commission recommended that there should be greater demarcation between private and public hospital beds, and that a common waiting list be established between public and private patients so that beds would be allocated on the basis of medical priority, not by ability to pay. It also recommended the abolition of tax relief for private insurance and the abolition of category three eligibility to health services so that all hospital services would be publicly available to all users. As examined in section three, some of these recommendations were implemented, at least partially. At the same time the Commission did not see a problem with private insurance as an individual choice. It did 'not consider it inequitable that private insurance should enable individuals to obtain speedier or otherwise unavailable treatment, *provided* that comprehensive and cost-effective publicly-funded health services are available within a reasonable period of time to all those assessed as in need of them' (Commission on Health Funding, 1989: 13). However, this proviso remains a core issue and the inequities of the two-tier system have persisted in the context of limited reform.

SECTION THREE

THE CONTEMPORARY SYSTEM: REFORM SINCE THE 1990s AND CONTINUING ISSUES AND CHALLENGES

Health is one of the social policy areas most subject to what Dunleavy and O'Leary (1987) call 'hyperactivism', not least in the Irish context. Policy developments since the 1990s have included two overall strategic plans; numerous reports dealing with issues of funding, staffing and organisational change; and several more reports dealing with the reorientation of the health services towards health promotion and addressing specific contemporary health problems, including chronic diseases, cancer, obesity, alcohol and drug use (see Box 8.3).

Box 8.3: Main health policy documents and developments since the early 1990s

1994   *Shaping a Healthier Future*

1999   *White Paper on Private Health Insurance*

2001   *Quality and Fairness: A Health System for you*

2001   *Primary Care: A New Direction*

2004   Health Act

2005   HSE established

2012   *Future Health: A Strategic Framework for Reform of the Health Service 2012–2015*

2013   *Healthy Ireland: A Framework for Improved Health and Wellbeing 2013-2025*

2014   *The Path to Universal Healthcare: The White Paper on Universal Health Insurance*

However, on balance and mirroring international trends and assessments, there is a pessimism about the extent of progressive reform achieved and the extent to which core problems in the health services have been addressed. Burke (2010) for example, sums up the situation as '"reform" without actual reform', capturing the ways in which near constant restructuring of health services coexists with the entrenched two-tier system. The organisation of services bears the growing imprint of new public management, while two-tier access and care, and the related entanglements of the private system with the public system, remain. The 2011-16 Fine Gael/Labour government committed to 'end the unfair, unequal and inefficient two-tier health system' by introducing universal health insurance (GoI, 2011: 31). Though many questions were raised about the effectiveness and equity of this model, this policy aspiration was arguably the most transformative one for the health services since the attempted reforms of the 1940s. However, the commitment is in abeyance, while privatisation and marketisation appear to be strengthening.

Before turning to examine contemporary developments in more detail we briefly set them in the context of overall trends in health expenditure. These indicate that the period from the 1990s is marked by a prolonged expansionary phase followed by austerity post-2008. While significant nominal increases in expenditure were achieved, especially from the late 1990s onwards (expenditure grew from €2.7bn in 1996 to a peak of €13.1bn in 2008), Irish expenditure as a percentage of GDP remained below the OECD average (see Figure 8.3). Besides the high GDP growth rate, below average expenditure also reflects the fact that increases in health expenditure served to repair the effects of austerity on the health system during the late 1980s and early 1990s (Burke et al, 2014). More recently, despite increasing as a percentage of GDP, major expenditure cuts took place in 2010 and 2011 and the health budget fell to €11.2bn in 2011 (DPER databank). Cutbacks were implemented by reducing staff numbers, shortening hospital stays and reducing public hospital bed capacity. While modest increases have since been made to the health budget, capacity within the public health system continues to be constrained. Corresponding with these recent trends, the proportion of out-of-pocket and of private expenditure has increased (see Figure 8.4).

Figure 8.3: Current health expenditure, Ireland and OECD average, 1990-2015

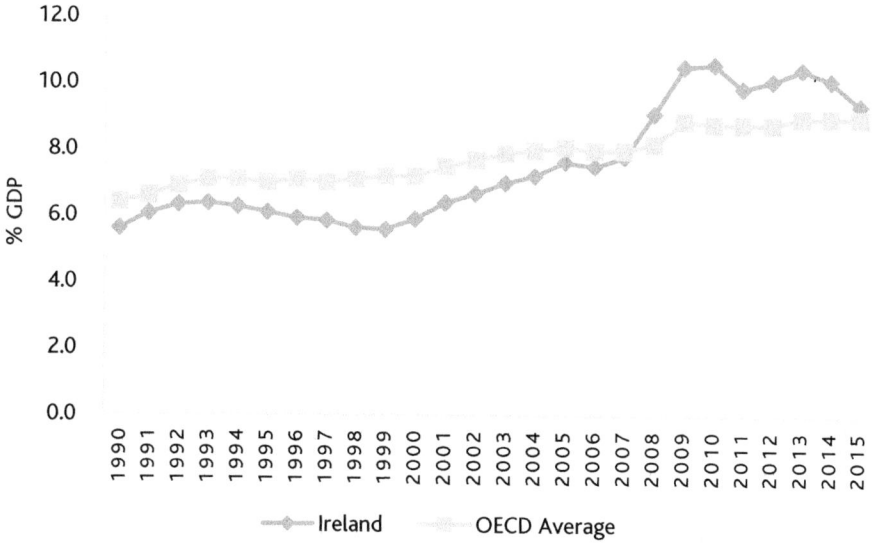

Source: OECD.Stat

Figure 8.4: Private, public and out-of-pocket share of current expenditure on health, 1990-2015

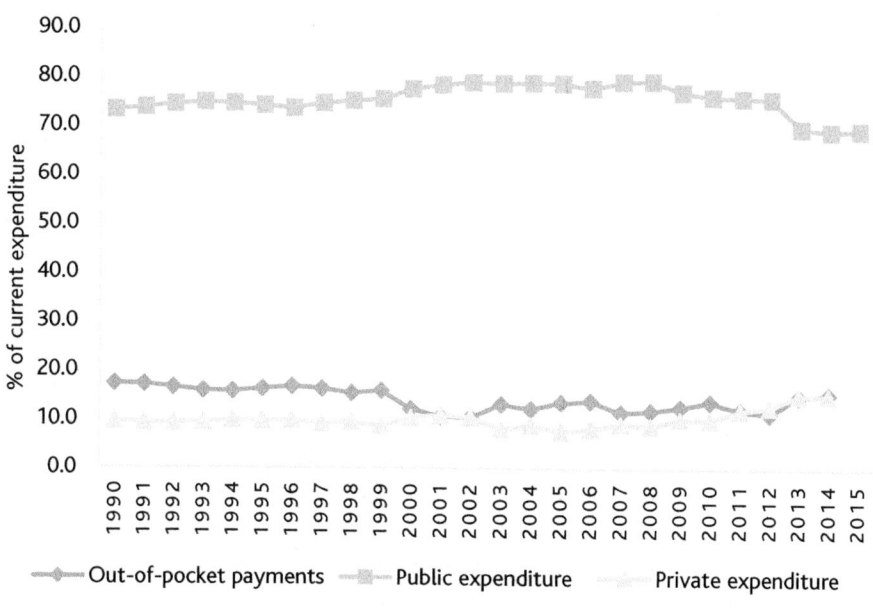

Source: OECD.Stat

Organisational reform: 'dynamics without change'?

The need for organisational reform had been recognised as far back as the 1989 Commission on Health Funding. Its major conclusion was that the solutions to healthcare lay in administration and management: 'the solution to the problem facing the Irish health services does not lie primarily in the system of funding but rather in the way that services are planned, organised and delivered' (Commission on Health Funding, 1989: 15). It recommended, among other things, the creation of a health executive authority that would have overall responsibility for managing the health services, separate from the Department of Health (DoH). This proposal was, however, too radical a step for the government to take at the time. Reflecting the growing influence of new public management, issues of managerial reform, accountability and quality appeared again in *Shaping a Healthier Future* (DoH, 1994) and in *Quality and Fairness: A Health System for You* (DHC, 2001a). Both documents raised the need for more effective and **evidence-based** decision-making procedures, and the need to improve financial, professional and organisational accountability.

Evidence-based decision making is an idea originating in medicine and now applied across the social sciences, but which is open to debate. It rests on the notion that decision making, policy and practice should be based on the best available research knowledge in order to improve quality and effectiveness.

After some restructuring in the Eastern Health Board region in 2001, wholesale change came in 2005 when the Health Boards were abolished and replaced with the Health Service Executive (HSE). Its establishment was triggered by a number of reports commissioned in the early 2000s by the Department of Health and Children (DHC). These were the Brennan Commission (Commission on Financial Management and Control Systems in the Health Service, 2003), the Prospectus Report (Prospectus, 2003) and the Hanly Report (National Task Force on Medical Staffing, 2003). By 2001 an upward trend in health expenditure was emerging and the Brennan Commission was given the remit of assessing health expenditure. It identified a 'management vacuum' in the sector and recommended the establishment of the HSE to manage services, while the DoHC would then focus more on health policy development (Commission on Financial Management and Control Systems in the Health Service, 2003). In other words, cost containment was to be achieved through managerial reform. The Prospectus Report (Prospectus, 2003) drew attention to the complicated and fragmented structures of the system and made similar recommendations. After hasty Dáil debate, which among other things neglected the issue of equity in how the structural reforms would proceed (Tussing and Wren, 2006), the passing of the Health Act 2004 saw the introduction of the HSE in 2005.

The new system created four regional HSE areas: West, South, Dublin Mid-Leinster and Dublin North East. Its service functions were divided into three core areas: National Hospitals Office; Primary, Community and Continuing Care;

and Population Health. In 2007 another major body, the Health Information and Quality Authority was established. Its role is to develop standards and to regulate the quality of care in healthcare settings and in social care services for older people, children and young people, and people with disabilities.

This reform process remains unsettled. Since it was established, the HSE has been subjected to a barrage of criticism, relating to for example, the adequacy of the health budget and the appropriateness of budgetary decisions, and for being overly centralised without clear lines of accountability, leading to administrative and other failures, highlighted by a number of high profile cases involving misdiagnoses and inappropriate care. In 2009 further internal restructuring took place to improve accountability and the integration of services. The National Hospitals Office and Primary, Community and Continuing Care were combined under Integrated Service Areas, reflecting the need to have greater integration between these services. Under the regional areas, 32 local health offices and eight hospital groups were formed and, also at regional level, new managers who would have overall responsibility for the healthcare budget for their area were installed.

Further deeper restructuring was envisaged in *Future Health 2012-2015* (DoH, 2012a), following the 2011 Programme for Government plan to abolish the HSE by 2015. However, the pace of transformation envisaged in that plan was deemed unworkable and the HSE continues to operate. Its abolition is still envisaged, with the 2016 Programme for Government committed to its dissolution and replacement with a Health Commission. In the meantime, following the publication of *The Establishment of Hospital Groups as a Transition to Independent Hospital Trusts* (DoH, 2013a), plans to reform how hospitals are organised are proceeding, albeit slowly, in a way which reflects the strengthening of new public management principles. The financing of hospitals is being transformed from a block grant system to activity-based funding where the 'money follows the patient'. Hospital groups, of which six were created in 2013, are to be transformed into stand-alone hospital trusts who will own their own assets. These hospital trusts will be expected to meet targets on performance indicators related to waiting times for inpatient, outpatient and emergency services, upon which activity-based funding will be allocated. Failure to manage budgets and outcomes, it is envisaged, will result in the temporary takeover of hospital management to restore it to effective functioning. All other parts of the health services are organised under nine Community Health Organisations. However, there is much administrative confusion as to how these will operate alongside the hospital groups; both sets of structures do not map directly on to each other (Burke, 2016a). A door to privatisation is also opened by the plan to constitute hospitals as hospital trusts. This makes them potentially easier to sell, or to increase private patient activity within the hospitals in the absence of sufficient public funding (Mercille and Murphy, 2015).

Reflecting swings in new public management practice internationally, Burke (2016a) remarks that constant change in the Irish system means that no plan is given enough time to become embedded in practice. More fundamentally, as

Byers (2010) notes, the managerial thrust of HSE reforms is focused on financial control. The wider principles of the health strategy *Quality and Fairness: A Health System for You* (DHC, 2001a), including equity, access, accountability and people-centredness, are not part of HSE functioning or institutional structure, having never been properly implemented, nor legislatively supported. Moreover, hospitals appear to consistently 'underperform' in relation to targets for waiting times service responsiveness, indicating that the targets are unachievable given current resources and healthcare need (Mesabbah and Arisha, 2016). While, as noted in section one, efficiency is a contested and difficult to measure concept, if we look at hospital activity, on this indicator hospitals appear to be performing efficiently. The occupancy rate for acute care in Ireland is 93.8% compared to 77.3% for the OECD average, and the average length of stay is six days, compared to 8.1 for the OECD average (OECD, 2016a).

Better management, more state control of the system, and greater accountability are not problems in themselves, especially in the context of the way the health services are subject to the vagaries of local political interests and to the power of the medical professions. However, modelling health activity on private business practices whose efficiency is open to question, and prioritising financial control in the context of under-resourced services and to the detriment of other health policy goals, such as access and equity, is problematic.

Equity of access and the evolution of two-tier health system.

Shaping a Healthier Future (DoH, 1994) was the first major strategic overview of the health service since the 1966 White Paper. The document was also significant for articulating, for the first time, an overall set of principles, namely quality, accountability and equity, and a mission for the health system (Byers, 2010). However, while the document was concerned with equity of access there was a lack of recognition of the effect of the private system on this. In 2001 a more far-reaching strategic policy document *Quality and Fairness: A Health System for You* was published (DHC, 2001). It made a much stronger statement about the problem of inequity of access and clearly acknowledged that the public/private mix was part of the problem, particularly in terms of hospital capacity and of how consultants allocated time between public and private patients. The strategy proposed four guiding principles for the health service, these included the three articulated by *Shaping a Healthier Future* (DoH, 1994), plus the goal of people-centredness. It translated the four principles into four national goals: better health for everyone (including health promotion, quality of life issues, and targeting and reducing health inequalities); fair access; responsive and appropriate care delivery; and high performance. These goals were converted into 121 actions to be met by 2010. Instead of transforming the public/private mix or the funding basis of the system, the strategy promised substantial investment in the public health system as a way of overcoming inequity of access. However the majority of its actions were not implemented (Burke, 2016a).

In 2011 the Fine Gael/Labour government made the ambitious commitment to achieve equity of access by introducing universal free GP care in 2015 and universal health insurance by 2016. Influenced by 2006 Dutch reforms, it planned to make social health insurance compulsory, via competing private providers and the state-owned VHI. A White Paper in 2014 set out (still vague) plans on what the system might entail, including the anticipation that the core health budget would still be tax financed; individuals would be required to purchase insurance for primary and hospital care; and insurance for those whom it was deemed unaffordable would be subsidised or paid in full by the state depending on means (DoH, 2014). However, the White Paper did not specify what might be in the 'basket of health services' covered by health insurance. A report on costings found that depending on what would be included, insurance would increase overall health expenditure by between 3.4% and 10.7% per annum and cost between €1,600 and €2,509 per person (Connolly and Wren, 2016). The report found that the major reason for the increase in costs would be the administrative costs associated with a multi-payer system, while marketing and profit margins would also contribute (Connolly and Wren, 2016). In reaction to these findings, political discourse shifted from universal health insurance to universal healthcare, a concept around which there is no clarity in terms of what it entails (Burke et al, 2016).

Health service eligibility

The current eligibility framework was set in 1991 when universal coverage of hospital care was achieved. Unlike earlier, when the eligibility framework was introduced in 1953 and extended in 1979, this time there was no opposition to the change being introduced. Consultants no longer perceived the extension of public hospital care as a threat to their private income, as the number of people opting for private health insurance was rising substantially. In any case, the government remained committed to the public private mix.

Box 8.4: Categories of entitlement to public health services

Category one: entitled, via a medical card, to all publicly provided health services free of charge, including GP care, dental, ophthalmic and aural services, public hospitals services, and maternity and infant care services. Medicines are subject to a limited co-payment. Eligibility is primarily determined by income (with different income limits for those under 70 and those aged 70 and over) and, in a limited number of cases, by discretion.

Category two: entitled to access to public hospital care, subject to capped overnight charges, and to maternity and infant care services. GP services are not included (except for those with GP Visit cards provided on a means-tested basis or on the basis of age). Category two users are eligible for subsidies under the Drugs Payment Scheme, if the cost of purchasing medicine exceeds a certain monthly threshold, and, in the case of chronic illnesses, for drugs free of charge or payment assistance under the Long Term Illness Scheme and High Tech Scheme. Tax relief is also available on medical costs.

The complexities of healthcare entitlements within category one and category two have grown over time. *Quality and Fairness: A Health System for You* (DHC, 2001a) promised to significantly increase the numbers of people eligible for a medical card by raising income thresholds, reviewing them annually, and prioritising families with young children and children with disabilities. However, what has evolved since then has been more haphazard. An unanticipated development, but one which recognised the extent of health needs of older people, occurred when medical card eligibility was extended to all people aged 70 and over (hereafter referred to as the over 70s) in 2001. Subsequently, instead of annually reviewing and increasing the income thresholds for full medical card eligibility, a more targeted expansion occurred in 2005 with the introduction of a means-tested GP Visit card for those on relatively low incomes but not low enough to be eligible for a full medical card. This card covers the cost of visiting a GP but not medical prescriptions. More recently GP Visit cards are being extended on a targeted basis (see Box 8.5).

By the late 2000s, one of the first austerity measures was the announcement in Budget 2009 of means-testing on medical cards for the over 70s. In response to swift protest by the over 70s, the proposal was altered to exclude only those with relatively high incomes on a self-assessment basis. The proportion of the population eligible for medical cards rose by default during the crisis because of falling incomes. However, rationing was applied to cards issued on an (already limited) discretionary basis to families where being without one would cause 'undue hardship' due to the costs of chronic illness or disability. In other ways the universality of healthcare is also being eroded by various 'out-of-pocket' payments (see Box 8.5), and in recent years there has been a shift in expenditure towards a greater share of out-of-pocket expenditure, reversing earlier trends (see Figure 8.4).

Eligibility for what? Limits to developments in primary and public hospital care

Historically, primary care has been a neglected and poorly resourced sector. It consisted mainly of self-employed GPs and a fragmented network of other health professionals. Although the significance of primary care gained ground in the 1980s, potentially significant reform and recognition did follow until *Primary Health Care: A New Direction* (DHC, 2001b). This proposed the creation of interdisciplinary primary healthcare teams comprising GPs, nurses and midwives, healthcare assistants, home helps, physiotherapists, occupational therapists and social workers, all working out of one location and serving populations of 3,000-7,000 people. In addition, a wider network of complementary professionals such as speech and language therapists, community welfare officers, and dentists, would serve a number of primary healthcare teams within a particular geographical area. This plan entailed significant investment in physical infrastructure and staffing,

Box 8.5: The expansion and contraction of healthcare entitlements

Expansion	Contraction
2001 Full medical cards for the over 70s	**2008-09** Inpatient hospital charge increased from €60 to €75 per night; Accident and Emergency charge increased from €60 to €100
2005 GP Visit cards introduced	**2008-14** Drugs Payment Scheme subsidy threshold gradually rose from €85 per month to €144 per month
2015 GP Visit cards for all children under six and the over 70s not entitled to full medical card	**2009** medical card for the over 70s subject to means testing
	2010-14 prescription charges introduced at 50c per item/maximum of €10 per family per month increased by 2014 to €2.50 per item/maximum of €24 per family (capped at €20 for the over 70s in 2017)

and it was originally envisaged that 400–600 primary healthcare teams would be needed by 2011, based on a projected population of 3.8 million. However, these reforms have been very slow to materialise and it is difficult to avoid the conclusion that the sector is still fragmented and under-resourced. By 2011, 425 primary care teams were in operation (HSE, 2012a). However, besides a third that could be said to be working effectively (Houston, 2012), other situations include a substantial proportion of teams amounting to GPs and a practice nurse only; many existing only as a virtual arrangement as opposed to working in a shared physical space; and many teams reporting that they were too fragmented to work successfully (Kelly, Garvey and Palcic, 2016).

Better primary care notwithstanding, access remains an issue in several ways. Concerns have been raised about how areas are targeted and prioritised for new primary care teams, arising from the fact that poorer areas are not well resourced in terms of GP services (CPA, 2007; Osborne, 2015). In addition while registration for primary care teams remains voluntary, it has been argued that it should be mandatory (CPA, 2007). This would be particularly beneficial for groups who have difficulty registering for GP services, including Travellers, asylum seekers, homeless people and refugees; groups which also have a greater likelihood of poor health. Finally, access to many primary care services is ambiguous. Access to services such as homecare, occupational therapy and community mental health services varies according to local policy decisions and there is little data available on inequalities in access (Burke, 2016a, 2016b).

In terms of hospital care, *Quality and Fairness: A Health System for You* (DHC, 2001a) proposed to increase the capacity of the public hospital system by adding 3,000 new hospital beds and to end waiting times of longer than three months for hospital treatment by the end of 2004. In relation to hospital beds, the total in 2001 was 22,658, a number which fell to 11,989 by 2014 (OECD.Stat). This mirrors a downward trend internationally, due, for example, to decreasing length of hospital stays and increasing numbers of day-cases. However, when measured as hospital beds per 1,000 population, Ireland falls below the OECD average (2.6 compared to the OECD average of 4.7 in 2014 (OECD.Stat)).

While the number of hospital beds is falling overall, private hospital capacity has grown, facilitated by tax incentives and by how waiting lists for public hospital services have been handled. The 2001 strategy stated that 'the government is committed to exploring fully the scope of the private sector to provide additional capacity' (DHC, 2001a: 102). Expanding the scope of the private sector began with the introduction of tax relief for private hospitals (as well as health clinics and nursing homes) in 2001 and 2002. A specific initiative of private 'co-located' hospitals was also announced in 2005 involving the construction of eight private hospitals, again with tax reliefs, on the grounds of existing public hospitals to provide more private beds and free up space in public hospitals. However, the plan attracted enormous criticism for potentially residualising the public system and it has not progressed, being further hampered by lack of private finance during the economic crisis. Besides co-located hospitals, the overall number of private hospitals in operation grew from two in the late 1980s to 24 by 2012 (OECD.Stat). As well as treating private patients, private hospitals have also benefited from the strategy of using private services for public patients as a way of managing waiting lists. A waiting list initiative for public patients was first introduced in 1993 and since then waiting list schemes have become an embedded characteristic of the public system and numbers waiting have, at best, fluctuated (Box 8.6). Policy efforts and funding to reduce them are sporadic, spurred by lists reaching crisis levels and by health scandals, such as the case of Susie Long who, in 2007, died from bowel cancer after waiting seven months for a colonoscopy. In addition to waiting list initiatives, a common waiting list system for both public and private patients, for outpatient diagnostic services (but not for treatment), was created in 2008. Yet the impact of this initiative has also been limited. In practice, private patients who have the ability to pay for their insurance cover can obtain a private diagnosis, enabling them to 'skip the queue' for treatment should it be needed (Burke and Pentony, 2011).

Box 8.6: Efforts to tackle waiting lists

1993 Waiting List Initiative

This initiative aimed to eliminate inpatient waiting times of over 12 months for adults and six months for children. Specific funding was allocated to public hospitals to carry out more elective procedures drawn from the waiting lists. Waiting list numbers, starting at almost 40,000 waiting over three months in 1993, subsequently fell to 26,000 in 2001 and rose to 29,000 in 2002 (Comptroller and Auditor General, 2003).

2002 National Treatment Purchase Fund (NTPF)

This fund, still in operation, shifted the focus from the public to the private system. It aims to reduce waiting times through the purchase of private treatment for public patients, on an individual basis, in private beds in public hospitals and from private hospitals in Ireland and the UK. While it did not succeed in meeting the 2004 target of no person waiting more than three months, until the onset of the economic crisis the NTPF appeared relatively successful in reducing in waiting times. By 2009 18,517 were waiting more than 12 months (NTPF, 2010).

2011 Special Delivery Unit

This Unit was created to work with the NTPF to tackle inpatient, outpatient and emergency department waiting times with greater use of performance management within the public hospital system and a reduced role for NTPF purchase of private care. New targets were set in 2012 of a maximum of eight months waiting time for adults and 20 weeks for children. These were subsequently revised upwards in 2015 to a maximum 15-month waiting time.

Cutbacks have seen waiting times escalate. By 2015, 41,433 people were waiting over three months and of these 13,351 were waiting longer than nine months.

Crucially, waiting times begin after a consultant referral. Consultant referrals are dependent upon an outpatient appointment. At the end of 2015, 227,664 people were waiting three months or longer for an appointment, and of these 37,197 were waiting longer than 12 months (NTPF, 2015). In effect this is pre-wait to get on another waiting list should treatment be required.

Besides fluctuating waiting-time numbers, the effectiveness of the NTPF fund on both efficiency and equity grounds is questionable. Essentially it involves the purchase of private care at the expense of investing in the public system. As the CPA (2007: 12) notes, the NTPF 'does not address the reasons behind the public system's inability to provide timely treatment in the first place, which should be the long term focus. ... Investing in public health services would gradually reduce the needs for the NTPF to operate on its present scale'. In addition, NESF (2002) pointed out the contradiction of using the private system to treat public patients while the public system used some of its capacity to treat private patients. Such a system also creates an incentive for consultants to convert public patient cases into private ones via self-referral. If public patients have to wait for three months or more then the likelihood of their treatment being covered by the NTPF increases, which represents a gain in terms of private income for a consultant. In order to curtail the potential for self-referral the NTPF was altered to limit the use of public facilities to 10%, which reduced but did not eliminate self-referrals. The limit was lifted in 2012 in the context of greater use of performance management of how public hospitals dealt with their waiting lists (Mullholland, 2016).

The public private mix and private insurance

The proportion of people privately insured peaked at 50.9% in 2008 and subsequently fell to 43.9% in 2014 before rising again (45.8% in 2015) (HIA, 2016). The relatively small contribution of private expenditure to overall expenditure on health has also been rising recently (see Figure 8.4). Depending on the type of insurance people take out, having insurance can mean people receive care in private hospitals and/or private care in public hospitals, with the latter situation at the crux of the two-tier system. While the proposed Universal Health Insurance aimed to create a single tier of access to the public system, its failure to progress has meant that private use of public resources is still a significant element of the system. This situation has long been encouraged as a source of funding for public hospitals. It is also promoted as a marker of individual responsibility, easing the burden of demand on public health services (McDonnell and O'Donovan, 2009). Private health insurance holders are also a significant political bloc for whom the status quo is beneficial; they continue to receive preferential and subsidised treatment which would not be the case under a social health insurance system (Finn and Hardiman, 2012).

There have, however, been some efforts to curtail public subsidisation of private insurance. The subsidisation of insurance premiums was reduced by limiting relief to the lower tax rate in 1997, and in 2014 the cost of premiums eligible for relief was capped at €1,000 per annum. The charge to insurers for patients in private beds in public hospitals also more than doubled between 2005 and 2013. This charge was extended to all beds in 2014, including public beds used by private patients but not previously charged to them (Turner, 2015). This was partly motivated by the aim of generating more revenue for the public health system. Charging all public hospitals beds used by private patients at a private rate also ended the bed designation system in place since 1991. That system aimed to keep a check on the level of private use in public hospitals by maintaining an 80:20 public:private bed ratio. In reality that ratio was frequently breached (O'Reilly and Wiley, 2010); however, the end of the designation system also further incentivises public hospitals to devote more capacity to private patients. At the same time, the full cost of private care is still subsidised as charges do not take into account costs associated with the use of public hospital equipment or premises (Finn and Hardiman, 2012). Within the public system greater demarcation of the public and private system was also intended with the introduction of a new consultants' contract in 2008. In contrast to previous contracts this agreement included the option of an exclusive public practice contract. However, there has been limited take-up of this type of contract; the majority of consultants in public hospitals, over 90%, continue to also practice privately (Moran et al, 2013). In a number of ways, therefore, policies to curtail the public subsidisation of private care and the public/private mix, have at best tinkered around the edges of this system. In addition, the introduction in 2015 of lifetime community rating represents something of a countermove, further embedding having private health insurance. Lifetime community rating is designed to encourage people to take out insurance at a younger age. Insurance companies may apply a higher charge to people who take out health insurance after the age of 35. This is intended to strengthen the insurance market by making it more financially sustainable, as, besides this 'late entry loading', premiums do not take account of health status or other risk factors.

Health inequalities

Inequities in the health system are part of a much broader context of health inequalities in Irish society. Differences in health status are marked by differences in socioeconomic position in particular and other health differences marked by ethnicity, geography and gender are 'generated by underlying socio-economic inequalities' (Farrell et al, 2008: 15). There have been some significant improvements at population level in recent years. For example, the standardised death rate per 100,000 of the population has been decreasing and life expectancy has been increasing, especially since the early 2000s (DoH, 2016a). However, significant health inequalities within the population remain. These inequalities can partly be attributed to problems with healthcare, particularly inequity of access: 'the inverse care law of inadequate provision for the most needy remains true' (Kelleher, 2007: 223).

Data on health inequalities in Ireland is limited and data collection and analysis is, as Houghton and Houghton (2015: 56) argue, 'systematically under-funded [and] routinely out of date'. Moreover, while it was significant that *Healthy Ireland* (DoH, 2013b: 34) included 'reducing health inequalities' as one of its four goals; this was not underpinned by a structural understanding of the socioeconomic foundations of health inequalities nor by any indication of how health inequalities might be tackled beyond an individualised approach to health promotion. The available research provides compelling evidence of unequal **mortality rates** and unequal patterns of **morbidity** across different

> **Mortality rate** refers to the death rate. The **mortality rate ratio** compares the death rate for one group with another.

> **Morbidity** refers to sickness. The **morbidity rate** can refer to both the incidence and prevalence of sickness and disease within a particular group.

socioeconomic groups. In essence those in the lower socioeconomic groups are more likely to get sick more often and to die younger. Furthermore, health status is marked by a **social gradient**: better income is positively related to better health.

Social gradient refers to the relationship between health status and socioeconomic group, whereby, for example, rising income or wealth is matched by improvements in health status.

Therefore, despite the fact that the standardised mortality rate has improved for the population as a whole, there are distinct social class differences (Balanda and Wilde, 2001; Layte et al, 2015). Layte et al (2015), for example, found that the differences in death rates between professional and manual workers actually increased between the 1980s and 2000s. This difference is also expressed in research on social class differences in life expectancy. Looking solely at the year 2006/07 the CSO (2010) found a gap of six years in life expectancy between professional and unskilled men and a gap of five years in the case of women. In addition, a social gradient can be observed for each sex (see Figure 8.5)

Morbidity follows a similar pattern of inequality across social groups (Layte et al, 2007). In the case of cancer inequalities for example, the National Cancer Registry (Walsh et al, 2016) found that for people diagnosed with cancer between 2008 and 2012, there is a 10% higher incidence in the case of men and 4% in the case of women in the areas of highest deprivation compared to those from the lowest areas of deprivation. Differences for specific cancers are higher again: 40% higher

Figure 8.5: Life expectancy at birth by sex and social class, 2006/07

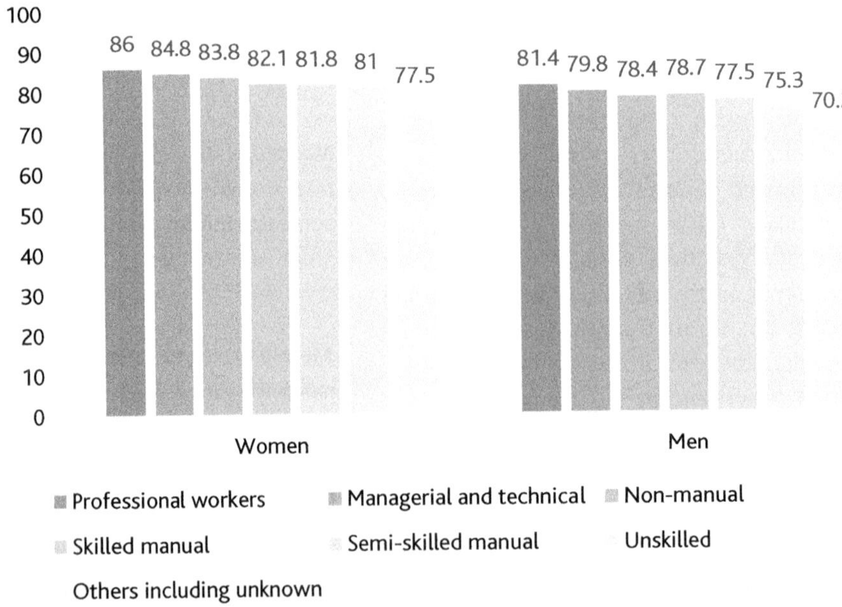

Source: CSO, 2010

in the case of stomach cancer and 60% for lung cancer. Those in deprived areas also have lower survival rates; mortality risk is 39% higher in the most deprived areas compared to the least deprived areas. Health inequalities in mortality and morbidity such as these raise serious challenges for the health service. As we have already noted, equity in healthcare is but one part of the broader range of policy responses considered necessary to address health inequalities. However, the fact that healthcare is inequitable in many ways exacerbates health inequalities and clearly is a matter of deep social injustice.

Chapter summary

- The first section of the chapter reviewed the main concepts associated with understanding health in a social policy context and which guide the development of health systems, namely health inequalities, equity and efficiency. The section also reviewed the main models of healthcare and the challenges facing all systems in recent decades. Of particular relevance is the tension between equity and efficiency in the context of rising costs and efforts at cost containment.
- The second section documented the development of the Irish healthcare system. It focused on the way the system evolved to produce a relatively unique two-tier system of private and public healthcare, and the various episodes in which opportunities to develop a more clearly defined social insurance-based or national health system failed to materialise.
- The consequences of this legacy for the contemporary healthcare system were discussed in section three. The issue of inequity of access has emerged as one of the most crucial issues in the Irish healthcare system. This section analysed a number of policy developments and areas of the healthcare system which continue to be significantly challenged by health inequities. Despite what appears to be greater political acknowledgement of the inequities of the two-tier health system, current reforms, dominated by financial control and managerial reform, fail to decisively address the problem. In many cases, such as the encouragement of privatisation and the continued incentivisation of private insurance, policy preferences continue to exacerbate two-tier healthcare.

Discussion points

- Trace the historical reasons why Ireland does not have a free GP service for all of the population.
- Explain the public/private mix in the Irish healthcare system and evaluate recent attempts to modify this system.

Further reading list

Barrington, R (1987) *The politics of health and medicine, 1900-1970*, Dublin: IPA

Burke, S (2009) *Irish apartheid: Healthcare inequality in Ireland*, Dublin: New Island

Burke, S and Pentony, S (2011) *Eliminating health inequalities: A matter of life and death*, Dublin: TASC

Burke, S, Normand, C, Barry, S and Thomas, S (2016) From universal health insurance to universal healthcare? The shifting health policy landscape in Ireland since the economic crisis, *Health Policy*, 120:3, 235–40

Wren, M-A (2003) *Unhealthy state: Anatomy of a sick society*, Dublin: New Island

nine

Education policy

Going to school is one of the first milestone experiences we have in childhood. Most of us have distinctive memories of school and our education on the whole can be quite a subjective experience; we remember teachers, schools and subjects we especially liked or disliked; we have nightmares about messing up major examinations. Our achievements or otherwise in the formal education system play a key role in determining our life chances thereafter. This is why equality – or more precisely equality of opportunity – is highly valued in education policy; it is important that education systems are seen to offer everyone an equal chance of doing the best they can. However, education systems are characterised by significant inequalities, which influence our participation to the effect that it is not simply a matter of individuals doing the best they can or failing to do so. The concept of equality of opportunity and this debate is the starting point for this chapter, which aims to look at the key issue of equality in education before examining the particular way in which the Irish education system developed and the current key issues and challenges it faces.

Chapter outline
- Section one discusses the concept of equality of educational opportunity and examines its evolving influence in education policy making.
- Section two examines the origins and development of education in Ireland, with particular reference to how the model of religious ownership with state funding evolved, and to how equality issues emerged and developed over time.
- Section three examines the contemporary Irish education system. Across preschool, primary and second level, and higher education we analyse policy developments since the early 1990s. We highlight issues such as the pressures of global economic competitiveness, changes to how the state manages education, fluctuations in funding, and the challenges of addressing economic disadvantage and multiple types of diversity. In the case of each issue we consider how it cross-cuts with equality of opportunity in the education system.

SECTION ONE
EQUALITY OF OPPORTUNITY AND EDUCATION POLICY

In Chapter Five we discussed the various meanings given to equality across the different political ideologies; in this chapter we apply these broader meanings to education. **Equality of opportunity** is the most commonly espoused concept associated with education policy. The concept has ambiguous and varied interpretations and thus has wide appeal. Equality of opportunity does not mean the same thing as equality; it is not a means of creating an equal society (however defined). Rather, it is a means of fairly allocating positions within society. This means that positions that confer wealth and privilege are not distributed according to ascribed characteristics such as gender or skin colour, but through acquired characteristics which everyone is given equal opportunity to obtain, such as educational qualifications. Allocation is based on **merit** and therefore, 'when equality of opportunity prevails, the assignment of individuals to places in the social hierarchy is determined by some form of competitive process, and all members of society are eligible to compete on equal terms' (Arneson, 2015). The concept therefore implies an acceptance of the existence of a social hierarchy or inequality, or as Lynch and Baker (2005: 132) puts it, equality of opportunity offers an 'equal opportunity of becoming unequal'. For some critics of equality of opportunity, including Lynch and Baker, this is the nub of the problem with equality of opportunity and they argue for alternative conceptions of equality.

> **Equality of opportunity** broadly refers to the notion that everyone is given an equal chance to succeed regardless of factors such as class, gender, 'race', or any other aspect of identity.

> **Meritocratic societies** are those in which achievement and success reflect ability and effort rather than factors such as class, 'race', religion, gender or family background and connections.

Equality of opportunity is a key tenet of liberalism. The basic idea underpinning liberal perspectives on equality is 'that people should in some sense have an equal chance to compete for social advantages' (Baker et al, 2009: 25). This accommodates different perspectives and interpretations. The key difference is between a conception of equality of opportunity which interprets equality in a minimal or formal way and one which promotes more generous interpretations of what constitutes minimum equality. The latter are known as maximalist or substantive interpretations of equality of opportunity. Despite these variations, because equality of opportunity is at base about fair or equal ways of arriving at hierarchy or inequality in society, liberal conceptions of equality define equality in ways that, at most, permit incremental and reformist rather than radical change.

Formal/minimalist equality of opportunity

Formal equality of opportunity stresses the equal eligibility of citizens 'for all positions, posts and public employments in accordance with their abilities' as expressed in Article 6 of the 1789 French Declaration of the Rights of Man (cited in Baker et al, 2009: 25). The hallmarks of education policy built upon formal equality of opportunity are access and non-discrimination. As long as there are no discriminatory barriers that prohibit access to education or advancement within education, then in this view, education functions in an equal opportunity way. Historical examples of inequality of educational opportunity under this definition include the prohibition of Catholics from education under the penal laws, and the denial of access to higher education to women. Formal equality of opportunity policies are favoured by Right-wing thinkers and governments, as a minimal conception of equality offers greater compatibility with individual freedom.

Substantive/maximalist equality of opportunity

Substantive definitions of equality of opportunity go beyond the assurance of access and non-discrimination, arguing that these are not sufficient to ensure equality of opportunity. In this view, formal opportunity is not the same as a genuine or real opportunity. For example, formal equality of access to university does not necessarily mean that a working-class person will have the same chance to attend as a middle-class person. Taking this kind of difference into account, 'a stronger form of equal opportunity insists that people should not be advantaged or hampered by their social background and that their prospects in life should depend entirely on their own effort and abilities' (Baker et al, 2009: 25). The most well-known substantive formulation of equality of opportunity is John Rawls' notion of 'equality of fair opportunity'. This prevails when 'any individuals who have the same native talent and the same ambition will have the same prospects of success in competitions that determine who gets positions that generate superior benefits for their occupants' (Arneson, 2015). To ensure equality of fair opportunity the task of education policy is to offset advantages of particular social groups through public measures. Here equality of access is presumed and is extended along a continuum which includes equality of participation and equality of success or outcome (Lynch, 1999). Equality of participation focuses on the equal participation of all social groups at all levels of the education system, while equality of outcomes aims for equal rates of achievement for all social groups. Instead of simply focusing on non-discrimination, education policy is more likely to be concerned with educational disadvantage and seeks to address it by affirmative action. So for example,

> if wealthy parents provide high-quality day care and nursery school and private tutoring for their children, society arranges public education practices so that children of non wealthy parents get the same or

equivalent advantages. ... The end result is that one can try to give one's own children a leg up in social competition, but whatever boost one provides will be met by a similar boost provided for other children whose native talent is the same as that of one's own children (Arneson, 2015).

This approach to equality of opportunity is more typical of social democratic thinking. In general, policies which strive for substantive equality of opportunity involve extra resources for particular groups or geographical areas, in an attempt to level the playing field. These groups and areas are treated differently in a positive or affirmative sense to try to ensure equal participation or equal rates of achievement. Irish examples include the Early Start preschool programme and Delivering Equality of Opportunity in Schools (DEIS), both of which are discussed in section three of the chapter.

Box 9.1: Key differences between formal and substantive equality of opportunity

Minimal/formal equality of opportunity	Maximal/substantive equality of opportunity
Focus on equality of access.	Focus on equality of participation and/or equality of outcome.
Concerned with discrimination.	Concerned with educational disadvantage.
Typical policies include formal statements stressing non-discrimination.	Typical policies include positive discrimination, including targets, quotas, and extra funding for particular groups, or schools in particular areas.

Critique of equality of opportunity: equality of condition and equality of respect

Critics of equality of opportunity argue that the concept is flawed because it assumes and accepts inequality, albeit inequality which is arrived at in a 'fair' way. Baker et al (2009: 27) suggest that this fairness is simply a 'forlorn hope'. This is because 'privileged parents will always find ways of advantaging their children in an unequal society' (Baker et al, 2009: 27). In an unequal society, those with the greater resources will have the means and the power to find ways to stay ahead of any policy measures designed to equalise opportunity. Moreover, as Baker (2003: 16) suggests, these are strategies that are 'perfectly rational ... in an unequal society ... which of us, rich or poor, would voluntarily expose our children to the risk of poverty?' Baker et al therefore propose an alternative form of equality called 'equality of condition'. This is underpinned by:

> the belief that people should be as equal as possible in relation to the central conditions of their lives. Equality of condition is not about trying to make inequalities fairer, or giving people a more equal opportunity to become unequal, but about ensuring that everyone has roughly equal prospects for a good life (Lynch and Baker, 2005: 132).

This involves tackling major inequalities both within and beyond the education system in order to challenge the key structures that reproduce inequality and oppression and impede real choices, including capitalism, patriarchy and racism.

However, a problem with equality of condition is that it is less well developed than the notion of equality of opportunity, particularly in terms of policy application (Lynch, 2000), and equality of opportunity has much greater political appeal. Marxist and feminist critiques of equality and of education have been influential in developing alternative conceptions of equality and here we look at two in particular, equality of economic condition and equality of cultural condition or respect. Both of these demonstrate ways in which liberal equality of opportunity fails in an educational context.

Equality of economic condition

Equality of economic condition and its relevance to education stems from 1970s Marxist scholarship. This perspective argues that equality in education cannot be isolated from equality in other spheres of life, hence equality of economic condition is necessary for education systems to perform in an egalitarian way. Equality of condition therefore 'aims at creating equality in the living conditions of all members of society. This refers to an ideal state where all goods, privileges and resources are distributed equally according to need' (Lynch, 1999: 39). In this context, educational institutions which pursue equality policies will not have their aims subverted by groups with more resources and power to confer advantages on their children. As Lynch mentions, this is an ideal and in practice no education system operates within a society where equality of condition prevails. The closest approximation is found among the Nordic welfare states which have relatively strong redistributive policies and a relatively strong egalitarian ethos in their education systems (West and Nikolai, 2013).

Equality of respect

Equality of respect refers to the cultural domain, and within education the concept illuminates ways in which education can perpetuate inequality through a cultural axis. Bourdieu and Passeron's (1977) examination of cultural transmission through the education system represents an early contribution to the importance of

> **Cultural capital** refers to attitudes and dispositions acquired within the family and community. It can include cultural goods such as books and formal academic qualifications.

culture in education. Bourdieu (1986) developed the notion of '**cultural capital**' which he used to show that it is not simply economic capital or resources that allowed certain children to succeed but also the cultural capital they have at their disposal. Perceptions of learning and education may differ significantly within a middle-class milieu as opposed to a working-class one. This difference becomes a problem when education institutions are for the most part staffed by middle-class people, and embody middle-class culture and values as the norm. For middle-class children the transition to this environment is relatively smooth whereas for working-class children this may not be the case. They are not 'at home' in this system and their ability to succeed in the system may therefore be hampered. Conversely, success for working-class students may be an ambivalent experience, representing a loss of a coherent, authentic sense of self-hood (Reay, 2001). Issues of culture and respect were taken further by feminist and other theorists of identity. This work has drawn attention to school culture including the curriculum which can transmit a gendered and racialised view of the world couched within a white, settled, male, heterosexual perspective. This has a negative effect on minority groups who are either rendered invisible or represented in stereotyped, negative ways. The need for equality of respect is being recognised somewhat in education systems in recent times through principles such as inclusion and interculturalism.

Equality of educational opportunity and the development of education policy

Ladders and talent pools

Prior to the twentieth century, there was little perceived need for a universal system of education once children had completed primary school. Further education was considered desirable only for an elite group of people with high intelligence, most of whom it was assumed already belonged to elite groups or the upper class. Post-primary education was made available on a paid basis and was, with the exception of a limited number of scholarships, inaccessible to those who could not afford to pay. Access to education via scholarships was compared to the rungs of a ladder, which only the most exceptional children of the lower classes had the ability to climb. The use of the ladder as a metaphor for educational access emerged in the 1870s when TH Huxley, who was influenced by Darwin's theory of evolution, proposed the notion of 'a great educational ladder, the bottom of which should be in the gutter and the top in the University and by which every child who had the strength to climb might, by using that strength, reach the place intended for him' (cited in Philpott, 1904: 153-4 in Sanderson, 1987: 77). Tied to this was the notion of talent pools, and 'the educational elite came to be known as the "pool" of talent, the nation's intellectual resources or the "pool of ability'" (Evetts, 1970: 425). It was assumed that the pool of talent among the working classes would not go to waste by facilitating a relatively small proportion of the most intelligent with an academic second-level education.

By the 1920s and 1930s, debates about equality and contributions from socialist theorists, such as RH Tawney, advanced the more radical egalitarian notion of equality of condition leading eventually to a classless society. Tawney forwarded the idea of equality not as 'equality capacity or attainment, but of circumstances and institutions and the manner of life' (Tawney, 1931: 50). Using this notion of equality Tawney (1922: 19) argued for free access to second-level education which would, in a generation, abolish 'the vulgar irrelevancies of class inequality'. Arguments such as these influenced the universalisation of access to post-primary education which occurred during the mid-twentieth century.

Human capital and affirmative action

By the 1950s ideas began to change and the fixed nature of IQ and the pool of talent were no longer accepted as immutable facts. The notion that these could be influenced by environmental or social factors and open to modification gained ground. It followed that if improvements were made in educational provision, intelligence and ability might also be improved across the population (Sanderson, 1987).

This changing interpretation of the talent pool was bolstered by new thinking about the relationship between the economy and education during the period of economic growth and industrial expansion from the 1950s onwards. If countries were to succeed in this expansionary phase then they would need to make the most of their workforce, and notions of fixed pools of talent did not help. The concept of 'human capital' (Schultz, 1961) offered a new way of thinking about education and its relationship with the economy. Schultz encouraged economists and education policy makers to think about human abilities in terms of human capital, a factor of production increasingly significant to economic growth. In 1961 it was agreed at an OECD conference to drop the concept of a pool of ability and take on board the significance of investing in human capital for economic growth. This had implications not just for the relationship between the economy and education, but also for the interpretation of equality of opportunity within education policy.

If talent or intelligence was now understood as a product in part at least of social experience then the onus was on educational opportunity policy to make the most of people's abilities. A shift occurred from defining equality of opportunity in formal terms to substantive terms, and during the 1970s focus moved from equality of access towards equality of participation and achievement. Equality of opportunity now entailed policies such as the 'comprehensivisation' of secondary education so that all children would have the same education rather than being segregated between technical and academically oriented schools.

Positive discrimination or affirmative action also became part of education policy (Evetts, 1970).

This new thinking also had an impact on the provision of higher education, which underwent a process of 'massification'. This meant universities and newly created institutes of higher education were no longer the preserve of an elite; they expanded to become part of a progression route for many on completion of second-level education. Mass access was accompanied by a process of diversification in the third-level sector. Influenced by the human capital perspective, it was argued that a new type of third-level education based more on teaching and professional training than research was needed to meet the needs of growing economies.

Knowledge capital and the 'race to the top'.

By the 1990s and early twenty-first century the educational landscape again changed and is now going through another phase of realignment with economic imperatives under the banner of economic globalisation. Human capital is now understood as knowledge capital and the central component of success in what are deemed knowledge or 'smart' economies. These economies signify the supposedly high-skill, high-wage transformations occurring in Western economies in the wake of industrial decline. According to this account, economic growth depends on economies being able to act fast, outwit their economic rivals, and thus reap the economic rewards. This is a process which applies not only to whole economies but to individual workers who need to be equipped by education systems that emphasise innovation and entrepreneurialism.

In its report *The Knowledge-Based Economy*, the OECD (1996) described education as a 'knowledge-intensive service sector' which is the key to future economic prosperity. In the process knowledge becomes a product that schools and universities are in the business of selling to students as consumers (Ball, 2013). The same themes are evident at EU level. The Lisbon Strategy sought to make the European economy the most competitive and knowledge-driven in the world. *Making a European Area of Lifelong Learning a Reality* (European Commission, 2001), issued as a contribution towards the Lisbon goal, emphasised the competitive advantages to be gained from investing in people and upgrading knowledge and competences. In the Lisbon Strategy's successor, Europe 2020, 'smart growth', that is, economic growth based on knowledge and innovation, is 'the follow-up to the concept "the knowledge-based economy"' (Lundvall and Lorenz, 2012: 334). Accordingly, one of Europe 2020's headline targets focuses on reducing early school leaving (from 15% to 10%) and increasing the proportion of the population aged 30-34 with a tertiary education (from 31% to 40%) across the EU. References to entrepreneurship and entrepreneurial skills are also becoming ubiquitous in how education policy is framed. Reflecting on the challenges Europe faces, the European Commission (2012: 2) for example states that

By 2020, 20% more jobs will require higher level skills. Education needs to drive up both standards and levels of achievement to match this demand, as well as encourage the transversal skills needed to ensure young people are able to be entrepreneurial and adapt to the increasingly inevitable changes in the labour market during their career.

Such thinking has implications in particular for higher education which as Peters (2003: 153) remarks, 'has become the new star ship in the policy fleet for governments around the world ... universities are seen to be a key driver towards the knowledge economy'. Higher education institutions, particularly as they expand into fourth-level education, are involved in a 'race to the top' because in knowledge capitalism the 'new rules of wealth creation rest on "out smarting" economic rivals' (Brown and Lauder, 2006: 26). Universities therefore strive to be identified as world class and compete on the basis of global ranking systems. These rankings are problematic for many reasons, not least because the wealthiest universities benefit from substantial private funding. However, ranking systems become a consumer indicator for how students engage with higher education. Under new public management or managerialist reforms governments are restructuring their higher education systems 'in the view that high ranked institutions are beacons for mobile investment and international talent – vital components for global competitiveness' (Hazelkorn, 2015: 6).

Brown and Lauder (2006), among others, are highly critical of policy rhetoric associated with the knowledge economy and new public management. They argue that it means that universities end up contributing to and reproducing inequalities rather than ameliorating them, and that it makes flawed assumptions about knowledge economies and the potential of high-skilled, high-wage employment for everyone. They identify an intensification of elitism in higher education, as universities shift their focus from massification to competition for elite students. This, in turn, is reinforced by the 'global war for talent' by multinational companies which, in a throwback to nineteenth-century ideas, perpetuates the idea that talent is a rare thing. This justifies greater rewards for the select few and creates a 'hyper-meritocracy' in which the 'winner takes all' (Brown and Tannock, 2009). Competition thus intensifies for top-earning jobs, which are won by those who have the greatest competitive advantages and greatest endowments of economic and cultural capital to perform well in the globalised and neo-liberalised higher education system. Instead of what Brown (2013: 685) calls the 'neo-liberal opportunity bargain' which posits that 'learning equals earning', the system is 'flattened into winners and losers'. This reflects trends, most evident in liberal economies such as the UK and the US, such as stagnant middle-class incomes and increasing competition for jobs that are high skill but low wage.

SECTION TWO
THE DEVELOPMENT OF EDUCATION POLICY IN IRELAND

Pre-independence

In Ireland and elsewhere, the earliest initiatives in education were voluntary in nature and usually motivated by religion. While the impetus for provision was voluntary, most education operated on a paid basis. Thus education was a private matter, accessible to the few who could afford to pay. Education was not of great importance in societies which were primarily agricultural and where little changed from generation to generation. In the Irish case, the lack of industrial development obviated the need for mass elementary education. Instead, policy was shaped by the nature of the colonial administration, and education provision was treated as an important tool of cultural control as opposed to industrial development.

Equality was not a major concern in nineteenth-century Irish debates about education. For the most part equality was mentioned in the context of Catholic and Protestant access to education; equality in terms of gender or class was of little concern. Second-level and third-level education were seen primarily as services for the middle classes, and which were to be paid for. Widening access to the lower classes was not contemplated; they were deemed only to need education in literacy and numeracy (Coolahan, 1981). Moreover, the same education was not seen as appropriate for men and women, particularly at second and third level. As Harford (2008: 1–2) notes, education was influenced by 'the doctrine of "separate spheres" … Men's sphere was the public world of work and commerce while woman's was the private world of the home, in her natural role as wife and mother'. This view was made all the more powerful by the Catholic Church whose (male) leaders were opposed to higher education for women.

Religious and state power intertwined in early provision. Colonial rule first concentrated on promulgating the Protestant faith and the English language by grant-aiding various schools with these aims, some of which 'out-churched the church' in their zeal to proselytise 'popish' children (Akenson, 1970: 33). Negative force was used through the implementation of Penal Laws from the late seventeenth century. These laws denied Catholics the freedom to send their children abroad to be educated, to set up schools in Ireland or to teach Catholic children. Clandestine hedge schools emerged under this regime, while wealthy Catholics still managed to emigrate for education despite the ban. The Penal Laws were gradually repealed during the 1780s and 1790s and this period saw the flourishing of religious voluntary education provision. The involvement of many Catholic orders which still play a prominent role in education provision, such as the Christian Brothers and the Loreto Sisters, can be traced back to this period.

From the state's point of view this system was fragmented with varying standards, and more significantly, the system posed a threat to colonial rule. Consequently

Ireland gained a state-supported national school system in 1831, while the equivalent in England did not occur until 1870. The 1831 initiative marks the origins of the primary school system and its main characteristics, in particular religious ownership of schools combined with state funding, stem from this time. Originally the aim was to teach children together for all subjects except religious instruction, and it was hoped that this would banish the proselytism associated with education at that time. The state promoted the idea of mixed denominational schooling and funding was to favour joint applications from the different churches. However, the various religious groups objected, and essentially the system as it evolved ran on denominational lines, with each denomination applying for money for their own schools either already in existence, including hedge schools, or new ones (Coolahan, 1981).

Provision of second-level education (known as intermediate education) was not as extensive as primary education in the nineteenth century. Again, early provision was dominated by religious groups and schools operated on a fee-paying basis. State intervention was prompted by inadequate financing as well as the problem of small numbers and poor standards. In 1878 an Intermediate Education Act was passed. This provided for the establishment of an Intermediate Board comprising representatives of the main religious denominations. The Board dispersed funds to second-level schools on the basis of examination results. During the preparatory stage of the legislation Catholic Church opposition to equal treatment of boys and girls in the intermediate system led to a campaign spearheaded by women prominent in the provision of education for girls, including Isabella Tod and Margaret Byers. This was successful in altering the proposed legislation to allow girls access to the intermediate examination system (Harford, 2005).

While the Intermediate Board ostensibly supported non-denominational schools, in practice the schools operated along denominational lines. A range of problems continued to hamper second-level education, including: negative consequences of the funding-by-results system used to fund schools; lack of trained teachers; poor pay and conditions; poor quality of schools and poor standards achieved. By the time of independence, therefore, 'it was a rickety and run-down intermediate education machine which the new independent Irish Free State inherited' (Coolahan, 1981: 73).

Technical or vocational education at second level remained undeveloped. As the Catholic Church took little interest in its development it proved the least controversial of all types of education. A Department of Agriculture and Technical Instruction was established in 1899 which liaised with local committees that developed technical education schemes funded by a combination of local and central funding. Demand for technical education was not as high as for intermediate education, as the status and employment opportunities flowing from intermediate education were seen as superior.

The establishment of Trinity College, the first Irish university, in 1591 predates any initiatives at first and second level. This is in line with developments across Europe, where universities were the first educational institutions to be established, usually under religious control (Collins, 2000). Trinity College operated as a fee-paying institution, heavily imbued with a Church of Ireland ethos. By the mid-nineteenth century demand for third-level education suitable for middle-class Catholics grew. This was met with the establishment of non-denominational colleges in Belfast, Cork and Galway, all of which opened in the 1840s with Queens University the awarding body for degrees offered by the colleges. Yet this was not the denominational education the Catholic Church wanted and it strenuously campaigned against these colleges. An alternative Catholic university was established by the Catholic Church in 1854 which subsequently became University College Dublin. By 1908, after decades of discussion, an Irish Universities Act 1908 was passed and the National University of Ireland (NUI) was established with three colleges, including the Queen's colleges at Cork and Galway, and the Catholic university in Dublin. Maynooth College (established in 1795 and mainly concerned with training seminarians for Catholic priesthood) joined the NUI in 1910. Queen's College Belfast became Queen's University Belfast, and Trinity also remained outside of the NUI. The creation of the NUI largely facilitated Catholic control of third-level education (Inglis, 1998). The 1908 Act also enabled local authorities to offer scholarships to students to attend university. However, a minority of students progressed to third level, only 5,000, for example, in 1914. University education continued to be an elite upper-class concern. It also remained predominantly male despite formal access being granted to women.

1920s-1950s

The education system changed very little in the first decades of independence. The main thrust of policy was to leave it in the hands of the Church. The tense relationship the Catholic Church had with the colonial administration changed as the new state's goals for education were in tune with those of the Church. The new state now had the opportunity to promote cultural nationalism. This had been gaining momentum prior to independence and essentially it meant building Irish national identity on native Irish culture. In this context education became significant as a vehicle for Irish language revival. Religious education also became highly important because of the connections made between religion and national identity (Williams, 1999). A Department of Education was created in 1924 but existing administrative and regulatory procedures were maintained. The tradition of decentralised school ownership and management continued while the state maintained centralised control of the curriculum, the inspection and examination process, and the financing of the system.

As for equality and access, while equality of opportunity 'as far as possible' (MacNeill 1924 cited in Farren, 1995: 106) was mentioned as a guiding principle of education, little was done to implement this principle. Primary education remained the only form of education that was free and only a small number of extra scholarships were granted for students to attend second level. Overall developments from the

1920s to the early 1960s may be understood as operating within a 'theocentric paradigm' (D O'Sullivan, 2005). In this paradigm the purpose of education is understood within a framework of Christian principles about human nature and its purpose, ownership and control is kept within religious authority and the state maintains a subsidiary role.

If anything, this meant a turn for the worse in the primary school system. A new curriculum was introduced in 1992 with fewer subjects and instruction in Irish, which replaced the broad range and child-centred focus of the curriculum in place since 1901. As Walsh (T Walsh, 2005: 259) comments 'the Irish language was perceived as the panacea for all problems and, as it was for the good of the nation, it was necessary for the child'. In addition, the School Attendance Act 1926, which made attendance in education compulsory for all those aged between 6 and 14, was 'promoted on the basis that a child needed to be in school to learn Irish' (T Walsh, 2005: 259). Little effort was made to change the system, and with the exception of some relatively minor revisions, the curriculum stayed in place until the 1970s. There was little concern about inequality, and programmes to deal with poverty, such as free school meals, free school books and the delivery of a school medical service, were minimal. Resource scarcity provides only a partial explanation for this lack of services, because, as Coolahan (1981: 45) notes, 'underlying it also was the social conservatism of the body politic and of the churches at that period'.

The overriding feature of second level was its academic, elitist and careerist focus, especially present in the Catholic secondary schools (D O'Sullivan, 2005). The influence of cultural nationalism also pervaded where, for example, Irish was made a compulsory subject and students were incentivised to use Irish by being awarded higher marks in examination papers if answered through Irish. This provision remains in place.

Second level remained private and fee-paying and few scholarships were available to 'bright' children. The focus was on the preparation of middle-class children to compete for middle-class jobs available in areas such as the civil service and semi-state companies for boys, and teacher training and nursing for girls. Secondary schools also existed in a hierarchical relationship, the school one attended reflected class distinctions and influenced one's future career possibilities. These class distinctions are well captured in James Joyce's *Portrait of an Artist as a Young Man*: 'Christian Brothers be damned! Said Mr. Dedalus. Is it with Paddy Stink and Mickey Mud? No, let him stick to the jesuits in God's name since he began with them. They'll be of service to him in after years. Those are the fellows who can get you a position' (Joyce cited in Ledden, 1999: 333).

Second-level schooling remained largely inaccessible. In 1960 for example, only 3.4% of students attending secondary schools were in receipt of scholarships (Coolahan, 1981). Some pupils attended by virtue of relatively low fees or because some schools offered poor pupils with potential a second-level education, not by virtue of state equality of opportunity policy. The Education Act 1944 in the UK, which introduced free second-level education and raised the school leaving age to 15, created some discussion about similar reforms and equality of opportunity in Ireland. However, political conservatism and financial restraint impeded any comparable moves, which were briefly considered in the late 1940s (Fleming and Harford, 2014).

Probably the most significant change to occur over this period was in the area of technical education. The Vocational Education Act 1930 facilitated the development of a network of vocational schools and Vocational Education Committees (VECs which in 2013 became Education Training Boards (ETBs)) were created which managed the schools. Vocational/technical schools were designed to prepare students for work in industry and agriculture, with the state reassuring the Catholic Church that the curriculum would not infringe on the secondary school curriculum (Farren, 1995). In any case these schools did not directly compete with other secondary schools because they came to represent preparation for lower-status occupations and were therefore seen as less prestigious (D O'Sullivan, 2005).

Few changes took place at university level. Access remained very limited. There were, for example, only 214 local authority scholarships for entry to third level in 1962-63 and no major growth in student numbers from the 1920s to the 1960s. The numbers of women attending university grew only slightly from 26% of full-time students in 1938 to 30% in 1960 (Coolahan, 1981). Once issues of control were settled in the 1908 legislation, a Catholic ethos pervaded the NUI universities. Catholic social thought was particularly evident in the content of subjects such as sociology and philosophy, frequently taught by members of the clergy and papal encyclicals were, for example, used as key texts (Fanning, 2008). By the 1950s demand for university education increased and the numbers of students at third level began to grow, to the extent that existing university facilities were unable to meet new demand. This set the scene for a major expansionary phase in Irish education in the 1960s and 1970s.

1960s-1980s

The 1960s witnessed a transformation in the thrust of education policy from an approach that was conservative, gradual and incrementalist to something briefly more radical and far-reaching. Following reforms that had taken place in many European countries a decade or two earlier, changes to education policy set about improving equality of opportunity by universalising second level and widening access to third level. Change was primarily motivated by the recognition of a changed world. The new direction of Irish economic policy in the late 1950s impacted upon education in terms of how it would prepare sufficient numbers of students with the requisite skills and knowledge for the changing economy, and for eventual membership of the European Economic Community (now EU). Denis O'Sullivan (2005) suggests that a paradigm shift occurred from a theocentric to a mercantile education system. In this transformation cultural nationalism, language revival and religious education all loosened their grip. These changes did not take place without a power struggle, and as Walsh (2012) documents, there was much Church resistance. In the mercantile paradigm the state takes on a managerial role, in contrast to its previous subsidiary and deferential role to the Church and it manages 'on behalf of the users and funders of education – parents, tax-payers, industry, employers' (D O'Sullivan, 2005: 121). While the mercantile paradigm has its roots in the 1960s, these changes continue to develop in what Denis O'Sullivan identifies as a predatory fashion in that the paradigm has the power to dominate all aspects of education.

The publication of *Investment in Education* (OECD, 1965), a joint Irish and OECD initiative, was also hugely influential. The report highlighted two major issues: (1) the existence of large social class and regional disparities in education participation rates and (2) the needs of the developing economy would not be met by the education system as it existed. These issues represented a dovetailing of equality of opportunity with economic necessity and the document became the fundamental driver of major expansion and change in the education system.

At primary level a new curriculum was introduced in 1971. Its introduction was deemed 'a seismic shift in state policy and attitude towards the education of children' though in practice its implementation was slow and variable (Walsh, 2016: 8). The notion of childhood as a distinct phase of development informed the new curriculum and new teaching methods, such as discovery-based learning, were intended to be more in tune with individual children's needs and abilities. Subjects were to be taught in an integrated as opposed to a compartmentalised manner and this applied also to religious instruction. The pervasiveness of religion in the curriculum became one of the catalysts for the emergence of an alternative multi-denominational, co-educational and democratically managed model of schooling. Starting with a single school in Dalkey in 1978, by 1984 the movement came under the banner of Educate Together (Hyland, 1996). The management structures of schools also began to open up. In 1975 primary schools were obliged to set up boards of management and include parent and teacher representatives, whereas previously schools were usually managed by a local cleric. Yet religious control was maintained as the patron's (usually the bishop) nominees formed a majority of the board. Similar changes to management occurred in second-level schools in 1985.

At second level, comprehensive and community schools were introduced in the early 1960s, mirroring the international trend of comprehensivisation. These schools sought to blur the academic–technical divide between secondary and vocational schools, and shift the system away from its heavy academic focus to become more responsive to new economic needs and opportunities. As such their introduction was framed in pragmatic rather than ideological terms. This had implications for how concerns about equality were realised, although as Clancy (2007: 107) notes, there was no 'detailed exploration of egalitarian principles, which questioned the invidious status distinctions between the education offered for mainly middle-class children in secondary schools and mainly working-class children in vocational schools'. As a result, these new schools left existing hierarchical relations undisturbed and simply became a middle tier in the system.

Access to second-level education was universalised in 1967–68 by the abolition of fees, and this change was introduced in conjunction with raising the compulsory school leaving age from 14 to 15 in 1972. Over time this made progression to second level the norm; until then many pupils simply remained in primary school until they were 14. Free transport was provided for those living beyond three miles of a school, and grants to offset educational cost were introduced on a means-tested basis. These changes, while very significant, did not have an equal impact. Participation rates increased across all social classes, but disparities remained, reflecting the fact that policy changes emphasised increasing participation rather than reducing inequality (Frawley, 2014). Children from professional, employer and managerial backgrounds continued to have the highest participation rates and children from semi- and unskilled backgrounds the lowest (Breen et al, 1990). By the early 1970s various reports highlighted continuing inequalities with regard to participation (see Fleming and Harford, 2014), however the reformist momentum of the 1960s had dissipated and educational inequalities were not seriously addressed again until the 1990s.

One of the continuing inequalities in the system rests with the existence of private secondary schools. For secondary schools the introduction of 'free fees' meant that the majority changed into schools that became non-fee-paying and 10% of secondary schools opted to remain fee-paying (Sheehan, 1979). Yet while these schools charge substantial tuition fees they continue to have their teacher salaries paid by the state and more recently have also benefited from public money for capital needs. As Clancy (2007: 108) argues these schools 'appear to have the best of both worlds. … what have become private schools use tuition fees to supplement the state's contribution. It is in effect a state-subsidised private system'. Those who can afford to attend private schools thus have the competitive advantages that this confers enhanced by state support, which is contrary to any form of equality of opportunity.

At third level the impetus of *Investment in Education* (OECD, 1965) combined with the *Report of the Commission on Higher Education* (1967) served to expand the system and widen access. The Commission on Higher Education documented severe inequalities, with participation heavily dominated by the middle classes. The Local Authority (Higher Education Grant) Act 1968 substantially expanded the means-tested grants available to attend third-level education. Greater emphasis was placed on technical education through the creation of Regional Technical Colleges (now Institutes of Technology), Dublin Institute of Technology, and two National Institutes of Higher Education in Limerick and Dublin (now University of Limerick and Dublin City University). Participation increased substantially at third level (by 129% from 1960 to 1970 and 92% from 1970 to 1980), yet inequalities in participation between social classes remained significant, something we return to in the contemporary context.

SECTION THREE
EDUCATION SINCE THE 1990s: AN OVERVIEW

The period since the 1990s has seen much activity and change within education. The predatory nature of the mercantile paradigm became stronger as the state has grown more active in the education field. International bodies, in particular the OECD, have also become more influential in how education policy and practice is steered. The primacy of education as human capital has become even more important and the wave of reform beginning in the early 1990s was strongly tied to the needs of the economy, whether expressed as the need to produce more enterprising workers or workers more appropriately skilled for the knowledge economy. At the same time widening access and addressing disadvantage has continued to be a core element of education policy. The legislative base of education, an area which had not seen significant change since the Vocational Education Act 1930, was also substantially augmented over the late 1990s and early 2000s (see Box 9.2).

Box 9.2: Key education policy and legislative developments

1991	OECD Report: *Review of National Policies for Education, Ireland*
1992	Green Paper: *Education for a Changing World*
1995	White Paper: *Charting Our Education Future*
1997	Universities Act
1998	Education Act
1999	*Ready to Learn: White Paper on Early Childhood Education*
2000	Education (Welfare) Act
2000	White Paper: *Learning for Life*
2004	OECD report: *Review of National Policies for Education: Review of Higher Education in Ireland*
2004	Education for Persons with Special Educational Needs (EPSEN) Act
2005/2008/2015	*National Plan(s) for Equity of Access to Higher Education*
2006	OECD report: *Review of National Policies for Education, Review of Higher Education in Ireland*
2011	*National Strategy for Higher Education to 2030*
2011	*Literacy and Numeracy for Learning and Life. The National Strategy to Improve Literacy and Numeracy Among Children and Young People 2011-2020*
2012	*The Forum on Patronage and Pluralism in the Primary Sector Report of the Forum's Advisory Group*
2012/2015	*Framework for Junior Cycle*
2016	*Investing in National Ambition: A Strategy for Funding Higher Education*

This policy activity was backed by greater investment in education. Between the mid–1990s and early 2000s Ireland ranked among the highest for countries with the largest increases in educational expenditure, though the scale of the increase reflected the fact that Ireland was coming from a low expenditure base (Drudy, 2009). By the late 2000s reductions in education expenditure due to the economic crisis impacted on services and student–teacher ratios across all levels of the system, particularly in higher education (see Figure 9.1). Provisions outside mainstream education such as services related to educational disadvantage and special education were particularly vulnerable to cutbacks. General government expenditure on education as a share of GDP in Ireland generally tracks below the EU average (see Figure 9.2).

Figure 9.1: Expenditure per student, 2005-13

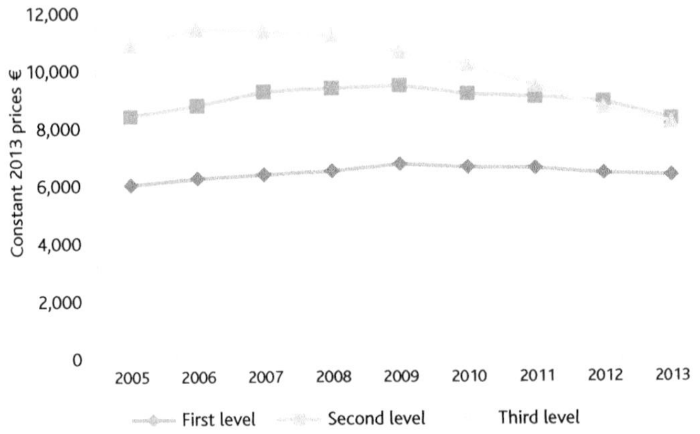

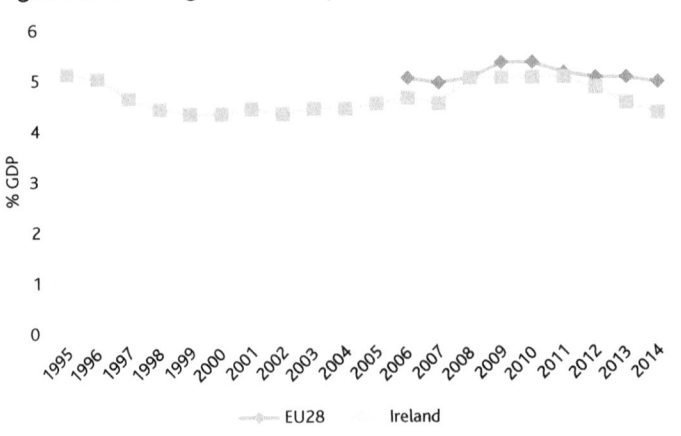

Data source: Department of Education and Skills, Education Statistics Database

Figure 9.2: General government expenditure on education, 1995-2014

Data source: Eurostat

Within this overall context a number of key trends and issues can be discerned. The first of these is the expansion of the education system, most especially at higher level. The scope of education has widened as lifelong education and early childhood education gained greater policy attention. Alongside expansion, the problem of educational disadvantage became a significant policy concern, and targeted programmes have proliferated at all levels of the system. Outside of the economic domain to which issues of educational disadvantage largely pertain, issues of inclusion related to diverse needs and identities have also become more significant. Thus children with special educational needs (SEN) and children of minority faith backgrounds and none, are gaining somewhat more recognition in the education system, as expressed through policy principles such as inclusion and interculturalism. Yet there are manifold limits to these changes, as we go on to explore in this section.

Preschool

Compulsory school attendance age in Ireland is six years of age. For children under six a variety of terms are used to refer to their education and care, including 'preschool' and 'early-years'. To make matters more confusing, the norm until recently in Ireland is that children attend 'infant classes' in primary school from age four onwards with almost all five-year-olds attending. In other countries such provision would be considered 'preschool', or 'pre-primary' (McKeown et al, 2015). The general term for provision for the under-sixes in the OECD and EU is early childhood education and care (ECEC) which implies an integration of education and care. In contrast, Ireland has a split system. This means that early education is the focus of provision for children aged three to six, while care is focus of services for the under-threes. The state typically supports childcare on a limited basis for disadvantaged families in order to facilitate parental employment. This split is more typical of liberal welfare states and considered problematic from the point of view of what is best for the child (O'Donoghue-Hynes and Hayes, 2011). Preschool services were traditionally run by the community and private sectors, and these include play groups and preschools, such as Montessori, Steiner and Naíonraí (Irish language) preschools, all of which typically cater for three-to-six-year-olds (Fallon, 2005). Approximately 70% of services are privately run (Hayes, 2016). Direct public provision is limited to the Early Start programme, a preschool service run in 40 urban disadvantaged areas, preschools for Traveller children, and a small number of special needs preschools. These initiatives were established in the mid-1990s and coincided with a growing interest in ECEC, culminating in the White Paper, *Ready to Learn* (GoI, 1999a). Factors which influenced growing interest included the rise in the female labour-force participation rate. Cognisance of mounting evidence of the importance of early intervention in a child's life and the benefits and cost-effectiveness of ECEC, in contrast to dealing with problems later such as early school leaving, also played a part. As such a human capital gains approach to ECEC dominates in Ireland.

This contrasts with an alternative, albeit less widespread, approach that emphasises social justice and rights and a more holistic approach to child well-being in the 'here and now' (Frawley, 2014). In any case, access and affordability remained critical issues in the 1990s and 2000s, especially for low-income families. Without committed state investment and regulation services were left to the market and were of variable quality (Hayes, 2007). Successive governments prioritised cash benefits over service provision, despite numerous recommendations (OECD, 2004a, 2006; NESF, 2005a, Hayes, 2008) to develop ECEC as a universal service.

Triggered by the fiscal crisis, a significant advance was made when the government abolished a short-lived cash benefit (Early Childcare Supplement) and replaced it in 2010 with a 'Free Pre-School Year', formally known as the Early Childhood Care and Education (ECCE) programme. The annual cost of this change was 65% less than the Early Childcare Supplement (Wolfe et al, 2013). Relying on the existing network of providers, the programme provides preschool for three hours a day, five days a week over 38 weeks of the year. The programme was extended to a second year of provision in 2016 so that all children from age three onwards may access the service. Participating services are expected to adhere to quality standards set out in *Síolta: The National Quality Framework for Early Childhood Education* (Centre for Early Childhood Development and Education, 2006) and *Aistear: The Early Childhood Curriculum Framework* (NCCA, 2009) and improve the professional qualifications of their staff; areas which were, and arguably still are, neglected (Hayes, 2016). The initiative means that Ireland's preschool landscape is now more convergent with international provision, and the enrolment rate of four-year-olds across preschool and infant primary school classes, which was historically low, has surpassed the OECD average. However, the sector is still under-resourced compared to infant classes in primary school and Ireland continues to spend well below the OECD average on pre-primary education (OECD, 2016b). Moreover, the service is not a formal right or entitlement but dependent on local availability (Wolfe et al, 2013). It is also part-time, meaning that full-time ECEC depends on ability to pay.

Although the benefits of early childhood education are indisputable (see Frawley, 2014) it is not a panacea for inequality, and specifically inequality in childhood. An early study on the child outcomes of children participating in the ECCE programme (McKeown et al, 2015) found that the gap remained between children with more or better skills, in areas such as social and emotional skills and language and cognitive development, and children with less, after participating in the service. Social class was found to be strongest influence on differences in skills. This, as McKeown et al (2015) argue, does not mean that preschool is not important in improving children's lives but it is only one part of a bigger task of tackling poverty and inequality that impact on child development.

Primary level and second level

The primary school system comprises 3,124 mainstream primary schools and 138 special schools. Approximately 90% of primary schools are under Catholic ownership/patronage. A limited number of private schools operate at primary level; these are not state funded, in contrast to the state-supported model of fee-paying schools at second level. At second level, 375 schools are secondary schools are in religious ownership and are predominantly Catholic, 265 are vocational schools and 95 are community and comprehensive schools (2015/16 figures) (DES, 2016).

Since the early 1990s curricula at both levels have been reformed and modernised under the advice of the National Council for Curriculum and Assessment (NCCA). Student-centred and active learning, inclusion and diversity, and human capital formation, in terms of acquiring skills for the knowledge economy, have permeated these reforms. At primary level a new curriculum was introduced in 1999 (GoI, 1999b) and revisions continued in areas such as languages and mathematics. After the 'PISA shock' in 2009 when Ireland performed poorly in the OECD Programme for International Student Assessment (PISA) rankings of reading, mathematical and scientific literacy, *The National Strategy to Improve Literacy and Numeracy among Children and Young People 2011-2020* (DES, 2011) was introduced encompassing all levels from early childhood to second level.

At second level the notion of education for the economy has been particularly influential. Reforms included the introduction of a transition year subsequent to completion of the Junior Certificate and two new senior-cycle programmes; the Leaving Certificate Vocational Programme (LCVP) in 1994 and the Leaving Certificate Applied Programme (LCAP) in 1995. In part, these new programmes were introduced as a result of greater numbers staying on at second level since the 1980s. The reforms were also driven by the view that second-level schooling was still too academic and needed to prepare students for the realities of the working world. The human capital orientation of the 1991 OECD education review (OECD, 1991) and the 1992 Green Paper *Education for a Changing World* (GoI, 1992) influenced this argument. These reports outlined a number of deficiencies relating to the predominance of factual knowledge over critical and entrepreneurial thinking and problem solving; and the failure to prepare students for the changing nature of work, particularly in terms of technology. Of the two Leaving Certificate programmes, the LCAP is considered the more radical innovation (Clancy, 2007), and its practical and applied nature allows students to progress to further education, such as post-leaving-certificate courses, but not higher education. It is also geared towards students who are at risk of leaving school early. Approximately 5% of students take the LCAP and 25% take the LCVP. While there are arguments for the LCAP and LCVP, they are also criticised for ingraining more distinct tracking into second level which impacts more heavily on working-class students and their chance of social mobility. Working-class students are disproportionately represented in the LCAP in particular and schools have been found to reinforce the effects of social class background in terms of how they intervene or don't intervene in student choice of programme (Banks et al, 2014).

At junior cycle, reform is also underway with the introduction of the *Framework for Junior Cycle* (DES, 2015). This is a revised version of 2012 proposals which met with teacher union opposition, particularly concerning how students would be assessed. The new junior cycle programme includes a new curriculum and modes of assessment, intended to strike a balance between acquiring subject knowledge, skill and thinking abilities, and between class-based assessment and a summative state examination. While the curriculum emphasises diversity, flexibility and creativity through the range of subjects and short courses involved, the changes also reflect the concerns of learning for the knowledge economy.

Though not as deeply impacted by managerialism as higher education, trends such as the practice of publishing Whole School Evaluation reports at both primary and second level since 2006, and the introduction of mandatory standardised testing in reading and mathematics at primary level in 2008, indicate its influence at these levels. The 'accountability' and competitive pressure generated by such practices lends itself to test-based teaching and greater use of ability grouping, which in turn has been found to validate the experiences and cultural capital of middle-class children over working-class children (Mac Ruairc, 2009). Such practices, therefore, are not only a matter of academic differentiation but also social differentiation, potentially further marginalising working-class and minority group children (Drudy and Kinsella, 2009). Moreover, though the production of league tables by the DES (Department of Education and Skills) has been resisted, the creation of second-level league tables by newspapers means that 'reputational criteria and entry to what is perceived as the "best" school becomes even more pronounced' (Grummell and Lynch, 2016: 224).

Educational disadvantage

The concept of educational disadvantage entered debates by the early 1990s and became a core feature of education policy and legislative developments. Educational disadvantage is strongly class-related; students from lower social class groups are more likely to be at a disadvantage in terms of participation and achievement in the education system (CPA, 2003). *Charting Our Education Future* (GoI, 1995) acknowledged educational disadvantage as a problem and signalled a shift in approaches to educational opportunity from ensuring equal access to trying to ensure equal participation and achievement. Subsequently educational disadvantage was formally defined in the Education Act 1998 as 'the impediments to education arising from social or economic disadvantage which prevent students from deriving appropriate benefit from education in schools' (Section 32(9)).

However, there are multiple ways in which educational disadvantage can be understood, which range from narrow understandings of disadvantage as a personal deficit, to radical understandings that see the problem as a product of unequal economic and power relations. Tormey (2010) suggests that Irish policy does not acknowledge that educational disadvantage is a political concept and open to a number of contested meanings and policy implications. Instead, these issues are obscured by a consensual approach and a focus on technical issues such as identifying indicators of disadvantage and which individuals and groups are 'at risk', and measuring how levels of educational disadvantage have changed over time.

In practice, educational disadvantage programmes, which since 2005 come under the umbrella of DEIS, focus on improving equality of participation and achievement. DEIS schools qualify as such on the basis of various indicators of socioeconomic disadvantage. Currently 19% of primary schools and 26% of second-level schools are DEIS schools. Urban DEIS schools are further differentiated, Urban Band 1 schools have a higher level of disadvantage than Urban Band 2 schools (Smyth et al, 2015). Typically, support under DEIS includes extra funding, extra numeracy and literacy supports, access to specific support programmes such as the Home, School Community Liaison and the School Completion programme, and, in the case of Urban Band 1 schools, reduced class sizes. DEIS does not address differences in family economic circumstances, but aims at developing children's cultural capital, such as cognitive and language abilities; and wider social capital, such as involving parents and the wider community and developing relationships which benefit children's educational development (DESc, 2005). Aspects of educational disadvantage were also addressed in the Education (Welfare) Act 2000, by raising the minimum school leaving age to 16 or the completion of three years of post-primary education; and by establishing a National Education Welfare Board in 2003 (which now operates under Tusla), whose role is to ensure that every child receives a minimum education and focuses on attendance and retention.

The success or otherwise of such initiatives is measured on the basis of what Tormey (2010) calls an output model, which typically specifies minimum targets for literacy and numeracy scores, school attendance, retention and progression. In these terms the performance of DEIS schools has, for the most part, improved (Smyth et al, 2015). However, Tormey (2010) suggests that such measures discount the competitive nature of education; setting minimum standards does not address the unequal positions of different groups in the system. Marked differences remain in areas such as test scores, rates of early school leaving and progression to higher education between DEIS and non-DEIS schools (Smyth et al, 2015). On the latter indicator, 24% of students from DEIS schools progress to higher level in comparison to 50% for all schools (HEA, 2015).

Given the relationship between educational disadvantage and social class, it can be argued that the solutions are not simply about pushing out the boundaries of equality of opportunity policy and reforming education policy. As discussed in section one, the general problem with equality of opportunity in terms of its acceptance of inequality is replicated in policies designed to address educational disadvantage. These policies remain detached from the bigger picture of inequality in society, and the role that the education system plays in perpetuating that inequality: enhancing the educational advantages of some. Irish policy, Tormey (2010: 195) suggests, is ultimately based on a politically conservative impulse, which

> focuses attention on the disadvantaged person while directing attention away from the possibility that processes of disadvantaging may be built into the educational system and … which identifies that it is willing to work towards increased attainment for working class children so long as this does not impact on the capacity of middle class parents to pass on wealth and power to their children.

Advantage is reproduced in numerous ways and often involves better resourced families choosing more selective schools for their children, and being well positioned to contribute to the resourcing of those schools by voluntary contributions. Private investment also takes place via extra tuition and private education in fee-paying primary and second-level schools (Lynch and Moran, 2006; Smyth, 2009). Within the fee-paying sector itself a hierarchy also exists: a select number of 'elite' schools at the top are central to reproducing inequality. Courtois (2015) identifies eight such schools which are prestigious, extremely expensive, focus on educating 'leaders' and admit a highly privileged interconnected group of pupils. The model of funding private schools came in for greater scrutiny during the economic crisis; however, only minor changes were made to how the state subsidises private schools. Issues such as these shape the uneven playing field on which policy to combat educational disadvantage operates and, in continuity with earlier reforms of the 1960s, the state's role is double-edged; it plays a role both in perpetuating inequality and in attempting to (modestly) modify it.

Diversity, inclusion and segregation

Since the early 1990s, greater awareness and commitment to principles of inclusion, equality and rights is also evident in the education system. Irish society is increasingly secular while at the same time the scale of immigration has given rise to a growing multi-ethnic population and groups with minority religious faiths. Such change poses a challenge to the existing model of education provision, particularly at primary level, which is dominated by Catholic patronage. The disability rights movement and the Traveller rights movement have also highlighted ways in which the education system has been unequal and exclusionary for minority groups. The beginnings of a response to these issues can be found in *Charting Our Education Future* (GoI, 1995) which sets out the principles which should underpin education; namely quality, equality, pluralism, partnership and accountability. Following this the Education Act 1998 placed an obligation on the minister for education and science to make available the support services, and a level and quality of education appropriate to meet the needs and abilities of every person, including children with SEN, and children from culturally diverse backgrounds. The Act also requires schools to have an admissions policy and school plan which must provide for equal access and participation. The Equal Status Acts 2000 and 2004 prohibit discrimination in relation to areas such as admission and access to courses. However, in a form of 'state-sanctioned exclusion' (Ledwith and Reilly, 2013: 321) exemptions allow schools preserve their religious ethos. Thus, meaning that schools can prioritise children whose religious background is in keeping with the religious ethos of the school and can refuse admission to children of other religious backgrounds. This is an indication of how slow, conservative and contradictory change can be with regard to realising diversity and inclusion.

Since the early 2000s greater numbers students with SEN are educated in mainstream schools or in special classes in mainstream schools (McConkey et al, 2016). At the same time, the number of children identified as having an intellectual disability also grew, possibly in part due to recent legislative developments. The Education for Persons with Special Educational Needs Act 2004 legally established the principle of inclusive education for children with SEN, stating that 'children with special educational needs have the same right to avail of, and benefit from, appropriate education as do their peers who do not have such needs' (Article 13.3b) and it provided for learning support/resource teachers in mainstream classes and special needs assistants for individual students. This dovetailed with the Disability Act 2005 which provided for assessment of pupils' SEN. However, neither Act has been fully implemented. Provisions in both Acts are curtailed by the inclusion of a resources clause meaning that the rights set out have not fully materialised and are subject to funding being available (Perry and Clarke, 2015).

In response to growing ethnic diversity, the NCCA (2005, 2006) developed guidelines on **interculturalism** in the curriculum at primary and post-primary level, which were followed up by an *Intercultural Education Strategy 2010-2015* (DES and OMI, 2010). However, echoing the lack of debate about what educational disadvantage means in the education system, there is a similar absence of any real debate on recognition of difference. Articulation of interculturalism within education policy tends to be primarily aspirational (D O'Sullivan, 2005), and in practice it has been left to individual teacher discretion (Parker-Jenkins and Masterson, 2013).

> **Interculturalism** in education is anti-discriminatory, based on respect for and engagement with cultural diversity, and the promotion of equality.

Evidence of segregation across schools also counters efforts develop inclusive and intercultural education. In particular admission policies, including the operation of waiting lists and the stipulation of catchment areas, may contribute to subtle forms of rejection of certain pupils. Parental choice, geographic factors and housing policy can also contribute to segregation, particularly in urban areas. Urban DEIS schools are more likely to have higher concentrations of immigrant children, children with physical disabilities, children with learning difficulties and Traveller children (Oireachtas Library and Research Service, 2015). The clustering of immigrant children was borne out in the 2013/14 DES census returns which found that two thirds of the enrolment in 20 schools came from children with a non-Irish background (Curry, 2016). The potentially segregating practices of schools is being addressed in the Education (Admissions to School) Bill 2016, which promises a fairer and more transparent admissions regime. If enacted, schools will not be allowed to employ waiting lists or charge admission fees, and where schools are not oversubscribed all students who apply must be admitted. However, schools will be permitted to continue to prioritise enrolment in accordance with religious denomination.

In 2011 a *Forum on Patronage and Pluralism in the Primary Sector* was established by the government which recommended that in selected areas where parental surveys indicated a preference for school choice, Catholic schools be divested (Coolahan et al, 2012). However, little progress has since been made and the Catholic Church in particular has been resistant to changing the status quo. Some progress occurred around the edges of the system: a new model of multi-denominational Community National Schools (CNS) under ETB management, brought about by the lack of school places for non-Catholic children in Dublin, was established in the mid-2000s. By 2016 there were 11 of these schools and the current ministerial preference is to see this school type grow. However, under the CNS model, pupils are still divided for religion classes to allow faith formation take place, which was a condition of Catholic Church support for the establishment of the schools (RTÉ, 2015). This model has thus been criticised for how it 'sanctions the segregation of young children' (Educate Together, 2016: 1). Despite the policy preference for CNSs, Educate Together schools, which admit children of all faiths and none, and teach ethical education instead of religious instruction, are the fastest-growing school type in areas where new schools are needed. Facilitated in part by changes to how the capital costs of schools are financed, this has also enabled the emergence of Educate Together schools at second level. However, while such change offers choice in some larger towns and urban areas, ensuring diversity is problematic in many areas where 'stand-alone' schools operate.

Beyond the lack of progress in diversifying patronage there are also broader issues with how change is being envisaged. As O'Toole (2015: 92) suggests, 'an alternative solution, namely one which would advocate creating common state schools for all children, irrespective of their religious background, is a perspective that is rarely heard in the patronage debate in Ireland, where denominationalism is considered the norm'. This would entail the creation of a secular education system: under state patronage, schools would accord equal treatment and parity of esteem to all children. Issues of faith and faith formation would belong to the private realm.

Higher education

Higher education is the part of the education system where the concept of the knowledge economy has had most impact. A human capital perspective and the links between education and economic growth have been influential in how higher education has been framed 'as a highway to economic salvation' (Walsh and Loxley, 2015: 1130) since the 1960s. These links intensified since the 1990s in the context of increasing globalisation, and again from the early 2010s as part of Ireland's economic recovery, with the contribution of higher education to the creation of a knowledge or 'smart' economy at the core. As such the social objectives of higher education, such as enhancing social citizenship and contributing to an open, democratic and equal society have been sidelined. Policies such as widening access and equalising opportunity have been increasingly justified on economic utilitarian grounds; that is, for the good of economic prosperity and competitiveness, and for the financial gains that accrue to the individual student.

Since the publication of *Education for a Changing World* (GoI, 1992) more pressure has been placed on higher education institutions to serve the needs of the economy. Subsequently they have been subject to new public management reforms that more explicitly steer and monitor institutions in line with national economic priorities. International policy actors have also been influential and in this regard, Grummell and Lynch (2016: 224) identify the OECD (2004b) invited review of higher education as 'a watershed in Irish higher education'. The review positioned higher education as fundamental to the creation of a successful knowledge economy in Ireland, particularly in terms of innovation and the creation of knowledge capital in areas such as science and technology. The review recommended that if the higher education sector was to meet its strategic objectives more effectively research activity needed to be expanded, and that this should include a significant expansion of 'fourth level' in the number of postgraduate students.

The concerns and recommendations of the OECD were broadly endorsed in domestic policy, most recently in the *National Strategy for Higher Education to 2030* (HEA, 2011), known as the 'Hunt Report' after chairman of the strategy group Colin Hunt. The Hunt Report ramped up the emphasis on the knowledge economy as the key to Ireland's prosperity. It noted the necessity of creating rather than applying knowledge; the need to continuously upskill the workforce; and, drawing on European Commission discourse on education and enterprise, emphasised the necessity of Irish graduates becoming 'job shapers and not just job seekers' (HEA, 2011: 37). The Report also addressed governance issues, recommending greater regulation and steering of the sector in the name of greater productivity, efficiency and accountability. In terms of funding and constraints on public resources, the Report recommended increased student contributions via an upfront fee, the payment of which could be deferred by a loan system. Since the Report's publication, the structural reform agenda has been gathering pace (Clancy, 2015). Reforms include the creation of performance contracts between individual institutions and the HEA (Higher Education Authority), which essentially drive institutions to perform more like businesses with productivity targets to meet, in terms of finance, student enrolment, research income and output. In addition, the higher education landscape is being rationalised and consolidated with the merger of smaller institutions and plans for the establishment of technological universities, based around clusters of existing Institutes of Technology.

Proposals to alter the funding base and to increase students' fees continue to be contentious and have been slower to progress. Ireland abolished third-level fees in 1995, following moves in earlier decades in most other European countries. At the time the government suggested that it would 'remove important financial and psychological barriers to participation at third level' (GoI, 1995: 101 in Clancy, 2005: 107). While a relatively small administration fee, known as the 'student contribution' was retained, the fee increased sharply (by 333%) between 2008 and 2015 (from €900 to €3,000). Following the Hunt Report's recommendations, an Expert Group on Future Funding of Higher Education was established by the government; its report (Expert Group on Future Funding Higher Education, 2016) is also known as the Cassells Report, after the group chairman Peter Cassells. It found that in the context of growing student numbers, difficulties families have paying the student contribution and the current underfunded state of the system, increased funding is required and it recommended three policy options. The first is a predominantly state-funded system, with increased state funding and the abolition of the student contribution; the second is increased state funding with continuing fees; and third, increased state funding with deferred payment of fees through income contingent loans. However, there appears to be political reluctance to address this issue and the current student contribution has become 'in effect, the tuition fee "that dare not speak its name"' (Hazelkorn, 2014: 1347), adding to the gradual process of converting the student into a consumer of higher education as a commodity. The current system also poses barriers to access, particularly for students who are just above the threshold for mean-tested support (SUSI grants), because of the very selective system of support. Elaborating on this point, participation and equality issues are next examined.

Overall participation has grown significantly in recent decades. In 1980 only one in five students entered third level (20%), and by 2011 this grew to just over one in every two students (52%) (HEA, 2015). Since the 1995 'free fees' initiative, more specific access and participation measures have been pursued. These began with the implementation of the Universities Act 1997 which, among other things, clearly obliged universities to promote equity. The approach that evolved has been one of targeting specific groups and addressing their under-representation, and the task is coordinated by National Access Policy Office (established in 2003 as the Office for Equity of Access to Higher Education). These groups include students from lower socioeconomic groups, and from other minority and non-traditional groups including mature students and students with disabilities. Periodic plans have been in place since 2005 which set targets to increase participation of under-represented groups (see Box 9.2). The current plan, the *National Plan for Equity of Access to Higher Education 2015-2019* (HEA, 2015) outlines specific targets in relation to students coming from the further education sector and sets a target for Traveller participation for the first time (see Table 9.1).

Table 9.1: Selected targets for participation in higher education

Target group	Current (2015)	Target (2019)
Non-manual worker (% of 18-20 cohort)	23%	30%
Semi/unskilled manual worker (% of 18-20 cohort)	26%	35%
Full-time mature students (% all new entrants)	13%	16%
Students with disabilities (% of all new entrants)	6%	8%
Students from the further education sector (% of new entrants)	6.6%	10%
Number of Irish Travellers	35	80

Source: adapted from HEA, 2015

The policy approach of setting targets represents a commitment to realise a substantive form of equality of opportunity. Achievements have been notable in terms of the increased participation of mature students and students with disabilities, whose participation as a percentage of all new entrants increased significantly from 4.5% and 0.9% respectively in 1998 (HEA, 2008). However, the targets of previous plans have not been met in the majority of cases, including for these student groups. The participation rate for the semi-/unskilled manual (working-class) group has hardly changed from the baseline figure of 23% in 1998 (HEA, 2008), despite higher targets being set. The broader picture of participation is still one where significant patterns of inequality of opportunity exist, as evident in a series of studies on participation at third level, which may be described as continuity with change (see Clancy 2015 for an overview). On the one hand more people are going to college. For the most part this includes more people from every socioeconomic group, and to some extent differentials are decreasing between groups. Yet continuity is also found by virtue of the fact that significant class inequalities remain. This is illustrated by participation rate data. Table 9.2 shows the estimated participation rate for each social class (calculated by dividing the number of first-year undergraduates aged 18–20 in each socioeconomic group by the numbers in the 17–19 years age cohort for each socioeconomic group in the 2011 Census). As the data is derived from two different data sets statistical anomalies arise, such as participation rates of over 100% for some groups. However, the results show wide class disparities.

Table 9.2: Estimated participation rate by socioeconomic background of new entrants to higher education in 2011

Socioeconomic group	Estimated participation rate
Employers and managers	64%
Higher professional	119%
Lower professional	48%
Non-manual workers	23%
Manual skilled workers	51%
Semi-skilled workers	24%
Unskilled workers	25%
Own account workers (self-employed)	146%
Farmers	166%
Agricultural workers	60%
Total	52%

Source: adapted from HEA, 2015

A particularly stark expression of class disparity can be found by looking at spatial inequalities in participation. For example, the Dublin postal districts with the two highest participation rates (99% and 84%), Dublin 6 and Dublin 4 respectively, are also two of the most affluent areas of the city. The districts with the lowest participation rates (15% and 16%), Dublin 17 and Dublin 10 respectively, are also the poorest areas of the city (HEA, 2015).

This pattern of inequality is not just evident in access to higher education but also within institutions with the greatest inequalities in participation to be found in the most prestigious fields of study. Thus for example, 44% of all those studying medicine/dentistry come from the same (higher professional) background (HEA, 2015). This is a reflection of the wider context of inequality of economic condition where groups with superior economic and cultural capital can use the education system to their advantage, and can subsequently benefit in terms of gaining the most advantageous positions in the labour market. Insights garnered from students from non-manual backgrounds (McCoy et al, 2010) further indicate how inequalities in social, economic and cultural capital mesh to create barriers to participation. McCoy et al (2010) found that students' experience of career guidance was that it tended only to be taken seriously for the 'honours' classes, while other groups were steered away from higher education. Financial barriers were also found to be significant as going to college poses a financial commitment not adequately covered by the student grant system. While issues such as these remain the case, even though equality of opportunity has had a significant impact in opening up education and improving social mobility, its goal of giving people 'an equal chance to compete for social advantages' (Baker et al 2009: 25) cannot be fully realised.

Chapter summary

- The opening section examined the concept of equality of opportunity in education and considered critiques of this concept from an equality of condition perspective. A major criticism of equality of educational opportunity is that it cannot be realised without some sort of equality of condition within wider society. However, equality of opportunity has been a key influence in the development of education policy over time. Recent trends, such as the imperative of educating for the needs of the knowledge economy, and the growing influence of new public management reforms, potentially dismantle efforts to achieve equality of opportunity.
- The second section considered the development of education policy in the Irish context, taking note of how equality issues have historically gained attention and also highlighting other significant characteristics of the system, most notably the origins of a school system that combines private religious ownership with public funding.
- The third section focused on the contemporary education system and discussed related policy issues. Equality of opportunity is now a core element of education policy and has contributed to the transformation of the education system particularly at second and third level, from an elitist system to one where access has opened up and participation has grown significantly. However, this section also highlighted the limits of this achievement, most notably in terms of continued inequalities of participation across the education system, which are tied to wider inequalities of social and economic condition in contemporary Ireland. Growing social and cultural diversity created a new set of challenges and the emerging policy responses also demonstrate the limits to recognising diversity.

Discussion points

- Think about the schools you attended. For each, consider who owns the school, their admissions policy, how they are funded, the choice of subjects taught, and the extent to which the school population exhibited diversity or homogeneity when you attended.
- What are the differences between equality of opportunity and equality of condition?
- Consider the arguments for and against third-level education fees. Which seem more convincing in your opinion?

Further reading list

Brown, P and Lauder, H (2006) 'Globalisation, knowledge and the myth of the magnet economy', *Globalisation, Societies and Education*, 4:1, 25-57

Clancy, P (2015) *Irish higher education: A comparative perspective*, Dublin: IPA

Irish Educational Studies Special Issue (2014) 'Investment in Education and the intractability of inequality', 33:2

ten

Housing policy

Housing is one of the most talked about topics in Irish society. It represents a microcosm of the changes that have taken place in Ireland since the 1990s, being deeply implicated in Ireland's boom and bust. Housing is also 'the most conspicuous sign of inequality' (Power, 1993: 8). This characteristic of housing is influenced by the fact that housing provision is delivered predominantly by the market, in contrast with other social services. For this reason Torgersen (1987) calls housing the 'wobbly pillar' of the welfare state. This means that while housing is a social need experienced by everyone, housing needs are more likely to be met through market provision. Buying or renting a home therefore represents more than the fulfilment of the need for shelter, it is also a source of profit to those in the housing industry, such as builders and landlords. Housing as a commodity and as a means of making money generates multiple inequalities and insecurities. The recent housing boom to bust brought the financial dimensions of housing into sharper focus, demonstrating the ways in which it can be a source of wealth for some and unsustainable debt and insecurity for others. Due to the problems generated by the housing market, state intervention also has an important role. State intervention can modify these inequalities, ensuring that the housing market operates efficiently and facilitating access. However, intervention does not always contribute to these goals and housing policy is an arena where competing actors and interests exert influence.

There has been a long history of state intervention in the Irish housing market to facilitate people buying their own homes, which, if measured solely in terms of owner-occupation, has been very successful. While the vagaries of the property market have dominated discussion about housing in Ireland in recent years, in general, housing policy and state intervention involves more than just addressing the issues raised by market provision of housing. The state is also a substantial provider of housing through the social housing sector, and it is involved in the regulation of a third sector, the private rental sector. However, in the Irish context these sectors have been overshadowed by the preoccupation with home ownership, to the extent that social housing plays a residual role and the private rental sector is weakly regulated and its occupants fare poorly in terms of security and affordability. The recent financial crisis and related housing crisis has generated many challenges and much debate about the overall direction of housing policy. While some potentially significant changes are in train, housing policy remains unsettled and reflects tensions between treating housing as a commodity and a secure home.

Chapter outline

- The first section examines housing policy in general. It discusses key themes such as tenure structure and housing systems across Europe. It also looks at the role of the state and the market in the provision of housing, and the issues of access, affordability and social segregation, and the role of housing in the global financial crisis.
- The second section charts the development of housing policy in Ireland from the nineteenth century to the mid-1990s. This section looks at the role of the state in housing over time and trends in housing provision, in particular the balance between the different tenures.
- The final section discusses the current state of Ireland's housing system in the context of the trajectory from the housing boom stemming from the late 1990s to the subsequent multifaceted housing crisis. We look at policy changes across the three tenures, taking account of the changing role of the state in terms of providing, financing and regulating housing and the changing interface between owner-occupied, private rented and social housing.

SECTION ONE
AN OVERVIEW OF HOUSING POLICY

Housing tenure: owner-occupation, private renting, social renting.

Housing is divided into different tenure types, and housing provision across countries varies according to **tenure** structure. The three main forms of tenure are owner-occupation, private renting and social renting.

Owner-occupied housing refers to housing owned by the occupier and it is usually paid for by acquiring a mortgage from a bank, building society or local authority. It is generally associated with a high level of security, choice and control provided that the owner can afford the property. Over much of the twentieth century the tendency was for the poorer European countries including Ireland, Portugal, Greece and Spain to have high levels of owner-occupation. Newer EU member states including Central and Eastern European countries have even higher levels of owner-occupation, which occurred in the context of rapid privatisation of formerly

Tenure comes from the French verb *tenir* meaning 'to hold'. Variations in tenure status refer to the ways in which people occupy or possess their homes, with varying levels of rights and security.

state-owned housing stock since the 1990s. Some suggest that the desire to own one's own home is a natural instinct and that over time the typical pattern is to see owner-occupation grow at the expense of renting (Saunders, 1990). However, this is a contested idea. As Forrest and Hirayama (2015: 235) note, 'the tenure carries a substantial, pervasive and powerful ideological and social baggage' in the way that it is promoted as a social project and associated with particular values such as social stability and responsibility.

Private rented housing refers to accommodation rented from a 'for-profit' landlord on the open market. This is generally considered the least secure tenure type. Levels of security vary from country to country with regard to issues such as tenancy rights and regulation of rents and leases. Particularly secure terms of tenure can be found in Germany and the Netherlands where unlimited lease agreements prevail and rent increases are regulated rather than being left to the market. Security can also have perceptual dimension and can be influenced by the extent to which renting is a cultural norm in a particular country (Hulse and Milligan, 2014). In the case of both owner-occupation and private renting, access and the type and quality of accommodation will be determined by individual ability to pay.

Social renting refers to renting in the social housing sector, where accommodation is provided by government, usually through local authorities, and other non-profit organisations. Rents are set below market levels and social renting is generally associated with a high level of security, with lifetime tenancies being typical. Social housing refers to both local authority housing and housing provided by other non-profit providers. Access to local authority housing is usually determined by bureaucratic allocation mechanisms to distribute housing to those most in need. Assessment criteria can include income level and evidence of living in overcrowded or unfit accommodation. Applicants are usually placed on a waiting list before receiving accommodation. Other non-profit providers include housing charities/associations, limited dividend companies and housing cooperatives. This type of provision may be state sponsored as many of these providers are funded by government, but the housing provided is not state owned or managed. There is a strong tradition of this type of provision in continental European countries in contrast to its weaker position in Ireland. Recently there has been an increase in a third type of social renting, that is where tenants who qualify for social housing assistance rent housing from for-profit landlords, but payment is largely subsidised by a state-provided housing payment.

Housing: a commodity, a social right, a matter of access?

One of the main ways in which housing systems differ across countries is in the balance between these three tenure types. This diversity can be due to historical, socioeconomic and policy factors, and not necessarily the level of wealth in a particular country. In policy terms, the diversity may be understood as a contrast between policy approaches which treat housing primarily as a commodity provided by the market, and approaches which treat housing as a social right, provided by the state. However, as Fitzpatrick (2012) notes, the meaning of a right to housing tends to be vague and can vary considerably in practice across different countries. The majority of Western European countries fall between the two extremes of state and market provision. While a right to housing is not individually guaranteed in these countries, most develop their housing policies around the right of access to adequate housing for all (Edgar et al, 2002). As such there is a greater mix between tenure types, and practically all housing is subsidised in some way so that access to owner-occupation is not purely left to market forces.

European housing regimes

Across Europe there are diverse patterns of housing tenure which don't neatly map onto the main welfare regimes (Edgar et al, 2002). Kemeny (1995, 2006) helps to distinguish between systems which are primarily market oriented and systems which are more concerned with access. His typology is based on the variations in the rental system in different countries. He suggests that social renting and private renting should not be treated as two entirely distinct housing tenures. Instead he identifies two different systems, which he calls dualist and integrated rental systems.

The dualist system keeps private and social renting separate and social rented accommodation is provided for those with low incomes only, through means-testing. Provision is primarily through the state via local authorities. Because of a lack of alternatives, high rates of home ownership also prevail in countries with this system, which include UK, Ireland, Norway and Finland.

The integrated system allows for competition between private renting and social renting, with many other social landlords besides local authorities providing social rented accommodation as opposed to mainly or only the state in the dualist system. Generally social renting is accessible to all regardless of income and the effect is to dampen market rental levels, as private landlords have competitors that are absent in the dualist system. The standard of accommodation is kept quite high because of competition. This policy regime also provides a viable alternative to home ownership. Writing about Germany, Austria and Switzerland, which are examples of this system, Behring and Helbrecht (2002 in Elsinga and Hoekstra, 2005: 406) suggest that 'there is really no necessity to enter into homeownership for the purposes of acquiring basic security and social acceptance ... people may prefer homeownership as a means of personal expression but there is no necessity to own'. However, providers, especially the non-government ones, may express a preference for more middle-class renters with stable jobs and incomes. Consequently poorer renters are left to the state-provided houses or drift to the private sector to cheap, low-quality accommodation. Thus social housing in this system may not adequately meet housing need, but concentrate on the needs of middle-income households (Kleinman, 1996).

Despite these distinctions, a number of commentators have pointed to neo-liberalisation as a driver which has blurred the boundaries between these housing systems (Aalbers, 2015; Ronald, 2013). Given differences in existing housing systems, neo-liberalisation does not impact on all countries in the same way or generate convergent outcomes. European welfare states seem to have gradually put greater emphasis on privatisation and marketisation, and have thus reoriented housing policy to prioritise home ownership and market solutions to housing problems across the tenures.

Recent housing policy reform in Europe

The 1950s and 1960s were the heyday of social housing provision in Europe (Priemus and Dieleman, 1999). States invested heavily in housing in response to severe housing shortages after the Second World War and large-scale housing provision was seen as a legitimate state activity. The term 'mass housing' is used to refer to the large-social housing estates that were built where an emphasis on quantity superseded concerns with quality (Power, 1993).

While not a uniform trend, there has been a decline in the share of social housing across Europe since the 1970s. Several factors influenced this decline. There was a sense that the housing provision of the 1950s and 1960s had served its purpose and that the needs of this era had been fulfilled. Incomes rose in the long period of economic prosperity following the Second World War, and this fuelled a preference for home ownership which, it was assumed, would be best served by private market provision (Edgar et al, 2002). The declining share of social housing must also be seen in the context of the wider fortunes of the welfare state since the 1970s, marked by fiscal crisis and the rise of neo-liberal thinking. As a result, the legitimacy of governments spending large amounts of money on building and managing housing was called into question. Since then, in comparison to other social services, Edgar et al (2002) suggest that housing policy has actually seen the most fundamental transformation in the context of welfare retrenchment, with the state withdrawing from provision and letting market solutions prevail. Yet paradoxically states remained substantially committed in terms of housing expenditure in facilitating market-based solutions and home ownership. This has resulted in both deeper 'state–market entanglements' (Aalbers and Engelen, 2015: 1602) and greater housing insecurity for low-income groups.

Market-based solutions include a switch in state housing expenditure from object to subject subsidies. Thus, instead of investing in bricks and mortar (social housing), individuals are given housing allowances to access housing in the private market. This policy was followed in France for example, from 1979 onwards. In Ireland, Rent Supplement (RS) was introduced in the late 1970s and grew substantially from the late 1980s when social housing was cut back (Norris, 2014). This policy solution still requires significant state expenditure, but the money is spent in what is seen as a more market-friendly way. The privatisation of social housing, giving tenants the option to buy their house below market prices, is another version of the shift from object to subject subsidies, while also reflecting the prioritisation of home ownership. The enactment of the 'right to buy' legislation in Britain in 1980 is a notable example, and it connects with the broader notion of asset-based welfare which became particularly strong in liberal welfare states. Asset-based welfare is based on the notion that the welfare of the poor is best served by encouraging saving and investing in property, which in turn compensates for declining social services, rather than redistribution via social security and taxation. As house prices rose, particularly in the 2000s, policy initiatives designed to aid lower-income households purchase their own homes also became popular, through various affordable house purchase schemes. In the UK, home-ownership rates grew from 50% in 1970 to 70% by 2005. Across Europe a similar trend occurred, with average home-ownership rates in the EU15 reaching 60% by 2007 (Ronald and Elsinga, 2012).

The allocation of the remaining social housing is much more targeted. The focus of social housing provision is now on those most in need and therefore with the lowest incomes, such as the unemployed. As such, social housing has assumed a much more distinct welfare role than in the past, when it served more broadly as a source of affordable housing for the working classes. In the UK this shift has been described as a turn to a 'social ambulance service' (Fitzpatrick and Pawson, 2011).

A shift in housing provision and management from the state to other non-profit providers is another example of state withdrawal from housing, evident in the UK, the Netherlands and to a lesser extent in Ireland. In other countries with a stronger tradition of non-state social housing, a shift away from the social market towards open-market-based structures can also be observed. Reforms in France and Germany, for example, allowed non-profit providers act as private landlords and exit social renting (O'Connell, 2005a).

Housing policy reform and the financial crisis

Changes in the state's role in housing provision and the elevation of home ownership connect with another set of 'state–market entanglements' concerning changes in housing finance and the role of housing in the increasing financialisation of economic growth since the 1990s. The liberalisation of banking activities meant that the mortgage market was no longer a 'sleepy industry' (Hannsgen, 2007: 11 in Forrest and Hirayama, 2015: 236) where profit was made simply from arranging mortgages for potential home owners. Mortgages were transformed into a complex financial product, residential mortgage backed securities, through which mortgages were 'sliced and diced' and traded globally. This fundamentally changed the nature of housing finance from a means to facilitate home ownership to something to profit from as a financial product. Moreover, low interest rates and lax lending practices under deregulation generated a growing sub-prime mortgage market, which extended home ownership to lower-income groups but made for very risky home ownership, particularly in the US. These trends led to the 'biggest bubble in history' (The Economist, 2005), which was also unprecedented in terms of its duration and the number of countries experiencing house price increases. Household debt also ballooned. Across the OECD it grew from an average of one year's household disposable income in 1996 to 170% by 2007 (André, 2010).

The collapse of this inflated wealth triggered by rising mortgage defaults generated a credit crunch culminating in the global financial crisis. Major bank bailouts ensued while various types of housing precarity, including mortgage defaults, negative equity and homelessness, also increased. While the impacts varied between and within countries, and the policy response is still unfolding, many note that there has not been a fundamental change in the dominant themes of housing policy. It is 'business as usual' (Forrest, 2015: 2). Under austerity and highly indebted welfare states, emphasis on home ownership and market-based solutions broadly remain, though these have exacerbated housing inequalities. Resources in many countries, albeit limited, were devoted via 'mortgage rescue programmes' to supporting households with repayment difficulties (Scanlon et al, 2011). More pressure has also been put on limited stocks of social housing, with demand not only stemming from the most vulnerable but also from 'mainstream households' out-stripping supply (Scanlon et al, 2015). Pressures to reduce public expenditure meant state investment in social housing declined, especially in the UK, the Netherlands, Spain and Ireland (Scanlon et al, 2015). Consequently the trend of social housing provision via private landlords is increasing. One of the more extreme austerity-led responses is evident in UK; the security of social housing tenure has been diminished by the introduction of 'affordable rent tenancies', fuelled not only by budgetary constraints but also the highly contested view that social housing for life encouraged dependency and 'worklessness' (Murie and Williams, 2015). Such tenancies bring social housing closer to conditions in the private rented sector by setting rents at up to 80% of market levels and stipulating fixed terms rather than lifetime tenancy.

Key problems and responses in contemporary housing policy

The reforms discussed above represent trends towards the treatment of housing primarily as a commodity. This policy shift has also resulted in the stronger presence of problems such as residualisation, social segregation, lack of access and affordability, which are typically associated with a policy regime which treats housing principally as something to be bought and sold. In this section we look broadly at how these problems are manifested across the tenures and how they have worsened since the financial crisis.

Social housing

Mass housing estates turned from 'visionary solutions' to fears that they would become ghettoes (Power, 1993: 389). A major problem with social housing from

> **Residualisation** primarily refers to the marginalisation of social housing within housing policy and provision, and the social exclusion of social housing tenants.

the 1970s onwards is captured in the term **residualisation**, which refers to a number of trends. These include the reduction in the size of the tenure and in the quality of social housing, as houses not bought by tenants tended to be those in the poorest condition and in the least preferred areas. Residualisation also refers to the way in which the role of social housing provision becomes a residual one in solving housing problems, as more housing needs are channelled through market-based policy instruments. Residualisation can also refer to the way in which the social profile of tenants became more concentrated in terms of poverty and disadvantage. Residualisation in turn is connected with the marginalisation of social housing tenants and more intense patterns of spatial segregation (Murie, 1997). A perceptual dimension to residualisation also occurs when tenants, who may have already been socially excluded due to unemployment and poverty, find themselves further marginalised by the stigma associated with living in social housing estates. Residualised social housing has also become associated with ethnic inequalities with 'ethnic minorities and immigrants ... overrepresented in social housing' (Scanlon et al, 2015: 5). Consequently ethnic inequalities become a prism by which social housing is perceived in negative terms. In France, for example, Ronald (2013: 7–8) notes that 'urban social housing estates are no longer seen as a triumph of post-war modernist architecture, but often the location of dangerous groups of impoverished people and the site of racial unrest'.

Regeneration and 'rescue' programmes became popular from the 1980s, with investment focused on upgrading existing social housing stock. By the 1990s attention turned again to shortages in social housing stock with an emphasis on smaller estates. Yet social housing provision remains more limited and targeted, and residualisation in all its forms remains a problem. There is need, as Ronald (2013: 8) notes, to 'rehabilitate social rental housing as a normal and viable tenure. While states have often contributed to the polarisation of tenure conditions and perceptions through policy and rhetoric, there is a sustained need for social housing'.

Private renting

In the private rented sector the influence of a strong market-based housing policy leads to problems of **segregation**, with divisions between high, middle and low segments of the market. The lower end of the rental market becomes concentrated in areas where cheap, low–quality accommodation is rented to low–income households and where minority ethnic groups, and especially new migrants, may cluster, accessing what may be the only accommodation

> **Segregation** in housing refers to the division of areas by tenure, social groups and social classes.

option open to them (Özüekren and van Kempen, 2003). In addition to migration, urban-related trends such as a return to inner-city living, demographic change, changing household composition and the transition from industrialisation to post-industrialisation resulted in a resurgence in private renting since the 1990s. Private renting is recognised as an important source of relatively cheap and flexible accommodation in post-industrial cities with higher levels of labour mobility. State encouragement of the sector has also been evident through tax incentives and direct subsidies.

Forrest and Hirayama (2015) suggest that a stronger financialised private landlordism has emerged with a renewed interest in investment in private renting. This takes advantage of both the declining property values and repossessed properties, and the growing demand for renting in the context of continued decline in social housing and obstacles to home ownership, which particularly affect younger cohorts. Ability to invest is also, of course, exclusive, and the result is a 'greater *concentration* of residential property assets with the property-poor paying market rents to the property-rich' (Forrest and Hirayama, 2015: 241). Segregation in the private rental sector is also potentially growing post-crisis because of the use of this sector to house vulnerable households in lieu of social housing (Scanlon et al, 2015).

Owner-occupied housing

For reasons similar to those related to private renting, owner-occupation is also subject to problems of segregation and accessibility, where the market responds not to need but ability to pay. Differences in the ability to pay for housing are manifested as spatial segregation, as private housing divides into high quality homes in good locations and poorer quality housing in less desirable and less accessible locations. The phenomenon of segregation is exacerbated by the processes of displacement and gentrification, as urban areas where the poor may have traditionally resided are redeveloped or '**gentrified**' and become areas that attract high-income homeowners.

> **Gentrification** refers to the redevelopment of areas and replacement of low-income housing with more expensive housing. This tends to attract higher-income groups thus 'crowding out' lower-income households.

During the boom, rising prices meant that the housing market became inaccessible for those earning insufficient incomes to generate large enough mortgages. Housing policy in many countries reinforced what was happening in housing finance in that it concentrated on facilitating access to the market, assisting people on lower incomes by providing subsidies to purchase their own homes. Consequently the concept of affordability entered the language of housing policy across European housing systems (Paris, 2007). The housing bust has continued problems of affordability and access and has sharpened inequalities generated by home ownership. In the initial aftermath of the crisis,

> **Negative equity** refers to the situation where the market value of a home is lower than what is owed on the mortgage taken out to pay for the home.

declining property values increased the risk of **negative equity** associated with home ownership. However negative equity is something that can be sat out if households have the means to do so; it becomes a problem if combined with some other stressor such as wages cuts, unemployment or relationship breakdown. In the longer term, with conditions of labour market precarity and income inequality meshing with tighter lending criteria there has been a decline in rates of home ownership across a number of countries. Ronald and Elsinga (2012) suggest there has been a 're-familisation of society' where familial financial support becomes more critical for younger people to accessing housing. Home ownership is thus becoming more exclusive with the new financial regime favouring the 'financially privileged' as the housing finance industry favours those who are well-resourced and low risk (Forrest and Hirayama, 2015).

SECTION TWO
THE HISTORICAL DEVELOPMENT OF HOUSING POLICY IN IRELAND

Pre-independence to the 1950s

The history of state intervention in social housing is tied to issues such as poverty and public health problems, which coincided with poor housing conditions. In Ireland social unrest was another factor, particularly in the case of rural housing provision (Fahey, 2001). This meant that social housing in Ireland started sooner and has a longer history than most other European countries (O'Sullivan, 2004). The process of land reform saw tenant farmers gaining their own farms. This did not extend to farm labourers for whom improved housing conditions served as a compensatory measure.

Generous provisions for the construction of local authority cottages for agricultural labourers began with the Labourers (Ireland) Act 1883. This Act enabled boards of guardians to provide houses for rent to labourers. By the time Ireland gained independence, a substantial local authority housing stock had been built amounting to 48,000 houses (Fahey, 2001). These houses offered a security of tenure not previously experienced by agricultural labourers under private landlords.

However, state support for housing did not extend as generously to urban areas. As outlined by Daly (1985: 122) reasons such as 'the relative political weakness of Irish cities; their stagnation during the nineteenth century, and an undefined feeling that the city was somehow alien to the true Irish identity' all played a part.

Moreover, state intervention in the provision of rural housing could be justified on the grounds that the Irish case was exceptional and similar claims in England could be resisted.

The working class and the poor in urban areas lived in tenements: large houses lived in by a number of families and a particular feature of late nineteenth- and early twentieth-century Dublin. Tenements were formerly the homes of the upper classes who moved from the centre to high-status suburbs when Dublin went into economic decline in the nineteenth century. Tenement conditions over time declined as they were let to the poor who could only afford the most basic accommodation and many were continuously subdivided. As a result, severe overcrowding, ill health and high death rates were the norm (Aalen, 1985).

State support for building social housing in urban areas originates in the Labouring Classes (Lodging Houses and Dwellings) Act 1866 which provided loans to urban local authorities and private companies towards the cost of constructing houses. At this time social housing was more likely to be built by private bodies. These included three types: philanthropic bodies, semi-philanthropic bodies, and companies building housing for their workers. Company housing was relatively rare; however, some was built by brewery companies such as Guinness and Watkins, and by Pims, a Quaker textile company. Semi-philanthropic bodies were more active, particularly the Artisans Dwelling Company, established in Dublin in 1876. It built houses in areas such as the Coombe, Rialto and Stoneybatter. In Cork, the Improved Dwellings Company built houses in schemes such as Prosperity Square, Industry Place and Prosperous Place, names suggestive of the attributes of the 'respectable working class' who were to be housed there (Cronin, 2006). An example of a philanthropic body providing housing was the Guinness Trust (now the Iveagh Trust and 'the oldest and largest, non-governmental housing body in Ireland' (Williamson, 2000: 642)). The Trust housed the poorer sections of the working class, building tenements up to five storeys high in inner-city Dublin.

Council housing built under the legislation for labourers' dwellings fared less well. Houses built in areas where uninhabitable slum housing had been cleared were not popular with intended tenants, and the council's poor housing management meant that much of this early social housing simply replicated the slums it had replaced. Local authority provision was strengthened by more generous financing in the Housing the Working Classes Act 1890 and more especially by the Housing Act 1908. These acts strengthened local authority provision, putting its output ahead of other social housing providers, for whom housing provision was becoming less financially viable. This trend ran contrary to many other European countries (Norris, 2005) and it was not until the 1990s that non-profit housing organisations re-emerged as significant providers of social housing (O'Sullivan, 2004). While local authority housing output did improve it failed to meet the scale of need in Dublin. A 1914 *Housing Inquiry* revealed that 14,000 houses were needed urgently to relieve congestion (Daly, 1985). However, action was stalled by the restrictions on spending during the First World War and the general situation of political unrest in Ireland as the decade went on.

After Ireland gained independence, state action on housing was a significant feature of social policy development. This action occurred on two fronts: there was a substantial social housing output, especially from the 1930s onwards; and substantial amounts of money were channelled towards the support of privately owned housing. As noted by O'Sullivan (2004: 332) 'the progress made in providing housing either directly by the State or indirectly via grants and subsidies in the first 40 years since independence, was remarkable in the context of the development of other welfare services and contributing largely to the predominance of owner-occupation'. This is not to say that all housing problems were resolved; however, in comparison to social security, health and education which were either left underdeveloped or in the hands of the Catholic Church, housing represented a particularly active area of state intervention.

The first initiative in the area of social housing was the Million Pound scheme in 1923. This provided new funding for urban local authority housing construction, where local authorities were required to provide £1 for every £2 of funding received from central government. Over time, the general pattern of development involved the spread of cottages in the suburbs, with a predominance of blocks of flats in more central locations. Private housebuilding got a major boost by the Housing (Building Facilities) Act 1924 which provided generous grants for private housing. The grants tended to favour financially better-off housebuilders who were in a position to build larger houses (O'Connell, 2005b), which they did mostly on the outskirts of cities.

The housing problems of the urban poor did not receive attention again until 1929 when a survey revealed the need for 40,000 new dwellings in urban areas in the wake of further slum clearance (Daly, 1985). The Housing (Financial and Miscellaneous Provisions) Act 1932 paved the way for a significant increase in local authority housing activity through the provision of funding to construct dwellings for the poor dislocated by slum clearance throughout the 1930s, 1940s and 1950s. New suburban housing estates, in areas such as Cabra and Crumlin in Dublin, and Gurranabraher and Farranferris in Cork, followed.

At the same time the push to enable private ownership did not decline. The 1932 legislation also provided further subsidies for private housing. Other measures introduced to encourage private ownership included a strengthening of the right of local authority tenants in rural areas to purchase their local authority houses. The Labourers Act 1936 obliged local authorities to sell off labourers' cottages at generous discounts. This turned out to be an extremely successful scheme and O'Connell (2005b: 30) suggests that overall tenant purchase of local authority housing was 'one of the most sustained and long running programmes of privatisation ever undertaken by the State in Ireland'. By 1964, 80% of rural local authority housing had been purchased (Fahey, 2001). Subsequently extended to urban areas in the 1960s, as discussed in the next section, tenant purchase has been identified as an early form of asset-based welfare in the Irish context (Norris and Fahey, 2011).

A 1948 white paper, *Housing: A Review of Past Operations and Immediate Requirements* (DLG, 1948), estimated that a further 100,000 new houses were needed in the ensuing decade. It divided this into 60,000 social houses and 40,000 private sector houses. The Housing (Amendment) Act 1948 provided for increased funding for local authorities to meet the target, and social housing output increased substantially over the following decade. Examples of social housing developments built include Ballyfermot in Dublin and Ballyphehane in Cork. However, social housing output was outpaced by the growth in private housing, which far exceeded predictions. The growth in private housing was assisted by provisions in the 1948 Act and subsequent amendments which provided for further financial assistance to private housebuilders. O'Connell (2005b: 26) argues that the 1948 White Paper set in train the 'institutionalisation of owner-occupation as the dominant tenure'. Table 10.1 shows the growing share of owner-occupation from the 1940s (when housing occupancy was first recorded in the 1946 census) to 1991 when it peaked, and also stood as one of the highest levels of home ownership in Western Europe (Drudy, 2006). Correspondingly the tenure share of private renting and social renting both declined over this period.

Table 10.1: Housing tenure, 1946-91

	1946 %	1961 %	1971 %	1981 %	1991 %
Local authority rented	Nav	18.4	15.5	12.5	9.7
Private rented	42.7	17.2	13.3	10.1	8.0
Owner-occupied	52.7	59.8	68.8	74.4	79.3
Other**	4.6	4.6	2.4	3.0	3.0
Total	100.0	100.0	100.0	100.0	100.00

Source: CSO, Census of Population, various years

Notes:
Nav: Not available.
* Local authority renting figures were included with privately rented dwellings in the 1946 census.
** 'Other': includes households living in employer-provided accommodation; caretaking a property; renting from a non-profit provider other than a local authority or not paying any rent.

1960s to the mid-1990s

While the output of social housing increased in the 1960s and 1970s, the role of social housing declined in favour of a greater emphasis on owner-occupation. Much of the legislative and policy developments in this period contributed to this trend. The main piece of housing legislation was the Housing Act 1966. This rationalised and reformed existing housing legislation, setting out the powers and duties of local authorities in relation to housing provision, and ending the tradition of separate legislation for urban and rural housing. As a consequence, the right to purchase one's local authority house was extended to urban tenants. Urban tenant purchase took off in the 1970s, when the incentives to do so were increased. This contributed to the growing share of owner-occupation in urban areas, which until then fell well behind rural areas. Owner-occupation in urban areas rose from 38% in 1961 to 65·6% in 1981. Increasing urbanisation was also a factor.

Social housing continued to be built and actually expanded in a major way by the 1970s. This was triggered in part by incidents in Dublin in the early 1960s including the death of an elderly couple caused by the collapse of a tenement house in Bolton Street in June 1963, and the death of two children in similar circumstances two weeks later. These tragedies revealed the poor and unsafe conditions of much of the housing stock and the incomplete eradication of slum buildings. A White Paper in 1964, *Housing Progress and Prospects* (DLG, 1964), considered tens of thousands of houses in the country unfit for human habitation. What followed was large-scale investment in the building of social housing which resulted in the development of large housing estates on the peripheries of towns and cities, where the tradition of low-density low rise houses continued. The only high-rise development built was Ballymun.

While the scale of social housing development was unprecedented, the construction of owner-occupied dwellings again outpaced it. As the main cities developed, the separation of areas into public and private housing became more defined. Private housing construction and prices boomed during the 1970s. Demand was accelerated by population growth, and the drive to encourage individuals to purchase their own houses was reinforced more strongly than ever. A housing policy document, *Housing in the '70s* (DLG, 1969), expressed the concern that private ownership was still not favoured enough over renting from local authorities. Accordingly, incentives to purchases one's own home were increased, particularly for first-time buyers. Echoing issues with building quality in the most recent housing boom, during this period, the quality of developments in both private and public estates left a lot to be desired. The quality of housing design, materials used, and construction methods were all extremely poor, and the condition of houses quickly deteriorated with problems such as dampness becoming apparent (Hourihan, 2006).

By the 1980s social housing was becoming increasingly residualised. Local authority housing estates became the physical receptors of many of the problems of the 1980s, such as long-term unemployment, homelessness and a rise in drug abuse, and the tenure's image as problematic and residual grew. Added to these problems, the economic difficulties of the 1980s meant investment in social housing declined so that social housing output fell sharply (see Figure 10.1).

Figure 10.1: Local authority houses completed and local authority houses sold to tenants, 1980-94

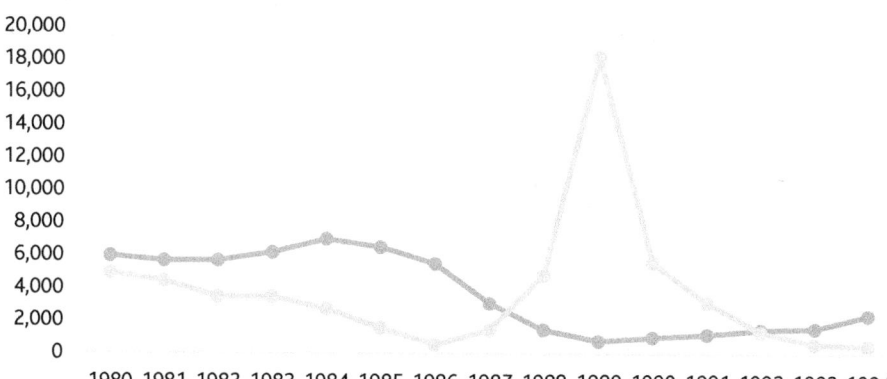

Data source: DEHLG Housing Statistics

* 1993 and 1994 figures include the number of local authority houses acquired (369, 467). Prior to that the figure was very small and not separately enumerated.

Policy attention shifted to making the most of existing social housing stock. Small-scale renewal schemes concentrated on the physical improvement of buildings although their impact was limited, given budgetary constraints. A Surrender Grant was introduced in 1984 to shore up existing stock; however, it contributed to the further residualisation of social housing. The grant was given to local authority tenants who opted to leave their local authority house and purchase a dwelling in the private market. The result was the loss of more well-off tenants, which impacted negatively on the local community and economy of the area, resulting in further marginalisation of those who remained. The surrender policy was abandoned in 1987. A new tenant purchase scheme was subsequently established, accounting for the dramatic rise in houses sold to tenants in 1989 (Figure 10.1).

The 1980s also saw difficult times for some owner–occupiers. Ability to service mortgages became a significant issue because of the escalation of interest rates, which peaked at 18%. An indication of the difficulty this caused was the rise in rent and mortgage supplement payments made under the Supplementary Welfare Allowance scheme, which grew substantially between 1980 and 1987 (Blackwell, 1990). The housing boom of the 1970s turned to a slump as output declined and new house prices fell by 27% in real terms between 1980 and 1987 (Blackwell, 1990).

Until the 1980s, homelessness was of little official concern and detached from the larger housing policy context. Homelessness was primarily understood as a personal condition: 'homeless people were seen as drop-outs, vagrants, tramps, anti-social people, for the most part unwanted elderly men' (Harvey, 1995:

76). The main form of accommodation offered was a bed in a county home, with voluntary agencies such as the Society of St Vincent de Paul also offering emergency accommodation. Newer voluntary agencies such as the Simon Community and Focus Point (now Focus Ireland) sought to challenge state inaction (Harvey, 2008). Research initiated by voluntary agencies indicated that homelessness was growing since the 1970s and that the traditional perception of homelessness obscured the fact that homeless was a structural problem affecting both men and women, and people of all ages including children (E O'Sullivan, 2005, 2008).

The Housing Act 1988 gave local authorities responsibility for homelessness, which previously had been the remit of health authorities. Yet while the legislation gave local authorities statutory responsibility to assist the homeless they were not required to house them. An obligation to carry out periodic assessments of homeless people and housing need was also included in the Act. These assessments began in 1989 and are carried out every three years.

In section 2 of the Act a person is defined as homeless if: 'there is no accommodation available which, in the opinion of the authority, he ... can reasonably occupy or remain in occupation of, or he is living in [an] institution, and is so living because he has no accommodation ... and he is ... unable to provide accommodation from his own resources.' This definition was well received because it highlighted homelessness as a problem linked to lack of accommodation, thus privileging structural factors over individual ones (Phelan and Norris, 2008). Yet implementation of the legislation was patchy at local level (Harvey, 1995) and homelessness actually grew over the 1990s.

The early 1990s also became the focus for a renewed interest in social housing and two policy documents, *A Plan for Social Housing* (DoE, 1991) and *Social Housing: The Way Ahead* (DoE, 1995), were published. Both policies aimed to address the shortage of social housing, to improve access to housing generally, and to deal with the divisions between private and social housing. These aims were to be achieved by: ending the building of large local authority housing estates; building mixed-tenure estates; facilitating greater involvement of other non-profit providers in the sector; and enabling tenant participation in the running of local authority housing estates. In addition these policies aimed to facilitate a greater range of housing options for lower-income households. These included the introduction of shared ownership (houses part owned by the occupier and part rented from the local authority), improving the terms of tenant sales, and introducing a Low Cost Housing Sites Scheme and a Mortgage Allowance Scheme to encourage social tenants to move out and buy in the private sector. However, the overall objectives of policy in relation to social housing did not change. Owner-occupation remained the key focus on the grounds that this would allow government to target social housing to the most needy. Social housing remained a residual sector.

SECTION THREE

IRISH HOUSING POLICY SINCE THE MID-1990s: CONTEMPORARY ISSUES AND DEVELOPMENTS

The most recent period of Irish housing policy has been dominated by the dramatic rise and fall of house prices. House prices began to increase from the mid-1990s onwards and the Irish housing boom became the steepest and longest one internationally (André, 2010). What followed was a similarly dramatic: 'Ireland experienced one of the deepest house market collapses on record' (Kitchin et al, 2015: 6). However, house prices were on the rise again from 2013, coupled with a rise the cost of private renting and rising homelessness (see Figure 10.2). The enduring crises in housing supply and affordability, and the severe lack of social housing, indicate the continual crisis-prone nature of Irish housing policy. Much has been written about the causes and the impact of the boom and bust (Drudy and Punch, 2005; Norris and Coates, 2014). Central to both periods is the treatment of housing as a commodity, the key role the market plays in housing provision, and the degree to which the housing system generates inequality and insecurity. The core problems of residualisation, social segregation, lack of accessibility and affordability already reviewed in the broader context of European housing reform are repeated in the Irish context. This is not to say that these problems did not exist before the housing boom and bust, but this section shows ways in which they have become particularly critical since then. This section

Figure 10.2: Annual average property prices, 1995-2015

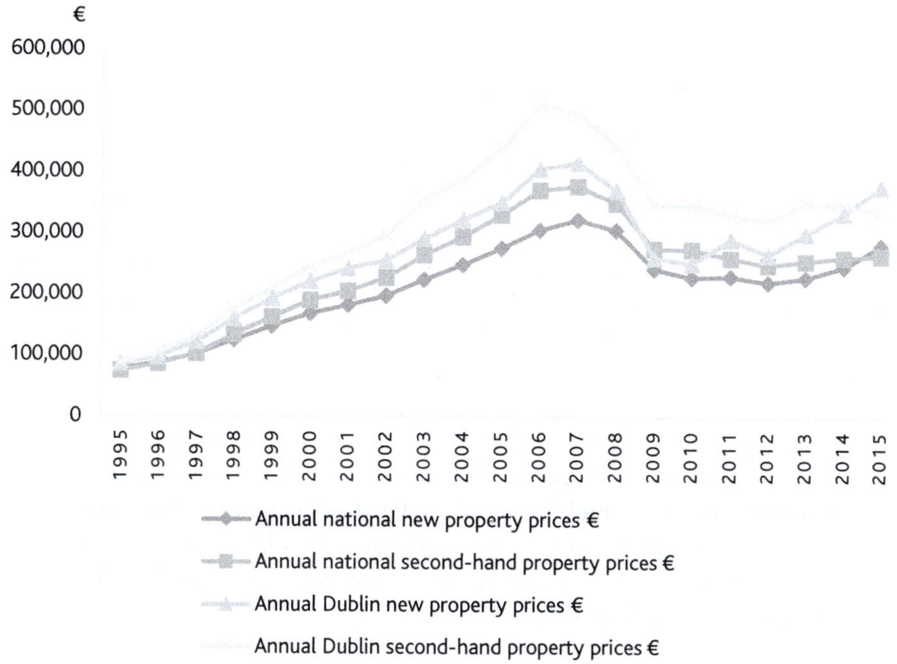

Annual national new property prices €

Annual national second-hand property prices €

Annual Dublin new property prices €

Annual Dublin second-hand property prices €

Data source: DHPCLG, Housing Statistics

reviews each tenure, the key problems and policy responses. First we set the section in context with an overview of tenure patterns since the mid–1990s and the broad thrust of housing policy over the same period.

The 1990s marked the start of a gradual shift in tenure trends that had prevailed for the previous half of century. From its 1991 peak (see Table 10.2) the share of owner-occupied housing declined to 69·7% by 2011 which aligns with the EU28 average (70% in 2014 (Eurostat)) leading to the question of whether the era of high levels of owner-occupation is now over in Ireland (NESC, 2014a; Norris, 2016). The biggest change occurred in the private rental sector, with a notable increase in the share of this tenure between 2006 and 2011. However, this category includes a substantial amount of state-funded social renting which grew in the context of the lack of social housing supply. Approximately one third of people in private renting receive state support (Housing Agency, 2016).

Table 10.2: Housing tenure, 2002-11

	2002 %	2006 %	2011 %
Local authority rented	6.9	7.2	7.8
Private rented	11.1	13.4	19.4
Owner occupied	77.4	74.7	69.7
Other	4.6	4.7	3.1
Total	100.0	100.0	100.0

Data source: CSO, Census of Population, various years

The dramatic boom to bust in house prices is indicative of the predominant emphasis on home ownership and the treatment of housing as a commodity in housing policy. This is complemented by factors such as a weakly regulated planning system and the credit boom, enabled by Ireland's light-touch approach to financial regulation. The role of housing in Ireland's economic crash and the continued crises in housing prompted a reappraisal of housing policy goals and policy instruments. The *Housing Policy Statement* (DECLG, 2011) made strong observations about the past thrust of housing policy and a more tenure neutral approach was signalled:

> Housing in Ireland has been characterised by a persistently hierarchical structure for several decades. … This structure and the value judgement that underlies it – which implicitly holds that the tenure which must ultimately be aspired to is homeownership – has had a considerable role in leading the Irish housing sector, Irish economy, and the wider Irish society to where they are today.

Our vision for the future of the housing sector in Ireland is based on choice, fairness, equity across tenures and on delivering quality outcomes for the resources invested. The overall strategic objective will be *to enable all households access good quality housing appropriate to household circumstances and in their particular community of choice* (DECLG, 2011: 2, emphasis in the original).

Yet in the immediate aftermath it seemed to be 'business as usual'. Given tight budgetary constraints, marketised solutions to housing shortages and housing need endured, with an emphasis on social renting via the private rental sector together with an expanded role for voluntary housing provision. The escalating scale of the housing shortage in high-demand urban areas, rising private rents and rising homelessness, prompted further policy developments since 2014 (see Box 10.1). The *Social Housing Strategy 2020* spoke of 'the realisation of a new vision: that, to the greatest extent possible, every household in Ireland will have access to secure, good quality housing suited to their needs at an affordable price and in a sustainable community' (DECLG, 2014a: 1). *Rebuilding Ireland* (GOI, 2016b) signalled a return to 'accelerated' social housing investment, building on commitments made in the *Social Housing Strategy 2020*. However, it remains to be seen whether the scale of provision envisaged will materialise, the extent to which social housing provision will continue to rely on market solutions, and whether signs of greater regulation of the housing and private rental market will be maintained.

Box 10.1: Key housing policy developments since 2000

2000	Part V of the Planning and Development Act
2000	*Homelessness – An Integrated Strategy*
2001	*Youth Homeless Strategy*
2002	*Homelessness Preventative Strategy*
2004	Residential Tenancies Act
2007	*Delivering Homes, Sustaining Communities*
2008	*The Way Home: A Strategy to Address Adult Homelessness in Ireland 2008-2013*
2011	*Housing Policy Statement*
2013	*Homelessness Policy Statement*
2014	*Social Housing Strategy 2020 Support, supply and reform*
2015	*Stabilising Rents Boosting Supply*
2015	Residential Tenancies (Amendment) Act
2016	*Rebuilding Ireland: Action Plan for Housing and Homelessness*

Social housing

Between the early 1990s until the economic crisis there was a slow increase in social housing output, yet social housing output during the 'boom' years was much lower than the output in the early 1980s (see Figure 10.3 and compare with Figure 10.1). Moreover, housing need has been mostly increasing since it was first measured in 1989. Tenant purchase remained steady until the crisis, though sales levels were not as high as the 1980s; and while voluntary housing provision was set to increase following increased support since the 1990s, its output did not greatly expand. During the boom local authorities continued to promote home ownership to lower-income households, so that they could get on the 'housing ladder', via affordable homes (houses sold at cost rather than market value by local authorities), shared ownership, and the mortgage allowance scheme. This had the effect of further residualising the remaining local authority population by 'creaming off' the top tier of housing applicants (Fahey and Watson, 1995: 10). The slow increase in social housing came to a halt during the economic crisis, as the capital budget for social housing was severely cut. Instead, in 2009 a switch was made to sourcing social housing via long-term private sector leasing, now called the Social Housing Current Expenditure Programme. This programme was designed to work alongside the National Assets Management Agency (NAMA) (Kitchin et al, 2012). NAMA was set up by the state in 2009 to relieve banks of their non-performing land and development loans and to operate with a commercial mandate. The bulk of social housing delivered by NAMA has been via long-term

Figure 10.3: Social housing output and local authority houses sold, 1995-2015

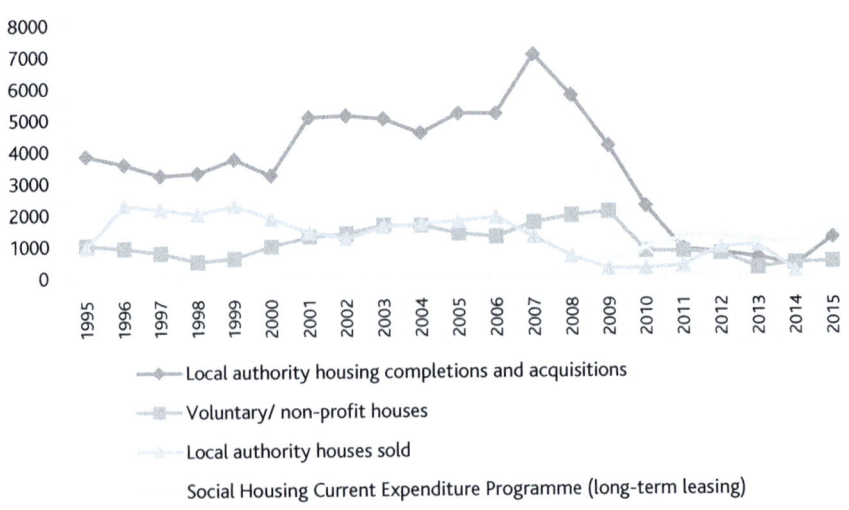

—◆— Local authority housing completions and acquisitions

—■— Voluntary/ non-profit houses

    Local authority houses sold

    Social Housing Current Expenditure Programme (long-term leasing)

Data source: DEHLG/DHPCLG Housing Statistics

leasing; local authorities, and in some cases voluntary housing bodies, lease the property for up to 20 years but do not acquire the asset as social housing stock.

As investment in social housing sharply declined and housing need grew, in addition to sourcing social housing via private sector leasing, the shift from 'object' to 'subject' subsidies took on increasing significance. The cost of RS, which was already a source of concern prior to the crisis, led to the introduction in 2005 of a new model of support, Rental Accommodation Supplement (RAS), and this has since been superseded by the Housing Assistance Payment (HAP) introduced in 2013. HAP is envisaged to house 75,000 households and to completely replace RS by 2020 (DECLG, 2015; GOI, 2016b). In contrast to RS, HAP is not withdrawn when the recipient finds work, instead a higher tenant contribution applies, thus removing the unemployment trap associated with RS. Tenancies are also longer-term and envisaged to provide better value for money for the state than RS arrangements. However, the increased role of private provision is to the detriment of security of tenure in the social rented sector. Unlike RS, RAS and HAP tenants are considered to have their long-term housing need met and are thus removed from the social housing waiting list. This means that they are no longer eligible for a local authority house which comes with lifetime and inheritable tenancy (Finnerty et al, 2016), though this permanency is a matter of practice rather than being established in law (O'Sullivan, 2012). Moreover, the problematic 'state–market entanglements' of this model are evident in the way that the state becomes reliant on private housing actors whose supply is ultimately motivated by profit-seeking. The private rental sector is heavily subsidised by the state, with 'over one half of all rents received by private landlords coming from RS, RAS or other schemes at an annual cost to the Exchequer of over €500m' (DECLG, 2014a: 47). Despite this level of subsidy many low-income tenants, especially those receiving RS, have faced 'economic eviction' in the context of recent private rental shortage and landlords seeking large rent increases which tenants cannot afford to pay (Drudy, 2016). This problem was compounded by a series of cuts to housing payments between 2008 and 2010. Serious concerns are thus raised about the marketisation of social renting in terms of access and security for tenants, and rather than regulating the market, the state is exposed to market volatility and rising rents.

A return to higher levels of social housing provision was envisaged in both the *Social Housing Strategy 2020* (DECLG, 2014a) and *Rebuilding Ireland* (GOI, 2016b), with the latter setting a target of 47,000 units by 2021. However, the bulk of provision is projected to come from HAP, followed by units acquired/leased, and social housing output is projected to increase to just over 5,000 units per year in 2021 (GOI, 2016b: 46). The highly residualised social housing sector therefore looks set to remain so. This is an inevitable effect of policy which targets only the most needy for social housing and encourages those with sufficient incomes to purchase their local authority house or leave the sector. Despite Ireland's economic prosperity, the relative position of areas with high concentrations of social housing remained the same, faring less well in terms of indicators such as unemployment, poverty and educational attainment (Fahey et al, 2011). Furthermore, despite efforts for more mixed-tenure estates, social housing estates remain highly spatially segregated. As Drudy (2006: 263) points out 'this is particularly obvious in the main urban centres and on the periphery were some estates contain up to 90 per cent Local Authority mainly low-income tenants'. The effect of high levels of spatial segregation is to 'divide, isolate and exclude rather than integrate urban communities' (Corcoran, 2000: 77). This has a negative effect on the quality of life of local authority tenants, though quality of life can vary both across and within different social housing estates. Research on a select number of estates found that the majority embody positive tenant experience, which is dependent on internal community cohesion (Fahey et al, 2011; Hearne, 2014).

Owner-occupation

Although owner-occupation tenure share peaked in 1991, the notion of owner-occupation as the preferred tenure, the buying and selling of houses, and the housing boom to bust has dominated public and policy debate about housing for much of the period since then. Various factors gave rise to increased demand by the late 1990s such as an increasing population, and in particular a rise in the number of young adults, smaller households and increasing wealth. By the early 2000s bubble conditions grew when the credit boom, combined with light-touch banking regulation, stimulated further house price growth. As prices rose, houses and land became more lucrative commodities and speculative demand pushed prices even higher. This in turn contributed to increasing inequality, as the housing market boom allowed developers and speculators to accrue 'unearned profits' on the basis of price rises. Many rural areas were left with vast amounts of oversupply, the legacy of which is high vacancy rates and unfinished estates, popularly known as ghost estates (Kitchin et al, 2012).

Although housing policy continued to prioritise owner-occupation and overstimulate market supply, there was at the same time a shift in policy supports since the 1970s from generous universal subsidisation of house purchase to targeting supports to first-time and low-income buyers (NESC, 2015). This shift, Norris (2016) suggests, marks a transition from a historic socialised form of home ownership to a marketised regime, where home ownership largely depends on one's ability to purchase without state assistance. Thus it is expected that owner-occupation will not return to its previous peak of tenure share in the aftermath of this boom-to-bust cycle, though it is perhaps too early to tell whether state support will entirely wane. On the other hand the shift to a stronger marketised regime brings new inequalities in terms of who can afford to acquire housing assets and those who can't.

During the housing boom, the problem of affordability became a major political issue. As wages did not increase in line with house prices, many socioeconomic groups who traditionally would have bought a house in the owner-occupied sector found themselves priced out of the housing market. Relatively minor efforts were made to dampen house price inflation in the late 1990s in response to a series of commissioned reports about the housing boom. However, the limited attempts to try to assist people in purchasing homes, such as reductions in stamp duty, had the opposite effect of fuelling house prices even further (Memery, 2001). The focus from the late 1990s turned towards the provision of 'affordable houses' built by local authorities, or transferred by developers to local authorities and sold at cost to low-income first-time buyers.

The first affordable housing scheme was launched in 1999, followed by a further scheme initiated under the provisions of Part V of the Planning and Development Act 2000, and a third scheme launched under *Sustaining Progress*, the social partnership agreement of 2003. The first scheme required property developers to transfer at cost price 20% of dwelling land, sites or finished houses to local authorities as a condition of planning permission, and this portion was to be provided as affordable, social and voluntary housing. In the Irish context this was a radical and progressive piece of legislation. It was in part an attempt to intervene and halt the escalating price of development land and the excessive profits generated from it. However, the legislation was opposed by property developers, who resisted the idea of mixed-tenure estates and argued that the legislation was unworkable and would damage them economically (Redmond, 2003). Their successful lobbying led to the Planning and Development (Amendment) Act 2002 . This allowed property developers to compensate local authorities with an equivalent monetary value of the sites, land or dwellings, or to provide these in an alternative area, or to combine both. The provision of alternative land was commonly used, with the result that little affordable housing was provided in urban areas where demand is highest. In any event, affordable housing output remained low throughout the 2000s (NESC, 2014a) and by the depths of the economic crisis affordable houses could not be sold; the house price crash meant that houses on the open market were often lower priced. Affordable housing schemes were suspended in 2011 and the *Housing Policy Statement* was particularly critical of the concept of 'affordable' housing, arguing that 'if the Government's approach to housing is successful in not repeating the mistakes of the past through over-stimulation of the market, there should be no need for national programmes of affordable housing provision by the State' (DECLG, 2011: 3). Part V of the Planning and Development Act 2000 was subsequently amended in 2015 by stipulating that 10% of developments should be designated on-site as social housing.

Despite their mantle as affordable homes, research on affordability during the 2000s found that those assisted into home ownership were actually those who subsequently experienced the biggest problems with affordability (Norris and Fahey, 2011). This included not only affordable homes but also other schemes such as shared ownership and local authority tenant purchase schemes, casting questions about the degree to which successive governments promoted home ownership at the cost of the financial security of low-income homeowners. Some 31% of local authority mortgages were in arrears for more than 90 days in 2013 (NESC, 2014a) and widespread defaults on loans have been reported in this sector (Kelly, 2013 in Stamp, 2016: 130).

In the mainstream housing market indebtedness also grew. Per capita mortgage debt rose from €7,000 to €33,000 between 1999 and 2009 (European Mortgage Federation, 2010 in Waldron and Redmond, 2014: 151) and 100% mortgages grew from 4% of mortgages taken out when they were introduced in 2004 to 12% by 2008 (Norris and Winston, 2011). The economic crisis thus brought a whole new set of affordability problems generated by wage cuts and job losses which led to significant mortgage arrears. As house prices fell, negative equity also became widespread. This is estimated to have affected 60% of borrowers who took out a mortgage between 2005 and 2010, with young first-time buyers most at risk (Duffy and O'Hanlon 2011 in Waldron and Redmond, 2014: 153). Mortgage arrears data shows that 26,000 or 3.3% of principal residence mortgages were in arrears for more than 90 days in September 2009, a figure which peaked at 99,189 (12.9%) in 2013 and has been in slow decline since (Central Bank of Ireland, 2016).

The fiscal crisis meant that relatively little financial support was offered to owner-occupiers in arrears, the main form being Mortgage Interest Supplement. The supplement subsidises mortgage interest and is restricted to unemployed home owners on a means-tested and short-term basis. The number of recipients grew from 3,712 in 2007 and peaked at 18,703 in 2011 (DSP, 2015). Instead policy emphasis was placed on bank forbearance, that is, restructuring loans in order to ease their repayment. By March 2016, 16% of principal residence mortgages were restructured, a much higher proportion of mortgages than those in arrears, though there is some overlap between the two categories, as 23% of restructured mortgages are also in arrears (Central Bank of Ireland, 2016). In addition a repossession moratorium of one year introduced in 2008 as part of the bank recapitalisation programme was extended to five years in 2010 for homeowners able to service two thirds of their mortgage interest repayments (Norris and Coates, 2014).

Repossessions have generally remained low in Ireland for a variety of reasons, including financial interests, because the capital base of the banks would be further eroded by selling repossessed houses in negative equity (Waldron and Redmond, 2014). This situation is made all the more complex because of the significant capital injections the state made to rescue the banking sector and the commercial role of NAMA. Thus, again because of deeper 'state–market entanglements' in how the economic crisis was managed, tensions exist for the state between seeing a return to higher property asset values and in the process protecting developer and financial interests, and ensuring affordable house prices in a stable housing market.

Mortgage indebtedness is likely to be a long-term problem for many owner-occupiers, not only for those in arrears, or with restructured mortgages, but also for those whose mortgage payments constitute a significant financial burden. These include households who continue to meet mortgage commitments but at considerable cost to their quality of life, and households who would prefer to sell their properties but cannot do so because of negative equity. These are the 'unrevealed casualties' of the crisis about which there is little information, but who are more likely to be first-time buyers who bought so-called 'starter homes' at the peak of the bubble (Waldron, 2016).

The limits of home ownership seem to be gaining policy acknowledgement in more recent times. *Rebuilding Ireland* (GOI 2016b: 26) stated that: 'The incomes of many households are such that aspiration to home ownership in the communities in which they came from and work is unlikely to be realisable ... Rates of home ownership continue to decline and this will have important implications for housing and related policies.'

Consequently there are some signs, albeit weak, that housing policy is turning towards the private rented sector and positioning it as a long-term, secure and affordable choice in contrast to prioritising home ownership. Stronger regulation of the housing market is also evident with the introduction of lending limits by the Central Bank in 2015, limiting mortgages to an 80% loan to value ratio or 90% in the case of first-time buyers and a multiple of 3.5 times annual income. Yet Budget 2017 introduced a new form of home ownership support, a 'Help to Buy' scheme 'to ensure availability of adequate, affordable mortgage finance or mortgage insurance for first-time buyers' (GOI, 2016b: 12). While it might assist first-time buyers to purchase housing, it raises questions about the degree to which it will counteract Central Bank attempts to moderate house prices, and the extent to which housing policy is moving on from promoting home ownership.

Private renting

The tenure share of private renting has increased since the early 1990s, a trend which mirrored the growth of buy-to-let investing by 'small-scale' investors during the housing and credit boom (NESC, 2015). The large jump in private renting's tenure share between 2006 and 2011 (see Table 10.3) also reflects the rise in affordability and access issues in owner-occupied and social housing over the same period. Inequalities in Irish housing are sharply evident in this sector and the system is tiered, between upper-middle-class, middle-class and low-income households who pay 'relatively high rents for low-quality dwellings' (Drudy and Punch, 2005: 81). The rise in buy-to-let properties is also indicative of inequalities in the sector as property was most likely to be bought by professionals and then let to lower social classes (NESC, 2014a). However, since the housing bubble burst, buy-to-let mortgages appear to be in greater trouble than principal residence mortgages, evidenced by higher levels of arrears (Central Bank of Ireland, 2016).

In policy terms, private renting was neglected for many years and deemed 'the forgotten sector' (O'Brien and Dillon, 1982). This neglect has gradually been addressed both in terms of supply and demand. However, on balance it would seem that supply-side actors such as property developers and landlords have been the main beneficiaries. Supply-side measures to boost the sector can be traced back to Section 23 of the Finance Act 1981, which provided generous tax relief to people who invested in accommodation for sale and for letting in 'designated areas'. This measure was applied to cities in an Urban Renewal Scheme beginning in 1986 and to rural areas in the late 1990s. The tax relief was successful in improving the supply of rental stock in areas where there may have been little incentive do so, especially neglected inner-city areas. However, it is also responsible for the oversupply of housing in rural areas, when, in some cases, whole counties were rezoned as designated areas. Tax reliefs of this type were eventually discontinued in 2006 (Norris et al, 2014).

Tax relief to renters was not introduced until the early 1990s (and since reduced during the crisis) along with a series of other measures giving a little more security to renters than heretofore. The Housing (Miscellaneous Provisions) Act 1992 provided that a minimum period of written notice (28 days) to quit must be given to a tenant, it also provided for regulations regarding accommodation standards, the provision of rent books and registration by landlords. The Commission on the Private Rented Residential Sector was set up in 1999 to address issues such as tenant security and the rights and responsibilities of landlords and tenants. The resulting Residential Tenancies Act 2004 improved security of tenure by entitling a tenant to occupy a dwelling for three and a half years, once a minimum continuous period of six months renting had passed. The Act also set 'open market rents' subject to review not more than once per annum and provided for the establishment of a Private Residential Tenancies Board. The Board deals with disputes, the registration of landlords, and the promotion of good practice. However, these provisions were still weak in relation to tenants' rights, and compared unfavourably to most European countries which, despite declining standards, continue to have much stronger security of tenure and rent regulation than Ireland (NESC, 2014b). And until the Equality (Miscellaneous Provisions) Act 2015 came into effect at the start of 2016 and introduced 'housing assistance' as a new discriminatory ground, landlords could discriminate against individuals seeking to rent a property with via state housing support.

Besides issues of security of tenure, affordability is a significant concern in the private rental sector and one which is generally overshadowed by the attention given to affordability in the owner-occupied sector. Issues of security and affordability rose to crisis levels again by the mid-2010s as housing supply became severely constrained in urban areas, and rents returned to peak levels of the mid-2000s. The rise in rents, together with the growing phenomenon of economic evictions impacting in particular on low-income workers and tenants renting with state support, forced government action in 2015 and measures were introduced in *Stabilising Rents, Boosting Supply* (DECLG, 2015) and the Residential Tenancies (Amendment) Act 2015. The preceding debate on rent regulation and the campaigning of various groups is again illustrative of the power of vested interests in Irish housing policy. A number of bodies, including NESC, and voluntary organisations including Simon and Threshold, advocated a system of rent regulation similar to Germany and Sweden, where rent increases are indexed against inflation or set by government. Moreover, as further measures to improve tenant security, NESC (2015) recommended indefinite tenancies and the removal of sale of property as a reason for vacant possession. On the other hand, as Drudy (2016) documents, property and mortgage interests groups, both Irish and international, campaigned against rent regulation. The outcome was 'rent certainty' with relatively minor modifications of the existing system. Rents are still set at market levels but landlords are permitted to increase them only every two years as opposed to each year. It is intended the system will revert to yearly reviews in 2019 (DECLG, 2015: 8). The minimum notice to quit was also raised to 90 days.

The international trend of financialised private landlordism is also beginning to have an impact on private rental supply in Ireland. Facilitated by the introduction of real estate investment trusts (REITs) which were legislated for in 2013, recent examples of investment include the purchase of 2,000 apartments from NAMA by an international landlord (Drudy, 2016), as well as purchases of land from NAMA by global real estate companies intending to build rental property (Byrne, 2015). As Drudy (2016: 4) comments 'companies whose sole objective is income and profit maximisation cannot be relied on to provide affordable and secure homes', though it remains to be seen how their role and influence will develop in the rental market over time. On other hand, housing policy since *Social Housing Strategy 2020* (DECLG, 2014a) has indicated the desirability of developing a cost rental segment in the private rented sector which would rent property on the basis of the costs of provision without seeking a profit and potentially pose as competition to for-profit landlords. *Rebuilding Ireland* (GOI, 2016b) has promised the introduction of an Affordable Rental Scheme along these lines. NESC (2015) recommended such a move as part of a shift from a dualist to an integrated rental sector which would also include stronger regulation of the sector overall, as it advocated, for example, in relation to rent regulation. Norris (2014) argues that taken as a whole, policy trends across the tenures indicate the emergence of a weak unitary model since the late 2000s. Yet as discussed throughout this section, there are conflicting trends and it remains to be seen how the current and unsettled phase of housing policy will evolve in the longer term.

Homelessness

Counts of homelessness over the 1990s and 2000s, which are based on local authority counts of households qualified for social housing at a point in time, reveal a fluctuating pattern (see Table 10.3). However, there are methodological issues that can affect the results, and voluntary agencies dealing with homelessness regularly disagree with the findings produced by the homeless assessments (Brownlee, 2008).

Table 10.3: Homeless households, 1989-2013

1989	1991	1993	1996	1999	2002	2005	2008	2011	2013
987	1,507	1,452	979	2,219	2,468	2,399	1,394	2,348	2,499

Data source: DEHLG and Housing Agency, Housing Statistics

A series of policies developed in the early 2000s (see Box 10.1) to address existing homelessness and prevent further homelessness signalled a greater effort to tackle homelessness on the part of statutory services in partnership with voluntary services. Policy emphasised the need to integrate the efforts of both sectors and to focus on a continuum from emergency to long-term responses, as well as responding to needs in the areas of health, education and employment. Part of the solution involved the creation of Homeless Fora in all local authorities, comprising statutory and voluntary representatives with responsibility for creating homeless action plans for their area. These changes were subsequently put on a statutory footing in the Housing (Miscellaneous Provisions) Act 2009. In Dublin the homeless forum has been replaced by the Homeless Agency. The implementation of these policies seemed to have been effective in reducing homelessness, particularly in Dublin, by the late 2000s.

A new homelessness strategy, *The Way Home: A Strategy to Address Adult Homelessness in Ireland 2008-2013* (DEHLG, 2008) consolidated existing efforts and optimistically aimed to eliminate long-term occupation of emergency services (defined as a stay of more than three months) and the need to sleep rough by the end of 2010. A third key aim was to prevent the occurrence of homelessness. These aims were to be principally achieved by placing greater emphasis on long-term solutions and mainstream housing, including both social housing and RAS, for persons moving out of emergency accommodation. This focus was made more explicit in the subsequent *Homelessness Policy Statement* 2013 in its adoption of a 'housing-led' approach to ending homelessness. This is described as 'accessing permanent housing as the primary response to all forms of homelessness. It includes the prevention of loss of existing housing, and it incorporates the provision of adequate support to people in their homes according to their needs' (DECLG, 2013: 3). This approach, also known as 'housing first', originated in the US and has since gained acceptance in responses to homelessness across the EU. It contrasts with the provision of temporary housing services (such as emergency and transitional accommodation) while getting people 'housing ready' (O'Sullivan, 2012). The backdrop to both these policy documents is the radically altered nature of the economy, and latterly the crisis in supply and cost of private rented accommodation, giving rise to economic eviction. Consequently the number of homeless households began to rise, a pattern captured in the collection of new data on homeless persons, as well as a breakdown of homeless families, accessing local-authority-managed emergency accommodation. This showed that the number of homeless families more doubled from 407 to 1,151 between December 2014 and August 2016; figures which included 880 and 2,363 children respectively (DHPCLG, nd). The rising figures pointed to a 'new homelessness dynamic' (GOI, 2016b: 34) created by unaffordable private rental accommodation, despite the fact that the individuals affected, principally working-class households, may be in receipt of a housing payment and/or in employment.

While the overall aims of recent iterations of homelessness policy might be fundamentally sound, they clash with the marketisation of social renting which, in the context of scarce private rental supply and rising rents, has led to the opposite of a housing-led outcome, namely a rise in the use of emergency accommodation. Families find themselves housed, over extended periods of time, in single rooms in hotels and bed and breakfasts, which has detrimental effects on their physical and mental well-being. *Rebuilding Ireland* (GOI, 2016b) aims reduce the use of emergency accommodation for families to 'limited circumstances' by mid-2017 and to address affordability and access by increasing the limits on RS and HAP payments as well as increasing supply via both HAP and social housing as previously discussed. In this context it is significant to note the views of homeless families who express a preference for local authority housing, seeing this as the only real affordable and permanent accommodation. Research into families' experiences of homelessness found that 'above all, [this] offered the security of tenure that they craved and which was absent from the private rented sector' (Walsh and Harvey, 2015: 40).

Chapter summary

- The first section outlined tenure trends across Europe and showed that while there are different approaches to housing policy, emphasis on privatisation and marketisation has grown over time. The thrust of housing policy reforms since the global financial crisis demonstrated that this policy emphasis has not fundamentally altered. In this context, long-standing policy issues and problems in each tenure, including housing inequality, social segregation, affordability and access were reviewed with a particular emphasis on how the financial crisis and its aftermath has impacted on these problems and has, in many instances, exacerbated them.
- The second section turned to Ireland to chart the origins and development of Irish housing policy. The key thread of this history is how, on gaining independence, successive governments promoted a shift from renting both in the private and social housing sector, to owner-occupation. While the state did play a substantial role as a social housing provider, the gradual privatisation of this sector has meant that it has become residualised and this process has diminished the status of the sector.
- The final section profiled developments and challenges in each of the housing tenures since the late 1990s, drawing on the key themes and wider housing policy context set out in the first section while also taking account of the heightened Irish version of housing market volatility and financial crisis. In particular the section showed that while the present period is one of considerable flux in tenure patterns and policy preferences, the treatment of housing primarily as a commodity and the reliance on privatised and marketised solutions continues to pose problems for an adequate supply of secure and affordable homes.

Discussion points
- Think about the accommodation you live in. Consider who owns it, how it is or was paid for, and what financial assistance from the state may have applied in the past or currently. Assess the design of the building and the surrounding area in relation to your needs and quality of life.
- Assess what you consider the most significant influences on the development of Irish housing policy and analyse their impact.
- Who are the 'winners' and 'losers' in the Irish housing system?
- Assess the advantages and disadvantages of each tenure type in the Irish context.

Further reading list
Norris, M (2016) *Property, family and the Irish welfare state*, Basingstoke: Palgrave Macmillan

Norris, M and Redmond, D (eds) (2005) *Housing contemporary Ireland: Policy, society and shelter*, Dublin: IPA

Sirr, L (ed) (2014) *Renting in Ireland: The social, voluntary and private sectors*, Dublin: IPA

PART IV
Analysing Irish social policy II: social groups, social policy and sustainability

eleven

Social policy and social groups: needs, rights and recognition

Welfare, well-being, and quality-of-life issues are intrinsically bound to the wider social policy approaches adopted to realise social rights. Earlier chapters demonstrated the impact of Catholic liberalism, subsidiarity and reliance on the voluntary sector and families in the development of the wider social care architecture of the Irish welfare state. However, despite these welfare legacies, the overarching role of the state in shaping and changing the nature and extent of social service provision, determining eligibility criteria and deciding on funding priorities should not be overlooked. This chapter and the next consider these issues from the vantage point of particular social groups whose recognition and rights were, and in some cases still are, neglected, delayed and problematised in various ways. Taken in this way, the chapter highlights only some of the major themes and policy issues in respect of the different groups, and therefore is not a comprehensive account of all the issues that arise.

Chapter outline
- The first section briefly scopes the issue of citizenship and difference and situates Ireland's poor record in realising social rights in this context.
- The chapter is then divided into four sections providing a brief overview of policy issues as they relate to the positions of children, older people, people with disabilities and the experiences of carers and caring.
- Each section critically examines some key aspects of social policy development as they relate to the recognition and realisation of rights of each group.

SECTION ONE
SOCIAL GROUPS, RECOGNITION AND CITIZENSHIP

The maturation of welfare capitalism and the concurrent development of social policy over the course of the twentieth century, while noteworthy in terms of the extension of citizenship rights in overall terms, re-enforced a certain social order regarding the position of particular social groups. The status of women is a case in point, as highlighted in various places throughout the book. This argument can also be made in respect of a number of other social groups for whom the social construction of their difference resulted in different, and often less favourable, treatment. As Christie (2004: 149) notes,

> Social policy both reflects and potentially challenges 'common-sense' notions of difference depending on how it formulates the social 'problem' and a policy response to it. The processes of differentiation that are part of social policy practice highlight the needs and abilities of groups, but often in ways that continue to privilege the needs of the dominant group.

Seen from the vantage point of the twenty-first century, this differentiation has had negative consequences for developing an inclusive framework of social rights. The path of citizenship rights initially developed in a way that catered most efficiently for the needs of able-bodied, adult, working men. The latter part of the twentieth century saw a significant challenge mounted to this historical bias in social policy. Chapter Four discussed the Marshallian model of citizenship. Marshall's account connected the nation state with social citizenship and proposed the welfare state as a community of belonging or creator of a 'great community' with a supra-local, supra-class and supra-ethnic vision of national consciousness (Wolfe and Klausen, 1997). As such, as Dwyer (2004: 37) notes, 'the notion of a national society within specified geographical boundaries with an imagined homogenous culture, linguistic, racial and ethnic community was increasingly the backdrop against which the social element of citizenship developed'. The 'false universalism' (Williams, 1992: 206) of this model and significant change in society over the last decades of the twentieth century and to date, mean that both hidden identities and new identities challenged this notion of citizenship and prompted new debates about citizenship rights and recognition.

Dominant influences on the development of the Irish welfare state, as documented in Chapter Two, left as much service provision as possible to families, charity and voluntary providers, with minimum interference or oversight by the state. The massive human costs of this 'hands-off' and 'see nothing' approach as demonstrated in respect of the experiences of children, and other groups such as unmarried mothers, as explored in Chapter Three, highlights the extent to which recognition and rights matter. Recent developments in social policy demonstrate varying degrees of effort to modernise and reform aspects of Irish social services, with some greater recognition of the diversity of groups and needs for which it must accommodate, although major work remains to be done.

The enduring weakness in the delivery of Irish social policy is its lack of proper appropriation of economic, social and cultural (ESC) rights (See Box 11.1) and the fact that not all such rights are protected in the Irish Constitution. The notion of 'struggle' and having to 'fight' for recognition and rights has been a consistent theme in the history of social policy for different social groups, especially where difference has been problematised, ignored or both. A myriad of campaigning and advocacy non-governmental organisations (NGOs) invest huge effort in highlighting issues and problems encountered across a wide range of groups and issues, as they have done over many years. However, as disability activist Donal Toolan (2003: 175) previously noted: 'modern Ireland's engagement with the concepts of rights seems at best uncomfortable. Any resolution of that discomfort seems to have been arrived at through the efforts of a perceived minority and their capacities to ultimately rely upon external forces to vindicate their lonely position.' The Irish state has also been challenged externally on matters of ESC rights as international human rights bodies have come more to the fore in issuing critical assessments of where Ireland has fallen short (UN Committee on Economic, Social and Cultural Rights, 2015).

Box 11.1: Economic, social and cultural rights

Economic, social and cultural (ESC) rights are those human rights relating broadly to issues such as healthcare, education, housing, standard of living, food, water and sanitation, education, social security, the workplace, family life and participation in cultural life. Along with civil and political rights, they are part of the international body of human rights.

ESC rights, and human rights law more broadly, are outcomes focused, but are also concerned with the process by which these outcomes are achieved. For example, ESC rights require the Government to take steps, over time, to deliver on those ESC rights outcomes identified in international law. They do not specify the specific policies which must be pursued to deliver on these rights but they require that the Government adopts appropriate processes for planning and decision-making and that decisions are made in a transparent, participatory manner, using reliable evidence.

Ireland has legal obligations to uphold ESC rights because it has ratified a range of both international and regional treaties which protect these rights.

Source: Amnesty International Ireland, 2014: 10

In terms of the contested nature of social rights, it is worth noting that a Constitutional Convention considered the issue of ESC rights in 2014; 85% voted in favour of strengthening the ESC rights provisions in the Constitution and 80% favoured constitutional protection for a full range of rights (Amnesty International Ireland, 2014). This aspect of the report on the Constitutional Referendum was to be referred to an Oireachtas committee for consideration in 2016. Amnesty International Ireland (2014: 68) argue that

> Ireland should take less than a minimalist approach and enshrine these rights in the Constitution to give them long-term protection. However, while preferable, there is no obligation as such under human rights law to give explicit constitutional protection to ESC rights. However, ESC rights do need to be given appropriate protection within the domestic legal order. There must be appropriate means of ensuring governmental accountability and for providing remedies and redress

At a practical level there is now greater awareness of the social exclusion, marginalisation and discrimination potentially experienced by different social groups. The level of recognition enjoyed by different groups varies; the point here is not to set groups in opposition but rather to acknowledge the reality of diversity of need, to explore the differing struggles for recognition and to examine the vindication of social rights in the Irish context. It is important to note in this context that there exists, in reality, many cross-cutting or intersectional issues; a person may be older and have a disability for instance, while risk of childhood deprivation is potentially compounded by experiences of anti-Traveller racism in the case of Traveller children. Our focus here and in Chapter Twelve is to present an account of the main social policy issues that arise in respect of different social groups for whom the contested nature of social rights in Ireland can present particular difficulties.

SECTION TWO
CHILDREN AND IRISH SOCIAL POLICY

Historically the position of children was seen, generally speaking, as a matter of private responsibility, with parents considered the sole and duty-bound providers of care and protection of their children. Apart from the Children's Allowance introduced during the 1940s, state support structures for the family remained weak, while state intervention was paternalistic and completely neglected the rights of children, and parents too, as outlined in Chapters Two and Three. Furthermore, the notion of the family was one of the traditional married nuclear form and there was little acknowledgement of other family types. Against the backdrop of the unremittingly grim history of children in Irish social policy about which we continue to learn, this section concentrates on the policy efforts made since the 1990s to improve child protection and welfare and enhance the rights of children, and notes some enduring problems that remain.

The 1990s undoubtedly marked a watershed in the recognition of the needs of children. There was a growing realisation that children needed and had the right to be protected, that earlier notions of the assumed welfare of children within the private domain was not adequate and that like all other people, children had the right to protection from abuse. From this crucial starting point there has been a substantial opening out of the debate about the position of children in society, their recognition and their rights. The ratification of the UN Convention on the Rights of the Child (UNCRC) by Ireland in 1992 was also significant. The Convention was agreed in 1989 and it sets out an international legally binding framework for delivering and realising the rights of children. Periodic reports are delivered to the UN Committee on the Rights of the Child, which monitors the implementation of the Convention in individual countries. The report issued on Ireland during the mid–1990s was critical of 'the absence of a focused Governmental approach to the needs of children' (Langford, 2007: 251) and this was among many issues which subsequent policy developments sought to address.

An emerging framework of social policy for children

The Child Care Act 1991 emerged as a landmark legislative development in child protection and it set the tone for a decade of much greater consideration children's needs and rights. The implementation of this Act, which took a number of years, coincided with much more public confrontation of child abuse during the 1990s, with the shortcomings of the child protection system brought into acute focus, heightening attention to the neglected position of children in Irish society. The Child Care Act 1991 continues to provide the legal framework for the operation of the child protection system and as such it is a crucial element of children's social policy in the vindication of the most basic of rights, that of protection. The Act is significant not least because it places a duty on Tusla, the Child and Family Agency (previously the HSE and Health Boards), to respond to children not receiving adequate care and protection and in so doing,

> must regard the welfare of the child as the first and paramount consideration, have regard to the rights and duties of parents, give due consideration to the child's wishes and have regard to the principle that it is generally better for children to be brought up in their own families (Barron, 1995: 10).

The Act also covered childcare emergencies and various care proceedings, children in care, regulation of preschool services and the registration of children's residential centres. In addition, the legislation requires provision of accommodation for children who are homeless.

A dedicated minister of state for children was appointed in 1994 and in 1997 the Department of Health was renamed the Department of Health and Children. The first ever *National Children's Strategy* was published in 2000. The adoption of 'the whole child perspective' in the Strategy was significant in its acknowledgement of children's own capacities, the recognition of various dimensions of children's development and the identification of the range of supports, formal and informal, on which children are reliant. The appointment of the first Ombudsman for Children in 2004 (hereafter the OCO (Ombudsman for Children's Office)) and the activities engaged in by that Office, the establishment of Dáil na nÓg (Youth Parliament) and Comhairle na nÓg (Youth Councils), provided new fora for children to participate and voice issues that concern them. By 2011 the Department of Children and Youth Affairs (DCYA) was established, with a full cabinet minister. Arguments had long been made that closer coordination of the various elements of social policy relevant to children was essential to the effective functioning of policy and its implementation. Notable developments in government/state structures sought to focus on meeting the needs of children in a more coherent way, with increased investment in services and the support of research on children (such as The Growing Up in Ireland national longitudinal study) along with policies designed with children's input into their needs (including *Ready, Steady, Play!* [National Children's Office, 2004] and *Teenspace* [Office of the Minister for Children, 2007]) represented advances in recognising the distinct needs and voices of children.

For all the policy developments of the 2000s (see Box 11.2), Ireland's child protection system continued to operate under considerable strain, with its worst shortcomings exposed in cases of children in state care who were not adequately protected and supported. The gravity of these issues is captured in the *Report of the Independent Child Death Review Group* (Shannon and Gibbons, 2012). The lack of coherent, coordinated and timely provision of services and supports has been a huge shortcoming for children in the care system. The establishment of Tusla in 2014, provided for its independence from the health services, of which it was part, has been described as 'a once in a generation opportunity to fundamentally reform children's services in Ireland' (DCYA, 2012: iii). The need for adequate investment, coherent collaboration between services and sustained attention to preventive and family support social work are among the issues (Buckley and Burns, 2015) that Tusla will need to navigate.

The children's referendum carried in 2012 repealed Article 42.5 of the Constitution and Article 42A was signed into law in April 2015. Legal analysis of Article 42A (Child Law Clinic, 2015: 2) clarifies its significance and potential limits

> The new Article explicitly recognizes and affirms the rights of all children; allows the Oireachtas to legislate for the adoption of marital children; and requires the Oireachtas to enact legislation requiring

decision-makers to consider the views and best interests of children in the context of a State intervention in child protection matters, and in adoption, guardianship, custody or access proceedings. The amendment clarifies how and when the State can intervene to protect the welfare of a child.

It provides for a child-focused approach by authorizing the State to intervene in a family where there has been a failure of parental duty such that the safety or welfare of the children is likely to be prejudicially affected. In addition, it prescribes that the State shall intervene by proportionate means as opposed to the former phrase 'appropriate means'.

Although some of the provisions stop short of giving full constitutional status to children's rights, they are important in that they promote the use of the law to express and protect children's rights.

The OCO (2016) makes similar observations about the extent to which Article 42A stops short, as outlined later.

The Children First Act 2015 puts aspects of the Children First guidelines on a statutory footing; organisations are required to keep children safe and have a Child Safeguarding Statement, defined (mandated) persons are required to report child protection concerns to Tusla, and are required to assist Tusla in their assessment if asked to do so. The Children First Interdepartmental Group is established on a statutory basis in this legislation which also abolishes the legal defence of reasonable chastisement in relation to corporal punishment. The Child and Family Relationships Act 2015 covers a number of family law reform measures including adoption, guardianship, custody, access, maintenance, succession and it sets out the factors which must be taken into account in considering the best interests of the child including obtaining the views of the child.

Box 11.2: Children: key policy and legislative developments

1991   Child Care Act

1992   Ireland ratifies UN Convention on the Rights of the Child

1999   Social Services Inspectorate (SSI) established/2007 given extended powers within Health Information and Quality Authority (HIQA)

1999   *Children First: National Guidelines for the Protection and Welfare of Children*/2011 Revised

2000   *National Children's Strategy: Our Children – Their Lives*

2001   Children Act

2001   Youth Work Act

2001   National Children's Office established

2001   *Youth Homelessness Strategy*

2003	Ombudsman for Children Act
2004	*National Play Policy (Ready, Steady, Play!)*
2005	Office of the Minister for Children established
2006	Irish Youth Justice Service established
2008	*National Youth Justice Strategy 2008-2010*
2010	Adoption Act
2010	National Review Panel established
2012	31st Amendment to the Constitution (repealed Article 42.5 and inserted Article 42A)
2013	Child and Family Agency Act
2014	*Action Plan on Bullying*
2014	*Youth Justice Action Plan 2014-2018*
2014	*Better Outcomes, Brighter Futures: the national policy framework for children and young people 2014-2020*
2015	*National Youth Strategy 2015-2020*
2015	*National Strategy on Children and Young People's Participation in Decision-making*
2015	Children First Act
2015	Child and Family Relationships Act
2015	Child Care (Amendment) Act
2015	Children (Amendment) Act
2016	Adoption (Information and Tracing) Bill
2016	Adoption (Amendment) Bill

Enduring challenges to realising the rights of all children

The vision outlined in *Better Outcomes, Brighter Futures: The National Policy Framework for Children and Young People 2014-2020,*

> is to make Ireland the best small country in the world in which to grow up and raise a family, and where the rights of all children and young people are respected, protected and fulfilled; where their voices are heard and where they are supported to realise their maximum potential now and in the future (DCYA, 2014a: 2).

It contains 163 commitments cutting across government departments and agencies and there is a particular emphasis on improving outcomes for children and young people. The real test will be whether the resources will be made available to match the ideals. For all the recent policy innovations there remain many significant problems that have clear implications for the vindication of the rights of children in Ireland. These include issues such as the persistence of child poverty; the variable quality and availability of early childcare and education services (see Chapter Nine); problems with timely access to certain important social services and family and mental health supports; the level and types of support available for children and young people in and leaving the care and youth justice systems;

and child and youth homelessness. The sharp rise in youth unemployment and the impact of the recent economic crisis on children and young people has been particularly acute.

Child poverty continues to be a very significant problem in Ireland, with children exposed to a higher than average risk of both consistent and relative income poverty (see Chapter Seven for an explanation of these measurements). Poverty data persistently indicates that children experience a higher risk of consistent poverty than the population as a whole. Furthermore, of all the age cohorts, children continue to be at highest risk of poverty and of deprivation (CSO, 2015). Ireland also compares poorly with the majority of the EU, having the ninth highest risk of poverty and social exclusion rate for children (Hearne and McMahon, 2016). The consequences which flow from the poverty and economic inequality experienced by children can extend in to all aspects of their lives. As TASC (Hearne and McMahon, 2016: 58) note

> Economic inequality is about more than just an inadequate income. It is about the situation of children in the context of the wider society in which they live, their levels of relative poverty, deprivation, their access to resources, education, health and their levels of happiness, anxiety, and perception of self-worth compared to others. It is about socioeconomic class inequalities and how children living at the bottom are differentially excluded and impacted through their childhood compared to those at the top, and how, as a result of inequality in childhood, their adult lives are also scarred by inequality.

The EU 2020 poverty targets set out in Chapter Seven have been updated to take account of increasing poverty since the targets were set and 97,000 children are to be lifted out of consistent poverty by 2020 (CRA, 2016). Both the UNCRC Committee (2016) and the OCO (2016) made strong recommendations for the state to do better in its efforts to tackle child poverty. It is widely recognised that children who experience sustained poverty are disadvantaged as a result, which can also impact negatively on their opportunities and life chances in adulthood. The lack of public and media scrutiny of the extent of child poverty, and poverty in general, underscores a particular ambivalence that social policy in Ireland must still go some way to challenge.

We now briefly turn our focus to some of the most vulnerable groups of children in order to draw attention to some of the most pressing issues that arise in realising rights for all children. Recent reports from the Ombudsman (OCO, 2015, 2016) highlight the ways in which children may experience breaches of their rights in the context of the principles of the UNCRC. Against this benchmark the findings raise very serious questions about the adequacy of services and supports available at present. While the Constitutional Amendment on the Rights of the Child passed in 2012 was a significant development, as discussed earlier, the Ombudsman (OCO, 2016: 2-3) notes that:

While the amendment is an important development in recognising children as rights holders, it falls significantly short of constitutional incorporation of the key principles of the UNCRC. With regard to the inclusion of the key principles of the UNCRC in the Constitution, the new provision in relation to best interests and voice of the child only apply in very specific judicial proceedings.

The Children's Rights Alliance (CRA) (2016: 12) assesses that the wording of the Amendment and argue that the proposed wording issued by the Joint Committee on the Constitutional Amendment on Children could have provided for 'greater constitutional protections to a wider range of children's rights'. The lack of a child-rights based approach to legislation in the areas of health and education, for example, is an issue raised by the Ombudsman (OCO, 2015, 2016), who recommends that steps be taken to incorporate fully the outstanding aspects of the UNCRC into Irish law.

A report conducted a decade ago (Kilkelly, 2007) found multiple barriers to the realisation of the social rights of children in the care system, children in the criminal justice system, homeless children, immigrant and asylum-seeking children, Traveller children, and children at risk of abuse and neglect. Other children identified as experiencing difficulty in the realisation of their rights included sick children and children with disabilities, mental health problems, and drug and alcohol abuse difficulties. Some progress has been made in respect of protecting the rights of some of these children but the position and experiences of most continue to feature prominently as being of continuing concern.

Regarding children at risk of abuse or neglect, the establishment of Tusla and the Children First Act 2015 mark potentially important developments in the move towards a more coherent framework for child protection in Ireland. However, Tusla will need to be adequately resourced; in 2016, it was not meeting its own targets for assessment of referrals in many cases (OCO, 2016). In relation to the implementation of the Children First Act 2015 the Ombudsman (OCO, 2016: 5) recommends that 'all necessary resources need to be put in place to ensure that Tusla can respond in a timely and effective manner to increase in reporting expected … and its impact on child protection services and practice should be subject to formal review'. The lack of adequate supports for children who have been abused, such as delays in accessing counselling and the closure of the specialist unit for forensic examination of children who have been sexually assaulted, are major shortcomings. An Emergency Out of Hours Service was recently established by Tusla, the objective of which 'is to co-operate with and support the Garda Síochána in the execution of their duties and responsibilities under Section 12(3) of the Child Care Act, 1991' (Tusla, 2015). This is a welcome development but it is not the nationwide out-of-hours' social work service that has long been sought, in that the Service must be accessed via the Gardaí. Wider issues also arise regarding supports available to families, particularly those in crisis and where domestic violence is occurring. The development of a national strategy to prevent and address all forms of violence against children has been recommended (OCO, 2015).

The number of children in the care of the state has risen in recent years (by 20%, for example, between 2008 and 2013) and 92.9% of these children live in foster families (DCYA, 2014b). Apart from the need to work in a more preventive way to minimise the number of children going into care in the first place and to ensure that, wherever possible, this is as short term as necessary, other difficulties arise for these children, such as problems in residential care, the risk of stigma, stress and bullying, the lack of input of children about decisions that affect their lives and their right to be kids (Kilkelly, 2007). The *Listen to Our Voices!* report (McEvoy and Smith, 2011) contains core messages from children in care: the importance of access to birth families; being treated as a member of the family in foster care; the need for assessment, vetting and training of foster families; the effects of multiple placements on their lives; the importance of having one person/ agency to be there for them; issues around privacy, constant record keeping and problems gaining consent for activities; the lack of information provided to them in care and in aftercare services and the inconsistency of its availability. The lack of visibility of children in the care system and inadequate acknowledgement of their right to be heard and to be consulted present additional obstacles to children in and leaving the care system (Carr, 2014; McEvoy and Smith, 2011; Daly, 2012a). The level of support made available to young people leaving the care system as adults, known as aftercare, is discretionary and variable by region. Daly (2012b) provides particular insight from young people leaving care about their experiences and the need for better aftercare planning, attention to social support needs and gaps in practical supports. The Child Care (Amendment) Act 2015, as mentioned above, may deliver more by way of supports to children leaving care but the age criteria and other eligibility restrictions are less inclusive than the definition of children and young people included in *Better Outcomes, Brighter Futures* (DCYA, 2014a) and fall short of what is likely to be needed to really support the transition to adulthood. Furthermore, it does 'not provide the young person with an entitlement to access services, only an entitlement to have a plan drawn up' (CRA, 2016: 84). The legislation has not yet been commenced.

The position of the Travelling Community and that of migrants and asylum seekers is dealt with in detail in the following chapter but breaches of the rights of these children are also of note here. The UNCRC Committee (2016: 6), for example, expressed its concern 'about the structural discrimination against Traveller and Roma children and their families, including alleged impunity for publicly expressed discriminatory remarks by public representatives'. The poorer health status of Traveller and Roma children was also highlighted. The vulnerable position of immigrant and asylum-seeking children has been a particular source of concern for almost two decades (see Chapter Twelve). The issue of homelessness as it relates to children (whether on their own or with their families) presents a series of difficulties quite apart from the emotional trauma including shortcomings in the appropriateness of emergency accommodation (for example, where bed and breakfasts are used – having to vacate the accommodation for the day) and a shortage of medium- and long-stay accommodation (see also Chapter Ten).

The higher profile of the needs and voice of children in Irish social policy over the last two decades gives ground for some optimism but not complacency. The policy advances have been considerable, resulting in much better awareness of the needs of children and how far social services and supports have fallen short. More extensive oversight of key social services and the child protection and care systems need to be matched by adequate resources to ensure they can deliver what is required to meet the needs and rights of children. And this is only half the battle; Ireland's failure to do enough to address enduring child poverty, and the disadvantage that accumulates, means that we fail to address the root cause of subsequent difficulties in many children's lives.

SECTION THREE
OLDER PEOPLE AND IRISH SOCIAL POLICY

The UN Principles for Older Persons – independence, participation, care, self-fulfilment and dignity – were adopted in 1991 and broadly endorsed, but are considered by many to now require updating. A UN Open Ended Working Group on Ageing was established in 2010 and is examining the need for a Convention on the Rights of Older People. There is no consensus, however, and some member states remain opposed to the development of such a Convention, which many NGOs contend would strengthen the human rights of older people.

There has been a significant growth in interest in issues of age, ageing and the life experiences of older people over the last decade. Traditional social constructions of ageing tended to see older persons as dependent and frail, which in large part neglected the contribution of older persons and their right to participate fully in society. Shifts in discourses of age and ageing challenged traditional theories of ageing but these have been largely overshadowed by somewhat patronising notions of active and positive ageing that have now come to dominate despite the fact that they remain ill-defined and largely problematic (see Timonen, 2016). Ireland's most recent policy statement regarding ageing and older people, *Positive Ageing Starts Now! National Positive Ageing Strategy* (DoH, 2013c: 3), states:

> Ireland will be a society for all ages that celebrates and prepares properly for individual and population ageing. It will enable and support all ages and older people to enjoy physical and mental health and well-being to their full potential. It will promote and respect older people's engagement in economic, social, cultural, community and family life, and foster better solidarity between generations. It will be a society in which the equality, independence, participation, care, self-fulfilment and dignity of older people are pursued at all times.

This vision statement does not yet have a timeline for the implementation of the specific policy targets it contains. There is not a single specific reference to the rights of older people in the objectives outlined in the Strategy.

Combating ageism, in contrast, is identified as one of the cross-cutting objectives of the National Positive Ageing Strategy. Its objectives include: promotion of activities to combat ageism, awareness raising campaigns, ensuring older people's needs are considered in any policies affecting them, promoting intergenerational solidarity and more inclusive approaches to policy consultation.

> **Ageism** refers to prejudicial attitudes and/or discrimination experienced by people on the grounds of age.

In terms of older people, **ageism** is often manifest in pervasive stereotypes and particular assumptions made about their roles and capacities by other members of society also sometimes reflected in media, for example (Fealy et al, 2012), and in social policy discourse more generally. The growing number of older people is frequently presented as a significant economic problem and social burden which largely ignores the 'demographic bounty' (O'Shea, 2006) that greater numbers of older people present. Driven in part by the changing demographics in Western countries and the implications for welfare states, more extensive consideration has been given to the employment rates of older people. However, persistently high rates of discrimination reported by people over 50 in relation to looking for work – 82% in 2004, 76% in 2010 and 87% in 2014 (DoH, 2016b) – highlight wider dimensions of the pervasiveness of ageism and the need for more robust social policies in this regard. Revised arrangements for monitoring the implementation of the National Positive Ageing Strategy are to include mechanisms for stakeholder consultation on key policy issues relevant to older people (McEntee, 2017). It remains to be seen as to how this mechanism and the other objectives on combating ageism will be implemented and how effective they will be.

Income, poverty and older people

Older people's income in Ireland is derived from a number of sources (the state pension, occupational pensions, returns on savings, continuing in employment). There is no set statutory retirement age in Ireland (outside of the public service) but in practice many workers have a retirement age (typically 65 years) included in their contracts of employment. Greater flexibility in retirement options has long been sought and this issue has become the focus of more attention in recent times. The state pension qualification age was increased without sufficient attention to this and related issues, around which further policy reform is likely. In reality, the state pension continues to be the primary income source for most older people. Almost two thirds (62.7%) of pensioners' incomes comes from state pensions and related transfers, private or occupational pensions account for 17.6% of incomes, while income from work/self-employment amount to 16.1% in 2011 (Hughes and Maher, 2016). Only in the top income quintile does the state pension not provide the majority income source for older people. The state pension (along with the other social transfers) therefore plays a vital role in minimising the risk of poverty for older people. The risk of income poverty was very high for older people during the economic boom years; almost one third (32.3%) of pensioners were at risk of poverty in 2003. Increases in the state pension have been very effective in reducing this poverty risk for older people, which by 2013 had reduced significantly to 7.5% (Hughes and Maher, 2016). However, older people experienced particular financial challenges associated with fixed and declining pension incomes over recent years. Cuts to the social transfers coupled with increased taxes and new service charges have had an impact. Particular groups of older people, including those living alone and those in ill health, are at particularly high risk of living in poverty (Connolly, 2015).

The importance of the public pension system to older people's income security in Ireland is often understated. Irish pension policy over several decades has sought to encourage individuals to supplement their state pensions by way of an occupational or personal pension. This policy preference has been incentivised via generous tax reliefs which have disproportionately benefited the better-off. However, less than half of workers have a private pension and generous tax benefits have not succeeded in increasing the overall rate of supplementary pension cover. Reform of the Irish pension system has been on the policy agenda for decades and it assumes more urgency as the demographic profile has begun to shift. Concerns about the long-term sustainability of the system have already resulted in increases in the state pension qualification age (from age 65 in 2011, to 66 in 2014, 67 in 2021 and 68 in 2028). Also, more stringent qualification criteria are to be applied to social insurance state pensions making it more difficult to qualify for a full state pension. Belated reform of the pension system will gather pace in the coming years and as it does, it is vital that the most effective aspect of the current system (state pensions) is not further undermined.

Box 11.3: Older people: key policy and legislative developments

1990	Health (Nursing Homes) Act
1998	*Health Promotion Strategy for Older People: Adding Years to Life and Life to Years*
2002	*Report of the Working Group on Elder Abuse: Protecting Our Future*
2007	Health Act
2008	Office for Older People established
2009	Nursing Home Support Scheme Act
2009	National Quality Standards for Residential Care Settings for Older People in Ireland/2016 Revised
2010	*Review of the Recommendations of Protecting Our Future: Report of the Working Group on Elder Abuse*
2013	*National Positive Ageing Strategy*

2014   *Irish National Dementia Strategy*

2014   Safeguarding Vulnerable Persons at Risk of Abuse: National Policy and Procedures

2015   Assisted Decision-Making (Capacity) Act

Care supports for older people

Home- and community-based care

Despite a common misconception to the contrary, the vast majority of older people continue to reside in their own home, and government policy since *The Care of the Aged Report* (Inter-Departmental Committee, 1968) has been to support and realise the preference of older people in this regard. The Health Act 1970 included provision for home help and, eligibility and discretion issues notwithstanding, the provision of state-funded home care did expand from the late 1970s onwards (Timonen and Doyle, 2008). *The Years Ahead: A Policy for the Elderly* (Working Party on Services for the Elderly, 1988) continued to emphasise the role of the family and the voluntary sector but overall the role of the state in the delivery and access to home-care provision has developed in an ad hoc and discretionary way. Demonstrated differences in the extent and type of help available, in the eligibility criteria applied and the practice of charging in some areas, highlighted the variable nature of home-care arrangements that existed (Lundström and McKeown, 1994). A decade later, the NESF (2005b: iv) also noted significant shortcomings, 'our under-developed community care system, which is crisis driven, lacks sufficient co-ordination and resources and does not afford older people the choice, independence and autonomy they seek and deserve'.

Pressure to address the wider hospital-bed shortage was a contributory factor in the notable expansion in home care during the 2000s. Public spending tripled between 2001 and 2008 and the proportion of over 65s in receipt of home-care services grew 3.7% in 2000 to 12.7% in 2009 (Timonen et al, 2012). Home Help Services were increased and the development of a new Home Care Package (HCP) Scheme accounted for a significant share of the increased investment. Introduced on a national basis in 2006, the HCP Scheme provides a set of services based on the specific needs of the person and can comprise nurses, home-care assistants, home helps, physiotherapists, occupational therapists and respite and day-care services. Eligibility for the scheme is based on a Care Needs Assessment and is not means-tested. However, it remains an administrative scheme of the HSE with no automatic right or entitlement to the scheme or its services (HSE, 2016a).

The expansionary shift of the 2000s halted by the end of that decade, and budget cutbacks since 2010 have allowed a build-up of more acute service challenges. While the number of HCPs granted has risen every year since their introduction, the number of people in receipt of home-help hours reduced by 14% between 2009 and 2014 (DoH, 2015). This is despite the fact the numbers of people aged 65+ and 80+ grew by 25% and 30% respectively over roughly the same period (2008-15) (Donnelly et al, 2016). The implications of this lack of funding and availability of home- and community-based services continues to be felt. Donnelly et al (2016: 5) found continuing disparities in entitlement and access to, and availability of, community-based supports, regularly meaning 'that older people did not receive the level of service that their care needs' assessment indicated'. A particular concern in this regard 'was unnecessary or premature admission to long-term residential care' (Donnelly et al, 2016: 5). The need to uphold the rights and dignity of older people and their involvement in decisions around their care would appear to be difficult in professional practice where suitable and appropriate services are in short supply.

Where services provided by the HSE fall short of what is actually required, older people and their families have increasingly had to make up that shortfall by way of extending family care arrangements where possible and/or via the purchase of additional home supports in the private sector. HSE home-care expenditure is estimated to account for 30% of the total market, with individuals and families procuring the remainder (McEntee, 2016), indicating the scale of market reliance in home-care services. There is also evidence of increased marketisation of the home-care sector within the HSE, which by 2014 had 60% of its HCPs provided by the private sector (DoH, 2015). However, neither the growth in the private home-care market nor calls for greater regulation to uphold the rights and dignity of service users across a wide range of services discussed in this chapter have spurred sufficiently robust policy in this area. HSE National Standards exist for home-care services but they are not subject to HIQA regulation or inspection, despite various calls for their development over recent years. A review of the regulation and financing of home-care services is due for publication in 2017.

Residential care

The Nursing Home Subvention Scheme, developed during the 1990s, increased capacity with greater numbers of private nursing homes, but its overall effectiveness was hampered by rising costs and a lack of consistency in the eligibility and in the levels of subvention granted to individuals and their families (Mangan, 2002; O'Shea et al, 2002). A new scheme subsequently paved the way for individual contributions towards the cost of nursing-home care regardless of whether it is public or privately provided, thus marking the introduction of an unprecedented charging structure for a core service within the Irish health system.

The Nursing Homes Support Scheme, more often known as the Fair Deal Scheme, was introduced in 2009. The scheme is operated by the HSE and covers nursing-home care only. Eligibility is determined via a Care Needs Assessment, it is not based on age but rather a confirmed requirement for long-term residential care. The financial contribution to be made is determined via an assessment of means. Individuals are required to contribute 80% of their assessable income and 7.5% of the value of any assets (above €36,000 per annum). There is a three-year cap, that is, 22.5% (11.25% in the case of couples where one remains in the family home), on the asset claim on one's principal residence, regardless of the length of time spent in nursing home care (HSE, 2016a).

Over 60% of health expenditure on services for older people is used to support long-term residential care (DoH, 2015). Long-term nursing-home care is now predominantly delivered via the private sector which provides 80% of the beds (DoH, 2015) compared with less than 30% in the early 1990s (O'Shea, 1994). The average individual contribution covers approximately 25% of the cost of care (DoH, 2015). Whether one has a legal right to nursing-home care outside of the Nursing Home Support Scheme remains unclear. According to the Irish Council for Civil Liberties (ICCL, 2016: 28):

> the Department of Health and HSE are of the view that, since the Nursing Home Support Scheme ... was introduced in 2009, people do not have a legal right to nursing home care. The Ombudsman has disagreed, suggesting that a right to nursing home care continues to be the case under the Health Act 1970.

In social policy terms, the scheme represents an erosion of the right of a particular group to utilise health services on the basis of differentiated need (albeit on less favourable terms than other need such as short-stay hospital care). The financial means assessment at the core of this scheme mark a distinctive shift in modes of welfare financing within the health service.

The care needs of older people, while gaining greater attention in recent years, continue to lack an official statutory entitlement on an equal assessment of need. Service users continue to lack information and certainty around the home supports available to them. These shortcomings mean that access to the available services is not secure on an equal basis for all older people. Overall the shifting, yet still discretionary, and increasingly market-based welfare mix in care supports for older people in the community need to be the subject of much more sustained public debate to inform a new coherent national policy strategy in this area.

Quality and regulation of services and the protection of older people

Media exposure of abuse experienced by people in Leas Cross nursing home in 2006 was ultimately influential in expanding the role of HIQA to cover older people's residential services (Timonen et al, 2012). Since 2009, all nursing homes, public and private, must be registered with HIQA and are subject to inspection by them. HIQA (2016: 4) sets out 35 National Standards which 'focus on outcomes which enhance the ability of people to participate in, and contribute to, daily life', including promoting people's rights, respecting people's right to dignity, privacy and autonomy, facilitation of independence and personal choice, safeguarding from abuse, providing information and assessing that appropriate supports are available.

In terms of vulnerable adult abuse more generally, research in the Irish context has been sparse until relatively recently and policies and practice continue to evolve. A dedicated Elder Abuse Service was established within the HSE during the 2000s with assigned senior case workers, an information line for persons concerned about elder abuse and the promotion of public awareness. National policy and procedures, Safeguarding Vulnerable Persons at Risk of Abuse (HSE, 2014), have been developed and the National Safeguarding Committee (2016: 5) is to support this work by 'encouraging an organisational and societal culture which promotes the rights of adults who may be vulnerable'. Phelan's (2014: 184) review of progress in this area notes, 'awareness of elder abuse in Ireland has progressed significantly … but complacency is not an option'.

While some services for older and vulnerable adults are now subject to much greater inspection and regulation than in the past, this is only one facet of a much more complex set of policy responses and practice changes required to safeguard and uphold the rights of all persons. In the case of older people, for example, the perpetrators are most frequently reported to be family members. Begley et al (2012) stress how making it clear that abuse of older people in all its forms is unacceptable is important to elder abuse prevention, is a core part of the response to it, as are information on abuse and the processes in place to deal with it. Maintaining health and social well-being via community and social networks and greater attention to personhood and autonomy of older people is also considered vital to effective policies and practices. A more robust approach to the human and social rights of older people in Ireland could undoubtedly contribute in this regard.

SECTION FOUR
PEOPLE WITH DISABILITIES AND IRISH SOCIAL POLICY

The UN Convention on the Rights of People with Disabilities (CRPD) was the first international human rights treaty of the twenty-first century. It seeks to protect and enhance the rights of all persons with a disability and equal rights in all areas of life. The Convention was adopted by the UN General Assembly in 2006 and Ireland signed the CRPD in 2007. As of early 2017, Ireland is the only EU member state that has not yet ratified the Convention. The tardiness of Ireland's commitment to ratifying the Convention is broadly in keeping with its limited achievements in enhancing the rights of people with disabilities over recent years, despite a plethora of policies and promises.

Almost 600,000 people in Ireland have a disability, 13% of the population, and the prevalence of disability increases with age (CSO, 2012a). The employment rate of working-age people with a disability is lower in Ireland than in other countries (Watson et al, 2013). Private adult living costs are estimated to be approximately one third higher than for those without a disability (Cullinan and Lyons, 2015).

Working-age adults with a disability and their children are also at greater risk of poverty and deprivation (Watson et al, 2016). Quality-of-life problems are also higher among adults with a disability and their children than other groups and, as Watson et al (2016: 87) note, 'the evaluation of progress in areas such as health and mental health service delivery and outcomes needs to take account of the complexity of the challenges facing those who are multidimensionally disadvantaged'. Acknowledgement of quality-of-life issues for people with disabilities has been notably absent from policy considerations until very recently. Much of the policy development that occurred over the last 20 years has been taken up with addressing major deficits in the areas of education and health, to which we now turn.

An emerging policy framework for people with disabilities?

The social policy landscape for people with disabilities has been evolving in Ireland since the late 1990s and much change has been recommended (see Box 11.4). Its inauspicious position is captured in the findings of the Commission on the Status of People with Disabilities (1996: 5) which stated:

> People with disabilities are the neglected citizens of Ireland. On the eve of the 21st century, many of them suffer intolerable conditions because of outdated social and economic policies and unthinking public attitudes. Changes have begun to come about, influenced by international recognition that disability is a social rather than a medical issue, but many of those changes have been piecemeal. Public attitudes towards disability are still based on charity rather than on rights, and the odds are stacked against people with disabilities at almost every turn. Whether their status is looked at in terms of economics, information, education, mobility, or housing they are seen to be treated as second-class citizens.

The Commission issued 402 recommendations, indicative of the scale of the shortcomings and monumental policy effort necessary to protect and promote the rights of people with disabilities in an altogether different way.

In terms of education, developments which began in the 1990s over time represented a radical improvement on the previous policy efforts to promote inclusion in education. A review in the early 1990s along with Ireland's adoption of the Salamanca Statement, which encouraged governments to adopt inclusive education with children to attend regular schools in the absence of compelling reasons not to, provided the impetus for considerable policy and legislative reform. There were only 70 Special Needs Assistants working in schools in Ireland in 1990; by 2000 there were 1,495 and in 2010 approximately 10,000 employed in schools across the country (M O'Sullivan, 2014). The substantial investment and improvement in supports for children with SEN arose from a remarkably low base at a time when demand for such educational rights continue to grow. However, the number of parents that sought to vindicate the rights of their children to an education through the courts during the 1990s and 2000s demonstrates the 'battle' that securing an appropriate education for children with disabilities has been. The Disability Strategy (DJELR, 2004) and the provisions contained in the Disability Act 2005 notwithstanding, the needs and rights of all persons with disability to access services remains problematic.

The Department of Justice and Equality is the coordinating department for government policy on disability. The National Disability Strategy as launched in 2004 had a number of components: the Disability Bill 2004, the Comhairle (Amendment) Bill 2004, sectoral plans and a commitment to multi-annual investment programme. Legislation was enacted (Disability Act 2005; Citizens Information Act 2007) but not all of it was commenced. Key provisions of the Disability Act 2005 were to include the delivery of an individual assessment of health and educational needs and a service statement of the provision to be provided. Sectoral plans were to be developed by six named government departments outlining how the needs of people with disabilities are met and plans for the future. Part 5 of the Act gave legal status to the 3% target for the employment of persons with disability in the public service (DJELR, 2005a). The Citizens Information Act 2007 included provision for a Personal Advocacy Service with a range of statutory powers to advocate with and on behalf of people with disabilities. The Education for Persons with Special Educational Needs Act 2004 (henceforth EPSEN Act) provides for the inclusive education of children with special educational needs and places certain responsibilities on schools in this regard. It also established the National Council for Special Education on a statutory basis.

Section 1 of the EPSEN Act 2004 provides the first statutory definition of special educational needs: 'a restriction in the capacity of a person to participate in and benefit from education on account of an enduring physical, sensory, mental health or learning disability, or any other condition which results in a person learning differently from a person without that condition'. This definition is considered broader than previously contained in the Education Act 1998 with potential implications for considering disability prevalence as well as the resources required to meet these children's needs (Banks and McCoy, 2011). Recent research from the Growing Up in Ireland data (Banks et al, 2016) provides more detailed insights into processes of SEN identification and how children with SEN view school, suggesting that more work is needed to enhance inclusive education in Ireland.

In terms of implementation, the EPSEN Act 2004 brought improvements in promoting inclusive education, backed up in practical terms by way of greater investment, and more special needs assistants and resource teachers were appointed. However, key sections of this Act were deferred in Budget 2009 because of the economic crisis. As of 2016, the following provisions have not been implemented: (1) an educational assessment for all children with special educational needs, (2) a statutory individual educational plan, (3) the delivery of services as outlined in the plan and (4) an independent appeals basis (Bruton, 2016). These core provisions would have made way for an entitlement to such services. The position such as it currently stands is that aspects of the EPSEN Act may be developed via policy developments but on a non-statutory basis initially (Bruton, 2016).

In the case of the Citizens Information Act 2007, the Personal Advocacy Service aspect of the Act was also deferred and a non-statutory National Advocacy Service (NAS) for people with disabilities was instead established in 2011, which is funded by the Citizens Information Board (Fitzgerald, 2015). The NAS provides representative advocacy which 'is a means of empowering people by supporting them to assert their views and claim their entitlements, and where necessary representing and negotiating on their behalf. It is not about making decisions for someone, mediation, counselling, care and support work or consultation' (Fitzgerald, 2015: 5). While the NAS has supported over 2,000 people in its role to date, both Fitzgerald (2015) and Inclusion Ireland (2013) note the limitations imposed by the absence of statutory powers at present and highlight the wider forms of advocacy which could be developed. Inclusion Ireland (2013: 16) argues that:

> the absence of a broad spectrum of advocacy supports impedes the right of significant numbers of people with disabilities to self determination and autonomy. It also affects their right to full and effective participation and inclusion in society, to attend social activities of their choice, and to have their say in the design and delivery of the services and supports they need.

The implementation of the Disability Act 2005 remains incomplete. Part 2 of the Act, which provides for Individual Assessments of Need, is available only to children born since June 2002. Furthermore, less than 60% of the applications for assessments made in 2015 were completed, and the average assessment time was 10.4 months despite the six-month timeframe specified in the legislation (Shanahan, 2016). Older children and adults still do not have access to an Individual Assessment of Need from the HSE. A new National Disability Inclusion Strategy is to be published in 2017.

Assessment of the Disability Act 2005 more generally included concern and disappointment about the lack of an overtly **rights–based approach**. De Wispelaere and Walsh (2007: 535) argued that the Act 'fails to meet the conditions for robust rights–based legislation in relation to disability services. The failure to provide secure access to public services is exacerbated by the fact that there is no genuine right to challenge assessment, service delivery or even the wider policy context, particularly resource commitments.' Finlay (2016) points out

> **A rights-based approach** is one which advocates a guaranteed level of social provision as a matter of right and entitlement. Inequities that often arise in discretionary and variable levels of social supports are thereby removed.

in his recent critique of the Act that 'the word rights never appears once' in the legislation. He notes numerous shortcomings in the Act, highlighting most especially the resource clause contained within it which ultimately, he argues, makes it 'the single most dishonest and fraudulent piece of legislation ever passed by the Oireachtas' (Finlay, 2016). Against this backdrop of resource-related contingencies built into core legislation on disability, significant ECS rights issues remain unresolved for people with disabilities. The stalling of key disability policy provisions during and since the economic crisis occurred alongside the development of plans to reform other aspects of the social care infrastructure which we now consider.

Box 11.4: People with disabilities: key policy and legislative developments

1991	*Needs and Abilities: A Policy for the Intellectually Disabled*
1992	Green Paper on Mental Health
1993	*Report of the Special Education Review Committee*
1996	*Report of the Commission on the Status of People with Disabilities: A Strategy for Equality*
2000	Establishment of the National Disability Authority
2001	Mental Health Act
2001	*Report of the Task Force on Autism*
2002	*Report of the Task Force on Dyslexia*
2004	Education for Persons with Special Educational Needs (EPSEN) Act
2004	*Disability Strategy*
2005	Disability Act
2006	*A Vision for Change: Report of the Expert Group on Mental Health Policy*
2007	Citizens Information Act
2011	*Time to Move on from Congregated Settings: A Strategy for Community Inclusion*
2011	*National Housing Strategy for People with a Disability 2011-2016*
2012	*New Directions: Personal Support Services for Adults with Disabilities*
2012	*Value for Money and Policy Review of Disability Services in Ireland*
2012	*National Review of Autism Services: Past, Present and Way Forward Report*
2013	National Standards for Residential Services for Children and Adults with Disabilities
2014	Safeguarding Vulnerable Persons at Risk of Abuse: National Policy and Procedures
2015	*Comprehensive Employment Strategy for People with Disabilities 2015-2024*
2015	Assisted Decision-Making (Capacity) Act

New directions and a person-centred approach?

A number of policy reports published during the 2010s point to some potentially significant directional shifts in the orientation, quality and regulation of services for people with disabilities with a more person-centred ethos evident in the proposals. The *Time to Move on from Congregated Settings: A Strategy for Community Inclusion* (HSE, 2011) proposes a new model of accommodation and support in the community for the over 4,000 people with disabilities living in congregated settings (ten or more residents). The vision of the Working Group (HSE, 2011: 12) for people living in congregated settings 'requires that this group of people will be actively and effectively supported to live full, inclusive lives at the heart of family, community and society. They should be able to exercise meaningful choice, equal to that of other citizens, when choosing where and with whom they will live'. The Working Group (HSE, 2011: 14) highlights how congregated provision is in breach of the UN CRPD, contrary to the mainstreaming policy in the National Disability Strategy and ultimately, they note that 'the ethical case to move people from isolation to community, and in some cases, from lives lived without dignity, is beyond debate'. It recommends the closure of all congregated settings over a seven-year timeframe with detailed consideration of the policy, including a transitioning programme required to facilitate a model of support 'based on the principles of person centeredness ... with supports tailored to their individual need' (HSE, 2011: 132). In 2015, 145 people moved from congregated to community living, a further 2,725 remain resident in congregated settings (HSE, 2016b). An overdue development, the implementation of this policy will require careful and considered consultation, planning, ongoing support and oversight.

The *Value for Money and Policy Review of Disability Services in Ireland* (DoH, 2012b) and the *New Directions: Personal Support Services for Adults with Disabilities* (HSE, 2012b) reports propose a shift towards a more personalised, user-led and individually funded system of support for people with disabilities. The results of the implementation of individualised funding piloted in four organisations capture the significant potential benefits to individuals alongside the challenges that can also arise (see Fleming, 2016). Following these developments, a Task Force on Personalised Budgets was established in September 2016 and will provide recommendations on the personalised budget model to be adopted in Ireland.

The Transforming Lives programme was established by the HSE (2016b) to oversee the implementation of the *Time to Move On* (HSE, 2011), *New Directions* (HSE, 2012b) and *Value for Money and Policy Review* (DoH, 2012b) policies. Taken together, these policy moves may, contingent on the specifics of their implementation, bring about substantial change in the nature and types of social support infrastructure available to people with disabilities in the future. The shift from a provider-led service to one led by the individual and designed to suit the individual's needs could potentially be transformative, although, the record in relation to the implementation of the National Disability Strategy gives little grounds for optimism. The situation is complicated further by the large number of service stakeholders involved, with different ways of working, ethos and perspectives, much will be required of these organisations, too, if real change is to be delivered (see Linehan et al, 2014). Important, too, will be the protection of personalised budgets and their adaptability to respond to changing needs and circumstances of individuals. The shift towards an increasingly private-market model evident in the home-care support sector for older people discussed earlier points to the necessity of rights-based entitlement to personalised budgets. It is also important to note that opinion on personalised budgets is divided, based on the experiences in the UK over recent years, particularly on the adequacy of funding (Beresford, 2016; Waters, 2016; and see Carter Anand et al, 2012 for an overview of assessments of personalised budgets introduced in various countries). The recommendations of the Task Force on Personalised Budgets are likely to be important in informing the model adopted and in shaping the nature of its benefits to the service user.

Mental health policy

Turning to mental health policy, developments during the 2000s including the Mental Health Act 2001, the establishment of the Mental Health Commission and the publication of *A Vision for Change* (Expert Group on Mental Health Policy, 2006) seemed to indicate that Ireland might finally have been coming of age in respect of its approach to mental health issues and in its delivery of mental health services. The updating of mental health legislation was widely welcomed, particularly with regard to changes in the legal rights of persons admitted to psychiatric hospitals. *A Vision for Change* provided a framework for the development of a comprehensive mental health service with accessible, community-based specialist services, and it adopts a biopsychosocial model with an emphasis on working towards recovery. The full implementation of *A Vision for Change* was expected to take seven to ten years and that would have represented radical progress. However, implementation remains incomplete and, despite considerable progress in some areas and significant commitment, funding and staff shortages remain a problem. Staffing levels in 2015 were approximately 75% of what was recommended in A Vision for Change and as the Mental Health Commission (2016: 7) Chairman notes, 'there is still a significant absence of psychology, social work, occupational therapy and other multidisciplinary team members and we will not have a recovery-orientated service unless staff make-up reflects the move from a purely medical model to a more holistic biopsychosocial one'. Other shortcomings, such as inadequate out-of-hours services, the inappropriate placement of children in adult facilities and the lack of a right to an advocate, remain. Child and Adolescent Mental Health Services are also under-resourced with negative consequences for children in need of their services who experience lengthy waiting times (HSE, 2015 in CRA, 2016: 59). Sapouna and Gijbels (2016: 1–2) refer to numerous other concerns regarding the mental health services including

> coercive practices, lack of treatment choices, abuse of professional power, overreliance on and excessive use of medication, discrimination and stigmatisation, inhumane physical conditions in hospital units, and the lack of meaningful community-based alternatives to hospitalisation.

Furthermore, while the language of 'recovery' and 'user involvement' feature quite prominently in mental health service provision, there are increasing concerns about these terms being assimilated in the current biomedical discourse, thus losing their transformative potential

Considerable problems remain in the availability of services, treatment choices, and supports provided in the Irish mental health services. Recent years have seen important progress in our collective ability to be more open about mental health issues; this has been largely led by individuals and advocacy groups, while state-provided mental health services remain under-resourced and in need of major investment and reform.

SECTION FIVE
CARING, CARERS AND IRISH SOCIAL POLICY

While care is fundamental to human well-being, conceptualising care and caring in social policy terms is a relatively recent endeavour. As welfare states expanded from the 1950s onwards, care and caring were largely taken for granted, as something that would just happen in the context of the family. This belief was later challenged, largely within feminist social policy, both in terms of the gendered assumptions underpinning the development of the welfare state itself and through which the male breadwinner model of welfare was built on the notion of male 'earning' female 'caring' dichotomy.

Much of the early literature that emerged on caring highlighted the negative consequences of caring, often to the neglect of care-receiver experiences. The disability movement in particular challenged this approach, drawing attention to its impact in re-enforcing a dependency status on care receivers for example. More recent exposition of carer issues brought greater clarity to the various dimensions of care. Tronto (1993), for example, saw care as both a disposition and an activity and stressed the relational aspect of care via a process that includes: caring about, taking care of, caregiving and care-receiving. The interdependence at the core of care relations became increasingly recognised in the literature and the feminist development of 'an ethic of care' (see Chapter Five) contributed to enhancing our ways of understanding care relations. Williams (2001), for example, advocates the development of a new ethic of care which could balance the long-established ethic of work as a new basis of welfare citizenship. For this to be realised in terms of citizenship means complementing the 'rational economic actor model of the citizen' with a 'Care-Full model of the citizen, one that recognises the centrality of care and love relations to the mental health and well-being of all members of society' (Lynch and Lyons, 2008: 183).

Lynch (2014: 177) develops the concept of affective equality in which attention is given to securing equality in both 'the distribution of the nurturing provided through love, care and solidarity relationships' and 'in the doing of emotional and other work involved in creating love, care and solidarity relations'. Based on the recognition of humans as relational, we live our lives in various stages of dependency and interdependency, are vulnerable, and have relational feelings and identities. The citizen is therefore both 'a carer and care recipient both in the public and the private domain of life' (Lynch, 2014: 177). Seen in this way, affective equality marks an important theoretical contribution to developing ways of thinking about receiving and giving care as central to human relations. It also provides a framework for the identification of long-standing affective inequalities: directly, where people do not receive the love, care and solidarity they need and where 'burdens and pleasures of care and love work are unequally distributed'; and indirectly, where 'people are not recognized economically, politically, and/or culturally ... and when love, care, and solidarity work is trivialized by omission from public discourse' (Lynch, 2014: 177). Recognition of affective inequalities forces us to think critically about the sustained neglect of these issues in social policy.

The relative decline of the male breadwinner model, reflected in the growing number of women occupied in the formal labour market and the intensification of policy measures aimed at maximising employment rates have, over time, led to the emergence of 'adult worker'- and 'dual earner'-centred models (Williams, 2010). One of the consequences of this shift has been its exposure of the role and extent of care in society, previously hidden in the private family domain. It also 'placed the issue of care more centrally on the political agenda, providing claims makers for social justice care with some new political opportunities' (Williams, 2010: 5). Care applies and is relevant to many different facets of life and occurs in many different contexts, which presents a considerable challenge to how we understand and accommodate care and care relations. Carers themselves are often conflicted by the term and its meaning for them; family carers are still mothers, sons, partners and many 'prefer to identify themselves by their relationship to the person "cared for" rather than by the tasks or duties of "caring"' (Care Alliance Ireland, 2015: 9). The wider question of how care and care relations are conceptualised, recognised and valued in society generally and in social policy in particular is also prescient.

The assumed place of care and caring in Irish social policy

The consequences of the long-standing neglect of issues of care and caring is acutely evident in the Irish policy context. The tradition of informal care arrangements coupled with the considerable role played by the voluntary sector (including the Church) in the provision of many of the personal social services has meant that in overall terms there is a long history of leaving care work to women within the home and to the informal and voluntary sectors. As Fanning (2006: 15) notes, 'the emphasis on the unpaid role of women as carers within the Irish welfare economy was sustained in part by discrimination.' The recognition afforded to women within the home in the Constitution was provided without reference to the choices, autonomy or social rights of women, drawn up as it was without consideration of the notion of gender equality. Seen in this way, women were denied choice regarding the basis of their participation in society, an issue which the feminist movement subsequently challenged. This is not to say that women did not want to care or did not value it, rather what feminists seek is that this activity actually be recognised and valued in a meaningful and respectful way. What is increasingly argued for is the right to care; both in the sense of providing and receiving care, as a critical element of all our social rights.

Carer specific welfare measures and supports in Ireland come primarily by way of the social protection system (see Box 11.5). The first acknowledgement of informal or family carers was in the late 1960s when the Prescribed Relatives Allowance was introduced and made payable to and in respect of persons aged over 70 years requiring full-time care. The Domiciliary Care Allowance, introduced in 1973, provides a monthly payment in respect of children up to 16 years who owing to a disability require continual care as per medical guidelines. It is not means-tested. The Carers Allowance replaced the Prescribed Relatives Allowance in 1990 and the terms of eligibility have since been broadened (allowing a number of hours of paid employment, for example) but it remains a means-tested payment. A social insurance-based Carers Benefit was introduced in 2001 and it provides for persons to take time off work (up to 104 weeks) to provide full-time care. The Carers Benefit is payable to the carer during this period. The take-up of this benefit has been low; there have been fewer than 2,000 recipients per annum since the late 2000s (DSP, 2015). A Carer's Support Grant (formerly the Respite Care Grant) is an annual payment made to recipients of the weekly carer-related payments outlined. Full-time carers not in receipt of a carer's payment may apply for the grant but there are strict eligibility criteria attached. Outside of the social protection system, the health service is crucial in the provision of community-based supports in sustaining the care provided in the home, as outlined in section two. Family carers do not receive any additional health-service rights in Ireland. This contrasts with the situation in Britain where full-time adult carers have a legal entitlement to assessment and support. Parent carers and young carers have similar assessment rights in Britain also. The voluntary sector remains a key source of support and advocacy for carers in Ireland.

Box 11.5: Carers and caring: key policy and legislative developments

1990   Carers Allowance

2001   Carers Benefit

2001   Carer's Leave Act

2012   *National Carers' Strategy: Recognised, Supported, Empowered*

Counting carers and the pursuit of recognition

The long-standing invisibility of family and informal carers is illustrated by the fact that little official data was collected about them until relatively recently. The first census data generated on the level and extent of caring was gathered in Census 2002. Subsequent censuses have included a question which refers specifically to 'a friend or family member with a long-term illness, a health problem or a disability' (including those associated with old age). Census 2011 found that 4.1% of the population (187,112) was engaged in regular unpaid caring activities in Ireland. Despite their also low visibility, male carers (72,999) account for 39% of carers in 2011 (CSO, 2012a). Older people (aged 70+) provided nearly 800,000 hours care per week in 2011. In this regard, the HSE (2015: 96) acknowledges that 'the fastest growing population group providing care is the older population where there is a greater risk of the carer having or developing health problems themselves. Such caring situations require greater supports from the state services and are at greater risk of sudden breakdown'. More generally, for people involved in significant family or informal care, studies point to issues related to limited employment opportunities; higher risk of poverty; greater social isolation; and risk of various adverse health impacts (Care Alliance Ireland, 2016). Children (under 15 years) were also including in questions related to caring in Census 2011. It found that 4,200 children provided nearly 40,000 hours of unpaid care per week in 2011 (CSO, 2012a). Little was known about the lives and experiences of young carers in Ireland until relatively recently. Fives et al (2010) document some important insights into the different experiences of children and young people providing care in the home. Their study finds both positive (greater connectedness to the person cared for, maturity; compassion) and negative (school absence, distraction at school, lack of time for leisure/friends leading to social isolation, illness, being 'on call' and worry, resentment and boredom) impacts of caring on their lives.

Carers and caring have only emerged on the Irish public policy agenda since the 2000s and even then it might be argued that this was primarily in response to the care gaps and pressures exposed primarily by women's greater labour-market participation and the economic imperatives therein. Following a government commitment to develop a National Carers Strategy, a series of consultation seminars was held with carers in 2007. The *Listening to Carers: Report on a Nation-wide Carer Consultation* (Carers Association et al, 2008) documented the key issues that arise for carers and provided an insight into the impact of neglect on this group. The report highlighted 'an urgent need for action' and the overarching message from the report was 'that carers in Ireland are seeking and need a whole new relationship and interface with the state and support services to maintain them in their caring role' (Carers Association et al, 2008: v). Inadequate availability of home and community care services and the tendency to take the availability of family care for granted were noted. The 'arm's length' approach (Carers Association et al, 2008: 5) to carers was evidenced by the poor availability of information, long delays, fragmentation and a lack of coordination, and a lack of respect for carers. In terms of the needs of carers, a series of recommendations was made regarding the development of services and supports (training for carers, respite, needs assessment for carers), income supports (adequate financial recognition, security for the future), employment and work/ life balance, and social inclusion. A three-pillar approach was advocated based on a fair shouldering of the caring responsibility by the state, adequate income support for carers and a range of supports that target and meet carers' needs. For this to be realised, a substantial overhaul of current health and personal social services practices would be required.

Publication of a National Strategy was subsequently cancelled owing to the economic crisis; it was finally launched in July 2012. Four National Goals outlined in the *National Carers' Strategy: Recognised, Supported, Empowered* (DoH, 2012c: 10) aim to

1. Recognise the value and contribution of carers and promote their inclusion in decisions relating to the person that they are caring for
2. Support carers to manage their physical, mental and emotional health and well-being
3. Support carers to care with confidence through the provision of adequate information, training, services and supports
4. Empower carers to participate as fully as possible in economic and social life

A total of 42 actions were to be achieved by the relevant government departments in the short to medium term, with progress reports issued on implementation. The detailed policy objectives developed in the Strategy raised awareness about the need to better acknowledge the role of carers and accommodate their input across relevant government agencies and departments. In formal policy terms, the Strategy is an important statement of recognition of carers and their contribution. However, the Strategy expressly does not commit any extra resources or confer any new rights on carers in Ireland. It lacks ambition and the qualifications it contains suggest that not only must economic circumstances improve but a future policy framework for carers is contingent on wider reforms in the health service. The long delay in its publication was compounded by the constraints outlined in its opening page which contained any sense of expectation, stating that 'it is difficult at this point to develop longer-term commitments or proposals for the future. The Strategy, therefore, concentrates on Actions for the short to medium term, which can, to the greatest extent possible, be achieved on a cost neutral basis' (DoH, 2012c: 4).

The poor pace of its implementation continues to be a source of frustration. The National Carers Strategy Monitoring Group (2016), comprising carer organisations and family carers, reports a very mixed picture in its assessment of the implementation of the Strategy for the period to September 2015. Of the 42 actions: one (annual carers' forum) had been implemented in full; 14 actions are considered to have made good progress with positive results for carers; initial progress has been made on a further seven; no progress is reported in respect of 17 actions and the situation regarding three (carers' involvement in discharge planning; flexible and person-centred respite options; identification of gaps in existing services and the development of performance indicators for the provision of respite services) actions are considered to have worsened since the Strategy was launched in 2012. The impact of recent austerity has effected carers and care recipients too (Care Alliance Ireland, 2016). In overall terms, disadvantages often experienced by family carers are exacerbated by the lack of robust social supports. Carers and their advocates have shown remarkable forbearance over the last decade; policy developments do not seem to have been matched by any significant service improvements to date.

The approach to care more broadly defined raises yet more issues. For instance, census information on caring excludes one of the most common caring activities; that of caring for children. Addressing this point, Lynch and Lyons (2008: 170) argue that:

> Even though it is no doubt unintentional, the failure to collect data on hours spent on child care work in the Census, means that child care, which is *the* major form of care work in Irish society, is not counted in terms of work hours. Yet it is the form of care work that women of all social classes and ages are significantly more likely to undertake than men. There is a deeply patriarchal set of assumptions hiding women's unpaid work in the household in this way; it is a form of institutionalised sexism that needs to be addressed.

While recent policies have brought about some improvements in the availability of early childcare and education provision as outlined earlier, Ireland continues to underinvest in childcare overall. Childcare costs in Ireland remain amongst the most expensive in the OECD, accounting for 27.4% of two-parent-family net income and 41.6% of lone-parent-family net income, compared to the 12.6% and 13.5% OECD averages respectively (OECD, 2016c). The prohibitive cost of childcare re-enforces gendered and familial caring expectations, with significant implications for equality and economic security for women in particular. A study conducted by the Irish Congress of Trade Unions (2016) found that 29% of respondents had extended family as their main form of childcare. McGarrigle and Kenny (2013) similarly report that one third of women aged 50-69 look after their grandchildren (on average 34 hours per month). There is therefore a huge reliance on the extended family to support the caring of children, but this reality is largely neglected in the formal policy domain.

The so-called 'sandwich generation' of women aged 50-69 with living parents and children are also heavily involved in a range of 'transfers of financial care and non-financial care between the generations' (McGarrigle and Kenny, 2013: 8). Furthermore, when the social protection arrangements for full-time carers are considered, especially those in receipt of Carer's Allowance, it is important to note that it remains a means-tested payment with particular employment rules. The overall impact of these rules require closer examination because as Murphy (2007: 113) notes: 'it has to be asked whether women (by far the primary recipients of carer's allowance) are being pushed towards a triple burden of childcare, adult care and paid employment and how this is related to the mental and physical health of these women.'

The Irish male breadwinner model legacy lives on, in what Murphy (2011: 47) describes as 'a gender differentiated model, like the Mother-Worker approach' underpinned by various fragmented tax and social protection provisions. Expectations of carers and of women in particular, remain deeply embedded in a largely implicit policy framework which preferences familial care but without adequate care supports. Where supports are available they remain a mix of limited state provision and increasingly market-based solutions, contingent on ability to pay. It is clear that carers, and by association the people receiving care, are still not adequately recognised or supported and affective inequalities are widespread. There is little robust public or political consideration of the consequences of these shortcomings. We are still faced with what Fanning and Rush (2006: 4) refer to as a 'social care infrastructure deficit', in which policy and its implementation has not kept pace with the challenges that arise. Addressing this requires that the priorities of the Irish welfare state are made explicit and include recognition of, and a vision for, the place of care in contemporary Irish society.

Chapter summary

- This chapter examined the ways in which social policy attends to the needs and rights of various social groups in society. The approach to difference and differentiated need has historically been problematised. Major policy developments are frequently overshadowed by a continuing reluctance to deliver a rights-based approach to social policy.
- Social policy for children has seen substantial development and innovation since the 1990s. The challenge now is to attend to persisting impediments such as child poverty and various social service shortcomings, particularly in meeting the needs of vulnerable children.
- Despite the early recognition of the needs of older people in terms of pensions, contemporary social policy is marked by a number of challenges. The existence of ageism, the lack of entitlement to home supports if required, and no coherent vision for these services present as considerable challenges to achieving a more 'age-friendly society'.
- The marginalisation of people with disabilities in the past has been significantly challenged. Advances have been made, although major issues remain in the lack of rights-based provision in education and health, and in terms of quality of life more generally. Recent policy initiatives indicate plans for a more person-centred approach, which may bring about radical reorientation in the delivery of supports, depending on the approach taken to their implementation. However, lessons from the shortcomings in the Disability Act 2005 require us to be vigilant.

- Caring remains one of the most vital yet neglected aspects of human well-being. The position of carers has largely been taken for granted. Old assumptions are increasingly challenged by circumstance and in the demands for carers to be recognised. As we now know, however, formal policy recognition does not necessarily rights provide.
- Emerging trends in the protection of the welfare of various groups include the greater role of regulation and inspection of services and standards, the influence of external monitoring and the stronger voice being given to social rights as a human rights issue in Ireland. For all of these developments, significant obstacles persist in the realisation of different needs and rights in the operation of Irish social policy.

Discussion points
- Analyse the notion of a 'rights-based' approach and discuss its implications with reference to any social group(s).
- Is Ireland an 'age-friendly' society?
- Assess the status and recognition of care and caring in Irish social policy and in Irish society.

Further reading list

CRA (Children's Rights Alliance) (2016) *Children's Rights Alliance report card 2016: Is government keeping its promises to children?*, Dublin: CRA [and consult the CRA website for periodic updates: www.childrensrights.ie]

Lynch, K (2007) 'Love labour as a distinct and non-commodifiable form of care labour', *The Sociological Review*, 55:3, 550-70

Moran, J (2013) *Unfinished business: Social policy for social care students in Ireland*, Dublin: Orpen Press

Walsh, K, Carney, GM and Ní Léime, Á (eds) (2015) *Ageing through austerity: Critical perspectives from Ireland*, Bristol: Policy Press

twelve

Social policy and social groups: issues of diversity and discrimination

This chapter continues the focus on social groups and social policy begun in the previous chapter. Here we focus on groups whose identities contribute to the diversity of Irish society, but whose recognition and realisation of rights has been problematic, and issues of discrimination arise in varying ways. The chapter initially concentrates on immigration and the policy responses to the unprecedented growth of ethnic diversity in Ireland. The chapter also discusses the position of Travellers in Irish society as an indigenous minority ethnic group, and the position of lesbian, gay, bisexual and transgender (LGBT) people, largely invisible minorities until recently.

All of these groups pose challenges to the dominant construction of Irish identity and citizenship reflecting a homogeneous nation built on being white, settled and heterosexual. They draw attention to how citizenship creates boundaries which include and exclude. As groups and identities which display greater diversity and difference have become more visible in Irish society, and to varying degrees have campaigned for rights and recognition, legislation, institutional structures and policies have grown around issues of equality, racism, integration and interculturalism. In particular these issues have influenced the language and design of social policy and social services; however, issues such as differential treatment and gaps between policy discourse and policy practice remain. Inequality, exclusion, racism and the privileging of heterosexuality therefore are problematic in various ways for the groups discussed in this chapter.

Chapter outline

- Section one focuses on the evolution of immigration policy and the treatment of immigrants as migrant workers, asylum seekers and refugees. The issue of differential treatment and its effects, both across and within these groups in relation to social policy, citizenship and integration is examined.
- Section two considers the concept of ethnicity in relation to Travellers and their overall status and well-being in Irish society. We review relevant social policy developments which, despite some minor improvements, have perpetuated Traveller disadvantage and discrimination.
- Section three considers the growing visibility of sexual and gender diversity and LGBT politics before going on to examine issues regarding LGBT rights, recognition and equality in Irish society.

SECTION ONE

IMMIGRATION AND IRISH SOCIAL POLICY

Immigration, racism and diversity

Since the mid-1990s, Ireland has experienced a period of significant transformation. A substantial part of this is related to **migration**, specifically **immigration**. Recent immigration does not spell the first instance of diversity and difference in Irish society. This is evident in the issues raised in discussion of other social groups in both this and the previous chapter; however, the scale of immigration brings a new dimension to issues of difference, diversity and racism. When large-scale immigration occurs quite rapidly and difference becomes more readily visible, this prompts greater questioning of issues such as Irish citizenship, who is Irish and who can be an Irish citizen, and what rights and entitlements are afforded to non-citizens.

> **Migration, immigration, emigration**: migration refers to movement from one country to live in another: immigration refers to movement into a country, and emigration to movement from a country.

Consequently the period since the mid-1990s has been a relatively intense one in terms of legislative change concerning immigration and citizenship. As Fanning (2012) suggests, responses to difference and differential state treatment cannot be explained away by xenophobia or 'fear of the stranger' by the fact that Ireland was a largely homogeneous country until recently. Rather, the crafting of migration policy needs to be understood in terms of how it codes or makes assumptions about 'race' and racial difference, inferiority and superiority.

These questions and issues are reflected in the wider context of understanding contemporary patterns of racism and racialisation in which the Irish case can be placed. Differential and hierarchical treatment can be tied to racist patterns of discrimination which can emerge in multiple forms, where immigrants en masse, or particular categories of immigrants such as asylum seekers, or particular nationalities, religious or ethnic minorities, are characterised by particular assumptions about 'race' and culture, from a white/Western vantage point. For Lentin (2008: xiii) 'racism cannot be understood without a parallel understanding of how and why we have come to live as citizens of defined states, based on the idea of a common ethnic and political heritage, territorially bound by legal frontiers and with limited membership'. In this regard, the foundations of contemporary citizenship regimes can be traced back to the late nineteenth and early twentieth centuries when countries first introduced legislation to control the movement of 'aliens' across national borders. Further rounds of rules around movement and membership can be observed in relation to refugee movement post-Second World War; the growth of rules around entry to the EU; and the related trends of neo-liberalism and economic globalisation associated with flows of labour from peripheral to core economic regions of the globe.

Racism is central to the regulation of migration and the related construction of national identity and rules of belonging. For Garner (2013: 175-6), for example, racism as a:

> set of ideas and practices ... functions in the ways people routinely think about groups of people who are 'not like us' and in how the 'us' is imagined, in the ways laws operate, and in the way people have differential access to resources and services. ... racism is about power differentials encapsulated in social systems.

Moreover, racism is built, not only nor even necessarily on physical difference, but increasingly on cultural difference. Explicit reference to race or racial difference is rare in public and political discourse. This is captured by concepts such as 'racism without race' (Lentin and McVeigh, 2006; Garner, 2009), which conveys the way in which racism is still highly salient but is, for the most part, politically and socially taboo. The salience of race and racism instead plays out in processes of racialisation; particular cultural characteristics or behavioural traits are associated with particular groups of people, which have the effect of racialising difference and creating hierarchies of entitlement and belonging. As Lentin (2008: xv) puts it,

> racialisation involves endowing the characteristics, appearances, traditions, and lifestyles attributed to groups of different 'others' with negative signifiers that are deemed to be natural and insurmountable. The development of a racialised discourse about a group of people provides justification for their discrimination. It puts into words the very thing about a particular group that is said to disturb us and pose a threat to our way of life.

Central to this process, in the context of economic globalisation and the competition and insecurity it engenders, is that fact that 'today's global racism divides the rich and poor worlds, and is no longer a simple black-and-white issue' (Lentin, 2008: xv). Economic fears and insecurities are meshed with assumptions about culture and cultural difference, and who belongs to a nation and has legitimate rights, and who doesn't. Migrants and their characteristics are judged and categorised predominantly on their economic merits; of how they contribute to alleviating labour shortages or how their 'talent' contributes to a country's economic prosperity. By the same logic migrants en masse or particular categories of migrants, such as asylum seekers, are framed as a drain on resources, and a threat to social cohesion and the national characteristics that, to channel Donald Trump, make a nation 'great'.

Returning to the specifics of the Irish case, prior to the 1990s immigration flows into Ireland were relatively small and did not produce a significant increase in diversity. The main groups that immigrated to Ireland were returning Irish emigrants, small numbers of high-skilled migrants, and people coming from continental Europe and the UK for countercultural reasons or to retire. Very small numbers of **programme refugees** came to Ireland including Hungarians in the 1950s, Chileans and Vietnamese in the 1970s, and Iranians in the 1980s (Fanning, 2012). Groups more associated with contemporary migration patterns were also present in smaller numbers, including Roma coming to do seasonal and temporary work, and Muslims, from a range of ethnic and national backgrounds, coming as students (Nasc, 2013; Carr and Haynes, 2015). For the most part, however, these forms of immigration consisted mainly of people who were not significantly 'different' from the existing Irish population. Their presence did not challenge existing interpretations of Irishness and Irish culture as white and Catholic, there were no major increases in demand for social services and user groups remained relatively homogenous.

> **Programme refugees** are refugees invited to a country by a government, already recognised as a refugee (that is, does not have to go through the asylum seeking process once in the country), usually on the basis of a humanitarian request.

By the late 1990s new immigration flows changed this equilibrium. The pace and scale of change was dramatic; Ireland became a multi-ethnic nation over a much shorter timescale compared to other European countries with longer histories of immigration. The bulk of the rise in immigration has been labour migration. The relatively small high-skills category of immigrants prior to the 1990s was significantly augmented by large numbers of both high- and low-skilled migrants coming to Ireland in response to labour shortages during the economic boom. The other main change in immigration is related to asylum seeking, which rose from a very small base. The recession halted these trends somewhat. Between 2010 and 2015 emigration outpaced immigration, beginning with people from elsewhere in the EU, followed by a rise in Irish people emigrating. More recently stronger immigration flows have returned, composed of a mix of returning Irish and other people, principally from non–EU countries (González Pandiella, 2016; see also Figure 12.1). Numbers seeking asylum (see Figure 12.2) have also begun

Figure 12.1: Emigration, immigration and net migration, 1990–2016

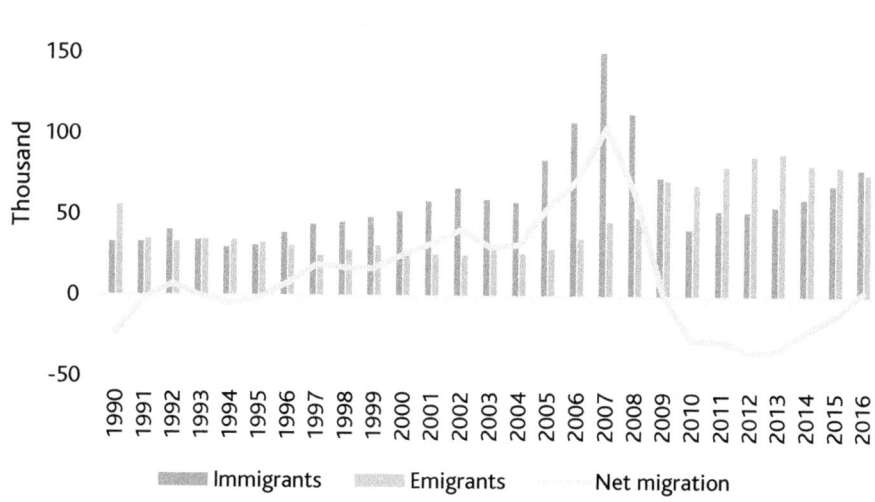

Source: CSO annual population estimates

Figure 12.2: Asylum-seeking trends, 1992–2015

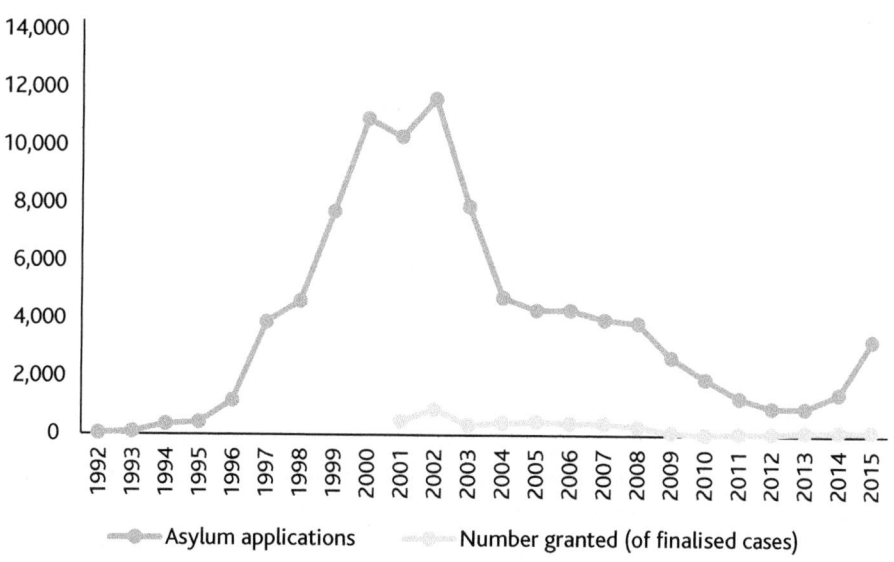

Source: ORAC annual reports (various years)

to rise, reflecting a global growth in asylum seeking arising from factors such as armed conflict and human rights abuses.

Since the 1990s, therefore, the composition of the Irish population has changed, with significant growth in the numbers whose nationality is not Irish. The proportion of non-Irish citizens grew from 5.8% of the population in 2002, the first time the Census included the question 'what is your nationality?', to 9.9% in 2006. Their share of the population continued to grow, albeit more slowly through the early years of the crisis, to 12% in 2011 (CSO, 2012b). The population also became more ethnically diverse. In 2006 the census included a question on cultural background for the first time. When results between 2006 and 2011 are compared, the greatest changes can be observed in the 'White Irish' and 'Any other White background' categories. The former category decreased from 87.4% to 84.5% of the population, while the latter grew from 6.9% to 9.1%. People born in Poland (122,585) and in the UK (112,759) were the two largest nationalities after Irish in the 2011 Census. There are therefore limits to how diverse Ireland has become since the 1990s, reflecting 'a diversification of whiteness' (Garner, 2013: 194). This in turn is related to shifting rules around migration, asylum seeking and citizenship. Across the board the rights and entitlements of immigrants, whether as workers, asylum seekers or refugees are calibrated and categorised, creating grades of exclusion and inclusion in Irish society. As we go on to examine in this section, much of this rests on the degree to which various immigrant groups are considered compatible with Ireland's economic interests and the degree to which they **assimilate** into Ireland's predominantly monocultural tribal notion of Irishness.

Assimilation refers to the absorption into a dominant majority of a usually smaller minority group which as a result loses its group specificity and awareness of itself as a group.

Box 12.1: Key immigration policy and legislative developments

1996	Refugee Act
1999	*Integration: A two way process*
1999/2003/2004	Immigration Acts
2000	Illegal Immigrants (Trafficking) Act
2000	Dispersal and Direct Provision Scheme
2001/2004	Irish Nationality and Citizenship Acts
2003/2006	Employment Permits Acts: **2014** Employment Permits (Amendment) Act
2004	Habitual Residence Condition
2005	*Planning for Diversity National Action Plan Against Racism 2005–2008*
2007	Establishment of the Office of the Minister for Integration: Renamed and restructured as the **2011** Office for the Promotion of Migrant Integration

2008	*Migration Nation Statement on Integration Strategy and Diversity Management*
2008/2010	Immigration, Residence and Protection Bills
2011	*Ireland's National Traveller/Roma Integration Strategy*
2015	*Working Group to Report to Government on Improvements to the Protection Process, Including Direct Provision and Supports to Asylum Seekers*
2015	International Protection Act

Immigration policy and labour migration

The Aliens Act 1935 was one of the early pieces of immigration legislation in Ireland and the basis for regulating migrant movement, residence and right to work within the state. Subsequently Ireland's entry to the EEC in 1973 changed the status of immigrants from other EEC countries due to the right to freedom of movement of workers that came with EEC membership. Freedom of movement was widened to citizens of European Economic Area (EEA) countries in 1992. The EEA includes all EU member countries, Iceland, Norway and Liechtenstein. In 1993 the Maastricht Treaty introduced the right to freedom of movement of all citizens of the EU. In general, EU citizens resident within Ireland have the same rights as Irish citizens to social services. With the expansion of the EU in 2004 to include ten new member states, existing member states were given the option to impose employment restrictions for up to seven years on citizens of new member states. In 2004 Ireland, the UK and Sweden were the only countries to immediately extend the right to work to citizens from the 2004 new member states. Romanians and Bulgarians were not given the right to work in Ireland when their countries joined the EU in 2007, while Croatians were when Croatia joined in 2013.

Immigration policy and non-EEA migrant workers

In contrast to EU residents in Ireland, a more complex and differentiated regime prevails for non-EEA immigrants, also referred to as Third Country Nationals. In the past Ireland had an ad hoc, liberal and employer-led approach to economic immigration (Ruhs, 2005). Employers were given the freedom to recruit, through work visas and permits, as many non-EEA workers as they needed for whatever job. These were generally issued on a guest-worker basis; permit holders were discouraged from taking up permanent residence in Ireland (Boucher, 2010). In anticipation of EU enlargement the state began to develop a more interventionist role, which has seen a gradual tightening of regulations and a focus on higher-paying jobs. At the same time, immigration policy is becoming more finely tuned in response to global competition for workers with particular skills, epitomised by the so-called global war for talent. This has led to more controls on low-skilled labour migration and greater distinctions between conditions, rights and incentives for high-skilled versus low-skilled workers.

Under the Employment Permits (Amendment) Act 2014, nine types of work permit are in operation, covering a range of situations such as intra-company transfers and being a dependant/partner/spouse. Across the range of permits, the principal distinction is between General Employment Permits and Critical Skills Employment Permits, formerly known as Green Cards. Critical Skills Employment Permits are determined by a regularly revised critical skills list that contains occupations which are in short supply, such as IT and healthcare. These permits are generally granted to those earning over €60,000 a year and dependant/ partner/spouse permits are immediately issued if required. Residency rules are designed to encourage permanent residency: the initial job tied to the permit must be two years in duration, after which time the permit holder may apply to reside and work in Ireland without requiring a permit. Further incentives favour very well-paid migrants. Thus high-income migrants (both Irish and non-Irish) with a salary of €75,000 benefit from the Special Assignee Relief Programme (SARP) introduced in 2009. Under the programme, 30% of one's income over €75,000 is disregarded for income tax. General Employment Permits are linked with jobs with lower earnings limits (generally at least €30,000) and apply to all jobs except those on an ineligible occupations list. A labour test is required (advertising a vacancy to test if it is taken up by an EU worker) and the permit lasts for two years, renewable for another three years, after which time the permit holder may apply for permanent residency.

Box 12.2: Roma in Ireland

The position of Roma in Ireland illustrates the complexities of migration policy.

Roma people comprise a very broad ethnic group and the term Roma in Europe encompasses a range of groups including Roma, Gypsies, Travellers, Sinti, Ashkali and others. Roma in Ireland refers to non-Traveller or migrant Roma, the majority of whom are from Romania, but also include some from Hungary, the Czech Republic and Poland. Up to 10,000 Roma are estimated to live in Ireland.

Prior to 2007, Roma from Romania could to come to Ireland either to work under Ireland's work permit scheme or as asylum seekers. On the accession of Romania and Bulgaria to the EU and under EU protocol, Roma, as EU citizens, were no longer permitted to seek asylum, and because Ireland did not extend the right to work to EU members from these countries until 2012, Roma were only allowed to reside in Ireland on the basis of being self-supporting/ self-employed or under work permit rules.

Regardless of their shifting migration status, which has often made access to social rights unclear, Roma in Ireland endure disproportionate levels of deprivation and anti-Roma racism. This includes institutional racism via state agencies such as the Gardaí and via legislation primarily targeted as Roma, such as the Criminal Justice (Public Order) Act 2011, which makes certain behaviours associated with begging an offence and is known as the 'Roma Begging Law' (Nasc, 2013; Logan, 2014).

Under the EU Framework for National Roma Integration Strategies 2011, each member state is required to produce a strategy on Roma integration. *Ireland's National Traveller/ Roma Integration Strategy* was published (DJE, 2011); however, in its review of EU members' strategies, the European Commission was pointedly critical of Ireland's lack of funding, targets and timelines. A new strategy is being prepared.

Discrimination and social rights

Besides a selective group of highly desired global workers, in general migrants fare less well than Irish nationals when it comes to rates of pay, poverty and unemployment; access to promotion and to professional and managerial occupations; and the likelihood of experiencing discrimination both in employment and searching for employment (Conroy and Brennan, 2003; MRCI, 2007; McGinnity and Lunn, 2011; Zimmermann et al, 2012; Kingston et al, 2015). These inequalities have been present during both Ireland's boom and bust, and they persist despite the fact that non–Irish nationals tend to be more highly educated; approximately 40% hold a third–level degree, compared to just over 30% of Irish nationals (González Pandiella, 2016).

General work permit holders have also been found at greater risk of discrimination and exploitation (DoJE, 2011); situations which are compounded by the fact that employment permits are tied to a particular job and employer. As the Migrant Rights Centre Ireland (MRCI) (MRCI, 2015: 12) has found,

> many workers have been and continue to be reminded by their employers that their stay in the country is dependent on their employment and particularly on the employment specified in the permit. As such, many workers are forced to accept exploitative conditions of employment in order to retain their work permit and remain documented in the State.

In addition, Pillinger (2006) documents gender–based discrimination for female migrant workers, especially denial of rights and entitlements in relation to pregnancy. These problems are compounded by high rates of non–compliance with labour law regarding conditions such as rates of pay and overtime, despite the fact that the National Employment Rights Agency was set up in 2008 to monitor compliance, partly in response to high-profile cases of migration worker exploitation.

The MRCI (2016) also points to a growing problem of undocumented migrants, generated by the tightening of the migrant permits regime. Between 20,000 and 26,000 undocumented migrants are estimated to reside in Ireland, the majority of whom are in precarious, low-paid work in sectors such as domestic work, catering and cleaning. Some progress was made, at least for migrant workers who previously had permits, with the introduction of Reactivation Permits in the Employment Permits (Amendment) Act 2014. These are granted to workers who find themselves without a permit through no fault of their own, due, for example, to employer exploitation or deception.

Social rights and habitual residence condition

All workers, Irish, EEA and non-EEA, have the same protection and entitlements under labour law regarding rights such as maternity leave, parental leave, the minimum wage, working time and holiday entitlements, and redundancy payments. Distinctions and gradations begin to apply when it comes to entitlements to social services. Non-EEA workers for example, are not entitled to apply for social housing, but they do have access to publicly provided healthcare and children of all migrants have the same access to education as Irish children aged under 18. Access to social security became particularly restricted on foot of EU enlargement in 2004 with the introduction of the Habitual Residence Condition (HRC). It was introduced to prevent the perceived risk that people would move to Ireland to avail of the social welfare system rather than to take up employment. Effectively racialising migrant workers, when announcing the HRC the minister for social and family affairs declared that: 'I will not allow our social welfare system to become overburdened and I will be taking the precaution of ring fencing that system of social protection ...We need to ensure that our social welfare system and other public services are not open to abuse' (DSFA, 2004).

More broadly referred to as 'benefit tourism' or 'welfare tourism', this concern has become more acute across Europe in the context of the post-2008 economic crisis and an increase in anti-immigrant sentiment, which, among other factors, contributed to 'Brexit' in the UK. However, the notion of welfare tourism is strongly contested and there is scant empirical evidence of its occurrence, either in Ireland (Corrigan, 2010) or elsewhere in the EU (Zimmermann et al, 2012).

The HRC stipulates that all applicants, regardless of nationality, have to satisfy a residency condition for social assistance payments. In general, an applicant who has been present in Ireland for two years or more, works and intends to remain in Ireland as their permanent home satisfies the condition. Amendments were made to the system after the European Commission found that the condition contravened EU law. Consequently EEA citizens working in Ireland and who have 'a history of working in the state' but not necessarily fulfilling the HRC became re-eligible for supplementary welfare allowance and family payments.

Despite this easing of some the severities of the HRC, deciding criteria are found to be open to ambiguous and speculative interpretation, particularly as to what constitutes 'a history of working in the state' and the intention to remain in Ireland (MRCI, 2006; González Pandiella, 2016). Consequently cases of denial of benefit entitlements as a result of misapplication of the HRC are a problem (Crosscare et al, 2012).

The HRC can have a particularly negative impact on work permit holders, contributing to workplace exploitation by locking a person into an undesirable job when there is no alternative but unemployment and no social welfare support. Work permit holders who cannot work because of illness or injury are also particularly vulnerable, and those without work are at high risk of homelessness. HRC notwithstanding, migrant workers have also been found reluctant to apply for social welfare support, fearful of the implications for their residency status which in some cases includes stipulations such as not posing a 'burden' on the state (Zimmerman et al, 2012).

Asylum seekers and refugees

An asylum seeker is a person who seeks to be recognised as a refugee in accordance with the terms of the 1951 UN Geneva Convention relating to the status of refugees. If an asylum-seeker's claim for refuge is recognised then that person's status moves from an asylum seeker to a refugee. A refugee is a person who

> owing to a well-founded fear of being persecuted for reasons of race, religion, nationality, membership of a particular social group or political opinion, is outside the country of his nationality and is unable or, owing to such fear, is unwilling to avail himself of the protection of that country; or who, not having nationality and being outside the country of his former habitual residence, is unable or owing to such fear, is unwilling to return to it (Article 1A(2) UN General Assembly, 1951).

Initially the Convention referred to Europe only and as Mac Éinrí (2006: 359) points out, 'it reflected a post-WWII Cold War perspective which tended to see refugees in Europe ... as heroic individuals fleeing from Communism'.

From the 1990s asylum-seeking trends were more strongly related to movement from underdeveloped Southern countries to wealthy Northern countries. As well as fleeing situations of war and conflict, reasons for leaving include poverty, famine and environmental disasters; situations not covered under the original convention. In some cases these reasons overlap with economic reasons as they involve situations where it is impossible to maintain a livelihood. However, economic refugees are also not recognised under the Convention. While reasons for seeking asylum have grown over time and in many cases are quite complex, policy developments run counter to these trends. States, as Mac Éinrí (2006: 359) notes, have 'gradually imposed new barriers designed to make it administratively difficult, if not impossible, for many would-be refugees to apply for asylum'.

Asylum and refugee policy

Ireland's first response to increased asylum seeking, the Refugee Act 1996, was 'hailed as progressive ... because it broadened the 1951 Geneva Convention definition of "refugee" to include "membership of a particular social group" extending to membership of a trade union, being either male or female, or having a particular sexual orientation' (Lentin and McVeigh, 2006: 43). However, its implementation was delayed and it was subsequently amended in a series of other Acts in the midst of what was termed an 'asylum crisis' in the late 1990s and early 2000s. The proposed broadening of the definition of a refugee never occurred and instead the Immigration Acts 1999, 2003 and 2004 and the Illegal Immigrants Trafficking Act 2000, have employed a more restrictive approach to asylum seeking. These acts deal with issues such as augmenting the state's powers in relation to deportation, the finger printing of asylum seekers, and the designation of 'safe countries' from which applications for asylum are disallowed.

During this period increasing emphasis was placed on the need to distinguish between 'genuine' refugees versus 'bogus' or 'illegal' asylum seekers. This had the effect of criminalising asylum seekers, all of whom under the Geneva Convention have a legal right to seek asylum, and the 'genuine' are only deemed genuine once they have been recognised as refugees. Such a perception was fuelled by ministers of the time. The minister for justice, equality and law reform, for example, opined that he 'would much prefer to have a system whereby we could interview people at the airport, find out their cock and bull story and say "You're going home on the next flight". Unfortunately, however the UN convention requires me to go through due process' (McDowell in Select Committee on Justice, Equality, Defence and Women's Rights, 2005).

In reality, examinations of the application process have found many problems with the system, which is stacked against asylum seekers. It takes an adversarial approach and asylum seekers' applications are treated with incredulity. This is compounded by lack of legal advice, and poor quality translation and interpretive services. The quality of these services are particularly crucial when recounting traumatic events such as rape and torture (Nasc, 2008; Conlan et al, 2012; IRC, 2015).

Thus, while the numbers seeking asylum increased in an unprecedented way, the number granted refugee status in the first instance, as decided by the Office of the Refugee Applications Commissioner (ORAC), has been extremely limited and well below EU norms (Colan et al, 2012; see Figure 12.2). In the case of certain refusals, asylum seekers may appeal the decision to the Refugee Appeals Tribunal and appeals at this stage tend to result in more positive results than the initial ORAC application, though the rate of successful appeal has also decreased over time (Fanning, 2012). On further refusal, a person may apply for subsidiary protection. Subsidiary protection was introduced by the EU Qualification Directive, which Ireland adopted in 2006. It allows asylum seekers to apply for subsidiary protection where they do not qualify as a refugee but face serious harm if returned to their country of origin. Upon a negative outcome at this point an applicant may apply for leave to remain on humanitarian grounds, a status granted at the discretion of the minister for justice and equality. When all avenues fail, asylum seekers are issued with a deportation order. As such the system is a myriad of lengthy and complex avenues of application, appeal and status categories. A single application procedure is being planned pending the implementation of the International Protection Act 2015, which we discuss later in this section.

Changes to Irish citizenship rules instigated in 2004 were also motivated by attempts to curb asylum seeking, effectively making entitlement to Irish citizenship more restrictive and a mechanism to separate the 'deserving' from the 'undeserving' immigrant. Until the Irish Citizenship and Nationality Act 2004, Irish citizenship was largely based on *jus soli*, meaning that anyone born on Irish soil had automatic entitlement to Irish citizenship. The minister for justice, equality and law reform claimed that this was unsatisfactory in a number of ways, principally because migrants, specifically women in the late stages of pregnancy were coming to Ireland as 'baby tourists' to take advantage of the system. The minister proposed that a residency requirement of three years be applied to non-national parents before their Irish-born child would become entitled to Irish citizenship. Though many of the minister's claims were hugely questionable (Brandi, 2007; Garner, 2007), the proposal was accepted by 80% of those who voted in the Citizenship Referendum 2004. The change introduced in the subsequent Act is an example of shift from 'unconditional to conditional *jus soli*' (Joppke, 2008: 8). This is part of a wider move 'not toward abandoning *jus soli* in total, but making it contingent on legal residence requirements of a parent' (Joppke, 2008: 8) occurring in immigrant-receiving states. This effectively also closed off the practice of granting asylum seekers leave to remain status on the basis of having an Irish-born child, which by the early 2000s was considered a legislative loophole (Glynn, 2014). The Citizenship Act 2004 thus effectively racialises particular immigrant groups. It principally affects migrants from outside the EU and EEA, and especially asylum seekers. Far from the sentiment of the 1951 Convention, asylum seekers as a whole have been ascribed particularly negative cultural traits, such as taking advantage of the welfare system and 'abusing' Irish citizenship laws. The thrust of policy is deterrence, not asylum.

Social policy provision for asylum seekers

Asylum seekers are at the bottom of the hierarchy when it comes to how migrants are categorised in relation to social rights and social policy provision. Social policy is essentially treated as a tool to deter asylum seeking. Prior to 2000 relatively generous conditions were in place as asylum seekers had access to Supplementary Welfare Allowance and Rent Supplement and for a brief period had the right to work. However, concerned that the social welfare system was operating as a 'pull factor for non-genuine asylum seekers' (Minister for Justice, Equality and Law Reform, 1999 in O'Connor, 2003: 8), a Dispersal and Direct Provision scheme was introduced in 2000. This scheme is administered by the DJE through the Reception and Integration Agency (RIA). Under Direct Provision (DP) bed and board is provided in accommodation centres run on a contract basis by private companies such as hotel and guest-house owners for the RIA, whose accommodation is not purpose-built to provide adequate space for families. Inspections by the RIA have been found to be inadequate and calls for an inspection system independent of the RIA have been resisted. Moreover, the RIA is a misnomer, there are no formal efforts to integrate asylum seekers who are excluded from integration policy.

The only monetary payment asylum seekers receive is a weekly allowance of €19.10 per adult, unchanged since 2000, and €15.60 per child, which includes a €6 increase agreed in 2016. Asylum seekers are entitled to apply for exceptional needs payments but otherwise have no access to social welfare, including Child Benefit. Rights are also denied across the other social services, other than basic education and healthcare. Asylum seekers are entitled to health services under the medical card scheme and children are entitled education until they reach 18, with the exception of children who have been in the school system for five years or more who became entitled to higher education grants in 2015. Asylum seekers are not entitled to work.

From the beginning, research has documented the overwhelmingly negative experiences of DP for asylum seekers. As O'Connor (2003: 40) pointed out, it leaves asylum seekers 'bored, isolated, socially excluded, impoverished, deprived of services, unaware of their entitlements, demoralized, deskilled and institutionalised' and has a detrimental effect on their human rights. Fanning and Veale (2004) highlighted the particularly damaging effects of the scheme on the lives of children growing up in such an environment; they live in extreme poverty and deprivation, and their parents are prohibited from basic elements of caring and parenting, such as cooking meals for their children. Moreover, the type of food provided bears little or no relation to ethnic preferences, which affects asylum-seeker well-being (Manandhar et al, 2006; Barry, 2014). Significant child welfare and child protection concerns were also raised in the first independent inspection of child welfare in DP carried out by HIQA (2015). Its findings described a system failing children and their parents and very serious issues such as accidents as a result of cramped physical conditions, lack of privacy, and parents whose vulnerable mental state and isolation left them ill-equipped to care for their children. The report calculated a child welfare and protection referral rate of 14% for asylum-seeking children in comparison to 1.6% for the general population, noting that in many cases the referrals were the result of living conditions that Tusla cannot address.

The unbearable conditions in accommodation centres and length of time spent in them awaiting decisions on their status generated a wave of protests by asylum seekers, including hunger strikes, in 2013-14. A Working Group on the Protection Process and Direct Provision was established in 2014 by the DJE and reported in 2015. Although the Working Group's report (DJE, 2015) gave cursory attention to the views of asylum seekers, its findings on asylum-seeker experiences mirrored previous research by highlighting issues such as lack of autonomy and privacy, and the uncertainty the system created. Despite sustained criticism of DP and calls for its abolition, the remit of the Working Group was limited to making recommendations focused on 'improving' rather than replacing the system, being conscious of budgetary realities and existing legislation. It made 173 recommendations, the majority of which have not (yet as of January 2017) been implemented. These include allowing asylum seekers to work, consistent with the EU Reception Conditions Directive 2003, which stipulates a right to work if an asylum seeker is still awaiting a decision after nine months in the system. Ireland opted out of this Directive. The recommendation to increase rates of support to €38.74 for an adult and €29.80 for a child materialised as a €6 increase in the child rate. Much of the report's attention focused on the time within the system as the main problem, thus bolstering plans already in train to introduce a single application procedure under the International Protection Act 2105. When fully implemented this will replace separate, sequential applications for refugee status and subsidiary protection, and align Ireland with normal practice in most other EU countries. While a single application procedure is the norm in many other EU countries, in Ireland it appears that it is presented as a political panacea for what is wrong with the system. Given the research discussed earlier, deeper questions need to be asked about why the majority of applications are refused refugee status in the first instance.

Social policy provision and refugees

Once an asylum seeker has been recognised as a refugee their social rights and entitlements are similar to those of Irish citizens and they are also exempt from the HRC. They are entitled to apply for family reunification, but as in the case of migrant workers, this is granted at the discretion of the minister for justice and equality. Refugees are entitled to apply to become an Irish citizen through naturalisation three years after the date of their asylum application. Individuals with subsidiary protection have similar rights. However, those with leave to remain status are prohibited from applying for family reunification unless they work and earn at least €30,000 per annum, and need five years residency before they can apply for citizenship.

Regardless of their status, life after asylum seeking and making the transition from direct provision can be difficult. A number of reports have documented the detrimental effects of DP, including a scarring effect in terms of employment due the time spent unable to work, pursue education or upskill, as well as the socially scarring effects of the stigma associated with asylum seeking (Conlan, 2014; E Kelly et al, 2016). Moreover refugees are ill-equipped for the basics of living and accessing services upon leaving DP. Ní Raghallaigh et al (2016) document the huge hurdles faced by new refugees, including the challenges faced in establishing claims for social welfare and rent allowance without an address, but not having the means to rent accommodation in order to acquire an address. Other than an information booklet, only made available following a recommendation made by the 2015 Working Group, no formal supports are available to assist refugee transition from DP.

Immigration and integration

While the discussion of immigration has so far concentrated on issues of differential rights, deterrence and discrimination, on the other hand, the concept of integration and the development of integration policy has also been notable since the late 1990s. There are, however, many problems with how integration policy has evolved. At the broadest level, several authors (Mac Éinrí, 2007; Boucher, 2008; Feldman, 2008; Fanning, 2012) have pointed out the stark contradiction of a state which, on the one hand, expresses a desire for integration, cohesion and anti-racism in relation to immigrant and new ethnic groups, while at the same time it categorises, discriminates, racialises, excludes and impoverishes these groups to varying degrees. If integration as a process is defined as 'flowing from the totality of policies and practices that allow societies to close the gap between the rights, status and opportunities of natives and immigrants and their descendants' (OECD, 2007: 13 in Feldman, 2008: 1–2) then it is clear that in practice policy in Ireland has in many instances widened the gap and reduced the potential for integration. This is also reflected in Ireland's standing in comparative indicators; the Migrant Integration Policy Index for European countries, for example, ranks Ireland poorly for its policy on family reunification and long-term residency. Decisions in these areas, as well as for citizenship via naturalisation, are ultimately at the discretion of the minister for justice and equality meaning that the rate of positive outcomes can ebb and flow, and clear standards and rights are not instituted in law (MIPEX, 2015). Successive Immigration, Residence and Protection Bills were drafted to address these issues (see Box 12.1); however, besides dealing with the protection component separately in the International Protection Act 2105, the broader issues have been stalled.

In addition, integration is quite a vague concept and models of integration vary. The Irish model rests on the concept of interculturalism, which is seen as preferable to multiculturalism. This is reflective of the critique of multiculturalism which sees it emphasising specific cultural identities at the expense of integration and risking division rather than integration (Montgomery, 2013). However, the concept of interculturalism also lacks precision and uses of the term in Ireland as elsewhere do not really go beyond the rhetorical. Little mention is made of equality, social justice or social rights (O'Toole, 2015). As a result buzzwords such as 'respecting and celebrating diversity' obscure the realities of unequal treatment of different groups of immigrants (and Travellers, who are also included in intercultural policies as discussed in the next section). Moreover, diversity still tends to be judged against a benchmark of a homogenous or monocultural Irish identity, and integration seems to imply assimilating with dominant cultural norms (Montgomery, 2013).

Integration policy has thus developed in a piecemeal way with no overarching vision of what integration means or how it is to be achieved. The idea of integration policy materialised with the publication of *Integration: A two-way process* (DJELR, 1999). Reflecting immigration trends of the late 1990s, the policy only applied to refugees and people granted leave to remain, and did not include asylum seekers or migrant workers. In 2005 the government produced a *National Action Plan Against Racism* (DJELR, 2005b). This plan, in place between 2005 and 2008, adopted a more comprehensive approach to integration and connected it more clearly with anti-racist and intercultural policies. However, for the most part policies were still targeted at particular groups, and this time Travellers and migrants (meaning primarily migrant workers) were included as well as refugees. At the same time, the Plan did not consider the differential rights and entitlements of migrant groups which cause barriers to intercultural integration, or as Fanning (2007: 237) puts it, create state sanctioned 'internal borders' in Irish society.

In 2007 the notion of integration gained somewhat greater attention with the appointment of a minister of state for integration and the creation of an Office of the Minister for Integration (OMI). The OMI subsequently published *Migration Nation Statement on Integration Strategy and Diversity Management* (OMI, 2008). While the statement lacked policy targets and funding, promised developments included an expert Commission on Integration, a Ministerial Council on Integration, and a Task Force on Integration. With the rapid onset of the economic crisis none of these were implemented. The OMI budget was cut and it has since become the Office for the Promotion of Migrant Integration. The same wave of austerity downgraded the Equality Authority and abolished the National Consultative Committee on Racism and Interculturalism, both of which were important in addressing migrant inequalities, racism and discrimination. Such issues are primarily left to migrant NGOs, who also do much of the integration work neglected by the state. At the same time they are dependent on the state for funding and access to policy-making fora which limits their dissent against government policy (Landy, 2015). While commitments to integration, that were ultimately mostly rhetorical, have stalled, issues such as second-generation integration, as anticipated by *Migration Nation* (OMI, 2008) are not being adequately addressed. As Boucher (2010) and Fanning (2011) suggest, the broader landscape of migration policy effectively underscores the intergenerational transmission of social exclusion.

SECTION TWO
TRAVELLERS AND IRISH SOCIAL POLICY

Travellers and ethnicity

Travellers are a minority ethnic group who occupy an unequal position in Irish society. Their status as Irish citizens is ascribed at birth, yet their realisation of citizenship rights has been for the most part denied. As a result, 'Travellers fare poorly on every indicator used to measure disadvantage: unemployment, poverty, social exclusion, health status, infant mortality, life expectancy, illiteracy, education and training levels, access to decision making and political representation, gender equality, access to credit, accommodation and living conditions' (O'Connell, 2002: 49).

The issue of Travellers' position in Irish society and their access to social rights is contested. Much rests on whether Travellers are recognised as an ethnic group commanding rights and respect on the basis of their ethnic identity; or whether they form a subculture of poverty and need to be absorbed back into mainstream, settled, Irish monocultural society, and avail of rights and services in the same way as the majority population. For Travellers the issue is primarily one of culture and identity, and denial of ethnic identity generates anti-Traveller racism which has material effects such as poverty and health inequality. As Pavee Point (2006: 1) puts it:

> a key issue in shaping social policy and practice has been the way in which Travellers' identity is conceptualized: who the Travellers are and what their place is in Irish society, in the eyes of policy makers, service providers and the majority population; and how Travellers themselves assert their identity.

The concept of ethnicity is complex and contested (Ratcliffe, 2004) and the notion of Travellers as an ethnic group has also generated debate (Equality Authority, 2006; McCann et al, 1994; McVeigh, 2007). The concept of ethnicity first came into use during the 1950s and replaced the flawed assumption that distinct races exist. However, theories about what constitutes ethnicity change over time and while on the one hand ethnicity and ethnic group formation has an elusive quality, on the other hand there is also a problem with attributing essential qualities to ethnic groups that 'freeze' them over time, and make it difficult to see issues in common; 'difference' becomes everything (Ratcliffe, 2004).

The core aspect of ethnicity is that it 'is a self-conscious and claimed identity' (Platt, 2008: 370), in other words, it is based on how an ethnic group understands itself, not on characteristics attributed to it by others. Cornell and Hartman (2007: 19) suggests that ethnic groups are based on three kinds of claims: 'a claim to kinship, broadly defined; a claim to a common history of some sort; and a claim that certain symbols capture the core of the group's identity'. Claims about common ancestry need not be founded in fact, though a small DNA study carried out for an RTÉ (2011) documentary series, *The Blood of the Irish*, suggested that Travellers are an historically distinct group. Furthermore, cultural claims do not have to be premised on actual practice. Travellers, for example, identify with a culture of nomadism, but not all Travellers are necessarily nomadic. And, as Cornell and Hartman (2007) suggest, one of ethnicity's defining features in recent decades is the fact that in many societies the cultural distinctiveness of ethnic groups has faded, while the sense of having a distinct identity remains strong.

According to McDonagh (2000), Travellers see themselves as an ethnic group based on the grounds that they are biologically self-perpetuating, share fundamental cultural values, make up a field of communication and interaction, have a membership which defines itself and is defined by others, and are subject to oppression. The notion of oppression is important for understanding Travellers' unequal position in Irish society and in relation to social policy and social rights. They are a minority not just numerically (2011 Census counted 29,495 Travellers, 0.6% of the population), but also in terms of power relations in Irish society. This is expressed through anti-Traveller prejudice or anti-Traveller racism. Travellers as a group are racialised in the sense that they associated with a raft of negative traits and considered inferior to the majority settled population. It is important to also be mindful of the fact that Travellers are not a homogenous group. As with any group in the population, there are different experiences and perspectives, in relation to, for example, gender and sexuality. Traveller women's attitudes towards gender roles, marriage and family size are also changing. For some there are also ambivalences about a settled versus traditional way of life and the consequences that has for identity. This is compounded by the accumulation of socioeconomic changes over the last number of decades which have eroded Traveller independence and self-reliance which, together with the corrosive effects of anti-Traveller racism, has generated a growing crisis of identity within the community (AITHS, 2010).

A multitude of international and national organisations such as the UN Committee on the Elimination of Racial Discrimination and the Irish Human Rights and Equality Commission frequently criticised the state's resistance to formally recognising Traveller ethnicity. Successive governments argued that there are no grounds for accepting that Travellers are a separate ethnic group, and that recognition would be too costly to implement in terms of the rights and protections that the state would be obliged to afford Travellers, in accordance with international human rights conventions and EU directives to which Ireland is committed. That stance appeared to change somewhat when then minister for justice and equality committed in 2011 to give 'serious consideration to the issue' (Shatter cited in Joint Committee on Justice, Defence and Equality, 2014: 5). Following this a government body, the Joint Oireachtas Committee on Justice, Defence and Equality 2014 in its *Report on the Recognition of Traveller Ethnicity* recommended that the state recognise Traveller ethnicity. In a subsequent report by the Joint Committee on Justice and Equality this recommendation was reiterated:

> The Committee is of the view that Travellers are, de facto, a separate ethnic group. This is not a gift to be bestowed upon them, but a fact the State ought to formally acknowledge, preferably by way of a statement by the Taoiseach to Dáil Éireann (Joint Committee on Justice and Equality, 2017: 20).

A statement was made to this effect in Dáil Éireann on 1st of March 2017, thus over-turning decades of state resistance to recognising Traveller ethnicity. This change alone is of enormous importance and the Joint Committee on Justice and Equality also recommended that the Statement be followed with a formal review of changes that might consequently be required in policy and legislation. It remains to be seen whether and how this recommendation will be implemented and what practical effects formal recognition will have. Ethnic recognition has long been a significant goal of the community; however, some Travellers question this goal, asking whether 'it would make a practical difference or whether it would reinforce the idea of an unbridgeable gap between settled people and Travellers' (Brandi, 2013).

Travellers in Irish society and Irish social policy prior to the 1960s

In premodern Ireland, nomadism was the norm rather than the exception for many groups of people, including Travellers. Helleiner (2000) suggests that this mobility, interpreted as 'uncivilised' behaviour, was initially suppressed by English colonialism, which associated settlement with civility, from the mid-sixteenth century onwards. Accordingly, early houses of industry, as discussed in Chapter One, were designed to punish various groups of vagrants, and Travellers would not have been distinguished from the larger mass of the wandering poor (Hayes, 2006). By the late nineteenth century nomadism was again discouraged, but this time, as MacLaughlin (1999: 137) argues, from a nationalist and nation-building perspective: 'Nomadism and "tinkers" in Ireland were regularly perceived as a threat to national progress by propertied sectors in Irish society. ... Travellers, like Gypsies in mainland Europe, were considered inferior to the propertied classes because they literally had no territorial stake in the nation-state'.

During the early decades of independence Travellers were excluded from the gradual expansion of social provision. Their lack of fixed abode precluded them from locally administered services such as local authority housing and Home Assistance. Lack of attendance at school was not considered a problem and compulsory attendance was not enforced for Traveller children. Travellers were occasionally debated in terms of issues such as the threat posed to rural class relations and to public health, but for the most part concerns were not acted upon.

In many respects lack of official concern about Travellers worked to their advantage; they occupied a niche position and relations with others were not overly negative. And, as McVeigh (2008: 93) argues, 'for ethnic nomads, being neglected by the state is often far less oppressive than being "protected" or "respected" by it'. As such, the deterioration of relationships between Travellers and the rest of the population and an increase in anti-Traveller racism can be traced back to the early 1970s when state intervention grew (Mac Gréil, 1977).

Box 12.3: Key policy and legislative developments with regard to Travellers

1963   Report of the Commission on Itinerancy

1983   Report of the Travelling People Review Body

1995   *Report of the Task Force on the Travelling Community*

1996   *National Strategy for Traveller Accommodation*

1998   Housing (Traveller Accommodation) Act

2002   *Traveller Health Strategy 2002-2005*

2002   Housing (Miscellaneous Provisions) Act

2002   *Guidelines on Traveller Education in Primary Schools/ Guidelines on Traveller Education in Second-Level Schools*

2006   *Report and Recommendations for a Traveller Education Strategy*

2007   *National Intercultural Health Strategy 2007-2012*

2010   *Intercultural Education Strategy 2010-2015*

2012   *Ireland's National Traveller/Roma Integration Strategy*

Traveller policy since the 1960s

By the 1950s complaints about issues such as trespass and wandering horses, and the siting of campsites increasingly came from urban politicians (Bhreatnach, 2006). This was the context in which the Commission on Itinerancy was established in 1960. This Commission, which reported in 1963, 'marked the beginning of an explicit settlement policy' (McVeigh, 2008: 94). The Commission reflected the prevailing view of the time that Travellers were a social problem, to be solved by absorption into the rest of the population to live 'a better way of life'. This absorption was possible because the Commission was of the view that there was nothing distinctive about them as a group, and specifically that they were not a distinct ethnic group.

Self-reform, rehabilitation and settling down was the ultimate vision of the Commission on Itinerancy (1963: 103): 'itinerants, by an improvement in their behaviour pattern and therefore in the public image and by settling in a district would come to be accepted more quickly by the settled community'. The crux of the Commission's recommendations rested on permanent settlement, whether in houses supplied by local authorities or in official campsites. This would become the foundation for availing of the same opportunities as settled people, including social services and conventional employment. As Fanning (2012: 153) puts it, 'Travellers were not to have equal rights to welfare unless they first ceased to be Travellers. The price of social citizenship, within the assimilationist logic of the social policies which emerged to address the "problem of itinerancy" included the surrendering of identity and difference'.

In the event the assimilationist thrust of the Commission's recommendations failed. There were two key problems. Settled people remained hostile and resistant to Travellers regardless of whether they were settled or nomadic. Consequently local provision of services proved politically unfeasible. Second, the majority of Travellers did not want to be permanently settled.

The Travelling People Review 1983 was the second official review of Travellers. The main issue was reframed: Travellers were no longer the problem requiring a solution, the key issue was the social problems or social deprivation Travellers experienced. In addition, the Review seemed to have moved on from a policy of assimilation: 'in light of experience and current knowledge the concept of absorption is unacceptable … it is better to think in terms of integration' (Travelling People Review Body, 1983: 6). However, it is clear from the report that those who remained nomadic were understood as a group who were choosing not to conform to the settled norms on which social services are delivered and were thus putting themselves at a disadvantage. Therefore, while the report offered a definition of Travellers that recognised their cultural distinctiveness, this did not have any bearing on how Traveller's social rights were understood. For example, the report recommended 'a house for all Traveller families who desire to be housed. Travellers who are not so accommodated cannot hope to receive an adequate education. Nor can they avail satisfactorily of services such as health and welfare which are of such significance in the life of all people' (Travelling People Review Body, 1983: 15).

Subsequent relevant legislative developments include the Housing Act 1988, which was the first piece of legislation to specifically make reference to Travellers. This was in the context of Local Authority responsibility for providing halting sites. The Prohibition of Incitement to Hatred Act 1989 included 'membership of the Travelling community' as a ground on which incitement to hatred is prohibited, but only after Traveller groups campaigned for inclusion in the legislation (McVeigh, 2007). However, this legislation has been largely symbolic. The grounds for prosecution have proven very ineffective, particularly around proof of intent, and its ability to deal with the growing trend of online racism is also inadequate.

More broadly, as Ní Shuinéar notes (1998: 14), 'sea changes took place between the 1983 publication of the Review Body Report and the setting up of the Task Force in 1993'. These changes can largely be attributed to the rise of the Traveller movement and the politicisation of Travellers (Bhreatnach, 2006; McVeigh, 2008). In particular the Irish Traveller Movement and Pavee Point have been significant in affording Travellers their own voice and participation in policy-making processes, such as the 1995 Task Force and subsequent policy developments.

1995 Report of the Task Force on the Travelling Community

This report seemed to represent a definite move forward in terms of understanding Traveller issues. Here for the first time discrimination was acknowledged:

> the 'Settled' community ... have to accept that their rejection of Travellers is counter-productive and that incidents of social exclusion and discrimination against the Traveller community, such as the refusal of service in hotels, public houses and other establishments and the segregation of Travellers in the provision of facilities, must end (Task Force on the Travelling Community, 1995: 58).

In addition the report linked discrimination to inequalities experienced by Travellers 'the recognition of the importance of concepts of culture, ethnicity, racism and discrimination has entered the debate about the situation of Travellers. This has resulted in a redefinition of the Traveller situation in terms of cultural rights as opposed to simply being a poverty issue' (Task Force on the Travelling Community, 1995: 63). However, the main report did not go so far as to recognise the claims of Travellers as a specific ethnic group and this has remained the case since at official state level. Nevertheless the report envisioned the development of an intercultural framework for the future development of social services in relation to Travellers.

An addendum to the main report signed by four members of the Task Force reflected views which remained much closer to the thrust of the 1963 and 1983 reports, and which might be said to have proven closer to the reality of the effects of policy development since the 1990s which have been moderated by lack of political will and growing anti-Traveller racism. In this regard the nomadic lifestyle was represented as 'inordinately expensive on the taxpaying community to maintain for the questionable benefit of a small section of population' (Task Force on the Travelling Community, 1995: 289).

The main report, however, took a different view. It dealt with relationships between Travellers and the settled community, culture, discrimination, accommodation, health, education and training, Traveller economy, Traveller women, and disability. Across the range of issues, the Task Force emphasised the need to respect Traveller culture. The bulk of the Task Force recommendations concerned education. The Task Force outlined a number of principles and objectives including equality of access, acknowledgement of cultural diversity, and the principle of integration.

Policy and problems since the 1995 Task Force on the Travelling Community

For the most part the Task Force Report was treated positively. McVeigh (2008: 91) for example speaks of it as the highpoint of interculturalism which pointed to a future 'of gentle if limited reformism and reform in state policy towards Travellers'. This was bolstered by the Employment Equality Act 1998 and the Equal Status Act 2000. Both Acts included membership of the Travelling community as a ground for recognising discrimination, but as a separate category to the race ground. However, a monitoring committee established to periodically examine progress on the Task Force recommendations reported in 2000 and 2005, and both times was generally quite pessimistic about improvements made since the Task Force report. In 2005 it stated that

> The bottom line is that despite the allocation of considerable financial and staff resources and some progress being achieved, Travellers continue to have lower life expectancy, lower education qualifications and, in many cases, unacceptable accommodation. Traveller culture is under threat, both from lack of recognition by the settled community, but also from internal changes within the community (Committee to Monitor and Co-ordinate the Implementation of the Recommendations of the Task Force on the Traveller Community, 2005: 6).

Since then, particularly since the economic crisis, the situation for Travellers has worsened in some respects. Harvey (2013: 2) documents the extent of austerity borne by Travellers: 'One can think of no other section of the community which has suffered such a high level of withdrawal of funding and human resources, compounded by the failure of the state to spend even the limited resources that it has made available'.

There is also evidence of a hardening of attitudes among the settled population. This is not helped by predominantly racialised media portrayal of Travellers and Traveller culture and a backlash against Traveller politicisation, exemplified in newspaper headings such as:

> Travellers get preferential treatment from State: paper (*Sunday Independent*, 2002)

> Travellers' rights fetishists are dictating the agenda (*Sunday Independent*, 2010)

Mac Gréil's (2010) *Emancipation of the Travelling People*, which updated attitudinal research carried out in the early 1970s and again in the 1980s suggests that anti-Traveller racism has grown in some respects. For example, 18.2% of respondents would deny Travellers citizenship, which is a significant increase on the 8.2% who shared this response in the 1980s survey. Here we look briefly at some of the limited progress and continuing problems with regard to accommodation, education and healthcare since the 1995 Task Force report.

Accommodation

A National Strategy for Traveller Accommodation was published in 1996 (DoE, 1996) and this was followed by the Housing (Traveller Accommodation) Act in 1998. The Act requires local authorities to produce five-year programmes on meeting existing and projecting future Traveller accommodation needs. Traveller accommodation includes standard houses, and accommodation which is Traveller-specific, that is, group housing schemes and permanent and transient halting sites. The legislation also provided for the creation of the National Traveller Accommodation Consultative Committee on a statutory basis and for the creation of Traveller accommodation consultative committees within local authorities. However, outcomes have not been satisfactory, stymied by lack of political will as evidenced by consistent underspending of Traveller accommodation budget allocations, and settled community opposition to Traveller accommodation developments. Efforts to progress housing policy in a way in which affords greater recognition of Traveller needs have also been counteracted by other policy initiatives. These include the criminalisation of Traveller families who continue to live at unauthorised sites under the introduction of the Housing (Miscellaneous Provisions) Act 2002, which made trespass illegal.

Norris and Winston (2005) note a paradox in how accommodation provision has been unfolding, observing that a greater proportion of Traveller-specific accommodation was actually provided from the 1960s to the 1980s when officially assimilationist thinking was much stronger. These trends are continuing, and are not necessarily a reflection of majority Traveller preference but of the type of accommodation local authorities are providing. Since the 1990s, the number of Traveller families living in private rented accommodation with assistance such as Rent Supplement or HAP has grown significantly, while the number on halting sites has declined. The number living in unauthorised halting sites declined significantly but has recently begun to grow again. This is partly a reflection of the general crisis in housing (see Chapter Ten), with Travellers who are unable to continue to afford private rental accommodation moving to halting sites. Travellers are also more vulnerable to discrimination by private landlords, as direct social housing provision has declined (Coates et al, 2015). Following a case made by the European Roma Rights Centre with the Irish Traveller Movement to the European Committee of Social Rights, the Committee ruled that the Irish state has violated the rights of Travellers in accordance with the European Social Charter in relation to accommodation, both in terms of the quantity of Traveller-specific accommodation and its quality. In particular the Committee noted that 'a not insignificant number of sites are in poor condition, lack maintenance and are badly located' (European Committee of Social Rights, 2016). The risk to Traveller lives in inadequate halting sites was made stark by the deaths in 2015 of ten Travellers, including a pregnant woman, at a halting site caravan fire in Carrickmines, Dublin. The site was designated as temporary but had been open for eight years and levels of overcrowding meant that the spacing of caravans breached fire safety regulations. The subsequent opposition settled communities mounted when the local council attempted to rehouse Travellers from the Carrickmines site illustrates the depth of hostility and anti-Traveller racism the community continues to face.

Education

The general move has been to end segregated education including separate schools for Travellers only and separate classes in mainstream schools, so that education services across the board are inclusive of all children. This is a key policy principle articulated across several policy documents concerning Travellers over the 2000s (see Box 12.3). At the same time, mainstream education is guided by intercultural policy developments, in theory at least, so that cultural diversity and all ethnic groups are respected. The White Paper in Education 1995 (GoI, 1995) set participation targets for Traveller children. These included a target of 100% completion rate at primary level within five years and, within ten years, a 100% completion rate at Junior Certificate level and a 50% completion rate at senior cycle. However, improvements and progress has been limited. Revised targets included in the *Report and Recommendations for a Traveller Education Strategy* (DESc, 2006a) were to move from an 85% to 100% completion rate at primary level, and again, a 100% completion rate at junior cycle and a 50% completion rate at senior cycle within five years (DESc, 2006a). However, Travellers do not have equality of opportunity in the Irish education system; in various ways they continue to experience inequality of access, participation and outcome.

Although segregated classes in primary schools were phased out by 2004 and full participation at primary level has been more or less achieved, outcomes regarding literacy and numeracy are poor (Smyth et al, 2015). At second level, while progression rates from primary level have increased, retention and attainment remains a problem, although participation has been gradually increasing. By the early 2010s, for example, 13% of Travellers remained in school until the Leaving Certificate compared to 6% in 2002. Issues of segregation and discrimination are still acute and testify to the lack of impact of policy developments which promote an interculturalism. Issues include being refused enrolment, being withdrawn from core subjects and being harassed by other pupils on the grounds of being a Traveller (DESc, 2006b; AITHS, 2010). Moreover, Traveller children are discouraged from remaining in education because of the high levels of unemployment in the Traveller community (84% in the 2011 Census) and experiences of employer discrimination.

Austerity under the mantle of mainstreaming has posed further setbacks to Traveller progress in the education system. Services to support Traveller children in mainstream education, including a visiting teacher service and resource teachers for Travellers were dismantled in 2011. In 2012 senior Traveller training centres catering for Travellers who left school early were shut down. Lack of supports within the mainstream system mean that Travellers who are not doing well or who have behavioural issues are quickly referred to Youthreach programmes, the mainstream equivalent of Traveller training centres (Harvey, 2013). As for higher education, participation by Travellers is very limited. However, for the first time since national plans for equity of access have been in place, the 2015–19 plan contains a specific target on Traveller participation, aiming to increase participation from 35 to 80 Travellers by 2019 (HEA, 2015). Overall, therefore, there are still very large gaps to be bridged before Traveller educational access, participation and outcomes reach levels comparable to the general population.

Health

In terms of policy developments since the 1995 Task Force report, a Traveller Health Advisory Committee was established in 1998 which includes representatives from the DoH, Traveller Organisations and the HSE. At a regional level Traveller health units have been set up and a Traveller-specific model of primary healthcare was developed, following the *Traveller Health Strategy 2002-2005* (DHC, 2002). This has involved a high degree of participation from Travellers, including training Traveller women as primary healthcare workers for their community. In 2007 the HSE published a *National Intercultural Health Strategy 2007-2012* (HSE, 2007). This contained recommendations for the further development of an intercultural approach to health policy design, access and delivery, as it pertains to Travellers, other ethnic minority groups, and immigrants. However, Traveller utilisation of health services continues to be an issue, especially where mainstream services lack an intercultural ethos. Poor relationships with health professionals, such as GPs and midwives, hamper access and affect the quality of care Travellers receive, including lack of referral to secondary services and overprescribing (Hodgins et al, 2006; Reid and Taylor, 2007; AITHS, 2010).

Travellers bear the brunt of severe health inequality. Two studies carried out on the health status of Travellers in the late 1980s (Barry and Daly, 1988; Barry et al, 1989) found stark health inequalities among Travellers compared to the rest of the population. Principally these related to stillbirths which were twice the national rate, a rate of infant mortality which was three times the national rate, and life expectancy levels 10 and 12 years below settled men and women respectively. Extensive data on Traveller health was not collected again until the All Ireland Traveller Health Study (AITHS) which got underway in 2007 and reported in 2010. Among its starkest findings were that infant mortality rates worsened since the 1980s, with Traveller infants now 3.6 times more likely to die than infants in the general population, while the gap in life expectancy for men had grown to

15.1 years. For Traveller women the gap had decreased slightly to 11.5 years. In the qualitative data gathered, besides factors such as material life circumstances and problems with health services, one of the most striking findings was the corrosive effects, particularly on mental health, of pervasive discrimination and living with a constant sense of stigma. This has also been highlighted by other health studies which have found high rates of depression in the Community, particularly among women, while the suicide rate is three times higher than the general population and is particularly high among younger and male Travellers (Walker, 2012; Hodgins and Fox, 2014). Related to these problems is growing alcohol and drug dependency as a way of coping (Van Hout, 2011).

In short, across the social services reviewed here and in other policy areas such as equality and anti-racism policy, the situation may be summarised, as McVeigh (2008: 99) puts it as 'reformism without much reform'. The range of new policies, consultative structures and organisations pertaining to Travellers significantly outweighs tangible outcomes for Travellers in terms of services. Little progressive or deep-seated change has occurred since the state first turned its attention to Travellers in the 1960s.

SECTION THREE
LGBT PEOPLE AND IRISH SOCIAL POLICY

Transgender or trans refers to gender variance, which occurs when a person's gender identity and expression differs from the sex assigned to them at birth. Transgender and trans are umbrella terms encompassing a range of identities including non-gendered people and people whose identity is gender fluid. How trans people relate to gender-identity terminology, or what terms trans people use to describe their experience and identity can also vary widely.

The diversity of sexualities and genders, and the recognition and rights of sexual and gender minorities, has gradually gained increasing attention in social policy analysis. Various and often quickly changing and contested acronyms are used to convey and include a range of identities and groups concerning gender and sexual diversity. In this section we use LGBT (lesbian, gay, bisexual and transgender) to reflect the current main range of debate, scholarship and policy development in the Irish context, and historically, where apposite we use the shorter acronym LGB. However, use of the term LGBT does not include the evolving range of identities and related, frequently contested, issues emerging, which maybe include but are not limited to, LGBTQQI, or lesbian, gay, bisexual, transgender, queer, questioning and intersex (Richardson and Monro, 2012).

Using the term sexualities rather than sexuality is reflective of the range of ways of being sexual and of related social change that is gradually pushing beyond a heterosexual framework. This also entails moving beyond the traditional equation of sexuality with sexual orientation which suggests fixed or natural types of sexual attraction (hetero/homo) and related identities. Recognition of **transgender or trans** identities, is reflective of a similar process of social change with respect to gender and a move beyond genderism, 'the ideology that there are, and should be only two genders that are inevitably tied to the gender assigned at birth' (Galupo et al, 2015: 549). In both cases therefore recognition of diverse genders and sexualities challenges binaristic thinking, that is, that gender diversity is limited to being either male or female and that sexuality is limited to being homosexual or heterosexual (Hines, 2009).

Following this, recent legislative changes related to gender recognition across a number of countries disrupts the assumed correspondence between sex and gender, allowing social and legal recognition on the basis of preferred gender identity rather than genital configuration (Richardson and Monro, 2012). While this can be considered a positive development, it is important to acknowledge that there are a variety of perspectives – medical, legal and social – that shape understandings of sexual and gender diversity. There are also varying political positions within LGBT movements in different national and international contexts. The politics of identity and recognition is not a straightforward path from invisibility to visibility, deviance to normality, or exclusion to inclusion; the range of actors and perspectives can also close down, differentiate and deny, as well as open up recognition of particular identities. There are also issues of homophobia and transphobia, or specific forms of discrimination and oppression directed at LGBT people.

The gradual normalisation of, at least some, sexual and gender diversity is occurring against a long held **heteronormativity** in social policy. In Ireland, for example, issues relating to sexuality have been dominated in recent decades by issues relating to abortion, divorce and contraception (see Chapter Three), all debated within an implicit heterosexual

> **Heteronormativity** refers to the ways in which heterosexuality is treated as the norm and the ways in which rules and practices in social and other public policy thus assume and privilege heterosexuality.

framework. Until the 1990s, homosexuality and issues of discrimination and rights in relation to the LGBT community garnered less attention. This is reflective of social policy and sexuality generally; sexuality has for a long time been ignored in policy analysis and only made 'an appearance when it is perceived as a problem – as in the case of homosexuality, lone motherhood, teenage pregnancy, under-age sex, prostitution, divorce, sexually transmitted infections (STIs) and sexual offences' (Carabine, 2004: 12). The problematisation of sexuality is built upon the construction of what is assumed to be normal sexuality. This privileges an ideal of heterosexual monogamous married relationships, which also become the privileged site of reproduction and childrearing. Other expressions of sexuality and sexual relations are rendered invisible or are treated as deviant to varying degrees. A similar dynamic can be observed in relation to gender norms: gender normativity has the effect of rendering trans people invisible and discriminated in legislation which specifies sex and gender binaries, as well as in a whole range of practices such as gender segregation in prisons and schooling.

More recently, sexuality has been discussed in the context of citizenship and debates have emerged around the notion of sexual politics and sexual citizenship. In a broad sense this may be defined as 'the terrain in which contemporary actors struggle for the right to self-determination as sexual beings, freedom of sexual and gender expression and the right to control one's own body' (Lind, 2013: 193). This is not confined simply to the concerns of what might be cast as sexual and gender minorities, rather 'all citizenship is sexual citizenship' (Bell and Binnie, 2000: 10 in Lind, 2013: 196) in the sense that all citizens are sexed and gendered by how their rights across a whole range of areas such as the family, health and disability, housing, education, work and social protection, and immigration are shaped by gender and sexual norms. Richardson (2000) suggests that sexual rights may be understood in three forms: claims to rights centring on sexual practice, broadly involving the right to have sex; claims to rights centring rights of self-definition and identity, for the right to be gay, to be recognised as such and not discriminated against for it; and claims to rights within social institutions, such as the validation of same-sex marriages. This partly mirrors the progress of LGBT politics, from the decriminalisation of homosexuality and legalising same-sex activity, to identity politics and anti-discrimination legislation, through to demands for the right to be married, and benefit from the rights and entitlements associated with marriage. These rights and entitlements relate to social security, pensions, taxation, inheritance and, in relation to children (guardianship, adoption, fostering, fertility treatment) and parenting.

However, these developments have provoked debate about what they mean for sexual citizenship. In particular, questions have been raised as to whether the basis on which claims to equality are made and met radically challenge heteronormativity, or conservatively represent a form of assimilation into heterosexual norms and culture. In the latter case a 'homonormative' dynamic is generated by which certain gay and lesbian identities are privileged over others (Lind, 2013). Such claims, as Richardson (2004) notes, tend to be made on the basis of sameness and of presenting the notion of the normal or 'good' lesbian/gay citizen who conforms to the notion of stable coupledom and who values family life. On the other hand the move can also potentially be interpreted as transformative. In this view, claims for equal rights may have 'the potential for reimagining concepts of marriage, family and citizenship, as new forms of knowledge about intimate relationships and "families of choice" enter the mainstream' (Richardson, 2004: 399). These issues remain open to question, and may not be, as Richardson suggests, a question of either/or but an uneven, complex process.

LGBT people in Irish society: from criminalisation to equality

Sex between men was first criminalised in Ireland under An Act for the Punishment of Vice of Buggery 1634. Part of the colonial project to civilise

Ireland, one of the first individuals to receive the death penalty in Ireland under the Act was John Atherton, the Bishop of Waterford and Lismore, who actually campaigned to have the law implemented in Ireland (Lacey, 2008). In the Offences Against the Person Act 1861, punishment for buggery was altered to a prison sentence, lasting anywhere from ten years to life imprisonment. In the Criminal Law Amendment Act 1885 the scope of illegal male homosexual activity was broadened from buggery to all sexual acts, referred to as 'gross indecency'.

In the early decades of independence these laws were mainly only applied in cases where minors were involved. However, homosexuality was cast as something foreign to Irish identity, with nationalist discourse displaying the same homophobia as colonialist discourse (Conrad, 2001). Hence LGB people were largely invisible in the construction of Irish citizenship. Sexual difference, like ethnic difference, was not acknowledged in the homogenous construction of nationhood and Irish identity.

The birth of the gay and lesbian movement in Ireland is part of the wider international movement emerging from the late 1960s. The Irish Gay Rights Movement was founded in 1974. The Lesbian movement became more formally organised after a conference in 1978 out of which Liberation for Irish Lesbians was formed (Rose, 1994). Internationally the transgender movement emerged in the 1990s 'merging – at least in name – with LGB activists' (Galupo et al, 2015: 552), and in Ireland transgender issues and rights did not gain attention until the late 1990s (Smyth, 2014), while the Transgender Equality Network Ireland (TENI) formed in 2006.

Box 12.4: Key LGBT legislative and policy developments

1993 Criminal Law (Sexual Offences) Act

2002 *Implementing Equality for Lesbians, Gays and Bisexuals* (Equality Authority)

2003 *Equality Policies for Lesbian, Gay and Bisexual People* (NESF)

2006 *The Rights of De Facto Couples* (Irish Human Rights Commission)

2006 *Rights and Duties of Cohabitants* (Law Reform Commission)

2006 *The All-Party Oireachtas Committee on the Constitution Tenth Progress Report: The Family*

2006 Working Group on Domestic Partnerships, Options paper on co-habiting couples

2010 Civil Partnership and Certain Rights and Obligations of Cohabitants Act

2011 *Report of the Gender Recognition Advisory Group*

2013 *Third Report of the Convention on the Constitution Amending the Constitution to Provide for Same-Sex Marriage*

2015 Child and Family Relationships Act

2015 Marriage Equality Act

2015 Gender Recognition Act

A core element of the movement during the 1970s and 1980s was the push to decriminalise homosexuality, or to claim rights around sexual practice or sexual conduct. This formally began with the establishment of the Campaign for Homosexual Law Reform in 1976. This led to a case being taken by David Norris in 1977 and after unsuccessful challenges in the Irish High Court and Supreme Court, Norris won his case at the European Court of Human Rights in 1988. This decision prompted a renewed wave of gay and lesbian activism to influence the legislative reform that would ensue in Ireland. An umbrella group, Gay and Lesbian Equality Network (GLEN), was set up and other groups acted in solidarity, including the Irish Council for Civil Liberties, the trade union movement, and various women's, Traveller and disability groups (Flynn, 1997). Against them were conservative Catholic groups, principally Family Solidarity, which was opposed to decriminalisation of any sort. In the event, homosexuality was finally decriminalised in the Criminal Law (Sexual Offences) Act 1993. This included a full repeal of existing legislation outlawing homosexuality and putting homosexuals on an equal footing with heterosexuals in relation to sexual rights such as age of consent and privacy codes, all of which was framed in the language of needing 'to recognise, respect and value difference' (Minister for Justice, 1993 in Rose, 1994: 57).

Since that time LGB groups and individuals have gained greater visibility in Irish society and have made gains in terms of equal treatment in various pieces of legislation. Having gained equal rights to sexual practice, the focus turned more firmly towards anti-discrimination and equal treatment in relation to identity and sexual orientation. In 1995 GLEN published a survey on discrimination and its impact on poverty and exclusion among the gay and lesbian community. It showed that fear of discrimination in particular was high in relation to for example, work and accessing services (GLEN and NEXUS, 1995).

Fuller recognition of sexual orientation appeared in the Employment Equality Act 1998 and Equal Status Act 2000, where sexual orientation, interpreted as 'heterosexual, homosexual or bisexual orientation' was included as a ground on which discrimination is prohibited. However section 37(1) of the Employment Equality Act allowed publicly funded religious bodies that provide religious, medical or education services an exemption from this discrimination ground on the basis of preserving their religious ethos. This exemption was particularly threatening for LGB teachers given the dominance of Catholic patronage in the school system (Fahie, 2016). This remained the case until section 37(1) was amended in the Equality (Miscellaneous Provisions) Act 2015 which significantly narrows the scope of the exemption and protects LGB people from discrimination in these contexts. In the early 2000s both the Equality Authority and NESF published reports focusing on equality issues for LGB people (see Box 12.4). Both reports focused on the need for greater attention to LGB needs in mainstream services and greater attention to the impact decisions made in government departments and agencies on LGB people.

Since the mid-2000s equality and rights discourses in relation to LGBT people have shifted more firmly to the third form of sexual citizenship rights as identified by Richardson (2000), namely claims to rights within social institutions, such as the validation of same-sex marriages and the right to gender recognition. Momentum was gained by a High Court Case taken by Katherine Zappone and Ann Louise Gilligan in 2004, a lesbian couple who married in Canada and who sought to have their marriage recognised in Ireland and be treated as a married couple for taxation purposes. Although that case was not successful, the subsequent broader mobilisation of the LGBT community, coupled with the effect of numerous reports that invoked the state to act on this issue (see Box 12.4) led to the introduction of civil partnership in 2010 (Ryan, 2014). For some campaigning groups, such as LGBT Noise and Marriage Equality, the civil partnership did not go far enough, and offered an inferior form of relationship status. For others such as GLEN, civil partnership was largely welcomed, with the exception of its implications for same-sex couples who co-parent because the model established did not offer joint legal rights in relation to children. While these might broadly represent 'equality in sameness' versus 'equality in difference' (Richardson and Monro, 2012) approaches to LGBT rights and recognition, in the event the LGBT movement united to mobilise and lobby for full marriage equality (Neary, 2016). This was achieved in a historic referendum in 2015 in which 62.07% voted in favour of same-sex marriage, and Ireland became the first country worldwide to achieve marriage equality by referendum (Y Murphy, 2016). A very broad 'Yes' campaign, which employed an extensive grassroots strategy and which had the support of all the main political parties, won out against a 'No' campaign, comprised, among others, of the Iona Institute, Mothers and Fathers Matter, and Stand Up for Marriage. When the Marriage Equality Act was enacted in November 2015, civil partnership was simultaneously no longer an option. While marriage equality was broadly welcomed there are questions, too, about how LGBT support for marriage leaves aside critique of the heteronormative institution of marriage and privileges sexual citizenship based on sameness or normality thus eradicating difference or any notion of equality based on LGBT difference (Neary, 2016). In the same year, wider issues relating to adoption, guardianship and assisted reproduction were dealt with in a separate legislative process culminating in the Children and Family Relationships Act 2015. The Act provided for the rights of children and parents in LGBT families, including second-parent adoption and guardianship.

The Gender Recognition Act was also passed in 2015, the origins of which can be traced back to Lydia Foy's application to the Registrar General in 1993 to have her gender identity recognised on her birth certificate having had gender reassignment surgery in 1992. After a continuing battle with the state, which denied her recognition, an eventual turnaround was initiated in 2010 with the setting up of a Gender Recognition Advisory Group. Preparation of the eventual legislation was also significantly altered following further transgender activism which succeeded, for example, in shifting proposals from a medical model (whereby gender identity would require medical verification) to a model of self-declaration. However, several issues remain problematic such as the exclusion of under–16s, and of intersex and non-binary individuals from the legislation.

> **Gender identity** refers to one's personal or internal sense of being female, male or other gender.
> **Gender expression** refers to one's outward/eternal presentation of their gender identity.

Protection from discrimination on the grounds of **gender identity** and **gender expression** are also issues in relation to equality legislation (TENI, 2016).

There is a growing body of research documenting the contemporary lives of LGBT people particularly in the areas of mental health and well-being, and in relation to experiences of discrimination, homophobia and transphobia (Minton et al, 2008; Mayock et al, 2009; Sharek et al, 2015; Higgins et al, 2016; Szydlowski, 2016). While stigma and discrimination continue to feature in the lives of LGBT in ways that affect their well-being, Bryan and Mayock (2012: 8) caution against constructing LGBT lives 'in terms of their vulnerability to bullying, their experiences of homophobic or transphobic violence, and their "at riskness" for depression, self-harm and suicidality'. Such discourses, they argue, individualise and pathologise LGBT people's experiences while neglecting the heteronormative processes that generate such problems. This point has implications for how LGBT-sensitive policies are developed. In the case of education, for example, where homophobic and transphobic bullying tends to be most pervasive (Bryan and Mayock, 2012) revised anti-bullying procedures were introduced for primary and second–level schools in 2013 which address identity-based bullying, specifically transphobia and homophobia. Such an approach, as Bailey (2016) argues, tends to isolate one negative aspect of LGBT experience while the wider heteronormative aspects of school culture and curricula are not questioned. Thus while great strides have been achieved for LGBT rights and recognition, the wider context is one where heteronormativity prevails.

Chapter summary
- This chapter focused on rights and recognition issues for groups who, in various ways, have been excluded from full and equal participation in Irish society, based on their difference from the established norms of Irish identity and citizenship.
- The chapter broadly discussed the theme of immigration, diversity and racism, and the differential rights afforded to various categories of immigrant. The implications of this differential treatment in social policy, integration policy and formal citizenship status was examined.
- Travellers were discussed as an indigenous minority ethnic group, also treated in racist ways by state and society, and whose inclusion in Irish society commanding respect and equal rights still remains a significant challenge.

- The position of LGBT people as minority groups in Irish society was examined in the final section of the chapter. This charted the gradual but occasionally rapid gains in terms of LGBT recognition and rights against a backdrop of tensions with heteronormativity in Irish social politics and policy making.

Discussion points

- Discuss the norms on which Irish citizenship has traditionally been based. How have these influenced the development of social provision?
- Discuss the notion of the 'deserving' versus the 'undeserving' immigrant. How is this manifest in Irish immigration policy?
- Discuss ways in which Irish social policy is used as an instrument of exclusion in relation to minority groups in Irish society.
- Why does anti-Traveller racism continue to be a problem in contemporary Irish society?
- In what ways have LGBT rights and recognition challenged the heteronormative basis of Irish citizenship?

Further reading list

Fanning, B (2012) *Racism and social change in the Republic of Ireland* (2nd edn), Manchester: Manchester UP

Garrett, PM (2015) 'Constraining and confining ethnic minorities: Impoverishment and the logics of control in neoliberal Ireland', *Patterns of Prejudice*, 49:4, 414-34

Leane, M and Kiely, E (eds) (2014) *Sexualities and Irish society: A reader*, Dublin: Orpen Press

thirteen

Social policy, the environment and sustainable development

The previous two chapters indicated how a focus on particular social groups demonstrates the scope of social policy beyond the social-service areas. This chapter also looks at how the boundaries of social policy are changing, this time as a result of the challenges posed by environmental issues and the need for sustainable development. Traditionally, social concerns and environmental concerns have been interpreted as being irreconcilable (Eames, 2006). Green arguments challenge economic thinking based on continued economic growth that equates welfare with consumption. The implications of this, as Barry (1998: 224) points out, are potentially 'dramatic for social policy, given that one of the central justifications for social policy is to reduce socio-economic inequality via the redistribution of income, goods and services generated from a growing economy'. However, environmental concerns and environmental politics are increasingly moving from the margin to mainstream, and are beginning to exert greater influence over policy debates and reform not just in relation to environmental protection policy but also social and economic policy. This is partly due to the fact that one environmental problem, climate change, has become increasingly urgent and has acute consequences for the future of human well-being. Accordingly the issue of climate change is threaded throughout this chapter.

The chapter looks at the relationship between sustainable development and social policy as a two-way challenge or relationship. On the one hand the increasingly accepted need for sustainable development challenges mainstream social policy in terms of its reliance on continued economic growth for the realisation of social goals, and in terms of models and forms of welfare provision that do not take account of their environmental impact. On the other hand, the core concerns of social policy in relation to inequality and equity challenge the design of environmental policies in terms of their impact on different groups in society. In exploring these issues this chapter comes with a number of qualifications and a health warning. It skims and hops over the surface of enormously broad, complex and interdisciplinary areas (sustainable development and climate change) and dips into one very small part of that overall picture (transport). Moreover, the picture painted is not particularly positive. This is not exactly an ideal ending for a book about welfare, but nonetheless it is a realistic assessment of the challenges posed by environmental change and the shortcomings of current policy responses.

Chapter outline

- Section one explores some of the links between the discipline of social policy and environmental concerns.
- Section two examines the concept of sustainable development and the issues and challenges of sustainable development as it relates to climate change.
- Section three looks at transport as one particular example of issues related to sustainable development and climate change. It draws together the specifics of the Irish situation with the broader literature on transport, social exclusion and environmental justice. Travel and transport policy are areas which go beyond the conventional boundaries of social policy; by focusing on them the aim is to demonstrate some of the connections between social policy and the environment.

SECTION ONE
SOCIAL POLICY AND ENVIRONMENTAL CONCERNS

Concern for the environment is often considered to have emerged during the 1960s and 1970s. It actually has a much longer history, which has parallels and connections with the emergence of social policy. As Cahill (1991: 19) suggests, social policy 'was born out of a dissatisfaction with, and documentation of, the damage wrought to individuals by industrialism'. This damage included poverty, ill health, poor housing, child labour and poor factory conditions. These problems intensified as industrialisation coincided with urbanisation, which saw large populations concentrated in small areas. Early environmental concerns had similar origins. Industrialism was criticised for damaging nature or the countryside, particularly in terms of use of raw materials and the rise in pollution, while the growth of urbanisation was criticised for being 'unnatural' and inhumane, and the cause of problems such as ill health, and the spread of disease and pollution (Macnaghten and Urry, 1996).

These problems led to both the development of modern social policy and many of the first 'environmental' groups. In many cases, concern for the welfare of species and habitat preceded concern for human welfare. Furthermore, many reformers and activists were members both of early environmental groups and social policy groups, suggesting that they didn't perceive major differences in being concerned about human welfare and the environment. One of the first examples of these types of groups is the Society for Prevention of Cruelty to

Animals (SPCA) founded in the UK in 1824, and 1866 in the US. Animal cruelty legislation was used to try the first case of child abuse taken to court in the US in the absence of legislation on child abuse. Societies for the Prevention of Cruelty to Children came later and modelled themselves on existing SPCAs (Parry and Parry, 2000). Edwin Chadwick, one of the early members of the UK SPCA, became well known for his later efforts in the public health movement. In 1842 he wrote the *Report on the Sanitary condition of the labouring population of Great Britain* (Chadwick, 1965[1842]) providing an account of the damage industrialism and urbanisation had wrought on the health and living conditions of the poor. He drew attention to the 'environmental bads' affecting the life of the poor: 'atmospheric impurities', bad housing, lack of light, poor ventilation, lack of clean water, build-up of waste and overall poor sanitation. This led to reform of governmental responsibility for 'environmental goods' such as clean water, clean air, safe food and general sanitation, which were first legislated for in the Public Health Act 1848. The mid-nineteenth century public health movement, as Dean (2002) notes, can be considered the first articulation of the environmental rights of citizenship, preceding the concerns of the 1970s discussed below.

However, over time mainstream social policy lost its connection with environmental concerns and became more firmly anthropocentric. A boundary thus formed between concern for humans and concern for wider environmental issues such as the use of natural resources, the physical environment and animal welfare. As Ferris (1991: 26) notes, 'post-enlightenment liberalism and socialism which shape the parameters of contemporary thinking about social policy were both premised on the conquest of nature'. Within social policy, human nature and its fulfilment, whether in liberal or socialist terms is perceived by what is economically and technically feasible, and therefore detached from ecological limits that were applied to the non-human organic world (Hewitt, 2000). Social policy and well-being, whether coming from a Right-wing or Left-wing perspective, is wedded to the logic of industrialism and the assumption that economic growth is open-ended and living standards will continuously improve. Within social policy, the outcome is the subject of distributive struggles which determine whether governments intervene in the standards of living so that different groups benefit relatively equally or whether one's standard of living is left to the market with a minimal state safety net. In the former case, where redistribution is achieved on the assumption of open-ended growth, this appears to be done in a 'painless' way (Fitzpatrick, 2011a: 62). No one is left worse off.

Furthermore as Fitzpatrick (1998) points out, in conventional social policy well-being is promoted in very economistic, or 'productivist' terms, which defines quality of life in materialistic terms. Productivism is based on a number of core ideas. These include the employment ethic, which is the idea that 'jobs should be the principal means by which income and status is distributed to the vast majority of people' (Fitzpatrick, 1998: 14), and so essential is the wage contract to our sense of self-worth and self-esteem that it is difficult to envisage anything else. A second element is 'the accumulative impulse' which is 'the notion that welfare equals material affluence' (Fitzpatrick, 1998: 15). As a result, an individualistic, consumption-based notion of welfare is promoted. The limits to pursuing welfare in productivist and materialist terms are becoming more apparent; however, the logic of productivism still dominates. Wilkinson and Pickett (2014: 2) for example, argue that, 'we see rich, developed societies as the peak of human achievement. But the truth is that, despite historically unprecedented levels of comfort and plenty, our societies have many serious social failings and are not efficient producers of well-being'.

By the 1960s and 1970s things were happening outside the discipline of social policy which challenged these assumptions and ways of achieving well-being. The environmentally disruptive effects of the growth model pursued were becoming increasingly apparent and the modern green movement emerged in response to problems such as the loss of wilderness, pollution such as acid rain, the impact of chemical pesticides and the risks of nuclear energy. In addition to these often quite localised environmental problems and movements, the notion that the world was in environmental crisis gained centre stage due to a number of pivotal reports. These included *The Limits to Growth* in which Meadows et al (1972: 23) argued that:

> if the present growth trends in world population, industrialisation, pollution, food production and resource depletion continue unchanged, the limits to growth on this planet will be reached sometime within the next 100 years. The most probable result will be a rather sudden and uncontrollable decline in both population and industrial capacity.

A special issue of the *Ecologist* magazine, *A Blueprint for Survival*, had a similar message. It argued that 'continued economic growth would end either against our will, in a succession of famines, epidemics, social crises, and wars, or because we want it to … in a series of thoughtful, humane and measured changes' (Goldsmith and Allen, 1972: 15). Both reports quantified the seriousness of environmental problems and presented them as global in nature as regards causes and solutions. It was argued that unless action was taken, these problems would worsen at an exponential rate, such that the earth would no longer be able to support humankind. Both reports also supported the idea of the limits to growth. This assumes that there is a trade-off between environmental protection and economic growth, and one can only be achieved at the expense of the other. These reports provoked a lot of criticism and backlash against environmental thinking. They were accused of being overly pessimistic, apocalyptic and lacking in concern for human welfare, but they did stimulate debate and they contributed to the beginnings of more serious treatment of environmental issues. And while the reports of the 1970s might be accused of catastrophism, the contemporary issue of climate change demonstrates the urgency of responding to environmental issues for the future of human welfare. The work of the **Intergovernmental Panel on Climate**

Change (IPCC) brings this into sharp focus, commenting in its most recent assessment that 'continued emission of greenhouse gases will cause further warming and long-lasting changes in all components of the climate system, increasing the likelihood of severe, pervasive and irreversible impacts for people and ecosystems' (IPCC, 2014: 8).

> The **Intergovernmental Panel on Climate Change**, established in 1988 by the UN Environment Programme and World Meteorological Association, comprises scientists and other experts from UN member nations. The IPCC produces periodic assessments of climate change from scientific, socioeconomic and technical perspectives, to support the work of the UN on climate change. Its fifth assessment report was published in 2014 and a sixth is due in 2022.

Social policy and modern environmentalism

For the most part, however, the discipline of social policy was slow to react to the implications of environmental thinking. In this sense social policy perhaps shared the traditional Left-wing sceptical response to environmentalism. This holds that it is a middle-class **post-materialist** concern and is typically about conservation, and a threat to improving the living conditions of the poor in both the developed and developing world (Foley, 2004). However, since the 1990s several strands of research within social policy have emerged which

> **Post-materialism** suggests once people have attained material security their priorities change and they become more concerned with values such as self-expression and quality of life.

address environmental issues. One strand includes consideration of the 'greening of social policy', the connections between social policy and sustainability and the implications of the green critique for social policy, including examination of ways in which social policy has not been 'green' in how it has developed (Cahill, 1991, 2002; Fitzpatrick, 1998, 2011b). This approach encompasses analysis of the sectoral areas of social policy, such as health and housing, from an environmental perspective. A second strand looks at resource issues such as water, food, energy and transport, which have not been part of mainstream social policy analysis but are now also being analysed from a social policy perspective (Huby, 1998, 2001; Cahill, 2010; Dukelow, 2016). This entails, for example, asking questions about the impact of policy in these areas on poor and vulnerable groups. In this sense the concepts of social inclusion and exclusion have widened to incorporate environmental issues that affect quality of life, and to include issues such as water poverty, travel poverty, fuel poverty and food poverty. These are issues brought together by Fitzpatrick (2014) under the term 'ecosocial poverty'. This term conveys the way in which the characteristics of poverty in contemporary developed countries need to include exclusion and deprivation related to 'socionatural resources', as well as to socioeconomic resources such as income, employment and core social services.

> **Environmental justice** highlights the fact that poor and minority groups suffer disproportionately from environmental 'bads' such as pollution and poor-quality living environments. Environmental justice seeks fairness in relation to the distribution of environmental 'goods' and 'bads', and equal access to and participation in environmental decision making.

A related area, and third strand, involves research about the environmental concerns of disadvantaged groups (Burningham and Thrush, 2001) and issues of **environmental justice** and environmental inequalities (Adebowale, 2008). In some respects these have parallels with issues arising in other contexts, such as the 'environmentalism of the poor' (Guha and Martinez-Alier, 1997). This looks at the materialist environmental basis for many development-induced conflicts, including water and land pollution, which threaten the livelihoods of the poor, particularly in developing countries. In addition, in the US the emergence of a grass-roots environmental justice movement has seen a convergence of environmental concerns and social justice based on the fact that minority groups such as Black people, Hispanics and the poor are at greater risk of environmental contamination and nuisances (Sarokin and Schulkin, 1994). This attention to justice has recently focused on climate justice as environmental justice. This highlights the ways in which climate change impacts most heavily both on the poorest regions of the world, and on the poorest within countries, such as is the case with exposure to flooding and vulnerability to its effects in the UK (Walker and Burningham, 2011). From a social policy perspective, the inequalities associated with climate change exemplify a double injustice of climate change: the poor contribute least to its causes and are impacted most by its effects (Gough, 2011).

A final broader strand examines environmental issues from the point of view of the politics of, and prospects for, welfare states. This has entailed examining how and what types of welfare states are likely to transition from 'welfare states' to 'ecostates' (Meadowcroft, 2005); why climate change matters to welfare states; and what policy options and policy routes might be taken to 'decarbonise' the welfare state (Gough and Meadowcroft, 2011; Gough, 2013, 2016; Bailey, 2015). Other related questions include what new social risks are generated by environmental change, what distributional conflicts they generate and what new social injustices they might cause (Büchs et al, 2011).

Thinking within social policy has therefore progressed from the traditional scepticism about implications of green thinking for social issues such as poverty and inequality. The common ground between these various strands is the point that if environmental issues are to be fully understood and addressed, they cannot be divorced from the social context in which they are generated and, in turn, impact upon. Within social policy, this may be understood as something of a two-way relationship. On the one hand the environmental critique poses a challenge to social policy for its contribution to unsustainable development. As Hoff and McNutt (2009: 295) point out 'traditional models of social welfare, based on models of the economy that do not take into account the key role of the resource base, have outlived their usefulness for guiding social policy making'. This invokes the need for the 'greening' of social policies. On the other hand the discipline of social policy can contribute to the integration of social and environmental issues, by bringing issues of inequality and equity, and the means to address them to attention, which is a vital part of achieving sustainable development. The next section unpacks some of these points by looking at the evolution of thinking about sustainable development and the continuing issues, conflicts and challenges, particularly as they relate to the issue of climate change.

SECTION TWO
SUSTAINABLE DEVELOPMENT AND CLIMATE CHANGE

The evolution of the concept of sustainable development

A UN Conference on the Human Environment, called *Only One Earth* was held in Stockholm in 1973. As Reid (1995: 36) suggests, this was the 'first major attempt to involve the nations of the world in a concerted, constructive response to environmental problems' and 'it is generally regarded as a milestone in the development of global responses to environmental issues'. Of major concern to the conference was how to manage resources at a global level in order to tackle the mounting problems of pollution beyond 'harmless' dispersal which was the taken for granted way of dealing with pollution. However, this concern did provoke some conflict as it was felt to reflect the interests of the Northern participant countries and to put obstacles in the way of the development priorities of Southern countries. These countries considered themselves to suffer from the 'pollution of poverty', an idea first articulated at this conference. For countries coming from this perspective, measures to tackle pollution would be a luxury, something to attend to once higher living standards had been attained.

> The **pollution of poverty** refers to the environmental problems that arise from a lack of development such as poor water quality, poor housing, malnutrition and disease.

One of the few things the conference achieved was the *Stockholm Declaration on the Human Environment* which articulated a number of important principles, including the idea of environmental human rights and of intergenerational equity, conceived as responsibility the present generation has towards future generations (Aiken, 1992; Hayward, 2005). However little headway was made with resolving the conflicts between developed and developing countries (Elliot, 2005) and this is an issue which has continued to hamper progress ever since.

Some conceptual advances were made at least when sustainable development, proposed by *Our Common Future*, also known as the Brundtland Report, gained widespread recognition after the report's publication in 1987 (WCED, 1987). The report was produced by a UN Commission, the World Commission on Environment and Development (WCED), established after the UN held a Stockholm +10 conference in Nairobi in 1982. The WCED was given the task of proposing long-term environmental strategies with an international cooperative focus between developing and developed countries.

Our Common Future was a breakthrough in terms of environmental thinking and policy making. It changed the way of thinking about the relationship between the economy, society and the environment, seeing them as the three pillars of sustainable development. In institutional terms it urged the replacement of environmental policy as a discrete area of government with the integration of environmental, social and economic policy. Compared to the reports of the early 1970s, it did not convey a message of doom and it modified the limits to growth thesis somewhat. This is perhaps one of the reasons why the concept of sustainable development became so attractive and endorsed by interests and groups coming from very different starting points regarding social, economic and environmental issues. Its much-quoted definition of sustainable development is 'development that meets the needs of the present without compromising the ability of future generations to meet their own needs' (WCED, 1987: 43). This definition is informed by two key ideas: needs and limitations. With respect to needs, it prioritised 'the essential needs of the world's poor' while its reference to limitations meant 'the idea of limitations imposed by the state of technology and social organisation on the environment's ability to meet present and future needs' (WCED, 1987: 43).

The report suggested that some limits could be expanded and that the carrying capacity of the earth's resource base could be enhanced by growth in knowledge and technology. However, this was not to detract from the need for equitable access to resources or from recognition of the fact that ultimate ecological limits do exist. The report therefore proposed the idea of changing the quality of growth. It suggested that Southern countries need growth to eradicate poverty and to develop in ways that are not environmentally destructive. However, if this growth were to be a duplication of the model pursued in developed countries then further environmental damage would ensue. All countries need to change the quality of their growth, by making it 'less material – and energy – intensive and more equitable in its impact' (WCED, 1987: 52). Northern countries in particular need to change the quality of their growth by more efficient use of materials and less use of energy. The report's reference to social organisation therefore involved an equitable distribution of resources. This means striving for intra-generational as well as intergenerational equity when it comes to issues of poverty, consumption and living standards:

> a world in which poverty and inequity are endemic will always be prone to ecological and other crises. Sustainable development requires meeting the basic needs of all and extending to all the opportunity to

satisfy their aspirations for a better life. Living standards that go beyond the basic minimum are sustainable only if consumption standards everywhere have regard for long-term sustainability. ... sustainable development requires the promotion of values that encourage consumption standards that are within the bounds of the ecological possible and to which all can reasonably aspire (WCED, 1987: 43-44).

This challenged the high-consumption countries of the North which consume a far greater share of the world's resources in proportion to its population size. Addressing this inequality within ecological limits requires redistribution. Living standards in poorer nations need to rise in order to meet basic needs and eradicate absolute poverty and the range of associated problems such as malnutrition, ill health and slum housing. The concept of the **ecological footprint** has probably become the most well-known way of understanding unequal use of resources, or of going beyond ecological limits in a localised way by different countries or regions (Littig and Grießler, 2005). Living within ecological limits, or within our ecological footprint involves social change; or 'changes in the understanding of well-being and what is needed to live a good life. Such change allows for necessary development in the South' (Baker, 2016: 59).

> **Ecological footprint** is a measure of human impact on the environment. It represents the natural resources (biocapacity) required for a particular population to maintain its current levels of consumption and waste disposal.

Since the early 1990s, policy developments attempting to realise sustainable development have gathered pace. The Brundtland Report and the concept of sustainable development it articulated became a catalyst for the mainstreaming of green thinking and environmental policy. At the same time sustainable development is a contested concept; it is broad enough to draw support from a wide range of actors, but what it precisely means and how to act upon it is contested, its status is both ubiquitous and ambiguous. At a surface level, sustainable development therefore is a concept that has gained widespread recognition and acceptance as something to favour. As Cahill (2003: 558) puts it, 'employers, government agencies, and pressure groups have all sprayed "sustainable" onto policies and titles'. However, while the concept provides a 'common language', different groups import different meanings to it.

Capturing this diversity Baker (2016) identifies four models on what she calls a sustainable development ladder: pollution control, weak sustainable development, strong sustainable development and an ideal model of sustainable development. These models or approaches to sustainable development involve different political scenarios and practical policy options, and are underpinned by differing attitudes towards nature and the relationship between nature and human beings. At the foot of the ladder is a minimal approach to environmental protection involving pollution control policies. On the next rung of the ladder is a weak model of sustainable development, which aims to integrate environmental concerns into the capitalist economy by economic instruments. By pricing environmental goods and bads, environmental problems are managed by market solutions and market–based interventions such as taxes and **tradeable quotas**.

Tradeable quotas in the context of environmental policy are a policy instrument designed to limit pollution, such as CO_2 emissions. Governing authorities allocate or sell permits for specific amounts of emissions to relevant bodies, such as industries, who can trade permits if not all permits are required by that particular company or if more are needed. The most well-known trading quota system is the EU Emission Trading Scheme.

The **precautionary principle** refers to the idea that the absence of scientific certainty should not be taken as a reason for failing to respond or to take precautionary measures against the occurrence of environmental risks.

A strong model of sustainable development gives more serious attention to environmental protection, understanding it as a necessary condition of economic development, with greater emphasis on the protection of natural resources and adopting the **precautionary principle** in the face of scientific uncertainty and risk. Market solutions alone are not seen as the answer to environmental problems and this model invokes stronger government intervention. This includes the participation of all in society to adopt environmentally friendly behaviour and consumption patterns. In terms of the technological changes required, this model focuses on changing the quality of economic growth via ecological modernisation. Ecological modernisation is defined as 'the ecological restructuring process of production and consumption' (Spaargaren and Mol, 1992: 335). In policy terms, this means that the development of economic and environmental policy is underpinned by the belief that a different kind of economic growth is possible through technological development that enables the production of low-polluting goods. In this way economic growth can 'decouple' from environmental degradation, while more efficient production processes mean less use of materials for the same level of output, known as 'dematerialisation'.

At the top of the ladder is what Baker (2016) refers to as the ideal model of sustainable development. For some of its proponents this involves a rejection of the concept of sustainable development, or at least the mainstream models of sustainable development. This model espouses something more radical and transformative, reflecting ecocentric principles, as discussed in Chapter Five, where the capitalist economic model is rejected, as is the anthropocentric attitude towards nature. In some instances this model of sustainable development is also considered compatible with, or can be integrated with a radical socialist transformation of societies and economies.

The aftermath of the Brundtland Report: sustainable development and climate change

Nested within the commitment to sustainable development are global agreements and related multilevel policy developments designed to tackle climate change (see Box 13.1). At a global level these developments can be traced to the first UN Earth summit held in Rio de Janeiro in 1992 (and which have since been held at ten-yearly intervals). The idea of holding an earth summit was recommended by the Brundtland Report to progress the implementation of sustainable development globally. The *Rio Declaration on the Environment and Development* (UN Environment Programme, 1992) included a number of principles to guide climate change policy, including the precautionary principle; the polluter pays principle; and the principle of 'common but differentiated responsibilities' between developed and developing countries. However, as with previous declarations, assessments of the practical influence of these principles are generally pessimistic (Gough, 2013).

The essence of the climate change problem is the build-up of 'greenhouse gases' (GHGs) in the atmosphere, hampering the atmosphere's ability to deflect heat from the sun's rays, thus leading to global warming. Though GHGs also include methane and nitrous oxide, the primary one is carbon dioxide (CO_2). CO_2 emissions are linked to the burning of fossil fuels, an activity which has been accelerating since the onset of industrialisation and whose negative effects have become increasingly apparent since the 1970s. The most recent assessment of the IPCC (2014: 2) therefore states that 'each of the last three decades has been successively warmer at the Earth's surface than any preceding decade since 1850'. From the period 1880 to 2012 the IPCC found that the global average temperate has increased by 0.85°C. In projecting future trends, the IPCC predicts a continuation of global warming under all scenarios, ranging from the smallest rise under stringent mitigation to the greatest rises in the absence of additional efforts to constrain emissions. Across this spectrum, average global surface temperature is predicted to rise by the end of the twenty-first century relative to 1986-2005, to between 0.3°C to 1.7°C under the best-case scenario, and to between 2.6°C and 4.8°C under the worst-case scenario. Regardless of what temperature rise occurs, the IPCC (2014: 10) suggests that 'it is *virtually certain* that there will be more frequent hot and fewer cold temperature extremes over most land areas on daily and seasonal timescales … It is *very likely* that heat waves will occur with a higher frequency and longer duration'.

Box 13.1: Climate change: key global, EU and national commitments

1992 Rio Summit – UNFCCC (United Nations Framework Convention on Climate Change), a UN treaty setting out (loose) obligations on climate change and emissions reductions on the part of UN members who signed the treaty. Detailed agreements are subsequently negotiated at meetings of the conference of parties (CoPs) and the Kyoto Protocol was agreed as a result of acknowledging that tighter obligations were needed than set out in the original UNFCCC.

1997 Kyoto Protocol – agreed after the third CoP held in Kyoto. Under the principle of common but differentiated responsibilities it set mandatory GHG targets for developed members, depending on their level of economic development. The protocol came into force in 2005 and has two commitment periods, 2008-12 and 2013-20. The overall target for the 2008-12 period was to reduce GHG emissions by 5% compared to 1990 levels.

The EU set a reduction target of 8%, under which Ireland was permitted to increase its GHGs by 13% above its 1990 levels in recognition of its underdeveloped economy at that time. Under the second period, the EU again agreed to make deeper cuts – a 20% reduction compared to 1990 levels. Under this Ireland is committed to reduce its GHGs (outside of the non-European Trading Scheme sectors, which the EU as a whole is responsible for) by 20% compared to 2005 levels.

2015 Paris Agreement – achieved at the 21st CoP, agrees to 'holding the increase in the global average temperature to well below 2°C above pre-industrial levels and pursuing efforts to limit the temperature increase to 1.5°C above pre-industrial levels' (UNFCCC, 2015: 5). It came into force in November 2016 after a sufficient number of member countries signed it. Commitments to meeting this goal, by both developed and developing countries are to be nationally determined and progress is to be assessed by five-yearly global stocktakes.

Prior to the Paris CoP, the EU set its contribution as a 40% reduction by 2030, as part of a longer-term goal of an 80% to 95% reduction by 2050. As of 2016, Ireland's targets under the EU plan are yet to be agreed. In 2014, however, Ireland set out a National Policy Position of an 80% reduction in CO_2 emissions by 2050.

Policy responses to global warming generally come under two types: adaptation and mitigation. Adaptation entails 'adjusting to climate change that is already underway' while mitigation refers to 'actions to slow the accumulation of GHG emissions in order to forestall further climate change' (Baker, 2016: 174). However, the bigger picture of the causes of global warming, the risks and the policy responses is one of entrenched inequalities which are tied up with the complexities and politics of sustainable development. The anthropogenic or human–related causes of climate change as well as the uneven impact of the risks associated with it expose the continued path of unsustainable development that has evolved since the 1970s. In reality earth summits, which involve up to 200 governments result in the 'law of least ambitious program' such that 'collective action will be limited to those measure acceptable to the least enthusiastic party' (Foryn, 2007 in Gough, 2013: 190). Progress towards sustainable development and mitigating climate change has therefore not materialised despite the Kyoto Protocol. Developing countries, rehearsing versions of the pollution of poverty argument, remain opposed to actions that would curb their opportunities for economic growth. Later industrialisers, such as China, India and Brazil are now the greatest contributors to rising GHG emissions; however, this does not negate the fact that developed countries are responsible for the bulk of historic emissions because of their longer histories of industrialisation. Developed nations, the US in particular, have similarly obstructed progress on agreements and their content. The obstructing role played by the US is in turn underpinned by corporate actors whose interests in fossil fuel-based industries would be threatened by far-reaching action on climate change. While the EU has been more progressive and set more ambitious targets than globally agreed ones, there are also divisions within EU institutions and among the member states about what EU targets should be (Skovgaard, 2014). The chief mechanisms used are market-based instruments, such as the EU Emissions Trading Scheme, and EU thinking has been informed at a stretch, by ecological modernisation. However, as Baker (2016: 57) suggests this model is 'silent on issues of social justice, the distribution of wealth and on society–nature relations'. It is also significant that EU15 countries achieved greater reductions in GHG emissions in 2009, at the height of the economic crisis, than in the previous 18 years combined. Any achievements therefore 'are less a result of conscious climate policy measures and much more the outcome of ad hoc events and crises' (ETUI, 2012: 82). The same can be said for the Irish case, which we turn to later. This lack of progress is reflected in the worsening of global warming. The Paris Agreement, settled only after several failed attempts to agree a successor agreement to the Kyoto Protocol, sets out a more ambitious plan, though considering that national commitments have yet to be determined and actually pursued leaves much open to question.

Underlying the politics of these agreements is a pattern of continued unsustainable development. The global ecological footprint, which includes among other elements, the earth's capacity to absorb carbon, has grown substantially since the 1970s, resulting in global overshoot. The WWF (World Wide Fund for Nature) estimates that in 2016, the equivalent of 1.6 'earths' was needed to account for all the resources used globally. The crux of this problem is that nations are not equally responsible for this overshoot, a small number of countries, who are also the poorest are 'ecological creditor countries', while the majority are 'ecological debtor countries' using more than their share of global resources; though the extent of overshoot varies substantially (WWF, 2016). This is also reflected in differences in per capita CO_2 emissions (see Table 13.1). It should be kept in mind that current accounting methods for CO_2 emissions are nation based. This means that with the global shift in manufacturing activity, some less-developed countries' CO_2 emissions are generated by the production of goods that are ultimately destined for consumption by the world's richer nations (Artaraz and Hill, 2016). Nation-based per capita measurements therefore do not fully capture responsibility for emission trends. Differences within countries are also significant. For example, using a consumption-based measure of emissions (and thus attributing the emissions related to the production of luxury goods to where the goods are exported) the richest 10% of people in the US emit 50 metric tonnes of CO_2 per capita, while the bottom 50% emit nine metric tonnes per capita (Oxfam, 2015, figures interpolated from bar chart).

Table 13.1: CO_2 emissions, per capita, selected countries and country blocs, 2013

Country/country bloc	CO_2 metric tonnes per capita
World	5.0
EU	6.7
Least developed countries, UN classification	0.3
US	16.4
China	7.6
India	1.6
Ireland	7.6

Data source: World Bank, www.data.worldbank.org

Returning to the concepts of climate justice and double injustice mentioned earlier in the chapter, it is clear that the developed world is responsible for the majority of climate change, while the poor bear the brunt of the risks (see Box 13.2). This is the case both between the developed and developing regions of the globe, and between the poorest and richest within countries, regardless of their levels of wealth. Risks include risk of death, ill health and disrupted livelihoods, as well as food insecurity from extreme weather events such as flooding, drought and heat waves, and from disrupted public services as a result of these events (IPCC, 2014). Responses also bear the prospect of a triple injustice (see Box 13.2). As Gough (2013: 196, emphasis in the original) asks, 'might the double injustice which characterises global environmental relations be converted into a *triple* injustice, whereby the poor emit less, suffer more, *and* bear the brunt of climate mitigation policies?'

Box 13.2: Connections between climate change and climate justice

i Responsibility for climate change is not equally distributed. Some groups and societies emit more GHG than others, an idea known as 'ecological debt'

ii Impacts will not affect all groups and societies equally: some are more vulnerable than others

iii The developed world has greater capacity to protect itself against climate change (adaptation)

iv Vulnerability is determined by political-economic processes that benefit some and disadvantage others, with the disadvantaged frequently being the most vulnerable

v Climate change will compound underdevelopment, given the factors above

vi   Policy responses may themselves create unfair outcomes by exacerbating, maintaining, or ignoring existing and future inequalities

vii   The developed world has more financial and technical ability to undertake mitigation effort

Source: modified from Barnett 2006: 115 in Baker, 2016: 180

From the point of view of social policy, and specifically in the context of the welfare states of the developed world, addressing such inequities, according to Gough (2013: 198) would mean 'taking seriously our responsibility for the historic development of carboniferous capitalism, accumulated GHGs and the major part of global warming thus far'. In something akin to an ideal model of sustainable development, this would entail a radical rethink of economic growth and a shift to de-growth or a steady-state model of the economy, which would 'very likely entail some move away from the consumption of commodities towards de-commodified production – reducing working hours and commodity purchases, developing "co-production" (comprising civic and household economies), and fostering preventive social behaviour' (Gough, 2013: 198 and see Gough and Meadowcroft, 2011 for further elaboration of these ideas and policy implications). The reality, however, is that policy developments in the developed world equate at best to a weak model of sustainable development, with perhaps some elements of a strong model, depending on national context. Though a sceptic might ask whether anything about the high consumption and (aspiration of) high growth model of contemporary capitalism equates with sustainable development and commitment to tackle climate change. Within this ambiguous and ambivalent context, in the following section we examine transport policy with specific reference to Ireland's attempt to achieve sustainable development and meet its climate change targets.

SECTION THREE
SOCIAL POLICY, TRANSPORT AND THE ENVIRONMENT

Transport trends and problems

Transport and transport policy is clearly a matter of environmental concern and 'how we travel has become a pressing ethical, environmental and social issue in the 21st century' (Cahill, 2011: 227). As a sector which is heavily dependent on fossil fuels, transport is one of the main contributors to GHG emissions as well as to other sources of air pollutants linked to ill health. In Europe, for example, transport contributes a quarter of GHG emissions, behind only the contribution from energy use. Within the transport sector, road transport accounts for more than 70% of GHG emissions (European Commission, 2016), and while emissions from other sectors have been declining since the 1990s, transport sector emissions continue to grow (Gössling and Cohen, 2014). Underlying this is the centrality of the car to the value and experience of mobility in modern society: 'car culture has developed into a dominant culture generating major discourses of what constitutes the good life and what is necessary to be a mobile citizen' (Urry, 2007: 117). If car ownership constitutes the good life and being on the move signifies social status and success, conversely use of public transport is often stigmatised. This perception of public transport was epitomised by a remark attributed to Margaret Thatcher: 'a man who, beyond the age of 26, finds himself on a bus can count himself as a failure' (cited in Milne, 2012: 65). This elevation of private over public transport in turn affects the social cohesion of communities, and as Barry (2002: 26 in Lucas, 2012: 109) puts it, 'the private car is the enemy of social solidarity in as much as public transport is its friend. The private car isolates people and puts them in competition with other road users'. However, the values attached to mobility, and the ethical and social issues attached to travel, are taboo subjects in politics and policy making (Gössling and Cohen, 2014). Policy is for the most part restricted to measures that don't fundamentally challenge private car ownership and car culture.

In Ireland the 1980s marks the end to what Tovey and Share (2000: 436) identify as 'ascetic developmentalism' and the gradual transition to a high-consumption society. As part of that transition, changes related to transport made up a large part of the changing picture of GHG emissions in Ireland. In 1990 transport contributed 9.1% of total emissions and by 2015 it contributed 19.8% (see Figure 13.1). The total number of vehicles exceeded 2.5 million for the first time in 2014, and 1.9 million of these vehicles are private (EPA, 2016). The increasing volume and usage of motor cars counter any gains made in cleaner car technologies. This is an example of the rebound effect, which raises questions about the efficiency premises of ecological modernisation (Baker, 2016). Thus greater consumption, in this case car use, outstrips any gains made by cleaner technologies, and indeed these may actually encourage greater car use. There are also questions about the validity of energy emissions data supplied by car manufacturers, and the discrepancy between emissions in real world conditions, which have been found to be up to 40% higher compared to laboratory tests (EPA, 2016). Ireland's economic downturn did temporarily halt the pattern of increasing car numbers, and with it, increases in nitrogen dioxide (NO_2) emissions; however, it is expected that economic recovery will reverse these trends (EPA, 2016).

In the Irish context, traffic volume and car use patterns are also directly connected with the ways in which land use and settlement patterns have evolved. In particular, the manner in which suburbanisation has unfolded poses serious environmental challenges due to the intensification of low-density urban sprawl throughout the housing boom of the mid-1990s to the mid-2000s. During that time there has been a proliferation of detached houses, which create larger footprints than other housing types, and which are spread out over wide areas.

Figure 13.1: Ireland's GHG emissions (total and transport), 1990-2015

National total ■ Transport

Data source: Environmental Protection Agency (www.epa.ie/irelandsenvironment/environmentalindicators)

Noting this trend, the European Environment Agency (2006) pointed to Dublin sprawl (along with Istanbul and Madrid) as 'a worst-case scenario' of urban planning. This type of development generated further car ownership, with McGoldrick and Caulfield (2015) finding that households living in houses built during the boom were more likely to have poor access to public transport and to own several cars. Public transport has not developed in tandem with housing sprawl and housing sprawl in itself becomes a reason not to provide public transport, because it is more costly to provide in comparison to transport which serves compact settlement areas.

A long-standing trend has been increasing car dependency as a means of travel to work (Figure 13.2). Even though the numbers commuting on foot, by bicycle and by train – all of which have less environmental impact than cars – have generally increased, the share of travel by car has continued to grow.

Transport is also a major contributor to poor urban air quality and therefore to health risks associated with poor air quality. While Ireland currently complies with the EU standards on air quality, in urban areas it exceeds air quality guidelines suggested by the World Health Organization, based on revised information on the relationship between air quality and health (EPA, 2016). Two pollutants in particular are associated with road traffic, particulate matter (PM_{10}) and NO_2. The inhalation of small particles is associated with respiratory and cardiopulmonary disorders, such as asthma, heart disease and lung cancer. Children, because of the immaturity of their lungs, and older people, who may already have respiratory or cardiopulmonary disorders, are particularly vulnerable to health problems due to exposure to air pollution. It is estimated that 1,200 people annually die

Figure 13.2: Means of travel to work and total share of car drivers, 1991-2011

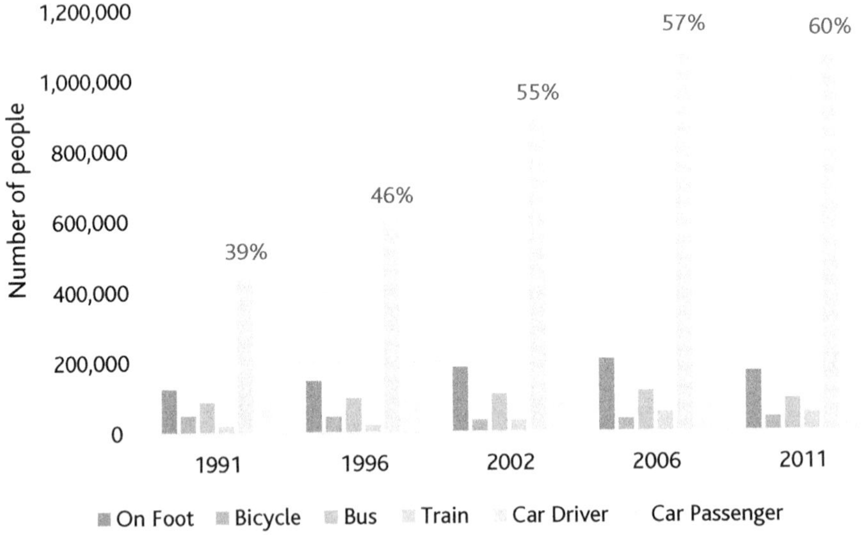

Data source: CSO

prematurely in Ireland because of air pollution, primarily due to strokes and heart disease attributable to air pollution (EPA, 2016). Low-income groups generally also bear the brunt of environmental inequalities associated with road traffic (Baeten, 2000). They are, for example, more likely to live near busy roads, and thus have greater exposure to air pollution and to noise pollution, and they are also more vulnerable to accidents because of where they live and their greater likelihood to walk or to cycle (Lucas et al, 2001).

Transport inequalities, travel poverty and social exclusion

Transport policy is primarily concerned with mobility as physical movement, and on improving the movement of those who are already mobile. This focus obscures the fact that transport is integral to social goals, such as social inclusion and improving quality of life. Those who don't have cars and whose access to public transport is non-existent or very limited, are socially excluded. Travel poverty covers a number of areas and dimensions (Box 13.3).

Box 13.3: Dimensions of travel poverty

Mobility poverty: A systemic lack of (usually motorised) transport that generates difficulties in moving, often (but not always) connected to a lack of services or infrastructures

Accessibility poverty: The difficulty of reaching certain key activities – such as employment, education, healthcare services, shops and so on – at reasonable time, ease and cost

Transport affordability: The lack of individual/household resources to afford transportation options, typically with reference to the car (in developed countries) and/or public transport

Exposure to transport externalities: The outcomes of disproportionate exposures to the negative effects of the transport system, such as road traffic casualties and chronic diseases and deaths from traffic related pollution

Source: Lucas et al, 2016: 355

Travel poverty, in particular its accessibility and mobility dimensions, can interact with broader patterns of change affecting public service delivery. For example, the necessity of transport to access healthcare and other social services is compounded when public services are in retreat (Nutley, 2000), such as the centralisation of hospital services. The spatial positioning of services is also determined by transport policy, as services tend to follow new roads, and therefore become located along major road networks and out-of-town centres. As a consequence, local communities lose localised services, such as doctor surgeries, banks, post offices and shops, which were more accessible for those without cars. Transport policy that assumes car ownership and is based on ease of movement for car drivers detracts from, rather than enhances, social sustainability and sustainable communities.

The social dimension of transport is not just about social exclusion, but quality of life and social capital. Mobility and transport can contribute to 'social capital and the building of networks and relationships between people, feelings of trust and mutual assistance or reciprocity' (Stanley and Lucas, 2008: 37). As such, mobility and access to transport 'gives people greater access to a wider range of interests and activities and allows them a higher degree of engagement with other like-minded members of the various communities to which they belong, thus enriching their lives and contributing to social and economic vitality' (Troy, 1996: 208 in Lucas, 2004: 10). On the whole, however, the role of transport in enhancing quality of life has been scarcely explored, and quality of life in debates about transport tend to be reduced to an economistic notion of time-saving, particularly for commuters.

Travel poverty in terms of its affordability dimension not only refers to those who don't own cars and who have little or no access to public transport, it is also concerned with those on low incomes who are dependent on cars for mobility. These people are 'forced' to own cars (Lucas et al, 2001). This means that in the absence of suitable public transport these people have little choice but to own a car to meet their essential needs such as access to employment, healthcare and shopping. This explains why there is still a high level of car ownership within low-income families. This is especially the case where low-income families live in isolated rural areas; or who work in shifts and/or at isolated locations on the edge of cities; or who have to make multipurpose trips under time constraints, which applies to women as mothers and carers in particular (Lucas et al, 2001). In addition, car ownership among low-income households to an extent exacerbates their poverty and social exclusion, as sacrifices are made in order to be able to run a car, and in comparison with wealthier car owners, fewer and shorter trips are made (Lucas et al, 2001).

Regarding rural transport and travel poverty, although car dependency is very high in rural Ireland and rural car-ownership is higher than urban car-ownership (CSO, 2012c), this obscures the problems experienced by those living in rural areas without access to cars. This includes people with disabilities, older people, women, lone parents and younger people (McDonagh, 2006; Irish Rural Link, 2016). Cloke (1993, in McDonagh, 2006) found, for example, that these people feel 'trapped either at home or away from home' because of their dependency on very limited public transport services or depending on neighbours for lifts. Furthermore, lack of transport is a significant factor contributing to the loneliness of older rural dwellers (Drennan et al, 2008). In addition McGrath's (1999) comparison of travel patterns between urban and rural car owners shows that the quality of rural life is not necessarily enhanced by car ownership. He found that rural dwellers spend far more time in their cars, often making trips 'to serve passenger' in the absence of public transport and general lack of accessible amenities in the countryside.

As for travel poverty in urban areas, lack of public transport contributes to the social segregation of particular areas; especially areas with high levels of social housing. If transport is a means by which other rights can be enjoyed, lack of public transport affects people's 'right to the city' (Harvey 2003 in Lucas et al, 2016) not only in terms of accessing employment, but fully participating in the social and cultural life of the city. Wickham (2004: 13) for example cites the example of Jobstown in Dublin, an area of high unemployment and a high proportion of social housing, but with very poor public transport links to other areas in the city: 'in Jobstown, those without a car were isolated: getting a job or even doing the shopping became major and sometimes insuperable logistical problems'. This pattern is repeated in other areas of the city: deprivation and poor public transport go together (Ahern et al, 2016). Moreover, people who live in disadvantaged areas who do have a job are the most likely to have the longest commute times, of 90 minutes or more, which is linked to lack of timely and accessible public bus transport (Rock et al, 2016).

Challenges for the development of sustainable transport policy

In common with the concept of sustainable development, the meaning of sustainable transport is open to diverse interpretations. As Steg and Gifford (2005: 60) note, 'it is generally accepted that ... sustainable transport involves finding a proper balance between (current and future) environmental, social and economic qualities. ... it is less clear which environmental, social and economic qualities should be guaranteed and balanced'. In practical terms sustainable transport policy involves a shift from a 'predict and provide' model to a 'predict and prevent' model, based on curbing escalating car use, and providing and encouraging alternative modes of transport which have a lesser impact on the environment. In the Irish context, where planning and transport policy are very heavily based on mobility by car, the transition to sustainable transport is a huge challenge. It is very difficult and costly to reverse decades of policy and provision based on urban sprawl, rural dispersion and car dependency. In addition it is evident that only the most minimal attention is given to social concerns in how sustainable transport policy is evolving.

During the celtic tiger period the 'predict and provide' model was dominant and large sums of money were spent on transport infrastructure which privileged private transport. In the National Development Plan 2000-2006 (GoI, 1999c), €4.7 billion was allocated to roads and €2.234 billion to public transport measures. This was followed with plans for investment of €34 billion in *Transport 21*, a programme of investment intended to cover the period 2006-15. However, the economic crisis meant that the programme of expenditure was cancelled midway in 2010. *Transport 21* recalibrated the balance between public and private transport expenditure somewhat, €18 billion was to be spent on roads and €16 billion between public transport and regional airports, and the policy appeared to embrace the idea of sustainable transport. However, the dominant thrust, according to Rau et al (2016), remained a car-centric, predict and provide model. Its replacement, *Smarter Travel 2009-2020* (DoT, 2009) is set in the context of radical cutbacks to the transport budget, so it is difficult to assess whether the policy signals a definitive paradigm shift to sustainable transport (Rau et al, 2016). Instead of large-scale projects, public or private, the policy focuses on low-cost and low-carbon modes of transport and reducing private car use. Moreover, the policy is framed by an acknowledgement that Ireland's travel and transport trends are unsustainable. However, even if the policy signals an actual shift in policy ideas and practice related to the environmental dimension of sustainability, it nevertheless has several shortcomings with regard to social sustainability. Besides broad references to social inclusion and an overall goal to 'improve quality of life and accessibility to transport for all and, in particular, for people with reduced mobility and those who may experience isolation due to lack of transport' (DoT, 2009: 27), these are not linked with any tangible actions or any explicit reference to poverty or transport poverty. The *Programme for a Partnership Government* (GoI, 2016c) seems to signal a return to 'business as usual' and a return to the 'predict and provide' model with increases in capital expenditure planned for road building and for light-rail projects in Dublin.

When measured against recent trends with regard to car dependency, GHG emissions and Ireland's overall efforts in relation to climate change, there are further reasons to doubt the shift to sustainable transport. While Ireland was projected to substantially overshoot its Kyoto targets for 2012 during the boom, the subsequent recession meant that it actually achieved compliance. Ireland thus met its target primarily because of the recession and decline in economic activity, not because of any conscious policy effort. Moreover, predictions for 2020 targets suggest that Ireland will not meet them. Along with emissions from agriculture, transport emissions, which are expected to increase by 10%–16% relative to 2014 levels, are also identified as a reason for this failure to meet targets (EPA, 2016). This makes the longer term goal of at least an 80% reduction in CO_2 emissions by 2050, as set out by Ireland's National Position Policy Position (DECLG, 2014b) more difficult to achieve, notwithstanding the fact that this target is considered the minimum Ireland should aspire to (Climate Change Advisory Council, 2016).

Ireland's GHG emissions and the question of appropriate reduction-targets fit within the bigger picture of Ireland's ecological footprint. On that measure it would appear that the country has been overshooting its national biocapacity since the 1970s, with fluctuations largely determined by the state of the economy (Figure 13.3). If Ireland's footprint was measured against its global share of biocapacity, which currently stands at 1.7 global hectares per person, then the overshoot is considerably greater. The issues reviewed here matter therefore, not only for future well-being and sustainable development within Ireland, but also for Ireland's global responsibilities in terms of sustainable development and climate justice.

Figure 13.3: Ireland's ecological footprint

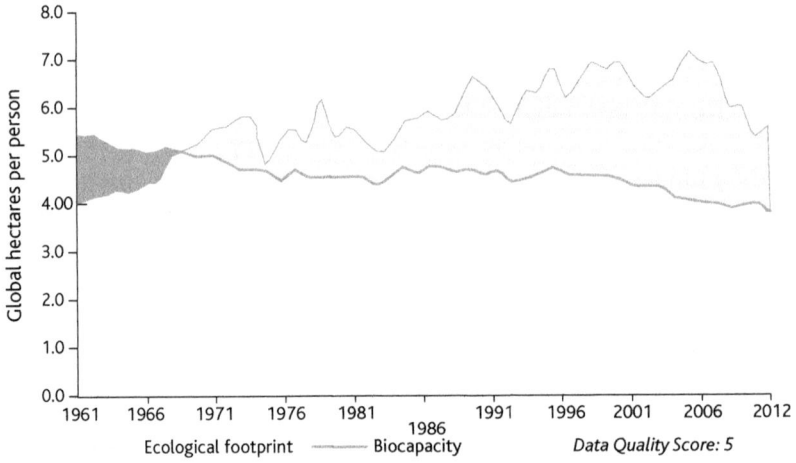

Source: © 2016 Global Footprint Network. www.footprintnetwork.org

Chapter summary

- This chapter has considered the issue of the environment and sustainable development and its implications for the discipline of social policy. As environmental concerns and the concept of sustainable development have entered mainstream policy discourse, and have increasingly centred on issues of social relevance such as environmental injustices, greater connections have been forged between social policy and the environment.
- Against this backdrop the chapter examined the evolution of the concept of sustainable development, looking in particular at efforts to address climate change within this framework. The realpolitik of climate change policy reveals the gap between the principles of sustainable development and their realisation, with the consequences evident in a range of climate change injustices.
- Turning specifically to themes of transport, climate change and environmental inequalities, the final section of the chapter examined these issues in the Irish context, documenting the ways the transport and transport policy in Ireland cannot be said to currently contribute to sustainable development nor mitigate climate change.

Discussion points

- Explore the reasons why social policy has traditionally been sceptical about environmentalism.
- In what ways are the emerging impacts of climate change in the developed world issues of environmental justice?
- Think about the area in which you live and how public transport serves that area. Consider its adequacy, who uses it and whether it contributes to sustainable travel patterns.

Further reading list

Aldred, R, Cahill, M, Ginsburg, N and MacGregor, S (guest eds) (2011) *Social justice, social policy and the environment*. Themed Issue of *Critical Social Policy*, 31:2

Baker, S (2016) *Sustainable development* (2nd edn), Abingdon: Routledge

Fitzpatrick, T (ed) (2011) *Understanding the environment and social policy*, Bristol: Policy Press

Lucas, K (ed) (2004) *Running on empty: Transport, social exclusion and environmental justice*, Bristol: Policy Press

References

Aalbers, M (2015) 'The great moderation, the great excess and the global housing crisis', *International Journal of Housing Policy*, 15:1, 43-60

Aalbers, M and Engelen, E (2015) 'The political economy of the rise, fall and rise again of securitization', *Environment and Planning A*, 47, 1597-605

Aalen, FHA (1985) 'The working-class housing movement in Dublin, 1850-1920', in MJ Bannon (ed) *The emergence of Irish planning, 1880-1920*, Dublin: Turoe Press, 131-88

Abel-Smith, B and Townsend, P (1965) *The poor and the poorest: A new analysis of the Ministry of Labour's family expenditure surveys of 1953-1954 and 1960*, London: Bell

Adebowale, M (2008) 'Understanding environmental justice: Making the connection between sustainable development and social justice', in G Craig, T Burchardt and D Gordon (eds) *Social justice and public policy: Seeking fairness in diverse societies*, Bristol: Policy Press, 251-75

Adler, K (2016) Is Europe lurching to the far right? *BBC News*, 28 April, www.bbc.com/news/world-europe-36150807

Ahern, A, Vega, A and Caulfield, B (2016) 'Deprivation and access to work in Dublin City: The impact of transport disadvantage', *Research in Transportation Economics*, 57, 44-52

Aiken, W (1992) 'Human rights in an ecological era', *Environmental Values*, 1:3, 191-203

AITHS (All Ireland Traveller Health Study) (2010) *All Ireland traveller health study: Our geels – Qualitative studies, Part A of technical report 3*, Dublin: School of Public Health, Physiotherapy and Population Science, UCD

Akenson, DH (1970) *The Irish education experiment: The national system of education in the nineteenth century*, London: Routledge Kegan Paul

Alber, J (1988) 'Is there a crisis of the welfare state? Cross-national evidence from Europe, North America, and Japan', *European Sociological Review*, 4:3, 181-207

Alford, RR (1972) 'The political economy of health care: Dynamics without change', *Politics & Society*, 2:2, 127-64

Alford, RR (1975) *Health care politics: Ideological and interest group barriers to reform*, Chicago, IL: University of Chicago Press

Allen, M (1998) *The bitter word: Ireland's job famine and its aftermath*, Dublin: Poolbeg

All-Party Oireachtas Committee on the Constitution, The (2000) *Fifth progress report: Abortion*, Dublin: Stationery Office

Amnesty International Ireland (2014) *Bringing ESC rights home: The case for legal protection of economic, social and cultural rights in Ireland*, Dublin: Amnesty International Ireland

Anderson, KM (2015) *Social policy in the European Union*, London: Palgrave

André, C (2010) *A bird's eye view of OECD housing markets*, OECD Economics Department Working Papers No. 746, Paris: OECD

Antoniades, A (2007) 'Examining facets of the hegemonic: The globalization discourse in Greece and Ireland', *Review of International Political Economy*, 14:2, 306-32

Anttonen, A and Sipilä, J (2012) 'Universalism in the British and Scandinavian social policy debates', in A Anttonen, L Häikiö and K Stefánsson (eds) *Welfare state, universalism and diversity*, Cheltenham: Edward Elgar, 16-41

Arneson, R (2015) 'Equality of opportunity', *The Stanford Encyclopedia of Philosophy* (2015 edn), EN Zalta (ed) https://plato.stanford.edu/entries/equal-opportunity/

Artaraz, K and Hill, M (2016) *Global social policy: Themes, issues and actors*, London: Palgrave

Arts, WA and Gelissen, J (2002) 'Three worlds of welfare capitalism or more? A state-of-the-art report', *Journal of European Social Policy*, 12:2, 137-58

Atkinson, AB (2015) *Inequality: What can be done?*, Cambridge, MA: Harvard UP

Bacik, I (2015) 'Abortion and the law in Ireland', in A Quilty, S Kennedy and C Conlon (eds) *The abortion papers Ireland: Volume 2*, Cork: Attic Press, 104-17

Baeten, G (2000) 'The tragedy of the highway: Empowerment, disempowerment and the politics of sustainable discourses and practices', *European Planning Studies*, 8:1, 69-86

Bailey, D (2015) 'The environmental paradox of the welfare state: The dynamics of sustainability', *New Political Economy*, 20:6, 793-811

Bailey, S (2016) 'From invisibility to visibility: A policy archaeology of the introduction of anti-transphobic and anti-homophobic bullying guidelines into the Irish primary education system', *Irish Educational Studies*, ahead of print: DOI: 10.1080/03323315.2016.1243066

Baker, J (2003) 'Poverty and equality: Ten reasons why anyone who wants to combat poverty should embrace equality as well', in CPA/Equality Authority, *Poverty and inequality applying an equality dimension to poverty proofing*, Dublin: CPA

Baker, J, Lynch, K, Cantillon, S and Walsh, J (2009) *Equality: From theory to action* (2nd edn), Basingstoke: Palgrave Macmillan

Baker, J, Lynch, K and Walsh, J (2015) 'Cutting back on equality', in R Meade and F Dukelow (eds) *Defining events: Power, resistance and identity in twenty-first-century Ireland*, Manchester: Manchester University Press, 181-199

Baker, S (2016) *Sustainable development* (2nd edn), Abingdon: Routledge

Balanda, KP and Wilde, J (2001) *Inequalities in mortality 1989-1998: A report on All-Ireland mortality data*, Dublin: IPH

Baldwin, R, Beck, T, Bénassy-Quéré, A, Blanchard, O, Corsetti, G, de Grauwe, P, den Haan, W, Giavazzi, F, Gros, D, Kalemli-Ozcan, S, Micossi, S, Papaioannou, E, Pesenti, P, Pissarides, C, Tabellini G and Weder di Mauro, B (2015) 'Rebooting the Eurozone, step 1: Agreeing a crisis narrative', *CEPR Policy Insight No 85*, CEPR, available at: http://voxeu.org/sites/default/files/file/Policy%20Insight%2085.pdf

Ball, S (2013) *The education debate* (2nd edn), Bristol: Policy Press

Banks, J and McCoy, S (2011) *A study on the prevalence of special educational needs: National Council for Special Education research report No. 9*, Trim, Co. Meath: NCSE

Banks, J, Byrne, D, McCoy, S and Smyth, E (2014) 'Bottom of the class? The Leaving Certificate Applied Programme and track placement in the Republic of Ireland', *Irish Educational Studies*, 33:4, 367–81

Banks, J, McCoy, S, Frawley, D, Kingston, G, Shevlin, M and Smyth, F (2016) *Special classes in Irish schools phase 2: A qualitative study, research report No. 24*, Trim, Co. Meath: NCSE

Banting, K and Kymlicka, W (2012) 'Is there really a backlash against multiculturalism policies? New evidence from the multiculturalism policy index', GRITIM Working Paper Series, 14, Barcelona: Pompeu Fabra University

Baradat, LP (2000) *Political ideologies: Their origins and impact* (7th edn), Mahwah, NJ: Prentice Hall

Barber, T (2016) 'Ireland may be Europe's comeback kid, but not thanks to Brussels', *Financial Times*, 4 February

Barbier, J-C (2004) 'Systems of social protection in Europe: Two contrasted paths to activation, and maybe a third', in J Lind, H Knudsen and H Jørgensen (eds) *Labour and employment regulation in Europe*, Brussels: Peter Lang, 233-54

Barr, N (2001) *The welfare state as piggy bank: Information, risk, uncertainty and the role of the state*, Oxford: Oxford UP

Barr, N (2004) *Economics of the welfare state* (4th edn), Oxford: Oxford UP

Barrington, R (1987) *The politics of health and medicine, 1900-1970*, Dublin: IPA

Barron, P (1995) 'The Child Care Act 1991: An overview', in H Ferguson and P Kenny (eds) *On behalf of the child: Child welfare, child protection and the Child Care Act 1991*, Dublin: A&A Farmar, 9-16

Barry, J (1998) 'Social policy and social movements: Ecology and social policy', in N Ellison and C Pierson (eds) *Developments in British social policy*, Basingstoke: Palgrave Macmillan, 218-32

Barry, J and Daly, L (1988) *Travellers' health status study census of Travelling People 1986*, Dublin: Health Research Board

Barry, J, Herity, B and Solan, J (1989) *The Travellers health status study: Vital statistics of the Travelling People, 1987*, Dublin: Health Research Board

Barry, K (2014) *What's food got to do with it? Food experiences of asylum seekers in direct provision*, Cork: NASC

Bauman, Z (2013) *150 years of German social democracy*, Social Europe Occasional Paper 2, Social Europe, available at: www.socialeurope.eu/book/op-2-150-years-of-german-social-democracy/

Beaumont, C (1997) 'Women and the politics of equality: The Irish women's movement, 1930-1943', in MG Valiulis and M O'Dowd (eds) *Women and Irish history*, Dublin: Wolfhound Press, 173-88

Begley, E, O'Brien, M, Carter Anand, J, Killick, C and Taylor, B (2012) 'Older people's views of support services in response to elder abuse in communities across Ireland', *Quality in Ageing and Older Adults*, 13:1, 48-59

Béland, D, Rocco, P and Waddan, A (2016) 'Obamacare and the politics of universal health insurance coverage in the United States', *Social Policy & Administration*, 50:4, 428-51

Berend, IT (2005) 'Foucault and the welfare state', *European Review*, 13:4, 551-6

Beresford, P (2016) 'Personal budgets don't work. So why are we ignoring the evidence?', *The Guardian*, 5 May

Berger, S (2002) 'Democracy and social democracy', *European History Quarterly*, 32:1, 13-37

Beveridge, W (1942) *Social insurance and allied services: Report by Sir William Beveridge*, London: HMSO

Bhreatnach, A (2006) *Becoming conspicuous: Irish Travellers, society and state, 1922-70*, Dublin: UCD Press

Blackwell, J (1982) 'Government, economy and society', in F Litton (ed) *Unequal achievement: The Irish experience 1957-1982*, Dublin: IPA, 43-60

Blackwell, J (1990) 'Housing finance and subsidies in Ireland', in P McLennan and R Williams (eds) *Affordable housing in Europe*, York: Joseph Rowntree Foundation, 101-27

Blair, T (1998) *The third way: New politics for the new century*, Fabian Pamphlet 588, London: Fabian Society

Blank, RH and Burau, V (2014) *Comparative health policy* (4th edn) Basingstoke: Palgrave Macmillan

Bloemraad, I (2011) 'The debate over multiculturalism: philosophy, politics, and policy', Migration Policy Institute, available at: www.migrationpolicy.org/article/debate-over-multiculturalism-philosophy-politics-and-policy

Bloom, DE and McKinnon, R (2010) 'Social security and the challenge of demographic change', *International Social Security Review*, 63:3/4, 3-21

Bochel, H and Powell, M (2016) 'The transformation of the welfare state? The Conservative-Liberal Democrat coalition government and social policy', in H Bochel and M Powell (eds) *The coalition government and social policy: Restructuring the welfare state*, Bristol: Policy Press, 1-25

Bochel, H, Bochel, C, Page, R and Sykes, R (2005) *Social policy: Issues and developments*, Harlow: Pearson

Böhmer, M, Funke, C, Sachs, A, Weinelt, H and Weiß, J (2016) *Globalization Report 2016: Who benefits most from globalization?*, Gütersloh: Bertelsmann-Stiftung

Bonoli, G (2007) 'Time matters: Postindustrialization, new social risks, and welfare state adaptation in advanced industrial democracies', *Comparative Political Studies*, 40:5, 495-520

Bonoli, G (2011) 'Active labour market policy in a changing economic context', in J Clasen and D Clegg (eds) *Regulating the risk of unemployment: National adaptations to post-industrial labour markets in Europe*, Oxford: Oxford UP, 318-32

Boucher, G (2008) 'Ireland's lack of a coherent integration policy', *Translocations*, 3:1, 5-28

Boucher, G (2010) 'The entrenchment of Ireland's laissez-faire integration policy', *Translocations*, 6:2, 1-7

Bourdieu, P (1986) 'The forms of capital', in JG Richardson (ed) *Handbook of theory and research for the sociology of education*, Westport, CT: Greenwood Press, 241-58

Bourdieu, P and Passeron, J-C (1977) *Reproduction in education, society and culture*, Sheffield: Sheffield Region Centre for Science and Technology

Brandi, S (2007) 'Unveiling the ideological construction of the 2004 Irish citizenship referendum: A critical discourse analysis approach', *Translocations*, 2:1, 26-47

Brandi, S (2013) 'The intra-Traveller debate on "Traveller ethnicity", in the Republic of Ireland: A critical discourse analysis', PhD thesis, University College Cork

Braveman, P (2006) 'Health disparities and health equity: Concepts and measurement', *Annual Review of Public Health*, 27, 167-94

Braveman, P and Gruskin, S (2003) 'Defining equity in health', *Journal of Epidemiology and Community Health*, 57:4, 254-58

Breen, R, Hannon, DF, Rottman, DB and Whelan, CT (1990) *Understanding contemporary Ireland: State, class and development in the Republic of Ireland*, Dublin: Gill & Macmillan

Brennan, C (2007) 'Facing what cannot be changed: The Irish experience of confronting institutional child abuse', *Journal of Social Welfare and Family Law*, 29:3-4, 245-63

Brennan, P (1982) 'Backlash and blackmail: How a tiny Catholic pressure group privately won a commitment to a constitutional amendment on abortion', *Magill*, July, 14-24

Brophy, CS and Delay, C (eds) (2015) *Women, reform and resistance in Ireland, 1850-1950*, Basingstoke: Palgrave Macmillan

Brown, P (2013) 'Education, opportunity and the prospects for social mobility', *British Journal of Sociology of Education*, 34:5/6, 678-700

Brown, P and Lauder, H (2006) 'Globalisation, knowledge and the myth of the magnet economy', *Globalisation, Societies and Education*, 4:1, 25-57

Brown, P and Tannock, S (2009) 'Education, meritocracy and the global war for talent', *Journal of Education Policy*, 24:4, 377-92

Brown, T (1981) 'Poverty, politics and policies', in S Kennedy (ed) *One million poor? The challenge of Irish inequality*, Dublin: Turoe Press, 145-63

Browne, N (1986) *Against the tide*, Dublin: Gill & Macmillan

Browne, V (ed) (1982) 'Will the last TD to leave the Dáil please switch off the light at the end of the tunnel', *Magill*, January, 21

Brownlee, A (2008) 'Paradise lost or found? The changing homeless policy landscape in Ireland', in D Downey (ed) *Perspectives on Irish homelessness: Past, present and future*, Dublin: Homeless Agency, 34–42

Bruton, R (2016) Written answers, Department of Education and Skills, Special Educational Needs Service Provision, Tuesday 19 July, available at: www.kildarestreet.com/wrans/?id=2016-07-19a.667

Bryan, A and Mayock, P (2012) 'Speaking back to dominant constructions of LGBT lives: complexifying "at riskness" for self-harm and suicidality among lesbian, gay, bisexual and transgender youth', *Irish Journal of Anthropology*, 15:2, 8–15

Bryson, V (2003) *Feminist political theory: An introduction* (2nd edn), Basingstoke: Macmillan

Buchanan, JM (2003) 'Public choice: Politics without romance', *Policy*, 19:3, 13–18

Büchs, M, Bardsley, N and Duwe, S (2011) 'Who bears the brunt? Distributional effects of climate change mitigation policies', *Critical Social Policy*, 31:2, 285–307

Buckley, H and Burns, K (2015) 'Child welfare and protection in Ireland: Déjà vu all over again', in A Christie, B Featherstone, S Quin and T Walsh (eds) *Social work in Ireland: Changes and continuities*, London: Palgrave Macmillan, 51–70

Burke, H (1987) *The people and the poor law in 19th century Ireland*, Dublin: Women's Education Bureau

Burke, S (2010) 'Boom to bust: Its impact on Irish health policy and health services', *Irish Journal of Public Policy*, 2:1, available at: http://publish.ucc.ie/ijpp/2010/01/burke/08/en

Burke, S (2016a) 'Reform of the Irish healthcare system: What reform?', MP Murphy and F Dukelow (eds) *The Irish welfare state in the twenty-first century: Challenges and change*, Basingstoke: Palgrave Macmillan, 167–91

Burke, S (2016b) 'Inequality and access to healthcare, Oireachtas Committee on the Future of Healthcare', 5 October, available at: http://www.oireachtas.ie/parliament/media/committees/futureofhealthcare/Dr-Sara-Burke,-Centre-for-Health-Policy-and-Management,-TCD.pdf

Burke, S and Pentony, S (2011) *Eliminating health inequalities: A matter of life and death*, Dublin: TASC

Burke, S, Thomas, S, Barry, S and Keegan, C (2014) 'Indicators of health system coverage and activity in Ireland during the economic crisis 2008–2014 – From "more with less" to "less with less"', *Health Policy*, 117, 275–8

Burke, S, Normand, C, Barry, S and Thomas, S (2016) 'From universal health insurance to universal healthcare? The shifting health policy landscape in Ireland since the economic crisis', *Health Policy*, 120:3, 235–40

Burningham, K and Thrush, D (2001) *Rainforests are a long way from here: The environmental concerns of disadvantaged groups*, York: Joseph Rowntree Foundation

Butler, J (1990) *Gender trouble: Feminism and the subversion of identity*, London: Routledge

Byers, V (2010) 'Irish healthcare: The evidence on communicating policy', paper presented at the Political Studies Association of Ireland Annual Conference, Dublin Institute of Technology, 8-10 October

Byrne, M (2015) 'Ireland's new transnational landlords', Ireland after NAMA blogpost, 9 September, available at: https://irelandafternama.wordpress.com/2015/09/09/irelands-new-transnational-landlords/

Cahill, M (1991) 'The greening of social policy', in N Manning (ed) *Social policy review, 1990-91*, Harlow: Longman, 9-23

Cahill, M (2002) *The environment and social policy*, London: Routledge

Cahill, M (2003) 'The environment and green social policy', in J Baldock, N Manning and S Vickerstaff (eds) *Social policy* (2nd edn), Oxford: Oxford UP, 553-76

Cahill, M (2010) *Transport, environment and society*, Maidenhead: Open UP

Cahill, M (2011) 'Transport', in T Fitzpatrick (ed) *Understanding the environment and social policy*, Bristol: Policy Press, 227-44

Callaghan, J (2003) 'Social democracy in transition', *Parliamentary Affairs*, 56:1, 125-40

Callan, T, Colgan, B, Logue, C, Savage, M and Walsh, JR (2015) *Distributional impact of tax, welfare and public service pay policies: Budget 2016 and budgets 2009-2016*, Dublin: ESRI

Callan, T, Nolan, B, Whelan, BJ, and Hannon, D with Creighton, S (1989) *Poverty, income and welfare in Ireland*, General Research Series, 46, Dublin: ESRI

Cantillon, B (2011) 'The paradox of the social investment state: Growth, employment and poverty in the Lisbon era', *Journal of European Social Policy*, 21:5, 432-49

Carabine, J (2004) 'Sexualities, personal lives and social policy', in J Carabine (ed) *Sexualities, personal lives and social policy*, Bristol: Policy Press with the Open University, 1-48

Care Alliance Ireland (2015) *Defining carers, discussion paper 1*, Dublin: Care Alliance Ireland

Care Alliance Ireland (2016) *Disadvantages faced by family carers*, Dublin: Care Alliance Ireland, available at: http://www.carealliance.ie/userfiles/file/Disadvantages%20Faced%20by%20Family%20Carers%20January%202016.pdf

Carers Association in partnership with Caring for Carers Ireland and Care Alliance Ireland (2008) *Listen to Carers: Report on a Nation-wide Carer Consultation*, available at: http://familycarers.ie/wp-content/uploads/2016/01/Listening-to-Carers-2008.pdf

Carey, S (2005) 'Land, labour and politics: Social insurance in post-war Ireland', *Social Policy and Society*, 4:3, 303-11

Carr, J and Haynes, A (2015) 'A clash of racializations: The policing of "race" and of anti-Muslim racism in Ireland', *Critical Sociology*, 41:1, 21-40

Carr, N (2014) 'Invisible from view: Leaving and aftercare provision in the Republic Of Ireland', *Australian Social Work*, 67:1, 88-101

Carter, N (2007) *The politics of the environment: Ideas, activism, policy* (2nd edn), Cambridge: Cambridge UP

Carter, N (2013) 'Greening the mainstream: Party politics and the environment', *Environmental Politics*, 22:1, 73-94

Carter Anand, J, Davidson, G, Macdonald, G, Kelly, B, Clift-Matthews, V, Martin, A, and Rizzo, M (2012) *The transition to personal budgets for people with disabilities: A review of practice in specified jurisdictions*, Dublin: NDA

Cassell, RD (1997) *Medical charities, medical politics: The Irish dispensary system and the poor law, 1836-1872*, Woodbridge: Boydell Press

Central Bank of Ireland (2016) *Residential mortgage arrears and repossessions statistics: Q1 2016, Statistical Release*, 10 June, available at: www.centralbank.ie/press-area/press-releases/Pages/ResidentialMortgageArrearsandRepossessionsStatisticsQ12016.aspx

Centre for Early Childhood Development and Education (2006) *Siolta - A national quality framework for early childhood education*, Dublin: Centre for Early Childhood Development and Education

Chadwick, E (1965[1842]) *Report on the sanitary condition of the labouring population of Great Britain*, Edinburgh: Edinburgh UP

Child Law Clinic (2015) 'Case study: The "children's referendum" 2012', Child Law Clinic, available at: https://www.ucc.ie/en/media/academic/law/childlawclinic/ChildrensReferendumBriefingNoteFinal8DecemberPDF.pdf

Christie, A (2004) 'Difference', in B Fanning, P Kennedy, G Kiely and S Quin (eds) *Theorising Irish social policy*, Dublin: UCD Press, 147-64

Clancy, P (2005) 'Education policy', in S Quin, P Kennedy, A Matthews and G Kiely (eds) *Contemporary Irish social policy*, Dublin: UCD Press, 80-114

Clancy, P (2007) 'Education', in S O'Sullivan (ed) *Contemporary Ireland: A sociological map*, Dublin: UCD Press, 101-19

Clancy, P (2015) *Irish higher education: A comparative perspective*, Dublin: IPA

Clark, A (2005) 'Wild workhouse girls and the liberal imperial state in mid-nineteenth century Ireland', *Journal of Social History*, 39:2, 389-409

Clark, D (2015) *The global financial crisis and austerity: A basic introduction*, Bristol: Policy Press

Clarke, J (2001) 'US welfare: Variations on the liberal regime', in A Cochrane, J Clarke and S Gewirtz (eds) *Comparing welfare states: Family life and social policy* (2nd edn), London: Sage (with The Open University), 113-52

Clarke, J and Piven, FF (2001) 'United States: An American welfare state?', in P Alcock and G Craig (eds) *International social policy: Welfare regimes in the developed world*, Basingstoke: Palgrave, 26-44

Clasen, J (1994) 'Social security: The core of the German employment-centred social state', in J Clasen and R Freeman (eds) *Social policy in Germany*, Hemel Hempstead: Harvester Wheatsheaf, 61-82

Clasen, J and Clegg, D (2011) 'Unemployment protection and labour market change in Europe: Towards "triple integration"?', in J Clasen and D Clegg (eds) *Regulating the risk of unemployment: National adaptations to post-industrial labour markets in Europe*, Oxford: Oxford UP, 1-12

Clegg, D (2015) 'The demise of tax credits', *The Political Quarterly*, 86:4, 493-9

Climate Change Advisory Council (2016) *First report*, Dublin: Climate Change Advisory Council

Coates, D, Anand, P and Norris, M (2015) *Capabilities and marginalised communities: The case of the indigenous ethnic minority Traveller community and housing in Ireland*, Open Discussion Papers in Economics, 80, Milton Keynes: Open University

Cochrane, A (1993) 'Comparative approaches and social policy', in A Cochrane and J Clarke (eds) *Comparing welfare states: Britain in an international context*, London: Sage, 1-18

Collins, ML (2013) 'Retraining and activating the "distant unemployed": New roles and measures for locally based ALMPs', paper presented at IWPLMS Conference Dublin, www.nerinstitute net/download/pdf/distant_unemployed_ iwplms_tcd_sep_2013 pdf

Collins, ML and Murphy, MP (2016) 'Activation: Solving unemployment or supporting a low-pay economy?', in MP Murphy and F Dukelow (eds) *The Irish welfare state in the twenty-first century: Challenges and change*, Basingstoke: Palgrave Macmillan, 67-92

Collins, R (2000) 'Comparative and historical patterns of education', in M Hallinan (ed) *Handbook of the sociology of education*, New York: Kluwer, 213-39

Commission on Financial Management and Control Systems in the Health Service (2003) *Report of the Commission on Financial Management and Control Systems in the Health Service*, Dublin: Stationery Office

Commission on Health Funding (1989) *Report of the commission on health funding*, Dublin: Stationery Office

Commission on Higher Education (1967) *Presentation and summary report*, Dublin: Stationery Office

Commission of Inquiry on Mental Handicap (1965) *Report*, Dublin: Stationery Office

Commission of Investigation (2009) *Report into the Catholic Archdiocese of Dublin*, Dublin: Government Publications

Commission of Investigation (2010) *Report into the Catholic Diocese of Cloyne*, Dublin: Government Publications

Commission on Itinerancy (1963) *Report of the Commission on Itinerancy*, Dublin: Stationery Office

Commission on Social Welfare (1986) *Report of the Commission on Social Welfare*, Dublin: Stationery Office.

Commission on the Status of People with Disabilities (1996) *A strategy for equality*, Dublin: Stationery Office

Commission on the Status of Women (1972) *Report of the Commission on the Status of Women*, Dublin: Stationery Office

Committee to Monitor and Co-ordinate the Implementation of the Recommendations of the Task Force on the Traveller Community (2005) *Second progress report of the Committee to Monitor and Co-ordinate the Implementation of the Recommendations of the Task Force on the Traveller Community*, Dublin: DJELR

Community Platform (2014) *Now you see us: The human stories behind poverty in Ireland*, Dublin: Community Platform

Comptroller and Auditor General (2003) *The waiting list initiative*, Dublin: GoI

Conlan, S (2014) *Counting the cost: Barriers to employment after direct provision*, Dublin: IRC

Conlan, S, Waters, S and Berg, K (2012) *Difficult to believe: The assessment of asylum claims in Ireland*, Dublin: IRC

Connolly, S (2015) 'Contextualising ageing in Ireland', in K Walsh, GM Carney and Á Ní Léime (eds) *Ageing through austerity: Critical perspectives from Ireland*, Bristol: Policy Press, 17–30

Connolly, S and Wren, M-A (2016) 'The 2011 proposal for universal health insurance in Ireland: Potential implications for healthcare expenditure', *Health Policy*, 120:7, 790–6

Connolly, T (2004) 'The Commission on Emigration, 1948-1954', in D Keogh, F O'Shea and C Quinlan (eds) *The lost decade: Ireland in the 1950s*, Cork: Mercier Press, 87–104

Conrad, K (2001) 'Queer treasons, homosexuality and Irish national identity', *Cultural Studies*, 15:1, 124–37

Conroy, P and Brennan, A (2003) *Migrant workers and their experiences*, Dublin: Equality Authority

Conroy-Jackson, P (1993) 'Managing mothers: The case of Ireland', in J Lewis (ed) *Women and social policies in Europe: Work, family and the state*, Aldershot: Edward Elgar, 72–91

Constitution of Ireland (1937) *Bunreacht na hÉireann*, Dublin: Stationery Office

Considine, M and Dukelow, F (2014) 'The role of national and international policy actors and influences in crisis times: the case of Ireland' in M Hill (ed) *Studying public policy: An international approach*, Bristol: Policy Press, 254–66

Cook, G (1986) 'Britain's legacy to the Irish social security system', in PJ Drudy (ed) *Ireland and Britain since 1922*, Cambridge: Cambridge UP, 65–85

Cook, G and McCashin, A (1997) 'Male breadwinner: A case study of gender and social security in the Republic of Ireland', in A Byrne and M Leonard (eds) *Women in Irish society: A sociological reader*, Belfast: Beyond the Pale, 167–80

Coolahan, J (1981) *Irish education: History and structure*, Dublin: IPA

Coolahan, J, Hussey, C and Kilfeather, F (2012) *The forum on patronage and pluralism in the primary sector*, Dublin: DES

Copeland, P (2015) 'The European Union and the "social deficit"', *Representation*, 51:1, 93–106

Copeland, P and Daly, M (2012) 'Varieties of poverty reduction: Inserting the poverty and social inclusion target into Europe 2020', *Journal of European Social Policy*, 22:3, 273–87

Copeland, P and Daly, M (2014) 'Poverty and social policy in Europe 2020: Ungovernable and ungoverned', *Policy & Politics*, 42:3, 351-65

Copelovitch, M, Frieden, J and Walter, S (2016) 'The political economy of the Euro crisis', *Comparative Political Studies*, 49:7, 811-40

Corcoran, M (2000) 'Local authority residents: An invisible minority', in M MacLachlan and M O'Connell (eds) *Cultivating pluralism: Psychological, social and cultural perspectives on a changing Ireland*, Dublin: Oak Tree Press, 75-91

Corcoran, P, Griffin, E, Arensman, E, Fitzgerald, A and Perry, I (2015) 'Impact of the economic recession and subsequent austerity on suicide and self harm in Ireland: An interrupted time series analysis', *International Journal of Epidemiology*, 44:3, 969-77

Cork Examiner, The (1847) 'City opposition to out-door relief', 14 May, https://viewsofthefamine.wordpress.com/1847/05/14/city-opposition-to-out-door-relief/

Cornell, S and Hartmann, D (2007) *Ethnicity and race: Making identities in a changing world* (2nd edn), Thousand Oaks, CA: Pine Forge Press

Corrigan, O (2010) 'Migrants, welfare systems and social citizenship in Ireland and Britain: Users or abusers?', *Journal of Social Policy*, 39:3, 415-37

Council of the European Union (2002) 'Fight against poverty and social exclusion: Common objectives for the second round of National Action Plans: Endorsement, SOC 508', Brussels, 25 November, available at: http://ec.europa.eu/employment_social/social_inclusion/docs/counciltext_en.pdf

Courtois, A (2015) '"Thousands waiting at our gates": Moral character, legitimacy and social justice in Irish elite schools', *British Journal of Sociology of Education*, 36:1, 53-70

Cousins, M (1999) 'The introduction of children's allowances in Ireland, 1939-1944', *Irish Economic and Social History*, XXVI, 35-53

Cousins, M (2000) 'From the white paper to the Commission on Social Welfare, 1949-1986', in A Lavan (ed) *50 years of social welfare policy*, Dublin: DSCFA, 31-7

Cousins, M (2003) *The birth of social welfare in Ireland, 1922-52*, Dublin: Four Courts Press

Cousins, M (2005a) *Explaining the Irish welfare state: An historical, comparative and political analysis*, New York: Edwin Mellen Press

Cousins, M (2005b) *European welfare states: Comparative perspectives*, London: Sage

Coyne, EJ (1951) 'Mother and child service', *Studies*, XL:158, 129-49

CPA (Combat Poverty Agency) (1987) 'Poverty budget', *Poverty Today*, 1:1, 12

CPA (Combat Poverty Agency) (2003) *Educational disadvantage in Ireland*, Poverty Briefing 14, Dublin: CPA

CPA (Combat Poverty Agency) (2007) *Health policy statement*, Dublin: CPA

CRA (Children's Rights Alliance) (2016) *Children's Rights Alliance report card 2016: Is government keeping its promises to children?*, Dublin: CRA

Crespy, A and Menz, G (2015) 'Commission entrepreneurship and the debasing of Social Europe before and after the Eurocrisis', *Journal of Common Market Studies*, 53:4, 753-68

Cromien, S (2011) 'The story of the first "Bórd Snip"', *Irish Journal of Public Policy*, 3:2, available at: http://publish ucc ie/ijpp/2011/02/Cromien/09/en

Cronin, M (2006) 'Place, class and politics', in JS Crowley, RJN Devoy, D Linehan, P O'Flanagan and M Murphy (eds) *Atlas of Cork city*, Cork: Cork UP, 202-08

Crosland, A (1956) *The future of socialism*, London: J Cape

Crosscare, Doras Luimní and NASC (2012) *Person or number? Issues faced by immigrants accessing social protection*, Dublin: Crosscare

Crossman, V (2006) *The poor law in Ireland 1838-1948*, Dundalk: Economic and Social History Society of Ireland

Crossman, V (2013) *Poverty and the poor law in Ireland, 1850-1914*, Liverpool: Liverpool UP

Crossman, V and Gray, P (2011) 'Introduction: poverty and welfare in Ireland, 1838-1948', in V Crossman and P Gray (eds) *Poverty and welfare in Ireland, 1838-1948*, Dublin: Irish Academic Press, 1-20

Crouch, C (2011) *The strange non-death of neoliberalism*, Cambridge: Polity

Crouch, C (2013) 'Class politics and the social investment welfare state', in M Keating and D McCrone (eds) *The crisis of social democracy in Europe*, Edinburgh: Edinburgh UP, 156-68

Crouch, C (2014) 'Introduction: Labour markets and social policy after the crisis', *Transfer*, 20:1, 7-22

Crowley, N (1999) 'Travellers and social policy', in S Quin, P Kennedy, A O'Donnell and G Kiely (eds) *Contemporary Irish social policy*, Dublin: UCD Press, 243-65

CSO (Central Statistics Office) (2006) *Women and men in Ireland*, Cork: CSO

CSO (Central Statistics Office) (2010) *Mortality differentials in Ireland*, available at: www.cso.ie/en/media/csoie/census/documents/Mortality_Differentials_in_Ireland.pdf

CSO (Central Statistics Office) (2012a) *Profile 8: Our bill of health*, Dublin: Stationery Office

CSO (Central Statistics Office) (2012b) *Profile 6: Migration and diversity*, Dublin: Stationery Office

CSO (Central Statistics Office) (2012c) *This is Ireland: Highlights from Census 2011, part 2*, Dublin: Stationery Office

CSO (Central Statistics Office) (2015) *SILC 2014 results*, Dublin: Stationery Office

Cullen Owens, R (1984) *Smashing times: A history of the Irish women's suffrage movement 1889-1922*, Dublin: Attic Press

Cullinan, J and Lyons, S (2015) 'The private economic costs of adult disability', in J Cullinan, S Lyons and B Nolan (eds) *The economics of disability: Insights from Irish research*, Manchester: Manchester UP, 58-73

Curry, J (1986) 'Symposium on the report of the Commission on Social Welfare', *Journal of the Statistical and Social Inquiry Society of Ireland*, XXV: IV, 1-7

Curry, J (2011) *Irish social services* (5th edn), Dublin: IPA

Curry, J (2016) 'Education, 2015', *Administration*, 63:4, 63-75

Curtin, C and Varley, T (1995) 'Community action and the state', in P Clancy, S Drudy, K Lynch and L O'Dowd (eds) *Irish society: Sociological perspectives*, Dublin: SAI and IPA, 379-409

Dáil Debates (2016) 'Written answers, Tuesday, 2 February 2016, Social Welfare benefits data', available at: http://oireachtasdebates.oireachtas.ie/debates%20 authoring/debateswebpack.nsf/takes/dail2016020200053

Dáil Éireann (1919) Volume 1: 21 January, 1919 *Democratic Programme*, available at: www.firstdail.com/?page_id=38

Daly, F (2012a) *"My voice has to be heard": Research on outcomes for young people leaving care in North Dublin*, Dublin: EPIC

Daly, F (2012b) 'What do young people need when they leave care? Views of care-leavers and aftercare workers in North Dublin', *Child Care in Practice*, 18:4, 309-24

Daly, H (1995) 'The steady state economy: Alternatives to growthomania', in J Kirby, P O'Keefe and L Timberlake (eds) *The Earthscan reader in sustainable development*, London: Earthscan, 331-42

Daly, M (1989) *Women and poverty*, Dublin: Attic Press (with the CPA)

Daly, M (2008) 'Whither EU social policy? An account and assessment of developments in the Lisbon social inclusion process', *Journal of Social Policy*, 37:1, 1-19

Daly, M (2015) *ESPN Thematic report on social investment: Ireland 2015*, Brussels: European Commission

Daly, M and Lewis, J (2000) 'The concept of social care and the analysis of contemporary welfare states', *British Journal of Sociology*, 51:2, 281-99

Daly, ME (1981) *Social and economic history of Ireland since 1800*, Dublin: The Educational Company

Daly, ME (1985) 'Housing conditions and the genesis of housing reform in Dublin, 1880-1920', in MJ Bannon (ed) *The emergence of Irish planning, 1880-1920*, Dublin: Turoe Press, 77-129

Daly, ME (2011) 'The Irish free state and the Great Depression of the 1930s: The interaction of the global and the local', *Irish Economic and Social History*, XXXVIII, 19-36

Daly, ME (2016) *Sixties Ireland: Reshaping the economy, state and society, 1957-1973*, Cambridge: Cambridge UP

Darvas, Z, Huettl, P, de Sousa, C, Terzi, A and Tschekassin, O (2014) *Austerity and poverty in the European Union*, Study for the EMPL Committee, Brussels: Directorate General for Internal Policies

Dawson, C (1910) 'The Children Act and the Oldham League', *Journal of the Statistical and Social Inquiry Society of Ireland*, XII, 388-95

DCYA (Department of Children and Youth Affairs) (2012) *Report of the task force on the Child and Family Support Agency*, Dublin: Government Publications

DCYA (Department of Children and Youth Affairs) (2014a) *Better outcomes, brighter futures: The national policy framework for children & young people 2014-2020*, Dublin: Government Publications

DCYA (Department of Children and Youth Affairs) (2014b) *State of the Nation's Children: Ireland 2014*, Dublin: Government Publications

Department of Finance (1958) *Economic Development*, Dublin: Department of Finance

Department of Health and Social Welfare (1984) *Towards a full life: Green paper on services for disabled people*, Dublin: Department of Health and Social Welfare

Department of Social Welfare (1949) *White paper containing proposals for social security*, Dublin: Stationery Office

Department of the Taoiseach (1999) *Green paper on abortion*, Dublin: Department of the Taoiseach

De Grauwe, P (2013) *Design failures in the Eurozone: Can they be fixed?*, LSE 'Europe in Question' Discussion Paper Series, LEQS 57, London: LSE

de la Porte, C and Heins, E (2015) 'A new era of European integration? Governance of labour market and social policy since the sovereign debt crisis', *Comparative European Politics*, 13, 8–28

De Wispelaere, J and Walsh, J (2007) 'Disability rights in Ireland: Chronicle of a missed opportunity', *Irish Political Studies*, 22:4, 517–43

Deakin, N and Wright, A (1995) 'Tawney', in V George and R Page (eds) *Modern thinkers on welfare*, Hertfordshire: Prentice Hall/Harvester Wheatsheaf, 133–48

Dean, H (2002) 'Green citizenship', in M Cahill and T Fitzpatrick (eds) *Environmental issues and social welfare*, Oxford: Blackwell, 22–37

Dean, H (2008) 'The socialist perspective', in P Alcock, M May and K Rowlingson (eds) *The student's companion to social policy* (3rd edn), Oxford: Blackwell, 84–90

Dean, H and Taylor-Gooby, P (1992) *Dependency culture: The explosion of a myth*, Hemel Hempstead: Harvester Wheatsheaf

DECLG (Department of Environment, Community and Local Government) (2011) *Housing policy statement*, Dublin: Stationery Office

DECLG (Department of Environment, Community and Local Government) (2013) *Homelessness policy statement*, Dublin: Stationery Office

DECLG (Department of Environment, Community and Local Government) (2014a) *Social housing strategy 2020: Support, supply and reform*, Dublin: Stationery Office

DECLG (Department of Environment, Community and Local Government) (2014b) *Climate action and low-carbon development: National policy position Ireland*, Dublin: Stationery Office

DECLG (Department of Environment, Community and Local Government) (2015) *Stabilising rents, boosting supply*, Dublin: Stationery Office

DEHLG (Department of Environment, Heritage and Local Government) (2008) *The way home: A strategy to address adult homelessness in Ireland 2008 - 2013*, Dublin: Stationery Office

DES (Department of Education and Skills) and OMI (Office of the Minister for Integration) (2010) *Intercultural education strategy 2010-2015*, Dublin: DES

DES (Department of Education and Skills) (2011) *Literacy and numeracy for learning and life. The national strategy to improve literacy and numeracy among children and young people 2011-2020*, Dublin: DES

DES (Department of Education and Skills) (2015) *Framework for Junior Cycle 2015*, Dublin: DES

DES (Department of Education and Skills) (2016) *Key statistics 2014/2015 and 2015/2016*, https://www.education.ie/en/Publications/Statistics/Key-Statistics/Key-Statistics-2015-2016.pdf

DESc (Department of Education and Science) (2005) *Delivering equality of opportunity in schools: An action plan for educational inclusion*, Dublin: DESc

DESc (Department of Education and Science) (2006a) *Report and recommendations for a traveller education strategy*, Dublin: DESc

DESc (Department of Education and Science) (2006b) *Survey of Traveller education provision*, Dublin: DESc

DG ECFIN (2003) *Statistical annex of the European economy 2003*, Brussels: European Commission

DG ECFIN (2011) *The Economic Adjustment Programme for Ireland: Spring 2011 Review*, Brussels: European Commission

DG EMPL (2007) *Joint report on social protection and social inclusion 2007*, Luxembourg: Office for Official Publications of the European Communities

Dhamoon, RK (2013) 'Feminisms', in G Waylen, K Celis, J Kantola and SL Weldon (eds) *The Oxford handbook of gender and politics*, Oxford: Oxford UP, 88-110

DHC (Department of Health and Children) (2001a) *Quality and fairness: A health system for you*, Dublin: DHC

DHC (Department of Health and Children) (2001b) *Primary health care: A new direction*, Dublin: DHC

DHC (2002) *Traveller health strategy 2002-2005*, Dublin: DoHC

DHPCLG (Department of Housing, Planning, Community and Local Government) (nd) Homelessness data, available at: www.housing.gov.ie/housing/homelessness/other/homelessness-data

Dieckhoff, M and Gallie, D (2007) 'The renewed Lisbon Strategy and social exclusion policy', *Industrial Relations Journal*, 38:6, 480-502

Dixon, J (1999) *Social security in global perspective*, London: Praeger

DJE (2011) *Ireland's national Traveller/Roma integration strategy*, Dublin: DJE

DJE (2015) *Working group to report to Government on improvements to the protection process, including direct provision and supports to asylum seekers*, Dublin: DJE

DJELR (Department of Justice, Equality and Law Reform) (1999) *Integration: A two-way process*, Dublin: DJELR

DJELR (Department of Justice, Equality and Law Reform) (2004) *National disability strategy 2004*, available at: www.justice.ie/en/JELR/Pages/National-Disability-Strategy

DJELR (Department of Justice, Equality and Law Reform) (2005a) Guide to the Disability Act, available at: www.justice.ie/en/JELR/DisabilityAct05Guide.pdf/Files/DisabilityAct05Guide.pdf

DJELR (Department of Justice, Equality and Law Reform) (2005b) *Planning for diversity: The national action plan against racism 2005-2008*, Dublin: DJELR

DLG (Department of Local Government) (1948) *Housing: A review of past operations and immediate requirements*, Dublin: DLG

DLG (Department of Local Government) (1964) *Housing progress and prospects*, Dublin: DLG

DLG (Department of Local Government) (1969) *Housing in the '70s*, Dublin: DLG

DoE (Department of Environment) (1991) *A plan for social housing*, Dublin: Stationery Office

DoE (Department of Environment) (1995) *Social housing the way ahead*, Dublin: Stationery Office

DoE (1996) *National strategy for traveller accommodation*, Dublin: Stationery Office

DoH (Department of Health) (1986) *Health the wider dimensions*, Dublin: Stationery Office

DoH (Department of Health) (1994) *Shaping a healthier future*, Dublin: Stationery Office

DoH (Department of Health) (2012a) *Future health: A strategic framework for reform of the health service 2012–2015*, Dublin: Stationery Office

DoH (Department of Health)(2012b) *Value for money and policy review of disability services in Ireland*, Dublin: DoH

DoH (Department of Health) (2012c) *National carers' strategy: Recognised, supported, empowered*, Dublin: DoH

DoH (Department of Health) (2013a) *The establishment of hospital groups as a transition to independent hospital trusts*, Dublin: Stationery Office

DoH (Department of Health) (2013b) *Healthy Ireland*, Dublin: Stationery Office

DoH (Department of Health) (2013c) *Positive ageing starts now! The national positive ageing strategy*, Dublin: DoH

DoH (Department of Health) (2014) *The path to universal healthcare: White paper on universal health insurance*, Dublin: Stationery Office

DoH (Department of Health) (2015) *Review of the nursing homes support scheme, A fair deal*, Dublin: DoH

DoH (Department of Health)(2016a) *Health in Ireland key trends 2015*, Dublin: Stationery Office

DoH (Department of Health) (2016b) *Positive ageing 2016: National indicators report*, Dublin: DoH

Donnelly, S, O'Brien, M, Begley, E and Brennan, J (2016) *"I'd prefer to stay at home but I don't have a choice": Meeting older people's preference for care: Policy, but what about practice?* Dublin: UCD

Donoghue, F (1998a) 'Defining the nonprofit sector: Ireland', in LM Salamon and HK Anheier (eds) *Working Papers of the Johns Hopkins Comparative Nonprofit Sector Project*, 28, Baltimore, MD: The Johns Hopkins Institute for Policy Studies

Donoghue, F (1998b) 'The politicisation of disadvantage in the Republic of Ireland: The role played by the third sector', paper presented at the International Society for Third Sector Research Conference, Geneva, 10 July

Donoghue, F (1999) *Uncovering the non-profit sector in Ireland: Its economic value and significance*, Dublin: The Johns Hopkins Institute for Policy Studies and National College of Ireland

Doorley, J (2015) *JobBridge: Stepping stone or dead end?* Dublin: National Youth Council of Ireland

Dorling, D (2010) *Injustice: Why social inequality persists*, Bristol: Policy Press

DoT (Department of Transport)(2009) *Smarter travel: A sustainable transport future – A new transport policy for Ireland 2009-2020*, Dublin: DoT

Drennan, J, Treacy, M, Butler, M, Byrne, A, Fealy, G, Frazer, K and Irving, K (2008) 'The experience of social and emotional loneliness of older people in Ireland', *Ageing and Society*, 28:8, 1113-32

Drudy, PJ (2006) 'Housing in Ireland: Philosophy, problems and policies', in S Healy, B Reynolds and M Collins (eds) *Social policy in Ireland: Principles, practice and problems* (2nd edn), Dublin: Liffey Press, 241-69

Drudy, PJ (2016) 'The housing problem and the case for rent regulation in the private rented sector: Submission to the Committee on Housing and Homelessness', available at: www.oireachtas.ie/parliament/media/committees/32housingandhomelessness/Drudy-Submision-to-Committee-on-Housing-and-Homelessness-May-2016.docx

Drudy, PJ and Punch, M (2005) *Out of reach: Inequalities in the Irish housing system*, Dublin: TASC at New Island

Drudy, S (2009) 'Education and the knowledge economy: A challenge for Ireland in changing times', in S Drudy (ed) *Education in Ireland: Challenge and change*, Dublin: Gill & Macmillan, 35-53

Drudy, S and Kinsella, W (2009) 'Developing an inclusive system in a rapidly changing European society', *International Journal of Inclusive Education*, 13:6, 647-63

Dryzek, JS (2005) *The politics of the earth: Environmental discourses* (2nd edn), Oxford: Oxford UP

Dryzek, JS and Schlosberg, D (eds) (2005) *Debating the earth: The environmental politics reader*, Oxford: Oxford UP

DSFA (Department of Social and Family Affairs) (2004) 'Mary Coughlan Minister for Social and Family Affairs to announce new social welfare code restrictions', Press Release, 24 February, available at: www.welfare.ie/en/pressoffice/Pages/pr240204.aspx

DSFA (Department of Social and Family Affairs) (2006) *Government discussion paper: Proposals for supporting lone parents*, Dublin: DSFA

DSFA (Department of Social and Family Affairs) (2008) *Statement of strategy 2008-2010*, Dublin: DSFA

DSP (Department of Social Protection) (2012) *High level issues paper emanating from a review of Department of Social Protection employment support schemes*, Dublin: DSP

DSP (Department of Social Protection) (2015) *Statistical information on social welfare services 2014*, Dublin: DSP

Duff, L (1997) *The economics of governments and markets: New directions in European public policy*, London: Longman

Duffy, PJ (2004) '"Disencumbering our crowded places": theory and practice of estate migration schemes mid-nineteenth century Ireland', in PJ Duffy (ed) *To and from Ireland: Planned migration schemes c. 1600-2000*, Dublin: Geography Publications, 79-104

Dukelow, F (2005) 'The path towards a more "employment friendly" liberal regime? globalisation and the Irish social security system' in B Cantillon and I Marx (eds) *International co-operation in social security – how to cope with globalisation?*, Antwerp: Intersentia, 125-54

Dukelow, F (2011) 'Economic crisis and welfare retrenchment: Comparing Irish policy responses in the 1970s and 1980s with the present', *Social Policy & Administration*, 45:4, 408-29

Dukelow, F (2016) 'Irish water services reform: Past, present and future', in MP Murphy and F Dukelow (eds) *The Irish welfare state in the twenty-first century: Challenges and change,* Basingstoke: Palgrave, 141-65

Dukelow, F (forthcoming) '"Some sort of super welfare state"? The "rediscovery of poverty" and Irish welfare state change in the 1970s', in E Eklund, M Oppenheimer and J Scott (eds) *The welfare state at the end of the long boom*, Bern: Peter Lang

Dukelow, F and Considine, M (2014a) 'Outlier or model of austerity? The case of Irish social protection reform', *Social Policy & Administration*, 48:4, 413-29

Dukelow, F and Considine, M (2014b) 'Between retrenchment and recalibration: The impact of austerity on the Irish social protection system', *Journal of Sociology & Social Welfare*, 41:2, 55-72

Dunleavy, P and O'Leary, B (1987) *Theories of the state*, London: Macmillan

Dwyer, P (2004) *Understanding social citizenship: Themes and perspectives for policy and practice*, Bristol: Policy Press

Eames, M (2006) *Reconciling environmental and social concerns –findings from the JRF research programme*, York: Joseph Rowntree Foundation

Earner-Byrne, L (2007) *Mother and child: Maternity and child welfare in Ireland, 1922-60*, Manchester: Manchester UP

Earner-Byrne, L (2015) '"Should I take myself and family to another religion [?]": Irish catholic women, protest, and conformity, 1920-1940', in CS Brophy and C Delay (eds) *Women, reform and resistance in Ireland, 1850-1950*, Basingstoke: Palgrave Macmillan, 77-100

Ebbinghaus, B (2015) 'The privatization and marketization of pensions in Europe: A double transformation facing the crisis', *European Policy Analysis*, 1:1, 56-73

Economist, The (1988) 'The poorest of the rich (Ireland survey)', *The Economist*, 16 January

Economist, The (2005) 'In come the waves', *The Economist*, 16 June

Edgar, B, Doherty, J and Meert, H (2002) *Access to housing: Homelessness and vulnerability in Europe*, Bristol: Policy Press

Educate Together (2016) Community national schools: An Educate Together position paper, January, available at: https://www.educatetogether.ie/sites/default/files/20160121_cns_et_positionpaper.pdf

Elliot, JA (2005) *An introduction to sustainable development* (3rd edn), London: Routledge

Elsinga, M and Hoekstra, J (2005) 'Homeownership and housing satisfaction', *Journal of Housing and the Built Environment,* 20:4, 401-24

Emmenegger, P, Häusermann, S, Palier, B and Seeleib-Kaiser, M (2012) 'How we grow unequal', in P Emmenegger, S Häusermann, B Palier and M Seeleib-Kaiser (eds) *The age of dualization: The changing face of inequality in deindustrializing societies*, Oxford: Oxford UP, 3-26

Emmenegger, P, Kvist, J, Marx, P and Petersen, K (2015) '*Three worlds of welfare capitalism*: The making of a classic', *Journal of European Social Policy*, 25:1, 3-13

Englander, D (1998) *Poverty and poor law reform in 19th century Britain, 1834-1914: From Chadwick to Booth*, London: Addison Wesley Longman

EPA (Environmental Protection Authority) (2016) *Ireland's environment: An assessment 2016*, Wexford: EPA

Equality Authority (2006) *Traveller ethnicity*, Dublin: Equality Authority

Esping-Andersen, G (1990) *The three worlds of welfare capitalism*, Cambridge: Polity

Esping-Andersen, G (1999) *Social foundations of postindustrial economies*, Oxford: Oxford UP

Esping-Andersen, G, with Gallie, D, Hemerijck, A and Myles, J (2002) *Why we need a new welfare state*, Oxford: Oxford UP

ETUI (European Trade Union Institute) (2012) *Benchmarking working Europe 2012*, Brussels: ETUI

European Commission (2001) *Making a European area of lifelong learning a reality*, Brussels: Commission of the European Communities

European Commission (2010) *Europe 2020: A strategy for smart, sustainable and inclusive growth: Communication from the Commission*, COM (2010) 2020 final, Brussels: European Commission

European Commission (2012) *Rethinking education: Investing in skills for better socio-economic outcomes*, Strasbourg: European Commission

European Commission (2015) 'Annual Growth Survey 2016: Strengthening the recovery and fostering convergence', COM(2015) 690 final, 26 November, Brussels: European Commission

European Commission (2016) 'Reducing emissions from transport: A European strategy for low-emission mobility', available at: http://ec.europa.eu/clima/policies/transport_en

European Committee of Social Rights (2016) Decision on the merits, European Roma Rights Centre v. Ireland, Complaint No. 100/2013, available at: http://hudoc.esc.coe.int/eng#{%22ESCDcIdentifier%22:[%22cc-100-2013-dmerits-en%22],%22ESCDcType%22:[%22DEC%22],%22ESCStateParty%22:[%22IRL%22]}

European Environment Agency (2006) *Urban sprawl in Europe: The ignored challenge*, Copenhagen: European Environment Agency

European Parliament (2004) 'European Parliament fact sheets: 4.8.1 Social and employment policy: General principles', available at: http://www.europarl.europa.eu/facts_2004/4_8_1_en.htm

Eurostat (nd) 'At risk of poverty rate across EU', available at: http://epp.eurostat.ec.europa.eu/tgm/tabledo?tab=table&init=1&plugin=1&language=en&pcode=tsisc030

Evason, E, Darby, J and Person, M (1976) *Social need and social provision in Northern Ireland*, Coleraine: New University of Ulster

Evetts, J (1970) 'Equality of educational opportunity: The recent history of a concept', *British Journal of Sociology*, 21:4, 425-30

Expert Group on Future Funding for Higher Education (2016) *Investing in national ambition: A strategy for funding higher education*, Dublin: Stationery Office

Expert Group on Mental Health Policy (2006) *A vision for change: Report of the Expert Group on Mental Health Policy*, Dublin: Stationery Office

Expert Working Group on the Integration of Tax and Social Welfare Systems (1996) *Integrating tax and social welfare*, Dublin: Stationery Office

Fahey, T (2001) 'Housing and local government', in ME Daly (ed) *County and town: One hundred years of local government in Ireland*, Dublin: IPA, 120-29

Fahey, T (2002) 'The family economy in the development of welfare regimes: A case study', *European Sociological Review*, 18:1, 51-64

Fahey, T (2012) 'Small bang? The impact of divorce legislation on marital breakdown in Ireland', *International Journal of Law Policy and the Family*, 26:2, 242-58

Fahey, T and Fitz Gerald, J (1997) *Welfare implications of demographic trends*, Dublin: Oak Tree Press with CPA

Fahey, T and McLaughlin, E (1999) 'Family and state', in AF Heath, R Breen and CT Whelan (eds) *Ireland, north and south: Perspectives from social science*, Oxford: Oxford UP, 117-40

Fahey, T and Watson, D (1995) *An analysis of social housing need*, Dublin: ESRI

Fahey, T, Norris, M, McCafferty, D and Humphrey, E (2011) *Combating social disadvantage in social housing estates: The policy implications of a ten-year follow-up study*, CPA Working Paper Series 11/02, Dublin: CPA

Fahie, D (2016) '"Spectacularly exposed and vulnerable": How Irish equality legislation subverted the personal and professional security of lesbian, gay and bisexual teachers', *Sexualities*, 19:4, 393-411

Fallon, J (2005) 'Targeting disadvantage among young children in the Republic of Ireland', *Child Care in Practice*, 11:3, 289-311

Fanning, B (2006) 'The new welfare economy', in B Fanning and M Rush (eds) *Care and social change in the Irish welfare economy*, Dublin: UCD Press, 9-25

Fanning, B (2007) 'Integration and social policy', in B Fanning (ed) *Immigration and social change in the Republic of Ireland*, Manchester: Manchester UP, 237-58

Fanning, B (2008) *The quest for modern Ireland: The battle of ideas 1912-1986*, Dublin: Irish Academic Press

Fanning, B (2011) *Immigration and social cohesion in the Republic of Ireland*, Manchester: Manchester UP

Fanning, B (2012) *Racism and social change in the Republic of Ireland* (2nd edn), Manchester: Manchester UP

Fanning, B (2016) 'Immigration, the celtic tiger and the economic crisis', *Irish Studies Review*, 24:1, 9-20

Fanning, B and Rush, M (2006) 'Introduction: Context, change, challenges and care', in B Fanning and M Rush (eds) *Care and social change in the Irish welfare economy*, Dublin: UCD Press, 1-8

Fanning, B and Veale, A (2004) 'Child poverty as public policy: Direct provision and asylum seeker children', *Child Care in Practice*, 10:3, 241-51

Farley, D (1964) *Social Insurance and social assistance in Ireland*, Dublin: IPA

Farnsworth, K (2004) 'Welfare through work: An audit of occupational social provision at the turn of the new century', *Social Policy & Administration*, 38:5, 437-55

Farnsworth, K and Irving, Z (eds) (2015) *Social policy in times of austerity: Global economic crisis and the new politics of welfare*, Bristol: Policy Press

Farrell, C, McAvoy, H, Wilde, J and the CPA (2008) *Tackling health inequalities: An all-Ireland approach to social determinants*, Dublin: CPA with the IPH

Farren, S (1995) *The politics of Irish education, 1920-65*, Belfast: Institute of Irish Studies, QUB

Fealy, G, McNamara, M, Tracey, M, Lyons, I (2012) 'Constructing ageing and age identities: a case study of newspaper discourses', *Ageing and Society*, 35, 85-102

Feldman, A (2008) 'Integration: Mapping the terrain', *Translocations*, 3:1, 133-41

Ferguson, H (2007) 'Abused and looked after children as "moral dirt": Child abuse and institutional care in historical perspective', *Journal of Social Policy*, 36:1, 123-39

Ferguson, H and O'Reilly, M (2001) *Keeping children safe: Child abuse, child protection and the promotion of welfare*, Dublin: A & A Farmar

Ferns Inquiry (2005) *The Ferns report*, Dublin: Government Publications

Ferragina, E and Seeleib-Kaiser, M (2015) 'Determinants of a silent (r)evolution: Understanding the expansion of family policy in rich OECD countries', *Social Politics*, 22:1, 1-37

Ferrera, M (1996) 'The "Southern Model" of welfare in Social Europe', *Journal of European Social Policy*, 6:1, 17-37

Ferrera, M (2008) 'The European welfare state: Golden achievements, silver prospects', *West European Politics*, 31:1-2, 82-107

Ferris, J (1991) 'Green politics and the future of welfare', in N Manning (ed) *Social Policy Review, 1990-91*, Harlow: Longman, 24-41

Ferriter, D (2004) *The transformation of Ireland 1900-2000*, London: Profile Books

Ferriter, D (2012) *Ambiguous republic: Ireland in the 1970s*, London: Profile Books

Fine Gael (1965) *Towards a just society*, Dublin: Fine Gael Party

Finlay, F (2016) 'Disability Act should be a shining example, but it's a shaming one', *Irish Examiner*, 22 November

Finn, C and Hardiman, N (2012) 'Creating two levels of healthcare', in N Hardiman (ed) *Irish governance in crisis*, Manchester: Manchester UP, 110-31

Finn, T (2012) *Tuairim, intellectual debate and policy formation: Rethinking Ireland, 1954-1975*, Manchester: Manchester UP

Finnane, M (1981) *Insanity and the insane in post-famine Ireland*, London: Croom Helm

Finnegan, F (2001) *Do penance or perish, a study of Magdalen asylums in Ireland*, Kilkenny: Congrave Press

Finnerty, J, O'Connell, C and O'Sullivan, S (2016) 'Social housing policy and provision: A changing regime?, in MP Murphy and F Dukelow (eds) *The Irish welfare state in the twenty-first century: Challenges and change*, Basingstoke: Palgrave Macmillan, 237-59

Fitzgerald, E (1981) 'The extent of poverty in Ireland', in S Kennedy (ed) *One million poor? The challenge of Irish inequality*, Dublin: Turoe Press, 13-34

Fitzgerald, E (2015) *Presentation to the Joint Oireachtas Committee on Health and Children*, 26 November, available at: www.oireachtas.ie/parliament/media/committees/healthandchildren/health2015/Opening-Statement-by-Ms.-Eileen-Fitzgerald.-Senior-Manager,-Citizens-Information-Board.pdf

Fitzpatrick, S (2012) 'Homelessness', in D Clapham, W Clark and K Gibb (eds) *The Sage handbook of housing studies*, London: Sage, 359-78

Fitzpatrick, S and Pawson, H (2011) *Security of tenure in social housing: An international review*, London: Shelter

Fitzpatrick, T (1998) 'The implications of ecological thought for social welfare', *Critical Social Policy*, 18:1, 6-26

Fitzpatrick, T (2001) *Welfare theory: An introduction*, Basingstoke: Palgrave

Fitzpatrick, T (2006) 'Fabian society', in T Fitzpatrick, H-J Kwon, N Manning, J Midgley and G Pascall (eds) *International encyclopedia of social policy*, Abingdon: Routledge, 443-4

Fitzpatrick, T (2011a) 'Challenges for social policy', in T Fitzpatrick (ed) *Understanding the environment and social policy*, Bristol: Policy Press, 61-89

Fitzpatrick, T (ed) (2011b) *Understanding the environment and social policy*, Bristol: Policy Press

Fitzpatrick, T (2014) *Climate change and poverty: A new agenda for developed nations*, Bristol: Policy Press

Fives, A, Kennan, D, Canavan, J, Brady, B and Cairns, D (2010) 'If I can make their life a little easier, then I'm happy', *Study of young carers in the Irish population*, Dublin: DCYA

Fleckenstein, T (2011) 'The politics of ideas in welfare state transformation: Christian Democracy and the reform of family policy in Germany', *Social Politics*, 18:4, 543-71

Fleming, B and Harford, J (2014) 'Irish educational policy in the 1960s: A decade of transformation', *History of Education*, 43:5, 635-56

Fleming, P (2016) *How personal budgets are working in Ireland: Evaluating the implementation of four individualised funding initiatives for people with a disability in Ireland*, available at: www.genio.ie/system/files/publications/PERSONAL_BUDGETS_IRELAND_MAY16.pdf

Flora, P (1981) 'Solution or source of crises? The welfare state in historical perspective', in WJ Mommsen (ed) *The emergence of the welfare state in Britain and Germany: 1850-1950*, London: Croom, 343-89

Flynn, L (1997) '"Cherishing all her children equally": The law and politics of Irish lesbian and gay citizenship', *Social and Legal Studies*, 6:2, 493-512

Foley, J (ed) (2004) *Sustainability and social justice*, London: IPPR

Forde, C, O'Byrne, D and Ó hAdhamaill, F (2016) 'Community development in Ireland under austerity and local government change: Policy and practice', in ISS21 Local and Community Development Working Group (ed) *The changing landscape of local and community development in Ireland: Policy and practice*, Cork: ISS21, UCC, 15-36

Forrest, R (2015) 'The ongoing financialisation of home ownership: New times, new contexts', *International Journal of Housing Policy*, 15:1, 1-5

Forrest, R and Hirayama, Y (2015) 'The financialisation of the social project: Embedded liberalism, neoliberalism and home ownership', *Urban Studies*, 52:2, 233-44

Fraser, D (1984) *The evolution of the British welfare state: A history of social policy since the industrial revolution* (2nd edn), London: Macmillan

Fraser, N (2009) 'Feminism, capitalism and the cunning of history', *New Left Review*, 56, 97-117

Fraser, N (2016) 'Contradictions of capital and care', *New Left Review*, 100, 99-117

Frawley, D (2014) 'Combating educational disadvantage through early years and primary school investment, *Irish Educational Studies*, 33:2, 155-71

Frazer, H (2007) 'Promoting social inclusion: The EU dimension', *Administration*, 55:2, 27-60

Freeman, R (2000) *The politics of health in Europe*, Manchester: Manchester UP

Fukuyama, F (1992) *The end of history and the last man*, Harmondsworth: Penguin

Galupo, MP, Stuart, JF and Siegel, DP (2015) 'Transgender, transsexual, and gender variant individuals', in JD Wright (ed) *International Encyclopedia of the Social and Behaviour Sciences* (2nd edn), Oxford: Elsevier, 549-53

Gamble, A (2009) *The Spectre at the feast: Capitalist crisis and the politics of the recession*, Basingstoke: Palgrave Macmillan

Gamble, A (2014a) *Crisis without end? The unravelling of Western prosperity*, Basingstoke: Palgrave Macmillan

Gamble, A (2014b) 'Ideologies of governance', in A Payne and N Phillips (eds) *Handbook of the international political economy of governance*, Cheltenham: Edward Elgar, 13-31

Gamble, A (2016) *Can the welfare state survive?*, Cambridge: Polity

Garner, R (1996) *Environmental politics*, London: Prentice Hall, Harvester Wheatsheaf

Garner, S (2007) 'Babies, bodies and entitlement: Gendered aspects of access to citizenship in the Republic of Ireland', *Parliamentary Affairs*, 60:3, 137-51

Garner, S (2009) *Racisms: An introduction*, London: Sage

Garner, S (2013) 'Reflections on race in contemporary Ireland', in JV Ulin, H Edwards and S O'Brien (eds) *Race and immigration in the new Ireland*, Notre Dame, IN: University of Notre Dame Press, 175-204

Garrett, PM (2013) 'A "catastrophic, inept, self-serving" church? Re-examining three reports on child abuse in the Republic of Ireland', *Journal of Progressive Human Services*, 24:1, 43-65

Garrett, PM (2015) 'Excavating the past: Mother and baby homes in the Republic of Ireland, *British Journal of Social Work*, DOI: 10 1093/bjsw/bcv116 ahead of print, 1-15

Garvin, T (2005) *Preventing the future: Why was Ireland so poor for so long?* Dublin: Gill & Macmillan

Geary, LM (2004) *Medicine and charity in Ireland 1718-1851*, Dublin: UCD Press

George, V and Wilding, P (1985) *Ideology and social welfare*, London: Routledge and Kegan Paul

George, V and Wilding, P (1994) *Welfare and ideology*, Hemel Hempstead: Harvester Wheatsheaf

Giddens, A (1994) *Beyond left and right: The future of radical politics*, Cambridge: Polity

Giddens, A (1998) *The third way: The renewal of social democracy*, Cambridge: Polity

Giddens, A (2000) *The third way and its critics*, Cambridge: Polity

Gilligan, R (2014) 'The "public child" and the reluctant state?', in M Luddy and JM Smith (eds) *Children, childhood and Irish society, 1500 to the present*, Dublin: Four Courts Press, 145-63

Ginsburg, N (1979) *Class, capital and social policy*, London: Macmillan

Ginsburg, N (2001) 'Globalization and the liberal welfare states', in R Sykes, B Palier and PM Prior (eds) *Globalization and European welfare states: Challenges and change*, Basingstoke: Palgrave, 173-91

Ginsburg, N (2003) 'The socialist perspective', in P Alcock, A Erskine and M May (eds) *The student's companion to social policy* (2nd edn), Oxford: Blackwell, 92-9

Girvin, B (2010) 'Before the celtic tiger: Change without modernisation in Ireland 1959-1989', *Economic and Social Review*, 41:3, 349-65

GLEN and NEXUS (Gay and Lesbian Equality Network and NEXUS Research Cooperative) (1995) *Poverty: Lesbians and gay men – the economic and social effects of discrimination*, Dublin: CPA

Glennerster, H (1995) *British social policy since 1945*, Oxford: Blackwell

Glyn, A (2006) *Capitalism unleashed: Finance, globalisation and welfare*, Oxford: Oxford UP

Glynn, I (2014) *An overview of Ireland's integration policies*, INTERACT RR 2014/10, Robert Schuman Centre for Advanced Studies, San Domenico di Fiesole (FI): European University Institute

Glynn, I with Kelly, T and Mac Éinrí, P (2015) *The re-emergence of emigration from Ireland: New trends in an old story*, Washington DC: Migration Policy Institute

GoI (Government of Ireland) (1958) *Programme for economic expansion*, Dublin: Stationery Office

GoI (Government of Ireland) (1966) *The health services and their further development*, Dublin: Stationery Office

GoI (Government of Ireland) (1970) *Reformatory and industrial schools systems report*, Dublin: Stationery Office

GoI (Government of Ireland) (1987) *Programme for National Recovery*, Dublin: Stationery Office

GoI (Government of Ireland) (1992) *Education for a changing world*, Dublin: Stationery Office

GoI (Government of Ireland) (1995) *Charting our education future*, Dublin: Stationery Office

GoI (Government of Ireland) (1997) *National anti-poverty strategy*, Dublin: Stationery Office

GoI (Government of Ireland) (1999a) *Ready to learn*, Dublin: Stationery Office

GoI (Government of Ireland) (1999b) *Primary school curriculum*, Dublin: Stationery Office

GoI (Government of Ireland) (1999c) *Ireland, national development plan 2000-2006*, Dublin: Stationery Office

GoI (Government of Ireland) (2007) *National action plan for social inclusion 2007-2016*, Dublin: Stationery Office

GoI (Government of Ireland) (2010) *National pensions framework*, Dublin: Stationery Office

GoI (Government of Ireland) (2011) *Programme for government 2011-2016*, available at: http://taoiseach.gov.ie/eng/Publications/Publications_Archive/Publications_2011/Programme_for_Government_2011.pdf

GoI (Government of Ireland) (2016a) *Pathways to work 2016-2020*, Dublin: Stationery Office

GoI (Government of Ireland) (2016b) *Rebuilding Ireland: Action plan for housing and homelessness*, Dublin: DHPCLG, available at: http://rebuildingireland.ie/Rebuilding%20Ireland_Action%20Plan.pdf

GoI (Government of Ireland) (2016c) *Programme for a partnership government*, available at http://www.merrionstreet.ie/MerrionStreet/en/ImageLibrary/Programme_for_Partnership_Government.pdf

Goldsmith, E and Allen, R (1972) *A blueprint for survival*, London: Penguin

González Pandiella, A (2016) *Migration in Ireland: Challenges, opportunities and policies*, OECD Economics Department Working Papers, 1292, Paris: OECD

Gössling, S and Cohen, S (2014) 'Why sustainable transport policies will fail: EU climate policy in the light of transport taboos', *Journal of Transport Geography*, 39, 197-207

Gough, I (1979) *The political economy of the welfare state*, London: Macmillan

Gough, I (2011) *Climate change, double injustice and social policy: A case study of the United Kingdom*, Geneva: UNRISD

Gough, I (2012) 'Reply to Michael Hill', *Social Policy & Administration*, 46:5, 587-91

Gough, I (2013) 'Climate change, social policy, and global governance', *Journal of International and Comparative Social Policy*, 29:3, 185-203

Gough, I (2016) 'Welfare states and environmental states: A comparative analysis', *Environmental Politics*, 25:1, 24-47

Gough, I and Meadowcroft, J (2011) 'Decarbonizing the welfare state', in JS Dryzek, RB Norgaard and D Schlosberg (eds) *Oxford handbook of climate change and society*, Oxford: Oxford UP, 490-503

Graham, H (2007) *Unequal lives: Health and socioeconomic inequalities*, Maidenhead: Open UP

Greve, B (2015) *Welfare and the welfare state: Present and future*, Abingdon: Routledge

Grimshaw, D and Rubery, J (2015) 'Neoliberalism 2.0: Crisis and austerity in the UK', in S Lehndorff (ed) *Divisive integration. The triumph of failed ideas in Europe – revisited*, Brussels: ETUI, 202-32

Gros, D and Alcidi, C (2015) 'Economic policy coordination in the euro area under the European Semester', *CEPS Special Report 123*, Brussels: CEPS

Grubb, D, Singh, S and Tergeist, P (2009) *Activation policies in Ireland*, OECD Social, Employment and Migration Working Papers, 75, Paris: OECD

Grummell, B and Lynch, K (2016) 'New managerialism: A political project in Irish education', in MP Murphy and F Dukelow (eds) *The Irish welfare state in the twenty-first century: Challenges and change*, Basingstoke: Palgrave Macmillan, 215-35

Guha, R and Martinez-Alier, J (1997) *Varieties of environmentalism: Essays North and South*, London: Earthscan

Guinnane, TW (1993) 'The poor law and pensions in Ireland', *Journal of Interdisciplinary History*, 24:2, 271-91

Hall, PA (2014) 'Varieties of capitalism and the Euro crisis', *West European Politics*, 37:6, 1223-43

Hall, PA (2015) 'Postscript: The future of the welfare state', in C Chwalisz and P Diamond (eds) *The predistribution agenda: Tackling inequality and supporting sustainable growth*, London: IB Tauris, 254-65

Hantrais, L (2000) *Social policy in the European Union* (2nd edn), Basingstoke: Macmillan

Hantrais, L (2008) 'Social policy and the European Union', in P Alcock, M May and K Rowlingson (eds) *The student's companion to social policy* (3rd edn), Oxford: Blackwell, 284-91

Harford, J (2005) 'The movement for the higher education of women in Ireland: Gender equality or denominational rivalry?', *History of Education*, 34:5, 473-92

Harford, J (2008) *The opening of university education to women in Ireland*, Dublin: Irish Academic Press

Harvey, B (1995) 'The use of legislation to address a social problem: The example of the Housing Act, 1988', *Administration*, 43:1, 76-85

Harvey, B (2003) *Guide to equality and the policies, institutions and programmes of the European Union*, Dublin: Equality Authority

Harvey, B (2008) 'Homelessness and the 1988 Housing Act, state policy and civil society', in D Downey (ed) *Perspectives on Irish homelessness: Past, present and future*, Dublin: Homeless Agency, 10-14

Harvey, B (2012) *Downsizing the community sector: Changes in employment and services in the voluntary and community sector in Ireland, 2008-2012*, Dublin: ICTU

Harvey, B (2013) *Travelling with austerity: Impacts of cuts on Travellers, Traveller projects and services*, Dublin: Pavee Point

Harvey, B (2014) *Scoping of need in social justice sphere*, Dublin: Philanthropy Ireland

Harvey, B (2016) 'Local and community development in Ireland: An overview', in ISS21 Local and Community Development Working Group (ed) *The changing landscape of local and community development in Ireland: Policy and practice*, Cork: ISS21, UCC, 7-14

Harvey, D (2005) *A brief history of neoliberalism*, Oxford: Oxford UP

Haugh, D (2016a) 'Ireland's economy: Still riding the globalisation wave', *OECD Observer 305*, January, available at: http://oecdobserver.org/news/fullstory.php/aid/5456/Ireland_92s_economy:_Still_riding_the_globalisation_wave.html

Haugh, D (2016b) 'Ireland...trading in the global talent pool', *OECD Ecoscope*, 5 April, available at: https://oecdecoscope.wordpress.com/2016/04/05/irelandtrading-in-the-global-talent-pool/

Hay, C, Riihelainen, JM, Smith, NJ and Watson, M (2008) 'Ireland: The outlier inside', in K Dyson (ed) *The Euro at 10: Europeanization, power and convergence*, Oxford: Oxford UP, 182-203

Hayek, FA (2006 [1960]) *The constitution of liberty*, Abingdon: Routledge

Hayes, M (2006) 'Indigenous otherness: Some aspects of Traveller social history', *Éire-Ireland*, 41:3/4, 133-61

Hayes, N (2007) 'Early childhood education and care: A decade of reflection, 1996-2006', in N Hayes and S Bradley (eds) *A decade of reflection: Early childhood care and education in Ireland 1996-2006*, Dublin: Centre for Social and Educational Research, 3-9

Hayes, N (2008) *The role of early childhood care and education: An anti-poverty perspective*, Dublin: CPA

Hayes, N (2016) 'Early childhood education and care: A neglected policy arena?', in MP Murphy and F Dukelow (eds) *The Irish welfare state in the twenty-first century: Challenges and change*, Basingstoke: Palgrave Macmillan, 193-214

Hayward, T (2005) *Constitutional environmental rights*, Oxford: Oxford UP

Hazelkorn, E (2014) 'Rebooting Irish higher education: Policy challenges for challenging times', *Studies in Higher Education*, 39:8, 1343-54

Hazelkorn, E (2015) *Rankings and the reshaping of higher education: The battle for world-class excellence* (2nd edn), Basingstoke: Palgrave Macmillan

HEA (Higher Education Authority) (2008) *National plan for equity of access to higher education 2008-2013*, Dublin: HEA

HEA (Higher Education Authority) (2011) *National strategy for higher education to 2030*, Dublin: HEA

HEA (Higher Education Authority) (2015) *National plan for equity of access to higher education 2015-2019*, Dublin: HEA

Hearne, R (2014) 'Communities and housing standards in Ireland: Tenants' experience of social rented housing', in L Sirr (ed) *Renting in Ireland: The social, voluntary and private sectors*, Dublin: IPA, 155-69

Hearne, R and McMahon, C (2016) *Cherishing all equally 2016: Economic inequality in Ireland*, Dublin: TASC

Helleiner, J (2000) *Irish Travellers and the politics of culture*, Buffalo, NY: University of Toronto Press

Hemerijck, A (2013) *Changing welfare states*, Oxford: Oxford UP

Hemerijck, A (2015) 'The quiet paradigm revolution of social investment', *Social Politics*, 22:2, 242-56

Hemerijck, A (2016) *New EMU governance: Not (yet) ready for social investment?*, Institute for European Integration Research Working Paper Series 1, Vienna: EIF

Hemerijck, A and Vandenbroucke, F (2012) 'Social investment and the Euro crisis: the necessity of a unifying social policy concept', *Intereconomics*, 47:4, 200-6

Hewitt, M (2000) *Welfare and human nature: The human subject in twentieth century social politics*, London: Macmillan

Heywood, A (2002) *Politics* (2nd edn), Basingstoke: Palgrave Macmillan

Heywood, A (2003) *Political ideologies: An introduction* (3rd edn), Basingstoke: Palgrave Macmillan

Heywood, A (2012) *Political ideologies: An introduction* (5th edn), Basingstoke: Palgrave Macmillan

HIA (Health Insurance Authority) (2016) *Annual report and accounts, 2015*, Dublin: HIA

Higgins, A, Doyle, L, Downes, C, Murphy, R, Sharek, D, DeVries, J, Begley, T, McCann, E, Sheerin, F and Smyth, S (2016) *The LGBT Ireland report: national study of the mental health and wellbeing of lesbian, gay, bisexual, transgender and intersex people in Ireland*, Dublin: GLEN and BeLonG To

Hill Collins, P and Chepp, V (2013) 'Intersectionality', in G Waylen, K Celis, J Kantola and SL Weldon (eds) *The Oxford handbook of gender and politics*, Oxford: Oxford UP 57-87

Hill, M (2003) *Understanding social policy* (7th edn), Oxford: Blackwell

Hill, M (2012) 'Re-reviews: The political economy of the welfare state, Ian Gough', *Social Policy & Administration*, 46:5, 582-7

Hines, S (2009) 'A pathway to diversity? Human rights, citizenship and the politics of transgender', *Contemporary Politics*, 15:1, 87-102

HIQA (Health Information and Quality Authority) (2015) *Report on the inspection of the child protection and welfare services provided to children living in direct provision accommodation under the National Standards for the Protection and Welfare of children, and section 8(1)(c) of the Health Act 2007*, available at: www.hiqa.ie/system/files/inspectionreports/706.pdf

HIQA (Health Information and Quality Authority) (2016) *National Standards for Residential Care Settings for Older People in Ireland 2016*, Dublin: HIQA

Hobson, B, Orloff, A, Daly, M, Michel, S and Williams, F (2015) 'Revisioning gender, an introduction', *Social Politics*, 22:4, 495-12

Hockerts, HG (1981) 'German post-war social policies against the background of the Beveridge Plan some observations preparatory to a comparative analysis', in MJ Mommsen (ed) *The emergence of the welfare state in Britain and Germany: 1850-1950*, London: Croom Helm, 315-39

Hodgins, M and Fox, F (2014) '"Causes of causes": Ethnicity and social position as determinants of health inequality in Irish Traveller men', *Health Promotion International*, 29:2, 223-34

Hodgins, M, Millar, M and Barry, M (2006) '"…it's all the same no matter how much fruit or vegetables or fresh air we get": Traveller women's perceptions of illness causation and health inequalities', *Social Science and Medicine*, 62:8, 1978-90

Hoff, MD and McNutt, JG (2009) 'Social policy and the physical environment', in J Midgley and M Livermore (eds) *The handbook of social policy*, Thousand Oaks, CA: Sage, 295-311

Holohan, C (2011) *In plain sight: Responding to the Ferns, Ryan, Murphy and Cloyne reports*, Dublin: Amnesty International Ireland

hooks, b (1982) *Ain't I a woman: Black women and feminism*, London: Pluto Press

hooks, b (2015) *Feminism is for everybody: Passionate politics* (2nd edn), New York: Routledge

Houghton, F and Houghton, S (2015) '"Say nothing for a wee while, and then say nothing at all": Still hiding the evidence on health inequalities in Ireland, *Radical Statistics*, 112, 56-69

Hourihan, K (2006) 'The suburbs', in J Crowley, R Devoy, D Linehan, P O'Flanagan and M Murphy (eds) *Atlas of Cork city*, Cork: Cork UP, 278-89

Housing Agency (2016) *Submission to the Committee on Housing and Homelessness*, 28 April, available at: www.oireachtas.ie/parliament/media/committees/32ho usingandhomelessness/Housing--Homelessness-Committee-HA-Combined-Submission-Revised.pdf

Houston, M (2012) 'Little progress on primary care teams says College CEO', *Irish Medical Times*, 16 May

HSE (2007) *National intercultural health strategy 2007-2012*, Kildare: HSE

HSE (2011) *Time to move on from congregated settings, A strategy for community inclusion: The report of the working group on congregated settings*, Dublin: HSE

HSE (Health Service Executive) (2012a) *Annual report and financial statements 2011*, Dublin: HSE

HSE (Health Service Executive) (2012b) *New directions: Personal support services for adults with disabilities,* Dublin: HSE

HSE (Health Service Executive) (2014) *Safeguarding vulnerable persons at risk of abuse: National policy & procedures, incorporating services for elder abuse and for persons with a disability*, Dublin: HSE

HSE (Health Service Executive) (2015) *Planning for health: Trends and priorities to inform health service planning 2016*, Dublin: HSE

HSE (Health Service Executive) (2016a) 'Nursing homes support scheme, a fair deal,' available at: http://hse.ie/eng/services/list/4/olderpeople/nhss/

HSE (Health Service Executive) (2016b) *Transforming Lives Programme to implement the recommendations of the 'Value for Money and Policy Review of the Disability Services in Ireland'*, Bulletin 1: July, Dublin: HSE, available at: http://www. inclusionireland.ie/sites/default/files/attach/basic-page/1014/time-move-bulletin-july-2016.pdf

Huby, M (1998) *Social policy and the environment*, Buckingham: Open UP

Huby, M (2001) 'The sustainable use of resources on a global scale', *Social Policy and Administration*, 35:5, 521-37

Hughes, G and Maher, M (2016) 'Redistribution in the Irish pension system: Upside down?', in MP Murphy and F Dukelow (eds) *The Irish welfare state in the twenty-first century: Challenges and change*, Basingstoke: Palgrave, 93-118

Hulse, K and Milligan, V (2014) 'Secure occupancy: A new framework for analysing security in rental housing', *Housing Studies*, 29:5, 638-56

Hunter, DJ (2016) *The health debate* (2nd edn), Bristol: Policy Press

Hutton, D (1991) 'Labour in the post-independence Irish state', in S Hutton and P Stewart (eds) *Ireland's histories: Aspects of state, society and ideology*, London: Routledge, 52-79

Hyland, A (1996) 'Multi-denominational schools in the Republic of Ireland 1975-1995', paper delivered at a conference, Education and Religion, organised by CRELA at the University of Nice, 21-2 June, available at: www.educatetogether. ie/node/1918

ICCL (Irish Council for Civil Liberties) (2016) *Know your rights: A guide for older people*, Dublin: ICCL

IHREC (Irish Human Rights and Equality Commission) (2015) *Ireland and the international covenant on economic, social and cultural rights*, Dublin: IHREC

Immervoll, H and Scarpetta, S (2012) 'Activation and employment support policies in OECD countries: An overview of current approaches', *IZA Journal of Labour Policy*, 1:9, 1-20

Inclusion Ireland (2013) *Implementing the National Disability Strategy: Inclusion Ireland position paper*, Dublin: Inclusion Ireland

Inglis, T (1998) *Moral monopoly: The rise and fall of the Catholic Church in modern Ireland*, Dublin: UCD Press

Inglis, T (2002) 'Sexual transgression and scapegoats: A case study from modern Ireland', *Sexualities*, 5:1, 5–24

Inglis, T (2005) 'Origins and legacies of Irish prudery: sexuality and social control in modern Ireland', *Éire-Ireland*, 40:3 & 4, 9–37

Inter-Departmental Committee (1968) *Report of the Inter-Departmental Committee on the Care of the Aged*, Dublin: Stationery Office

Inter-Departmental Committee (2013) *Report of the Inter-Departmental Committee to establish the facts of State involvement with the Magdalen laundries*, Dublin: Department of Justice and Equality

IPCC (Intergovernmental Panel on Climate Change) (2014) *Climate change 2014 synthesis report summary for policymakers*, available at: www.ipcc.ch/pdf/assessment-report/ar5/syr/AR5_SYR_FINAL_SPM.pdf

IRC (Irish Refugee Council) (2015) *The Working Group and the time factor: A missed opportunity*, available at: www.irishrefugeecouncil.ie/wp-content/uploads/2015/10/The-Working-Group-and-the-time-factor-a-missed-opportunity_Oct2015.pdf

Irish Congress of Trade Unions (2016) *Who cares? Report on childcare costs and practices in Ireland*, Dublin: ICTU

Irish Fiscal Advisory Council (2014) *Pre-budget 2015 statement*, Dublin: Irish Fiscal Advisory Council

Irish Rural Link (2016) *Poverty and social inclusion: The case for rural Ireland*, Moate: Irish Rural Link

Irish Times (1968) 'Controversial group wants action on housing, aims of DHAC explained', *Irish Times*, 17 June

Irish Times (2009) 'The savage reality of our darkest days', *Irish Times*, 21 May

Jackson, T (2009) *Prosperity without growth?*, London: Sustainable Development Commission

Jaeger, M and Kvist, J (2003) 'Pressures on state welfare in post-industrial societies: Is more or less better?', *Social Policy & Administration*, 37:6, 555–72

Jenkinson, H (1996) 'History of youth work', in P Burgess (ed) *Youth and community work: A course reader*, Centre for Adult and Continuing Education, Cork: Cork UP, 35–43

Jensen, C (2008) 'Worlds of welfare services and transfers', *Journal of European Social Policy*, 18:2, 151–62

Jenson, J (2012) 'A new politics for the social investment perspective', in G Bonoli and D Natali (eds) *The politics of the new welfare state*, Oxford: Oxford UP, 21–44

Jenson, J (2015) 'The fading goal of gender equality: Three policy directions that underpin the resilience of gendered socio-economic inequalities', *Social Politics*, 22:4, 539–60

Joint Committee on Justice and Equality (2017) *Report on the recognition of Traveller ethnicity*, Dublin: Houses of the Oireachtas, available at: http://www.oireachtas.ie/parliament/media/committees/justice/Report-on-the-Recognition-of-Traveller-Ethnicity-20-01-17.pdf

Joint Committee on Justice, Defence and Equality (2014) *Report on the recognition of Traveller ethnicity*, Dublin: Houses of the Oireachtas, available at: www.oireachtas.ie/parliament/media/committees/justice/Report-onTraveller-Ethnicity.pdf

Jones, K (2000) *The making of social policy in Britain: From the poor law to New Labour* (3rd edn), London: The Athlone Press

Jones, T (1910) 'Pauperism and poverty', *Journal of the Statistical and Social Inquiry Society of Ireland*, XII, 358-70

Joppke, C (1999) 'How immigration is changing citizenship: a comparative view', *Ethnic and Racial Studies*, 22:4, 629-52

Joppke, C (2008) 'Comparative citizenship: A restrictive turn in Europe?', *Law and Ethics of Human Rights*, 2:1, 1-41

Juncker, JC (2014) 'A new start for Europe', Opening statement in the European Parliament plenary session, Strasbourg, 15 July, available at: http://europa.eu/rapid/press-release_SPEECH-14-567_en.htm

Juncker, JC with Tusk, D, Dijsselbloem, J, Draghi, M and Schultz, M (2015) *Completing Europe's Economic and Monetary Union,* Brussels: European Commission

Kaim-Caudle, PR (1967) *Social security in Ireland and Western Europe*, Dublin: ESRI

Kalyvas, SN and van Kersbergen, K (2010) 'Christian democracy', *Annual Review of Political Science* 13, 183-209

Kangas, O and Kvist, J (2013) 'Nordic welfare states', in B Greve (ed) *The Routledge handbook of the welfare state*, Abingdon: Routledge, 148-60

Karanikolos, M, Heino, P, McKee, M, Stuckler, D and Legido-Quigley, H (2016) 'Effects of the global financial crisis on health in high-income OECD countries: A narrative review', *International Journal of Health Services*, 46:2, 208-40

Katz, M (1996) *In the shadow of the poorhouse: A social history of welfare in America* (rev. edn), New York: Basic Books

Keating, A (2015) 'Administrative expedience and the avoidance of scandal: Ireland's industrial and reformatory schools and the inter-departmental committee of 1962-3', *Estudios Irlandeses – Journal of Irish Studies*, 10, 95-108

Keating, M and McCrone, D (2013) 'The crisis of social democracy', in M Keating and D McCrone (eds) *The crisis of social democracy in Europe*, Edinburgh: Edinburgh UP, 1-13

Kelleher, C (2007) 'Health and modern Irish society: The mother and father of a dilemma', in M Cousins (ed) *Welfare policy and poverty*, Dublin: IPA and CPA, 201-28

Kelly, E, McGuinness, S, O'Connell, P, González Pandiella, A and Haugh, D (2016) *How did immigrants fare in the Irish labour market over the Great Recession?* OECD Economics Department Working Papers, 1284, Paris: OECD

Kelly, J (1999) 'The emergence of scientific and institutional medical practice in Ireland, 1650-1800', in E Malcolm and G Jones (eds) *Medicine, disease and the state in Ireland, 1650-1940*, Cork: Cork UP, 21-39

Kelly, M (2009) 'The Irish credit bubble', Dublin: Centre for Economic Research Working Paper Series WP09/32, Dublin: Centre for Economic Research

Kelly, N, Garvey, J and Palcic, D (2016) Health policy and the policymaking system: A case study of primary care in Ireland, *Health Policy*, 120, 193-9

Kemeny, J (1995) *From public housing to the social market*, London: Routledge

Kemeny, J (2006) 'Corporatism and housing regimes', *Housing, Theory and Society*, 23:1, 1-18

Kennedy, F (2001) *Cottage to crèche: Family change in Ireland*, Dublin: IPA

Kennedy, KA, Giblin, T and McHugh, D (1988) *The economic development of Ireland in the twentieth century*, London: Routledge

Kennedy, S (ed) (1981) *One million poor? The challenge of Irish inequality*, Dublin: Turoe Press

Keogh, D (1987) 'The Irish constitutional revolution: An analysis of the making of the Constitution', *Administration*, 35:4, 4–84

Kerrigan, G (1983) 'The moral civil war', *Magill*, September, 6-15.

Keskinen, S, Norocel, OC, Jørgensen, MB (2016) 'The politics and policies of welfare chauvinism under the economic crisis', *Critical Social Policy*, 36:3, 321-9

Kildal, N and Kuhnle, S (2005) 'The Nordic welfare model and the idea of universalism', in N Kildal and S Kuhnle (eds) *The normative foundations of the welfare state: The Nordic experience*, Abingdon: Routledge, 13-33

Kilkelly, U (2007) *Barriers to the realisation of children's rights in Ireland*, commissioned by the Ombudsman for Children 2007, available at: www.oco.ie/wp-content/uploads/2014/03/Barrierstorealisationofchildren_x0027_srights.pdf

Kingston, G, McGinnity, F and O'Connell, P (2015) 'Discrimination in the labour market: Nationality, ethnicity and the recession', *Work, Employment and Society*, 29:2, 213-32

Kirby, P (2010) 'Lessons from the Irish collapse: Taking an international political economy approach', *Irish Studies in International Affairs*, 21, 43-55

Kirby, P and Murphy, MP (2008) *A better Ireland is possible: Towards an alternative vision for Ireland*, Galway: Community Platform

Kirby, P and Murphy, MP (2011a) *Towards a second republic: Irish politics after the celtic tiger*, London: Pluto

Kirby, P and Murphy, MP (2011b) 'Globalisation and models of state: Debates and evidence from Ireland', *New Political Economy*, 16:1, 19–39

Kitchin, R, Hearne, R and O'Callaghan, C (2015) *Housing in Ireland: From crisis to crisis*, NIRSA Working Paper Series, 77, Maynooth: Maynooth University

Kitchin, R, O'Callaghan, C and Gleeson, J (2012) *Unfinished estates in post-celtic tiger Ireland*, NIRSA Working Paper Series, 67, Maynooth: Maynooth University

Kleinman, M (1996) *Housing, welfare and the state in Europe: A comparative analysis of Britain, France, and Germany*, Aldershot: Edward Elgar

Kleinman, MA (2002) *A European welfare state? European Union social policy in context*, Basingstoke: Palgrave

Koopmans, R (2013) 'Multiculturalism and immigration: A contested field in cross-national comparison', *Annual Review of Sociology*, 39, 147-69

Korpi, W (1983) *The democratic class struggle*, London: Routledge and Kegan Paul

Korpi, W and Palme, J (1998) 'The paradox of redistribution and strategies of equality: Welfare state institutions, inequality, and poverty in the western countries', *American Sociological Review*, 63:5, 661-87

Krippner, GR (2005) 'The financialiszation of the American economy', *Socio-Economic Review*, 3:2, 173-208

Krugman, P (2009) 'Erin go broke', *The New York Times*, 19 April

Kvist, J, Fritzell, J, Hvinden, B and Kangas, O (eds) (2012) *Changing social equality: The Nordic welfare model in the 21st century*, Bristol: Policy Press

Kwon, HJ (1997) 'Beyond European welfare regimes: Comparative perspectives on East Asian welfare systems', *Journal of Social Policy*, 26:4, 467-84

Laeven, L and Valencia, F (2012) *Systemic banking crises database: An update*, IMF Working Paper WP/ 12/163, Washington: IMF

Lacey, B (2008) *'Terrible queer creatures': Homosexuality in Irish history*, Dublin: Wordwell Books

Laffan, B and Tonra, B (2010) 'Europe and the international dimension', in J Coakley and M Gallagher (eds) *Politics in the Republic of Ireland* (5th edn) London: Routledge & PSAI Press, 407-33

Landy, D (2015) 'Challengers in the migrant field: Pro-migrant Irish NGO responses to the Immigration, Residence and Protection Bill', *Ethnic and Racial Studies*, 38:6, 927-42

Langford, S (2007) 'Delivering integrated policy and services for children', *Journal of the Statistical and Social Inquiry Society of Ireland*, XXXVI, 250-60

Lapavitsas, C (2011) 'Theorizing financialization', *Work, Employment and Society*, 25:4, 611-26

Larragy, J (2014) *Asymmetric engagement: The community and voluntary pillar in Irish social partnership*, Manchester: Manchester UP

Lavalette, M (2006) 'Marxism and welfarism', in M Lavalette and A Pratt (eds) *Social policy: Theories, concepts and issues* (3rd edn), London: Sage, 46-65

Lawson, N (2013) *Europe as a good society: The joint transformation of the social democratic and European projects*, Social Europe Occasional Paper 1, Social Europe, available at: www.socialeurope.eu/book/op-1-europe-as-a-good-society/

Lawson, N (2014) 'Social democrats face irrelevance at best, extinction at worse', *New Statesman*, 8 December, available at: www.newstatesman.com/politics/2014/12/social-democrats-face-irrelevance-best-extinction-worse

Layte, R, Banks, J, Walsh, C and McKnight, G (2015) 'Trends in socio-economic inequalities in mortality by sex in Ireland from the 1980s to the 2000s', *Irish Journal of Medical Science*, 184:3, 613-21

Layte, R, Nolan, A and Nolan, B (2007) *Poor prescriptions, Poverty and access to community health services*, Dublin: CPA

Ledden, PJ (1999) 'Education and social class in Joyce's Dublin', *Journal of Modern Literature*, 22:2, 329-36

Ledwith, V and Reilly, K (2013) 'Accommodating all applicants? School choice and the regulation of enrolment in Ireland', *The Canadian Geographer*, 57:3, 318-26

Lee, JJ (1979) 'Continuity and change in Ireland, 1945-70', in JJ Lee (ed) *Ireland 1945-70*, Dublin: Gill & Macmillan, 166-77

Lee, JJ (1989) *Ireland 1912–1985 Politics and society*, Cambridge: Cambridge UP

Lee, P and Raban, C (1988) *Welfare theory and social policy: Reform or revolution?*, London: Sage

LeGrand, J, Propper, C and Robinson, R (1992) *The economics of social problems* (3rd edn), London: Macmillan

Leibfried, S (1992) 'Towards a European welfare state? On integrating poverty regimes into the European community', in Z Ferge and JE Kohlberg (eds) *Social policy in a changing Europe*, Frankfurt am Main: Campus Verlag, 245-80

Lemass, S (1963) Dáil Debates, vol 202, col 305, 24 April 1963

Lenaghan, J (1997) 'Health care rights in Europe: A comparative discussion', in J Lenaghan (ed) *Hard choices in health care*, London: BMJ Publishing, 177-200

Lentin, A (2008) *Racism: A beginner's guide*, London: Oneworld

Lentin, R and McVeigh, R (2006) *After optimism? Ireland, racism and globalisation*, Dublin: Metro Éireann

Leoni, T (2015) Welfare state adjustment to new social risks in the post-crisis scenario: A review with focus on the social investment perspective, Working Paper 89, WWWforEurope project, available at: http://www.wifo.ac.at/jart/prj3/wifo/resources/person_dokument/person_dokument.jart?publikationsid=57899&mime_type=application/pdf

Lewis, J (1992) 'Gender and the development of welfare regimes', *Journal of European Social Policy*, 2:3, 159-73

Lewis, J (1997) 'Gender and welfare regimes: Further thoughts', *Social Politics*, 4:2, 160-77

Lewis, J (1999) 'The voluntary sector in the mixed economy of welfare', in D Gladstone (ed) *Before Beveridge: Welfare before the welfare state*, London: Civitas, 10-17

Lewis, J and Åström, G (1997) 'Equality, difference and state welfare: Labour market and family policies in Sweden', in C Ungerson and M Kember (eds) *Women and social policy: A reader* (2nd edn), London: Macmillan, 25-40

Liang, CS (ed) (2007) 'Europe for the Europeans: The foreign and security policy of the populist radical right', in CS Liang (ed) *Europe for the Europeans: The foreign and security policy of the populist radical right*, Farnham: Ashgate, 1-32

Lightman, ES and Riches, G (2001) 'Canada: one step forward, two steps back?' in P. Alcock and G. Craig (eds) *International social policy: Welfare regimes in the developed world*, Basingstoke: Palgrave, 45–63

Lind, A (2013) 'Heteronormativity and sexuality', in G Waylen, K Celis, J Kantola and SL Weldon (eds) *The Oxford handbook of gender and politics*, Oxford: Oxford UP, 189-213

Linehan, C, O'Doherty, S, Tatlow-Golden, M, Craig, S, Kerr, M, Lynch, C, McConkey, R and Staines, A (2014) *Mapping the National Disability Policy landscape*, Dublin: School of Social Work and Social Policy, TCD

Lister, R (ed) (1996) *Charles Murray and the underclass: The developing debate*, The IEA Health and Welfare Unit Choice in Welfare, 33, London: Civitas

Lister, R (2003) *Citizenship: Feminist perspectives* (2nd edn), Basingstoke: Palgrave Macmillan

Lister, R (2004) *Poverty*, Cambridge: Polity

Lister, R (2010) *Understanding theories and concepts in social policy*, Bristol: Policy Press

Lister, R (2015) '"To count for nothing": Poverty beyond the statistics', *Journal of the British Academy*, 3, 139-65

Littig, B and Grießler, E (2005) 'Social sustainability: A catchword between political pragmatism and social theory', *International Journal of Sustainable Development*, 8:1/2, 65-79

Litton, F (1982) *Unequal achievement: The Irish experience 1957-1982*, Dublin: IPA

Logan, E (2014) Garda Síochána Act 2005 (Section 42) (Special inquiries relating to Garda Síochána) Order 2013 Report of Ms Emily Logan, available at: www.justice.ie/en/JELR/Emily%20Logan%20report.pdf/Files/Emily%20Logan%20report.pdf

Lord, S (2015) 'The Eight Amendment: Planting a legal timebomb', in A Quilty, S Kennedy and C Conlon (eds) *The abortion papers Ireland: Volume 2*, Cork: Attic Press, 90-103

Lucas, K (2004) 'Locating transport as a social policy problem', in K Lucas (ed) *Running on empty: Transport, social exclusion and environmental justice*, Bristol: Policy Press, 7-13

Lucas, K (2012) 'Transport and social exclusion: Where are we now?', *Transport Policy*, 20, 105-13

Lucas, K, Grosvenor, T and Simpson, R (2001) *Transport, the environment and social exclusion*, York: Joseph Rowntree Trust

Lucas, K, Mattioli, G, Verlinghieri, E and Guzman, A (2016) 'Transport poverty and its adverse social consequences', *Transport*, 169: TR6, 353-65

Luddy, M (1999) '"Angels of mercy": Nuns as workhouse nurses, 1861-1898', in E Malcolm and G Jones (eds) *Medicine, disease and the state in Ireland, 1650-1940*, Cork: Cork UP, 102-17

Luddy, M (2002) 'Women and politics in Ireland, 1860-1918', in A Bourke, SM Kilfeather, M Luddy, M Mac Curtain, G Meaney, M Ní Dhonnchadha, M O'Dowd and C Wills (eds) *The field day anthology of Irish writing, volume v Irish women's writings and traditions*, Cork: Cork UP, 69-74

Luddy, M (2011) 'Unmarried mothers in Ireland, 1880-1973', *Women's History Review*, 20:1, 109-26

Luddy, M (2014) 'The early years of the NSPCC in Ireland', in M Luddy and JM Smith (eds) *Children, childhood and Irish society, 1500 to the present*, Dublin: Four Courts Press, 100-20

Lund, B (2002) *Understanding state welfare: Social justice or social exclusion?*, London: Sage

Lund, B (2006) 'Distributive justice and social policy', in M Lavalette and A Pratt (eds) *Social policy: Theories, concepts and issues* (3rd edn), London: Sage, 107-23

Lundström, F and McKeown, K (1994) *Home help services for elderly people in Ireland*, National Council for the Elderly Report, 36, Dublin: National Council for the Elderly

Lundvall, B and Lorenz, E (2012) 'From the Lisbon Strategy to Europe 2020', in N Morel, B Palier and J Palme (eds) *Towards a social investment state? Ideas, policies and challenges*, Bristol: Policy Press, 333-51

Lupton, R with Hills, J, Stewart, K and Vizard, P (2013) *Labour's social policy record: Policy, spending and outcomes 1997-2010*, London: CASE, LSE

Lynch, K (1999) *Equality in education*, Dublin: Gill & Macmillan

Lynch, K (2000) 'Research and theory on equality and education', in MT Hallinan (ed) *Handbook of the sociology of education*, New York: Kluwer, 85-105

Lynch, K (2007) 'Love labour as a distinct and non-commodifiable form of care labour', *The Sociological Review*, 55:3, 550-70

Lynch, K (2010) 'From a neo-liberal to an egalitarian state: Imagining a different future', *TASC Annual Lecture*, Royal Irish Academy, Dublin, 17 June, available at: http://researchrepository.ucd.ie/handle/10197/2468

Lynch, K (2014) 'Why love, care, and solidarity are political matters: Affective equality and Fraser's model of social justice', in AG Jónasdóttir and A Ferguson (eds) *Love: A question for feminism in the twenty-first century*, New York: Routledge, 173-89

Lynch, K and Baker, J (2005) 'Equality in education: An equality of condition perspective', *Theory and Research in Education*, 3:2, 131-64

Lynch, K and Lyons, M (2008) 'The gendered order of caring', in U Barry (ed) *Where are we now? New feminist perspectives on women in contemporary Ireland*, Dublin: TASC at New Island, 163-83

Lynch, K and Moran, M (2006) 'Markets, schools and the convertibility of economic capital: the complex dynamics of class choice', *British Journal of Sociology of Education*, 27:2, 221-35

Lyons, P (1972) 'The distribution of personal wealth in Ireland', in AA Tait and JA Bristow (eds) *Ireland: Some problems of a developing economy*, Dublin: Gill & Macmillan, 159-85

Mac Éinrí, P (2006) 'Migration in Ireland: A changing reality', in S Healy, B Reynolds and M Collins (eds) *Social policy in Ireland: Principles, practice and problems*, Dublin: Liffey Press, 357-83

Mac Éinrí, P (2007) 'Integration models and choices', in B Fanning (ed) *Immigration and social change in the Republic of Ireland*, Manchester: Manchester UP, 214-36

Mac Gréil, M (1977) *Prejudice and tolerance in Ireland*, Dublin: Research Section, College of Industrial Relations

Mac Gréil, M (2010) *Emancipation of the Travelling people,* Maynooth: NUIM

Mac Laughlin, J (1999) 'Nation building, social closure and anti-Traveller racism in Ireland', *Sociology*, 33:1, 129-51

Mac Ruairc, G (2009) 'Language, socio-economic class and educational underachievement', in S Drudy (ed) *Education in Ireland: Challenge and change*, Dublin: Gill & Macmillan, 118-35

Mac Sharry, R (2000) 'The challenge of 1987', in R Mac Sharry and P White (with J O'Malley), *The making of the celtic tiger: The inside story of Ireland's boom economy*, Cork/Dublin: Mercier, 42-74

Mackay, F (2015) *Radical feminism*, Basingstoke: Palgrave Macmillan

Macmillan, H (1938) *The middle way: A study of the problem of economic and social progress in a free and democratic society*, London: Macmillan

Macnaghten, P and Urry, J (1996) *Contested natures*, London: Sage

MacSweeney, AM (1915) 'A study of poverty in Cork City', *Studies*, 4:13, 93-104

Magill (1977) 'Two-thirds now favour divorce', *Magill*, December, 27

Magnusson, L (2010) *After Lisbon: Social Europe at the crossroads?* Brussels: ETUI

Maguire, M (1986) 'Ireland', in P Flora (ed) *Growth to limits – the Western European welfare states since World War II: Volume 2, Germany, United Kingdom, Ireland, Italy*, Berlin: Walter de Gruyter, 241-384

Maguire, MJ (2002) 'Foreign adoptions and the evolution of Irish adoption policy, 1945-52', *Journal of Social History*, 36:2, 387-404

Maguire, MJ (2009) *Precarious childhood in post-independence Ireland*, Manchester: Manchester UP

Mair, P and Weeks, L (2005) 'The party system', in J Coakley and M Gallagher (eds) *Politics in the Republic of Ireland* (4th edn), London: Routledge with PSAI Press, 135-59

Maître, B, Nolan, B and Whelan, CT (2006) *Reconfiguring the measurement of deprivation and consistent poverty in Ireland*, Dublin: ESRI

Malcolm, E (1999) '"The house of the strident shadows": The Asylum, the family and emigration in post-famine rural Ireland', in E Malcolm and G Jones (eds) *Medicine, disease and the state in Ireland, 1650-1940*, Cork: Cork UP, 177-91

Manandhar, M, Share, M, Friel, S, Walsh, O and Hardy, F (2006) *Food, nutrition and poverty among asylum-seekers in North West Ireland*, CPA Working Paper 06/01, Dublin: CPA

Mangan, I (2002) *Older people in long stay care: Report for the Irish Human Rights Commission*, available at: www.ihrec.ie/download/pdf/research_elderly_in_institutions_200304.pdf

Marmot, M (2015) *Status syndrome: How your place on the social gradient directly affects your health* (new edn), London: Bloomsbury

Marshall, TH (1949/1964) 'Citizenship and social class', in TH Marshall, *Class, citizenship and social development: Essays by TH Marshall*, New York: Double Day, 65-122

Martin, JP (2015) 'Activation and active labour market policies in OECD countries: Stylized facts and evidence on their effectiveness', *IZA Journal of Labour Policy*, 4:4, 1-29

Martínez-Alier, J, Pascual, U, Vivien, F-D, Zaccai, E (2010) 'Sustainable de-growth: Mapping the context, criticisms and future prospects of an emergent paradigm', *Ecological Economics* 69, 1741-7

Mayock, P, Bryan, A, Carr, N and Kitching, K (2009) *Supporting LGBT lives: A study of the mental health and well-being of lesbian, gay, bisexual and transgender people*, Dublin: GLEN and BeLong To

McAvoy, S (1999) 'The regulation of sexuality in the Irish free state, 1929-1935', in E Malcolm and G Jones (eds) *Medicine, disease and the state in Ireland, 1650-1940*, Cork: Cork UP, 253-66

McCann, M, Ó Síocháin, S and Ruane, J (eds) (1994) *Irish Travellers: Culture and ethnicity*, Belfast: Institute of Irish Studies, QUB

McCarthy, A (2004) 'Aspects of local health in Ireland in the 1950s', in D Keogh, F O'Shea and C Quinlan (eds) *The lost decade: Ireland in the 1950s,* Cork: Mercier Press, 118-34

McCashin, A (2004) *Social security in Ireland,* Dublin: Gill & Macmillan

McCashin, A and O'Shea, J (2007) 'The Irish welfare system', in K Schubert, S Hegelich and U Bazant (eds) *The handbook of European welfare systems*, Abingdon: Routledge, 260-76

McConkey, R, Kelly, C, Craig, S and Shevlin, M (2016) 'A decade of change in mainstream education for children with intellectual disabilities in the Republic of Ireland', *European Journal of Special Needs Education*, 31:1, 96-110

McCoy, S, Byrne, D, O'Connell, PJ, Kelly, E and Doherty, C (2010) *Hidden disadvantage? A study on the low participation in higher education by the non-manual group*, Dublin: HEA

McDonagh, J (2006) 'Transport policy instruments and transport-related social exclusion in rural Republic of Ireland', *Journal of Transport Geography*, 14:5, 355-66

McDonagh, M (2000) 'Ethnicity and culture', in E Sheehan (ed) *Travellers: Citizens of Ireland – our challenge to an intercultural Irish society in the 21st century*, Dublin: The Parish of the Travelling People, 26-31

McDonnell, O and O'Donovan, Ó (2009) 'Private health insurance as a technology of solidarity? The myth of "community" in Irish healthcare policy', *Irish Journal of Sociology,* 17:2, 6-23

McDonough, T and Dundon, T (2010) 'Thatcherism delayed? The Irish crisis and the paradox of social partnership', *Industrial Relations Journal*, 41:6, 544-62

McEntee, H (2016) Seanad Debates Health (Amendment) (Professional Home Care) Bill 2016: Second Stage, 9 November, available at: https://www.kildarestreet.com/sendebates/?id=2016-11-09a.227&s=speaker%3A476

McEvoy, O and Smith, M (2011) *Listen to our voices! Hearing children and young people living in the care of the state*, Dublin: DCYA

McGarrigle, C and Kenny, RA (2013) *Profile of the sandwich generation and intergenerational transfers in Ireland*, Dublin: The Irish Longitudinal Study on Ageing

McGing, C (2014) 'The Children's Referendum 2012', *Irish Political Studies*, 29:3, 471-9

McGinnity F and Lunn, P (2011) 'Measuring discrimination facing ethnic minority job applicants: An Irish experiment', *Work, Employment and Society*, 25:4, 693-708

McGoldrick, P and Caulfield, B (2015) 'Examining the changes in car ownership levels in the Greater Dublin Area between 2006 and 2011', *Case Studies on Transport Policy*, 3:2, 229-37

McGrath, B (1999) 'The sustainability of a car dependent settlement pattern: An evaluation of new rural settlement in Ireland', *The Environmentalist*, 19:2, 99-107

McGregor, C (2014) 'Why is history important at moments of transition? The case of 'transformation', of Irish child welfare via the new Child and Family Agency', *European Journal of Social Work*, 17:5, 771-83

McGuinness, S, O'Connell, PJ and Kelly, E (2013) *Carrots, no stick, no driver: The employment impact of job search assistance in a regime with minimal monitoring and sanctions*, Geary WP2013/08 Dublin: UCD Geary Institute

McKee, E (1986) 'Church-state relations and the development of Irish health policy: The mother-and-child scheme, 1944-53', *Irish Historical Studies*, 25:98, 159-94

McKeown, K, Haase, T and Pratschke, J (2015) 'Determinants of child outcomes in a cohort of children in the Free Pre-School Year in Ireland, 2012/2013', *Irish Educational Studies*, 34:3, 245-63

McLaughlin, J (2003) *Feminist social and political theory: Contemporary debates and dialogues*, Basingstoke: Palgrave Macmillan

McLoughlin, D (1990) 'Workhouses and Irish female paupers, 1840-70', in M Luddy and C Murphy (eds) *Women surviving: Studies in Irish women's history in the 19th and 20th centuries*, Dublin: Poolbeg Press, 117-47

McVeigh, R (2007) '"Ethnicity in denial" and racism: The case of the government against Irish Travellers', *Translocations*, 2:1, 90-133

McVeigh, R (2008) 'The "final solution": Reformism, ethnicity denial and the politics of anti-Travellerism in Ireland', *Social Policy & Society*, 7:1, 91-102

Mead, L (1992) *The new politics of poverty: The nonworking poor in America*, New York: Basic Books

Meadowcroft, J (2005) 'From welfare state to ecostate' in J Barry and R Eckersley (eds) *The state and the global ecological crisis*, Cambridge MA: MIT Press, 3-23

Meadows, DH, Meadows, DL, Randers, J and Behrens III, WW (1972) *The limits to growth*, New York: Universe Books

Meehan, C (2013) *A just society for Ireland? 1964-1987*, Basingstoke: Palgrave Macmillan

Memery, C (2001) 'The housing system and the celtic tiger: The state response to a housing crisis of affordability and access', *European Journal of Housing Policy*, 1:1, 79-104

Mental Health Commission (2016) 'Progress made on mental health service provision, but it's time for a formal review of A Vision for Change, according to the Mental Health Commission', Annual report press release, 20 June, available at: http://www.mhcirl.ie/File/2015-Annual-Report-Press-Release.pdf

Mercille, J and Murphy, E (2015) *Deepening neoliberalism, austerity and crisis: Europe's treasure Ireland*, Basingstoke: Palgrave Macmillan

Mesabbah, M and Arisha, A (2016) 'Performance management of the public healthcare services in Ireland: a review', *International Journal of Health Care Quality Assurance*, 29:2, 209-35

Millar, J (2009) 'Introduction: The role of social security in society', in J Millar (ed) *Understanding social security: Issues for policy and practice* (2nd edn), Bristol: Policy Press, 1-10

Millet, K (1970) *Sexual politics*, London: Virago

Milne, E (2012) 'A public health perspective on transport policy priorities', *Journal of Transport Geography*, 21, 62-9

Minas, R (2014) 'One-stop shops: Increasing employability and overcoming welfare state fragmentation?', *International Journal of Social Welfare*, 23:S1: S40-S53

Minton, SJ, Dahl, T, O'Moore, AM and Tuck, D (2008) 'An exploratory survey of the experiences of homophobic bullying among lesbian, gay, bisexual and transgendered young people in Ireland', *Irish Educational Studies*, 27:2, 177-91

MIPEX (Migrant Integration Policy Index) (2015) Migrant Integration Policy Index 2015 Ireland, available at: www.mipex.eu/ireland

Mishra, R (1990) *The welfare state in capitalist society: Policies of retrenchment and maintenance in Europe, North America and Australia*, New York: Harvester Wheatsheaf

Mjøset, L (1992) *The Irish economy in a comparative institutional perspective*, Dublin: NESC

Mokyr J and Ó Gráda, C (1988) 'Poor and getting poorer? Living standards in Ireland before the Famine', *Economic History Review*, 41:2, 209-35

Monbiot, G (2016) 'Neoliberalism: The ideology at the root of all our problems', *The Guardian*, 15 April

Montgomery, V (2013) 'Multicultural Ireland? Muslim women and integration in Ireland', *Irish Political Studies*, 28:3, 434-49

Mooney, G (1998) 'Remoralizing the poor?: Gender, class and philanthropy in Victorian Britain', in G Lewis (ed) *Forming nation, framing welfare*, London: Routledge with OUP, 49-91

Moran, G (2004) *Sending out Ireland's poor: Assisted emigration to North America in the nineteenth century*, Dublin: Four Courts Press

Moran, M (1999) *Governing the health care state: A comparative study of the United Kingdom, the United States and Germany*, Manchester: Manchester UP

Moran, M (2000) 'Understanding the welfare state: The case of health care', *British Journal of Politics and International Relations*, 2:2, 135-60

Moran, V, Normand, C and Smith, A (2013) 'Ireland', in L Siciliani, M Borowitz and V Moran (eds) *Waiting time policies in the health sector: What works?*, Paris: OECD

Morel, N, Palier, B and Palme, J (eds) (2012) *Towards a social investment welfare state? Ideas, policies, challenges*, Bristol: Policy Press

Moynihan, M (ed) (1980) *Speeches and statements by Eamon de Valera, 1917-73*, Dublin: Gill & Macmillan

MRCI (Migrants Rights Centre Ireland) (2006) *Social protection denied: The impact of the habitual residence condition on migrant workers*, Dublin: MRCI

MRCI (Migrants Rights Centre Ireland) (2007) *Realising integration: Migrant workers undertaking essential low-paid work in Dublin city*, Dublin: MRCI

MRCI (Migrants Rights Centre Ireland) (2015) *Workers on the move: Past lessons and future perspectives on Ireland's labour migration*, Dublin: MRCI

MRCI (Migrants Rights Centre Ireland) (2016) *Ireland is home*, available at: www.mrci.ie/wp-content/uploads/2016/05/Ireland-is-Home-2016-Infographic-FINAL.pdf

Mudge, S (2008) 'What is neo-liberalism?, *Socio-Economic Review*, 6:4, 703–31

Mudge, S (2014) '"Critiquing a shadow" roundtable on "the limits of neo-liberalism"', *Renewal: A Journal of Social Democracy*, 22, 3/4, available at: www.renewal.org.uk/articles/the-limits-of-neo-liberalism

Mullard, M and Spicker, P (1998) *Social policy in a changing society*, London: Routledge

Mullholland, P (2016) 'The return of the NTPF', *The Medical Independent*, available at: www.medicalindependent.ie/95385/return_of_the_ntpf

Murie, A (1997) 'The social rented sector, housing and the welfare state in the UK', *Housing Studies*, 12:4, 437–61

Murie, A and Williams, P (2015) 'A presumption in favour of home ownership? Reconsidering housing tenure strategies', *Housing Studies*, 30:5, 656–76

Murphy, MP (2007) 'Working-aged people and welfare policy', in M Cousins (ed) *Welfare policy and poverty*, Dublin: IPA and CPA, 101–37

Murphy, MP (2011) 'Making Ireland a caring society', *Studies: An Irish Quarterly Review*, 100:397, 43–53

Murphy, MP (2012) 'Interests, institutions and ideas: Explaining Irish social security policy', *Policy & Politics*, 40:3, 347–65

Murphy, MP (2014) *Forty years of EU influencing social policy in Ireland: A glass half full?*, Politics Power and Society Working Paper Series, 27 July, Maynooth: Maynooth University

Murphy, MP (2015) *JobBridge: Time to start again?* Dublin: Impact Trade Union

Murphy, MP (2016) 'Low road or high road? The post-crisis trajectory of Irish activation', *Critical Social Policy*, 36:3, 432–52

Murphy, Y (2016) 'The marriage equality referendum 2015', *Irish Political Studies*, 31:2, 315–30

Murray, C (1984) *Losing ground: American social policy, 1950-1980*, New York: Basic Books

Murray, T (2016) 'Socio-economic rights and the making of the 1937 Constitution', *Irish Political Studies*, 31:4, 502-24

Nasc (2008) *Hidden Cork: The perspectives of asylum seekers on direct provision and the asylum legal system*, Cork: Nasc

Nasc (2013) *In from the margins: Roma in Ireland*, Cork: Nasc

Natali, D (2013) 'Future prospects: *Vademecum* to address EU policy and political challenges', in D Natali and B Vanhercke (eds) *Social developments in the European Union 2012,* Brussels: ETUI, 245-64

National Carers Strategy Monitoring Group (2016) *Family carers' scorecard: Assessing the government's third National Carers' Strategy report from the perspective of family carers*, available at: http://familycarers.ie/wp-content/uploads/2016/07/Third-Scorecard-20162.pdf

National Children's Office (2004) *Ready, steady, play! A national play policy*, Dublin: Stationery Office

National Children's Strategy (2000) *The national children's strategy: Our children – their lives*, Dublin: Stationery Office

National Safeguarding Committee (2016) *National Safeguarding Committee Strategic plan 2017-2021*, Dublin: National Safeguarding Committee

National Task Force on Medical Staffing (2003) *Report of the National Task Force on Medical Staffing*, Dublin: DoHC

National Youth Policy Committee (1984) *The National Youth Policy Committee final report*, Dublin: Stationery Office

NCCA (National Council for Curriculum and Assessment) (2005) *Intercultural education in the primary school: Guidelines for schools*, Dublin: NCCA

NCCA (National Council for Curriculum and Assessment) (2006) *Intercultural education in the post-primary school: Guidelines for schools*, Dublin: NCCA

NCCA (National Council for Curriculum and Assessment) (2009) *Aistear, The early childhood curriculum framework*, Dublin: NCCA

Neary, A (2016) 'Civil partnership and marriage: LGBT-Q political pragmatism and the normalization imperative', *Sexualities*, 19:7, 757-79

NESC (National Economic and Social Council) (1991) *The economic and social implications of emigration*, Dublin: NESC

NESC (National Economic and Social Council) (2005) *The developmental welfare state*, Dublin: NESC

NESC (National Economic and Social Council) (2011) *Supports and services for unemployed jobseekers: Challenges and opportunities in a time of recession*, Dublin: NESC

NESC (National Economic and Social Council) (2014a) *Homeownership and rental: What road is Ireland on?*, Dublin: NESC

NESC (National Economic and Social Council) (2014b) *Social housing at the crossroads: Possibilities for investment, provision and cost rental*, Dublin: NESC

NESF (National Economic and Social Forum) (2002) *Equity of access to hospital care*, Forum Report 25, Dublin: NESF

NESF (National Economic and Social Forum) (2005a) *Early childhood education and care*, Forum Report 31, Dublin: NESF

NESF (National Economic and Social Forum) (2005b) *Care for older people*, Forum Report 32, Dublin: NESF

Ní Shuinéar, S (1998) '"Solving itinerancy": Thirty-five years of Irish government commissions', available at: www.history.ul.ie/heatravinit/documents/pdf/solving-itinerancy-final.pdf

Ní Raghallaigh, M, Foreman, M and Feeley, M (2016) *Transition from direct provision to life in the community*, Dublin: UCD

Nicaise, I and Schepers, W (2013), 'Social investment: The new paradigm of EU social policy?' *Belgisch Tijdschrift voor Sociale Zekerheid*, available at: http://ec.europa.eu/europe2020/pdf/contributions/nicaisescheperssocialinvestmentbtsz.pdf

Nicholls, G (1856) *A History of the Irish poor law*, London: John Murray

Nolan, B (2013) 'What use is "social investment"?', *Journal of European Social Policy*, 23:5, 459-68

Nolan, B, O'Connell, PJ and Whelan, CT (eds) (2000) *Bust to boom? The Irish experience of growth and inequality*, Dublin: IPA

Norris, M (2005) 'Social housing', in M Norris and D Redmond (eds) *Housing contemporary Ireland: Policy, society and shelter*, Dublin: IPA, 160-82

Norris, M (2014) 'Policy drivers of the retreat and revival of private renting: Regulation, finance, taxes and subsidies', in L Sirr (ed) *Renting in Ireland*, Dublin: IPA, 19-36

Norris, M (2016) 'Varieties of home ownership: Ireland's transition from a socialised to a marketised policy regime', *Housing Studies*, 31:1, 81-101

Norris, M and Coates, D (2014) 'How housing killed the celtic tiger: Anatomy and consequences of Ireland's boom and bust', *Journal of Housing and the Built Environment*, 29:2, 299-315

Norris, M and Fahey, T (2011) 'From asset based welfare to welfare housing? The changing function of social housing in Ireland', *Housing Studies*, 26:3, 459-69

Norris, M and Redmond, D (eds) (2005) *Housing contemporary Ireland: Policy, society and shelter*, Dublin: IPA

Norris, M and Winston, N (2005) 'Housing and the accommodation of Irish Travellers: From assimilationism to multiculturalism and back again', *Social Policy and Administration*, 39:7, 802-21

Norris, M and Winston, N (2011) 'Transforming Irish home ownership through credit deregulation, boom and crunch', *International Journal of Housing Policy*, 11:1, 1-21

Norris, M, Gkartzios, M and Coates, D (2014) 'Property-led urban, town and rural regeneration in Ireland: Positive and perverse outcomes in different spatial and socio-economic contexts', *European Planning Studies*, 22:9, 1841-61

Nozick, R (1974) *Anarchy, state and utopia*, Oxford: Basil Blackwell

NSPCC (National Society for the Prevention of Cruelty to Children) (nd) *A pocket history of the NSPCC*, London: NSPCC

NTPF (National Treatment Purchase Fund) (2010) *Annual report 2009*, Dublin: NTPF

NTPF(National Treatment Purchase Fund) (2015) '2015/Inpatient/Day Case/ National Numbers, available at: www.ntpf.ie/home/inpatient.htm

Nutley, S (2000) 'Rural transport: Time for action?', *Geography*, 5:1, 85-7

Ó Cinnéide, S (1969) 'The development of the home assistance service', *Administration*, 17:3, 284-308

Ó Cinnéide, S (1970) *A law for the poor: A study of home assistance in Ireland*, Dublin: IPA

Ó Cinnéide, S (1972) 'The extent of poverty in Ireland', *Social Studies, Irish Journal of Sociology*, 1:4, 381–400

Ó Cinnéide, S (2000) 'The 1949 White Paper and the foundations of social welfare', in A Lavan (ed) *50 years of social welfare policy*, Dublin: DSCFA, 18-30

Ó Cinnéide, S (2010) 'From poverty to social inclusion: The EU and Ireland in EAPN', in EAPN (ed) *Ireland and the European Social Inclusion Strategy: Lessons learned and the road ahead*, Dublin: EAPN, 18-35

Ó Gráda, C (1997) *A rocky road: The Irish economy since the 1920s*, Manchester: Manchester UP

Ó Gráda, C (2002) '"The greatest blessing of all": The old age pension in Ireland', *Past and Present*, 175, 124-61

Ó hÓgartaigh, M (1999) 'Dr Dorothy Price and the elimination of childhood tuberculosis', in J Augusteijn (ed) *Ireland in the 1930s new perspectives*, Dublin: Four Courts Press, 67-82

Ó Riain, S (2014) T*he rise and fall of Ireland's celtic tiger: Liberalism, boom and bust*, Cambridge: Cambridge UP

O'Brien, G (1999) 'State intervention and medical relief of the Irish poor, 1787-1850', in E Malcolm and G Jones (eds) *Medicine, disease and the state in Ireland, 1650-1940*, Cork: Cork UP, 195-207

O'Brien, L and Dillon, B (1982) *Private rented: The forgotten sector*, Dublin: Mount Salus Press

O'Callaghan, M (2002) 'Women and politics in independent Ireland, 1921-68', in A Bourke, S Kilfeather, M Luddy, M Mac Curtain, G Meaney, M Ní Dhonnchadha, M O'Dowd, C Wills (eds) *The field day anthology of Irish writing: Volume V. Irish women's writings and traditions*, Cork: Cork UP, 120-35

O'Connell, C (2005a) 'The collective home? Recent experiences of social housing in Europe', in P Herrmann (ed) *Utopia between corrupted public responsibility and contested modernisation: Globalisation and social responsibility*, New York: Nova Science, 77-90

O'Connell, C (2005b) 'The housing market and owner occupation in Ireland', in M Norris and D Redmond (eds) *Housing contemporary Ireland: Policy, society and shelter*, Dublin: IPA, 19-43

O'Connell, J (2002) 'Travellers in Ireland: An examination of discrimination and racism', in R Lentin and R McVeigh (eds) *Racism and anti-racism in Ireland*, Belfast: Beyond the Pale, 49-62

O'Connor, C (2003) *Direct discrimination? An analysis of the scheme of direct provision in Ireland*, Dublin: Free Legal Advice Centres

O'Connor, J (1973) *The fiscal crisis of the state*, New York: St. Martin's Press

O'Connor, J (1995) *The workhouses of Ireland: The fate of Ireland's poor*, Dublin: Anvil Books

O'Connor Lysaght, D (1991) 'A Saorstát is born: How the Irish Free State came into being', in S Hutton and P Stewart (eds) *Ireland's histories: Aspects of state, society and ideology*, London: Routledge, 36-51

O'Donoghue-Hynes, B and Hayes, N (2011) 'Who benefits from early childcare subsidy design in Ireland?', *Journal of Poverty and Social Justice*, 19:3, 277-88

O'Hanlon, G (2004) 'Population change in the 1950s: A statistical review', in D Keogh, F O'Shea and C Quinlan (eds) *The lost decade: Ireland in the 1950s*, Cork: Mercier Press, 72-9

O'Hearn, D (1997) 'The celtic tiger: The role of the multi-nationals', in E Crowley and J Mac Laughlin (eds) *Under the belly of the tiger: Class, race, identity and culture in the global Ireland*, Dublin: Irish Reporter Publications, 21-34

O'Hearn, D (2011) 'What happened to the "Celtic Tiger"?', *Translocations*, 7:1, 1-8

O'Mahony, C (2005) *Cork's poor law palace: Workhouse life 1838-1890*, Cork: Rosmathún Press

O'Mahony, C (2016) 'Falling short of expectations: The 2012 children amendment, from drafting to referendum', *Irish Political Studies*, 31:2, 252-81

ORAC (Office of the Refugee Applications Commissioner) (various years) Annual report, Dublin: ORAC

O'Reilly, J and Wiley, M (2010) 'Who's that sleeping in my bed? Potential and actual utilization of public and private in-patient beds in Irish acute public hospitals', *Journal of Health Services Research and Policy*, 15:4, 210-14

O'Riordan, T (1981) *Environmentalism* (2nd edn), London: Pion Books

O'Shea, E (2006) *Towards a national strategy for older people in Ireland*, Older and Bolder Campaign, available at: http://web.archive.org/web/20071118175900/ http://www.olderandbolder.ie/documents/1_Older&Bolder.pdf

O'Shea, E, with Convery, J and Larragy J (2002) *Review of the Nursing Home Subvention Scheme*, Dublin: Stationery Office

O'Sullivan, D (1979) 'Social definition in child care in the Irish Republic: Models of the child and child-care intervention', *Economic and Social Review*, 10:3, 209-29

O'Sullivan, D (2005) *Cultural politics and Irish education since the 1950s*, Dublin: IPA

O'Sullivan, E (2004) 'Welfare regimes, housing and homelessness in the Republic of Ireland', *European Journal of Housing Policy*, 4:3, 323-43

O'Sullivan, E (2005) 'Homelessness', in M Norris and D Redmond (eds) *Housing contemporary Ireland: Policy, society and shelter*, Dublin: IPA, 245-67

O'Sullivan, E (2008) 'Researching homelessness in Ireland: Explanations, themes and approaches', in D Downey (ed) *Perspectives on Irish homelessness: Past, present and future*, Dublin: Homeless Agency, 16-23

O'Sullivan, E (2012) *Ending homelessness: A housing-led approach*, available at: www. homelessdublin.ie/sites/default/files/publications//Eoin_O_Sullivan_Housing_ Led_Approach_May_2012.pdf

O'Sullivan, E (2014) 'Child welfare services, 1970-80: From the Kennedy Committee to the task force', in M Luddy and JM Smith (eds) *Children, childhood and Irish society, 1500 to the present*, Dublin: Four Courts Press, 121-44

O'Sullivan, E (2015) 'The Ryan Report: Reformatory and industrial schools and twentieth century Ireland', in R Meade and F Dukelow (eds) *Defining events: Power, resistance and identity in twenty-first-Ireland*, Manchester: Manchester UP, 200-17

O'Sullivan, E and O'Donnell, I (2012) *Coercive confinement in post-independence Ireland: Patients, prisoners and penitents*, Manchester: Manchester UP

O'Sullivan, M (2014) 'Leading and managing the Special Needs Assistant working in the primary school environment', presentation at the IPPN Conference 23-4 January, Dublin

O'Sullivan Committee (1980) *The development of youth work services in Ireland*, Dublin: Stationery Office

O'Toole, B (2015) '1831-2014: An opportunity to get it right this time? Some thoughts on the current debate on patronage and religious education in Irish primary schools', *Irish Educational Studies*, 34:1, 89-102

O'Toole, F (1988) 'Highbrow robbery', *Magill*, April, 22-26

Obinger, H and Starke, P (2014) *Welfare state transformation: Convergence and the rise of the supply side model*, TranState Working Papers, 180, available at: https:// www.econstor.eu/bitstream/10419/93095/1/778925676.pdf

OCO (Ombudsman for Children's Office) Ireland (2015) *Report of the Ombudsman for Children to the UN Committee on the Rights of the Child on the occasion of the examination of Ireland's consolidated Third and Fourth Report to the Committee*, Dublin: OCO

OCO (Ombudsman for Children's Office) Ireland (2016) *Submission for the 25th Session of the Working Group on Universal Periodic Review*, 31 March, available at: www.oco.ie/wp-content/uploads/2014/03/Final-OCO-Submission-UPR-2016-31Mar16.docx

OECD (Organisation for Economic Co-operation and Development) (1965) *Investment in education*, Dublin: Stationery Office

OECD (Organisation for Economic Co-operation and Development) (1987) *Financing and delivering health care: A comparative analysis of OECD countries*, Paris: OECD

OECD (Organisation for Economic Co-operation and Development) (1991) *Review of national policies for education, Ireland*, Paris: OECD

OECD (Organisation for Economic Co-operation and Development) (1996) *The knowledge-based economy*, Paris: OECD

OECD (Organisation for Economic Co-operation and Development) (1999) *OECD historical statistics 1960-1997* (1999 edn), Paris: OECD

OECD (Organisation for Economic Co-operation and Development) (2004a) *Early childhood education and care policy: Country note for Ireland*, Paris: OECD

OECD (Organisation for Economic Co-operation and Development) (2004b) *Review of national policies for education: Review of higher education in Ireland*, Paris: OECD

OECD (Organisation for Economic Co-operation and Development) (2006) *Early childhood education and care policy: Country note for Ireland,* Paris: OECD

OECD (Organisation for Economic Co-operation and Development) (2007) *Health at a glance 2007: OECD Indicators*, Paris: OECD

OECD (Organisation for Economic Co-operation and Development) (2008) *OECD health data 2008*, Online Version, available at: www.sourceoecd.org

OECD (Organisation for Economic Co-operation and Development) (2011) *Doing better for families*, Paris: OECD

OECD (Organisation for Economic Co-operation and Development) (2015a) *Pensions at a glance 2015: OECD and G20 indicators*, Paris: OECD

OECD (Organisation for Economic Co-operation and Development) (2015b) *Health at a glance 2015: OECD indicators*, Paris: OECD

OECD (Organisation for Economic Co-operation and Development) (2016a) 'Health policy in Ireland', available at: www.oecd.org/ireland/Health-Policy-in-Ireland-February-2016.pdf

OECD (Organisation for Economic Co-operation and Development) (2016b) *Education at a glance 2016: OECD indicators*, Paris: OECD

OECD (2016c) Childcare costs are around 15% of net family income across the OECD, in *Society at a Glance 2016*, OECD Publishing, Paris. DOI: http://dx.doi.org/10.1787/soc_glance-2016-graph14-en

Oesch, D (2013) *Occupational change in Europe: How technology and education transform the job structure*, Oxford: Oxford UP

Offe, C (1982) 'Some contradictions of the modern welfare state', *Critical Social Policy*, 2:5, 7-16

Offe, C (1984) *Contradictions of the welfare state*, London: Hutchinson

Office of the Minister for Children (2007) *Teenspace: National recreation policy for young people*, Dublin: Stationery Office

Oireachtas Library and Research Service (2015) 'Choosing segregation? The implications of school choice', *Spotlight*, 1 of 2015, available at: www.oireachtas.ie/parliament/media/housesoftheoireachtas/libraryresearch/spotlights/SpotlightSchoolchoice290915_101712.pdf

OMI (Office of the Minister of Integration) (2008) *Migration nation: Statement on integration strategy and diversity management*, Dublin: OMI

Osborne, B (2015) *Irish general practice: Working with deprivation*, Dublin: Irish College of General Practitioners

Oxfam (2015) 'Extreme carbon inequality: Why the Paris climate deal must put the poorest, lowest emitting and most vulnerable people first', Oxfam media briefing, 2 December, available at: www.oxfam.org/sites/www.oxfam.org/files/file_attachments/mb-extreme-carbon-inequality-021215-en.pdf

Özüekren, AS and van Kempen, R (2003) 'Special issue editors' introduction: Dynamics and diversity: Housing careers and segregation of minority ethnic groups', *Housing, Theory and Society*, 20:4, 162-71

Page, R (2005) 'From democratic socialism to New Labour' in H Bochel, C Bochel, R Page and R Sykes (eds), *Social policy: Issues and developments*, Essex: Pearson Education, 268–91

Palier, B and Martin, C (2008) 'From "a frozen landscape" to structural reforms: The sequential transformation of Bismarckian welfare systems', in B Palier and C Martin (eds) *Reforming the Bismarckian welfare systems*, Oxford: Blackwell, 1-20

Palier, B and Thelen, K (2010) 'Institutionalizing dualism: Complementarities and change in France and Germany', *Politics & Society*, 38:1, 119-48

Paris, C (2007) 'International perspectives on planning and affordable housing', *Housing Studies*, 22:1, 1-9

Parker-Jenkins, M and Masterson, M (2013) 'No longer "Catholic, white and Gaelic": Schools in Ireland coming to terms with cultural diversity', *Irish Educational Studies*, 32:4, 477-92

Parry, J and Parry, N (2000) 'The equality of bodies: Animal exploitation and human welfare', in K Ellis and H Dean (eds) *Social policy and the body*, London: Macmillan, 160-79

Pavee Point (2006) *Assimilation policies and outcomes: Travellers' experiences*, Dublin: Pavee Point

Peña-Casas, R (2013) 'Desperately seeking the European Employment Strategy in the new economic governance of the European Union', in D Natali and B Vanhercke (eds) *Social developments in the European Union 2012*, Brussels: ETUI, 123-45

Pepper, D (1996) *Modern environmentalism*, London: Routledge

Perry, S and Clarke, M (2015) 'The law and special educational needs in Ireland: Perspectives from the legal profession', *European Journal of Special Needs Education*, 30:4, 490-504

Peters, M (2003) 'Classical political economy and the role of universities in the new knowledge economy', *Globalisation, Societies and Education*, 1:2, 153-68

Phelan, A (2014) 'Elder abuse: A review of progress in Ireland', *Journal of Elder Abuse & Neglect*, 26:2, 172-88

Phelan, E and Norris, M (2008) 'Neo-corporatist governance of homeless services in Dublin: Reconceptualization, incorporation and exclusion', *Critical Social Policy*, 28:1, 51-73

Pierson, P (1994) *Dismantling the welfare state? Reagan, Thatcher and the politics of retrenchment*, Cambridge: Cambridge UP

Pierson, P (1996) 'The new politics of the welfare state', *World Politics*, 48:2, 143-79

Pierson, P (2001) 'Post-industrial pressures on the mature welfare states', in P Pierson (ed) *The new politics of the welfare state*, Oxford: Oxford UP, 80-104

Piketty, T (2014) *Capital in the twenty-first century*, Cambridge, MA: Harvard UP

Pillinger, J (2006) *An introduction to the situation and experiences of women migrant workers in Ireland*, Dublin: Equality Authority

Pinker, R (2008) 'The conservative tradition', in P Alcock, M May and K Rowlingson (eds) *The student's companion to social policy* (3rd edn), Oxford: Blackwell, 69-76

Piven, FF and Cloward, RA (1993) *Regulating the poor: The functions of public welfare* (3nd edn), New York: Vintage Books

Platt, L (2008) '"Race" and social welfare', in P Alcock, M May and K Rowlingson (eds) *The student's companion to social policy* (3rd edn), Oxford: Blackwell, 369-77

Powell, FW (1989) 'Vagrancy and deterrence', *Social Policy & Administration*, 23:1, 72-83

Powell, FW (1992) *The politics of Irish social policy 1600-1990*, New York: Edwin Mellen Press

Powell, FW, Geoghegan, M, Scanlon, M and Swirak, K (2013) 'The Irish charity myth, child abuse and human rights: Contextualising the Ryan Report into care institutions', *British Journal of Social Work*, 43:1, 7-23

Powell, M (2008) 'Third Way perspectives', in P Alcock, M May and K Rowlingson (eds) *The student's companion to social policy* (3rd edn), Oxford: Blackwell, 91-8

Power, A (1993) *Hovels to high rise: State housing in Europe since 1950,* London: Routledge

Power, N (2009) *One dimensional woman*, London: Zero Books

Pratt, A (2006a) 'Neo-liberalism and social policy', in M Lavalette and A Pratt (eds) *Social policy: Theories, concepts and issues* (3rd edn), London: Sage, 9-25

Pratt, A (2006b) 'Towards a "new" Social Democracy', in M Lavalette and A Pratt (eds) *Social policy: Theories, concepts and issues* (3rd edn), London: Sage, 26-45

Pratt, J (2006) 'Citizenship, social solidarity and social policy', in M Lavalette and A Pratt (eds) *Social policy: Theories, concepts and issues* (3rd edn), London: Sage, 124-40

Preston, M (1998) 'Discourse and hegemony: Race and class in the language of charity in nineteenth-century Dublin', in T Foley and S Ryder (eds) *Ideology and Ireland in the nineteenth century*, Dublin: Four Courts Press, 100-12

Priemus, H and Dieleman, F (1999) 'Social housing finance in the European Union: Developments and prospects', *Urban Studies*, 36:4, 623-33

Prospectus (2003) *Audit of structures and functions in the health system*, Dublin: Stationery Office

Puirséil, N (2007) *The Irish Labour Party 1922-73*, Dublin: UCD Press

Quilty, A, Kennedy, S and Conlon, C (2015) 'Abortion: A legal timeline', in A Quilty, S Kennedy and C Conlon (eds) *The Abortion Papers Ireland: Volume 2*, Cork: Attic Press, 1-11

Raffass, T (2016) 'Work enforcement in liberal democracies', *Journal of Social Policy*, 45:3, 417-34

Raftery, M and O'Sullivan, E (1999) *Suffer the little children: The inside story of Ireland's industrial schools*, Dublin: New Island

Ratcliffe, P (2004) *Race, ethnicity and difference: Imagining an inclusive society*, Maidenhead: Open UP

Rau, H, Hynes, M and Heisserer, B (2016) 'Transport policy and governance in turbulent times: Evidence from Ireland', *Case Studies on Transport Policy*, 4:2, 45–56

Rayle, R (2015) 'What happened to EU subsidiarity?', *World Economic Forum*, 11 December, available at: www.weforum.org/agenda/2015/12/what-happened-to-eu-subsidiarity/

Reay, D (2001) 'Finding or losing yourself? Working class relationships to education', *Journal of Education Policy*, 16:4, 333–46

Redmond, D (2003) 'Defeat for tenure mix', *Cornerstone*, April, 12–13

Reich, R (2015) 'Friction is now between global financial elite and the rest of us', *The Guardian*, 11 November

Reid, B and Taylor, J (2007) 'A feminist exploration of Traveller women's experiences of maternity care in the Republic of Ireland', *Midwifery*, 23:3, 248–59

Reid, D (1995) *Sustainable development: An introductory guide*, London: Earthscan

Reidy, T (2016) *The Irish general election of 2016: Winners, losers and policy implications*, London: FES

Rein, M (1982) 'The social policy of the firm', *Policy Science*, 14:2, 117–35

Reissl, S and Stockhammer, E (2016) 'The Euro crisis and the neoliberal EU policy regime: Signs of change or more of the same?', Near Futures Online 1, Europe at a Crossroads, available at: http://nearfuturesonline.org/the-euro-crisis-and-the-neoliberal-eu-policy-regime-signs-of-change-or-more-of-the-same/

Rice, D (2013) 'Beyond welfare regimes: From empirical typology to conceptual ideal types', *Social Policy & Administration*, 47:1, 93–110

Richardson, D (2000) 'Constructing sexual citizenship: Theorising sexual rights', *Critical Social Policy*, 20:1, 105–35

Richardson, D (2004) 'Locating sexualities: From here to normality', *Sexualities*, 7:4, 391–411

Richardson, D and Monro, S (2012) *Sexuality, equality and diversity*, Basingstoke: Palgrave Macmillan

Ritschel, D (1995) 'Macmillan', in V George and R Page (eds) *Modern thinkers on welfare*, Hemel Hempstead: Prentice Hall/Harvester Wheatsheaf, 51–68

Robins, JA (1960) 'The Irish hospital: An outline of its origins and development', *Administration*, 8:2, 145–65

Robbins, G and Lapsley, I (2008) 'Irish voluntary hospitals: An examination of a theory of voluntary failure', *Accounting, Business and Financial History*, 18:1, 61–80

Rock, S, Ahern, A and Caulfield, B (2016) 'The economic boom, bust and transport inequity in suburban Dublin, Ireland', *Research in Transportation Economics*, 57, 32–43

Ronald, R (2013) 'Housing and welfare in Western Europe: Transformations and challenges for the social rented sector', *LHI Journal of Land, Housing and Urban Affairs*, 4:1, 1–13

Ronald, R and Elsinga, M (2012) 'Beyond home ownership: An overview', in R Ronald and M Elsinga (eds) *Beyond home ownership: Housing, welfare and society*, Abingdon: Routledge, 1-27

Rose, K (1994) *Diverse communities: The evolution of lesbian and gay politics in Ireland*, Cork: Cork UP

Rosenhaft, E (1994) 'The historical development of German social policy', in J Clasen and R Freeman (eds) *Social policy in Germany*, Hemel Hempstead: Harvester Wheatsheaf, 21-41

Rowbotham, S (1994) 'Interpretations of welfare and approaches to the state, 1870-1920', in A Oakley and AS Williams (eds) *The politics of the welfare state*, London: UCL Press, 18-36

RTÉ (Raidió Teilifís Éireann) (2011) *The blood of the Irish*, documentary series, Dublin: RTÉ

RTÉ (Raidió Teilifís Éireann) (2015) 'State gave commitments to Catholic Church on education', 10 November, available at: www.rte.ie/news/special-reports/2012/0328/315388-educationfoi/

Ruane, F and Görg, H (1997) *Reflections on Irish industrial policy towards foreign direct investment*, Trinity Economic Paper Series, 97/3, Dublin: TCD, available at: www.tcd.ie/Economics/TEP/1997/1997%20Policy%20Papers/973p.pdf

Ruhs, M (2005) *Managing the immigration and employment of non-EU nationals in Ireland*, Dublin: The Policy Institute, TCD

Ruhs, M and Quinn, E (2009) Ireland: from rapid immigration to recession, Profile, 1 September, Migration Policy Institute, available at: www.migrationpolicy.org/article/ireland-rapid-immigration-recession

Ryan, P (2014) 'The pursuit of gay and lesbian sexual citizenship rights, 1980-2011', in M Leane and E Kiely (eds) *Sexualities and Irish society: A reader*, Dublin: Orpen Press, 101-26

Salonen, T (2001) 'Sweden: Between model and reality', in P Alcock and G Craig (eds) *International social policy: Welfare regimes in the developed world*, Basingstoke: Palgrave, 143-60

Sanderson, M (1987) *Educational opportunity and social change in England*, London: Faber & Faber

Sandford, C and Morrissey, O (1985) *The Irish wealth tax: A case study in economics and politics*, Dublin: ESRI

Sapouna, L and Gijbels, H (2016) 'Social movements in mental health: The case of the Critical Voices Network Ireland', *Critical and Radical Social Work*, 4:3. 397-402

Saraceno, C (2015) 'A critical look to the social investment approach from a gender perspective, *Social Politics*, 22:2, 257-69

Sarokin, DJ and Schulkin, J (1994) 'Environmental justice: Co-evolution of environmental concerns and social justice', *The Environmentalist*, 14:2, 121-9

Saunders, P (1990) *A nation of home owners*, London: Unwin Hyman

Scanlon, K, Fernández Arrigoitia, M and Whitehead, C (2015) 'Social housing in Europe', *European Policy Analysis*, 17, 1-12

Scanlon, K, Lunde, J and Whitehead, CME (2011) 'Responding to the housing and financial crises: Mortgage lending, mortgage products and government policies', *International Journal of Housing Policy*, 11:1, 23-49

Scharpf, FW (2002) 'The European Social Model: Coping with the challenges of diversity', *Journal of Common Market Studies*, 40:4, 645-70

Schultz, TW (1961) 'Investment in human capital', *The American Economic Review*, 51:1, 1-17

Seguino, S (2011) 'Financialization, distribution, and inequality', paper presented at DAWN Development Debates, 18-20 January, Mauritius, available at: www.uvm.edu/~sseguino/pdf/Finance.pdf

Select Committee on Justice, Equality, Defence and Women's Rights (2005) Vote 19: Justice, Equality and Law Reform (revised) 18 May, available at: http://oireachtasdebates.oireachtas.ie/debates%20authoring/debateswebpack.nsf/committeetakes/JUS2005051800003?opendocument

Sen, A (1999) *Development as freedom*, Oxford: Oxford UP

Shanahan, C (2016) 'HSE fails to assess 2,500 kids for disability', *Irish Examiner*, 21 November

Shannon, G and Gibbons, N (2012) *Report of the independent child death review group*, Dublin: DCYA

Sharek, DB, McCann, E, Sheerin, F, Glacken, M and Higgins, A (2015) 'Older LGBT people's experiences and concerns with healthcare professionals and services in Ireland', *International Journal of Older People Nursing*, 10:3, 230-40

Sheehan, J (1979) 'Education and society in Ireland, 1945-70', in JJ Lee (ed) *Ireland 1945-70*, Dublin: Gill & Macmillan, 61-72

Siim, B (2000) *Gender and citizenship: Politics and agency in France, Britain and Denmark*, Cambridge: Cambridge UP

Sinfield, A (2013) 'Fiscal welfare', in B Greve (ed) *The Routledge handbook of the welfare state*, Abingdon: Routledge, 20-9

Skehill, C (2011) 'The origins of child welfare under the poor law and the emergence of the institutional versus family care debate', in V Crossman and P Gray (eds) *Poverty and welfare in Ireland, 1838-1948*, Dublin: Irish Academic Press, 115-26

Skovgaard, J (2014) 'EU climate policy after the crisis', *Environmental Politics*, 23:1, 1-17

Smith, JM (2007) *Ireland's Magdalen laundries and the nation's architecture of containment*, Notre Dame, IN: University of Notre Dame Press

Smyth, A (1993) 'The women's movement in the Republic of Ireland 1970-1990', in A Smyth (ed) *Irish women's studies reader*, Dublin: Attic Press, 245-69

Smyth, A (2014) 'The struggle for LGBT rights in Ireland, interview with Ailbhe Smyth', *Irish Marxist Review*, 3:11, 28-35

Smyth, E (2009) 'Buying your way into college? Private tuition and the transition to higher education in Ireland', *Oxford Review of Education*, 35:1, 1-22

Smyth, E, McCoy, S and Kingston, G (2015) *Learning from the evaluation of DEIS*, Dublin: ESRI

Social Welfare Benchmarking and Indexation Group (2001) *Final report of the social welfare benchmarking and indexation group*, Dublin: DSFA

Spaargaren, G and Mol, APJ (1992) 'Sociology, environment and modernity: Ecological modernisation as a theory of social change', *Society and Natural Resources*, 5:4, 323-44

Spicker, P (2011) *How social security works: An introduction to benefits in Britain*, Bristol: Policy Press

Stamp, S (2016) 'Personal finance: Financial services, access to credit and debt management', in MP Murphy and F Dukelow (eds) *The Irish welfare state in the twenty-first century: Challenges and change*, Basingstoke: Palgrave Macmillan, 119-39

Standing, G (2014) *The precariat: The new dangerous class*, London: Bloomsbury

Stanley, J and Lucas, K (2008) 'Social exclusion: What can public transport offer?', *Research in Transportation Economics*, 22:1, 36-40

Steg, L and Gifford, R (2005) 'Sustainable transportation and quality of life', *Journal of Transport Geography*, 13:1, 59-69

Stevenson, J (1984) 'From philanthropy to Fabianism', in B Pimlott (ed) *Fabian essays in socialist thought*, London: Heinemann, 15-26

Stiglitz, JE (2012) *The price of inequality: How today's divided society endangers our future*, New York: WW Norton

Stockhammer, E (2010) *Financialisation and the global economy*, Working Paper Series 240, Amherst, MA: Political Economy Research Institute, available at: http://content.csbs.utah.edu/~mli/Economics%207004/Stockhammer-WP240.pdf

Streeck, W (2014) *Buying time: The delayed crisis of democratic capitalism*, London: Verso

Streeck, W (2015) 'The rise of the European consolidation state', MPIfG Discussion Paper 15/1, Cologne: Max Planck Institute for the Study of Societies

Street, A (2015) 'Tax-based financing of the NHS is better than the alternative', *The Conversation,* 23 April, available at: http://theconversation.com/tax-based-financing-of-the-nhs-is-better-than-the-alternative-40494

Study Group on the Development of the Psychiatric Services (1984) *The psychiatric services: Planning for the future*, Dublin: Stationery Office

Swank, J (2010) 'Globalization', in FG Castles, S Leibfried, J Lewis, H Obinger and C Pierson (eds) *The Oxford handbook of the welfare state*, Oxford: Oxford UP, 318-30

Sweeney, P (1999) *The celtic tiger: Ireland's continuing economic miracle* (2nd edn), Dublin: Oak Tree Press

Swift, A (2014) *Political philosophy: A beginners' guide for students and politicians* (3rd edn), Cambridge: Polity

Szydlowski, M (2016) 'The rights to health and health care of vulnerable populations: Reducing the existing barriers to health equity experienced by transgender people in Ireland', *Journal of Human Rights Practice*, 8:2, 239-63

Tampke, J (1981) 'Bismarck's social legislation: A genuine breakthrough?', in WJ Mommsen (ed) *The emergence of the welfare state in Britain and Germany: 1850-1950*, London: Croom Helm, 71-83

Task Force on the Travelling Community (1995) *Report of the Task Force on the Travelling Community*, Dublin: Stationery Office

Tawney, RH (1922) *Secondary education for all: A policy for Labour*, London: Allen & Unwin

Tawney, RH (1931) *Equality*, London: Allen & Unwin

Taylor-Gooby, P (2001) 'Preface', in P Taylor-Gooby (ed) *Welfare states under pressure*, London: Sage, ix-x

Taylor-Gooby, P (2002) 'The silver age of the welfare state: Perspectives on resilience', *Journal of Social Policy*, 31:4, 597-621

Taylor-Gooby, P (2004) 'New social risks and welfare states: New paradigm and new politics?', in P Taylor-Gooby (ed) *New risks, new welfare: The transformation of the European welfare state*, Oxford: Oxford UP, 209-38

Taylor-Gooby, P, Gumy JM and Otto, A (2015) 'Can "new welfare" address poverty through more and better jobs?', *Journal of Social Policy*, 44:1, 83-104

Teasdale, A (2012) 'Lisbon Strategy and Europe 2020', *The Penguin Companion to European Union*, available at: http://penguincompaniontoeu.com/additional_entries/lisbon-strategy-and-europe-2020/

TENI (Transgender Equality Network Ireland) (2016) *Activity report 2015*, Dublin: TENI

Thane, P (1996) *Foundations of the welfare state* (2nd edn), Harlow: Longman

Thomson, S, Jowett, M and Mladovsky, P (eds) (2014) *Health system responses to financial pressures in Ireland*, Copenhagen: WHO/European Observatory on Health Systems and Policies

Timonen, V (2003) *Restructuring the welfare state: Globalization and social policy reform in Finland and Sweden*, Cheltenham: Edward Elgar

Timonen, V (2016) *Beyond successful and active ageing: A theory of model ageing*, Bristol: Policy Press

Timonen, V and Doyle, M (2008) 'From the workhouse to the home: Evolution of care policy for older people in Ireland', *International Journal of Sociology and Social Policy*, 28:3/4, 76-89

Timonen, V, Doyle, M and O'Dwyer, C (2012) 'Expanded, but not regulated: Ambiguity in home-care policy in Ireland', *Health and Social Care in the Community*, 20:3, 310-18

Titmuss, R (1968) *Commitment to welfare*, London: Allen & Unwin

Titmuss, R (1987 [1956]) 'The social division of welfare: Some reflections on the search for equity', in B Abel-Smith and K Titmuss (eds) *The philosophy of welfare: Selected writings of Richard M Titmuss,* London: Allen & Unwin, 39-59

Tong, R (2007) 'Feminist thought in transition: Never a dull moment', *The Social Science Journal*, 44:1, 23-39

Toolan, D (2003) 'An emerging rights perspective for disabled people in Ireland: An activist's view', in S Quin and B Redmond (eds) *Disability and social policy in Ireland*, Dublin: UCD Press, 171-81

Torgersen, V (1987) 'Housing: The wobbly pillar under the welfare state', in B Turner, J Kemeny and L Lundqvist (eds) *Between state and market: Housing in the post-industrial era*, Stockholm: Almqvist & Wiksell International, 116-26

Tormey, R (2010) 'The silent politics of educational disadvantage and the National Anti-Poverty Strategy', *Irish Educational Studies*, 29:2, 189-99

Toth, F (2010) 'Healthcare policies over the last 20 years: Reforms and counter-reforms', *Health Policy*, 95:1, 82-9

Tovey, H and Share, P (2000) *A sociology of Ireland*, Dublin: Gill & Macmillan

Trattner, WI (1999) *From poor law to welfare state: A history of social welfare in America* (6th edn), New York: Free Press

Travelling People Review Body (1983) *Report of the Travelling People Review Body*, Dublin: Stationery Office

Trench, B (1987) with additional reporting by Herbert, C and Fitzgerald, W, 'Short cuts to misery', *Magill*, September, 4-6

Trench, B and Brennan, P (1980) 'Poverty in Ireland', *Magill*, April, 10-31

Tronto, JC (1993) *Moral boundaries: A political argument for an ethic of care*, London: Routledge

Turner, B (2015) 'Unwinding the state subsidisation of private health insurance in Ireland', *Health Policy*, 119, 1349-57

Tusla (2015) Emergency out of hours service briefing information, Dublin: Tusla, available at: www.tusla.ie/uploads/content/EOI_EOHS_Briefing_Information.pdf

Tussing, AD and Wren, M-A (2006) *How Ireland cares: The case for health care reform*, Dublin: New Island

UN Committee on Economic, Social and Cultural Rights (2015) *Concluding observations on the third periodic report of Ireland*, 8 July, Geneva: UN

UN Environment Programme (1992) *Rio declaration on environment and development*, available at http://www.unep.org/documents.multilingual/default.asp?documentid=78&articleid=1163

UNCRC (United Nations Committee Convention on the Rights of the Child) (2016) *Concluding observations on the combined third and fourth periodic reports of Ireland*, 1 March, Geneva: UNCRC

UNFCCC (United Nations Framework Convention on Climate Change) (2015) *Paris Agreement*, available at: http://unfccc.int/files/essential_background/convention/application/pdf/english_paris_agreement.pdf

UN General Assembly (1951) *Convention relating to the status of refugees*, 28 July, United Nations, Treaty Series, volume 189, 137

UNHRC (United Nations Human Rights Committee) (2014) 'Concluding observations on the fourth periodic report of Ireland', www.ihrec.ie/download/pdf/un_hrc_concluding_observations_on_ireland_and_iccpr_24_july_2014.pdf

Urry, J (2007) *Mobilities*, Cambridge: Polity

Valiulis, MG (2011) 'The politics of gender in the Irish Free State, 1922-1937', *Women's History Review,* 20:4, 569-78

Van der Zwan, N (2014) 'Making sense of financialization', *Socio-Economic Review,* 12:1, 99-129

Vanhercke, B and Zeitlin, J with Zwinkels, A (2015) *Further socializing the European Semester: Moving forward for the 'Social Triple A'?* Report prepared for the Luxembourg Presidency of the Council of the European Union, Brussels: European Social Observatory

Van Hout, MC (2011) 'Travellers and substance use in Ireland: Recommendations for drug and alcohol policy', *Drugs: Education, Prevention and Policy,* 18:1, 53-9

Van Kersbergen, K (2013) 'What are welfare state typologies and how are they useful, if at all?', in B Greve (ed) *The Routledge handbook of the welfare state,* Abingdon: Routledge, 139-47

Van Kersbergen, K, Vis, B and Hemerijck, A (2014) 'The Great Recession and welfare state reform: Is retrenchment really the only game left in town?', *Social Policy & Administration,* 48:7, 883-904

Van Kersbergen, K and Vis, B (2015) 'Three worlds' typology: Moving beyond normal science?', *Journal of European Social Policy,* 25:1, 111 –23

Vaughan-Whitehead, D (2014) 'Is Europe losing its soul? The European social model in times of crisis', in D Vaughan-Whitehead (ed) *The European social model in times of economic crisis and austerity policies,* Geneva: ILO, 9-60, available at: http://www.ilo.org/brussels/information-resources/publication/WCMS_236720/lang--en/index.htm

Verdun, A (2013) 'Small states and the global economic crisis: An assessment', *European Political Science,* 12:1, 276–93

Verdun, A (2015) 'A historical institutionalist explanation of the EU's responses to the euro area financial crisis', *Journal of European Public Policy,* 22:2, 219-37

Vertovec, S and Wessendorf, S (eds) (2010) *The multiculturalism backlash: European discourses, policies and practices,* Abingdon: Routledge

Waldron, R (2016) 'The "unrevealed casualties" of the Irish mortgage crisis: Analysing the broader impacts of mortgage market financialisation', *Geoforum,* 69, 53-66

Waldron, R and Redmond, D (2014) 'The extent of the mortgage crisis in Ireland and policy responses', *Housing Studies,* 29:1, 149-65

Walker, G and Burningham, K (2011) 'Flood risk, vulnerability and environmental justice: Evidence and evaluation of inequality in a UK context', *Critical Social Policy,* 31:2, 216-40

Walker, MR (2012) 'An explorative study of episodes of suicide between 2000 and 2006 within Traveller culture', *Irish Journal of Anthropology,* 15:2, 28-32

Walsh, AM (1999) 'Root them in the land: Cottage schemes for agricultural labourers', in J Augusteijn (ed) *Ireland in the 1930s: New perspectives,* Dublin: Four Courts Press, 47-66

Walsh, J (2007) 'Monitoring poverty and welfare policy 1987-2007', in M Cousins (ed) *Welfare policy and poverty,* Dublin: IPA and CPA, 13-58

Walsh, J (2012) 'Ministers, bishops and the changing balance of power in Irish education 1950-70', *Irish Historical Studies*, 38:149, 108-27

Walsh, J and Loxley, A (2015) 'The Hunt Report and higher education policy in the Republic of Ireland: "An international solution to an Irish problem?"', *Studies in Higher Education*, 40:6, 1128-45

Walsh, K and Harvey, B (2015) *Family experiences of pathways into homelessness*, Dublin: Housing Agency

Walsh, PM, McDevitt, J, Deady, S, O'Brien, K and Comber, H (2016) *Cancer inequalities in Ireland by deprivation, urban/rural status and age: A National Cancer Registry report*, Cork: National Cancer Registry

Walsh, T (2005) 'Constructions of childhood in Ireland in the twentieth century: A view from the primary school curriculum 1900-1999', *Child Care in Practice*, 11:2, 253-69

Walsh, T (2016) '100 years of primary curriculum development and implementation in Ireland: A tale of a swinging pendulum', *Irish Educational Studies*, 35:1, 1-16

Waters, J (2016) 'Personal budgets allow people to control their own support and their own lives', *The Guardian*, 27 May

Watson, D and Maître, B (2013) *Social transfers and poverty alleviation in Ireland: An analysis of the Survey on Income and Living Conditions 2004-2011*, Social Inclusion Report 4, Dublin: DSP and ESRI

Watson, D, Kingston, G and McGinnity, F (2013) *Disability in the Irish labour market: Evidence from the QNHS Equality Module 2010*, Dublin: Equality Authority and the ESRI

Watson, D, Maître, B, Whelan, CT and Russell, H (2016) *Social risk and social class patterns in poverty and quality of life in Ireland: An analysis of the CSO Survey on Income and Living Conditions, 2004 to 2013*, Social Inclusion Report 6, Dublin: DSP and the ESRI

WCED (World Commission on Environment and Development) (1987) *Our Common Future*, Oxford: Oxford UP

Wendt, C (2013) 'Healthcare', in B Greve (ed) *The Routledge handbook of the welfare state*, Abingdon: Routledge, 347-57

Wendt, C (2014) 'Changing healthcare system types', *Social Policy & Administration*, 48:7, 864-82

Wendt, C, Frisina, L and Rothgang, H (2009) 'Healthcare system types: A conceptual framework for comparison', *Social Policy & Administration*, 43:1, 70-90

West, A and Nikolai, R (2013) 'Welfare regimes and education regimes: Equality of opportunity and expenditure in the EU (and US)', *Journal of Social Policy*, 42:3, 469-93

Whelan, T (1987) 'The new emigrants', *Newsweek*, 10 October

WHO (World Health Organization) (1998) *Monitoring equity in health: A policy-oriented approach in low-and-middle-income countries*, Geneva: WHO

WHO (World Health Organization) (2008) *Closing the gap in a generation: Health equity through action on the social determinants of health, Final Report of the Commission on Social Determinants of Health*, Geneva: WHO

Whyte, JH (1971) *Church and state in modern Ireland 1923-1970*, Dublin: Gill & Macmillan

Wickham, J (2004) *Public transport and urban citizenship*, Working Paper 9, Dublin: The Policy Institute, TCD

Wilensky, HL (1975) *The welfare state and equality: Structural and ideological roots of public expenditures*, Berkeley, CA: University of California Press

Wilkinson, R and Pickett, K (2009) *The spirit level: Why more equal societies almost always do better*, London: Allen Lane

Wilkinson, R and Pickett, K (2014) *A convenient truth: A better society for us and the planet*, London: Fabian Society

Williams, F (1989) *Social policy: A critical introduction: issues of race, gender and class*, Cambridge: Polity

Williams, F (1992) 'Somewhere over the rainbow: Universality and diversity in social policy', in N Manning and R Page (eds) *Social Policy Review 4*, Canterbury: SPA, 200-19

Williams, F (2001) 'In and beyond New Labour: Towards a new political ethics of care', *Critical Social Policy*, 21:4, 467-93

Williams, F (2010) *The making and claiming of care policies: The recognition and redistribution of care*, Geneva: UNRISD

Williams, F (2016) 'Critical thinking in social policy: The challenges of past, present and future', *Social Policy & Administration*, 50:6, 628-47

Williams, K (1999) 'Faith and the nation: Education and religious identity in the Republic of Ireland', *British Journal of Educational Studies*, 47:4, 317-31

Williamson, A (2000) 'Housing associations in the Republic of Ireland: Can they respond to the government's challenge for major expansion?', *Housing Studies*, 15:4, 639-50

Wolfe, A and Klausen, J (1997) 'Identity politics and the welfare state', *Social Philosophy and Policy*, 14:2, 231–55

Wolfe, T, O'Donoghue-Hynes, B and Hayes, N (2013) 'Rapid change without transformation: The dominance of a national policy paradigm over international influences on ECEC development in Ireland 1995-2012', *International Journal of Early Childhood*, 45:2, 191-205

Working Party on Services for the Elderly (1988) *The years ahead - A policy for the elderly*, Dublin: Stationery Office

Wren, MA (2003) *Unhealthy state: Anatomy of a sick society*, Dublin: New Island

WWF (World Wide Fund for Nature) (2016) *Living planet report: Risk and resilience in a new era*, Gland: WWF International

Yeates, N (1997) 'Gender and the development of the Irish social welfare system', in A Byrne and M Leonard (eds) *Women and Irish society*, Belfast: Beyond the Pale, 145-66

Yeates, N (2004) 'A dialogue with "global care chain analysis": Nurse migration in the Irish context', *Feminist Review*, 77, 79–95

Yeates, N (2007) 'Globalization and social policy', in J Baldock, N Manning and S Vickerstaff (eds) *Social Policy* (3rd edn) Oxford: Oxford UP, 627-53

Young, IM (1989) 'Polity and group difference: A critique of the ideal of universal citizenship', *Ethics,* 99:2, 250-74

Zeitlin, J and Vanhercke, B (2015) 'Economic governance in Europe 2020: Socialising the European Semester against the odds?', in D Natali and B Vanhercke (eds) *Social Policy in the European Union: State of play 2015*, Brussels: ETUI and OSE, 65-95

Ziliak, ST (2004) 'Self-reliance before the welfare state: Evidence from the Charity Organisation Movement in the United States', *The Journal of Economic History*, 64:2, 433-61

Zimmermann, KF, Kahanec, M, Giulietti, C, Guzi, M, Barrett, A and Maître, B (2012) *Study on active inclusion of migrants*, Bonn: IZA

Index

Note: Page numbers in *italics* indicate tables, figures and boxes. Page numbers followed by 'n' indicate end-of-chapter notes.

A

Abel-Smith, B. 47, 95
'able-bodied' poor 10, 12, 15–16
abortion 58, 62–63, 73–74
accessibility poverty *388–389*, 389
accommodation 359–360
  see also housing policy
activation 103–104, 185, 197–200
active labour-market policies (ALMPs) 103–104
activism 46, 65–66, 83–85, 95
  see also disability rights movement; gay and
    lesbian movement; labour movement;
    women's movement
adaptability 153
adaptation 382
ADC (Aid to Dependent Children) 95
adoption 35
advocacy 46, 323
affective equality 327–328
affluence, disease of 212–213
affordable housing 293
ageing 183–184, 212, 314
  see also demographic pressures; life expectancy
ageism 315
agrarianism 31, 187
air pollution 387–388
Amsterdam Treaty 153
Annual Growth Survey (AGS) 156, 162
anthropocentrism 137
anti-establishment sentiment 116–117, 169
'architecture of containment' 32
asset-based welfare 276
assimilation 340
asylum seekers 338, 339–340, *339*, 345–349
asylums 14
austerity 42, 69–72, 97, 105–108, *106-108*
  carers 332
  health policy 224, 230
  housing policy 277
  immigration 351
  'permanent austerity' 104, 150–151, 183,
    192–197
  Travellers 358, 361
automatic stabilisers 158

B

banking crisis *see* financial crisis
banking sector 61–62
beggars 10, 12
'benefit tourism' 344
Beveridge Report 90–91, 92, 94, 188
bipartisan strategy 59
Blackrock Clinic 222
Booth, Charles 85–86
Britain
  austerity 107
  Conservatives 122
  emigration to 15, 42–43
  healthcare 216–217
  New Labour 100–101, 131
  New Right 97–98
  poor law 15–16
  social policy developments 23
  trade unions 85
  welfare provision 88, 91–93
Browne, Noël 40, 41, 42, 219
Brundtland Report 377–378
bullying 368
Burke, PJ 30–31
Butler, Judith 134–135

C

capitalism 128, 131
capitalist patriarchy 133
car ownership 386, 387, 389–390
care 148, 317–320, 327–328
CARE (Campaign for the Care of Deprived
    Children) 46
carers 328–333, *329*
Cassells Report 266
Catholic Church
  child abuse 64, 72–73
  education 13, 248, 249, 250, 264
  healthcare 40, 41, 217, 218–219
  orphanages 11
  social change 45
  social control 33–35, 36, 57–58
  social protection 187
  social services 21–22, 32

Chadwick, Edwin 15–16, 373
Charitable Infirmary 12, 28n
charities 12, 18, 21, 83–85
  see also philanthropy; voluntary hospitals;
    voluntary organisations
child abuse 63–64, 72–73, 373
  see also child protection
child care 332
Child Care Act 1991 63, 307–308
child labour 82
child poverty 202, 311
child protection 88, 307–309, 312
  see also child abuse
child welfare 24, 71, 72–73
children
  abandonment 11
  born outside of marriage 34–35, 57
  in care 46, 313
  as carers 330
  healthcare 39–42
  homelessness 313–314
  industrial and reformatory schools 22, 35, 45,
    49–50, 64, 72
  key policy and legislative documents 309–310
  social policy 306–314
  Travellers 313
  workhouses 20
Children's Allowance 39, 46, 187
  see also Child Benefit
Child Benefit 195, 196, 348
  see also Children's Allowance
Children's Charter 24, 88
children's referendum 72, 308
children's rights campaigners 65
Christian democracy 123–124
chronic illness 213
citizenship 93–94, 102, 304
  and care 327
  and immigration 336, 347, 349
  and sexuality 364
  Travellers 352
civil partnership 367
civil rights 93
climate change 376
  and climate justice 384–385
  key global, EU and national commitments
    381–382
  mitigation 382
  and sustainable development 381–385
climate justice 376, 384, 384–385
CO2 emissions 383–384, 384
'coercive confinement' 32, 72
collectivist approach 92, 93
Commission on Itinerancy 355–356
Commission to Inquire into Child Abuse
  (CICA) 64, 72
communalism 139
communitarianism 131
community activism 46, 65–66

community development 71, 95
Community Employment (CE) 197, 199
community living 325
Community National Schools (CNS) 264
community-based care 49, 317–318
competition state 165
conditionality 184
Congested Districts Board 24–25
conservatism 121–123
consistent poverty 201–202
'containment, architecture of' 32
contested concept 67
contraception 46, 50, 57–58, 62
contracting out 98
contributory programmes see social insurance
control 10, 11, 14, 32–33
Cork 11, 12
corporate tax 61
COS (Charity Organisation Society) 84
cost containment 184, 194, 212, 214, 215, 221,
  226
county homes 32, 49
county hospitals 217, 219, 220
County Infirmaries Act 1765 13
credit crunch 68–69
  see also financial crisis
cultural capital 244
cultural control 14
Cumann na nGaedheal 30–31, 36
  see also Fine Gael
cycle of poverty 86

D

Daly, Herman 138
decommodification 147, 148
DEIS (Delivering Equality of Opportunity in
  Schools) 261, 263–264
democracy 85
  see also Christian democracy; social democracy
demographic pressures 54–55, 145–146,
  183–184, 212
Denmark 87
'dependency politics' 99
deprivation 70, 201
'deserving' poor 11, 12, 21, 24, 31
Developmental Welfare State, The (NESC, 2005)
  68
Dignan plan 188
disabilities, people with 56
  intellectual disabilities 49, 263
  key policies and legislative developments 324
  social policy 320–327
  see also special educational needs (SEN)
Disability Act 2005 322, 323–324
disability rights movement 65, 327
Disabled Persons Maintenance Allowance 189
discrimination 66, 94–95
  immigrants 343–344

LGBT (lesbian, gay, bisexual and transgender)
people 366, 368
Travellers 51, 313, 357, 358–359, 360
disease of affluence 212–213
dispensaries 13, 14, 19–20, 49, 216, 220
Disraeli, Benjamin 122
distributive justice *see* social justice
diversity 262–264, 338–340, 350–351
see also multiculturalism
divorce 58, 62
domestic policy *see* national policy
'double ageing' 184
Dr Steeven's Hospital 12
dualisation 179
dualism 68, 102, 170
Dublin 11, 12
Dublin Foundling Hospital 11

E

Early Childhood Care and Education (ECCE)
programme 258
early childhood education and care (ECEC)
257–258
ecocentrism 139
ecological footprint 379, 383, *392*
ecological modernisation 380
economic, social and cultural (ESC) rights *305*,
305–306
Economic and Monetary Union (EMU) 61,
101, 153, 157–162, 166
economic change 82–83
economic conservatism 30–32
economic crisis 54–55, 58–59, 68–70, 95–96
social protection 191–192, 194–195
see also financial crisis
economic cycle 166
economic dependency 55
economic expansion 43–44
economic failure 42
economic globalisation 143, 163–165, 166–167,
338
economic growth 60–62, 246, 374, 378, 380
economic liberalism 121
economic protectionism 36, 42
economic state intervention 90
economy
frailties 51
history 14
'ecosocial poverty' 375
'ecostates' 376
'eco-welfare state' 129
education 2–3, 13, 65
Britain 91
bullying 368
equality of opportunity 240–247, 250,
267–268
expenditure 256, *256*
higher 246–247, 249–250, 252, 254, 265–268,
267, *268*

historical policy development 48, 248–254
key policy and legislative developments *255*
national school system 14, 249
policy trends 255–268
special educational needs (SEN) 263, 321–323
Travellers 360–361
see also schools
Education Act 1998 262–263
Education for Persons with Special Educational
Needs Act 2004 (EPSEN Act) 322–323
educational disadvantage 260–262
efficiency 208
elder abuse 320
emigration 15, 19, 42–43, 55, 56, 61, 70, 336,
339
employment 60, 82, 103, 154
Community Employment (CE) 197, 199
see also underemployment; unemployment
Employment Permits (Amendment) Act 2014
342
environmental concerns 372–377
sustainable development 377–385
transport 385–392
see also greenism
environmental justice 376
environmentalism 375–377
see also greenism
environmentalism of the poor 376
equality 71, 112, 115, 118, 207, 248
affective 327–328
social 115, 125
see also gender equality; inequality
equality agenda 66, 67–68
Equality Authority 66, 67, 71
equality legislation 66
equality of condition 243
equality of economic condition 243
equality of opportunity 101, 115, 130, 240
critique 242–244
education 240–247, 250, 267–268
formal 241, *242*
substantive 241–242, *242*
see also educational disadvantage
equality of outcome 115, 125
equality of participation 241
equality of respect 243–244
Esping-Andersen, G. 89, 103, *147*
ethnicity 352–354
EU subsidiarity 152, 156
Euro crisis 157–162, *161*, 166
Europe 2020 155–156, *155–156*, 162, 202,
246–247
European Economic Area (EEA) 341
European Economic Community (EEC) 47, 49,
151, 341
European Employment Strategy (EES) 153
European Financial Stability Facility (EFSF) 159
European semester 159–160, 162
European Union (EU)

anti-establishment sentiment 117
anti-poverty programmes 166
austerity 107
  climate change *382*, 383
  housing policy reform 275–276
  housing tenure 274–275
  membership 61, 165–167
  migration 341
  social investment (SI) 149
  social policy 151–157
  social protection 191–192
  welfare reform 101–102
evidence-based decision making 226
exclusion *see* inclusion; social exclusion

F

Fabian socialism 125–127
Fabian Society 86, 127
Fabianism 86
Fair Deal Scheme 318–319
  see also nursing homes
families
  Catholic Church 32
  homelessness 298, 299
family allowances 91
family planning *see* abortion; contraception
family policy 38, 103, 124
family structures 184
farmers 31
far-Right 123
feminism 132–136, 148
feminist ethic of care 136
Fianna Fáil 35–39, 43, 54, 58, 59, 188
  health policy 39–42, 50, 218, 220
financial crisis 68–69, 157–158
  housing policy 276–277, 290, 294
  ideological debate 116
  impact on welfare states 105–108
  see also austerity
financial services 61
financialisation 69, 143–145
Fine Gael 35, 36, 45, 54, 56
  in government 41, 43, 47, 224, 229
  'Tallaght Strategy' 59
fiscal welfare 181–182
Fitzgerald Report 220
Five Presidents' Report (Juncker et al, 2015)
  159–160
formal equality of opportunity 241, *242*
'foundling hospitals' 11
France 101–102, 153, *213*, 278
Fraser, Nancy 135
freedom 114–115, 125
friendly societies 83

G

Gay and Lesbian Equality Network (GLEN)
  366
gay and lesbian movement 365–366

gender 134–135
  see also women
gender diversity 362–364
gender equality 26
  care work 329
  labour market 38–39, 46
  social protection 46, 49, 94, 343
  see also feminism
gender expression 368
gender identity 367–368
General Medical Services Scheme (GMS) 49,
  220
gentrification 279
Germany
  Economic and Monetary Union (EMU) 153
  employment law 82
  family policy 124
  health expenditure *213*
  male bread winner model 94
  multiculturalism 105
  pensions 101–102
  poor relief 80–81
  rent regulation 296–297
  rented sector 272, 274, 276
  social insurance 87, 179
  welfare reform 101–102
global ecological footprint 383
global financial crisis 68–69, 157–158
  housing policy 276–277, 290, 294
  ideological debate 116
  impact on welfare states 105–108
  see also austerity
global financial services 61
global warming *see* climate change
globalisation 142–145, 163–165, 166–167, 338
'golden age' of welfare 93, 130, 182
Gough, I. 128–129, 376, 381, 384, 385
Great Famine 18–19
greenhouse gas (GHG) emission 381, 385–386,
  387, 391–392
greenism 136–139
  see also environmentalism; environmental
  concerns
gross domestic product (GDP) 44, 60, 69

H

Habitual Residence Condition (HRC) 344–345
Hayek, Friedrich von 119
Health (Family Planning) (Amendment) Act
  1985 57–58
Health Act 1970 48, 220–221
health equity 206–207
health expenditure 212, *213*, 214, 215, 220,
  221, 224–225, *225*, 226
health inequality 206, 235–237, 361–362
health inequity 206
Health Information and Quality Authority
  (HIQA) 73, 227, 309, 318, 319, 348
health insurance 25, 217, 219

private 211, 234–235
social 210–211, 229
health promotion 221
health service eligibility 229–234
Health Service Executive (HSE) 226, 227
healthcare
mother and child scheme 39–42
poor law 19–20
Travellers 361–362
healthcare entitlements 230, 229–230, 231
healthcare systems
Britain 92
continuum 209
efficiency 208
historical development 48–49, 215–223
investment 65
see also health expenditure
Ireland 212
reform 223–225, 224
equity of access 228–234
organisational 226–228
two-tier health system 222–223, 234–235
trends and pressures 212–215
typologies 208–212
heteronormativity 363
high dependency ratio 55
higher education 48, 246–247, 249–250, 252,
254, 265–268, 267, 268
home assistance 31–32, 49, 187
Home Care Package (HCP) 317
home ownership 37, 48, 276
see also owner-occupation
home-based care 317–318
homelessness 285–286, 297–299, 298, 313–314
homonormativity 364
homosexuality 62, 363, 365, 366
see also LGBT (lesbian, gay, bisexual and
transgender) people
horizontal redistribution 178
hospital beds 232
hospitals
closures 58, 221
county 217, 220
efficiency 208
performance 228
private 222, 222–223, 232
public 217–219, 221, 222
reform 227–228, 232
rural 13
voluntary 12–13, 216, 218, 219, 221
workhouses 19, 20, 215, 217
house of industry 11
house prices 287, 292–293, 294
household structures 184
Housing Act 1988 356
housing action groups 46
Housing Assistance Payment (HAP) 291
'housing first' 298
housing policy

contemporary issues 277–280, 287–299
Europe 275–276
Fianna Fáil 36–37
financial crisis 276–277, 290, 294
historical development 24–25, 48, 280–286
key policy developments 289
Travellers 359–360
housing tenure 272–273, 283, 288, 288
Europe 274–275
human capital 245, 265
Hunt Report 265
Huxley, TH 244

I

ideological ambiguity 167–169
ideologies 112–114
Christian democracy 123–124
conservatism 121–123
contemporary context 116–117
feminism 132–136
greenism 136–139
liberalism 117–121, 148
social democracy 129–132
socialism 124–129
'illegitimate' children 34–35, 57
immigrants
citizenship 102
discrimination 343–344
segregation 264
social rights 94, 105, 344–345
see also asylum seekers; immigration; refugees
immigration 45, 61, 336, 339
diversity 262
integration 350–351
key policy and legislative documents 340–341
labour migration 338, 341–342
racism and diversity 336–340
see also immigrants
inclusion 262–264
see also social exclusion
income inequality 101
individualism 80–82, 118
indoor relief see workhouses
industrial policy 44
industrial schools 22, 35, 45, 49–50, 64, 72
industrialisation 82–83, 372
inequality
health 206, 235–237, 361–363
income 101
transport 388–390
wealth 47
see also equality
infant mortality 217, 361
infirmaries see hospitals
institutional control 32
institutional discrimination 94
insurance
health 25, 210–211, 217, 219, 229, 234–235
national 25, 186

social 25, 87, 178–179, 192
integration 350–351
intellectual disabilities, people with 49, 263
interculturalism 263, 350
Intergovernmental Panel on Climate Change (IPCC) 374–375
International Financial Services Centre 61
intersectionality 134
Invalidity Pensions 189–190
Investment in Education (OECD, 1965) 253
Irish Constitution 1937 38
Irish Labour Party 37, 41, 43, 45, 168, 167, 168, 169, 188
Irish language 251
Irish National Organisation for the Unemployed (INOU) 65
Irish Poor Relief Extension Act 1847 18

J

JobBridge 199
Jobstown 390
Jones, T. 16
justice *see* climate justice; social justice

K

Keynes, JM 90
Keynesian economics 90, 95, 130
knowledge capital 246
knowledge economy 246–247, 265

L

labour market changes 142
labour migration 338, 341–343
labour movement 85
Labourers' Acts 25
land use 24–25
Left- and Right-wing ideologies 112–115, *114*
lesbian movement 365–366
'less eligibility, principle of' 16
LGBT (lesbian, gay, bisexual and transgender) people 362–364
  from criminalisation to equality 364–368
  discrimination 366, 368
  key policy and legislative documents *365*
liberal feminism 133
liberalism 117–121, 240
libertarianism 118–119
liberty *see* freedom
life expectancy 145, 184, 212, 218, 236, *236*
  Travellers 361–362
lifestyle diseases 212–213
Lisbon Strategy 153–154, 246
local authority houses *285*, *290*
  see also social rented housing
Local Government (Temporary Provisions) Act 1923 31
lone parents 49, 195, 198
longevity *see* life expectancy
lunatic asylums 14

Lyons, Patrick 47

M

Maastricht Treaty 153
Magdalen homes 21–22
male bread winner model 25, 38, 94, 124
marginalised groups *see* minority groups
marketisation 98
marriage 34–35
marriage bar 38, 49
Marshallian citizenship 93–94, 304
Marxism 85, 125, 127, 243
Mater Private 222
maternity leave 191–192
maximalist equality of opportunity 241–242, *242*
McElligott, JJ 187
media 44–45
medical cards 230
Medical Charities (Ireland) Act 1851 19–20
mental health 362
mental health policy 326–327
mental health services 56
mercantile education system 252–253
Mercer's Hospital 12
meritocratic societies 240, 247
Migrant Integration Policy Index 350
Migrant Rights Centre Ireland (MRCI) 343, 344
migrants *see* immigrants
migration 45, 61, 336, *339*
  see also emigration; immigration
Million Pound Scheme 282
minimalist equality of opportunity 241, *242*
minimum wage *106*
minority groups 49, 71, 231–232
mobility poverty *388*, *389*
modern environmentalism 375–377
morality 20, 32, 33–34, 57, 95
Moran, M. 209, 210
morbidity 235
morbidity rate 236–237
mortality rate 235–237
mortality rate ratio 235
mortgage debt 293–295
Mother and Baby homes 34–35
mother and child scheme 39–42
motherhood 34–35, 103
multiculturalism 102–103, 105, 123, 350
  see also interculturalism
mutual aid 83

N

National Advocacy Service (NAS) 323
National Anti-Poverty Strategy (NAPS) 65, 194, 198, 201–202
National Asset Management Agency (NAMA) 290–291, 297
National Carers's Strategy (DoH, 2012c:10) 331

National Economic and Social Council (NESC) 47
national health service (NHS) 92
national health systems 210, 214
national insurance 25, 186
National Insurance Act 1911 25
national policy 145–146, 164
national school system 14, 249
National Treatment Purchase Fund (NTPF) 233–234, *233*
National University of Ireland (NUI) 250
nationalism 123
negative equity 280, 294
negative freedom 115, 118
neo-conservatism 123
neo-liberalism 116, 120–121, 131, 135, 183, 247
neo-Marxism 127–129
New Labour 100–101, 131
new public management 98, 247
New Right 97–100, 183
new social risk groups 184
new social risks 103
New Zealand 87, 210
news media 44–45
Nicholls, George 16–17
nomadism 354, 356, 357
non-statutory payments 182
North Charitable Infirmary 12, 28n
Norton, William 188
Nozick, Robert 118
nursing homes 318–319
  see also Fair Deal Scheme

O

O'Brien, G. 12
occupational benefits 82
Occupational Injuries scheme 189
occupational schemes 197, 199–200
occupational welfare 182
Old Age Pension Act 1908 23–24
old age pensions 23–24, 31, 87, 190
old social risks 103, 146
older people
  abuse 320
  ageism 315
  care 317–320
  as carers 330
  employment 315
  income and poverty 315–316
  key policy and legislative documents *316–317*
  social policy 49, 56, 314–315
  UN Principles for Older Persons 314
one-nation conservatism 122
open method of coordination (OMC) 154
oppression 353
orphans 11

Our Common Future (World Commission on Environment and Development, 1987) 377–378
outdoor relief 15, 18–19, 21, 31, 187
overcrowding 24
owner-occupation 272–273, 279–280, 283–284, 285, 288, 292–295, 294
  see also home ownership

P

parenting *see* lone parents; motherhood
participatory democracy 138
patriarchy 30, 133
pensions 23–24, 31, 36, 82–83, 87, 189–190, 196, 315–316
  reform 146
people with disabilities 56
  key policies and legislative developments *324*
  social policy 320–327
  see also special educational needs (SEN)
people with intellectual disabilities 49, 263
permanent residency 342
personalised budgets 326
person-centred approach 324–326
philanthropy 12, 83–85, 281
  see also charities; voluntary organisations
Political Economy of the Welfare State (Gough, 1979) 128–129
political ideologies 112–114, 167–169
  Christian democracy 123–124
  conservatism 121–123
  contemporary context 116–117
  feminism 132–136
  greenism 136–139
  liberalism 117–121, 148
  social democracy 129–132
  socialism 124–129
political rights 93
pollution of poverty 377
pools of talent 244–245
poor law 10–12, 15–21, 80–82, 187
poorhouses 81
  see also workhouses
population ageing *see* ageing; demographic pressures
populism 123
positive freedom 115
post-industrialisation 142
post-materialism 375
poverty *202*
  attitudes towards 15, 23, 31, 39
    see also 'deserving' poor; 'undeserving' poor
  children 202, 311
  consistent 201–202
  cycle of 86
  ecosocial 375
  EU anti-poverty programmes 166
  National Anti-Poverty Strategy (NAPS) 65, 194, 198, 201–202

older people 316
pollution of 377
primary 86
relative 201
relative income 201–202
research 46–47, 85–86
secondary 86
and social protection 201–203
travel 388–390, *388–389*
women 55
working poor 55, 182
poverty rates 202
poverty traps 197–198
precariat 178, 184
precautionary principle 380
preschool 195, 257–258
Prescribed Relative Allowance 189
primary care 208, 230–232
primary poverty 86
primary school 249, 250–251, 253, 254,
    259–264, 360
'principle of less eligibility' 16
private health insurance 211, 234–235
private healthcare 214, 221–223, *225*
private hospitals 222, *222–223*, 232
private pensions 146
private rented housing 359
  contemporary issues 278–279, 288, 291,
    295–297
  Europe 274
  Travellers 273
private schools 254, 262
private sector 67, 318
privatisation 97
productivism 373–374
Programme for Economic Expansion (GoI, 1958)
    43–44
programme refugees 338
property prices *287*, 292–293, 294
protectionism 36, 42
protest 45–46
Protestantism 11, 13
public choice theory 119–120
public expenditure 58–59, 64–65, 67
  see also social expenditure
public health 83, 216
public health services 229–230
public lunatic asylums 14
public transport 386, 387, 390, 391

Q

Quakers 18
quasi-markets 98, 214

R

racism 66, 134, 336–340, 353
radical feminism 133–134
radical greenism 137–139
radical Right 123

radicalism 45–46
Rawls, John 241
recession *see* economic crisis
redistribution 177, 182, 379
  horizontal 178
reformatory schools 22, 35, 49–50, 64, 72
reformist greenism 137
refugees 345–347
  programme refugees 338
  social policy provision 349–350
relative income poverty 201–202
relative poverty 201
rent regulation 296–297
Rent Supplement (RS) 275, 291
Rental Accommodation Supplement (RAS) 291
rented housing 273
  see also private rented housing; social rented
    housing
replacement ratio 182
reproductive rights *see* abortion; contraception
residency rules 342, 344–345
residential care 318–319
residualisation 278, 290
retirement age 315
Right- and Left-wing ideologies 112–115, *114*
rights-based approach 323
*Rio Declaration on the Environment and
    Development* (UN Environment Programme,
    1992) 381
roads 391
Roma *342–343*
Rome, Treaty of 151
Rowntree, Seebohm 85–86
rural development 24–25
rural hospitals 13
rural transport 390
Ryan Report 72

S

same-sex marriage 367
schools
  Community National Schools (CNS) 264
  industrial and reformatory 22, 35, 45, 49–50,
    64, 72
  national school system 14, 249
  preschool 195, 257–258
  primary 249, 250–251, 253, 254, 259–264,
    360
  private 254, 262
  secondary 91, 245, 251–252, 254, 259–264,
    360
  technical and vocational 48, 245, 249, 252,
    253, 254, 259
  see also education
secondary care 208
secondary poverty 86
secondary school 91, 245, 251–252, 254,
    259–264, 360
segregation 263–264, 278–279, 292, 360

selectivism 179
Sen, Amartya 114
Senior, Nassau 15–16
sexual abuse 64
sexual diversity 362–364
sexual rights 364
sexuality 34, 362–364
single parents *see* lone parents
Smallholders Assistance 189
Smith, Adam 117
Social Action Programme 151
social assistance 179–180
social care *see* care
social change 44–47, 62–64, 72–74, 82–85
    conservatism 122
    feminism 133–134
    limits to 50–51, 57–58
    sexual diversity 362–363
    sustainable development 379
social control 10, 11, 32–33, 128
    Catholic Church 33–35, 36, 57–58
social democracy 129–132
social equality 115, 125
social exclusion 65, 66, 102, 375, 388–390
    see also inclusion
social expenditure 48, 70, 71, 96, 177, 195,
    196–197, *196*
    see also public expenditure
social gradient 236
social health insurance 210–211, 229
social insurance 25, 87, 178–179, 192
social investment (SI) 149–151
social investment states 100, 185–186
social justice 119, 177
social market economy 123–124
social norms 94
Social Open Method of Coordination (OMC)
    154–155, 166
social partners 59
social partnership 59, 61, 66, 163
social policy 1–2
    after 1800 13–22
    early social policy 10–13
    late 19th and early 20th century 23–26
social protection
    challenges and reform 182–186
    definition 176–177
    historical development 186–192
    summary of measures *190*
    migrants 344–345
    and poverty 201–203
    redistribution and social justice 177
    reform 192–200, *193*
    types of 177–181, *181*
    women 25, 49, 51, 94, 186, 189, 191–192,
    343
social rented housing 273, *290*
    contemporary issues 277–278, 288, 290–292
    Europe 274

financial crisis 277, 290
    historical development 280–286
    housing policy reform 275, 276
social rights 93
social risks 83, 103, 146
social sciences 17
social welfare *see* social protection; welfare
socialism 124–129
socialist feminism 133, 135
Society for Prevention of Cruelty to Animals
    (SPCA) 372–373
Society of Friends 18
sociodemographic trends 183–184
soup kitchens 18
Special Delivery Unit *233*
special educational needs (SEN) 263, 321–323
Stability and Growth Pact (SGP) 153
state pensions 36, 146, 196, 315–316
statutory payments 182
steady state economy 138
stigma 180
Stockholm Declaration on the Human Environment
    377
'sturdy beggars' 10
subsidiarity 36, 152, 156
substantive equality of opportunity 241–242,
    242
suffrage 26
Supplementary Welfare Scheme 49
'supply-side welfare state' 104
sustainable development 377–380
    and climate change 381–385
sustainable transport 390–392
Sweden
    health expenditure *213*
    immigration policy 341
    labour-market policies 94, 103–104
    national health service 214
    rent regulation 296–297
    social insurance 87
    Third Way 130
    welfare 88–89

T

talent pools 244–245
'Tallaght Strategy' 59
Tawney, RH 245
tax credits 182
tax relief 296
technical schools 48, 245, 249, 252, 253, 254
technology 139
television 44–45
tenants' groups 46
tenements 281
tenure types 272–273, 288, *288*
    Europe 274–275
tertiary care 208
Thatcher, Margaret 97
Third Country Nationals 341–342

Third Way 100–101, 116, 130–132
Three Worlds of Welfare Capitalism (Esping-Andersen, 1990) *147*
Titmuss, Richard 126
Tormey, R. 260–262
Townsend, P. 47, 95
trade unions 85, 98
tradeable quotas 380
transgender (trans) identities 362, 363
transgender movement 365
transport affordability 389–390, *389*
transport externalities *389*
transport inequalities 388–390
transport policy 390–392
transport trends and problems 385–388
travel, means of *388*
travel poverty 388–390, *388–389*
Traveller movement 356–357
Travellers
　1995 Report of the Task Force on the Travelling Community 357–358
　austerity 361
　children 313
　discrimination 51, 313, 357, 358–359, 360
　education 257, 360–361
　ethnicity 352–354
　healthcare 361–362
　key policy and legislative documents *355*
　social policy 49, 51, 56, 354–357
　unemployment 360
　see also Roma
Treaty of Rome 151
Treaty on European Union 153
Trinity College 249–250
tuberculosis 217, 219–220
Tús 199
Tusla 71, 72, 73, 261, 307, 308, 309, 312, 348
two-tier health system *222–223*, 234–235

U

UN Convention on the Rights of People with Disabilities (CRPD) 320
UN Convention on the Rights of the Child (UNCRC) 307, 311–312
UN Principles for Older Persons 314
'underclass' 99
underemployment 70
'undeserving' poor 11, 12, 21, 31
undesirability 10
unemployment 42, 55, 60–61, 70, 98, 183
　Irish National Organisation for the Unemployed (INOU) 65
　Travellers 360
　see also employment
unemployment assistance 37, 187, 191
unemployment traps 197–198
universal payments 180–181
universal provision 92, 93
universities 247, 249–250, 252

University College Dublin 250
Unmarried Mothers Allowance 49
urban sprawl 386–387
urbanisation 45, 82–83
US
　child abuse 373
　climate change 383
　environmental justice 376
　health expenditure 212
　health insurance 211
　New Right 99
　poorhouses 81
　welfare provision 89, 95, 98

V

Van der Zwan, N. 144
vertical distribution 179
Vision for Change, A (Expert Group on Mental Health Policy, 2006) 326
vocational schools 249, 252, 253, 259
Voluntary Health Insurance (VHI) 219
voluntary hospitals 12–13, 216, 218, 219, 221
voluntary organisations 18, 50, 83–85, 286
　see also charities
vulnerable adult abuse 320

W

waiting lists 232, *233*
wealth inequality 47
welfare 4, 23, 70, 80–86
　asset-based 276
　children 24, 71, 72–73
　fiscal 181–182
　'golden age' 93, 130, 182
　occupational 182
　worlds of *147-148*
　see also social protection
welfare capitalism 127–128
welfare chauvinism 105
welfare dependency 30–31, 99, 122, 183
welfare dualism *see* dualism
welfare regimes *147–149*
welfare states 3, 68
　emergence of 87–96
　environmental concerns 376
　ideological ambiguity 169–170
　libertarianism 119
　reform 96–105
　'supply-side' 104
　typologies 147–149
'welfare tourism' 344
women
　as carers 322–323, 328–329
　Catholic Church 33, 34–35, 57
　education 248, 249
　emigration 19, 42
　home assistance 31–32
　Magdalen homes 20–21
　poverty 55

in public life 25–26
social insurance 178
social protection 25, 49, 51, 94, 186, 189,
  191–192, 343
Travellers 353
work 38–39, 60, 103, 148, 154, 166
workhouses 20
see also feminism
women's movement 25–26, 46
work permits 341–342
work-based pensions 82–83
workfare 99
workhouse hospitals 19, 20, 215, 217
workhouses 11, 12, 16, 17–18, 20, 31
working age 185
working conditions 82, 85
'working poor' 55, 182
Workmen's Compensation Act 1897 23
work-related benefits 82
World Health Organisation (WHO) 206–207

Y

young people
  activation 200
  Amsterdam Treaty 153
  as carers 330
  emigration 55, 70
  leaving care 313
  precariat 178, 184
  rights 310
  social welfare/social protection 59, 71
youth policy 56, 66